Spirit Christology
in the Christian Tradition

From the Patristic Period to the Rise of
Pentecostalism in the Twentieth Century

Herschel Odell Bryant

CPT Press
Cleveland, Tennessee

Spirit Christology in the Christian Tradition
From the Patristic Period to the Rise of Pentecostalism in the
Twentieth Century

Published by CPT Press
900 Walker ST NE
Cleveland, TN 37311
USA
email: cptpress@pentecostaltheology.org
website: www.cptpress.com

Library of Congress Control Number: 2014956053

ISBN-10: 1935931474
ISBN-13: 9781935931478

Copyright © 2014 CPT Press

All rights reserved. No part of this book may be reproduced or translated in any form, by print, photoprint, microfilm, microfiche, electronic database, internet database, or any other means without written permission from the publisher.

Spirit Christology in the Christian Tradition
From the Patristic Period to the Rise of
Pentecostalism in the Twentieth Century

To my wife and children
Elizabeth Ann Bryant
William Odell Bryant
Joel Isaac Bryant
John Paul Bryant

Contents

Preface xii
Abbreviations xv

Chapter 1
Introduction 1
   A Survey of the Modern Discussion 2
      The First Phase: Revisionist Spirit Christologies 2
         G.W.H. Lampe 3
         Piet Schoonenberg 7
         James D.G. Dunn 10
      The Second Phase: Trinitarian Spirit Christologies 16
         David Coffey 16
         Jürgen Moltmann 22
         Clark Pinnock 28
   Pentecostal Contributions 33
      Amos Yong 34
      S.D.L. Jenkins 35
      Sang-Ehil Han 35
      Sammy Alfaro 36
   The Need, Purposes, and Methodology of this Inquiry 38

Part One
Spirit Christology from the Apostolic Fathers to the Fifth Ecumenical Council

Chapter 2
The Apostolic Fathers 47
   Ignatius of Antioch 47
   The Epistle of Barnabas 52
   The Shepherd of Hermas 59
   The Second Epistle of Clement to the Corinthians 59
   Conclusion 62

Chapter 3
The Early Apologists 63
Aristides of Athens 64
Justin Martyr 66
Melito of Sardis 72
Conclusion 75

Chapter 4
Voices from the Margins 78
Gnosticism 78
    The Gospel of Truth 82
    Testimony of Truth 84
    The Gospel of Philip 86
Ebionism 91
Monarchianism 95
    Dynamic Monarchianism 96
        Theodotus 96
        Paul of Samosata 97
    Modalist Monarchianism 98
        Noetus of Smyrna 98
        Praxeas 99
        Sabellius 101
New Prophecy 102
    Montanus 105
    Tertullian 106
Conclusion 111

Chapter 5
The Later Apologists 113
Irenaeus 113
Hippolytus of Rome 118
Clement of Alexandria 125
Origen 130
Conclusion 138

Chapter 6
Eastern Writers 140
Arius 140
Eustathius of Antioch 146
Marcellus of Ancyra 151
Aphrahat the Persian 158

Photinus 162
Cyril of Jerusalem 163
Athanasius 169
Apollinarius of Laodicea 176
The Cappadocian Fathers 181
Nestorius 189
Conclusion 198

Chapter 7
Western Writers 201
Hilary of Poitiers 202
Marius Victorinus 210
Ambrose of Milan 216
Augustine 220
Conclusion 227

Chapter 8
Setting the Boundaries 229
The Council of Ephesus (431) 229
The Council of Chalcedon (451) 249
The Council of Constantinople II (553) 261
Conclusion 267

Chapter 9
Summary/Conclusion to Part One 269

Part Two
Spirit Christology from the Fifth Ecumenical Council
to the Rise of Pentecostalism

Chapter 10
Eastern Writers 275
The Council of Constantinople III (680) 275
The Council of Nicea II (787) 277
Byzantine Mystical Tradition 278
  Symeon the New Theologian 279
  Gregory Palamas 282
  Nicholas Cabasilas 283
The Fall of Constantinople (1453) 285
The Ethiopian Tradition 286
Conclusion 298

Chapter 11
Western Writers 300
- The Venerable Bede 301
- Elipandus 306
- Bonaventure 309
- Conclusion 315

Chapter 12
Protestant Writers 317
- The Protestant Tradition of Conservative Self-Criticism 318
  - Richard Sibbes 319
  - John Owen 325
- The Protestant Tradition of Liberal Self-Criticism 334
  - Friedrich Schleiermacher 337
  - Gottfried Thomasius 343
  - Hermann Gunkel 348
- Conclusion 352

Chapter 13
Voices from the Margins 355
- Armenian Paulicians 357
- Russian Nonconformists: Khlysty and Skoptsy 363
- Conclusion 372

Chapter 14
Summary/Conclusion to Part Two 374

Part Three
The Rise of Pentecostalism

Chapter 15
Proto-Pentecostals 379
- Molokan-Jumpers (*Pryguny*) 379
- Edward Irving 392
- Conclusion 411

Chapter 16
The Emergence of Pentecostalism from Holiness Revivalism 412
- The Development of the Fourfold Full Gospel 412
  - Albert Benjamin Simpson 418
- The Unfolding of the Fivefold Full Gospel 432

Contents xi

    Ralph Cecil Horner 432
    George Douglas Watson 436
    Benjamin Hardin Irwin 440
    Charles Fox Parham..450
    William Joseph Seymour 456
  Conclusion 461

Chapter 17
Early Pentecostal Periodical Literature 464
  The Fivefold Gospel Stream 465
    Apostolic Faith...466
    The Bridegroom's Messenger...469
    The Church of God Evangel 473
    The Whole Truth..478
    The Pentecostal Holiness Advocate..480
  The Fourfold Gospel Stream 487
    The Latter Rain Evangel..487
    The Pentecost 490
    The Pentecostal Testimony..493
    Oneness Pentecostalism...498
  Conclusion 506

Chapter 18
Summary/Conclusion to Part Three 509

Chapter 19
Contributions and Implications 512
  Contributions 512
  Implications for Pentecostal Theology 516

Bibliography 521

Index of Biblical and Other Ancient References 565

Index of Names 577

Preface

The concept for this monograph was conceived in me by the Spirit during my MDiv studies at the Church of God Theological Seminary (now the Pentecostal Theological Seminary). It developed through graduate seminars at Regent University, and it came to fruition as a PhD thesis at Bangor University. This monograph is an expanded and revised version of this PhD thesis which did not include significant portions of this present work: neither the survey of the modern discussion located in the introductory chapter, nor the material contained in chapters eleven, twelve, thirteen, fourteen, and sixteen made it into the final version of the thesis.

The journey has been long and arduous, and without the assistance, kindness, patience, and love of certain people, as well as those who have invested part of themselves in my life, the work would not have progressed this far. I readily acknowledge these debts, realizing that words are feeble currency for recompense.

I begin by giving praise to my Lord and Savior, Jesus Christ, who has taken a farm boy and transformed him from a lost, hurting, angry, and vindictive person to one who loves God and neighbor, a preacher of the full gospel, and shepherd of God's people. Accordingly, I recognize the spiritual formation instilled in me as a young man by the saints of the Pentecostal community. In response to the multitude of questions filling my mind about God, the saints replied: 'you do not need theology; you need kneeology'. Attending to God in prayer, however, multiplied the questions, deepened the divine mystery, and intensified my desire to know God. So, I gratefully acknowledge the influence of the prayer-warriors – especially my father-in-law, Tom Bowlin – who taught me how to pray, setting me on a theological quest to peer into the divine mystery.

My context of ministry for the past thirty-one years has been serving as a Pentecostal pastor. Thanks are due to those congregants who have encouraged me in my academic pursuits and prayed for my success. Appreciation is expressed for the support and patience of the members of the Glad Tidings Church of God, in

Clanton, AL where I have served as pastor while writing the monograph.

A special debt of gratitude is owed to Wade H. Phillips, Presiding Bishop of Zion Assembly, for sharing with me his copies of various Holiness periodicals: *Way of Faith*, *Tongues of Fire*, and *Live Coals of Fire*. Several libraries have given much assistance in this research. Bangor University's library in Wales was accessible via the internet. Beeson School of Divinity library located on the campus of Samford University in Birmingham, Alabama has been a valuable resource. William G. Squires Library along with the Dixon Pentecostal Research Center in Cleveland, Tennessee has provided access to several Holiness and Pentecostal publications which were out of print. Furthermore, the interlibrary loan department of Squires Library supplied me with several sources which were difficult to find. Much of the early Pentecostal periodical literature was gathered via the internet from the Flower Pentecostal Heritage Center in Springfield, Missouri. Of course, the Center for Pentecostal Theology in Cleveland, Tennessee has provided assistance in acquiring sources and on occasion a place to write and sleep overnight.

I gratefully acknowledge the time, effort, and investment of those who have taught me and helped me along the journey. I express thanks to French L. Arrington who served as my supervisor during MDiv studies and has become a dear friend; during the writing of this monograph, he has always been willing to check my Greek translations for accuracy. I should also mention that Terry L. Cross was kind enough to assist me regarding Latin translations. Lee Roy Martin's friendship is invaluable, as a fellow Pentecostal pastor, preacher, and scholar; his technical assistance is much appreciated. Stanley Burgess and Vinson Synan have greatly influenced me concerning historical theology and Pentecostal studies; the time spent with them provided much insight and inspiration. Moreover, I happily express gratitude to the professors who have taught me in various biblical and theological seminars: Steven J. Land, R. Hollis Gause, Rickie D. Moore, Kimberly Erwin Alexander, Kenneth J. Archer, Cheryl Bridges Johns, Jackie D. Johns, Graham H. Twelftree, Petrus J. Gräbe, Frank D. Macchia, Veli-Matti Kärkkäinen, and John Christopher Thomas.

This research would not have been possible without the consent and supervision of John Christopher Thomas through the PhD thesis. He found me in academic despair, disgust, and disillusionment and rescued me, agreeing to guide me through the process. In my mind, it is inconceivable to think of a better supervisor than Chris. He is a genuine mentor in every sense of the word. His generous and hospitable spirit – always willing to give his time, attention, fellowship, and energy – ability to encourage, and critical eye, providing criticism with kindness, has set an example of discipleship that will be difficult for anyone to match. For his superb supervision, I express my heartfelt gratitude.

The deepest sense of gratitude and obligation of recompense, however, extends to my wife, Ann, and my sons, William, Joel, and John; the debt for their sacrifices can never be repaid. Ann's love, devotion, encouragement, and occasional gentle 'push' forward has sustained me through the years it took to complete this project. Her invaluable assistance in the pastoral role of the church has enriched the church, but at times, she has borne more of the load than is reasonable, yet remarkably she did it without complaint. The greatest loss caused by this project is the time sacrificed, not spent with my wife and children, which can never be recovered. Though William and Joel are married and have their own family responsibilities, occasionally, grown men still need their dads, and grandchildren need their grandparents; furthermore, grandparents need to hold and spoil their grandchildren. Since John is a senior in high school and has grown up with this project, perhaps, he has most severely felt the hardships and disruptions. Here, words are the feeblest comforters; all I can do is offer apologies to my wife and sons for our loss of time together and dedicate this work to them: Ann, William, Joel, and John.

Abbreviations

Holiness Periodicals

AF (Baxter Springs)	*Apostolic Faith (Baxter Springs)*
AF (Topeka)	*Apostolic Faith (Topeka)*
TF	*Tongues of Fire*

Early Pentecostal Periodicals

AF	*Apostolic Faith*
COGE	*The Church of God Evangel*
LRE	*The Latter Rain Evangel*
PHA	*The Pentecostal Holiness Advocate*
PT	*The Pentecostal Testimony*
TBM	*The Bridegroom's Messenger*
TWT	*The Whole Truth*
WE	*The Weekly Evangel*
WW	*Word and Witness*

Nag Hammadi Tractates

Ap. John	*Apocryphon of John*
Gos. Phil.	*Gospel of Philip*
Gos. Truth	*Gospel of Truth*
Hyp. Arch.	*Hypostasis of the Archons*
Orig. World	*On the Origin of the World*
Testim. Truth	*Testimony of Truth*
Thom. Cont.	*Book of Thomas the Contender*
Treat. Res.	*Treatise on Resurrection*
Tri. Trac.	*Tripartite Tractate*

Early Christian Literature and Modern Sources

AARD	Dissertation Series – American Academy of Religion
AARAS	American Academy of Religion Academy Series
ABD	*The Anchor Bible Dictionary*
ABRL	The Anchor Bible Reference Library
ACW	Ancient Christian Writers
Ambrose of Milan, *Fid.*	*On the Christian Faith*

Ambrose of Milan, *Incarn.*	*The Sacrament of the Incarnation of Our Lord*
Ambrose of Milan, *Spir.*	*On the Holy Spirit*
ANF	*Ante-Nicene Fathers*
Aphrahat, *Dem.*	*Demonstrations*
AsTJ	*Asbury Theological Journal*
Athanasius, *C. Ar.*	*Four Discourses against the Arians*
Athanasius, *Ep. Serap.*	*Letters to Serapion concerning the Holy Spirit*
Athanasius, *Prax.*	*Against Praxeas*
Athanasius, *Syn.*	*De synodis*
Athanasius, *Tom.*	*Tomus ad Antiochenos*
ATR	*Anglican Theological Review*
Augustine, *Enchir.*	*Enchiridion on Faith, Hope, and Love*
Augustine, *Tract. Ev. Jo.*	*Tractates on the Gospel of John*
Augustine, *Praed.*	*The Predestination of the Saints*
Augustine, *Trin.*	*The Trinity*
BA	*The Biblical Archaeologist*
BAGD	Walter Bauer, William F. Arndt, F. William Gingrich and Frederick W. Danker, *A Greek-English Lexicon of the New Testament and Other Early Christian Literature*
Barn.	*The Epistle of Barnabas*
Basil of Caesarea, *DSS*	*De Spiritu Sancto*
Bijdr	*Bijdragen: Tijdschrift voor filosofie en theologie*
BJS	Brown Judaic Studies
CChr	Corpus Christianorum
CH	*Church History*
CHC	*The Cambridge History of Christianity*
Chrysostom, *Hom. Jo.*	*Homiliae in Joannenm*
Chrysostom, *Hom. Matt.*	*Homiliae in Matthaeum*
Chrysostom, *Hom. Phil.*	*Homiliae in epistulam ad Philippenses*
Clement, *Paed.*	Clement of Alexandria, *Christ the Educator*
Clement, *Protr.*	Clement of Alexandria, *Exhortation to the Greeks*
Clement, *Strom.*	Clement of Alexandria, *Miscellanies*
Clement of Rome, 1 *Clem.*	*The First Epistle of Clement to the Corinthians*
Clement of Rome, 2 *Clem.*	*The Second Epistle of Clement to the Corinthians*

CSChO	Corpus scriptorum christianorum orientalium
CSS	Cistercian Studies Series
CW	*The Collected Writings of Edward Irving*
CWS	The Classics of Western Spirituality
Cyprian, *Idol.*	*That Idols Are Not Gods*
Cyril, *Ep. Nestorius*	Cyril of Alexandria, *Letter to Nestorius*
Cyril, *Monks*	Cyril of Alexandria, *Letter to the Monks of Egypt*
DBI	*Dictionary of Biblical Interpretation*
DLNT	*Dictionary of the Later New Testament & Its Developments*
Didymus, *Trin.*	*De Trinitate*
ECF	The Early Church Fathers
Epiphanius, *Pan.*	*The Panarion*
Eusebius, *Hist. eccl.*	*Ecclesiastical History*
EvQ	*Evangelical Quarterly*
ExpTim	*Expository Times*
FC	Fathers of the Church
GBWW	Great Books of the Western World
GOTR	*Greek Orthodox Theological Review*
HCS	A History of Christian Spirituality
HCL	The Higher Christian Life
Hermas, *Man.*	*Mandate*
Hermas, *Sim.*	*Similitude*
Hermas, *Vis.*	*Vision*
HeyJ	*Heythrop Journal*
Hilary of Poitiers, *Syn.*	*De Synodis*
Hilary of Poitiers, *Trin.*	*De Trinitate*
Hippolytus, *Haer.*	*The Refutation of all Heresies*
Hippolytus, *Noet.*	*Against the Heresy of One Noetus*
Hippolytus, *Trad. ap.*	*The Apostolic Tradition*
HTR	*Harvard Theological Review*
Ignatius, *Eph.*	*Letter to the Ephesians*
Ignatius, *Magn.*	*Letter to the Magnesians*
Ignatius, *Phld.*	*Letter to the Philadelphians*
Ignatius, *Pol.*	*Letter to Polycarp*
Ignatius, *Rom.*	*Letter to the Romans*
Ignatius, *Smyrn.*	*Letter to the Smyrnaeans*
Ignatius, *Trall.*	*Letter to the Trallians*
IJST	*International Journal of Systematic Theology*
Irenaeus, *Epid.*	*Demonstration of the Apostolic Preaching*

Irenaeus, *Haer.*	*Against Heresies*
JAAR	*Journal of the American Academy of Religion*
JBL	*Journal of Biblical Literature*
JEH	*Journal of Ecclesiastical History*
JEPTA	*Journal of the European Pentecostal Association*
JES	*Journal of Ecumenical Studies*
JPT	*Journal of Pentecostal Theology*
JPTSup	*Journal of Pentecostal Theology*, Supplement Series
JSJ	*Journal for the Study of Judaism in the Persian, Hellenistic and Roman Period*
JSNTSup	*Journal for the Study of the New Testament*, Supplement Series
JSPSup	*Journal for the Study of the Pseudepigrapha*, Supplement Series
JSOT	*Journal for the Study of the Old Testament*
JTS	*Journal of Theological Studies*
Lactantius, *Inst.*	Lactantius, *The Divine Institutes*
LCC	The Library of Christian Classics
LCL	The Loeb Classical Library
LQ	*Lutheran Quarterly*
NHL	*Nag Hammadi Library*
NIDPCM	*The New International Dictionary of Pentecostal and Charismatic Movements*
NovT	*Novum Testamentum*
NovTSup	Novum Testamentum, Supplement Series
NPNF	*Nicene and Post-Nicene Fathers*
NTL	New Testament Library
ODCC	*The Oxford Dictionary of the Christian Church*
OECS	Oxford Early Christian Studies
OECT	Oxford Early Christian Texts
Origen, *Princ.*	*First Principles*
Origen, *Cels.*	*Against Celsus*
Origen, *Comm. Jo.*	Commentary on the Gospel according to John
Origen, *Comm. Matt.*	Commentary on the Gospel according to Matthew
OSHT	Oxford Studies in Historical Theology
OTM	Oxford Theological Monographs

OTT	Orthodox Theological Texts
PG	J.P. Minge (ed.), *Patrologia cursus completus ... Series Graeca* (166 vols.; Paris: Petit-Montrouge, 1857–83)
Pneuma	*Pneuma: The Journal of the Society for Pentecostal Studies*
ProEccl	*Pro Ecclesia*
PTMS	Princeton Theological Monograph Series
SBLWGRW	Society of Biblical Literature Writings from the Greco-Roman World
Socrates, *Hist. eccl.*	Socrates Scholasticus, *Ecclesiastical History*
Sozomenus, *Hist. eccl.*	Sozomenus, *Ecclesiastical History*
SR	*Studies in Religion*
Studpb	Studia post-biblica
SVTQ	*St. Vladimir's Theological Quarterly*
TDNT	*Theological Dictionary of the New Testament*
Tertullian, *Apol.*	*Apology*
Tertullian, *Carn. Chr.*	*The Flesh of Christ*
Tertullian, *Marc.*	*Against Marcion*
Tertullian, *Prax.*	*Against Praxeas*
Theodoret, *Hist. eccl.*	*Ecclesiastical History*
Theophilus, *Autol.*	*To Autolycus*
ThTo	*Theology Today*
TS	*Theological Studies*
TTCH	The Transformation of the Classical Heritage
TUGAL	Texte und Untersuchungen zur Geschichte der Altchristlichen Literatur
USQR	*Union Seminary Quarterly Review*
VC	*Vigiliae Christianae*
VCSup	Vigiliae Christianae, Supplement Series
Victorinus, *Ad. Ar.*	Victorinus, *Against Arius*
Victorinus, *Ad. Cand.*	Victorinus, *Against Candidus*
WTJ	*Westminster Theological Journal*

1

INTRODUCTION

The goal of this inquiry is to contribute to three fields of study: Historical Theology, Spirit Christology, and Pentecostal Theology. The research involved in this project, therefore, surveys the historical presence of Spirit Christology and its relationship with doctrinal development in the Christian tradition, beginning with the Patristic Period and continuing through the various epochs of church history to the rise of Pentecostalism in the early twentieth-century. When one embarks of such a journey certain questions immediately appear. What is Spirit Christology? How is it distinguished from the traditional Logos form of Christology? Are these two forms of Christology compatible with one another, or do they exist in an antithetical relationship? Historically, did Spirit Christology only exist in the early church, or did it appear in other epochs of the Christian tradition? Of course, these are not original questions regarding the subject of Spirit Christology, nor are they the only questions that arise; indeed, they are inherent to the field of study, so these questions are presented here to pique the interest and alert the reader to these forthcoming issues. By way of introducing the reader to the subject and field of Spirit Christology, this chapter consists of two parts. Part One supplies an overview of the modern discussion of Spirit Christology. Part Two offers a few observations regarding the modern discussion, and it delineates the need, purposes, and methodology of this inquiry into Spirit Christology in the Christian tradition.

A Survey of the Modern Discussion

This survey of the modern discussion regarding Spirit Christology contains three sections. Since its appearance in the early twentieth-century, Spirit Christology has received attention from an extensive and diverse array of theologians; furthermore, Spirit Christology inherently encompasses many complex issues. Consequently, the first and second sections survey two phases of development in the modern discussion of Spirit Christology. Here, the focus rests on acquainting the reader with selected major proponents and their writings, which have shaped the contours of the modern discussion, and essential elements of these theologians' Spirit Christology. The third section concisely presents Pentecostal contributions, which either use Spirit Christology by integrating it into Pentecostal theology or attempt to build various contextual Pentecostal theologies on Spirit christological foundations. Here, the focus rests on acquainting the reader with the lie of the land as it presently exists in the modern discussion among Pentecostals.

The First Phase: Revisionist Spirit Christologies

Spirit Christology first appeared in the modern era among theologians of the liberal Protestant tradition attempting to reconstruct a Christology amicable to the mind of humans living in modern culture. These theologians re-opened christological discussion by rejecting triune doctrine, the doctrine of the incarnation, and virginal conception. Consequently, they attempted to move the christological discussion from speaking of Christ's two *natures* to affirming two *stories*, human and mythological. The human story asserted Christ's genuine human nature, while mythological claims to literal incarnation of deity were dismissed as docetic misinterpretations of the story.[1] In considering how to express Jesus' relationship with deity,

---

[1] 'A literal incarnation doctrine, expressed in however sophisticated a form, cannot avoid some element of docetism, and involves the believer in claims of uniqueness which seem straightforwardly incredible to the majority of our contemporaries.' Francis Young, 'A Cloud of Witnesses', in John Hick (ed.), *The Myth of God Incarnate* (Philadelphia: Westminster Press, 1977), p. 32. For discussion of these issues see, John A.T. Robinson, *Honest to God* (Philadelphia: Westminster Press, 1963); John A.T. Robinson, *The Human Face of God* (Philadelphia: Westminster Press, 1973); Maurice Wiles, 'Does Christology Rest on a Mistake?', in Stephen Sykes and John Powell Clayton (eds.), *Christ, Faith and History: Cambridge Studies in Christology* (London: Cambridge University Press, 1972), pp. 3-12; Peter R. Baelz, 'A Deliberate Mistake?', in Stephen Sykes and John Powell

a turn to Spirit Christology appeared among some of these theologians: Jesus was a human inspired by the divine Spirit.

G.W.H. Lampe

G.W.H. Lampe[2] critiques problems which he believes are inherent in Logos Christology and recovers Spirit Christology, stemming from the concept of God as Spirit, in order to answer these problems.[3] Following liberal Protestant theology, Lampe denies the historical fall of humanity into sin; rather, the fall portrays every human under the temptation to be as God.[4] Accordingly, Lampe

---

Clayton (eds.), *Christ, Faith and History: Cambridge Studies in Christology* (London: Cambridge University Press, 1972), pp. 13-34; S.W. Sykes, 'The Theology of the Humanity of Christ', in Stephen Sykes and John Powell Clayton (eds.), *Christ, Faith and History: Cambridge Studies in Christology* (London: Cambridge University Press, 1972), pp. 53-72; Maurice Wiles, 'Christianity without Incarnation?', in John Hick (ed.), *The Myth of God Incarnate* (Philadelphia: Westminster Press, 1977), pp. 1-10; D.M. Baillie, *God Was in Christ: An Essay on Incarnation and Atonement* (New York: Scribner, 1955).

[2] Geoffrey William Hugo Lampe (1912–80) was educated at Blundell's School (1926–31) and Exeter College (1935–36). Lampe served the Anglican Church as priest and member of the General Synod of the Church of England. Lampe dedicated his life to theological teaching and research, while holding such prestigious positions as Ely Professor of Divinity at the University of Cambridge (1960–70) and Regius Professor (1970–79). Lampe published several monographs and was renowned for his dictionary of patristic Greek, *A Patristic Greek Lexicon*. His publications about Spirit Christology are primarily found in his Brampton Lectures (1976) which were published as *God as Spirit* (1977) and an earlier article 'The Holy Spirit and the Person of Christ' (1972). For a helpful overview and analysis of Lampe's life, theological context, development as a theologian, and Spirit Christology, see David A. Dorman, 'The Spirit Christology of Geoffrey Lampe: A Critical Analysis' (PhD dissertation, Fuller Theological Seminary, 1992).

[3] Norman Hook's monograph *Christ in the Twentieth Century* was an early contribution to the discussion which preceded Lampe; however, his work was not as influential as Lampe's; those who have followed this trajectory either interact or build on Lampe's work. According to David Dorman, 'But it is clear at any rate that the proposal articulated in *God as Spirit* is to be viewed as one expression of a groundswell of sorts which occurred in the third quarter of the century. As it happened, the depth and erudition of Lampe's own effort was to provide a particularly catalytic effect for Spirit Christology, permitting a new intentionality in the general use of the term'. Dorman, 'The Spirit Christology of Geoffrey Lampe', p. 28. Hook's primary contributions to the discussion include Norman Hook, *Christ in the Twentieth Century*; Norman Hook, 'A Spirit Christology', *Theology* 75 (1972), pp. 226-32. Lampe's work is also foreshadowed by Hendrikus Berkhof in Hendrikus Berkhof, *The Doctrine of the Holy Spirit* (Richmond, VA: John Knox Press, 1964); Hendrikus Berkhof, *The Christian Faith: An Introduction to the Study of Faith* (Grand Rapids: Eerdmans, 1979), pp. 267-337.

[4] G.W.H. Lampe, *God as Spirit* (Oxford: Clarendon Press, 1977), p. 19.

teaches an integration of creation and evolutionary theory: creation is a continual process moving toward perfection in God. Thus, humans exist as spiritual beings, so that God as Spirit inspires them in progression toward perfection, deification.[5] Christ, then, is not the 'Second Adam'; rather, Christ is the *genuine* Adam in whom God's plan for humanity comes to full realization.[6] Jesus, moreover, is the son of God, representing humanity living in obedience and unbroken fellowship with God. Creation and salvation, therefore, is a single continuous divine act of inspiration or incarnation of God as Spirit in the spirits of humans, in which Jesus is its archetype and fulfillment;[7] it is one theandric operation.[8]

According to Lampe, Logos/Son Christology fails to do justice to Jesus' relationship with God.[9] Lampe, accordingly, brings the Chalcedonian confession of Christ's two natures under scrutiny. The inherent problem is the hypostatic union of the *preexistent* Logos – who coexists with God and acts as mediator between God and his creation – with the human Jesus.[10] Hence, Lampe asserts his central concept that God is Spirit: 'Essentially, it is God himself who is pre-existent, for he is eternal and it is his purpose which is realized in the developing process of his creativity'.[11] The Patristic Fathers, according to Lampe, recognized in Scripture that Logos, Wisdom, and Torah were terms describing the preexistence of God as Spirit; consequently, Logos Christology retroactively read the

---

[5] Lampe, *God as Spirit*, pp. 34-60.

[6] Lampe, *God as Spirit*, p. 19.

[7] Lampe, *God as Spirit*, pp. 17-33. 'In this continuous incarnation of God as Spirit in the spirits of men the Jesus represented to us by the Gospels holds his unique place. The Pauline imagery of Adam is appropriate, for Jesus is what man (Adam) is meant to be: son of God, made in God's image, "being in the form of God". The "sonship" of Jesus thus means that he is truly and fully human: man as the creator has designed him, that is, in unbroken fellowship with God. In Jesus the incarnate presence of God evoked a full and constant response of the human spirit. This was not a different divine presence, but the same God the Spirit who moved and inspired other men, such as the prophets. It was not a different kind of human response, but it was total instead of partial.' Lampe, *God as Spirit*, pp. 23-24. Cf. Lampe, *God as Spirit*, pp. 52-53, 95, 142-44, 161.

[8] 'It is not inappropriate to apply to all human experience of inspiration by God's Spirit at every level, and not only at the highest (in the person of Christ), the Monothelite phrase, "one Theandric operation."' Lampe, *God as Spirit*, p. 46.

[9] Lampe, *God as Spirit*, p. 142.

[10] 'The door is opened to the Arian denial that the Son or Logos whom men encounter in Jesus is the fullness of deity.' Lampe, *God as Spirit*, p. 140.

[11] Lampe, *God as Spirit*, p. 120.

preexistence of the Logos/Son into these creative activities of God as Spirit.[12] Thereupon, the idea of preexistent deity in Christ is defined as Spirit.[13] Furthermore, the concept of a mediator is unnecessary: 'It is God himself, disclosed to us and experienced by us as inspiring and indwelling Spirit (or Wisdom or Word), who meets us through Jesus and can make us Christ-like'.[14]

According to Lampe, the doctrine of the enhypostatic union of the Logos in Jesus is docetic in nature and ignores Christ's true humanity.[15] In fact, Lampe understands incarnation in terms of inspiration rather than hypostatic union. So, Lampe portrays Jesus as a man uniquely inspired of the Spirit standing in the succession of prophets, yet completing and fulfilling the work of all the prophets.[16] Because the Spirit inundates all of Jesus' life and ministry and does not pertain to a particular point of his life, such as baptism, Lampe affirms that he avoids the danger of adoptionism.[17] The Spirit's inspiration in Jesus was unique because it was total and not partial: a full incarnation of the presence of deity, a deification of man.[18]

Lampe, also, supports a realized eschatology. So, he denies that Jesus has a post-existence as the Christ.[19] Jesus was neither resurrected in human flesh nor did he ascend into heaven: Christ is the Spirit. The Spirit is the single reality that signifies the one God in his relations to humanity, and he comes to us as the Christ. Since the Christ-Spirit continues to inspire and make persons into sons of God, bodily resurrection occurs in a visible community of reconcili-

---

[12] Lampe, *God as Spirit*, pp. 123-25, 140. Cf. G.W.H. Lampe, 'The Holy Spirit and the Person of Christ', in Stephen Sykes and John Powell Clayton (eds.), *Christ, Faith and History: Cambridge Studies in Christology* (London: Cambridge University Press, 1972), pp. 111-15. The terms are interchangeable. Lampe, *God as Spirit*, pp. 116-18.
[13] Lampe, *God as Spirit*, pp. 114-16, 120-44.
[14] Lampe, *God as Spirit*, p. 144.
[15] For Lampe this is an abstraction that is far removed from biblical theology. Lampe, 'The Holy Spirit and the Person of Christ', pp. 119-23.
[16] Lampe, *God as Spirit*, p. 97.
[17] Lampe, 'The Holy Spirit and the Person of Christ', p. 125.
[18] Lampe, *God as Spirit*, pp. 23-24. 'Incarnation and "inspiration" are not in fact two quite different alternative models for Christology ... Incarnation, unless understood in inspirational terms, is equally inadequate.' Cf. Lampe, 'The Holy Spirit and the Person of Christ', pp. 117-18, 121-30; Lampe, *God as Spirit*, pp. 12-13.
[19] Lampe, *God as Spirit*, pp. 145-75.

ation and forgiveness.[20] In this context, Lampe examines and critiques Pentecostalism's view of Spirit baptism as a second blessing, concluding that it delineates a poor concept of God as Spirit.[21]

Lampe's Spirit Christology represents the Protestant tradition's desire to formulate a Christology amicable to the modern mind and culture. Regarding his contributions in shaping the modern discussion, the following observations emerge. First, Lampe delineates a Spirit Christology based on the concept of God as Spirit. Second, his concept of soteriological history as evolution with a continual incarnation of divine Spirit in the human spirit, through the Spirit's inspiration, places Jesus' unique inspiration of the Spirit at the apex of the salvific process. Thus, Lampe illuminates the potential of Spirit Christology to depict alternative anthropologies and redemptive formulas. Third, his critique of Logos Christology being docetic in nature pushes him to affirm the Spirit's inspiration as being synonymous with incarnation; hence, his Christology attests to Christ's genuine humanity and the Spirit's integral relation in Jesus' life and mission, so that the Spirit entirely permeates them. Fourth, Lampe's realized eschatology affirms that Christ is the Spirit; there is no distinction of presence. Although Lampe denies his christological formulation supports a Christology of inspiration, the core of his Spirit christological trajectory reflects this position.[22]

---

[20] Lampe, *God as Spirit*, pp. 155-60.
[21] Lampe, *God as Spirit*, pp. 198-201.
[22] Other theologians that follow this revisionist trend are, Paul W. Newman, *A Spirit Christology: Recovering the Biblical Paradigm of Christian Faith* (Lanham, MD: University Press of America, 1987); John Hick, 'An Inspiration Christology for a Religiously Plural World', in Stephen T. Davis (ed.), *Encountering Jesus: A Debate on Christology* (Atlanta: John Knox, 1988), pp. 5-29; John Hick, *The Metaphor of God Incarnate: Christology in a Pluralistic Age* (Louisville, KY: Westminster/John Knox Press, 1993); John Hick, 'Jesus and the World Religions', in John Hick (ed.), *The Myth of God Incarnate* (Philadelphia: Westminster, 1977), pp. 167-85; John Hick, *Disputed Questions in Theology and the Philosophy of Religion* (New Haven: Yale University Press, 1993), pp. 35-57; Roger Haight, 'The Case for Spirit Christology', *TS* 53 (1992), pp. 257-87; Olaf Hansen, 'Spirit Christology: A Way out of the Dilemma?', in Paul D. Opsahl (ed.), *The Holy Spirit in the Life of the Church: From Biblical Times to the Present* (Minneapolis: Augsburg, 1978), pp. 172-203; also Michael Lodahl Spirit christological proposal of a Shekhinah Christology is similar, see Michael Lodahl, *Shekhinah/Spirit: Divine Presence in Jewish and Christian Religion* (New York: Paulist Press, 1992).

Piet Schoonenberg

Piet Schoonenberg[23] constructs a metaphysical theology on the biblical basis of creation and covenant.[24] According to Schoonenberg, the notion that conflict exists between human and divine causality is a false dilemma; in fact, creation is in covenant relationship with God, and through God's transcendent initiative divine and worldly causality concur.[25] Via the mediation of creatures, God's covenantal grace is active in creation, calling persons to their own vocation and mission. Schoonenberg, therefore, affirms that God's grace is mediated to humanity through humanity: 'This is true in the highest

---

[23] Piet J.A.M. Schoonenberg (1911–99) was born in Amsterdam and educated in Holland and the Biblical Institute in Rome. Schoonenberg served the Catholic Church as professor of theology at the Jesuit Scholasticare of Maastricht and professor of dogmatic theology at the Catechetical Center of Nijmegen. Also, he distinguished himself as an architect and collaborator of the Dutch Catechism. As an author he published several books, including a series on the Articles of Faith, and contributed numerous articles to scholarly journals. On several occasions, he received warnings from Rome regarding his christological teachings. Piet Schoonenberg's writings include two christological documents, a monograph and an article, which will be the focus of this section. *The Christ* is his central christological treatise, while his journal article 'Spirit Christology and Logos Christology' provide an overview of the rise, fall, and restoration of Spirit Christology in the modern era, as well as a comparison of Spirit Christology and Logos Christology. Schoonenberg interacts and builds on the earlier pneumatological emphasis in the writings of Matthias Scheeben and Heribert Mühlen: Matthias Joseph Scheeben, *Die Mysterien Des Christentums* (Freiburg: Herder, 1941); Heribert Mühlen, *Der Heilige Geist Als Person* (Münster Westfalen: Aschendorffsche Verlagsbuchhandlung, 1963); Heribert Mühlen, *Una Mystica Persona* (Paderborn: Ferdinand Schöningh, 1964).

[24] Metaphysics can be 'the expression of the mystery that our real world does not conceal behind it, but is itself ... Then it is an unravellment of the question of God and world. It is in this sense that I have attempted here an exercise in metaphysical theology'. Cited according to the translation of Della Couling, Piet J.A.M. Schoonenberg, *The Christ: A Study of the God-Man Relationship in the Whole of Creation and in Jesus Christ* (New York: Herder and Herder, 1971), p. 13. For a thorough explication of his view regarding this subject, see Piet J.A.M. Schoonenberg, *Covenant and Creation* (Notre Dame: University of Notre Dame Press, 1969).

[25] Schoonenberg, *The Christ*, pp. 19-22. Cf. Schoonenberg, *Covenant and Creation*, pp. 99-111.

degree in Jesus Christ'.[26] From this theology of covenant and creation and human meditation, Schoonenberg revises Christology.[27]

Schoonenberg's criticism of Chalcedon, confessing two natures in Christ, regards the confusion caused by the terms nature and person.[28] At issue is how Christ's human nature existed. Did Christ's humanity *enhypostatically* subsist within the eternal person of the Logos,[29] or was his an existence of *anhypostasia*?[30] Considering both of these proposals inadequate, Schoonenberg presents his own solution: a Christology of God's presence.[31]

The christological starting point directly informs how one understands the relation of divinity and humanity in Christ. Because Schoonenberg's 'thinking moves from the world to God, and can never move in the opposite direction,'[32] his starting point is from below.[33] Hence, neither the Trinity nor the preexistent Logos is a valid starting point because the content of Christ's preexistence can be understood only by his earthly and glorified life.[34] Schoonenberg, thereupon, begins with the biblical version of the Spirit conceiving Jesus in Mary's womb; Jesus was a man anointed and filled with the Spirit, a God-bearing man.[35]

---

[26] Schoonenberg, *The Christ*, pp. 44-45. 'God's creation is thus evolution and history. And God's covenant in it is salvific history.' Schoonenberg, *The Christ*, p. 46.

[27] Schoonenberg, *Covenant and Creation*, pp. 112-49. For a helpful critique of Schoonenberg, see Ralph Del Colle, *Christ and the Spirit: Spirit-Christology in Trinitarian Perspective* (New York: Oxford University Press, 1994), pp. 150-52, 217-19.

[28] Schoonenberg, *The Christ*, pp. 61-66.

[29] This is Schoonenberg's real target. Schoonenberg, *The Christ*, pp. 57-58. Basically, Schoonenberg will turn this concept on its head.

[30] 'Then Jesus Christ is again not a man, for what is a man who is not a person.' Schoonenberg, *The Christ*, p. 73.

[31] Schoonenberg, *The Christ*, pp. 91-96, 114-16, 146.

[32] Piet J.A.M. Schoonenberg, 'Trinity-the Consummated Covenant: Thesis on the Doctrine of the Trinity', *SR* 5 (1975–76), thesis 1, p. 111. Cf. Schoonenberg, *The Christ*, pp. 82-83.

[33] Piet J.A.M. Schoonenberg, 'Spirit Christology and Logos Christology', *Bijdr* 38 (1977), pp. 362-65.

[34] Schoonenberg, 'Trinity-the Consumated Covenant', theses 3; 4, p. 111. Schoonenberg, *The Christ*, pp. 105-75.

[35] Schoonenberg, 'Spirit Christology and Logos Christology', pp. 362-63. For Schoonenberg's discussion of the Spirit's anointing, see Schoonenberg, 'Spirit Christology and Logos Christology', pp. 356-58. In making room for Spirit Christology, while avoiding it becoming nothing more than an appendix to Logos Christology, Schoonenberg desires 'to introduce more of the Bible's own theolo-

In order to present his Christology of God's presence, affirming Christ's deity no less than Logos Christology, Schoonenberg inverts the doctrine of the hypostatic union: the divine nature became enhypostatic in Jesus' human nature.[36] The question, then, becomes: 'How can the divine person of the Spirit mediate between the other divine person of the Logos and his humanity without interrupting their hypostatic union?'[37] According to Schoonenberg, this is an invitation to rethink the concept of personhood in trinitarian doctrine, specifically, the Son and Spirit.

Schoonenberg revises triune doctrine through the idea of 'extension of person'.[38] According to Schoonenberg, this concept is found in the Hebrew Bible; the person of God extends in his name to indwell the temple, the nation, the angel of Yahweh, and notably the Spirit, Word, and Wisdom. So, through the Father's extension of person, the Spirit conceived Jesus and the Logos became flesh; in other words, the Christ event brought the Trinity into existence. Because of the Logos' presence in him, the human Jesus became the second divine person of the Trinity.[39] The Holy Spirit, however, became the third person of the Trinity, 'Only in connection with the risen Christ, as gift of his glorification'.[40] Spirit, thus, can mediate between the Logos and Jesus' humanity because the Logos did

---

gy into dogmatics'. Schoonenberg, 'Spirit Christology and Logos Christology', p. 360.

[36] Schoonenberg, 'Spirit Christology and Logos Christology', pp. 364-65; Schoonenberg, *The Christ*, pp. 87-89. 'Because the Spirit is equally divine as the Logos, the Spirit too is not only present in Jesus, but also embraces, contains and sustains his human reality, although we do not say that it is enhypostatic in the Spirit. In Spirit Christology as well, the Spirit is connected with Jesus not only functionally but also ontologically, because function is the expression of being and being includes function.' Schoonenberg, 'Spirit Christology and Logos Christology', p. 365.

[37] Schoonenberg, 'Spirit Christology and Logos Christology', p. 366.

[38] Schoonenberg, 'Spirit Christology and Logos Christology', pp. 367-70.

[39] Schoonenberg, 'Trinity-the Consumated Covenant', theses 30-33, p. 115. This is possible because 'in Jesus this mode of God's being becomes person. Therefore we can speak of an *en*hypostasis of Jesus in the Logos (in classical fashion, but without any sort of *an*hypostasis). Conversely, too, one can speak of an enhypostasis of the Logos in the man Jesus. The mode of God's being as Logos thereby becomes divine person in the fullest sense of the word'. Schoonenberg, 'Trinity-the Consumated Covenant', thesis 32, p. 115.

[40] Schoonenberg, *The Christ*, p. 182. 'Again on God's inner life apart from the salvific history brought about by him we have no knowledge, but on the other hand we can name God himself in his own depth and eternity no other than as he has given himself.' Schoonenberg, *The Christ*, p. 182.

not become divine person until Christ's resurrection, and the Spirit did not become divine person until Pentecost. Consequently, during Christ's earthly life and mission, he lived and functioned as a human filled with God's presence.

Piet Schoonenberg represents the trajectory within Catholicism which critically engages its dogmatic tradition to formulate a model of Spirit Christology. The following contributions of Schoonenberg to the modern discussion should be noted. First, Schoonenberg aims to revise Chalcedon's Christology of duality – divine and human – replacing it with a Christology of the fullness of God's presence, which is Spirit.[41] Thus the basis of his Spirit Christology, God as Spirit, accords with his concept of Christ's two natures: Spirit and flesh. Second, his doctrine regarding the unity of creation and covenant mediated through humanity, places Jesus' Spirit anointed humanity in the front of the conversation; thus, Schoonenberg presses past the doctrine of appropriation; the Spirit has a distinct function apart from the Logos in Christ's life and mission. Third, Schoonenberg integrates Logos Christology into Spirit Christology, inverting Chalcedon, by asserting the Logos' enhypostatic subsistence in Jesus' humanity. To accomplish this, Schoonenberg opts for an economic view of the Trinity: the Logos became the triune person of the Son in the resurrection, and the Spirit became the person of the Holy Spirit at Pentecost. Schoonenberg, accordingly, constructs a Spirit christological trajectory of divine presence.[42]

James D.G. Dunn

James Dunn[43] has constructed his pneumatic Christology in dialogue with nineteenth-century Protestant Liberalism and the

---

[41] Schoonenberg, *The Christ*, p. 123.

[42] Although Roger Haight's Spirit christological proposals are similar to Lampe's, there are also affinities with Schoonenberg's Christology of divine presence. Roger Haight, *Jesus, Symbol of God* (Maryknoll, NY: Orbis Books, 1999). Cf. William P. Loewe, 'Two Revisionist Christologies of Presence; Roger Haight and Piet Schoonenberg', in Michael Horace Barnes and William P. Roberts (eds.), *A Sacramental Life: A Festschrift Honoring Bernard Cooke* (Milwaukee: Marquette University Press, 2003), pp. 93-115.

[43] James Dunn (born 1939) received his higher education from the University of Glasgow (MA and BD degrees) and the University of Cambridge (PhD and DD degrees). A leading and influential New Testament scholar, Dunn served as the Lightfoot Professor of Divinity at the University of Durham until his retirement; also, Dunn has received numerous honors and held prestigious positions, such as the president of the Studiorum Novi Testamenti Societas. Dunn has writ-

twentieth-century way of eschatology;[44] the former focused on Jesus' consciousness of sonship, and the latter addressed the issue of his consciousness of the Spirit. Dunn recognizes that diversity exists in the New Testament between the kerygmatic Christ (Christ of faith) and the historical Jesus.[45] Dunn, however, argues for unity in diversity as well as continuity on the basis of Jesus' sense of sonship and his experience of the Spirit.[46] Dunn's exegesis locates Jesus' sense of sonship in his custom of addressing God as Abba in his prayers, expressing the language of experience rather than formal address, indicating Jesus' intimate relationship with God as Father.[47] Moreover, Jesus' eschatological consciousness stemmed from the presence of the Spirit in him and its power performing mighty works through him; the eschatological kingdom of God was already present, yet not fully consummated.[48] Dunn, therefore, asserts: 'Jesus' consciousness of Spirit is the eschatological dimension to Jesus' ministry Liberalism missed'.[49] Likewise, the quest for the charismatic Jesus ignored 'Jesus' consciousness of sonship and

---

ten extensively regarding Christian origins and what has become known as the New Perspective on Paul. Here, the concern is with Dunn's writings as they speak to the issues of Spirit Christology. James Dunn is one of the most prolific writers in the area of Spirit Christology. This overview of Dunn's Spirit Christology will focus on his work *Jesus and the Spirit* and will integrate other sources which speak to the issues at hand.

[44] Dunn follows Hermann Gunkel, *The Influence of the Holy Spirit*, Albert Schweitzer, *The Mysticism of Paul the Apostle* (trans. William Montgomery; New York: Macmillan, 1956), and Wilhelm Bousset, *Kyrios Christos: A History of the Belief in Christ from the Beginnings of Christianity to Irenaeus* (trans. John E. Steely; Nashville: Abingdon, 1970). However, he takes his point of departure from Adolf Deissmann, *The Religion of Jesus and the Faith of Paul: The Selly Oak Lectures, 1923, on the Communion of Jesus with God & the Communion of Paul with Christ* (trans. William Ernest Wilson; London: Hodder and Stoughton, 1923). Cf. James D.G. Dunn, *Jesus and the Spirit: A Study of the Religious and Charismatic Experience of Jesus and the First Christians as Reflected in the New Testament* (NTL; London: S.C.M. Press, 1975), pp. 12-67.

[45] James D.G. Dunn, *Unity and Diversity in the New Testament: An Inquiry into the Character of Earliest Christianity* (Philadelphia: Westminster Press, 1977), pp. 17-33. This diversity, according to Dunn, exists because the kerygmatic Christ represented a broad scope of development and different understandings of the Christ event. Dunn, *Unity and Diversity*, pp. 232-45.

[46] Dunn, *Unity and Diversity*, pp. 202-205, 228-32, 246-47.

[47] Dunn, *Jesus and the Spirit*, pp. 21-40.

[48] Dunn, *Jesus and the Spirit*, pp. 43-53. Cf. James D.G. Dunn, 'Spirit and Kingdom', *ExpTim* 82 (1970–71), pp. 36-40.

[49] Dunn, *Jesus and the Spirit*, pp. 41-43, 90.

overemphasized his consciousness of Spirit'.[50] Dunn's thesis is clear; the claims of Christianity for Jesus and Jesus' self-consciousness must correlate: 'It is the transcendent otherness of Jesus' experience of God which roots the claims of Christianity in history'.[51] Dunn, consequently, constructs a Spirit-Christology which integrates the historical Jesus with the Christ of faith.

According to Dunn, Jesus' consciousness of the Spirit was primary to Jesus' experience of God, his sense of sonship, and his understanding of mission.[52] Jesus' experience of the Spirit and sonship are not two separate events, but two sides of the same coin.[53] In fact, Dunn suggests that the Jordan event[54] – Jesus' Spirit baptism – is 'understood to be Jesus' adoption as Son'.[55] Moreover, Dunn

---

[50] Dunn, *Jesus and the Spirit*, p. 90.

[51] Dunn, *Jesus and the Spirit*, p. 92.

[52] James D.G. Dunn, *Christology in the Making: A New Testament Inquiry into the Origins of the Doctrine of the Incarnation* (Philadelphia: Westminster Press, 1980), pp. 22-31. Cf. Dunn, *Jesus and the Spirit*, pp. 53-62. 'Basic to Jesus' experience of God, to his self-consciousness and to his understanding of mission, was his sense of *sonship* and his consciousness of *Spirit*'. Dunn, *Jesus and the Spirit*, p. 62.

[53] Dunn, *Jesus and the Spirit*, pp. 62-67.

[54] This phrase will be employed frequently throughout this work, so it may require some explanation: it refers to the event in Jesus' life recorded in the Gospels: Mt. 3.16-17; Mk 1.9-11; Lk. 3.21-22; Jn 1.32-33. Comprehensively, the Jordan event encompasses Jesus' baptism in water by John the Baptist and the epiphany: the rending of the heavens, the appearance of the Holy Spirit descending from heaven upon Jesus, and the Father speaking from heaven. More specifically, when I use the phrase, the Jordan event, I am referring to Jesus' reception of the Spirit, his Spirit baptism.

[55] Dunn, *Jesus and the Spirit*, p. 65. Moreover, Jesus' anointing with the Spirit at the Jordan initiated a pivotal epoch in salvation-history: it marked a transition into the messianic age. James D.G. Dunn, *Baptism in the Holy Spirit: A Re-Examination of the New Testament Teaching on the Gift of the Spirit in Relation to Pentecostalism Today* (London: S.C.M. Press, 1970), p. 25. The Jordan event initiated the new covenant; therefore, for Jesus 'it is not a second experience of the new covenant or of Jesus within the new covenant. It is in fact the event which begins the new covenant for Jesus'. Dunn, *Baptism in the Holy Spirit*, p. 25. In Dunn's *Baptism in the Holy Spirit*, he critiques the Pentecostal doctrine of Spirit baptism: an experience subsqent to conversion-initiation. Dunn firmly joins Spirit baptism and conversion-initiation; therefore, Dunn has functioned as a dialogue partner with Pentecostals regarding these issues. Cf. Howard M. Ervin, *Conversion-Initiation and the Baptism in the Holy Spirit: A Critique of James D.G. Dunn, Baptism in the Holy Spirit* (Peabody: Hendrickson, 1984); Roger Stronstad, *The Charismatic Theology of St. Luke* (Peabody: Hendrickson, 1984); Robert P. Menzies, *The Development of Early Christian Pneumatology: With Special Reference to Luke-Acts* (JSNTSup 54; Sheffield: JSOT Press, 1991); Robert P. Menzies, *Empowered for Witness: The Spirit in Luke-Acts* (JPTSup 6; Sheffield: Sheffield Academic Press, 1994); James D.G. Dunn, 'Baptism in the Holy Spirit: A Response to Pentecostal Scholarship on

concludes: 'If we can indeed properly speak of the "divinity" of the historical Jesus, we can only do so in terms of his experience of God: his "divinity" means his relationship with the Father as son and the Spirit of God in him'.[56] Moreover, Jesus' consciousness of mission came to fruition during the Jordan event, when the Spirit descended upon Jesus.[57] Dunn, consequently, depicts Jesus as a charismatic: Jesus accomplished his mission as a man inspired, empowered, and dependent on the Spirit.[58]

At Jesus' resurrection, according to Dunn, the Holy Spirit became the Spirit of Christ; then, if Christ is experienced, it must be in the Spirit. This is an important statement, but what does it mean? For Dunn, this statement is significant for three primary reasons: to explain (1) resurrection as Jesus' transformation, (2) the continuity of Christ's presence in the church, and (3) his concept of the Trinity.

Luke-Acts', *JPT* 3 (1993), pp. 3-27; Robert P. Menzies, 'Luke and the Spirit: A Reply to James Dunn', *JPT* 4 (1994), pp. 115-38; William Atkinson, 'Pentecostal Responses to Dunn's Baptism in the Holy Spirit: Luke-Acts', *JPT* 6 (1995), pp. 87-131; William Atkinson, 'Pentecostal Responses to Dunn's Baptism in the Holy Spirit: Pauline Literature', *JPT* 7 (1995), pp. 49-72; Frank D. Macchia, 'Salvation and Spirit Baptism: Another Look at James Dunn's Classic', *Pneuma* 24 (Spring 2002), pp. 1-6; William P. Atkinson, *Baptism in the Holy Spirit: Luke-Acts and the Dunn Debate* (Eugene, OR: Wipf and Stock, 2011).

[56] Dunn, *Jesus and the Spirit*, p. 92. Dunn considers the doctrine of the incarnation as a theology of the church's doctrine of Christ. Because Dunn views Pauline theology through the prism of Romans 1.3-4 and 1 Corinthians 15.44-45, he does not allow for any three-stage Christology. In fact, the only explicit Pauline reference to preexistence is when Paul identifies Jesus with preexistent Wisdom (1 Cor 1.24, 30; 8.6, Col 1.15). 'Strictly speaking it is Wisdom alone which is pre-existent. The earthly Jesus was not pre-existent: Jesus was the man that Wisdom became (so also, probably, Phil 2.6 cf. John 1.14).' James D.G. Dunn, 'Jesus-Flesh and Spirit: An Exposition of Romans 1.3-4', *JTS* 24 (1973), p. 59. Cf. Dunn, *Christology in the Making*, pp. 176-95; James D.G. Dunn, 'Christology', *ABD*, I, pp. 983-84. Furthermore, according to Dunn, the author of John's Gospel might have just appropriately explicated the incarnation of the logos by reference to Spirit or Wisdom. Dunn, *Christology in the Making*, pp. 239-47. Dunn, therefore, presents the following challenge to theologians, 'A theology which reckons seriously with the ἐγένετο of John 1.14 must reckon just as seriously with the ἐγένετο implied in I Cor 15.45b'. James D.G. Dunn, '1 Corinthians 15.45 – Last Adam, Life-Giving Spirit', in Barnabas Lindars and Stephen S. Smalley (eds.), *Christ and the Spirit in the New Testament* (Cambridge: Cambridge University Press, 1973), p. 139. Cf. James D.G. Dunn, 'Incarnation', *ABD*, III, pp. 397-404.

[57] Dunn, *Jesus and the Spirit*, pp. 62-65.

[58] Jesus' notoriety, the miracles he worked, his words, his prophetic role, and authority are given in charismatic terms. Dunn, *Jesus and the Spirit*, pp. 68-84.

First, according to Dunn, the resurrection appearances of Jesus were not corporal manifestations; instead, they presented Christ's new mode of existence as spiritual body (1 Cor. 15.44-45).[59] Jesus, therefore, is no longer in the flesh, but as the last Adam he became a life-giving Spirit; consequently, 'it was *in and by the resurrection* that Jesus fully "took over" the Spirit, ceased to be a man dependent on the Spirit, and became Lord of the Spirit'.[60] This is the crux of Dunn's concept of Spirit Christology: the resurrection definitely transformed Jesus; the Spirit-inspired eschatological prophet became the life-giving Spirit.[61] The Spirit has become the Spirit of Jesus.[62]

Second, the Christian community, accordingly, experiences the Spirit as the continuity of Christ's presence; their experience of Christ and the Spirit are synonymous.[63] So, the early church's consciousness of sonship and Spirit are congruous with Jesus'. Paul's

---

[59] James D.G. Dunn, *The Evidence for Jesus* (Philadelphia: Westminster Press, 1985), pp. 53-76. Paul, therefore, had rejected the physical resurrection. 'Paul, faced with the problem of how to present resurrection faith in a Hellenistic context, resolved it by driving a wedge between *sarx* and *sōma*; he diverted Hellenistic aversion to the material wholly on to the "flesh", and successfully neutralized the concept of "body", so that "body" could be used on both sides of the antithesis between "spirit" and "flesh" or "spirit" and "soul". So resurrection, including the resurrection of Jesus, could be presented not as a restoration of the physical, but as a transformation, a quite new mode of existence – as a *spiritual body* (σῶμα πνευματικόν) in contrast to *natural body* (σῶμα ψυχικόν).' Dunn, *Jesus and the Spirit*, p. 121. Cf. Dunn, *Jesus and the Spirit*, pp. 114-34; James D.G. Dunn, *The Theology of Paul the Apostle* (Grand Rapids: Eerdmans, 1998), pp. 62-73. Furthermore, these appearances were 'spiritual experiences', which convinced the recipients that Jesus was alive and gave them a sense of mission and calling. Dunn, *Christology in the Making*, pp. 107-14.

[60] Dunn, 'Jesus-Flesh and Spirit', p. 67.

[61] Dunn, *Christology in the Making*, pp. 159-61. Cf. Dunn, 'Life-Giving Spirit', pp. 127-41.

[62] Dunn, *Jesus and the Spirit*, pp. 301-42.

[63] 'The point for us is that *Paul equates the risen Jesus with the Spirit who makes alive* ... He deliberately says that Jesus by his resurrection became that Spirit which believers experience as the source and power of their new life and new relationship with God. As from his resurrection Jesus may be known by men only as life-giving Spirit ... But so far as the religious experience of Christians is concerned Jesus and Spirit are no different. The risen Jesus may not be experienced independently of the Spirit, and any religious experience which is not in character and effect an experience of Jesus Paul would not regard as a manifestation of the life-giving Spirit.' Dunn, *Jesus and the Spirit*, pp. 322-23. Cf. James D.G. Dunn, '2 Corinthians 3.17 "the Lord Is the Spirit"', *JTS* 21 (1970), pp. 309-20; Dunn, 'Christology', pp. 984-85.

writings, consequently, depict the early church as a charismatic community, experiencing the charismata and functioning in charismatic authority.⁶⁴ This motif of continuity, consequently, leads Dunn to compare Jesus' and the early church's charismatic experiences to modern Pentecostalism.⁶⁵

Third, in the resurrection, the character of the Spirit is molded and shaped by Jesus: 'as the Spirit was the "divinity" of Jesus, so Jesus became the personality of the Spirit'.⁶⁶ Jesus was a human inspired and entirely determined by the divine Spirit, but now Jesus' character has become the clearest expression of the Spirit. Dunn, thus, grounds the doctrine of the Trinity in the experience of the Spirit. Early Christians did not experience the Trinity: 'they experienced *Spirit*, who made them conscious of their dual relationship as men of Spirit'.⁶⁷ Dunn, accordingly, advises trinitarian theologians to consider the primacy of early Christian experience of the Spirit, 'and return to it rather than old dogmas as the starting point for fresh definitions'.⁶⁸ Arguably, James Dunn presents a non-incarnational two-stage Spirit Christology of inspiration.

James Dunn has been a major voice and contributor to the contemporary Spirit christological discussion, representing the modern commitment of interpreting Scripture and constructing Christology according to the principles of historical criticism. Hence, the following observations emerge. First, because Dunn's theological method from below focused on Jesus' experience of the Spirit, his exegetical

---

⁶⁴ Dunn, *Jesus and the Spirit*, pp. 136-96. 'In other words, *the earliest Christian community was essentially charismatic and enthusiastic in nature, in every aspect of its common life and worship, its development and mission.*' Dunn, *Jesus and the Spirit*, p. 194. Cf. James D.G. Dunn, 'Spirit, Holy Spirit', *NIDNTT*, III, pp. 693-707. In fact, the charismatic community is identifiable by the Spirit depicting the character of Christ, and charismatic manifestations marking the community as the body of Christ. Dunn, *Jesus and the Spirit*, pp. 319-21.

⁶⁵ He affirms some facets of Pentecostalism and critiques other practices. For his comparison with Pentecostalism, see Dunn, *Jesus and the Spirit*, pp. 68, 150-51, 161-62, 189-93, n. 91, p. 399, n. 113, p. 405, n. 41, p. 431. Dunn even addresses the issue of whether Jesus spoke in tongues. Dunn, *Jesus and the Spirit*, p. 86. Regarding his discussion of the charismatic features of the early church, see Dunn, *Jesus and the Spirit*, pp. 136-318.

⁶⁶ Dunn, *Jesus and the Spirit*, p. 325. Cf. Dunn, *Christology in the Making*, pp. 159-61; James D.G. Dunn, 'Jesus – Flesh and Spirit: An Exposition of Romans 1.3-4', *JTS* 24 (1973), pp. 40-68.

⁶⁷ Dunn, *Jesus and the Spirit*, p. 326.

⁶⁸ Dunn, *Jesus and the Spirit*, p. 326. Cf. Dunn, *Christology in the Making*, p. 268.

work has elucidated a valid basis for integrating the Christ of faith and the historical Jesus. Second, Dunn presents a two-stage Christology. The environs of the first stage portray Jesus functioning in his life and mission as a human inspired of the Spirit; the Spirit is the agent of his sense of sonship, empowerment for mission, and deity. The second stage began with Jesus' resurrection: his transformation into spiritual body. In this exaltation, Jesus became Lord and synonymous with the Spirit. Third, Dunn has accentuated continuity between the risen Christ and the church, allowing for contemporary charismatic experience.

So, the contours of the first phase of the discussion were primarily shaped by theologians proposing revisionist Spirit Christologies. In doing so, they looked back to the early church to find ancient christological models which might validate their modern christological proposals.

The Second Phase: Trinitarian Spirit Christologies

Since the initial phase of the modern discussion produced Spirit Christologies which significantly revised the Chalcedonian christological confession and triune theology, this was unacceptable to traditional trinitarian theologians. The second phase of the modern discussion, therefore, emerged as various scholars, among both Protestant and Catholic scholarship, attempted to formulate trinitarian Spirit Christologies which complement Logos Christology.

David Coffey

David Coffey[69] represents a trinitarian Spirit Christology which methodologically begins with ascending Christology and integrates

---

[69] David Coffey (born 1934) was educated at Manly, Australia and Munich, Germany. He has served as priest of the Archdiocese of Sydney, Australia, as well as professor in the Pontifical Faculty of Theology and Principal of the Catholic Institute of Sydney. Coffey seems to follow and build on the work of Matthias Scheeben and Karl Rahner, and one can detect a considerable amount of Eastern Orthodox influence. Walter Kasper's Spirit christological work predates Coffey's and to some extent seems to have contributed to Coffey's thinking, see Walter Kasper, *Jesus Der Christus* (Mainz: Matthias Grunewald-Verlag, 1974). Cf. Thomas Pertriano's PhD dissertation, 'Spirit Christology or Son Christology?: An Analysis of the Tension between the Two in the Theology of Walter Kasper' (Fordham University, 1998). Philip Rosato was another Catholic theologian developing Spirit Christology influenced by Kasper, which probably influenced Coffey, see Philip J. Rosato, 'Spirit Christology: Ambiguity and Promise', *TS* 38 (1977), pp. 423-49. The Spirit christological trajectory which Coffey delineates carries the thinking bequeathed to him by his predecessors to another level.

descending Christology.[70] Coffey's hermeneutical starting point agrees with Piet Schoonenberg's: theological reflection proceeds from reality to God, so that it moves from christological revelation to Trinity.[71] Coffey, therefore, posits three trinitarian models: biblical, immanent, and economic. According to Coffey, the NT neither contains the concept of metaphysical incarnation nor the doctrine of immanent Trinity. Instead, the NT reveals a biblical Trinity: Jesus' sonship is functional and not yet an ontological divine reality, and the Spirit functions as an impersonal power entirely filling and empowering Christ. Subsequently, the church's doctrine of the immanent Trinity grew out of the biblical doctrine of the Trinity, thus, attaining the ontological divine order: Father, Son, and Holy Spirit. The economic Trinity was produced when the biblical data integrated with the immanent Trinity.[72] Traditional Western Logos Christology, however, has delineated what Coffey labels the procession

---

[70] Coffey claims that his model, 'at the level of the immanent Trinity provides the appropriate Trinitarian context of the data of ascending Christology and indeed all ascending theology'. David Coffey, 'The Holy Spirit as the Mutual Love of the Father and the Son', *TS* 51 (1990)', p. 219. Ralph Del Colle follows Coffey's method and discusses it extensively in his own treatment of Spirit-Christology. Ralph Del Colle, *Christ and the Spirit: Spirit-Christology in Trinitarian Perspective* (New York: Oxford University Press, 1994), pp. 91-140.

[71] 'All our thinking moves from the world to God, and can never move in the opposite direction.' Schoonenberg, 'Trinity-the Consumated Covenant', thesis 1, p. 111. Walter Kasper in developing his Christology affirms Schoonenberg's starting point, 'He starts out from the principle which has guided my own reflections up to now; "Our whole thinking moves from reality towards God and can never move in the opposite direction ... In no respect do we conclude from the Trinity to Christ and to the Spirit given to us, but always the other way round"'. Cited according to the translation of V. Green, Walter Kasper, *Jesus the Christ* (New York: Paulist Press, 1976), p. 180. Kasper, however, does not agree with Schoonenberg's conclusions and points out several contradictions in his Christology. Kasper, *Jesus the Christ*, pp. 180-81. Coffey agrees with this starting point but critiques Schoonenberg and Kasper as only half correct in that they move from Scriptural revelation to the immanent Trinity, but they are incorrect in that they do not allow a return from the immanent Trinity to Scripture to formulate the doctrine of the economic Trinity; rather, they proceed only from the economic to the immanent Trinity. Coffey also critiques Karl Rahner's dictum of the simple identity of the economic and immanent Trinity. David Coffey, *Deus Trinitas: The Doctrine of the Triune God* (New York: Oxford University Press, 1999), pp. 14-16.

[72] Coffey, *Deus Trinitas*, pp. 14-26; Coffey, 'Mutual Love', pp. 194-95; David Coffey, 'Spirit Christology and the Trinity', in Bradford E. Dabney Hinze, D. Lyle (ed.), *Advents of the Spirit: An Introduction to the Current Study of Pneumatology* (Milwaukee: Marquette University Press, 2001), pp. 323-24.

model: it begins with the unity of persons, then spirates outward through the procession of the Son from the Father, and the Spirit from the Father and Son.[73] For Coffey, this traditional descending model has 'absolutized what was in fact only a relative model of the Trinity'.[74] Because his 'return model' is an ascending Christology extrapolated from Scripture, Coffey asserts that it is a more appropriate trinitarian model, because it moves from the correct epistemological order to the ontological order: biblical Trinity, immanent Trinity, economic Trinity.[75]

Coffey's 'return model' is based on Augustine's 'mutual-love' hypothesis: the Holy Spirit is the mutual love of the Father and the Son.[76] In this model, the Holy Spirit is the love the Father radically bestows on Christ in the event of incarnation, bringing about Jesus' divine sonship.[77] The Spirit, accordingly, created Jesus' humanity, sanctified it, and united it to the divine Son. Here, Coffey affirms the traditional doctrine of the enhypostatic union; then, building on

---

[73] Coffey, *Deus Trinitas*, pp. 28-35, 46-48; David Coffey, 'A Proper Mission of the Holy Spirit', *TS* 47 (1986), pp. 230-31.

[74] Coffey, 'Proper Mission', p. 231.

[75] David Coffey, *Grace: The Gift of the Holy Spirit* (Manly: Catholic Institute of Sydney, 1979), pp. 11-32, 111-14; Coffey, *Deus Trinitas*, pp. 46-65. 'Outreach does not imply return, but return does involve outreach. Hence, a trinitarian model based on outreach, i.e. Logos Christology will be partial, whereas one based on return texts, i.e. Spirit Christology will be comprehensive.' Coffey, 'Spirit Christology', p. 325. The results produce a thoroughgoing trinitarian Spirit Christology. According to Ralph Del Colle, Coffey's constructive proposals 'in my judgment bespeak a mature Spirit-christology in trinitarian perspective'. Del Colle, *Spirit-Christology*, p. 6. In his earlier writings, Coffey designated his theory the 'bestowal model' and later renamed it the 'return model'. Coffey, 'Proper Mission', p. 228.

[76] Coffey, 'Mutual Love', pp. 193-229; Coffey, *Deus Trinitas*, pp. 35-45; Coffey, 'Spirit Christology', pp. 325-38. Of course, Coffey derives his theory from Augustine; however, after Coffey examines Augustine's rendition of the mutual love theory, he concludes it lacks Scriptural support, so Coffey seeks to provide scriptural support for the theory. Coffey, 'Mutual Love', pp. 193-218. For a positive critique and results of this theory see, Del Colle, *Spirit-Christology*, pp. 118-28. Yves Congar, however, examines the mutual love theory and rejects it as an acceptable model for the Trinity. Yves Congar, *I Believe in the Holy Spirit* (3 vols.; New York: Seabury, 1983), I, pp. 85-92. Coffey refutes Congar's objections, Coffey, 'Mutual Love', pp. 223-26.

[77] Coffey, 'Mutual Love', pp. 201-205. 'The starting point of Christological reflection must be the giving of the Son by the Father and the self-giving of the Son to the Father and for the many, rather than the generation of the Son by the Father.' Cited according to the translation of Matthew J. O'Connell, Walter Kasper, *The God of Jesus Christ* (New York: Crossroad, 1994), p. 189.

Karl Rahner's argument for created human nature's supernatural potency for hypostatic union with divinity,[78] he reverses the concept of enhypostasis: the Logos subsists in Christ's human nature.[79] This means that Christ is human in a divine way and divine in a human way; regarding the *communicatio idiomata*, there exists in Christ one theandric nature, and a single theandric act of existence.[80] The Spirit, thus, mediates Jesus' relationship with the Father and the enhypostatic union.[81]

The Holy Spirit is also Jesus' answering love for the Father.[82] The Holy Spirit empowered every aspect of his ministry. Noteworthily, Coffey does not distinguish the incarnation from the Spirit anointing Jesus, during the Jordan event; this is not a secondary anointing: 'The Incarnation and the anointing are two ways of presenting the same event, the one in the perspective of descending, the other in the perspective of ascending, Christology'.[83] The Spirit

---

[78] David Coffey, 'The Theandric Nature of Christ', *TS* 60 (1999), pp. 411-14. 'Hence we can say that human nature as *potential obedientialis* for hypostatic union is realized absolutely in the case of Christ, and relatively in the case of others. There are therefore two ways of being divine: the simply given divinity of the transcendent God, and the divinity achieved by divine grace in humanity.' Coffey, 'Theandric Nature', p. 413.

[79] 'If one may assert that the human nature of Christ subsists in the person of the divine Word, we may also assert that the divine Word subsists in the human nature of Christ. This reversibility serves to contain the mystery of Christ within his human nature which was the intention of Rahner and the Dutch-writing theologians. Further, it makes his human nature theandric, and it allows him a single theandric operation in the Pseudo-Dionysian sense.' Coffey, 'Theandric Nature', pp. 417-18. For his complete discussion of enhypostasis, see Coffey, 'Theandric Nature', pp. 414-18. Coffey is careful to distinguish his reversal of the concept of enhypostasis from Piet Schoonenberg's similar reversal. Coffey, 'Theandric Nature', p. 418.

[80] Coffey, 'Theandric Nature', pp. 419-22, 424-25.

[81] 'What I expressed earlier as the ontological communication from the divine to the human nature in Christ, beginning with the communication of the *esse*, can now be re-expressed as the Father's communication of his being through the Holy Spirit to Jesus in and at the inception of his life so that he comes into existence as God's only-begotten Son. This places Jesus in a unique ontological, psychological, and spiritual relationship with the Father, mediated from the Father to him and from him to the Father, by the Holy Spirit. This is indeed the Jesus whom we meet in the Gospels.' Coffey, 'Theandric Nature', pp. 424-25.

[82] Coffey, 'Mutual Love', pp. 205-18.

[83] Coffey, 'Proper Mission', p. 241. I agree with Yves Congar who sharply disagrees with Coffey at this point. 'This is the anointing which makes Jesus the "Christ" or Messiah. The New Testament knows of no other anointing. Many of the Fathers as well as the scholastics and Thomas Aquinas situated this anointing at Jesus' conception and attributed it to the Word, calling it the hypostatic union.

anointed Jesus in the incarnation, so his theandric nature remained entirely filled with the Spirit throughout his life.[84] Here, Coffey posits the Spirit's anointing as part of the Spirit's proper mission apart from the Logos, and not merely by appropriation.[85] Finally, Jesus' love for the Father is perfected – in becoming the suffering servant – in the supreme act of obedience and love, surrendering his life to the Father through the Spirit.[86] The Holy Spirit, then, is bestowed or returned to the Father as the reciprocity of Jesus' love.

After the resurrection, Jesus bestows the Spirit upon his followers as his own love for humanity. According to Coffey, during Christ's earthly sojourn, the Holy Spirit became incarnate in Christ's human love, as love for God and neighbor.[87] Following James Dunn, Coffey believes 'the character of the Spirit has taken its "shape" from the impress of Jesus' own relationship with God';[88] consequently, as the church experiences the Spirit as the presence

---

In their opinion, Jesus possessed everything for that moment onwards ... What we have, then, in the anointing of Jesus at the time of his baptism is a new act in which his divine sonship was made present – the act that made him and declared him to be "Christ". Before that event, it was not known that he had those gifts which he was able from then onwards to use. He was able to express in an entirely new way, in the perspective of his mission, his consciousness, at the human level, of his quality as the Son of God and of his condition as the Servant.' Yves Congar, *The Word and the Spirit* (San Francisco: Harper & Row, 1986), pp. 87-88.

[84] 'Christ's supernatural operations flow not from habitual grace as with us, but directly from the hypostatic union itself. There is no room in this scheme for a habitual grace in Christ ... If Jesus' human nature was theandric, there was no place in him for habitual grace, for the radical sanctification of his human nature by the Holy Spirit terminated in its union with the divine Son.' Coffey, 'Theandric Nature', pp. 426-27.

[85] Coffey, 'Proper Mission', pp. 227-50.

[86] Coffey, 'Mutual Love', pp. 209-11. There is some similarity between Moltmann and Coffey. For Coffey's assessment of their similarity, see Coffey, *Deus Trinitas*, pp. 110-30. Cf. Ralph Del Colle, 'A Response to Jürgen Moltmann and David Coffey', in Bradford E. Dabney Hinze, D. Lyle (ed.), *Advents of the Spirit: An Introduction to the Current Study of Pneumatology* (Milwaukee: Marquette University Press, 2001), pp. 339-46.

[87] Coffey believes that the Holy Spirit became incarnate – not in the sense of a divine being – in Jesus' human love for God and his love for humanity. David Coffey, 'The "Incarnation" of the Holy Spirit in Christ', *TS* 45 (1984), pp. 466-80. 'Thus, as I have already argued, whereas our love for God and our fellow human beings is a human love *in* the Holy Spirit, that is, charity, the corresponding love in Christ is identical with the person of the Holy Spirit, divine love incarnate in human love.' Coffey, 'Theandric Nature', p. 426. Cf. Del Colle, *Spirit-Christology*, pp. 126, 139.

[88] Coffey, '"Incarnation" of the Holy Spirit', p. 466. Coffey is quoting James Dunn; see Dunn, *Jesus and the Spirit*, p. 320.

of Christ, it is drawn into union and returns to God in the Spirit.[89] If Jesus can return the Holy Spirit as his own love to the Father and bestow the Spirit on the church as his love for humanity, this proves his divinity and equality with the Father. Also, the Holy Spirit must be divine and equal to the Father and the Son in every respect.[90] Thus, the proper inner-trinitarian title of the Holy Spirit is the mutual love of the Father and the Son, and the proper mission of the Holy Spirit is Christ's love for the brethren.[91] David Coffey, therefore, delineates a Spirit Christology faithful to the Catholic tradition which incorporates Logos Christology and trinitarian theology.

David Coffey represents the interests of Catholic theologians seeking to push the pneumatological boundaries in traditional dogmatic theology and harmonize Spirit Christology and triune theology; hence, Coffey has made several contributions to the modern discussion. First, his Spirit christological framework presents the lineaments of a triune theology which accords with traditional trinitarian concepts. His methodology moves his Spirit Christology beyond the trajectories of non-incarnational Spirit Christologies of pneumatic inspiration and Schoonenberg's Spirit Christology of divine fullness. Second, Coffey's contribution of Augustine's mutual love theory has provided much leverage for subsequent Spirit Christology. Third, Coffey breaks through the concept of appropriation; the Holy Spirit has a proper mission in Christ's incarnation, life, and ministry. Thus, the Spirit mediates the creation, sanctification, and union of Jesus' human nature to the Son, as well as the relationship of the Father and Son. Fourth, Coffey affirms that the Spirit became incarnate in Christ's love for God and neighbor; thus, the Spirit takes its personality and character from Christ. Moreover, after Christ's death and resurrection, the bestowal of the Spirit is the presence of Christ among believers. David Coffey, therefore, delineates a Spirit christological trajectory faithful to the Catholic

---

[89] Coffey, 'Mutual Love', pp. 211-13.
[90] 'Thus is acquired the mutual-love theory in its original and primitive form as a theology of the biblical doctrine of the Trinity.' Coffey, 'Mutual Love', p. 219.
[91] Coffey, 'Proper Mission', p. 239.

tradition which incorporates Logos Christology and trinitarian theology.[92]

Jürgen Moltmann

Jürgen Moltmann[93] has constructed a triune model of Spirit Christology which complements Logos Christology.[94] Indeed, Moltmann delineates a Christology established within the lineaments of the 'eschatological history' of Jesus and the triune God;[95] in other

---

[92] Ralph Del Colle builds his trinitarian Spirit Christology from Coffey's proposals; see Del Colle, *Spirit-Christology*. Cf. Del Colle, 'A Response', pp. 339-46. Del Colle was part of the charismatic movement among Catholics and a member of the Society for Pentecostal Studies. Regarding his Spirit christological contributions among Pentecostals, see Ralph Del Colle, 'Spirit Christology: Dogmatic Foundations for Pentecostal-Charismatic Spirituality', *JPT* 3 (1993), pp. 91-112; Ralph Del Colle, 'Oneness and Trinity: A Preliminary Proposal for Dialogue with Oneness Pentecostalism', *JPT* 10 (1997), pp. 85-110. For theologians following a similar trajectory, see Kilian McDonnell, 'A Trinitarian Theology of the Holy Spirit', *TS* 46 (1985), pp. 191-227; Adrian D. Day, 'The Spirit in the Drama: Balthasar's *Theo-Drama* and the Relationship between the Son and the Spirit' (PhD dissertation, Marquette University, 2001).

[93] Jürgen Moltmann was born in Hamburg, Germany (1926). After serving in the German military in WWII and spending time as a prisoner of war, he studied theology at the University of Göttingen; the professors at Göttingen were significantly influenced by the theology of Karl Barth. Moltmann received his doctorate at Göttingen (1952), subsequently, serving as pastor of the Evangelical Church of Bremen-Wasserhorst (1952–57). He began his theological teaching career at Bonn University (1963–67); then, he was appointed Professor of Systematic Theology at the University of Tübingen, where he remained until his retirement (1967–94). During his distinguished career, Moltmann has served as a member of the Faith and Order Committee of the World Council of Churches (1963–83) and the Robert W. Woodruff Distinguished Visiting Professor of Systematic Theology at Candler School of Theology at Emory University in Atlanta, Georgia (1983–93); he delivered the Gifford Lectures at the University of Edinburgh (1984–85) and won the Louisville Grawemeyer Award in Religion (2000). Moltmann has produced numerous books; however, the focus of this inquiry rests on his writings regarding Spirit Christology.

[94] 'In volume one of this series, *The Trinity and the Kingdom of God*, I presented the Holy Spirit in its trinitarian communion with the Father and Son. In volume two, *God in Creation*, I looked at the Spirit as the power and life of the whole creation. In volume three, *The Way of Jesus Christ*, I developed a Spirit christology designed to be a necessary complement – not an alternative – to Logos christology.' Cited according to the translation of Margaret Kohl, Jürgen Moltmann, *The Spirit of Life: A Universal Affirmation* (Minneapolis: Fortress, 1992), p. 17.

[95] 'Here we shall try to put forward the outline of a *christology in the eschatological history of God*. We are giving the name "eschatological" to the coming redemption of the world, which is to be found in the universal messianic kingdom of peace, and in the perfection of creation to become the kingdom of glory. By "eschatological history" we mean the history which is aligned towards this future ... A

words, history's movement, toward its redemptive future, in light of Jesus' relationship with the Spirit: the Spirit-history of Jesus Christ.[96]

Jesus' Spirit-history, therefore, is central to Moltmann's Spirit Christology. This history did not originate with Jesus himself, rather, it commenced with the creative breath of God (Gen. 2.7, Ps. 104.29-30), the *ruach,* which is the divine energy of all life and God's confronting presence among his people;[97] thereupon, Jesus came forth as the anointed Christ, fulfilling the messianic promises.[98] Moreover, Jesus' birth focuses neither on Mary nor the concept of the virgin birth; rather, it rests on the power of the Spirit: the motherhood of the Spirit.[99] Accordingly, because Wisdom and Spirit are feminine modes of the divine appearance, and they are interchangeable terms, Spirit-Christology is also Wisdom Christology. Since in the messianic tradition the Spirit anointed messiah is the Son of God, Spirit Christology is the premise for every Son of God Christology.[100]

---

christology of this divine eschatological history with the world discerns the person of Jesus as the Christ who is on the road, and in all the movements and changes of this history. God's eschatological history with the world is at heart God's history with Jesus, and Jesus' history with God. To be more precise: it is *the trinitarian history* of the Father, the Son, and the Spirit.' Cited according to the translation of Margaret Kohl, Jürgen Moltmann, *The Way of Jesus Christ: Christology in Messianic Dimensions* (Minneapolis: Fortress Press, 1993), pp. 70-71.

[96] 'In the introductory chapters, we talked generally about "the eschatological history of Jesus Christ". We are now giving this more specific designation, calling it the Spirit-history of Jesus Christ: the coming, the presence, and the efficacy of the Spirit in, through and with Jesus, is the hidden beginning of the new creation of the world.' Moltmann, *The Way of Jesus Christ*, p. 73. Cf. Moltmann, *Spirit of Life*, p. 58.

[97] Moltmann, *The Way of Jesus Christ*, pp. 73-74. Cf. Moltmann, *Spirit of Life*, pp. 39-47. There were six leading Pentecostal theologians from five continents that critiqued Moltmann's *The Spirit of Life: A Universal Affirmation*. These theologians found quite a bit to disagree with Moltmann and these articles are very helpful in defining a Pentecostal position; see: Mark W.G. Stibbe and et al., 'A Global Pentecostal Dialogue with Jurgen Moltmann's *the Spirit of Life: A Universal Affirmation*', *JPT* 4 (1994), pp. 5-70.

[98] Moltmann, *The Way of Jesus Christ*, pp. 3-10, 73-74, 91-93. Cf. Moltmann, *Spirit of Life*, pp. 58-59.

[99] Moltmann, *The Way of Jesus Christ*, pp. 78-87.

[100] Moltmann, *The Way of Jesus Christ*, p. 74. In fact, according to Moltmann, 'The notion that there is an antithesis between an adoptionist and a pre-existence Christology is a nineteenth-century invention'. Moltmann, *The Way of Jesus Christ*, p. 74.

24   Spirit Christology

Even though Jesus was conceived, born, and lived his early life through the power of the Spirit,[101] during the Jordan event, he subsequently experienced Spirit baptism, anointing him to fulfill his ministry as the Christ.[102] Through the power of the Spirit, Jesus proclaimed the eschatological kingdom had come near, as he demonstrated the signs of it breaking into spatial reality: the sick were healed and the oppressed were liberated.[103] In the Spirit, Jesus lived out his intimate relationship with the Father as son, affectionately referring to God as Abba;[104] in fact, the Spirit mediated this relationship.[105] According to Moltmann, Jesus' Spirit baptism delineated the *kenosis* of the Spirit – God's creative and vital energy, saving power, and the Shekinah – taking up its indwelling in Jesus Christ. The Spirit, consequently, not only guided Jesus, succored him in temptations, functioned as the agent through whom Christ was offered as a sacrifice for sins, and raised Christ from the dead,[106] the Spirit also participated in Jesus' weakness, suffering, and

---

[101] 'It was not only Jesus' ministry which was *in* the power of the Holy Spirit. He springs from the very beginning *from* the power of the Most High, the Holy Spirit. There was no time and no period of his life when Jesus was not filled with the Holy Spirit.' Moltmann, *The Way of Jesus Christ*, p. 81. Cf. Moltmann, *The Way of Jesus Christ*, p. 142.

[102] Moltmann, *The Way of Jesus Christ*, pp. 87-94. Cf. Moltmann, *Spirit of Life*, p. 60.

[103] Moltmann, *The Way of Jesus Christ*, pp. 91-102.

[104] Moltmann, *The Way of Jesus Christ*, p. 90, writes:

According to the tradition of Israel's messianic promise, it is evident that all this leads to the divine Sonship of the one so anointed and endowed. With the indwelling of Yahweh's *ruach*, Jesus' relationship to God becomes one of sonship, and perceives that God's relationship to him is one of fatherhood. This too is entirely in accordance with Israel's messianic tradition. But something new is added: a new revelation of the name of God. Until the hour in Gethsemane, Jesus in his prayers always addressed God exclusively and with incomparable intimacy as 'Abba', my Father.

Cf. Moltmann, *Spirit of Life*, p. 61; Moltmann, *The Way of Jesus Christ*, pp. 142-45.

[105] 'The divine Spirit who indwells Jesus, initiates and makes possible the relationship of the Father to the Son, and of the Son to the Father. In the Spirit, God experiences Jesus as the messianic child, and Jesus experiences God as "Abba."' Moltmann, *The Way of Jesus Christ*, p. 92. Cf. Moltmann, *Spirit of Life*, p. 61.

[106] Moltmann, *The Way of Jesus Christ*, pp. 178-80, 248-49. For the significance of the cross in the resurrection, see: Jürgen Moltmann, *The Crucified God: The Cross of Christ as the Foundation and Criticism of Christian Theology* (Minneapolis: Fortress, 1993), pp. 179-87; Moltmann, *The Way of Jesus Christ*, pp. 151-273.

death, so that the Spirit was bound to Christ's destiny and in the resurrection became the Spirit of Christ.[107]

The Spirit, therefore, gives the new birth and new creation;[108] also, in the Spirit, Christ is experienced in the community of faith as the risen Lord.[109] The present experience of the Spirit, ergo, mediates between Christ and the eschatological kingdom of God, so that the community of faith becomes a charismatic community; the down-payment of the new creation of all things.[110] Since Moltmann presents Jesus as the messianic prophet of the poor, the eschatological charismatic community lives in the liberative ethic of the kingdom of God: extending liberation to the oppressed, prophetically protesting abuses and evil heaped upon humanity and the environment.[111]

Jesus' Spirit-history is also trinitarian history. Though Moltmann does not reject Logos Christology, he asserts that the *filioque* should be dropped from triune theology because it subordinates the Spirit to the Son, and this trinitarian structure has restricted pneumatology to following the model of Logos Christology. Furthermore, the trinitarian structure revealed in Jesus' Spirit-history was very distinct from the traditional trinitarian view.

> But if instead we note the experience of the Spirit out of which Christ himself comes and acts, and ask about the trinitarian structure which can be detected in that, we discover that the Spirit proceeds from the Father and determines the Son, rests on the Son and shines through him. The roles of Son and Spirit are then exchanged. The Son proceeds from the Father and has the impress of the Spirit. We might say that Christ comes *a patre spirituque*, from the Father and the Spirit – though in fact it is better

---

[107] Moltmann, *The Way of Jesus Christ*, pp. 91-94. Cf. Moltmann, *Spirit of Life*, pp. 61-65.

[108] The presence of the Spirit working in and through Christ is the beginning of the new creation of the world. Moltmann, *The Way of Jesus Christ*, pp. 252-59. Cf. Jürgen Moltmann, *God in Creation: A New Theology of Creation and the Spirit of God* (Gifford Lectures; 1984-85; Minneapolis: Fortress, 1993), pp. 7-13.

[109] Moltmann, *The Way of Jesus Christ*, pp. 76-78. 'The risen Christ lives from, and in, the eternal Spirit, and that the divine Spirit of life acts in and through him. Through this reciprocal perichoresis of mutual indwelling Christ becomes the "life-giving Spirit" and the Spirit becomes the "Spirit of Jesus Christ"'. Moltmann, *Spirit of Life*, p. 67.

[110] Moltmann, *Spirit of Life*, pp. 69, 73-77.

[111] Moltmann, *The Way of Jesus Christ*, pp. 94-104, 274-312

to avoid any undifferentiating 'and' in the trinitarian structure altogether.[112]

So, Moltmann posits a triune structure in which the Son and Spirit coinstantaneously proceed from the Father.[113] Though there are distinctions in relations, the eternal generation of the Son from the Father and eternal procession of the Spirit from the Father are neither parallel nor sequential; instead, according to the concept of perichoresis, they are *in* one another.[114]

According to Moltmann, the unity of the immanent Trinity is seen in the perichoretic relationship of the divine persons;[115] consequently, he forms a social model of the Trinity by using the paradigm of perichoresis. By mutually indwelling and emptying themselves into each other, the perichoretic relationship becomes a divine kenotic relationship: if you see or know one divine person, you also see and know the other two persons.[116] Because this paradigm understands the three divine persons to be 'co-original,' the issue of procession is overcome.[117] Moltmann, therefore, rejects the concept of the *filioque* on this basis: if the Holy Spirit proceeded from the Father and the Son, 'This would make the Son another Father'.[118] However, the dangers of tritheism and modalism are overcome through the perichoretic relationship maintaining a constant balance between persons and community.[119]

---

[112] Moltmann, *Spirit of Life*, p. 71.

[113] 'The one does not precede the other. We shall be talking about the Spirit if we talk about the eternal birth of the Son from the Father. We shall be talking about the Son if we think of the "procession" of the Spirit from his Father.' Moltmann, *Spirit of Life*, p. 72.

[114] Moltmann, *Spirit of Life*, pp. 71-73.

[115] Jürgen Moltmann, *The Trinity and the Kingdom: The Doctrine of God* (Minneapolis: Fortress, 1993), pp. 177-78; Jürgen Moltmann, 'The Trinitarian Personhood of the Holy Spirit', in Bradford E. Hinze, Dabney, D. Lyle (ed.), *Advents of the Spirit: An Introduction to the Current Study of Pneumatology* (trans. D. Lyle Dabney; Milwaukee: Marquette University Press, 2001), pp. 310-11.

[116] Moltmann, *Spirit of Life*, p. 312. 'Their eternal kenotic existence is the condition for the possibility of the temporal kenosis of the Son.' Kasper, *The God of Jesus Christ*, pp. 310-11.

[117] Moltmann, 'Trinitarian Personhood', p. 311.

[118] Moltmann, 'Trinitarian Personhood', p. 313. Cf. Moltmann, *Spirit of Life*, pp. 306-309.

[119] Moltmann, 'Trinitarian Personhood', pp. 312-13. It is significant that this paradigm, also, rejects the Augustinian definition of the Holy Spirit as the mutual bond of love between the Father and the Son: 'the Holy Spirit "eksists" *in* the mutual love of the Father and the Son, but it is not the love itself, because this

Jürgen Moltmann represents a trajectory of Spirit Christology which complements Logos Christology, within a revised triune structure, apprehending Jesus as the messianic prophet. His contributions to the modern discussion are numerous. First, Moltmann's concept of Jesus' Spirit history conjoins the agency of the Spirit in creation, God's historical redemptive movement, the messianic promises, and Christ's life and ministry; therefore, the Spirit-history of Jesus is one salvific journey in God to the *Parousia*. Second, placing his Christology within the environs of Jewish eschatological expectations, Moltmann depicts Jesus' coming in fulfillment of the messianic promises, as one anointed by the Spirit. Third, Moltmann stresses the significance of Jesus' Spirit baptism: through this experience Jesus realizes his filial role with the Father, it empowers Jesus to fulfill his salvific mission, and it signifies the in-breaking of the eschatological kingdom of God and the initiation of new creation. Although Jesus was filled with the Spirit from the incarnation, Jesus' Spirit baptism was a subsequent endowment of the Spirit. Fourth, the significant turn in Moltmann's trinitarian theology is his concept of perichoresis,[120] allowing Moltmann to posit the co-original procession of the Son and Spirit, thus removing the hint of the Spirit being subordinate to the Son. This perichoretic relationship provides for the *kenosis* of the Spirit in Jesus, so in the resurrection the Spirit became the Spirit of Christ. Fifth, he extends the perichoretic relationship to creation and history. Through the Spirit, creation and redemption conjoin in Christ's resurrection; consequently, all of creation is caught up in the process of deification. Sixth, the church is a charismatic community:[121] the presence of the

---

mutual love is already there in the mutual relationships of the Father and the Son'. Moltmann, 'Trinitarian Personhood', p. 313.

[120] Laurence W. Wood, 'From Barth's Trinitarian Christology to Moltmann's Trinitarian Pneumatology: A Methodist Perspective', *AsTJ* 48 (Spring 1993), pp. 53-56. Apparently, Moltmann is attempting a synthesis between the Eastern and Western trinitarian views using the paradigm of perichoresis. He acknowledges that a similar attempt was made at the Council of Florence (1438–45). Moltmann, 'Trinitarian Personhood', pp. 311-12.

[121] It is important to note that for Moltmann the charismata are not limited to the church; all of life is charismatically endowed. 'There is no such thing as unendowed life. There is only the social undervaluation of certain gifts, and the preference given to others.' Moltmann, *Spirit of Life*, p. 180. It is significant for Pentecostals to note that Moltmann affirms that glossolalia accompanied the birth of the church. Moltmann, *Spirit of Life*, p. 185.

eschatological power of new creation extending its liberative ethic in the earth.[122]

Clark Pinnock

Clark Pinnock[123] has constructed a Spirit Christology, within a triune framework, which complements Logos Christology.[124] In his social trinitarian doctrine, the designation Spirit refers both to the common essence of deity and divine person, the Holy Spirit.[125] Within this social Trinity, person signifies relationality, existing in a social matrix of Father, Son, and Holy Spirit; the persons are constituted by their *perichoretic* relations to one another: 'the Spirit is the love that bonds the Father and Son, mediating the relationship and evoking its ecstasy'.[126]

From this community of trinitarian love, creation and redemption flow as triune events, in which the Spirit mediates God's presence and power.[127] The Spirit is the Lord and giver of life, vivifying

---

[122] Similarly, Denis Edwards posits a Spirit-anointed Wisdom Spirit Christology; Denis Edwards, *Breath of Life: A Theology of the Creator Spirit* (Maryknoll: Orbis Books, 2004).

[123] Clark Pinnock (1937–2010) was born and reared in Toronto, Canada. Pinnock received his undergraduate degree in Ancient Near Eastern Studies at the University of Toronto (1960). While studying under the supervision of F.F. Bruce at the University of Manchester, England, Pinnock earned his PhD. Pinnock served on the faculty of the New Orleans Baptist Theological Seminary (1965–69), Trinity Evangelical Divinity School, Deerfield, Illinois (1969–74), Regent College, Vancouver, Canada (1974–77), and at McMaster Divinity College (1977–2002). Pinnock was a prolific author, exploring Reformed, Arminian, Eastern Orthodox, Roman Catholic, and Pentecostal streams of thought. This inquiry will focus on his monograph *Flame of Love* to explore his Spirit christological thought.

[124] Clark H. Pinnock, *Flame of Love: A Theology of the Holy Spirit* (Downers Grove, IL: InterVarsity, 1996), p. 91, argues:

> My point is that Spirit Christology and Logos Christology are complementary, not antithetical. One complements without replacing the other. Logos Christology is ontologically focused, while Spirit Christology is functionally focused, but the two work together. Generally speaking, Logos addresses the Person of Jesus while Spirit addresses his work.

[125] Pinnock, *Flame of Love*, pp. 25-29, 32.

[126] Pinnock, *Flame of Love*, p. 37. Regarding the Spirit's triune mediation, see Pinnock, *Flame of Love*, pp. 39-40. Pinnock does affirm the full personhood of the Spirit; therefore, he is in agreement with Moltmann that the Spirit is not reduced to just a 'fostering environment of love'. Pinnock, *Flame of Love*, pp. 40-42.

[127] Pinnock, *Flame of Love*, p. 60, writes:

> Spirit is the ecstasy by which God, without leaving himself, can enter the world and be present. The world, created by God through the Son, is also a result of the breathing of the Spirit. Spirit mediates the presence of God in

all of creation and directing history toward its teleological goal, new creation. Since creation and redemption conjoin, creative acts are the basis of redemptive acts: the goal is union of the creature with God.¹²⁸ Because the Spirit is present in all of creation, everything manifests his power; Pinnock establishes the Spirit's universal presence and power in the prevenient grace of God. This is significant. By grounding the cosmic activity of the Spirit in prevenient grace, Pinnock affirms the universal nature of Christ's atonement, while maintaining Christianity's salvific claims for Christ.¹²⁹ Moreover, by appropriating Irenaeus' analogy of the two hands of God, Pinnock preserves the Spirit's and the Son's unity and distinction of missions in creation and redemption.¹³⁰

Pinnock's Spirit Christology affirms principles of *kenosis* Christology. Anointing by the Spirit, therefore, figures prominently in Pinnock's Spirit Christology; in fact, it is essential to understand the person and work of Jesus Christ.¹³¹ Moreover, the title 'Christ' signifies anointing:

---

creation and enables the creature to participate in God. The creature, distinct from the Father in the Son, is united to God by the Spirit ... As the Spirit mediates the relationship between Father and Son, he also mediates the relationship between creatures and God. The goal is that we may enjoy the responsive relationship that the Son enjoys with the Father.

¹²⁸ Pinnock, *Flame of Love*, pp. 49-58. 'The process of nature involves sacrifices. Nature is unfinished and groans in the pangs of childbirth. A cross is woven into its creation.' Pinnock, *Flame of Love*, p. 72.

¹²⁹ Pinnock, *Flame of Love*, pp. 61-63, states:

Spirit prepares the way for Christ by gracing humanity everywhere. In such global activities Spirit supplies the prevenient grace that draws sinners to God and puts them on the path toward reconciliation. What one encounters in Jesus is the fulfillment of previous invitations of the Spirit ... One does not properly defend the uniqueness of Jesus Christ by denying the Spirit's preparatory work that preceded his coming.

Pinnock, *Flame of Love*, p. 63. It is important to note the difference between common grace and prevenient grace. The former is God's universal non-saving grace that bestows on humanity blessings of substance, pleasure, and beauty as expressions of God's goodness. The latter is the grace of God that goes before and enables one to choose to further cooperate with grace. Thomas C. Oden, *John Wesley's Scriptural Christianity* (Grand Rapids: Zondervan, 1994), p. 169; Albert C. Outler, *John Wesley* (New York: Oxford University Press, 1964), p. 273; Randy L. Maddox, *Responsible Grace: John Wesley's Practical Theology* (Nashville: Kingswood, 1994), pp. 29, 75, 84, 99, 123, 132, 159-61, 224, 228-29, 241, 245-46, 249.

¹³⁰ Pinnock, *Flame of Love*, pp. 58-60.
¹³¹ Pinnock, *Flame of Love*, p. 79.

It was anointing by the Spirit that made Jesus "Christ," not the hypostatic union, and it was the anointing that made him effective in history as the absolute Savior.[132]

Pinnock's Spirit-Christology, accordingly, depicts Jesus as the Son of God emptying himself of divine attributes, in incarnation, in order to live in solidarity with humanity; thus, he lived as one dependent on the Holy Spirit.[133] In fact, the Spirit anoints every aspect of Jesus' life and ministry; consequently, Jesus' virgin birth accentuates the giving of Jesus as gift of the Holy Spirit and points forward to Pentecost and new creation.[134] Though from infancy to adulthood, Jesus lived as a human anointed by the Spirit, during the Jordan event, Spirit baptism brought Jesus' consciousness of his filial relationship with the Father and empowerment to fulfill his mission.[135] The Spirit enabled Jesus, subsequently, to resist temptations. Christ's miracles attested to the Spirit's power working in him, demonstrating the presence of the eschatological kingdom of God.[136] Jesus' death and resurrection were also in the power of the Spirit.[137] Jesus' salvific journey and mission, therefore, transpired through the anointing of the Spirit.

Connecting the concept of anointing to Irenaeus' theory of recapitulation is integral to Pinnock's Spirit Christology: 'it offers a "last Adam Christology" in which Jesus is empowered by the Spirit to recapitulate the human journey and bring about humanity's fulfillment'.[138] This has significant consequences for soteriology, par-

---

[132] Pinnock, *Flame of Love*, p. 80. 'Let us see what results from viewing Christ as an aspect of the Spirit's mission, instead of (as is more usual) viewing Spirit as a function of Christ's.' Pinnock, *Flame of Love*, p. 80.

[133] Pinnock, *Flame of Love*, pp. 85-91. 'He was the Son of God who nevertheless emptied himself to live in solidarity with others, as dependent on the Spirit as any of them.' Pinnock, *Flame of Love*, p. 85. 'In becoming dependent, the Son surrendered the independent use of his divine attributes in incarnation.' Pinnock, *Flame of Love*, p. 88. 'The Son came in veiled glory, emptied of divine prerogatives, dependent on the power of the Spirit.' Pinnock, *Flame of Love*, p. 100.

[134] Pinnock, *Flame of Love*, p. 86. Pinnock agrees with Moltmann that Wisdom and Spirit are synonymous terms. Pinnock, *Flame of Love*, p. 53.

[135] Pinnock, *Flame of Love*, pp. 27, 85-89.

[136] Pinnock, *Flame of Love*, pp. 89-90.

[137] Pinnock, *Flame of Love*, pp. 90-91.

[138] Pinnock, *Flame of Love*, p. 80. 'The incarnation represents the true divine likeness, and the resurrection signifies what humans are called to become.' Pinnock, *Flame of Love*, p. 100. Cf. Pinnock, *Flame of Love*, pp. 93-98.

ticularly, atonement theory.[139] Salvation becomes more than a change of status; it becomes a participatory journey in *union* with the divine nature.[140] As a result, 'God is not primarily an angry judge needing satisfaction but a passionate lover seeking at-one-ment'.[141] This union with God, according to Pinnock, occurs at the moment of receiving the Spirit during water baptism;[142] also, this is the incipient event of Spirit baptism.[143] The church, accordingly, exists dependent on the Spirit, as the continuation of the Spirit's anointing which rested on Jesus Christ. The charismatic dimension of Christ's

---

[139] Pinnock, *Flame of Love*, pp. 80-83. 'Spirit Christology helps us to take seriously the motif of the last Adam's tracing of our human path and directs our attention to a participatory model of atonement, in which the central motif is union with Christ.' Pinnock, *Flame of Love*, p. 97.

[140] Pinnock, *Flame of Love*, p. 102, writes:

> The goal is that we be brought into unity with God and be enabled to share the divine glory. Spirit Christology invites us to view the cross differently, in the context of recapitulation and participatory journey. It gives us the opportunity to celebrate the centrality of resurrection, conceptualize the cross in terms of recapitulation and give the Spirit back its role in the work of atonement.

Regarding Pinnock's discussion of salvation as participatory union, see Pinnock, *Flame of Love*, pp. 149-83. This is not an ontological union, but it is a personal union. Pinnock, *Flame of Love*, pp. 149-50, 154.

[141] Pinnock, *Flame of Love*, p. 156.

[142] Pinnock, *Flame of Love*, p. 100, explains:

> With a view to atonement, the Father gave the Spirit to the Son, that he might complete a representative journey on our behalf. The Risen One now gives us the Spirit, which had previously been given to him, in order to bring us along with him on the journey that leads to God. All humanity has the potential to be the children of God, because all were included in his representation. What remains is for everyone to be reconciled to God personally and subjectively.

[143] Pinnock, *Flame of Love*, pp. 124-25. 'Baptism is the moment when the Spirit is imparted and when people open themselves to gifts of the Spirit. Baptism is an expression of the obedience of faith and the moment when God gives the Spirit ... Proper initiation is water baptism coupled with Spirit baptism.' Pinnock, *Flame of Love*, p. 124. 'There is not a dichotomy between water baptism and Spirit baptism.' Pinnock, *Flame of Love*, p. 167. Pinnock affirms that Spirit baptism is received during water baptism; however, he acknowledges that the charisms may not be present at this time, so he supports the position that these gifts are actualized at a later date. Although a sympathetic supporter of Pentecostalism, he rejects Pentecostalism's doctrine of Spirit baptism as a 'second blessing'; furthermore, he attests to the significance of glossolalia, but not as initial evidence. Pinnock, *Flame of Love*, pp. 166-73. Nonetheless, his conjoining of water baptism and Spirit baptism along with including the charismatic dimension of Christian experience sounds somewhat similar to the sacramental claims of Oneness Pentecostalism.

ministry, therefore, continues in the church; the church fulfills its mission through the Spirit's anointing and power.[144]

Pinnock delineates a trajectory of Spirit Christology which complements Logos Christology, established in the structure of social trinitarianism.[145] Regarding Pinnock's contributions to the modern discussion, the following observations arise. First, his social trinitarian doctrine allows Pinnock to see Spirit both as the divine essence and a divine person in the social matrix of the Godhead: Spirit is the bond of love between the Father and Son. Second, Pinnock recovers Irenaeus' concept of the Logos and Spirit functioning as the two hands of God in creation and redemption, joining their missions, while maintaining their distinction: the Father creates and redeems through the Son; the Spirit mediates creation and redemption. Third, he accentuates the cosmic activity of the Spirit as God's prevenient grace, working in and through all things, preparing creation for its fulfillment in Christ and new creation. Fourth, Pinnock's Spirit-Christology connects *kenosis* Christology to Logos Christology. *Kenosis* speaks of self-emptying or dependence. Dependency implies relying on something outside of oneself. The incarnation, therefore, made the Son dependent on the Spirit: the Spirit enabled him to live as a human. Thus, Jesus has demonstrated that true humanity depends solely on the Spirit of God. Fifth, Pinnock reintroduces Irenaeus' atonement theory of recapitulation. The Spirit mediates Jesus' salvific journey as the head of new creation; responding in faith to Christ, humans join this salvific journey in union with God. This offers a more dynamic atonement theory, than seeing Jesus' redemptive function simply as a propitiation or vicarious sacrifice for sin. Sixth, Pinnock advocates a Spirit ecclesiology, in

---

[144] Pinnock, *Flame of Love*, pp. 129-47. Pinnock affirms the Pentecostal dimension of this monograph, *Flame of Love*: 'it is charismatic in celebrating Pentecostalism as a mighty twentieth-century outpouring of the Spirit. I think of this as the most important event in modern Christianity'. Pinnock, *Flame of Love*, p. 18.

[145] Myk Habets, a Baptist theologian, also constructs a Spirit Christology which complements Logos Christology within a trinitarian framework. Habets' work offers a good introduction to the field of Spirit Christology and is one of the most recently published monographs. Habets Myk Habets, *The Anointed Son: A Trinitarian Spirit Christology* (PTMS 129; Eugene, OR: Wipf and Stock, 2010); Myk Habets, 'Spirit Christology: Seeing in Stereo', *JPT* 11 (2003), pp. 199-234. Cf. Steven M. Studebaker, 'Integrating Pneumatology and Christology: A Trinitarian Modification of Clark H. Pinnock's Spirit Christology', *Pneuma* 28 (2006), pp. 5-20.

which the charismatic dimension integrates into the church's liturgy, offices, and sacraments. The church is recognized by the power of the Spirit; it functions as the continuation of Jesus' Spirit baptism, fulfilling its mission in the Spirit's power.[146] Pinnock's Spirit Christology, therefore, connects *kenosis* Christology with Logos Christology.

The contours of the second phase were shaped by attempts to formulate trinitarian Spirit Christologies which complement Logos Christology. Similar to the first phase, they looked back to the early church to find ancient christological models which might validate and form their modern christological proposals, demonstrating the fluid nature of Spirit Christology in the early church.

Pentecostal Contributions

Albeit early Pentecostals stood on the theological margins, during the early part of the twentieth-century, protesting the dominant culture and the institutional church's desiccation and theological liberalism, in the 1960's the experience of Spirit baptism transcended denominational barriers with the emergence of the Charismatic renewal among the churches of the central tradition, including Catholicism, producing a global revival of Pentecostal/Charismatic experience and influence.[147] Among Protestant and Catholic theologians, this influence prompted a pneumatological shift toward restoring a proper pneumatic emphasis in doctrine. Though Pentecostals did not directly engage in the early part of the modern discus-

---

[146] 'The church may be viewed in many different ways: as institution, sacrament, herald, servant, body of Christ, colony and more. Here let us view it from the standpoint of the Spirit. Let us see it as a continuation of the Spirit-anointed event that was Jesus Christ.' Pinnock, *Flame of Love*, p. 113.

[147] As Pentecostalism moved from the margins into the central stream (1940's) and experienced its second wave of revival among traditional and Catholic churches, the Charismatic Renewal (beginning in the 1960's), pneumatological research increased regarding every major Christian doctrine, producing a plethora of monographs and articles focusing on the Spirit. Peter D. Hocken, 'Charismatic Movement', *NIDPCM*, pp. 477-519; Vinson Synan, *The Century of the Holy Spirit: 100 Years of Pentecostal and Charismatic Renewal, 1901–2001* (Nashville: Thomas Nelson Publishers, 2001); Walter J. Hollenweger, *Pentecostalism: Origins and Developments Worldwide* (Peabody, MA: Hendrickson Publishers, 1997); Walter J. Hollenweger, *The Pentecostals: The Charismatic Movement in the Churches* (Minneapolis: Augsburg, 1972); Allan Anderson, *An Introduction to Pentecostalism: Global Charismatic Christianity* (Cambridge: Cambridge University Press, 2004); Bradford E. Hinze and D. Lyle Dabney, *Advents of the Spirit: An Introduction to the Current Study of Pneumatology* (Milwaukee: Marquette University Press, 2001), pp. 17-19.

sion, it appears that Pentecostalism's global significance has influenced and even provided some impetus for the emergence of the modern discussion of Spirit Christology.[148] In point of fact, Pentecostalism has been an impetus, either implicitly or explicitly, in every phase of the modern discussion. This is evident in the first phase by Lampe addressing Pentecostal issues, and Dunn's dialogue with Pentecostal theology. Though David Coffey did not explicitly deal with Pentecostal topics, Jürgen Moltmann and Clark Pinnock happily integrated Pentecostal issues and theological concepts in the second phase.[149]

Pentecostals have contributed to the modern discussion by either *using* Spirit Christology and integrating it into their theology or building contextual theological proposals on the foundation of Spirit Christology.[150] They use Spirit Christology to speak to their various theological and social contexts. Since formulating a general model of Spirit Christology is not their concern, and they follow the Spirit christological concepts of their predecessors in the modern discussion, this survey will concisely depict several contributions of Pentecostal scholars, rather than repeating these various Spirit christological concepts and issues. The intent of this section is to acquaint the reader with Pentecostal contributions to the modern discussion.

Amos Yong

Amos Yong's work has extensively *used* Spirit Christology in developing a systematic trajectory for Pentecostal theology. In doing so,

---

[148] For Pentecostalism's influence on the emergence of Spirit Christology, see Philip J. Rosato, 'Spirit Christology: Ambiguity and Promise', *TS* 38 (1977), p. 423; Harold D. Hunter, 'Spirit Christology Dilemma and Promise (1)', *HeyJ* 24 (1983), p. 127; Harold Hunter, 'The Resurgence of Spirit Christology', *European Pentecostal Theological Association Bulletin* 11 (1992), pp. 50-57; Dorman, 'The Spirit Christology of Geoffrey Lampe', p. 10.

[149] Scholars who build on Coffey's work such as Ralph Del Colle did engage Pentecostal issues and theology.

[150] Other than James Dunn's exegetical work, there seems to be a dearth of biblical scholarship focusing on Spirit Christology. Some examples of contributions made by biblical scholars, suggesting the need for more comprehensive research regarding Spirit Christology in Scripture, include John Christopher Thomas, 'The Spirit in the Fourth Gospel: Narrative Explorations', in Terry L. Cross and Emerson B. Powery (eds.), *The Spirit and the Mind: Essays in Informed Pentecostalism* (Lanham: University Press of America, 2000), pp. 157-74; Gary M. Burge, *The Anointed Community: The Holy Spirit in the Johannine Tradition* (Grand Rapids: Eerdmans, 1987).

Yong has integrated Irenaeus' concept of the two hands of God and the perichoretic relations of triune persons into David Coffey's Spirit christological paradigm.[151] In his attempt at forming a global Pentecostal theology, he structures it within the Pentecostal hermeneutic of Luke-Acts, so that Spirit Christology serves as the basis for pneumatic soteriology and dialogue with Oneness Pentecostals.[152]

S.D.L. Jenkins

S.D.L. Jenkins is a Pentecostal theologian who has attempted to formulate a Pentecostal incarnational Spirit Christology, by systematizing Pentecostal experience and doctrine in the ethos of the fivefold gospel. To accomplish this, Jenkins provides a cursory overview of the rise of Pentecostalism in the USA and early Pentecostal periodical literature. Here, Jenkins finds Pentecostalism's ecclesial identity; however, deciding that early Pentecostals lacked adequate depth of christological reflection, regarding the relationship of Jesus and the Spirit, Jenkins has integrated early Pentecostal spirituality and doctrine into the structure of Edward Irving's experience and doctrines of Spirit baptism, glossolalia, eschatology, and incarnational theology. Desiring ecumenical dialogue, Jenkins incorporates Pentecostal intuitions along with insights gained from Irving, Dunn, and Barth into Coffey's Spirit christological model, to construct his trajectory for a Pentecostal incarnational Spirit Christology.[153]

Sang-Ehil Han

Sang-Ehil Han is a Pentecostal scholar who has constructed a contextual Korean Spirit Christology, rooted in trinitarian perichoresis and Wesleyan theology. Connecting Christ's soteriological mission,

---

[151] Amos Yong, *Spirit-Word-Community: Theological Hermeneutics in Trinitarian Perspective* (Aldershot, England: Ashgate, 2002), pp. 50-72.

[152] Amos Yong, *The Spirit Poured out on All Flesh: Pentecostalism and the Possibility of Global Theology* (Grand Rapids: Baker, 2005), pp. 86-88, 109-12, 203-204. Frank Macchia is a Pentecostal theologian who constructs Pentecostal theology from an implicit Spirit christological basis. Frank D. Macchia, *Baptized in the Spirit: A Global Pentecostal Theology* (Grand Rapids: Zondervan, 2006); Frank D. Macchia, *Justified in the Spirit: Creation, Redemption, and the Triune God* (Pentecostal Manifestos; Grand Rapids: Eerdmans, 2010).

[153] See S.D.L. Jenkins, 'The Human Son of God and the Holy Spirit: Toward a Pentecostal Incarnational Spirit Christology' (PhD dissertation, Marquette University, 2004). It should be noted that Jenkins is heavily dependent on David Coffey's work, and Ralph Del Colle served as Jenkins' PhD director.

specifically, with the Korean cultural emotive concept of *han* and its accompanying sense of guilt, Han depicts its affinity with sin and suffering. After juxtaposing how traditional Christian theological approaches and Minjung theology have addressed soteriological issues, in light of Korean socio-economic and political issues, Han proposes his own Wesleyan model of 'sanctificationist soteriology' to address the issues of sin and suffering endemic in the Korean cultural context of *han*. Understanding salvation as love of God and neighbor, Han's soteriology posits a holistic integration of orthopathy, orthodoxy, and orthopraxis. Compassion, therefore, becomes the emotion amicable to Christian discipleship.[154]

Sammy Alfaro

Sammy Alfaro has laid the foundation for building a contextual Hispanic Pentecostal theology on the basis of Spirit Christology by integrating early Pentecostal spirituality and doctrine with his version of Hispanic Pentecostal liberation theology and Hispanic spirituality. Methodologically, Alfaro's proposal flows through four stages. First, Alfaro surveys early Pentecostal literature to demonstrate that Spirit Christology was present among early Pentecostals. Second, Alfaro accentuates the recent shift among Pentecostals, from simply adopting evangelical Christology, to Spirit Christology. Third, Alfaro seeks to establish a Christology relevant to Hispanic culture. Following the work of Hispanic Pentecostals in liberation theology among the poor, the *barrio*, Alfaro integrates the liberative aspect into his Spirit christological foundation. Alfaro, therefore, depicts Jesus as the prophet of social change, and Jesus' death on the cross as his ultimate solidarity with the suffering of the poor

---

[154] See Sang-Ehil Han, 'A Revisionist Spirit-Christology in Korean Culture' (PhD dissertation, Emory University, 2004). Cf. Sang-Ehil Han, 'Journeying into the Heart of God: Rediscovering Spirit-Christology and Its Soteriological Ramifications in Korean Culture', *JPT* 15 (2006), pp. 107-26; Sang-Ehil Han, 'Weaving the Courage of God and Human Suffering: Reorienting the Atonement Tradition', in John Christopher Thomas, Rickie Moore, and Steven J. Land (eds.), *Passover, Pentecost, and Parousia: Studies in Celebration of the Life and Ministry of R. Hollis Gause* (JPTSup 35; Blandford Forum: Deo, 2010), pp. 171-90. It should be noted that Minjung theology means 'the people's theology': Scripture and church history are interpreted from the perspective of the people. Developed by Korean Protestant theologians, Minjung theology interprets Scripture in light of the Asian struggle for liberation. For Han's discussion of Minjung theology and how it relates to his own proposal, see Han, 'A Revisionist Spirit-Christology in Korean Culture', pp. 92-133.

and oppressed, and Christ's resurrection manifests the triumph of justice for everyone. Fourth, he forms the foundation for his contextual Hispanic Pentecostal Christology, by combining the foregoing concepts with aspects of Hispanic spirituality found in Hispanic testimony, sermon, and song. In Hispanic spirituality, Jesus is a miracle worker and the answer for humanity's needs. Through the Spirit, therefore, Hispanic spirituality experiences Jesus as the Divino Compañero, the divine companion, accompanying them on this journey and identifying with their sufferings.[155]

The first two phases of the modern discussion were distinct in focus and purpose. On the one hand, the first phase focused on affirming Christ's genuine humanity and the inspiration of the divine Spirit in his life and ministry to construct a Spirit Christology acceptable to the modern mind and culture. On the other hand, the second phase focused on the agency of the Spirit in Christ's life and ministry and trinitarian theology to construct a Spirit Christology which complements Logos Christology. Contributions by Pentecostal scholars to the modern discussion, however, do not attempt to construct Spirit Christology; rather, focusing on Pentecostal issues, these scholars either integrate Spirit Christology into Pentecostal theology or attempt to construct Pentecostal theology on the basis of Spirit Christology.[156] As attempts to build theology on Spirit

---

[155] Sammy Alfaro, *Divino Compañero: Toward a Hispanic Pentecostal Christology* (PTMS 147; Eugene, OR: Wipf and Stock, 2010).

[156] Although he does not attempt to build a contextual Christology, Clifton Clarke has examined the Christology of Akan African Indigenous Churches, as well as Pentecostalism's impact. Here, it is noteworthy that these churches bear Spirit christological characteristics in several ways. For example, they have a functional Christology, in which Christ's significance lies in his ability to impact the present world by empowering believers and delivering them from evil powers. See Clifton Roy Clarke, 'Faith in Christ in Post-Missionary Africa: Christology among Akan African Indigenous Churches in Ghana' (PhD thesis, University of Birmingham, 2002), pp. 305, 309-10. Albeit Savior, Messiah, and Lord are eminent umbrella christological titles, Christ as healer is the paramount christological title. Clarke, 'Faith in Christ in Post-Missionary Africa', pp. 128-66. It is in the integration of the salvific roles of Christ and the Spirit as healer that Spirit christological language explicitly emerges: 'Christ is understood as subsumed in God as the source of all power and the Holy Spirit is the medium that transmits the power of God into a person'. Clarke, 'Faith in Christ in Post-Missionary Africa', p. 215. In answer to Western missionary criticism that they seriously denigrate the person and work of Christ by overemphasizing the role of the Holy Spirit, Akan AIC Christology responds by affirming that Christ is assimilated in the term God, and Christ's present demonstration and work in Spirit takes precedence over

christological foundations increase,[157] this trend may well be recognized as a third phase in the modern discussion; if so, Pentecostals appear to be leading the way.

The Need, Purposes, and Methodology of this Inquiry

Although Spirit Christology is a modern notion, its heritage has ancient roots. With the rise of Spirit Christology in the latter part of the twentieth-century, scholars turned their attention to early Christologies bearing certain pneumatological characteristics. The distinctive nature of these early Christologies marked the Spirit with Christ's inspiration, empowerment, deity, and preexistent state; in other words, they were functional Christologies focusing on the Spirit's agency and relationship in Christ's life and mission. Noteworthily, these early Christologies neither designated their models nor used the phrase Spirit Christology; this is the nomenclature of the modern discussion. Spirit Christology, therefore, is a concept representing the christological issues and interests of modern theologians and ancient Christologies with certain inherent pneumatic traits.[158]

Christ's historical work in the days of his flesh. Clarke, 'Faith in Christ in Post-Missionary Africa', pp. 92-94. According to Clarke, whereas traditional missionary Christology was at odds with the Akan AIC spirituality and worldview, Pentecostal spirituality and Christology was not only amicable, but it thrived, and a large number of indigenous churches transformed into Pentecostal/Charismatic Churches. Clarke, 'Faith in Christ in Post-Missionary Africa', pp. 99-102. I suggest that this ability of Pentecostalism to enculturate with indigenous spirituality stems from the inherent presence of Spirit Christology in the heart of Pentecostal spirituality. Cf. Clifton Roy Clarke, 'Towards a Functional Christology among Aics in Ghana', *Mission Studies* 22 (2005), pp. 287-318.

[157] Lucy Peppiatt has constructed a contextual Spirit christological trajectory for mission in the culture she defines as post-Christendom Europe. After examining various contemporary Spirit Christologies and delineating the inherent issues, Peppiatt argues that the dual missions of the Son and Spirit in the world, which are integral to trinitarian Spirit Christologies, provide solid ground to build a contemporary theology of mission. In comparing the NT model of mission and various historical models, Peppiatt argues for a Spirit christological model of mission based on the concepts of incarnation and anointing; the Spirit's anointing of Jesus Christ becomes a model for Spirit-filled missionaries. Lucy Peppiatt, 'Spirit Christology and Mission' (PhD thesis; Otago, NZ: University of Otago, 2010).

[158] J.N.D. Kelly appears to be the first to make the historical application for the concept of Spirit Christology. J.N.D. Kelly, *Early Christian Doctrines* (San Francisco: Harper & Row, 1960), pp. 142-45. Norman Hook and G.W.H. Lampe are

Introduction   39

The dilemma confronting anyone seeking to understand Spirit Christology is the lack of unanimity among contemporary scholars regarding either a definition or model of Spirit Christology.[159] In fact, two disparate paradigms of thought exist. One paradigm asserts that the deity of Christ consists of the presence of divine Spirit in Jesus, bringing it into tension with Logos Christology.[160] For example, G.W.H. Lampe argues that this model of Spirit Christology preserves the humanity of Christ while positing that Logos Christology is docetic in nature, represents the Hellenization of the gospel, and irreconcilable with biblical monotheism.[161] James Dunn, accordingly, states, 'If we talk properly of a *Spirit-christology* in the NT we are talking about a *two-stage christology*.'[162]

> A Spirit-christology would therefore in the first place be an attempt to understand Jesus of Nazareth in terms of *inspiration* rather than of *incarnation* ... But in the second place a Spirit-christology has also to be seen as an attempt to understand Christ *as one alive from the dead*, who, on the one hand, still encounters believers through the Spirit and as Spirit, but who also, on the other hand, is not wholly identified with the Spirit ... In short, the Spirit-christology of the NT writers involves and implies Jesus' post-existence (after death) but does not seem to imply or presuppose Jesus' pre-existence (before birth).[163]

So, these scholars support a non-incarnational paradigm of Spirit Christology.

---

some of the earliest twentieth-century Spirit Christologists. Cf. Hook, *Christ in the Twentieth Century*; Lampe, *God as Spirit*.

[159] 'Spirit Christology ... is not a precisely definable christological construction. As one enters into its arena it seems various theological problems begin to multiply.' Del Colle, *Christ and the Spirit*, p. 5. Harold Hunter also recognizes the lack of a definition among Spirit Christologists, but he proceeds to set forth several characteristics. Hunter, 'Spirit Christology Dilemma and Promise (1)', pp. 127-28.

[160] According to Roger Haight, 'Spirit Christology ... "explains" how God is present and active in Jesus, and thus Jesus' identity, by using the biblical symbol of God as Spirit, and not the symbol Logos'. Haight, 'The Case for Spirit Christology', p. 257. According to Paul Newman, 'Spirit Christology entails a relational unity between Jesus and God rather than ontological identity of Jesus and God'. Newman, *A Spirit Christology*, p. 65.

[161] Lampe, 'The Holy Spirit and the Person of Christ', pp. 119-23.

[162] Dunn, *Christology in the Making*, p. 160.

[163] Dunn, *Christology in the Making*, p. 161.

The other paradigm supports an incarnational Christology,[164] which affirms the preexistence of Christ as the divine Son of God, emphasizing the Spirit's agency in the conception, mission, death, resurrection, and continuing ministry of Christ. Clark Pinnock depicts this position.

> When I refer to Spirit Christology, I do so in an orthodox way that preserves the trinitarian distinctions. Spirit Christology enriches but does not replace Logos Christology. It enriches Logos Christology by doing greater justice to the role of the Spirit in Christ. It gives better recognition to the missions of both the Son and Spirit. It neither exaggerates nor diminishes the role of either Person.[165]

This paradigm, thus, attempts to establish a pneumatological emphasis in christological reflection by accenting the complementarity between Logos Christology and Spirit Christology.

Though Spirit Christology's nature is intrinsically fluid and diverse, paradigmatic classification according to inherent traits brings some clarification to the issues. Although these disparate christological models disallow a precise definition, a consensus appears to emerge: Spirit Christology focuses on how the Spirit relates to Christ's identity and soteriological mission; specifically, it elucidates Jesus' genuine humanity and the Spirit's agency in his life and ministry.[166]

Most overviews of Spirit Christology are very concise and tend to depict Spirit Christology as scarce, antithetical to Logos Christology, and dropping out of view sometime around the Council of

---

[164] 'To ponder the Spirit's role as author of the incarnation is to do a form of Spirit Christology.' Edwards, *Breath of Life*, p. 66.

[165] Pinnock, *Flame of Love*, p. 92.

[166] Michael Lodahl, who supports an inspirational form of Spirit Christology, states, 'A Spirit Christology ... affirms that the Spirit is the root, cause and empowerment of the event of Jesus as the Christ'. Lodahl, *Shekhinah/Spirit*, p. 154. In support of the incarnational view Ralph Del Colle affirms, 'Spirit Christology focuses theological reflection on the role of the Holy Spirit in Christology proper. It seeks to understand both "who Christ is" and "what Christ has done" from the perspective of the third article of the Creed: "I believe in the Holy Spirit, the Lord and Giver of Life".' Del Colle, *Spirit-Christology*, p. 3. Also, Jürgen Moltmann declares, 'Spirit Christology allows us to discover that the efficacy of the divine Spirit is the first facet of the mystery of Jesus'. Moltmann, *The Way of Jesus Christ*, p. 73.

Chalcedon;[167] thus, there is a need for a historical theological inquiry to determine the veracity of these assumptions. This inquiry, thus, seeks to further a historical theological overview of Spirit Christology by tracing the development of Spirit Christology, or lack thereof, in the Christian tradition, beginning with the Apostolic Fathers and extending to the rise of Pentecostalism in the twentieth-century.

Since modern theologians have identified certain ancient Christologies as Spirit Christologies because they bear distinctive pneumatological emphases, it is reasonable to assume that the Christologies of other writers in the Christian tradition may also bear these characteristics. Hence, a need exists for a more comprehensive historical identification of various groups, writers, and their primary writings representing Spirit Christology through the various stages of the Christian tradition. This inquiry, accordingly, attempts to identify the various historical streams of Spirit Christology and classify them paradigmatically.

Pentecostals have actively participated in the contemporary discussion of Spirit Christology. This is important to this author because my faith, testimony, worldview, and christological confession have been formed within the pneumatic experience and context of Pentecostalism. Therefore, I readily admit the presuppositions formed within my context. When I came to know Jesus as my Savior, Sanctifier, Spirit Baptizer, Healer, and King through the eschatological presence of the Spirit, it was among Pentecostals. Moreover, while serving as pastor of a Pentecostal church for thirty-one years, in the Church of God (Cleveland, TN), I have observed that among grass-roots Pentecostals, they readily recognize Christ's deity, and they accentuate the Spirit's anointing and empowerment of Jesus' genuine humanity for mission as a model of their own Spirit baptism. Certainly, these are Spirit christological issues integral to

---

[167] After considering NT literature, their attention primarily rested on the period beginning with the Apostolic Fathers and extending through the third-century, and with lesser degree until Chalcedon. Hunter, 'Spirit Christology Dilemma and Promise (1)', pp. 127-40; Harold D. Hunter, 'Spirit Christology Dilemma and Promise (2)', *HeyJ* 24 (1983), pp. 266-77; Habets, *The Anointed Son*, pp. 53-88; Del Colle, *Spirit-Christology*, pp. 39-59, 141-84; Rosato, 'Spirit Christology: Ambiguity and Promise', pp. 423-49; Schoonenberg, 'Spirit Christology and Logos Christology', pp. 350-75; Hook, 'A Spirit Christology', pp. 61-79.

Pentecostal experience.[168] So, this inquiry examines Pentecostalism's early periodical literature to identify the presence of Spirit Christology in these writings and determine how well Spirit Christology correlates with early Pentecostal theology. Moreover, the inquiry's conclusions will be assessed for their possible implications for Pentecostal theology.

Whereas a need exists for a more comprehensive historical theological overview of Spirit Christology in the Christian tradition, the goal of this inquiry is to contribute to this lacuna in the fields of Historical Theology, Spirit Christology, and Pentecostal Theology. I propose the following thesis statement for this project: Spirit Christology is very fluid in nature and transcends rigid boundaries, so several paradigms are necessary to account for its presence in the Christian tradition, and not all Spirit christological paradigms are antithetical to Logos Christology; moreover, certain Spirit christological paradigms have existed in amicable relationships with some forms of early Pentecostal theology.

Consisting of three parts, this monograph focuses on discovering writings which bear Spirit christological characteristics.[169] First, it begins with the earliest Patristic writings and extends to the fifth ecumenical council. Second, it examines the intervening period between the fifth ecumenical council and the rise of Pentecostalism in the twentieth-century. Third, it recognizes certain proto-Pentecostal writers; it depicts the rise of Pentecostalism as it emerged from the *ethos* of Holiness revivalism; and it searches early Pentecostal periodical literature and determines how well Spirit Christology has correlated with early Pentecostal theology. Methodologically, these sections proceed by identifying the theologians or groups whose writings support a form of Spirit Christology, citing their primary texts, and hermeneutically employing a synchronic method of interpretation: permitting the texts to stand as presented and hearing each voice in its context. Later, after being heard in its context, each

---

[168] Since I am willing to risk these presuppositions, I do not think they are a hindrance to interpretation; on the contrary, they may place me in a hermeneutical position to see the Spirit's relationship with Christ in ways not previously apparent.

[169] Although the periodization of a historical theological inquiry is at best arbitrary, the reasons for these particular divisions will become clear as the inquiry progresses.

distinct voice can enter dialogue with other voices.[170] Through each part, the fundamental purposes are to trace Spirit Christology's presence, or lack thereof, and to identify the Spirit christological paradigms and their relationships with doctrinal development in the Christian tradition.

---

[170] Although the survey attempts to examine the texts in chronological order according to the dates they were written, there will be some overlap among the various groups.

PART ONE

SPIRIT CHRISTOLOGY FROM THE APOSTOLIC
FATHERS TO THE FIFTH ECUMENICAL COUNCIL

2

THE APOSTOLIC FATHERS

The earliest extant writings, apart from the documents that formed the canon of Scripture, bequeathed to the Christian church came from the pens of a group of writers known as the Apostolic Fathers.[1] These writers received this designation because of their association with the apostles; it was presumed that they lived before the last apostle died and derived their teachings from the apostles. Their literary nature lacked homogeneity and systematization;[2] they were pastoral in character and developed their theology, in the soil of Hellenistic culture, from a Hebraic worldview.[3] Several of these ancient writings, which among some Christians attained the status of Scripture, made references to Spirit Christology.

Ignatius of Antioch

Among the Apostolic Fathers, the first references to Spirit Christology come from Ignatius, bishop of Antioch,[4] who wrote seven

---

[1] For an overview of this collection of writings, see Clayton N. Jefford, *The Apostolic Fathers: An Essential Guide* (Nashville: Abingdon Press, 2005), pp. 5-26.

[2] 'Nevertheless, they present a unified world of ideas that gives us a picture of the Christian doctrine at the turn of the century.' Johannes Quasten, *Patrology* (4 vols.; Christian Classics, Notre Dame, IN. Ave Maria Press repr.; Utrecht: Spectrum Publishers, 1950), I, p. 40.

[3] For an overview of Jewish influence on the Apostolic Fathers, see Jean Daniélou and John A. Baker, *The Theology of Jewish Christianity* (London: Darton Longman & Todd, 1964), pp. 29-44.

[4] Clement of Rome is probably the first Apostolic Father to provide a reference to Spirit Christology (96); however, since this text primarily deals with the preexistent state, it falls outside the parameters of this survey. Clement quotes Ps.

epistles while journeying toward martyrdom in Rome.[5] Six epistles were addressed to Christian communities – Ephesus, Magnesia, Tralles, Rome, Philadelphia, and Smyrna – and Polycarp, bishop of Smyrna received the seventh epistle.[6] Besides the immediate request that no one would rob him of martyrdom's honor, Ignatius wrote these epistles with three purposes in mind. First, the bishop of Antioch expressed solicitude for the future of the church at Antioch. Second, the unity of the Church concerned Ignatius; thus, each epistle consistently ascribed the highest authority to local bishops: when believers deferred to the bishop, they submitted to Christ. Third, Ignatius resolved to unmask the schismatic groups' teaching as heresy.[7] Primarily, Ignatius attempted to refute two unacceptable

---

34.11-17 to affirm that Christ 'through his Holy Spirit calls us' (1 Clem. 22.1-8). Cited according to the translation of Kirsopp Lake, *The Apostolic Fathers* (trans. Kirsopp Lake; LCL; 2 vols.; London: Heinemann, 1912); I, p. 49. Wolfson uses this text to assert that 'before he was born Christ existed in the form of the Holy Spirit' and spoke as the Holy Spirit through the Scriptures. Harry Austryn Wolfson, *The Philosophy of the Church Fathers: Faith, Trinity, Incarnation* (Structure and Growth of Philosophic Systems from Plato to Spinoza; 3 vols.; Cambridge: Harvard University Press, 3rd, rev. edn, 1970), I, p. 188. *Second Clement* contains similar references to Spirit as Christ's preexistent deity, and it is more extensive in its discussion. It should be noted that unless it is designated otherwise, all dates in this inquiry derive from the Common Era (CE).

[5] Kirsopp Lake mentions that, according to Eusebius, Ignatius' martyrdom was in Rome during the tenth year of Trajan's reign (108), but Lake asserts that this date is by no means certain; the date of origin falls somewhere during Trajan's reign (98–117). Lake, *Apostolic Fathers*, I, p. 166. For overviews about the issues involved in setting a date for these epistles see, Quasten, *Patrology*, I, pp. 63-64; Philip Schaff, *History of the Christian Church* (8 vols.; Grand Rapids: Eerdmans, 1910), II, pp. 653-56; Paul Foster, 'The Epistles of Ignatius of Antioch', in Paul Foster (ed.), *The Writings of the Apostolic Fathers* (London: T. & T. Clark, 2007), pp. 84-89. Although Paul Foster places the date as late as 125–50, it is doubtful that the evidence supports this late date.

[6] For years a controversy existed about the number of letters Ignatius authored. At one point as many as thirteen letters circulated under the name of Ignatius. Eventually, scholarship agreed on these seven as authentic. For concise summaries of this controversy, see Schaff, *History*, II, pp. 660-64; William R. Schoedel, *Ignatius of Antioch: A Commentary on the Letters of Ignatius of Antioch* (Hermeneia – A Critical and Historical Commentary on the Bible; Philadelphia: Fortress Press, 1985), pp. 1-7. For a detailed discussion of this issue, see J.B. Lightfoot, *The Apostolic Fathers: A Revised Text with Introductions, Notes, Dissertations, and Translations* (trans. J.B. Lightfoot; 2 parts in 5 vols.; Peabody, MA: Hendrickson, 1984), part 2, *Ignatius*, I, pp. 70-134.

[7] This sequence of presenting Ignatius' purposes does not reflect the order of their importance, but it smoothes the transition to the present focus of inquiry. Lake agrees with my assessment of the purposes. Lake, *Apostolic Fathers*, I, pp. 166-67. Cf. Cyril Charles Richardson, *Early Christian Fathers* (New York: Macmil-

christological teachings: the Judaizing influence that depicted Jesus as simply a moral teacher within the structure of Judaism (*Magn.* 8-10, *Phld.* 6.1),[8] and the Hellenistic influence, which considered matter evil, which led to a Docetic denial of Christ's incarnation (*Trall.* 10.1, *Smyrn.* 2, 5).[9] Against the former, Ignatius postulated the preexistence and deity of Christ. Against the latter, Ignatius asserted Christ's physical lineage, birth, life, ministry, death, and resurrection.[10]

In this context of christological conflict, Ignatius asserts unity; there is one Christ who unites divinity and humanity, Spirit and flesh, and requires the unity of the church. Nonetheless, the question remains: how does Ignatius understand the Spirit's relationship with Christ in this unity? Six passages in Ignatius' writings merit examination. First, speaking of the deity of Jesus Christ, Ignatius affirms 'there is one God, who manifested himself through Jesus Christ his son, who is his Word [λόγος] proceeding from silence, who in all respects was well-pleasing to him that sent him' (*Magn.* 8.2).[11] Second, Ignatius uses trinitarian terminology – Son, Father, and Spirit – to stress that the laity should submit to the bishop, following Jesus Christ's example of submitting to the Father, 'in order that there may be a union of both flesh and S/spirit' (*Magn.* 13.1-

---

lan, 1970), pp. 75-77. For the theological context of Ignatius' writings, see Virginia Corwin, *St. Ignatius and Christianity in Antioch* (Yale Publications in Religion, 1; New Haven: Yale University Press, 1960), pp. 52-87.

[8] John Lawson identifies Ebionite tendencies among these teachers. John Lawson, *A Theological and Historical Introduction to the Apostolic Fathers* (New York: Macmillan, 1961), pp. 121-23, 133.

[9] Cf. Lawson, *Introduction*, pp. 126-27, 137-38, 147.

[10] For an examination of Ignatius' reaction to these opponents, see Justo L. González, *A History of Christian Thought: From the Beginnings to the Council of Chalcedon* (3 vols.; Nashville: Abingdon Press, 1970), I, pp. 73-75; Foster, 'Ignatius', pp. 88-93; Corwin, *Ignatius*, pp. 103-104.

[11] Cited according to the translation of Kirsopp Lake, *Apostolic Fathers*, I, p. 205. There is a variant reading of the phrase 'who is his Word proceeding from silence'; both Lake and Lightfoot examine the phrase and agree that ὅς ἐστιν αὐτοῦ λόγος ἀπὸ σιγῆς προελθών is the preferred reading of the text. When considering the temporal aspects of this statement, Lightfoot discusses whether this procession speaks of the eternal divine generation of the λόγος from the Father or the incarnation of God in human flesh. Lightfoot decides in favor of the latter possibility. Lightfoot, *Apostolic Fathers*, part 2, Ignatius, *Magn.*, II, pp. 127-28; Lake, *Apostolic Fathers*, I, p. 204.

2).¹² Third, Ignatius bids this church 'farewell in godly concord and may you possess an unhesitating S/spirit, for this is Jesus Christ' (*Magn.* 15).¹³ Fourth, speaking of the incarnation of Christ, Ignatius states: 'There is one Physician, who is both flesh and S/spirit, born and yet not born, who is God in man' (*Eph.* 7.2).¹⁴ Fifth, Ignatius sets forth the human and divine lineage of Jesus Christ, 'for our God, Jesus the Christ, was conceived by Mary by the dispensation of God "as well of the seed of David" as of the Holy Spirit' (*Eph.* 18.2).¹⁵ Sixth, Ignatius affirms the corporeal resurrection of Jesus Christ: 'And after his Resurrection he ate and drank with them as a being of flesh, although he was united in S/spirit to the Father' (*Smyrn.* 3.1-3).¹⁶

Several conclusions emerge from these passages regarding Ignatius' understanding of the Spirit's relationship with Christ. First, Ignatius affirms the union of Christ's dual natures, human and divine. Second, Ignatius' primary designation for Christ's deity is Spirit; flesh and Spirit constitute the christological union.¹⁷ Third, the Spirit is the medium of the conception and virgin birth, incarnate life,

---

¹² Lake, *Apostolic Fathers*, I, p. 211. The designation S/s signifies that although in Lake's translation the letter 's' is lower case, in my translation I use caps to depict deity.

¹³ (ἀδιάκριτον πνεῦμα) Lake, *Apostolic Fathers*, I, p. 211. Lake suggests, 'The translation "a spirit that knows no division" is possible, and perhaps suits the context better than "unhesitating," but the latter rendering seems to be justified by Trallians 1.1'. Lake, *Apostolic Fathers*, I, n. 1, p. 211. Lightfoot asserts that 'unity is the prominent idea in these passages'. Lightfoot, *Apostolic Fathers*, part 2, Ignatius, *Magn.*, II, p. 140. Following Lightfoot, Holmes translates the phrase as 'an undivided spirit'. Michael W. Holmes, *The Apostolic Fathers in English* (trans. Michael W. Holmes; after the earlier version of Lightfoot, J.B. and Harmer, J.R. repr.; Grand Rapids: Baker Book House, 3rd edn, 2006), p. 107.

¹⁴ Lake, *Apostolic Fathers*, I, p. 181. Cf. Aloys Grillmeier, *Christ in Christian Tradition: From the Apostolic Age to Chalcedon (451)* (trans. John Bowden; 2 vols.; Atlanta: John Knox Press, Second Revised edn, 1975), I, pp. 87-89.

¹⁵ Lake, *Apostolic Fathers*, I, p. 191-92. For the significance of Jesus' reception of the Spirit during the Jordan event, see Kilian McDonnell, *The Baptism of Jesus in the Jordan: The Trinitarian and Cosmic Order of Salvation* (Collegeville: Liturgical Press, 1996), pp. 30-33.

¹⁶ Lake, *Apostolic Fathers*, I, p. 255. Holmes translates this, 'spiritually he was united with the Father'. Holmes, *Apostolic Fathers*, p. 122.

¹⁷ See Bousset, *Kyrios Christos*, p. 285; Henry P. van Dusen, *Spirit, Son, and Father: Christian Faith in the Light of the Holy Spirit* (New York: Charles Scribner's Sons, 1958), p. 74.

resurrection, and present ministry of Christ.[18] Fourth, the unity of the church is based on obedience and union with the Spirit. Fifth, Ignatius uses trinitarian terminology to speak of the Godhead: Father, Son, and Holy Spirit. Sixth, Ignatius also employs Son and λόγος as synonymous designations for Christ's deity; the one God has manifested himself (φανερώσας ἑαυτόν) through Jesus Christ his Son (διὰ Ἰησοῦ Χριστοῦ τοῦ υἱοῦ αὐτοῦ) who is his Word (ὅς ἐστιν αὐτοῦ λόγος),[19] so an early form of Logos Christology seems to emerge in Ignatius' writings. Seventh, Although Ignatius clearly distinguishes the Father and Son (*Smyrn.* 8.1),[20] diversity between Logos and Spirit remains ambiguous.[21] Spirit, Logos, and Son, therefore, are synonymous designations for Christ's deity.

Ignatius delineates a Spirit christological paradigm of pneumatic incarnation which integrates an incipient Logos Christology. Ignatius avows that the Spirit designates Christ's deity in incarnation, ministry, death, resurrection, and present ministry; Christ is the union of flesh and Spirit. Ignatius, nonetheless, attests to the manifestation of the divine Logos in Christ, who is the eternal Son of the Father, acknowledging a nascent Logos Christology. Ignatius has no compunction in assigning either Spirit or Logos to Christ's identity and soteriological mission.

---

[18] Cf. *Eph.* 9.1. Ignatius had a strong sense of the present ministry of Christ. In the introduction to each epistle, Ignatius bears the epitaph God-bearer (θεοφόρος), and he testifies to manifesting gifts of the Spirit; for example, the Spirit had anointed Ignatius to prophesy (*Phld.* 7.1-2). Furthermore, the church at Smyrna had 'obtained mercy in every gift' (*Smyrn.* Superscription), and Ignatius instructs Polycarp to 'pray that the invisible things may be revealed to you, that you lack nothing and abound in every gift' (*Pol.* 2.2). Lake, *Apostolic Fathers*, I, pp. 245-47, 251, 271.

[19] *Magn.* 8.2. Cf. Thomas F. Torrance, *The Doctrine of Grace in the Apostolic Fathers* (Grand Rapids: Eerdmans, 1960), pp. 57-59. William Schoedel and Reinhold Seeberg reject the notion of any form of Spirit Christology in Ignatius' writings. Schoedel, *Ignatius*, pp. 20, 60, 132-33; Reinhold Seeberg and Charles Ebert Hay, *Text-Book of the History of Doctrines* (trans. Charles E. Hay; 2 vols.; Eugene, OR: Wipf and Stock, 1997 repr.; Philadelphia: Lutheran Publication Society, 1905), I, pp. 64-65.

[20] Ignatius, accordingly, affirms Jesus Christ's eternal personal preexistence with the Father (*Magn.* 6.1) and identifies him as the divine Son of the Father (*Rom.* Superscription) who came from the Father, returned to the Father, and is with the Father (*Magn.* 7.2).

[21] See *Smyrn.* Superscription; *Magn.* 9.1-2. Cf. Robert R. Williams, *A Guide to the Teachings of the Early Church Fathers* (Grand Rapids: Eerdmans, 1960), pp. 19-20.

The Epistle of Barnabas

The next set of references to Spirit Christology is found in *The Epistle of Barnabas*. Although ancient tradition ascribes this document[22] to Barnabas, a companion of the apostle Paul, its authorship remains anonymous, and its satisfactory determination is not likely.[23] The date of composition[24] and provenance, likewise, present conundrums for historians. Though resolving these issues are arduous tasks, an Egyptian origin is probable since its hermeneutical method bears strong affinities with the allegorical style of Alexandrian interpretation.[25] After an introductory chapter – in which the author greets the readers and sets forth his purpose for writing: 'that your knowledge may be perfected along with your faith' (1.5)[26] – the missive falls into two sections that broach a discussion about the Christian's relationship with Judaism and the Hebrew Scriptures. First, an exegetical section repudiates a literal interpretation of the Hebrew Scriptures and accentuates the allegorical method of exegesis that interprets them christologically (chs. 2–17). According to the author, the Jews have misunderstood the Scriptures, so they have failed to receive the promises and the covenant, but Christ has salvifically fulfilled them and has bestowed these blessings on believers rather than the Jews.[27] The second section describes the two

---

[22] Concerning the genre of the document, there is some discussion as to whether it should be classified as a homily, expository discourse, or an epistle. See Lawson, *Introduction*, pp. 198-99; James Carleton Paget, 'The Epistle of Barnabas', in Paul Foster (ed.), *The Writings of the Apostolic Fathers* (London: T. & T. Clark, 2007), pp. 75-76.

[23] Holmes, *Apostolic Fathers*, p. 174; Paget, 'Barnabas', p. 74.

[24] Possible dates range from 70 to 138. Cf. Lightfoot, *Apostolic Fathers*, part 1, Barnabas, II, pp. 509-12; Schaff, *History*, II, p. 168; Lake, *Apostolic Fathers*, I, p. 338; Quasten, *Patrology*, I, pp. 90-91. The date probably rests somewhere at the end of the first century or the beginning of the second century.

[25] Lawson, *Introduction*, pp. 199-200; Schaff, *History*, II, p. 677; Henry Barclay Swete, *The Holy Spirit in the Ancient Church: A Study of Christian Teaching in the Age of the Fathers* (Eugene, OR: Wipf and Stock, 1997 repr.; London: Macmillan, 1912), p. 18; Robert A. Kraft, *The Apostolic Fathers: A New Translation and Commentary* (6 vols.; London: Thomas Nelson, 1965), III, pp. 45-48.

[26] Cited according to the translation of Kirsopp Lake, *Apostolic Fathers*, I, pp. 341-42.

[27] Quasten, *Patrology*, I, pp. 85-86.

ways set before humanity – good and evil, life and death – so that believers' moral duties become clear (chs. 18–21).[28]

The first section contains two references to Spirit Christology, which are set within the theological context of Christ fulfilling various soteriological types in the Hebrew Scriptures. One reference regards Christ's sacrificial death.

> The Lord commanded this because he himself was going to offer the vessel of the S/spirit as a sacrifice for our sins, in order that the type established in Isaac, who was offered upon the altar, might be fulfilled (7.3).[29]

Here, the author recognizes Christ's dual natures, Spirit and flesh, so that Christ fulfills Isaac's proleptic sacrifice by offering his flesh, the vessel of the Spirit, as a sacrifice for humanity's sins. The other reference emphasizes Christ fulfilling the typology of several symbols that depict water baptism and the cross.[30] According to the author, although the Jews have refused the baptism that remits sins, forsaken the living fountain of waters, and favored cisterns of death, the images of the cross and water conjoin so that living water flows in fulfillment of God's salvific promises to those who hope in Jesus (11.1, 2, 8).

> The land of Jacob was praised above every land. He means to say that he is glorifying the vessel of his Spirit (11.9).[31]

This passage, accordingly, depicts Christ releasing the salvific benefits of the cross through the Spirit upon all who hope on Jesus and participate in the waters of baptism (11.10-11).[32]

The interpretation of these references hangs on how the author understands Spirit and vessel. In *Barn.* 7.3, the author clearly establishes the vessel of the Spirit as the human body of Christ that

---

[28] For a discussion concerning the two ways and its relationship in *Barnabas* and *The Didache*, see Kraft, *Apostolic Fathers*, III, pp. 4-16.

[29] Lake, *Apostolic Fathers*, I, p. 365.

[30] 'The Lord took pains to foretell the water of baptism and the cross' (11.1). Lake, *Apostolic Fathers*, I, p. 379. 'Mark how he described the water and the cross together' (11.8). Lake, *Apostolic Fathers*, I, p. 381.

[31] Lake, *Apostolic Fathers*, I, pp. 381-383.

[32] The author uses a variety of sources to reach this conclusion: Isa. 66.12; Ps. 1.3-6; Jer. 2.13; Ezek. 47.1; 7, 12; Jn. 4.1-11; 7.37-39. For a discussion of these sources, see Kraft, *Apostolic Fathers*, pp. 116-17; Lawson, *Introduction*, pp. 211-12.

becomes a sacrifice for sins.³³ The identity of Spirit, however, is questionable since the author refers to the deity in Christ as the Son of God in 7.2 and Spirit in 7.3. Are these identities synonymous? Examining the issue of preexistence elucidates a response to this question; notwithstanding the writer's affirmation of the Son's preexistence (5.5; 6.12), in their role of inspiring the Hebrew Scriptures (6.14; 5.6; 9.2), distinctions do not appear between Son and Spirit. In fact, the lack of distinction continues in the incarnation; the human flesh of the Son of God is a vessel of the Spirit.³⁴

Another matter of interpretation, furthermore, concerns how one understands the phrase 'the praised land' and connects it to the phrase 'vessel of his Spirit' (11.9).³⁵ More than likely, this passage has a double meaning: (1) Christ is the vessel of the Spirit, and (2) believers become the praised land, vessels of the Spirit, through which the Spirit flows.³⁶ The latter view garners support from the surrounding context; the Spirit is poured out on believers (1.1-3) and God dwells in them (16.6-8), so that the author considers the charismata and the indwelling of the Spirit normative for believers (16.9).

The author supports a Spirit Christology of pneumatic incarnation. The author sharply distinguishes between the divine and human natures: Spirit is united to human flesh. Christ's ministry, also, continues in the church through the Spirit. In other words, as the vessel of the Spirit, Christ salvifically fulfills these soteriological

---

³³ σκεῦος, BAGD, p. 754.

³⁴ 'Christ is the *Kyrios*, the Lord of the whole world (5.5), and has a divine nature. For the body is the "vessel of the spirit" (7.3 and 11.9), an expression which, despite all its ambiguity in the time when it was written, is here to be understood of the divine nature. For the body, as the vessel, and the spirit are sharply contrasted.' Grillmeier, *Christian Tradition*, I, p. 57.

³⁵ Christian Maurer suggests that the actual land of Jacob becomes the vessel of the Spirit. Christian Maurer, 'σκεῦος', TDNT, VII, p. 367. Yet the author consistently ascribes to believers the blessings which flow from Christ fulfilling prophetic types and refuses to ascribe these to the Jews. So Maurer misses the mark here.

³⁶ According to Kraft, 'the "praised land" (11.9) is probably the new creation in which the Lord dwells, although it could also be argued that, Jesus, come in the flesh is in view'. Kraft, *Apostolic Fathers*, III, p. 117.

types so that believers may enjoy their eschatological fulfillment as vessels of the Spirit[37] and partake of the salvific mission.

The Shepherd of Hermas

The next set of references to Spirit Christology is found in the writing of Hermas. Hermas composed an apocalyptic book,[38] the *Shepherd*, and named it after an angel who mediated revelations to Hermas. Several aspects of its composition, however, remain uncertain; for example, the authorship and date of composition lack satisfactory determination.[39] Probably, the *Shepherd* was the handiwork of a single author, Hermas, who composed it within the social context of Roman Christianity[40] and developed it over an extended period of time (92–140). The arrangement of the book consists of three sections of revelations: (1) 5 visions, (2) 12 mandates, and (3) 10

---

[37] 'The body of the baptized, as in Christ himself, is to be considered as the vessel, or the dwelling place of the Spirit.' Stanley M. Burgess, *The Holy Spirit: Ancient Christian Traditions* (Peabody, MA: Hendrickson, 2002), p. 22.

[38] Carolyn Osiek asserts that Hermas meets the criteria for apocalyptic literature. According to Osiek, the key to recognizing it as apocalyptic is not separating its form from its function, for Hermas employs changing needs in changing situations. Carolyn Osiek, 'The Genre and Function of the Shepherd of Hermas', *Semeia* 36 (1986), pp. 113-21. Edith Humphrey provides a summary of literature and an insightful discussion for classifying the *Shepherd* of Hermas as apocalyptic literature. Edith McEwan Humphrey, *The Ladies and the Cities: Transformation and Apocalyptic Identity in Joseph and Aseneth, 4 Ezra, the Apocalypse and the Shepherd of Hermas* (JSPSup 17; Sheffield: Sheffield Academic Press, 1995), pp. 119-26.

[39] Although the work bears Hermas' name, various issues concerning authorship are uncertain. For a discussion of these possibilities, see Hermas, *The Pastor of Hermas*, ANF, II, pp. 6-7; John Christian Wilson, *Toward a Reassessment of the Shepherd of Hermas: Its Date and Its Pneumatology* (Lewiston, NY: Mellen Biblical Press, 1993), pp. 10-23. Prospective dates of origin range from late first century to mid-second century. On the one hand, Hermas indicates that Pope Clement commissions him to write the book which places the date about 92. On the other hand, the Muratorian Canon implies that the author writes the Shepherd during the *time* of Pope Pius around 140. Wilson argues for an early date (80). Wilson, *Reassessment*, pp. 24-61. Cf. Kirsopp Lake, *The Apostolic Fathers* (trans. Kirsopp Lake; LCL; 2 vols.; London: W. Heinemann, 1913), II, p. 3.

[40] According to Osiek, there is a strong Jewish element, yet primarily the church draws its members from the Greek-speaking common people of the city who have a limited literary education; therefore, the specific context is predominantly an oral culture. Carolyn Osiek and Helmut Koester, *Shepherd of Hermas: A Commentary* (Hermeneia – A Critical and Historical Commentary on the Bible; Minneapolis: Fortress Press, 1999), pp. 20-23.

similitudes. The first section prophetically calls attention to the salvific necessity of repentance.[41] The second section delineates the believer's ethical duties. The third section conjoins the teachings of the visions and commandments. The majority of the book, therefore, develops the doctrine of repentance.[42]

The *Similitudes* contain two important Spirit christological texts. One pericope sets within a parable concerning a vineyard (*Sim.* 5.5.1-5). This parable includes several important symbols: a proprietor of a vineyard, vines, fences, weeds, a servant, and the proprietor's son. The owner commissions a servant to tend the vineyard and promises to reward the servant for obedient service. During the owner's absence, because the servant removes the weeds from the vineyard, the servant not only meets the proprietor's expectations but also exceeds them. The proprietor, therefore, declares the servant co-heir with his son, thus rewarding the servant.

As the Shepherd begins revealing the symbolism of the parable to Hermas, the theological emphasis of the allegory is disclosed. The proprietor represents the creator of everything, God. The vines typify the people of God, and the weeds that the servant removes from the vineyard portray their iniquities. The fences surrounding the vineyard depict angels who protect it and serve as friends and counselors of the proprietor and son. Ambiguity arises, however, as the Shepherd reveals the identities of the son and servant; according to the Shepherd, 'The servant is the Son of God' (5.5.2).[43] Hermas,

---

[41] According to Lake, Hermas' prophetic burden stems from the problem and question of believers committing post-baptismal sins. 'In the circle to which Hermas belonged the belief obtained that Christians after baptism were capable of leading sinless lives, and that if they fell they could not again obtain forgiveness.' Lake, *Apostolic Fathers*, II, p. 2. Osiek denies that this is the basis of the discipline of penance. Osiek carefully examines the word μετάνοια and consistently translates it as conversion; therefore, she insists that the change Hermas desires to inculcate is a fundamental personal change in the sinning Christian and not a ritual or repetitive action. Osiek and Koester, *Hermas*, pp. 28-30.

[42] Lake, *Apostolic Fathers*, II, p. 3. Along with repentance, Joseph Verheyden includes sin and the Church as key topics. Joseph Verheyden, 'The Shepherd of Hermas', in Paul Foster (ed.), *The Writings of the Apostolic Fathers* (London: T. & T. Clark, 2007), pp. 66-68.

[43] It is worth noting a textual problem. Lake notes that the Vulgate Latin version adds, 'the Son is the Holy Spirit' (filius autem spiritus sanctus est), but the phrase is absent in the text that Lake follows. Lake, *Apostolic Fathers*, II, n. 1, p. 164. According to Wilson, this phrase does not appear in any of the other versions, major manuscripts, fragments, and patristic quotations; nevertheless, he

then, presses the revelation along by asking: 'why ... is the Son of God in the parable given the form of a servant' (5.5.5)? The Shepherd responds, 'The Son of God is not given the form of a servant, but is given power and lordship' (5.6.1).[44] Furthermore, the Son has cleansed the sins of the people (5.6.2). Then, attention turns to the role of the Holy Spirit.

> The Holy Spirit which goes forth, which created all creation, did God make to dwell in the flesh which he willed. Therefore this flesh, in which the Holy Spirit dwelled, served the Spirit well, walking in holiness and purity, and did not in any way defile the S/spirit. When, therefore, it had lived nobly and purely, and had laboured with the Spirit, and worked with it in every deed, behaving with power and bravery, he chose it as companion with the Holy Spirit; for the conduct of this flesh pleased him, because it was not defiled while it was bearing the Holy Spirit on earth. Therefore he took the Son and the glorious angels as counselors, that this flesh also, having served the Spirit blamelessly, should have some place of sojourn, and not to have lost the reward of its service. For all flesh in which the Holy Spirit has dwelt shall receive a reward if it be found undefiled and spotless (5.6.6-7).[45]

Several important points emerge from this text. First, it sets within the theological context of a parable that emphasizes the activity of the Holy Spirit in Christ's salvific work. Second, concerning the deity manifest in Christ, apparently Hermas attributes it to the Holy Spirit; Hermas delineates the christological union of human flesh and the preexistent Holy Spirit, the original son of the parable with great power.[46] Third, the identities of the Son of God and Holy

---

examines the problem and concludes that the phrase is authentic. Wilson, *Reassessment*, pp. 107-109. Since the evidence for this phrase is inconclusive, this inquiry will not bring it into the discussion.

[44] These three successive references are cited according to the translation of Kirsopp Lake, *Apostolic Fathers*, II, pp. 165-67.

[45] Lake, *Apostolic Fathers*, II, pp. 167-69.

[46] According to Pelikan, 'The use of "Spirit" for the divine in Christ was most prominent in those early Christian writers which still showed marks of the Jewish origins of Christianity; at the same time even these writings also echoed the trinitarian language of the church'. Pelikan, *Christian Tradition*, I, pp. 185-86. J.N.D. Kelly agrees and cites these texts in Hermas as an example to describe Spirit Christology during this time period, 'By this is meant the view that in the histori-

58 Spirit Christology

Spirit seem to coalesce. Fourth, a nascent form of adoptionistic Christology seems to emerge: the servant (flesh) becomes another son and companion of the Spirit.[47]

Regarding the issue of adoptionism in Hermas, because Hermas mixes his metaphors – son, servant, Holy Spirit, and Son of God – and uses them interchangeably, this ambiguous language has led some scholars to an ambivalent position: adoptionism is difficult to prove or disprove.[48] Also, considering the soteriological context, Lage Pernveden has suggested that Hermas' use of Son of God does not imply an ontological attribution, but rather it depicts a soteriological concept.[49] Hermas, nevertheless, seems to use adoptionistic language to indicate that at some point, probably the resurrection, God exalts the obedient servant and declares him Son of God.[50]

In the other pericope, Hermas begins to summarize the revelations he has received thus far and bring together the messages of the visions and similitudes; hence, the Shepherd sets the theological

---

cal Jesus Christ the pre-existent Son of God, Who is divine Spirit, united himself with human nature'. Kelly, *Doctrines*, p. 143. Reinhold Seeberg disagrees: 'The pre-existent Christ was not "the Holy Spirit," but a pre-existent holy spiritual being'. Seeberg and Hay, *History* I, p. 59.

[47] Martin Dibelius stresses the blending of Spirit Christology and adoptionistic Christology. Martin Dibelius, *Der Hirt Des Hermas* (Die Apostolischen Väter; 4 vols.; Tübingen: Mohr, 1923), IV, p. 573. Adolf Harnack states that, in Hermas, adoptionistic Christology and Spirit Christology 'came very near each other when the Spirit of God implanted in the man Jesus was conceived as the pre-existent Son of God ... Yet, in spite of all transitional forms, the two Christologies may be clearly distinguished'. Adolf von Harnack, *History of Dogma* (trans. Neil Buchanan; 7 vols.; Eugene, OR: Wipf and Stock, 1997 repr.; Boston: Little, Brown, 3rd edn, 1901), I, pp. 193-94.

[48] Pelikan, *Christian Tradition*, I, p. 175; Lawson, *Introduction*, pp. 252-53. 'It is unlikely that even Hermas was an adoptionist in the strict sense.' Kelly, *Doctrines*, p. 143.

[49] Lage Pernveden concludes that Hermas stresses the pneumatic attribution in the work of Christ and not any consubstantial nature of the Son. 'This means that the term Son of God is a purely soteriological concept with a content which is thought of dynamically rather than statically and ontologically.' Lage Pernveden, *The Concept of the Church in the Shepherd of Hermas* (Lund: C.W.K. Gleerup, 1966), p. 49.

[50] Harnack, *Dogma*, I, p. 191, n. 3. Wilson suggests, 'The adaptable pneumatic Christology of Sim. V:6:5-7 and Sim. IX:1:1 serves as a bridge between the adoptionistic Christology of Sim. V and the pre-existent Christology of Sim. IX'. Wilson, *Reassessment*, p. 127. Cf. Grillmeier, *Christian Tradition*, I, pp. 54-56.

context of this important Spirit christological text by reaching back to the revelation of the Church, in *Vis.* 3.

> After I had written the commandments and parables of the shepherd, the angel of repentance, he came to me and said to me: I wish to show you what the Holy Spirit which spoke with you in the form of the Church showed you, for that Spirit is the Son of God (*Sim.* 9.1.1).[51]

In *Vis.* 3, a lady reveals to Hermas the building of a tower from different types of stones. The lady explains to Hermas that the stones depict the repentant that comprise the church, and the tower represents her, the Church (*Vis.* 3.3.3), but now, in *Sim.* 9.1.1, the lady is revealed as the Holy Spirit, and the Holy Spirit is also the Son. The context of this passage, therefore, accentuates the soteriological role of the Holy Spirit in repentance and placing believers (stones) into the church (the tower).

Hermas delineates a Spirit christological paradigm of pneumatic incarnation. In the incarnation preexistent Spirit united with human flesh, identifying Christ as Son of God and savior, so that Son and Spirit are synonymous designations identifying Christ's deity. In Christ's soteriological mission the flesh cooperates with the Spirit, cleansing humanity's iniquities, and becomes another Son through the indwelling of the Spirit. According to Hermas, believers also become sons by the indwelling of the Spirit; in fact, if believers bear the name of the Son but not his power, they bear his name in vain (*Sim.* 9.13.2-5). For Hermas, Spirit is essential to Christ's identity and salvific mission.

The Second Epistle of Clement to the Corinthians

Owing to the high esteem in which Clement of Rome was held, several pseudonymous documents were attributed to Clementine authorship, including *The Second Epistle of Clement to the Corinthians*.[52] Clement had previously written to the church at Corinth to settle an

---

[51] Lake, *Apostolic Fathers*, II, p. 217.
[52] Along with *2 Clement*, there are three documents attributed to Clement which originated in the early third century: *The Two Letters Addressed to Virgins*, *The Twenty Homilies*, and *The Ten Books of Recognitions*. For a concise overview of these three latter writings, see Quasten, *Patrology*, I, pp. 58-63.

internal dispute (about 96). Since conflict again arose in their midst, around 150, an elder within the Corinthian Church wrote 2 *Clement* and attributed it to Clement to bolster its authority.[53] Because of its literary nature, many scholars have come to classify the document as a homily rather than an epistle.[54]

As with most sermons, the introduction defines the subject and context: 'Brothers, we must think of Jesus Christ as of God, as of "the Judge of the living and the dead" and we must not think little of our salvation' (1.1).[55] According to the author, in the light of deity becoming flesh to save humanity and the future resurrection, believers have an ethical responsibility to live a life in the flesh that honors Christ. In fact, this call to ethical responsibility motivates the author's christological and soteriological statements. Although some evil teachers among them 'prefer the pleasures of the present to the promises of the future' (10.3),[56] the author assures believers that what they do in the flesh affects their salvific relationship with God. The author, therefore, reminds the audience that they have received salvation while in a fleshly state, and the flesh will be judged and will rise again; consequently, they should guard the flesh as a temple of God (9.1-3).

---

[53] This document was preserved along with 1 *Clement* in the Corinthian Church which strengthened a claim of Clementine authorship. For a brief discussion of this introductory material, see *2 Clem.* Lake, *Apostolic Fathers*, I, pp. 125-27; Clement, *The Second Epistle of Clement*, ANF, VII, pp. 511-15. For a more thorough discussion, see Lightfoot, *Apostolic Fathers*, part 1, 2 Clem., II, pp. 191-210. Karl Donfried goes against the prevailing view and posits a date about 98–100. Karl Paul Donfried, *The Setting of Second Clement in Early Christianity* (NovTSup 38; Leiden: E.J. Brill, 1974), pp. 1-19.

[54] Paul Parvis, '2 Clement and the Meaning of the Christian Homily', in Paul Foster (ed.), *The Writings of the Apostolic Fathers* (London: T. & T. Clark, 2007), pp. 34-35. Donfried contends that the term homily is vague and ambiguous; instead he suggests the use of hortatory address. Donfried, *Setting*, pp. 19-48.

[55] Cited according to the translation of Kirsopp Lake, *Apostolic Fathers*, I, p. 129.

[56] Lake, *Apostolic Fathers*, I, pp. 143-45. Parvis notes that these teachers display typical second-century Gnostic and docetic tendencies. Parvis, '2 Clement', p. 38. Lightfoot agrees with this observation. Lightfoot, *Apostolic Fathers*, part 1, 2 Clem., II, p. 203.

> If Christ, the Lord who saved us, though he was originally S/spirit, became flesh and so called us, so also we shall receive our reward in this flesh (9.5).[57]

The author, furthermore, extends the soteriological value of Christ's flesh and identifies it with the Church which has also pre-existed with Christ.

> Now if we say that the flesh is the Church, and the Spirit is Christ, of course he who has abused the flesh, has abused the Church. Such a one therefore will not receive the Spirit, which is Christ (14.4).[58]

Several conclusions can be drawn from these texts. First, the author attests to Christ's dual natures, human and divine. Second, the context emphasizes the preexistence of the Spirit, Christ, and the Church; probably, in response to teachers disseminating ideas with Gnostic characteristics, the soteriological and ethical implications of their fleshly manifestations for believers are accentuated.[59] In other words, how one responds to the flesh, the Church, represents that person's response to the Spirit which is Christ. Third, these passages attribute the deity of Christ to the Spirit;[60] the divine nature pre-existed as Spirit and was incarnated in human flesh.

The author's Spirit Christology supports a paradigm of pneumatic incarnation. The author, however, accentuates the significance of Christ's flesh in salvific mission: in the reality of human flesh, Christ redeemed humanity; thus, believers must honor Christ in their flesh. The preexistent Spirit, accordingly, united to flesh in Christ to save humanity.

---

[57] Lake, *Apostolic Fathers*, I, p. 143. The adjective πρῶτον stands in the attributive position to πνεῦμα, ascribing the preexistent mode of Christ to Spirit.
[58] Lake, *Apostolic Fathers*, I, p. 153. The author identifies the Spirit (τοῦ πνεύματος) with Christ (ὅ ἐστιν ὁ Χριστός).
[59] Lawson, *Introduction*, p. 187; Richardson, *Fathers*, pp. 183, 188, 199.
[60] Wolfson, *Church Fathers*, I, p. 188; Robert M. Grant, Graham, Holt H., *The Apostolic Fathers: A New Translation and Commentary* (6 vols.; London: Thomas Nelson, 1965), II, pp. 120, 125-26. Seeberg concedes that as 'The passage stands it appears to identify Christ with the Holy Ghost,' but he insists there is a distinction. Seeberg and Hay, *History* I, n. 1, p. 77.

Conclusion

Even though these Apostolic Fathers support a form of Spirit Christology, they speak with distinct voices; they agree and differ among themselves.[61] They agree, for example, that Christ is present in the church through the Spirit. These Fathers, also, agree that Spirit concerns the manifestation of deity in the salvific mission, but they differ about the identity of the manifestant. This important observation accentuates two methods along which Spirit Christology proceeds from the Apostolic Fathers. On the one hand, it moves along the path of pneumatic incarnation. This method, however, allows for two possible identifications of the divine Spirit incarnate in Christ: (1) the Holy Spirit, and (2) the nature of God which is Spirit. On the other hand, Spirit Christology progresses along the path which allows for its integration with an incipient Logos Christology.[62] This method recognizes Spirit and λόγος as the identity of deity manifest in Christ and acknowledges the dynamic activity of the Holy Spirit as the medium of the salvific mission, a move toward a Spirit Christology of pneumatic mediation which integrates Logos Christology. Although both modes of Spirit Christology continue, the latter will receive more attention from the next group of writers.

---

[61] For a discussion of the factors that contribute to this diversity, see Jefford, *Apostolic Fathers*, pp. 69-70.

[62] Hendrik Berkhof acknowledges only a pneumatic Christology among these Fathers. Berkhof, *The Doctrine of the Holy Spirit*, p. 20.

3

THE EARLY APOLOGISTS

Because of the nature and purpose of their writings, the next group of authors earned the epithet, Apologists, as they attempted to define, express, and defend Christianity during the political and social struggles of their time. Owing to pagans misunderstanding and misrepresenting Christian beliefs and practices, Christians faced a number of fallacious charges; for example, the accusations of incest, licentiousness, cannibalism, anarchy, and atheism aroused the ire of culture and state against the Christian church. These defenders of the Christian faith, therefore, engaged popular culture and Roman emperors in order to dispel these calumnies and dissipate persecution. Since these Apologists were children of their age, they appropriated the terms and symbols of Greek philosophy as tools to defend Christian practices, to attack pagan beliefs, and to explain rationally to their antagonists and earnest inquirers the fundamental monotheistic Christian beliefs about the revelation of God in Christ.[1]

---

[1] For information concerning the historical, cultural, political, and philosophical influences motivating the Early Greek Apologists see Robert M. Grant, *Greek Apologists of the Second Century* (Philadelphia: Westminster Press, 1988), pp. 9-43; González, *Christian Thought*, I, pp. 97-100; Louis Berkhof, *The History of Christian Doctrines* (2002 repr.; Carlisle, PA: Banner of Truth Trust, 1937), pp. 56-59; Quasten, *Patrology*, I, 186-89; Roger E. Olson, *The Story of Christian Theology: Twenty Centuries of Tradition & Reform* (Downers Grove, IL: InterVarsity, 1999), pp. 54-57.

Aristides of Athens

Among the Greek Apologists of the second century, Aristides of Athens bequeathed to posterity the first references to Spirit Christology in an apology that he addressed to the Roman emperor Hadrian. Aristides probably presented his defense of the Christian faith to Hadrian when he visited Athens (124–25), during his eleven year imperial tour.[2] The apology contains four movements. First, relying on typical apophatic theological concepts derived from Middle Platonic philosophy, Aristides related the nature of the true God, who has no beginning, end, composition, needs, passions, and infirmities (ch. 1). Second, Aristides demonstrated how the polytheistic worship of the Chaldeans, Greeks, and the Egyptians was contrary to sound reason; these false Gods neither have power to protect themselves nor their worshippers, and they exemplify licentiousness (chs. 2–13). Third, although the Jews rightly affirmed the monotheistic worship of the true God, they succumbed to idolatry by worshipping angels and Jewish laws rather than God; furthermore, the Jews failed because they denied the deity of Christ (ch. 14). Fourth, above all the people of the earth, the Christians have found the truth which induces them to live righteously, love one another, and preserve the world through their prayers: God, the creator of all things, is revealed in Jesus Christ (chs. 15–17).

As Aristides begins to explicate this revelation, three passages in chapter fifteen narrate pneumatic christological relationships.

> Christians trace their origin from the Lord Jesus Christ. And He is acknowledged by the Holy Spirit to be the son of the most high God, who came down from heaven for the salvation of men. And being born of a pure virgin, unbegotten and immacu-

---

[2] Aristides' contribution, therefore, represents the earliest extant apology of the Christian faith. For a concise overview of the issues involved in assigning a date to this apology, see Aristides, 'The Apology of Aristides', ANF, IX, p. 261; Grant, *Apologists*, p. 35, 38-39; Schaff, *History*, II, p. 709. J.R. Harris places the date early in the reign of Antoninus Pius, about 160. J. Rendel Harris and J. Armitage Robinson (eds.), *The Apology of Aristides on Behalf of the Christians: From a Syriac MS. Preserved on Mount Sinai, with an Appendix Containing the Main Portion of the Original Greek Text* (Piscataway, NJ: Gorgias Press, 2004), pp. 7-17.

late, He assumed flesh and revealed himself among men (ch. 15).³

The connections in the text suggest that in the incarnation the Holy Spirit confesses (ὁμολογεῖται) the deity of Christ, and the Son of God descends from heaven by the Holy Spirit (ἐν πνεύματι ἁγίῳ ἀπ' οὐρανοῦ καταβὰς). Of course, it is possible to translate this excerpt as J.N.D. Kelly does: 'it is confessed that this Son of the most high God descended from heaven as holy S/spirit'.⁴ On this reading of the text, in the incarnation the Spirit unites with human flesh and reveals Christ as the savior of humanity.

> For they know God, the Creator and Fashioner of all things through the only-begotten Son and the Holy Spirit (ch. 15).⁵

In this passage, Aristides affirms that God reveals himself through the divine Son and the Spirit. It appears that in this instance Aristides distinguishes between the identities of the Son and Spirit. Nonetheless, it is possible that Aristides makes this distinction only after the incarnation, so that the Holy Spirit declares Christ the Son of God at his birth.⁶ If this is the case, then, in the preexistent state the Son and Spirit are designations of the same divine personality. So Aristides' meaning remains equivocal.

The last text of interest affirms that because Christ has risen from the dead, Christians 'call themselves brethren not after the

---

³ Cited according to the translation of D.M. May, Aristides, 'Apology', ANF, IX, p. 276. There have been three renditions of Aristides' apology discovered: (1) an Armenian version, (2) a Syriac version, and (3) a Greek version. Several concise overviews discuss the history of these documents' discovery and translation. Quasten, *Patrology*, I, p. 192; Aristides, 'Apology' ANF, IX, pp. 260-61; Robert M. Grant, 'Aristides', *ABD*, I, p. 382; 'Aristides', *ODCC*, p. 101. J.A. Robinson juxtaposes all three translations of this christological passage and concludes that the Greek 'represents the original Apology much more faithfully than the Syriac does'. Aristides, Harris, and Robinson (eds.), *Aristides*, pp. 78-79. For the Greek text without translation, see Aristides, Harris, and Robinson (eds.), *Aristides*, p. 110.

⁴ Kelly, *Doctrines*, p. 145.

⁵ Aristides, 'Apology', ANF, IX, p. 277. Cf. Aristides, Harris, and Robinson (eds.), *Aristides*, p. 110.

⁶ Wolfson advocates this view. 'There is still no trinity before the birth of Jesus. Before that birth there was only one God and a preexistent Christ, who is called either Logos or Holy Spirit.' Wolfson, *Church Fathers*, I, p. 186.

flesh but after the Spirit' (ch. 15).[7] Since his exaltation, Christ no longer dwells corporeally among believers; instead, his presence dynamically abides among them as the Holy Spirit. The identifying characteristic of a Christian, henceforth, has nothing to do with ethnicity; the characteristics of the Spirit identify Christians. As the Spirit of holiness, the Holy Spirit sanctifies believers, engraving the commands of Christ in their hearts, and enables them to live righteously even now in the presence of God's judgment.

The identities and roles of the Son and Spirit so closely relate that it becomes difficult to distinguish them; thus, one can easily infer that Aristides supports a Spirit Christology of pneumatic incarnation. Assuredly, the Holy Spirit functions as the medium of the salvific mission and the agent of the continuing presence of Christ among believers.

Justin Martyr

Justin Martyr's writings transmit the next references to Spirit Christology; specifically, they are found in Justin's *First Apology* and his *Dialogue with Trypho*.[8] The martyrdom of Polycarp (155–56) probably prompted the writing of the *First Apology*,[9] which he addressed to the emperor Antoninus Pius. It requests that the emperor rationally examine Christianity and form his own judgment about Christian beliefs and practices (chs. 1–3). Next, Justin boldly protests against the judicial practice of arbitrarily punishing anyone, without collaborating evidence of wrongdoing, who confesses the Christian faith. According to the enemies of Christianity, the epithet 'Christian' stands as a metonym for atheism, immorality, and sedition. Justin refutes these charges by asserting that Christians are not atheists, but are monotheists; thus, Christians worship the one true God,

---

[7] Aristides, 'Apology', IX, p. 277. Cf. Aristides, Harris, and Robinson (eds.), *Aristides*, p. 111.

[8] Along with these two documents, Justin also wrote a *Second Apology* which possibly was a later addition to the *First Apology*. Scholars agree that Justin wrote these documents; however, the authorship of several other documents that are associated with Justin stand in question. For information about Justin's writings, and their date of origin, see L.W. Barnard, *Justin Martyr: His Life and Thought* (Cambridge: Cambridge University Press, 1967), pp. 14-26; Schaff, *History*, II, pp. 716-19.

[9] This places the date of origin about 155–57. Rome is probably the place of origin. Grant, *Apologists*, pp. 52-54.

and the polytheistic veneration of deity is against reason. Furthermore, Christians live in an eschatological expectation of the Second Advent of Christ and judgment; consequently, Christian rectitude is impeccable, and because Christians do not look for a human kingdom, they are not a threat to the state (chs. 4–12). In the remainder of the apology, Justin attempts to set forth Christianity as a reasonable religion and the true philosophy (chs. 13–68). According to Justin, the prophecies contained in the Hebrew Scriptures antedated the writings of all the Greek philosophers; Plato and Socrates, therefore, borrowed from Moses (ch. 59). In fact, these philosophers partook of the same Logos that inspired the prophets, but they only partially knew the Logos. These prophecies, furthermore, accurately predicted and proved that the Logos was incarnated in Jesus Christ; therefore, Christians know the fullness of the Logos (chs. 33–53). In other words, through the concept of the divine Logos, Justin could claim that Christianity is as old as creation, and anything is Christian that reveals the true God, goodness, and virtue among other traditions and their literature.[10] Justin's doctrine of God, therefore, uses the Logos concept to bridge Greek philosophy and Christianity.

Christians, according to Justin, worship God as Father, Son, and prophetic Spirit (6.1-2). Justin depends on two diverse sources to explicate this view of God. On the one hand, drawing from his Scriptural convictions, Justin affirms the idea of the living God, the Creator, and compassionate Father who is immanently involved with the welfare of humanity.[11] On the other hand, drawing from

---

[10] 'We have been taught that Christ is the first-born of God, and we have suggested above that He is the logos of whom every race of men and women were partakers. And those who lived with the logos are Christians' (*1 Apology*, 46.2-3). Cited according to Leslie Barnard's translation in Justin, *The First and Second Apologies* (trans. Leslie W. Barnard; ACW 56; New York: Paulist Press, 1997), p. 55. A.W.F. Blunt provides the Greek text without translation, see A.W.F. Blunt, *The Apologies of Justin Martyr* (Eugene, OR: Wipf and Stock, 2006 repr.; Cambridge: Cambridge University Press), p. 70. Cf. Grillmeier, *Christian Tradition*, I, pp. 89-94.

[11] For an overview of Judaism and the Christian tradition's influence on the formation of Justin's theology, see Barnard, *Life and Thought*, pp. 39-74. The following sources provide helpful inquires into Justin's use of OT and NT Scriptures, as well as his exegetical method. Oskar Skarsaune, 'Justin and His Bible', in Sara Parvis and Paul Parvis (eds.), *Justin Martyr and His Worlds* (Minneapolis: Fortress Press, 2007), pp. 53-76; Oskar Skarsaune, *The Proof from Prophecy: A Study in Justin Martyr's Proof-Text Tradition: Text-Type, Provenance, Theological Profile* (NovTSup

his philosophic training in Middle Platonism, Justin accentuates that God is utterly transcendent and unknowable to humanity.[12] To traverse this chasm between God's immanence and transcendence, Justin posits his doctrine of the divine Logos.[13] According to Justin, the Father begets the Logos, the preexistent Son, who serves as the agent of creation and revelation to humanity (ch. 63); thus, the Logos mediates between the Father and creation, preserving the Father's transcendence (64.5).[14] Justin's attempt to coalesce God's transcendence and immanence in the Logos concept, consequently, causes his trinitarian language to resound with a ring of subordinationism: Christians worship God rationally holding the Father in first place, the Son second, and the prophetic Spirit in third rank (13.3).

In their relationship, nevertheless, the Logos stands in essential unity of nature with the Father but distinct in personality; accordingly, through the incarnation of the Logos in Jesus Christ the transcendent God has drawn near to humanity. In their relationship, the Logos and the prophetic Spirit, also, appear to stand in essential unity of nature and identity.

55; Leiden: E.J. Brill, 1987); Willis A. Shotwell, *The Biblical Exegesis of Justin Martyr* (London: SPCK, 1965); A.J. Bellinzoni, *The Sayings of Jesus in the Writings of Justin Martyr* (NovTSup 17; Leiden: E.J. Brill, 1967).

[12] Barnard, *Life and Thought*, pp. 27-38.

[13] According to Jaroslav Pelikan, as the Apologists began to give greater precision of thought to Christology, they moved from identifying the divine in Christ as Spirit and took up two titles which were present in Christian nomenclature since the New Testament: Logos and Son of God. Pelikan, *Christian Tradition*, I, p. 186. 'The Logos-idea of the New Testament was more influential in forming the general philosophical notions of the church at this time, than was the department of secular philosophy itself.' William G.T. Shedd, *A History of Christian Doctrine* (2 vols.; Eugene, OR: Wipf and Stock, 1999 repr.; New York: Charles Scribner, 1864), I, p. 130. Whether Justin's Logos concept is his own or an extension of Hellenistic philosophy or Philo's theology is uncertain. On the one hand, Barnard argues that Justin's equation of the Logos with Jesus differentiates his thought at once from the speculations of Philo, Stoicism, and Middle Platonism. Barnard, *Life and Thought*, pp. 92-99. Barnard also asserts, 'However much he was indebted to Stoicism for the term *logos spermatikos*, the idea of the logos – Christ sowing seeds in people – was, I believe, in essence his own'. Justin, *Apologies*, p. 16. On the other hand, Erwin Goodenough contends that Justin is wholly dependent on Philo for his Logos concept. Erwin Ramsdell Goodenough, *The Theology of Justin Martyr: An Investigation into the Conceptions of Early Christian Literature and Its Hellenistic and Judaistic Influences* (Amsterdam: Philo Press, 1968), pp. 139-75.

[14] 'In short, the Logos is the means by which God is immanent in the world.' Shotwell, *Exegesis*, p. 109.

The Spirit and the Power from God cannot therefore be understood as anything else than the Word, who is also the first-begotten of God, as Moses the afore-mentioned prophet testified; and it was this which, when it came upon the virgin and overshadowed her, caused her to conceive not by intercourse, but by power (33.6).[15]

In fact, the functions of the Logos and Spirit are synonymous; for example, in 33.2 the prophetic Spirit inspires prophecy concerning Christ, yet in 36.1 Justin attributes this function to the Logos. Correspondingly, in 33.5 the Holy Spirit is the agent of the incarnation, whereas in 46.5 and 66.2 Justin ascribes the activity to the Logos.[16] For Justin, then, the Logos is a designation for the preexistent divine Son, the prophetic Spirit, and the Holy Spirit. Justin's doctrine of God, therefore, conjoins a nascent form of Logos Christology with Spirit Christology.

The *Dialogue with Trypho* contains Justin's two-day discussion, at Ephesus, with a well-educated Jew, shortly after the Jewish revolt in 132–35. Sometime later, while in Rome, Justin composed this document and dedicated it to Marcus Pompeius as a defense against Judaism (155–61).[17] The apology comprises four parts. First, it recounts Justin's search for truth, philosophical background, and conversion to Christianity; also, it sets the limits of the debate. Justin begins by placing his theological cards on the table: Jesus Christ is the promised messiah of Hebrew prophecy, and Christianity is

---

[15] Cited according to the translation of Leslie Barnard, Justin, *Apologies*, p. 46. Cf. Blunt, *Apologies*, pp. 53-54. Another translation asserts, 'It is wrong, therefore, to understand the Spirit and the power of God as anything else than the Word'. Justin Martyr, 'The First Apology of Justin', ANF, I, p. 174. 'Justin does not clearly distinguish between the πνεῦμα and the λόγος.' Blunt, *Apologies*, p. p. 53, n. 18.

[16] Blunt, *Apologies*, p. xxviii. Skarsaune concludes that the text probably indicates 'a causal relationship between Jesus' status as God's Son and his supernatural conception by the Spirit'. Skarsaune, *Prophecy*, p. 273.

[17] Discussions about the provenance, date, and purpose are provided by Michael Slusser (ed.), *St. Justin Martyr: Dialogue with Trypho*, FC, III, p. xv; Craig D. Allert, *Revelation, Truth, Canon and Interpretation: Studies in Justin Martyr's Dialogue with Trypho* (VCSup 64; Leiden: E.J. Brill, 2002), pp. 32-61. There is some discussion concerning Justin's dialogue partner; it is possible that Trypho is a fictitious opponent that Justin uses to demonstrate the superiority of Christian revelation over Greek philosophy, to engage Jews in a discussion about Hebrew Scriptures, and to reinforce the premise that Christianity has supplanted Judaism as the New Israel. Slusser (ed.), *Dialogue*, pp. 12-13.

the true philosophy. Trypho, nevertheless, contends that observance of the *torah* is the true way to serve God (chs. 1–8). Second, it presents the Christian view of the Mosaic Law. Although the moral requirements continue eternally, the ceremonial laws are temporary; they were given because of the Jews' proclivity to sin. Through Christ, however, Christians have inherited the new and eternal law that is for all humanity (chs. 9–31).[18] Third, from exegetically examining Hebrew prophecies, Justin sets forth the significance of Jesus Christ as the fulfillment of the prophetic witness. In this section, Justin discusses with Trypho the importance of the incarnation, virgin birth, the dual nature of Christ, crucifixion, and the resurrection (chs. 32–110). Fourth, it depicts Jews and Gentiles coming to God through Jesus Christ; these are the true chosen people of God, the new Israel (chs. 111–42).

The third section contains two references to Spirit Christology. One passage sets within the context of Justin's attempt to answer Trypho's challenge, 'prove to us that the prophetic Spirit ever admits the existence of another God, besides the Creator of all things' (55.1).[19] Consequently, to assuage Trypho's doubts, Justin exegetes numerous Scriptures, which seem to imply that Wisdom and Word depict a divine personality, and narrates several theophanies that various patriarchs have experienced: a unique angel appears to Abraham, Jacob, Joshua, and Moses who beholds the glory of God (chs. 56–63). Accordingly, Justin again turns to his Logos theology to vindicate his position;[20] these theophanies were manifestations of the preexistent Logos who was begotten from the Father.[21]

> God has begotten of himself a certain rational power as a beginning before all creatures. The Holy Spirit indicates this power by various titles, sometimes *the Glory of the Lord*, at other times *Son*, or *Wisdom*, or *Angel*, or *God*, or *Lord*, or *Word* ... The Word of Wisdom, who is this God begotten from the Father of all, and who is Word and Wisdom and Power and Glory of him who begot him (61.2-3).[22]

---

[18] For a discussion of this topic, see Allert, *Revelation*, pp. 168-74.
[19] Cited according to the translation of Thomas Falls Slusser, *Dialogue*, p. 82.
[20] Allert, *Revelation*, pp. 175-76.
[21] Skarsaune provides an overview of the theophanies and the second God. Skarsaune, *Prophecy*, pp. 409-24.
[22] Slusser (ed.), *Dialogue*, p. 94.

These various theophanies, accordingly, reveal that the Logos is a divine personality distinct from the Father but not distinct in divine essence, unity, and will;[23] indeed, the incarnation of this deity in Jesus Christ is the greatest revelation. Along with Angel, Wisdom, and Son, it appears that Logos and Spirit are synonymous terms for the deity incarnate in Jesus Christ (ch. 63).[24]

The other passage rests in the context of Justin's attempt to answer Trypho's query: if the preexistent God is incarnate in Christ, why is he, at his baptism, endowed with the gifts of the Holy Spirit as though he had lacked them (87.2)? Justin responds that Jesus needed neither baptism nor the descent of the Spirit upon him (88.4).[25] Christ received the Spirit at the Jordan for two reasons: (1) so the gifts of the Spirit would cease among the Jews, and (2) after Christ's ascension, the gifts of the Spirit would come upon Christians (87.5).

> In another prophecy it said: And it shall come to pass after this, I will pour out My Spirit on all flesh, and on My servants, and on My handmaids, and they shall prophesy. Now it is possible to see amongst us women and men who possess gifts of the Spirit of God (87.6–88.1).[26]

In other words, Christ's reception of the Spirit was a transitional marker in salvific history, from Old Covenant to New Covenant, so

---

[23] Justin attempted to preserve the unity of the divine essence by asserting that the Logos was begotten from the Father as fire from fire (*Dialogue*, 61.2).

[24] Cf. Goodenough, *Theology*, p. 176; Barnard, *Life and Thought*, pp. 104-106. See the comment of Moltmann, *The Way of Jesus Christ*, p. 74:

> Spirit christology is also Wisdom christology; for in the Israelite tradition Spirit and Wisdom were initially closely related, and in later Wisdom literature they can even be used as interchangeable terms. Spirit and Wisdom are incidentally feminine modes of the divine appearance. Spirit or Wisdom christology is the premise of every Son of God christology.

'Angel is a very old designation for Christ (see Justin's Dial.) which maintained itself up to the Nicean controversy ... and as the Logos doctrine gradually made way, the designation "Angel" became harmless and vanished' (Harnack, *Dogma*, I, p. 185, n. 3).

[25] Recognizing a Son of God motif present in the discussion, Skarsaune asserts, 'Jesus was not *made* or *established* God's Son in his baptism, but he was proved to be God's Son'. Skarsaune, *Prophecy*, p. 392. Skarsaune also explores the concept of the Spirit anointed messiah, see Skarsaune, *Prophecy*, pp. 273-77.

[26] Cited according to the translation of A. Cleveland Coxe, Justin Martyr, 'Dialogue with Trypho, A Jew', ANF, I, p. 243.

that Christians will become the rightful heirs of the Spirit's presence, power, and gifts as the people of God.[27]

No disparity exists between Justin's Logos Christology and Spirit Christology, so that they conjoin as one. The identities and functions of the Logos and Spirit are synonymous in the preexistent state and the incarnation, as well as in Christ's ministry, death, resurrection, and ascension. Through Christ the Spirit is poured out on believers, so that to receive the Spirit is to receive Christ, and to experience the power of the Spirit is to experience the gift of Christ. What can be said of one, can be said of the other.

Melito of Sardis

Melito, bishop of Sardis — who was esteemed by the ancient church as a prophet, and 'lived altogether in the Holy Spirit'[28] — taught a form of Spirit Christology. Although Melito was a prolific author, most of his writings survived only as fragments,[29] until the discovery of an almost complete homily, *Peri Pascha*.[30] *Peri Pascha* and a text

---

[27] 'The work of the Spirit in Dialogue 87 was primarily geared toward his desire to validate the church's legacy as the rightful heir to Israel's traditions.' Susan Wendel, 'Interpreting the Descent of the Spirit: A Comparison of Justin's Dialogue with Trypho and Luke-Acts', in Sara Parvis and Paul Parvis (eds.), *Justin Martyr and His Worlds* (Minneapolis: Fortress Press, 2007), p. 103. Cf. McDonnell, *The Baptism of Jesus in the Jordan*, pp. 24-25, 43-44, 46, 111-13; Kilian McDonnell and George T. Montague, *Christian Initiation and Baptism in the Holy Spirit: Evidence from the First Eight Centuries* (Collegeville, MN: Liturgical Press, 1990), p. 120.

[28] Eusebius, *Hist. eccl.* 5.24.5, NPNF, Second Series, I, p. 242. Cf. Schaff, *History*, II, p. 736.

[29] For example, Melito composed an apology (170–76) and addressed it to the emperor Marcus Aurelius which was preserved by Eusebius. See Grant, *Apologists*, pp. 93-95; Quasten, *Patrology*, I, p. 242. For a discussion of the fragments attributed to Melito, see Stuart George Hall (ed.), *Melito of Sardis: On Pascha and Fragments* (OECT; Oxford: Clarendon Press, 1979), pp. xiii-xvi.

[30] During the years of 1932–40, this document was discovered and identified through the efforts of Frederic Kenyon and Campbell Bonner. Bonner was the first to publish this document in Campbell Bonner, *The Homily on the Passion by Melito, Bishop of Sardis, and Some Fragments of the Apocryphal Ezekiel* (SD; Philadelphia: University of Philadelphia Press, 1940). Stuart Hall's work, however, provides a more recent and complete text and translation. For introductory issues concerning the homily's discovery, identification, and date of origin, see Hall (ed.), *Pascha*, pp. xvii-xxii; Alistar Stewart-Sykes, *The Lamb's High Feast: Melito, Peri Pascha and the Quartodeciman Paschal Liturgy at Sardis* (VCSup 42; Leiden: E.J. Brill, 1998), pp. 2-7; Lynn H. Cohick, *The Peri Pascha Attributed to Melito of Sardis: Setting, Purpose, and Sources* (BJS 327; Providence: Brown Judaic Studies, 2000), pp. 4-6.

that is part of three recently discovered fragments, which are known as the *New Fragments*, provide the next set of references to Spirit Christology.[31]

Following the Quartodeciman practice of some early Christians in Asia Minor, Melito probably preached *Peri Pascha* at Sardis (160–70) during the annual celebration of the Lord's resurrection, which occurred on the Jewish Passover.[32] The homily offers a typological interpretation of the Passover event: the slaying of the lambs and the corollary phenomena model Christ's salvific mission. The homily consists of four parts. First, it introduces the mystery of the Pascha (*Peri Pascha*, 1-10). Second, it asserts that all paschal events – the slaying of the first Passover lamb, the death of Egypt's firstborn, and the blood that saved Israel – portend Christ's sacrifice (*Peri Pascha*, 11-45). Third, it sets forth humanity's need of salvation and the models from Hebrew Scripture that prophetically augur the Lord's sufferings (*Peri Pascha*, 46-65). Fourth, it portrays the Lord's coming and passion, Israel's unbelief and punishment, Christ's victory over death and exaltation, and the salvific merits Christ offers to all humanity (*Peri Pascha*, 66-105).

Melito provides three Spirit christological texts that fall under the purview of this survey.

> It is he who, coming from heaven to the earth because of the suffering one, and clothing himself in that same one through a virgin's womb, and coming forth a man, accepted the passions of the suffering one through the body which was able to suffer and dissolved the passions of the flesh; and by the Spirit which could not die he killed death the killer of men. For, himself led as a lamb and slain as a sheep, he ransomed us from the world's service as from the land of Egypt, and freed us from the devil's slavery as from the hand of Pharaoh; and he marked our souls

---

[31] Apparently, the *New Fragments* represent part of a lost homily of Melito. These fragments were discovered and published, in 1972, from a Georgian homiliaria of the tenth century by M. van Esbroeck. Hall (ed.), *Pascha*, p. xxxix.

[32] Hall sets this date. Hall (ed.), *Pascha*, pp. 21-22. For provenance issues, see Stewart-Sykes, *Feast*, pp. 11-24; Cohick, *Pascha*, pp. 33-37. Quartodecimanism observed Easter on the fourteenth day of the Jewish month of Nisan, regardless of the day of the week it fell on. Stewart-Sykes, *Feast*, pp. 141-53. Cohick suggests that the homily rests in the context of a Jewish and Christian dialogue about the proper understanding of Jesus instead of the Quartodeciman controversy. Cohick, *Pascha*, pp. 22-31, 152-53.

with his own Spirit and the members of our body with his own blood (*Peri Pascha*, 66-67).[33]

Several conclusions emerge from this text. First, Melito taught Christ's dual natures, divine and human;[34] Spirit clothed himself with human flesh. Second, Christ's body suffered for human salvation, but the Spirit remained impassible. Third, through the salvific mission the Spirit defeated death and delivered the believer from bondage. Fourth, as the Spirit has revealed Christ, so the Spirit identifies Christians.[35] According to Melito, therefore, the divine nature incarnated in Christ was Spirit.[36]

In coherence with *Peri Pascha*, the *New Fragments* stress Christ's preexistence and deity. As with most of the Apologists, Melito advocates a form of Logos theology. The pericope of interest in the *New Fragments* brings Logos Christology into close relationship with Spirit Christology: 'For he is the Word of the Father, and the Spirit of his power' (*New Fragment*, 20).[37] So, similar to Justin, Melito makes no distinction between Logos and Spirit, but the philosophical concepts of Middle Platonism that lead Justin to speak of a second God are not present in Melito's writings. In point of fact, for Melito only one God exists, Christ.

> For he is all things: inasmuch as he judges, Law; inasmuch as he teaches, Word; inasmuch as he saves, Grace; inasmuch as he begets, Father; inasmuch as he is begotten, Son; inasmuch as he suffers, Sheep; inasmuch as he is buried, Man; inasmuch as he is raised, God. This is Jesus the Christ, to whom be glory for ever and ever. Amen (*Peri Pascha*, 9-10).[38]

This lack of distinguishing divine identities, thus, extends to the Father, so that Melito addresses his doxologies to Christ rather than

---

[33] Cited according to the translation of Stuart George Hall, *Pascha*, pp. 35-37.
[34] Cf. *Peri Pascha*, 8; 100; Grillmeier, *Christian Tradition*, I, pp. 95-98.
[35] The Spirit marked (ἐσφράγισεν, Aorist active indicative third person singular) the souls of Christians. The verb refers to the act of marking with a seal as a means of identification. Σφραγίζω, BAGD, p. 796.
[36] According to J.N.D. Kelly, 'For Melito He was "by nature God and man"; He had "clothed himself with the man", His divine element being described as "spirit."' Kelly, *Doctrines*, p. 145.
[37] Cited according to the translation of Hall (ed.), *Pascha*, p. 94.
[38] Hall (ed.), *Pascha*, p. 7. Cf. *Peri Pascha*, 47; *Fragment*, 15; *New Fragment*, II, 4; McDonnell, *The Baptism of Jesus in the Jordan*, pp. 38-39, 50-52.

the Father (*Peri Pascha*, 45, 65, 105; *Fragment*, 15; *New Fragment*, II, 23). Melito's emphasis on the preexistence and deity of Christ, consequently, brings his Christology close to modalism.[39]

Although Melito's Christology has been understood as 'Christocentric monotheism' by some scholars,[40] perhaps, monotheistic pneumatic Christology is a more apt description. The theology of *Peri Pascha*, the *Fragments*, and *New Fragments* present a fairly coherent Christology. The Creator took on the garment of flesh and was parthenogenetically born. Concerning the dual natures of Christ, they are Spirit and human body; God and the human the Lord became. Although concepts of substitutionary sacrifice are not expressed, they are present through Melito's typological interpretation of the Pascha. In fulfilling these types, there is the unity of flesh and Spirit in the corporeal reality of Christ's passion; death releases the divine Spirit that destroys death and resurrects Christ, and with him humanity. Now, Christ reigns as the sovereign Lord of history, the *Alpha* and *Omega*, and judge of all (*Peri Pascha*, 105), who marks the people of God by the Spirit. The point is, for Melito, in identity and mission no distinction exists between Christ and Spirit. Christ is God and the essence of God is Spirit. As with several of the Apostolic Fathers, Melito presents Spirit as the deity of Christ, a pneumatic incarnation.

Conclusion

These early Greek Apologists' paradigms of Spirit Christology have demonstrated continuity with the Apostolic Fathers and theological development of thought. Four congruent lines of thought flow through them from their predecessors. First, while maintaining a monotheistic view of God, the Apologists declared the deity and humanity of Christ: God was revealed in Jesus Christ. Second, the

---

[39] Bonner, *Homily*, pp. 27-28, argues:

Melito's theology, as far as this homily reveals it, is dominated by the conception of the divinity and the pre-existence of Christ ... But this emphasis upon his divinity and pre-existence made it natural and almost inevitable that in naïve, unguarded speech the personal distinction between God the Father and God the Son should be obscured.

Pelikan suggests that much of the early church's language of adoration sounds like modalistic Monarchianism. Pelikan, *Christian Tradition*, I, p. 177.

[40] Hall (ed.), *Pascha*, p. xliii.

76   Spirit Christology

twofold method for doing Spirit Christology continued. Aristides and Melito supported a model of pneumatic incarnation, while Justin advocated an incipient Logos Christology that coalesced with Spirit Christology, demonstrating their compatibility, and both forms of Christology seemed to be developing together.[41] Third, they all agreed that the Spirit functioned as the agent of the salvific mission, but with Justin the Logos also functioned in this role. Fourth, after his exaltation, Christ now abides among believers through the dynamic presence of the Spirit that brings them into union with God, identifies them as Christians, sanctifies and enables them to live righteously, and endows them with the charismata.[42]

The most significant development of thought occurred with Logos Christology. Justin used philosophical concepts to posit clearly a second divine personality within the Godhead who mediated between the Father and creation. Justin's theological legacy will take two courses of direction. First, the immediate successors to Justin's Spirit christological paradigm and theological method – Tatian, Athenagoras, and Theophilus – will develop the Logos concept into an early trinitarian formula of three divine personalities.[43] Second, although Justin carefully attempted to prevent any allusion

---

[41] 'The adherents of the pneumatic Christology partly made a definite distinction between the pre-existent Christ and the Holy Spirit ... and partly made use of formulae from which one could infer the identity of the two.' Harnack, *Dogma*, I, p. 197, n. 1. Harnack adds the following:

> The pneumatic Christology accordingly meets us wherever there is an earnest occupation with the Old Testament, and wherever faith in Christ as the perfect revealer of God occupies the foreground. The future belonged to this Christology because the current exposition of the Old Testament seemed directly to require it, because it alone permitted the close connection between creation and redemption ... and finally, because it had room for the speculations about the Logos (Harnack, *Dogma*, I, pp. 197-98).

[42] 'Every individual was, or at least should have been conscious, as a Christian, of having received the πνεῦμα θεοῦ.' Harnack, *Dogma*, I, p. 141. Cf. p. 151-52, n. 2.

[43] Theophilus was the first to use the word Trinity (τριάς) to describe God (*Autol.* 2.15). All three of these Fathers allude to Spirit Christology. For example, Tatian speaks about the Logos enlightening the human soul so that it salvifically unites with the Holy Spirit (*Address to the Greeks*, chs. 13; 15); Theophilus identifies the Logos as Spirit of God (*Autol.* 2.10); and Athenagoras affirms that the common deity of the Father and Son is Spirit (*A Plea for the Christians*, ch. 10). In these references they do not discuss the role of the Logos or Spirit in Christ's salvific mission; therefore, these references do not fall within the parameters of this inquiry.

to a division of divine nature in the Godhead, his Logos concept will lead toward subordinationism. Melito also integrates Logos Christology with Spirit Christology, but he omits any philosophical concepts that permit any hint of a second divine personality. For Melito, there is only one God, Jesus Christ, in whom the Father, Son, and Holy Spirit is revealed. Melito's theological legacy will proceed in the christological direction of modalism.

Spirit Christology's legacy, then, will develop and progress down two diverse paths. On the one hand, it journeys along with the doctrinal development of the Logos Christology in the central Christian tradition. On the other hand, it progresses among groups on the periphery of the institutional church. Now, the survey turns its attention to the latter group of writers.

4

VOICES FROM THE MARGINS

During the second and third centuries, certain christological questions began to press for attention: What was the Son's relationship with the Father and the Spirit? Was Christ divine? How should Christians explain Christ's deity? Could the developing Logos Christology and trinitarian doctrine be reconciled with Jewish monotheism? What inheritance did Christianity receive from Judaism and the Hebrew Scriptures? Several groups of dissonant voices spoke from the margins about christological development to help define and shape the responses to these questions. The presence of these voices serves as a reminder of the variety, vigor, and complexity of early christological thought among a broad range of Christian groups. Since some of these groups' writings are not extant, their voices cannot be heard directly, but their echo reverberates in the fragments of their witness that are preserved in the works of their opponents. So in these cases the survey will depend on these secondary sources to gain a hearing of the first cacophony of voices that come from the margins of christological development.

Gnosticism

Although the term Christian Gnostic could include anyone who has accessed and understood the truth of God revealed through Jesus Christ,[1] attention will focus on the groups, which flourished during

---

[1] This designation applied to several teachers and writings of the early church; for example, Clement of Alexandria, and Origen were called Christian Gnostics.

the second century and remained influential into the sixth century, that stood on the margins of doctrinal development and claimed a special knowledge, gnosis, of this truth. The origin of Gnosticism remains uncertain because of its syncretistic nature.² Gnostic teachers imbibed from many wells – Persian dualism, Babylonian astrology and magical arts, Greek philosophy, Philonic theology, Oriental mysticism, and certain forms of Judaism – and incorporated their contents into Gnostic systems.³ This confluence of Christian concepts and Hellenistic culture caused various schools of Christian Gnosticism to arise – named after their founders, activities, worship, and doctrines – with differing variations of this gnosis.⁴

Schaff, *History*, II, p. 445. Also, Evagrius Ponticus authored a book about the ideal monk entitled *The Gnostic*. Socrates Scholasticus, *Ecclesiastical History*, 4.23, NPNF 2nd Series, II, p. 107.

² There remains a debate about Gnosticism's origin and its relationship to Christianity. James M. Robinson states, 'This debate seems to be resolving itself, on the basis of the Nag Hammadi Library, in favor of understanding Gnosticism as a much broader phenomenon that the Christian Gnosticism documented by the heresiologists'. 'Introduction', in James M. Robinson (ed.), *NHL*, p. 6. Robert Grant suggests that Gnosticism has it roots in the apocalyptic-eschatological hopes of certain forms of Judaism, and Gnosticism arises from the debris of these hopes after the destruction of the Jerusalem temple: 'Only after these disasters do we encounter Gnosticism in its various systematic forms'. Robert McQueen Grant, *Gnosticism and Early Christianity* (New York: Columbia University Press, 2nd edn, 1966), pp. viii; cf. pp. 13-38. Pelikan, however, probably comes closer to the mark when he states, 'It is not altogether clear whether there was a pre-Christian as well as an extra-Christian Gnosticism and a post-Christian Gnosticism'. Pelikan, *Christian Tradition*, I, p. 82.

³ Hans Jonas examined the different historical phases of Hellenistic cultural development and concluded that Hellenism had synthesized these various teachings into its culture which produced a general religion, during the first and second century, that was a dualistic transcendent religion of salvation, which provided the cultural and spiritual climate for the rise of Gnosticism. Hans Jonas, *The Gnostic Religion: The Message of the Alien God and the Beginnings of Christianity* (Boston: Beacon Press, 2nd edn, 1963), pp. 3-32. 'Gnosticism is, therefore, the grandest and most comprehensive form of speculative religious syncretism known to history.' Schaff, *History*, II, p. 448. Cf. Kurt Rudolph, *Gnosis: The Nature and History of Gnosticism* (trans. Robert McLachlan Wilson; 1987 repr.; San Francisco: Harper & Row, 1977), pp. 275-94; Seeberg and Hay, *History*, I, pp. 91-102.

⁴ This confluence prompts Harnack to declare 'that the Gnostic systems represent the acute secularising or hellenising of Christianity'. Harnack, *Dogma*, I, p. 227. A comprehensive overview of the various Gnostic schools along with translations of their texts is provided by Robert McQueen Grant, *Gnosticism: A Source Book of Heretical Writings from the Early Christian Period* (New York: Harper & Row, 1961). For more concise overviews of these schools, see Rudolph, *Gnosis*, pp. 294-326; Schaff, *History*, II, pp. 459-508; Quasten, *Patrology*, I, pp. 255-77.

Nonetheless, certain common soteriological characteristics appeared; their *leitmotiv* doctrine was the redemption of the spirit through knowledge: 'He who is to have knowledge in this manner knows where he comes from and where he is going' (*Gos. Truth*, 22.13-15).[5] Gnostics, therefore, knew that they were originally spiritual beings that dwelt in the spiritual world above with the transcendent God. From this perfect primal divine source, several divine emanations (aeons) generated to constitute the divine fullness, pleroma.[6] Since the divine source was incomprehensible, a limit was established in the pleroma concerning understanding and speaking of the source; nevertheless, a certain aeon attempted to grasp the incomprehensible which resulted in its fall from the pleroma. After this aeon fell in a state of ignorance it produced angelic beings, corporeal creation, and humanity.[7] Material creation, therefore, exists in a fallen condition and is basically evil (*Gos. Phil.* 66.7-23; 75.2-11). The human condition, also, languishes in a quandary; albeit a spark of the divine nature, the human spirit is imprisoned in corporeality, and it is ignorant of its origination, descent, and the way of ascending back to the divine source (*Thom. Cont.* 138.19-21). Humanity, consequently, stands in need of redemptive knowledge. Because human flesh partakes of non-redeemable corporeality, gnosis cannot come by natural means; hence, the spirit within the person must receive a revelation from a divine revealer, a Savior (*Treat. Res.*, 44.14-19; *Thom. Cont.* 138.1-7). Gnosticism, therefore, bases its theology, cosmology, anthropology, and soteriology on the cosmic

---

[5] Cited according to the translation of Harold W. Attridge and George W. MacRae, in James M. Robinson (ed.), *NHL*, p. 42.

[6] There are some variations concerning the divine source from which all supernatural entities emanate. On the one hand, some Gnostics posited a masculine monadic source. On the other hand, some Gnostics posited a masculine-feminine dyadic source. The author of *Tri. Trac.* (51.1-57.8) provides an example of the former, and *Ap. John* (1.1-5.22) furnishes a specimen of the latter. Among Gnostic teachers, the number of aeons varies that constitute the pleroma.

[7] Typically, Gnosticism distinguishes between the transcendent God and the creator who is a lesser God. According to *Ap. John*, 9.26-19.15, *Hyp. Arch.*, 94.5-19, and *Orig. World*, 98.7-100.9, the aeon that fell was Sophia, but in *Tri. Trac.*, 74.17-80.11 the aeon is identified as the Logos. Irenaeus' exposition of Gnosticism is similar to the *Ap. John* (Irenaeus, *Haer.*, 1.1-6). Jonas also provides an overview of the system in the *Ap. John*. Jonas, *Gnostic Religion*, pp. 199-205.

redemption of the spirit through a divine revelation, gnosis. (*Tri. Trac.*, 80.12-138.27; *Ap. John*, 19.16-32.8).[8]

The sources for Gnostic research consist of both secondary and primary sources.[9] Until the nineteenth century, the polemical writings of several early Fathers – Irenaeus, Tertullian, Hippolytus, Epiphanius, and Clement of Alexandria – provided the main sources of Gnostic thought. The last two centuries, however, have yielded a plethora of primary sources.[10] For instance, in 1945 a fourth century Gnostic library was unearthed in a large jar near Nag-Hammadi in Upper Egypt.[11] The library consists of twelve codices and eight leaves from a thirteenth codex, containing fifty-two separate tractates, yet due to duplications there are forty-five separate titles.[12] The Nag Hammadi Library contains several passages that support a form of Spirit Christology; attention focuses on three representative tractates: *The Gospel of Truth*, *The Testimony of Truth*, and *The Gospel of Philip*.

---

[8] According to Harnack, Gnostics were 'the Theologians of the first century. They were the first to transform Christianity into a system of doctrines'. Harnack, *Dogma*, I, p. 228. Cf. Jonas, *Gnostic Religion*, pp. 42-47. This self-recognition, for Gnosticism, is the essence of the process of salvation. Majella Franzmann, *Jesus in the Nag Hammadi Writings* (Edinburgh: T. & T. Clark, 1996), p. 99; Grant, *Gnosticism and Early Christianity*, pp. 8-9. For an extensive discussion about the Gnostic idea of self–knowledge being the knowledge of God, see Elaine H. Pagels, *The Gnostic Gospels* (New York: Random House, 1979), pp. 119-41. Kurt Rudolph provides a comprehensive overview of the various aspects of Gnostic doctrine. Rudolph, *Gnosis*, pp. 59-272.

[9] For an extensive discussion of Gnostic sources, see Rudolph, *Gnosis*, pp. 9-52.

[10] During the nineteenth century several primary Gnostic writings turned up. For example, *Pistis Sophia* became available; the most important discovery occurred in 1895 when the Berlin museum bought a fifth century papyrus codex that contained the *Gospel of Mary*, the *Apocryphon of John*, and the *Sophia of Jesus Christ*. Grant, *Gnosticism and Early Christianity*, pp. 3-4.

[11] Rudolph, *Gnosis*, pp. 34-52; Floyd V. Filson, 'New Greek and Coptic Gospel Manuscripts', *BA* 34 (1961), pp. 2-8; Jonas, *Gnostic Religion*, pp. 37-42; Grant, *Gnosticism and Early Christianity*, pp. 3-6; Donald C. Ziemke, 'Echoes of the Ancient Gnostic Heresy', *LQ* 14 (1962), pp. 148-49.

[12] These tractates are primarily Coptic translations of original Greek texts. Robinson discusses such introductory issues as the state of the writings, the texts the library contains, the identity of the group and their purpose for burying the writings in a jar, and the fourth century date, as well as a description of the discovery. Robinson, 'Introduction', in Robinson (ed.), *NHL*, pp. 1-28.

The Gospel of Truth

Given the Valentinian affinities of the text, *The Gospel of Truth* is quite possibly the same text that Irenaeus mentions by this name (*Haer.*, 3.1.9). Assuming the validity of this hypothesis, it is likely that Valentinus authored this tractate, between 140–60, to introduce his Gnostic soteriological concepts to the church.[13] The tractate's structure consists of an introduction and three subsequent sections.[14] The introduction presents the tractate's thesis: the Word is the Savior that comes forth from the pleroma to redeem those who are ignorant of the primal divine source, the Father (16.31-17.4). In Gnostic fashion, the first section begins with the generation of Error from the Father. Next, the text immediately sets forth Jesus Christ as revealing the gnosis of the Father's essence, the origin and destiny of the redeemed, and the means of overcoming the powers of Error (17.4-24.9).[15] The second section depicts the upshot of the revelation: the awakening of the spirit from ignorance to wakefulness and joy, and the way of return to the Father (24.9-33.32). The third section accentuates the process of return and its ultimate goal, rest in the Father (33.33-43-24).[16]

---

[13] The provenance is uncertain; however, the date of origin falls between Valentinus' arrival in Rome about 136–40 and his death around 160. For discussions about these issues, see Irenaeus, *Haer.*, 3.4.3; Quasten, *Patrology*, I, pp. 260-61; Schaff, *History*, II, pp. 472-73; Attridge and MacRae's introduction to *Gos. Truth*, in Robinson (ed.), *NHL*, p. 38; Filson, 'Manuscripts', pp. 9-10; W.H.C. Frend, *The Rise of Christianity* (Philadelphia: Fortress Press, 1984), p. 207; Jonas, *Gnostic Religion*, pp. 309-10; Elliot R. Wolfson, 'Inscribed in the Book of the Living: *Gospel of Truth* and Jewish Christology', *JSJ* 38 (2007), pp. 239-40; Patricia Cox Miller, 'Words with an Alien Voice', *JAAR* 57 (1989), p. 447.

[14] Along with other apocryphal gospels, a debate has arisen about classifying these tractates that bear the name gospel, in the Nag Hammadi Library, in the genre of gospel. Franzmann, *Jesus*, pp. 7-19. Wolfson notes the possibility and the hermeneutical implications of labeling this tractate as sermon. Wolfson, 'Gos. Truth', pp. 241-42. Otto Piper suggests that the *Gos. Truth* should be regarded as an attempt 'to present the gospel in a new light and with a different scope'. Otto A. Piper, 'Change of Perspective', *Interpretation* 16 (1962), p. 402.

[15] Cf. Frend, *Christianity*, p. 198; Piper, 'Change of Perspective', pp. 403-404.

[16] Cf. Attridge and MacRae's introduction to *Gos. Truth*, in Robinson (ed.), *NHL*, pp. 38-39; Grant, *Gnosticism and Early Christianity*, pp. 128-34; Jonas, *Gnostic Religion*, pp. 310-19. A comprehensive discussion of introductory concerns, the structure of the text, as well as the Coptic version of the text with an English translation is provided in James M. Robinson (ed.), *The Coptic Gnostic Library: A Complete Edition of the Nag Hammadi Codices* (trans. The Institute of Antiquity and Christianity, 5 vols.; Leiden: Brill, 2000), I, pp. 55-122.

There are four Spirit christological texts that explain the process of revelation in the salvific mission. The first text clarifies Jesus' mission.

> Jesus, the Christ, enlightened those who were in darkness through oblivion. He enlightened them; he showed (them) a way; and the way is the truth which he taught them (18.16-21).[17]

The author leaves no doubt; gnosis flows through the teachings of Jesus Christ. The second text delineates the emanation of the gnosis from the Father.

> The Father reveals his bosom. – Now his bosom is the Holy Spirit. He reveals what is hidden of him – what is hidden of him is his Son – so that through the mercies of the Father the aeons may know him (24.10-16).[18]

In the same manner that the aeons within the pleroma acquire gnosis of the Father, humanity also receives the secret gnosis: the Father reveals the Holy Spirit, and the Holy Spirit reveals the Son. The third text asserts that Christ and the Spirit join the pneumatics[19] to the Father.

> The truth is the mouth of the Father; his tongue is the Holy Spirit – he who is joined to the truth is joined to the Father's mouth by his tongue, whenever he is to receive the Holy Spirit (26.35-27.4).[20]

The context seems to indicate that the phrase 'mouth of the Father' refers to Jesus' oral communication of the hidden gnosis through his teachings, and the Holy Spirit as the 'perfect power' (26.30-32) inspires Jesus' words and joins the redeemed to the truth: they

---

[17] Cited according to the translation of Harold W. Attridge and George W. MacRae, in Robinson (ed.), *NHL*, pp. 40-41. Cf. Wolfson, 'Gos. Truth', p. 242; Miller, 'Alien Voice', pp. 471-72.

[18] Robinson (ed.), *NHL*, p. 43.

[19] This identification agrees with other writings of the Valentinian school of thought; the reception of the gnosis or lack thereof reveals three classes of humans: materialists, psychics, and pneumatics. The materialists are non-Christians who reject the Savior. The psychics are ordinary Christians who are capable of receiving the gnosis. The pneumatics represent the Gnostics who immediately recognize the Savior and receive the gnosis. See *Tri. Trac.* 118.14-122.12; Frend, *Christianity*, pp. 199-200.

[20] Robinson (ed.), *NHL*, p. 44. Cf. Wolfson, 'Gos. Truth', pp. 244-45, 254-55.

receive the Holy Spirit. The fourth text depicts the results of receiving the redemptive gnosis.

> The Spirit ran after him, hastening from waking him up. Having extended his hand to him who lay upon the ground, he set him on his feet, for he had not yet risen. He gave them the means of knowing the knowledge of the Father and the revelation of the Son (30.17-26).[21]

According to this passage's context, receiving the gnosis is a dynamic pneumatic event of deliverance from ignorance akin to someone awaking from sleep, the blind receiving their sight, and the healing of the lame so that they stand and walk (29.27-30.16).[22]

From the preceding discussion of these Spirit christological texts, some conclusions can be drawn. First, in their preexistent state, Christ and the Holy Spirit emanate from the Father in a reciprocal relationship of revelation. Second, in their redemptive mission this relationship of reciprocity continues, so that it becomes difficult to distinguish one from the other: mouth and tongue, word and message. Third, because Christ comes to reveal gnosis to the pneumatics, his essential form of entry into the world and mission is spiritual, although present in the form of flesh. The *Gospel of Truth*, therefore, presents a Spirit Christology of pneumatic inspiration.

Testimony of Truth

The title, Testimony of Truth, draws its name from the author's concern to set forth the true faith and praxis, strengthen the convictions of the pneumatics, and to oppose those who speak from the center of the Christian tradition.[23] Owing to internal evidence, Birger Pearson has suggested that the author was originally influenced by Alexandrian Valentinianism but had departed from this tradition; thus, he points to Julius Cassianus as a strong possibility for authorship.[24] Although the issue of authorship remains questionable, an Alexandrian provenance and a date of origin between 189 and 232

---

[21] Robinson (ed.), *NHL*, pp. 45-46.
[22] Cf. Anne McGuire, 'Conversion and Gnosis in the Gospel of Truth', *NovT* 28 (1986), pp. 346, 353; Miller, 'Alien Voice', pp. 469-70.
[23] Pagels, *Gnostic Gospels*, pp. 110-11.
[24] 'As it happens, Clement of Alexandria has provided us with information about a gnostic teacher who fits the situation of our author very well: Julius Cassianus.' Birger A. Pearson's introduction to *Testim. Truth*, in Robinson (ed.), *NHL*, p. 449. Cf. Quasten, *Patrology*, I, pp. 274-75.

are certainly plausible.²⁵ The homily's structure consists of two sections. The first section begins with an address to the pneumatics (29.6-9). Then, the author's attitude toward human corporeality becomes evident as he polemically attacks the Torah's command to procreate (29.9-31.22), the concept of martyrdom,²⁶ and the idea of a physical resurrection of believers (31.22-38.27),²⁷ as well as contrasting the sexual defilement of marriage and procreation with Jesus' virgin birth (38.27-41.4). The section concludes with the Gnostic version of salvation: the self-knowledge of one's origin and destination (41.4-45.6). The second section consists of a discussion of Jesus' virgin birth (45.6-22), an interpretation of the Genesis account of the serpent and the Creator's relationship with humanity (45.23-49.10),²⁸ a contrast between the pneumatics and other Christians (49.10-50.11), and a refutation of any groups that disagree with the author's theology (55.1-74.30).

The first section contains a fragmented Spirit christological reference in which two events are coalesced: (1) Christ taking flesh from a virgin, and (2) the descent of the Holy Spirit upon Christ at the Jordan.

> [... word ...] upon the [Jordan river] [*sic*] when he came [to John at] the time he [was baptized]. The [Holy] Spirit [came] down upon him [as a] dove [...] accept for ourselves that [he] was born of a virgin [and] he took flesh; he [... having] received power (39.24-40.1).²⁹

---

²⁵ Birger A. Pearson, 'Truth, Testimony of', *ABD*, VI, p. 669. Pearson also discusses these introductory issues and provides a translation of the Coptic text in Robinson (ed.), *The Coptic Gnostic Library*, V, pp. 101-203.

²⁶ Pagels, *Gnostic Gospels*, pp. 91-93.

²⁷ For Gnostics, resurrection is a spiritual event, which occurs in this life, of receiving the Spirit, gnosis. Pagels discusses the Gnostic rejection of Christ's physical resurrection. Pagels, *Gnostic Gospels*, pp. 3-27.

²⁸ According to the author, the serpent typifies Christ as the revealer of life and knowledge, and God the Creator is depicted as an ignorant demon. Birger Pearson provides a helpful examination of the tractate's use of the Hebrew Scriptures. Birger A. Pearson, 'Gnostic Interpretation of the Old Testament in the Testimony of Truth (NHC IX, 3)', *HTR* 73 (1980), pp. 311-19. Although there is some question whether or not Marcion's theology completely fits a Gnostic profile, the Gnostic distinction between the benevolent Father and the malevolent creator becomes full-blown in his writings.

²⁹ Cited according to the translation of Soren Giverson and Birger A. Pearson, 'The Testimony of Truth', in James M. Robinson (ed.), *NHL*, p. 452.

A brief look at two parallel passages will aid the interpretation of this passage. The first pericope contrasts what the Jordan symbolizes – bodily senses, passions, and the desire for sexual intercourse – with the power that overcomes it (30.18-31.5). According to the author, the Jordan typifies natural human birth, and the power of the Holy Spirit that descends with Christ at his birth overcomes the defilement of human procreation. The second pericope contrasts John the Baptist's and Christ's births (45.6-18). On the one hand, John was begotten in Elizabeth and born through natural means. On the other hand, Christ was supernaturally conceived and passed through a virgin's womb, yet he appeared in the clothes of human flesh (32.22-24). It appears, therefore, that Jordan signifies the natural order of human procreation into corporeality, and Christ's virgin birth has circumvented the process; Christ as the Word descended (39.22-23) into Mary's womb and passed through it without having received anything of her human nature, the Jordan did not touch the Son of Man.[30]

Some conclusions can be drawn from the foregoing examination of the author's Spirit Christology. First, since the Holy Spirit was the power that descended, as a dove, upon Christ at the Jordan, the Holy Spirit was the power of the salvific mission. Second, because Christ descended as the Word, and the Holy Spirit descended upon Christ, the author has attempted to integrate Spirit Christology with a form of Logos Christology. Third, the author stresses that Christ enters the world by passing through the virgin while maintaining his transcendent spiritual nature; Christ does not acquire a human nature from Mary. In other words, the author's Spirit Christology focuses on the spiritual nature inspiring the vessel which bears it.

The Gospel of Philip

Several facets of *The Gospel of Philip* present a conundrum. For instance, the author is unknown; the tractate may simply bear this title because Philip is the only apostle the text mentions by name (73.8), and Gnostics hold him in high esteem.[31] Even though the late third century presents a plausible date for the original Greek version of the text, the date of origin is doubtful. Nevertheless, a Syrian prov-

---

[30] Franzmann, *Jesus*, pp. 52-54.
[31] Gnostics held that Jesus placed Philip in a favored position to record Jesus' words and deeds. Filson, 'Manuscripts', p. 11.

enance seems more certain because of the author's interest in Syrian words.³² The tractate's structure presents the most problematic analysis of the text; the sequence of thought is rambling, disjointed, and abruptly changes. Some continuity of thought, however, can be searched out by observing how the author links similar ideas, series of contrasts, and catchwords.³³ For example, the recurring themes of the sacraments, the human predicament, and life after death find their true meaning and value in a Gnostic worldview which delineates the results of humanity's fall as the differentiation of the sexes and death (68.22-26). The purpose of Christ's salvific mission, accordingly, purposes to reunite Adam and Eve, so that Christ brings about the reunion of humanity in the bridal chamber, which is a sacramental event, similar to a husband and wife uniting (70.10-22).³⁴ This document, consequently, stands as a compilation of statements about these concerns with a pneumatic christological interpretation.

There are four Spirit christological texts in the *Gospel of Philip* that elucidate a Gnostic version of Jesus Christ's virgin birth. The first text names Mary as the mother or Jesus, but by way of contrast to the canonical tradition it asserts that she did not conceive by the Holy Spirit.

---

³² Wesley W. Isenberg, 'Philip, Gospel of ', *ABD*, V, p. 312; Filson, 'Manuscripts', pp. 11-12. Jeffrey Siker suggests that the tractate reflects the earlier tensions in the Ignatian epistles, so that the Gospel of Philip provides evidence for relations among Jewish, Gnostic, and Christian communities around second century Antioch. Jeffery S. Siker, 'Gnostic Views on Jews and Christians in the Gospel of Philip', *NovT* 31 (1989), pp. 274-88.

³³ Wesley W. Isenberg's introduction to *Gos. Phil.*, NHL, pp. 139-41; R. McL. Wilson, *The Gospel of Philip: Translated from the Coptic Text, with an Introduction and Commentary* (London: A.R. Mowbray & Co., 1962), pp. 1-11; Isenberg, '*Gos. Phil.*', *ABD*, V, p. 313. Isenberg provides an introduction and translation of the Coptic text in Robinson (ed.), *The Coptic Gnostic Library*, II, pp. 129-215.

³⁴ Cf. Jorunn Jacobsen Buckley, 'A Cult-Mystery in the Gospel of Philip', *JBL* 99 (1980), pp. 570-73; Filson, 'Manuscripts', pp. 12-13. April DeConick posited that the heavenly bridal chamber represented the Holy of Holies in which Christ was begotten by the Father and the Holy Spirit. Human marriage, therefore, should reflect this heavenly marriage and be controlled by pure thought rather than sexual desire for someone outside of marriage. April D. DeConick, 'The True Mysteries', *VC* 55 (2001), pp. 246-47. Cf. Buckley, 'Cult-Mystery', pp. 574-75; Frend, *Christianity*, p. 200.

> Some said, 'Mary conceived by the [H]oly [S]pirit'. They are in error. They do not know what they are saying. When did a woman ever conceive by a woman (55.23-26)?[35]

This text, therefore, implies the femininity of the Holy Spirit,[36] and it raises the questions of the source of Mary's virginity and Jesus' parentage. First, the author affirms that Mary's virginity stands in relation to her knowledge of the Truth (55.18-22), which has preserved her as 'the virgin whom no power defiled' (55.27-28). Second, the author implies that Jesus has two fathers: 'And the lord [would] not have said "My [father who is in] heaven" (Mt. 16.17) unless [he] had had another father, but he would have said simply "[My father]"' (55.32-36).[37] Christ, therefore, had a set of earthly parents, Joseph (73.14-15) and Mary, and a heavenly Father.

The other Spirit christological texts seem to imply the concept of dual parentage, heavenly and earthly.[38] Thus, the author refers to Christ's first and second birth.

> Jesus appeared [...] Jordan – the [fullness of the kingdom] of heaven. He who [was begotten] before everything was begotten anew. He [who was] once [anointed] was anointed anew. He who was redeemed in turn redeemed (others) (70.34-71.3).[39]

Apparently, Christ's reception of the Spirit signals Christ's rebirth, re-anointing, and redemption, through the activity of the Father and the Holy Spirit, which is a paradigm for the rebirth, anointing, and redemption of the pneumatics.[40] Since this text points beyond this

---

[35] Cited according to the translation of Wesley W. Isenberg, 'The Gospel of Philip', in James M. Robinson (ed.), *NHL*, p. 143.

[36] Pagels, *Gnostic Gospels*, pp. 51-52; Stanley M. Burgess, 'Holy Spirit, Doctrine of: The Ancient Fathers', in Stanley M. Burgess and Ed M. Van der Maas (eds.), *NIDPCM* (Grand Rapids: Zondervan, Rev. and expanded edn, 2002), p. 732.

[37] Robinson (ed.), *NHL*, p. 143.

[38] Franzmann, *Jesus*, pp. 49-52.

[39] Robinson (ed.), *NHL*, p. 152.

[40] 'Through the [H]oly [S]pirit we are indeed begotten again, but we are begotten through Christ in the two. We are anointed through the Spirit. When we are begotten, we are united' (69.4-8). Robinson (ed.), *NHL*, p. 151. The emphasis is not on water baptism; the author asserts that the Father anointed the son; therefore, 'The charism is superior to baptism for it is from the word "chrism" that we are called "Christians," certainly not because of the word "baptism." And it is because of the chrism that "the Christ" has his name' (74.11-16). Robinson (ed.), *NHL*, p. 153. Furthermore, 'If one go [*sic*] down into the water and come up without having received anything and says, "I am a Christian," he has borrowed

event to a preexistent heavenly birth, before everything, the following text seems to depict the concept of a set of heavenly parents.

> The father of everything united with the virgin who came down, and a fire shone for him on that day. He appeared in the great bridal chamber. Therefore his body came into being on that very day. It left the bridal chamber as one who came into being from the bridegroom and the bride (71.4-11).[41]

Previously, the author has affirmed the femininity of the Holy Spirit, so it is reasonable to infer that the heavenly parents are the heavenly Father and the Holy Spirit.[42] The Holy Spirit descends hence as the heavenly virgin that comes down to rebirth Christ in the human body which his earthly parents had given birth.[43] The next text reiterates the idea of dual parentage.

> Adam came into being from two virgins, from the [S]pirit and from the virgin earth. Christ, therefore, was born from a virgin to rectify the fall which occurred in the beginning (71.16-21).[44]

True to Gnostic convictions, the author alludes to the origin of the human spirit from its heavenly mother, the divine Spirit, and

---

the name at interest. But if he receives the [H]oly [S]pirit, he has the name as a gift' (64.22-27). Robinson (ed.), *NHL*, p. 148. Those who are reborn and receive the unction are 'no longer called a Christian but a Christ. The lord [did] everything in a mystery, a baptism and a charism and a eucharist and a redemption and a bridal chamber' (67.9-30). Robinson (ed.), *NHL*, p. 150. The Pneumatics, then, are anointed by the Holy Spirit. Eric Segelberg, 'The Coptic-Gnostic Gospel According to Philip and its Sacramental System', *Numen* 7 (1960), pp. 189-200. Furthermore, the pneumatic is one who has already experienced resurrection through the Spirit. Michael A. Williams, 'Realized Eschatology in the Gospel of Philip', *ResQ* 14 (1971), pp. 1-17.

[41] Robinson (ed.), *NHL*, p. 152. The Word is Christ's preexistent spiritual body (55.11-13; 57.4-7).

[42] The author confirms this inference in 52.24 and 59.35-60.1. Symbols of the Holy Spirit that the author uses include: water, fire, chrism, and perfect light (58.8-12). 'It is from water and fire and light that the son of the bridal chamber (came into being). The fire is the chrism, the light is the fire' (67.3-6). Robinson (ed.), *NHL*, p. 150. During his descent, the powers could not see Christ because he was clothed in perfect light (70.6-9).

[43] The rebirth of the pneumatic, therefore, 'mirrors the spiritual birth of the aeon Jesus who had been conceived through the union of the Virgin or Holy Spirit and the Father in the Pleroma bridal chamber'. DeConick, 'True Mysteries', pp. 229.

[44] Robinson (ed.), *NHL*, p. 152.

descent into corporeality; therefore, Christ was also born from dual parentage, heavenly and earthly, to fulfill his salvific mission.[45]

With regard to the interpretation of these passages, it appears that the author's pneumatic Christology posits dual movements of Christ's entry and stages of being in the world, spiritual and earthly. In the spiritual movement Christ descended into the earth from his heavenly parents in the spiritual body of the Word and changed his appearance according to the context of the revelation (57.28-58.10). In the earthly movement Jesus experienced an ordinary birth from his earthly parents in human flesh. These two Christs merged during the rebirth of Christ from the Spirit, so that Christ had put on human flesh as clothing (57.6-8; 67.9-21). After they merged, however, the author did not seem to make any distinctions between Jesus and Christ.[46] In fact, it seems the author's concept of dual parentage serves as a basis to teach the dual natures of Christ: flesh and Spirit. Of course, the author does not teach an incarnational Christology; instead, the author appears to posit an adoptionist form of pneumatic Christology.

According to these three Gnostic witnesses, the protagonist of the Gnostic soteriological system is a salvific Spirit.[47] Salvation, receiving the gnosis, consequently, is a dynamic pneumatic event: a redemption, spiritual resurrection, new birth, reunion in a bridal chamber, and an anointing. The anointing of the Spirit, therefore, permeates all soteriology categories, so that those who possess the Spirit become known as the pneumatics. Furthermore, the essential form of entrance into the world and mission of Christ was spiritual; the anointing of the Spirit at Jordan is the significant event. Gnosticism devalues Christ' humanity by denying Christ's incarnation in human flesh, but it accentuates the salvific Spirit that anoints and

---

[45] Jesus accomplished this 'by bringing through his own birth, the divine bridal chamber to earth'. DeConick, 'True Mysteries', p. 253.

[46] 'There is no differentiation intended between Jesus and the Christ after the event of Jesus' rebirth. The fact that the Christ is said to be Jesus' body does not imply that he is thereby an "extra" added on the person of Christ.' Franzmann, *Jesus*, p. 50, n. 3.

[47] Marcion was an important contemporary voice, but his docetic Christology falls outside the parameters of this survey. Although Marcion stated that Jesus Christ descended from heaven as the saving Spirit (Tertullian, *Marc.* 1.19), he denied that Christ had a physical body; Christ was a phantom that appeared in the form of a man (Tertullian, *Marc.* 3.8).

inspires Christ; therefore, these voices from the margins present a Spirit Christology of pneumatic inspiration.

Ebionism

In the process of working out the early church's relationship with its Hebrew heritage various groups formed; among them were certain marginal groups: in particular, the Ebionites.[48] Although Ebionism probably originated during the first century, the term first appeared in Irenaeus' writings around 180 (*Haer.* 1.26.2). The epithet means the poor; however, it is uncertain whether this signifies a term of derision designating mental and spiritual deficiency, or a term of endearment denoting the inheritors of the kingdom of heaven (Mt. 5.3), the practice of voluntary poverty, or their piety of life.[49] Along with several reliable secondary patristic sources – Irenaeus, Tertullian, Hippolytus, Origen, Eusebius, Epiphanius, and Jerome – that provide fragments of Ebionite writings,[50] the Pseudo-

---

[48] Similar groups included the Nazarenes and the Elkasaites. Epiphanius, *Pan.* 29; Pelikan, *Christian Tradition*, I, p. 24; Schaff, *History*, II, pp. 431-34; Seeberg and Hay, *History*, I, pp. 87-90; Daniélou and Baker, *Jewish Christianity*, pp. 7-10; Hans-Joachim Schoeps, *Jewish Christianity: Fractional Disputes in the Early Church* (Philadelphia: Fortress, 1969), pp. 9-13; Ray Pritz, *Nazarene Jewish Christianity: From the End of the New Testament Period Until Its Disappearance in the Fourth Century* (Studpb 37; Leiden E.J. Brill, 1988). These groups supported a form of Spirit Christology; however, since the Elkasaites taught a blended form of Gnostic Christology, and the Nazarenes' Christology bore strong similarities with Dynamic Monarchianism, the survey will not discuss these groups.

[49] Epiphanius, *Pan.* 30.17.1-3; Daniélou and Baker, *Jewish Christianity*, pp. 55-56; Schoeps, *Fractional Disputes*, pp. 10-11; Joseph A. Fitzmyer, 'The Qumran Scrolls, The Ebionites, and Their Literature', in Krister Stendahl and James H. Charlesworth (eds.), *The Scrolls and the New Testament* (New York: Crossroad, 1992), pp. 209-10; Stephen Goranson, 'Ebionites', *ABD*, II, pp. 260-61. The description of the community's piety sounds remarkably similar to the one given by Raymond Brown concerning the Anawim community: 'Although this title "Poor Ones" may have originally designated the physically poor (and frequently still included them), it came to refer more widely to those who could not trust in their own strength but had to rely in utter confidence upon God'. Raymond Edward Brown, *The Birth of the Messiah: A Commentary on the Infancy Narratives in the Gospels of Matthew and Luke* (ABRL; New York: Doubleday, New updated edn, 1993), pp. 351-52.

[50] These fragments refer to such documents as the *Gospel of the Hebrews*, the *Gospel of the Ebionites*, the *Preaching of Peter*, the *Journeys of Peter*, and the translation of the Hebrew Scriptures by Symmachus. Schoeps, *Fractional Disputes*, pp. 13-17; Daniélou and Baker, *Jewish Christianity*, pp. 58-63. Although most scholars include Symmachus' translation of the Hebrew Scriptures as Ebionite literature, recent

Clementine literature preserve a couple of primary sources: *Recognitions* and *Homilies*.

Concerning early Christianity's relationship with its Jewish heritage, Ebionism represented a unique position; based on its views of the Hebrew Scriptures and messianic expectations, it called for a reform of the Mosaic Law.[51] First, they critically analyzed the Hebrew Scriptures and found evidence of redaction and falsification of certain texts (*Homilies* 2.38–52).[52] According to Ebionism, these interpolated texts included uninspired prophetic texts, anthropomorphic statements about God, and demeaning characterizations of the patriarchs; furthermore, they provided the basis for the illegal institution of animal sacrifices, the Jerusalem temple, and the monarchy. Second, Ebionism expected the messiah, the true prophet, to reform the law by revealing and repealing these falsifications (*Homilies* 3.50–57).[53] The true prophet's reformed version of the law, correspondingly, taught a better righteousness which included abstinence from meat, voluntary poverty, ceremonial washings to purge uncleanness, and instead of animal sacrifices water baptism initiated recipients into the kingdom of God (*Homilies* 8.15; 15.7–10; 9.23;

---

scholarship has called this into question. Thus, David Wright summarizes, 'Symmachus' alleged Ebionitism contributes nothing to any understanding of this strand of Jewish Christianity'. David F. Wright, 'Ebionites', *DLNT*, pp. 313-17.

[51] There has been some discussion about the appropriateness of using the term Jewish Christianity. Harnack posits that Jewish Christianity and Ebionism are synonymous terms; furthermore, he contends that the designation Jewish Christianity is only appropriately applied to a group that maintains 'the national and political forms of Judaism and the observance of the Mosaic law in its literal sense, as essential to Christianity'. Harnack, *Dogma*, I, p. 289. Cf. Georg Strecker, Appendix I, in Walter Bauer, Robert A. Kraft, and Gerhard Krodel, *Orthodoxy and Heresy in Earliest Christianity* (Philadelphia: Fortress Press, 1971), pp. 241-85. With the publication of texts from the Dead Sea Scrolls, the possible relationship between the Qumran sect and the Ebionites has received some attention from scholars. For a comparison of the Qumran sect and the Ebionites, see Fitzmyer, 'Ebionites', pp. 214-31.

[52] According to the Ebionites, this falsification occurred over a period of one thousand years in three phases: (1) Moses orally transmitted the law of God to seventy wise men to be handed down, but after his death, someone placed the law in writing; (2) the document was lost, but about five hundred years later it was rediscovered in the Temple; (3) approximately five hundred years after this reform, the document was carried away and destroyed under Nebuchadnezzar and was later rewritten (*Homilies* 3.47).

[53] Cf. Schoeps, *Fractional Disputes*, pp. 74-94; Shedd, *Doctrine*, I, pp. 106-12; Daniélou and Baker, *Jewish Christianity*, pp. 60-61; Epiphanius, *Pan.* 16.4-7; 18.7.

Recognitions 1.69).[54] Salvation, therefore, came through strict adherence to a reformed version of the law.

The Pseudo-Clementine literature contains an Ebionite version of Spirit Christology, specifically, the *Recognitions* and the *Homilies*. These documents were pseudonymously attributed to Clement of Rome and probably written in Syria during the early third century.[55] They are dyadic forms of a novel depicting Clement's journey of faith – from searching for truth in the philosophical schools of Rome, to finding faith in Christ, and becoming one of the Apostle Peter's disciples in Caesarea – and his search for his mother, two brothers, and father. Finally, through Peter's aid, Clement finds these relatives, and they recognize one another; hence, *Recognitions* furnishes the title for one version of the novel. The largest part of the documents, however, concerns Peter's sermons and his debates with the sorcerer Simon Magus;[56] accordingly, *Homilies* supplies the title for the companion volume.[57]

These documents delineate its Spirit Christology under Ebionism's rubric of the messianic true prophet. According to the author, beginning with Adam and continuing through anointed servants God revealed himself through a succession of true prophets (*Homi-*

---

[54] Cf. Schoeps, *Fractional Disputes*, pp. 99-109; Epiphanius, *Pan*. 30.15.3. It is worth noticing the similarity between Ebionism's concept of the 'true prophet' and the Samaritan eschatological expectation concerning the messianic figure of the 'Taheb'. According to this Samaritan view, there are four stages of history; there are two stages of divine disfavor and two stages of divine favor. The first stage of disfavor, which extends from Adam to Noah, is followed by the first stage of favor, extending from Noah to Samson; then, the second stage of disfavor begins with Eli and continues until the arrival of the prophet like Moses, the Taheb. Since the word taheb means to return or the one who restores, with the arrival of the Taheb, true and proper worship and divine favor will return, and the Samaritans will be vindicated. R.J. Coggins, *Samaritans and Jews: The Origins of Samaritanism Reconsidered* (Atlanta: John Knox Press, 1975), pp. 145-47.

[55] Quasten, *Patrology*, I, pp. 59-62; Harnack, *Dogma*, I, p. 311; Schaff, *History*, II, p. 442; F. Stanley Jones, 'Clementines, Pseudo', *ABD*, I, p. 1061. For a review of modern research and textual concerns of the *Recognitions* 1.27-71 and a translation of these texts, see F. Stanley Jones, *An Ancient Jewish Christian Source on the History of Christianity: Pseudo-Clementine Recognitions 1.27-71* (Atlanta: Scholars Press, 1995).

[56] It has been suggested that Peter's arch rival here is not actually Simon Magus but the apostle Paul. Epiphanius, *Pan*. 30.16.8-9; Schaff, *History*, II, pp. 437-38; Schoeps, *Fractional Disputes*, pp. 47-58; Jones, 'Clementines', pp. 1061-62.

[57] There is as much homiletic material in the *Recognitions* as there is narrative and recognitions in the *Homilies*; often long verbatim passages parallel one another. Fitzmyer, 'Ebionites', pp. 213-14.

lies 2.12–17; Epiphanius, *Pan.* 30.18.4-6).[58] The advent of the messianic true prophet, however, brought the definitive revelation of God's will (*Recognitions* 1.16). So that the people might recognize the prophet whom Moses foretold, following Moses' pattern, signs and miracles certified the messianic credentials of the true prophet (*Recognitions* 1.40; 5.10; 8.59; 10.51). The author's Spirit Christology, thereupon, elucidates Jesus as the true prophet.

> I do not speak of Moses, but of Him who, in the waters of baptism, was called by God His Son. For it is Jesus who has put out, by the grace of baptism, that fire which the priest kindled for sins; for, from the time when He appeared, the chrism has ceased, by which the priesthood or the prophetic or the kingly office was conferred (*Recognitions* 1.48).[59]

This Spirit christological passage presents three matters of interpretation. First, how does the author apply the designation Son of God to Jesus? Although *Recognitions* 1.45 seems to affirm the preexistent divine nature of the Son, the author in unambiguous monotheistic terms declares that the Son is not of the same substance as the divine Creator (*Homilies* 16.15–17; *Recognitions* 2.56–60). It appears, then, that Jesus becomes the adopted Son of God during his baptism at the Jordan.[60] Second, concerning the grace of baptism extinguishing the fire kindled for sins, this event referred to the true prophet replacing animal sacrifices with water baptism as the means of forgiveness of sins (*Recognitions* 1.47; 1.49). Third, what was the chrism that conferred the offices of prophet, priest, and king, and why did it cease? According to the author, chrism was an anointing

---

[58] The concept of pairs was important in Ebionism's theology; for example, juxtaposed with the appearance of a true prophet came their counterpart, a false prophet, who opposed their revelation of God (*Recognitions* 1.24; 3.24; 3.59–61; 5.9; 8.55). Cf. Epiphanius, *Pan.* 30.16.2. Often the author expressed these differences between the true and false prophets as male and female false spirits (*Homilies* 3.22–27).

[59] Cited according to the translation of Thomas Smith, Clement, 'Recognitions of Clement', ANF, VIII, p. 90. There are only a few minor variations in Stanley's translation. Jones, *Pseudo-Clementine Recognitions*, p. 80.

[60] Epiphanius, *Pan.* 30.14.4. In Ebionism he was not 'the only begotten Son of God, but a mere prophet within the sequence of prophets. He was no longer the Savior, but simply an element – sometimes secondary – of the action of God within the age'. González, *Christian Thought*, I, p. 125. 'They regarded Jesus as merely human.' Bauer, Kraft, and Krodel, *Orthodoxy and Heresy in Earliest Christianity*, p. 201. Cf. Kelly, *Doctrines*, p. 139.

that placed someone into these offices, and the designation Christ drew its meaning from this anointing (*Recognitions* 1.45). Moreover, Christ and the anointing emerge as synonymous concepts; throughout history Christ reappeared in the world as the anointing of the Spirit that inspired and constituted a true prophet (*Homilies* 3.20; *Recognitions* 1.47; Epiphanius *Pan.* 30.3.4-5). The Spirit, accordingly, filled and anointed Jesus (*Homilies* 3.15; Epiphanius *Pan.* 30.3.6). The chrism ceased because the lineage of prophetic succession culminated with Jesus; therefore, he became the archetypical Christ of whom Moses had prophesied, the messianic true prophet (*Recognitions* 1.43).

According to Ebionism, Jesus, like his predecessors, was a person anointed with the Holy Spirit; the last in a sequence of bearers of the Spirit. The anointing of the Holy Spirit, thus, constituted Jesus as the Christ, the true prophet, the bearer of the definitive revelation and will of God, and the Son of God at his baptism in the Jordan.[61] Through the anointing of the Spirit Jesus performed miracles and signs, verifying his messianic credentials. Ebionism's paradigm of the messianic true prophet, therefore, delineates a Spirit Christology of pneumatic inspiration.

Monarchianism

As the name implies, Monarchianism included monotheistic groups, which flourished during the late second and third centuries, which sought to preserve and protect the concept of the Father's divine monarchy. Originally, Monarchianism arose as a voice asserting the unity of God against Gnostic polytheism and Marcion Docetism. Since they suspected that the specter of Gnosticism stood behind the Logos concept developing at the center of Christology, this marginal voice spoke in opposition to Logos Christology; thus, nascent Monarchianism became known as the alogoi.[62] This group,

---

[61] The Ebionites used Ps. 2.7 to 'support their teaching that Jesus was a man endowed with special powers of the Spirit'. Pelikan, *Christian Tradition*, I, p. 176.

[62] The alogoi originated about 170 in Asia Minor. Epiphanius was the first to use the term because they rejected the Logos doctrine, the Fourth Gospel, and the Apocalypse; according to the alogoi, the Gnostic Cerinthus wrote the Fourth Gospel (Epiphanius, *Pan.* 51.3.1-6). Cf. Schaff, *History*, II, p. 573; Burgess, *The Holy Spirit: Ancient Christian Traditions*, p. 46. Along with opposing Docetism, Har-

accordingly, rejected trinitarian teaching as blatant tritheism and declared it incompatible with their monotheistic view of the Father's undivided essence.[63] This remained a central tenet of Monarchian theology as it developed past the alogoi into two similar but diverse branches: Dynamic Monarchianism and Modalistic Monarchianism.

Although Monarchianism's primary works are not extant, their opponents' writings have preserved fragments of Monarchian teaching: Hippolytus, Malchion, Tertullian, Epiphanius, Eusebius, Athanasius, and Basil. The survey will depend on these secondary sources to examine the Spirit christological references found in the prominent leaders' teachings of both branches of Monarchianism.

Dynamic Monarchianism

Theodotus

Theodotus, who came from Byzantium to Rome while Victor was bishop,[64] has furnished the earliest Spirit christological reference among Dynamic Monarchians. According to the record preserved by Hippolytus (222),[65] Theodotus' Christology was inherently pneumatic.

> Jesus was a (mere) man, born of a virgin, according to the counsel of the Father, and that after he had lived promiscuously with all men, and had become pre-eminently religious, he subsequently at his baptism in Jordan received Christ, who came from above and descended (upon him) in form of a dove. And this was the reason, (according to Theodotus,) why (miraculous) powers did not operate within him prior to the manifestation in him of that Spirit which descended, (and) which proclaims him to be the Christ (*Haer.* 7.32).[66]

---

nack states that the alogoi also resisted Montanist prophecies, and they affirmed Christ's virgin birth. Harnack, *Dogma*, III, pp. 14-19.

[63] 'Monarchianism', *ODCC*, p. 1102; González, *Christian Thought*, I, 143-44; Seeberg and Hay, *History*, I, pp. 162-63.

[64] This places his arrival in Rome around 192–202. At some point during this time Victor excommunicated Theodotus. Schaff, *History*, II, p. 574; 'Theodotus', *ODCC*, p. 1602.

[65] This date is according to Quasten. Quasten, *Patrology*, II, p. 168.

[66] Cited according to the translation of J.H. MacMahon, Hippolytus, 'The Refutation of all Heresies', ANF, V, pp. 114-15. Epiphanius recorded that Theodotus was a well-educated man. At some point, during a persecution of Chris-

According to this text, Jesus was born of a virgin; nonetheless, Jesus remained a normal person. Although Jesus' virgin birth came by a special decree of the Father and through the agency of the Holy Spirit, neither deity nor miraculous powers resided or operated in him. After Jesus' piety of life was tested, and he demonstrated righteousness that excelled all humans, the Holy Spirit descended upon him at the Jordan; this anointing and empowering for the messianic mission constituted and revealed him as the Christ. The Spirit's presence in Jesus, however, did not justify calling him God; Jesus was a man anointed and inspired by the Spirit, the impersonal power of God.[67]

Paul of Samosata

Paul of Samosata, while serving as bishop of Antioch (260–68), taught a form of Spirit Christology similar to Theodotus.[68] According to Malchion, who was instrumental in deposing Paul from the bishopric, Paul had erred from the faith.

> He does not wish to acknowledge that the Son of God came down from heaven. And this is a statement which shall not be made to depend on simple assertion; for it is proved abundantly by those memoranda which we sent you, and not least by that passage in which he says that Jesus Christ is from below (ch. 3).[69]

---

tians in Constantinople, Theodotus denied Christ. After he moved to Rome, the people recognized him as one who had denied Christ, so to vindicate himself, he claimed, 'I did not deny God, I denied a human being'. Cited according to the translation in Epiphanius, *The Panarion of St. Epiphanius, Bishop of Salamis: Selected Passages* (trans. Philip R. Amidon; New York: Oxford University Press, 1990), 54.1.1-7, p. 192.

[67] According to Epiphanius, Theodotus perceived Christ as a prophet like Moses: a man anointed by the Spirit (Epiphanius, *Pan.* 54.3.1). Cf. Harnack, *Dogma*, III, pp. 20-32; Kelly, *Doctrines*, pp. 115-17; Seeberg and Hay, *History*, I, pp. 163-64; Pelikan, *Christian Tradition*, I, p. 176. Some of Theodotus's followers affirmed that Jesus was made God after the resurrection from the dead (Hippolytus, *Haer.* 7.32). However, not all of his successors agreed with this supposition.

[68] Epiphanius, *Pan.* 65.1.3-4; 'Paul of Samosata', *ODCC*, p. 1242; Quasten, *Patrology*, II, pp. 140-41.

[69] Cited according to the translation of S.D. Salmond, Malchion, 'The Epistle Written by Malchion, in the Name of the Synod of Antioch, against Paul of Samosata', ANF, VI, p. 170. This is recounted in Eusebius, 'The Church History of Eusebius', NPNF, Second Series, I, 7.30.11, p. 315. The importance of the Council of Antioch, which deposed Paul, in the development of Christology is discussed by Robert Sample, 'The Christology of the Council of Antioch (268) Reconsidered', *CH* 48 (1979), pp. 18-26.

This statement concerned Paul's concept of the Son of God, and his view of Jesus Christ. In his triadic language – Father, Logos, and Spirit – Paul used the term ὁμοούσιος[70] to indicate the unity and undivided essence of deity and to deny any subsistence in God. Paul, accordingly, preserved the Father's monarchy by asserting that the Logos and Spirit were impersonal powers or spiritual energies of the one divine essence (Athanasius, *C. Ar.* 4.30-36; Epiphanius, *Pan.* 65.1.5-8). Through the Spirit's power Jesus was born of a virgin, and at the Jordan the Logos/Spirit anointed and empowered Jesus' mission. In Jesus the Logos of God dwelled, but it dwelled in a greater degree than it did in Moses and the prophets; he was fully inspired of the Spirit and given the dignity of a name above all names: Jesus became the Son of God from below (Athanasius, *Syn.* 26).[71]

Dynamic Monarchianism attempted to preserve a monotheistic view of one undivided divine essence by postulating that the divinity in Christ was an impersonal power, but this by no means implied that Jesus was divine. Jesus was a human uniquely inspired by the Spirit as the messianic redeemer; therefore, Dynamic Monarchianism posited a Spirit Christology of pneumatic inspiration.

Modalistic Monarchianism

Noetus of Smyrna

Noetus of Smyrna, who probably served as bishop and was condemned by a synod of that city around 200, produced the first Spirit Christological references among Modalist Monarchianism (Hippolytus, *Haer.* 9.2).[72] Noetus concerned himself with expressing the full

---

[70] Basil the Great and Hilary of Poitiers discuss the distinction between Paul of Samosata's use of ὁμοούσιος and its use at the Council of Nicea in 325 (Basil, *Letters*, 52; Hilary, *On the Councils*, 81-91). Cf. Atanasije Jevtich, 'Between the "Nicaeans" and the "Easterners": The Catholic Confession of Saint Basil', *SVTQ* 24 (1980), 235-52.

[71] Cf. Harnack, *Dogma*, III, pp. 37-47; González, *Christian Thought*, I, pp. 248-52; Seeberg and Hay, *History*, I, pp. 164-66; Kelly, *Doctrines*, pp. 117-19; Schaff, *History*, II, pp. 575-76; Frend, *Christianity*, p. 344; Shedd, *Doctrine*, I, p. 257; Berkhof, *Christian Doctrines*, p. 78; Pelikan, *Christian Tradition*, I, p. 176; Burgess, *Ancient Christian Traditions*, p. 47; Brian E. Daley, 'One Thing and Another: The Persons in God and the Person of Christ in Patristic Theology', *ProEccl* 15 (2006), pp. 29-332.

[72] Cf. Harnack, *Dogma*, III, p. 57; Kelly, *Doctrines*, pp. 120-21; Burgess, *Ancient Christian Traditions*, p. 47. According to Hippolytus, Noetus followed the tenets of the philosopher Heraclites. Since Heraclites taught the harmony of all antitheses

divinity of Jesus Christ while maintaining the unity of God. Although Noetus affirmed that the divine Logos became incarnate in Jesus Christ, he contended that this was the Father (Hippolytus, *Haer.* 9.5).

> There is one Father and God, the Creator of the universe, and that this (God) is spoken of, and called by the name of Son, yet that in substance He is one Spirit. For Spirit, as the Deity, is, he says, not any being different from the Logos, or the Logos from the Deity (Hippolytus, *Haer.* 10.23).[73]

According to Noetus, because the essence of deity is Spirit, no distinction exists within the divine nature; the Logos and Holy Spirit were manifestations of the one God, the Father (Epiphanius, *Pan.* 57.2.9). The designations Father and Son, furthermore, did not indicate real distinctions; they were simply names applicable in various times. When Noetus acknowledged Christ's deity, consequently, he affirmed that the Father was born of a virgin, assumed human flesh, suffered in crucifixion for humanity's sin, and raised himself from the dead (Hippolytus, *Noet.* 2).[74] Because this form of Monarchianism affirmed the Father's suffering in Christ, it became known as patripassianism; nevertheless, since Spirit is the substance of Deity in Noetus' theology, perhaps, monotheistic pneumatic Christology is as valid a designation for his Christology.

Praxeas

Praxeas was the first teacher to import this branch of Monarchianism into Rome from Asia, probably around 200, while Victor was

---

– the universe was divisible and indivisible, generated and un-generated, mortal and immortal – Noetus assumed that God was capable of combining opposite attributes in the divine nature (Hippolytus, *Haer.* 9.4-5).

[73] Cited according to the translation of J.H. MacMahon, Hippolytus, 'Refutation', ANF, V, p. 148. In this passage Hippolytus demonstrates that Noetus's disciples became known as Noetians because they closely adhered to this view of God as their starting point.

[74] When Noetus' beliefs were examined by the local presbytery, he responded, 'What have I done wrong in glorifying one God? I know one God and none other beside him, the one who was born, suffered, and died' (Epiphanius, *Pan.* 57.1.8). Cited according to the translation of Philip Amidon, Epiphanius, *Pan.*, p. 199. Cf. Pelikan, *Christian Tradition*, I, pp. 178-80; Daley, 'One Thing and Another', pp. 24-26; Seeberg and Hay, *History*, I, pp. 167-68; González, *Christian Thought*, I, p. 145; Schaff, *History*, II, pp. 578-79; Berkhof, *Christian Doctrines*, pp. 78-79.

Bishop.[75] Subsequently, Praxeas taught his doctrine in opposition to Montanism, effectively persuading the Roman bishop to reject the New Prophecy's doctrines (Tertullian, *Prax.* 1). Tertullian's polemic response to this action, *Against Praxeas*, has preserved valuable information about Praxeas' teachings since his writings are not extant.

Praxeas' hermeneutic maintained the monarchy of the Father by placing all Scripture under the rubric of Isa. 45.5, Jn 10.30, and Jn 14.9-10 (Tertullian, *Prax.* 20); correspondingly, Praxeas' Spirit Christology made no distinction in the divine essence.

> But you insist upon it that the Father Himself is the Spirit, on the ground that 'God is Spirit,' just as if we did not read also that there is 'the Spirit of God;' in the same manner as we find that as 'the Word was God,' so also there is 'the Word of God' (Tertullian, Prax. 27).[76]

Praxeas, thus, affirmed Spirit and Father as synonymous designations for the substance of deity. Allowing for use of the terms Logos and Holy Spirit, he asserted that these names were merely designations of the Father (Tertullian, *Prax.* 9–10). The deity, therefore, manifested in Jesus Christ was the Father (Tertullian, *Prax.* 2; 5; 7; 15). Praxeas, however, distinguished between the Father and the Son to avoid the implications of the Father expiring during the crucifixion; it was not deity that died but the Son of God (Tertullian, *Prax.* 29). According the Praxeas, in the incarnation the divine Spirit assumed human flesh, so that the Father dwelled in the Son as the human spirit dwelled in flesh; in other words, Jesus' human flesh constituted the Son of God, and the Father was the divine Spirit that conceived the Son in Mary's womb and dwelled in the Son (Tertullian, *Prax.* 27).[77] Thereupon, Praxeas' Spirit Christology predicates that the divine essence, the Spirit, became incarnate in Jesus Christ, a pneumatic incarnation.

---

[75] It has been suggested that Praxeas was a nickname for Noetus, Epignous, or Callistus, but this has failed to convince a number of scholars. Harnack, *Dogma*, III, pp. 59-61; 'Praxeas', *ODCC*, p. 1315.

[76] Cited according to the translation of Dr. Holmes, Tertullian, 'Against Praxeas', ANF, III, p. 624.

[77] Cf. Harnack, *Dogma*, III, pp. 65-68; Seeberg and Hay, *History*, I, p. 167; Pelikan, *Christian Tradition*, I, pp. 179-80; Schaff, *History*, II, p. 577; Kelly, *Doctrines*, p. 121; Daley, 'One Thing and Another', pp. 126-29.

Sabellius

Sabellius was the next proponent of this form of Spirit Christology. Sabellius remains an obscure figure; knowledge of his life and teachings must be gleaned from a few select passages of his opponents' writings. Sabellius probably was a Libyan who came to Rome during Zephyrinus' bishopric (198–217) and gained the confidence of Callistus before he became bishop (217–22).[78] Sometime during Callistus' bishopric, Callistus turned against Sabellius and excommunicated him. Nevertheless, his teaching spread into the East; subsequently, Dionysius, bishop of Alexandria, excommunicated him around 260.[79]

Though he maintained Monarchianism's central tenet, the monarchy of the Father, Sabellius gave a more extensive role to the Holy Spirit and developed a form of trinitarian doctrine. Spirit Christology was central to this paradigm.

> Sabellius also raves in saying that the Father is Son, and again, the Son Father, in subsistence One, in name Two; and he raves also in using as an example the grace of the Spirit. For he says, As there are 'diversities of gifts, but the same Spirit,' so also the Father is the same, but is dilated into Son and Spirit (Athanasius, *C. Ar.* 4.25).[80]

Sabellius begins by affirming the unity of divine essence (Epiphanius, *Pan.* 62.1.4; Athanasius, *C. Ar.* 4.2-3; Basil, *Letters*, 52.3). Then, he moves to discussing the plurality of manifestations as the Father expands into the Son and Spirit.[81] Sabellius' example of the gifts of the Spirit seems to indicate that the Spirit so expands and unfolds in the gifts that the Spirit does not remain as an element behind them but completely merges in them; the manifestation of the various gifts is the Spirit. In the same manner the Father expands or

---

[78] Basil the Great recorded that Sabellius came from Libya (Basil, *Letters*, 9.2).

[79] Schaff, *History*, II, p. 581; Kelly, *Doctrines*, p. 121. Sabellius presented a more systematic and advanced paradigm of doctrine than his predecessors, so that this branch of Monarchianism later became known as Sabellianism. Harnack, therefore, doubts that this was actually Sabellius that Dionysius excommunicated. 'Sabellius can hardly have been alive, yet it was under his name that the heresy was promoted.' Harnack, *Dogma*, III, p. 83.

[80] Cited according to the translation of Archibald Robertson, Athanasius, 'Four Discourses Against the Arians', NPNF, Second Series, IV, p. 443.

[81] He uses the word πλατυσμός which means extension, enlargement, or expansion. πλατυσμός, BAGD, p. 667.

unfolds through the Son and Spirit.[82] This unfolding occurs sequentially in three manifestations and phases of revelation. The first phase begins with the revelation of the Father as the Creator, and law-giver. The second phase begins with the incarnation and reveals the Son as the redeemer. The third phase continues today revealing the Holy Spirit as the agent of believers' regeneration and sanctification (Epiphanius, *Pan.* 62.1.6-9).[83] After each phase of revelation concludes, the extension of the divine manifestation returns into unity 'like a ray sent by the sun which speeds back up to the sun' (Epiphanius, *Pan.* 62.1.8; Athanasius, *C. Ar.* 9; 13–17). So Sabellius uses trinitarian language and distinguishes between manifestations of deity, but these manifestations lack permanence (Basil, *Letters* 236.5–6).[84] Deity simply extends as an active power in the Son and Holy Spirit and then contracts, so that the divine substance remains undivided. Since Sabellius uses Father and Spirit as interchangeable terms for the divine substance incarnate in Christ, he delineates a Spirit Christology of pneumatic incarnation.

This branch of Monarchianism taught a monotheistic pneumatic Christology. Although they used trinitarian language – Father, Son, and Holy Spirit – to designate the historical revelations of deity, Modalist Monarchianism attempted to preserve the essential unity of deity by positing that these were manifestations of the one undivided divine essence which was incarnated in Jesus Christ, the Spirit. Therefore, their Spirit christological paradigm depicts a pneumatic incarnation.

New Prophecy

The New Prophecy began as a prophetic movement in the region of Phrygia. About 155, a man named Montanus converted to Christianity and was baptized. Probably sometime between 155 and 175, Montanus claimed that he had become possessed of the Holy Spirit; allegedly, receiving the promised Johannine Paraclete, he subse-

---

[82] Harnack, *Dogma*, III, p. 88.
[83] 'Sabellius now made histories of the world and salvation into a history of the God who revealed himself in them.' Harnack, *Dogma*, III, p. 87.
[84] Cf. Harnack, *Dogma*, III, pp. 83-88; Schaff, *History*, II, pp. 581-83; Kelly, *Doctrines*, p. 122; Seeberg and Hay, *History*, I, p. 168; Pelikan, *Christian Tradition*, I, p. 179; Frend, *Christianity*, pp. 343-44; Berkhof, *Christian Doctrines*, p. 79; Burgess, *The Holy Spirit: Ancient Christian Traditions*, p. 48.

quently began to prophesy.⁸⁵ Two prophetesses, Priscilla and Maximilla, who also had received this experience of the Spirit, soon joined Montanus. This small group of prophets quickly developed into a movement as its prophecies attracted a considerable number of followers. In making reference to this movement, its detractors often named the group after the region of its origin, a city associated with the movement, or one of its prominent prophetic figures; thus, the group was commonly known as Phrygians, Cataphrygians, Pepuziani, Montanism, Priscillianists, Quintillians, and even Tertullianists.⁸⁶ Its adherents, however, preferred the designation New Prophecy.

The group identified themselves as the New Prophecy because the movement proclaimed a new epoch of the Spirit had arrived. Through the inspired prophetic utterances of its charismatic prophets, the Paraclete was bestowing new revelations, which were the final revelations to humanity, and leading them into all truth in light of the eschaton.⁸⁷ The available sources imply that these new revelations included at least six points.⁸⁸ First, because of the church's moral laxity, the gifts of the Spirit were becoming scarce; therefore, they required stringent holiness codes. Second, since the church often neglected fasting, they emphasized fasting and instituted new fasts. Third, they prohibited second marriages for widows and widowers. Fourth, they rejected flight from martyrdom and stressed martyrdom as a favored form of death. Fifth, the small Phrygian

---

⁸⁵ The date is by no means certain, see Pelikan, *Christian Tradition*, I, p. 97; Timothy D. Barnes, 'The Chronology of Montanism', *JTS* 21 (1970), pp. 403-408; William Tabbernee, *Montanist Inscriptions and Testimonia: Epigraphic Sources Illustrating the History of Montanism* (Macon, GA: Mercer University Press, 1997), pp. 17-19; Christine Trevett, *Montanism: Gender, Authority, and the New Prophecy* (Cambridge: Cambridge University Press, 1996), pp. 26-45.

⁸⁶ Schaff, *History*, II, pp. 418-19; Trevett, *Montanism*, pp. 8-9, 73-76, 159-65, 168-70, 202, 265-66.

⁸⁷ According to Trevett, it was common for Asian Christianity to associate the work of the Paraclete with Christian prophetism: 'then we do not have to look far for explanation of why the work of the Three and the activity of the Paraclete should have been linked'. Trevett, *Montanism*, pp. 93-94. For a discussion of the role of the Paraclete in continuing revelation, see Cecil M. Robeck, *Prophecy in Carthage: Perpetua, Tertullian, and Cyprian* (Cleveland, Ohio: Pilgrim Press, 1992), pp. 140-45.

⁸⁸ Pelikan, *Christian Tradition*, I, pp. 100-101; 'Montanism', *ODCC*, pp. 1107-108; Burgess, *The Holy Spirit: Ancient Christian Traditions*, pp. 49-53; Tabbernee, *Inscriptions*, p. 20; Trevett, *Montanism*, pp. 77-150.

towns of Pepuza and Tymion became known as Jerusalem.[89] Sixth, apostolic succession and prophetic succession conjoined, so that only the church of the Spirit could forgive sins and not the church consisting of a number of bishops. The New Prophecy, thus, primarily advocated an orthodox theology, an apocalyptic asceticism, and an egalitarian experience of spiritual empowerment for all Christians; 'your sons and daughters shall prophesy'.[90] The New Prophecy's teachings are accessible through several patristic sources that oppose the movement[91] and the writings of Tertullian after his conversion to the movement.[92]

---

[89] The movement arose in a region near Philadelphia. Trevett suggests an interesting point: the New Prophecy adherents saw themselves as the heirs of the promise the seer of the *Apocalypse* gave to the church at Philadelphia; therefore, 'they would bear the name of God's holy city, new Jerusalem, and the name of God himself'. Trevett, *Montanism*, pp. 23-26. Cf. Epiphanius, *Pan.* 51.33.1-3. David Wright, however, suggests that Montanus probably named the town after the Jerusalem of the Book of Acts, rather than the heavenly Jerusalem. 'The important point is his designating the places "Jerusalem" by virtue of their present character or function, whether in pious or self-important advertisement or by pentecostal precedent, rather than in the context of a future event'. David F. Wright, 'Why Were the Montanists Condemned?', *Themelios* 2 (1976), p. 20.

[90] Schaff, *History*, II, pp. 421-27; McDonnell and Montague, *Christian Initiation*, pp. 116-21.

[91] The movement demonstrated certain characteristics that discomforted the Catholic Church: its exclusiveness, stringent holiness codes, the mode of prophesying in a state of ecstasy accompanied with strange speech, and the clericalisation of women. Wright contends that the revelation of the Paraclete focuses more on the development of ethics than doctrine. Wright, 'Montanists ', p. 19. 'Tertullian argued that the Spirit introduced no *new* or *novel* teachings, but rather illuminated existing knowledge.' Robeck, *Prophecy in Carthage*, p. 141. According to Trevett, the movement did not have to defend itself against the charge of heresy until about fifty years after its inception. David Wright discusses 11 issues that concern the condemnation of Montanism. Wright, 'Montanists', pp. 15-22. Cf. Trevett, *Montanism*, p. 73. The movement disintegrated sometime around 527–31 after the edict of Justinian which enforced the conversion of the movement, allowed the destruction of its places of worship, and the burning of most of its literature. Trevett, *Montanism*, pp. 227-31.

[92] Ronald Heine has gathered all of the texts from the various sources, with the Greek and Latin texts juxtaposed beside an English translation, and arranged into three sections: (1) The Montanists' Oracles, (2) Testimonia from the Second and Third Centuries, (3) and Testimonia from the Fourth Century and Later. Ronald E. Heine, *The Montanist Oracles and Testimonia* (Macon, GA: Mercer University Press, 1989). William Tabbernee has provided access to New Prophecy historical information through the movement's epigraphy. Tabbernee, *Inscriptions*.

Montanus

Epiphanius has preserved two texts, which are considered authentic oracles of Montanus, which relate to Spirit Christology. According to Epiphanius, in a Modalist Monarchian fashion, Montanus confuses the identities of the Paraclete and God the Father: 'I am the Lord God, the Almighty dwelling in man . . . Neither angel nor envoy, but I the Lord God the Father have come' (*Pan.* 48.11).[93] Accordingly, other patristic witnesses quote a similar form of these oracles. For example, Hippolytus and Pseudo-Tertullian incriminate the movement for depicting Christ as the Father and the Son.[94] Furthermore, two fourth century writings, one which supposedly preserves a debate about this issue and Didymus of Alexander's *On the Trinity*, inculpate the movement as modalistic because Montanus says: 'I am the Father, and I am the Son, and I am the Paraclete'.[95] It appears, according to these witnesses, that the New Prophecy movement teaches a Spirit christological paradigm similar to Modalist Monarchianism.

To confirm or annul this deduction, the survey now turns its attention to Tertullian's New Prophecy writings which have preserved the only extant writings of this movement.[96] It is uncertain whether

---

[93] Cited according to the translation of Ronald Heine, *Oracles*, p. 3. Maximilla prophesies in a similar fashion: 'I am word, and spirit, and power' (Eusebius, *Hist. eccl.* 5.16.17). Heine, *Oracles*, p. 3.

[94] Hippolytus charges the New Prophecy with, 'agreeing with the heresy of the Noetians, say that the Father himself is the Son, and that he has experienced birth, suffering, and death' (Hippolytus, *Haer.* 8.19; 10.25-26). Heine, *Oracles*, p. 57. 'They add this also, that Christ himself is Son and Father' (Pseudo-Tertullian, *Haer.* 7). Heine, *Oracles*, p. 59. Sometimes the location of these texts, which Heine gives, varies from the location in the ANF. For example, the former text appears in Hippolytus, 'Refutation ', 8.12, ANF, V, pp. 123-24.

[95] *Debate of a Montanist and an Orthodox Christian*, in Heine, *Oracles*, pp. 117-21. The adherents of the movement 'rave irrationally that there is one person of the three divine hypostases. For Montanus says, he said: "I am the Father, and the Son, and the Paraclete"' (Didymus of Alexandria, *Trin.* 3.41). Heine, *Oracles*, p. 141.

[96] Tertullian, a native of Carthage, who was a lawyer and gained a reputation as an advocate in Rome, converted to Christianity around 193, and he joined the New Prophecy movement around 207. Quasten places Tertullian's literary activity between 195 and 220. For overviews of Tertullian's life and writings, see Quasten, *Patrology*, II, pp. 246-319; Geoffrey D. Dunn, *Tertullian* (ECF; London: Routledge, 2004), pp. 3-12; Timothy David Barnes, *Tertullian: A Historical and Literary Study* (2005 repr.; Oxford: Clarendon Press, 1971), pp. 3-59; Lloyd David Franklin, 'The Spiritual Gifts' in Tertullian' (PhD dissertation, St. Louis, St. Louis University, 1989), pp. 12-42; David Rankin, *Tertullian and the Church* (Cambridge:

Tertullian's New Prophecy writings represent the movement's normative views. Nonetheless, it is certain that he became an advocate for this movement. So it seems unlikely that he would have joined a movement that adversely relates to his theological positions.[97] Allowing for diversity within the group, at the least, this survey accepts Tertullian as one voice, among others, representing the movement's views, and perhaps, at the most, its greatest theologian.

Tertullian

About 213, Tertullian wrote *Against Praxeas*, which depicted his understanding of the New Prophecy's relationship with modalism, as a rebuttal to Praxeas' opposition to the New Prophecy.[98] Apparently, Praxeas disagreed with the New Prophecy's views of God and expressions of the charismata because Tertullian introduced this apology by stating that the bishop of Rome had given approval to the movement's prophecies and sent out letters affirming their validity, but Praxeas was directly responsible for changing the bishop's mind. Tertullian, therefore, declared that 'Praxeas did a twofold service for the devil at Rome: he drove away prophecy, and brought in heresy; he put to flight the Paraclete, and he crucified the Father' (ch. 1).[99] After this introductory chapter, through the remaining

---

Cambridge University Press, 1995), p. xiv. David Rankin provides eight characteristics that determine Tertullian's writings after his conversion to the New Prophecy. Rankin, *Tertullian*, p. xv. For a list of these writings, see Trevett, *Montanism*, pp. 72-73; A. Cleveland Coxe, 'Tertullian, Introductory Note', ANF, III, p. 11; Rankin, *Tertullian*, pp. 15-17.

[97] Rankin, *Tertullian*, pp. 41-43; Trevett, *Montanism*, pp. 2, 7; Barnes, *Tertullian*, pp. 130-42. David Franklin examines spiritual gifts in Tertullian's pre-Montanist and post-Montanist writings and concludes that spiritual gifts play an essential part in establishing the apostolic tradition; thus, Tertullian is defending apostolic tradition and authority. Franklin, 'Spiritual Gifts', pp. 43-97. 'We do not know much about early Montanism, and what we do know comes from Tertullian (and we do not know the extent to which he recast Montanism to suit his own inclinations).' Dunn, *Tertullian*, p. 6. Cf. McDonnell and Montague, *Christian Initiation*, pp. 121-32.

[98] Quasten, *Patrology*, II, p. 284; Robeck, *Prophecy in Carthage*, pp. 124-27. 'The *Adversus Praxean* exemplifies a paradox: Tertullian helped to rescue the Catholic Church from theological heresy precisely because he was a Montanist.' Barnes, *Tertullian*, p. 142.

[99] Cited according to the translation of Dr. Holmes, Tertullian, 'Against Praxeas', ANF, III, ch. 1, p. 597. Cf. Heine, *Oracles*, p. 89. According to David Franklin, Tertullian reacted, in this manner, to the bishop's decision 'because it deviated from the apostolic tradition as Tertullian understood it'. Franklin, 'Spiritual Gifts', p. 10. Franklin writes:

thirty chapters, Tertullian structured his argument against Praxeas around three interrelated tenets of Praxeas' theology. First, Praxeas asserted the unity of divine essence and the monarchy of the Father; Tertullian, however, affirmed the one divine substance has existed as three persons: Father, Son, and Holy Spirit (ch. 2).[100] Second, Praxeas insisted that the deity incarnated in Christ was the Father, and the Son was the flesh of Christ; thus, Tertullian discussed the generation of the divine Son from the Father, thereby distinguishing them (chs. 8; 10; 14–17). Third, by way of contrast to Praxeas Tertullian differentiated the Holy Spirit from the Father and Son (ch. 25). Hermeneutically, because Praxeas denied any distinction in the divine substance by placing all Scripture under the rubric of Isa. 45.5, Jn 10.30, and Jn 14.9-10, Tertullian adduced the Fourth Gospel to prove the plurality of the divine persons while maintaining their essential unity (ch. 20).[101]

Arguably, this struggle between Praxeas and Tertullian accentuates contending Spirit christological paradigms. The following Spirit christological passage sets forth the nexus of this debate: the Son of God's identity.

> See, say they, it was announced by the angel: 'Therefore that Holy Thing which shall be born of thee shall be called the Son of God.' Therefore (they argue,) as it was the flesh that was born, it must be the flesh that is the Son of God. Nay, (I answer,) this is spoken concerning the Spirit of God. For it was certainly of the Holy Spirit that the virgin conceived; and that which He conceived, she brought forth; that is to say, the Spirit, whose 'name should be called Emmanuel which, being interpreted, is, God

---

Praxeas's dissuasion, and the bishop's reversal of his endorsement, are regarded by Tertullian as the rejection of the continuing role of the Paraclete. Tertullian's approach to spiritual gifts is holistic – the spiritual gifts are neither more nor less important than baptism, repentance, and the other elements of the apostolic tradition (Franklin, 'Spiritual Gifts', p. 99).

Furthermore, 'The bishop's action is interpreted by Tertullian as a break with the apostolic tradition and practice, and a rejection of spiritual gifts.' Franklin, 'Spiritual Gifts', p. 117.

[100] Cf. chs. 3; 8; 9; 12; 13. In fact, Tertullian insists in opposition to Praxeas' modalism that the doctrine of the Trinity constitutes the difference between Judaism's and Christianity's view of God (ch. 31). According to Quasten, 'Tertullian is the first of the Latin authors to use *trinitas* as a technical term'. Quasten, *Patrology*, II, p. 286.

[101] Cf. chs. 21–24; 26–28.

with us.' Besides the flesh is not God, so that it could not have been said concerning it, 'That Holy Thing shall be called the Son of God,' but only the divine being who was born in the flesh … Now what Divine Person was born in it? The Word, [*sic*] and the Spirit which became incarnate with the Word by the will of the Father. The Word, therefore, is incarnate; and this must be the point of our inquiry: How the Word became flesh, – whether it was by having been transfigured, as it were, in the flesh, or by having really clothed Himself in the flesh. Certainly it was by a real clothing of himself in flesh (ch. 27).[102]

Since human flesh does not consist of divine substance, Tertullian rejects the notion that it designates the Son of God; only one who subsists in the divine nature can be the Son of God. For Tertullian, then, the basic query of the debate becomes: how did deity become flesh? Unambiguously, Tertullian asserts the Holy Spirit's agency of the incarnation; however, his postulate that the Logos and the Spirit became incarnate confuses his exposition a bit. This statement after all comes close to the supposition Praxeas advances: the Holy Spirit and the Logos are manifestations of the one undivided deity which is Spirit. The inquiry, then, becomes a Spirit christological question: what distinctions does Tertullian make between the designations Father, Spirit, Holy Spirit, Logos, and Son of God in Christ's identity?

To reach a conclusion, the text must be placed in the full context of Tertullian's train of thought. First, Tertullian agrees that the one divine substance is Spirit, so that the divine nature incarnate in Christ may aptly be regarded as Spirit (ch. 7).[103] Second, there is no

---

[102] Cited according to the translation of Dr. Holmes, Tertullian, 'Against Praxeas', ANF, III, p. 623.

[103] See Tertullian's exposition of the Spirit's role in the incarnation (Lk. 1.35):
Now by saying 'the Spirit of God' (although the Spirit of God *is God*,) and by not directly naming God, he wished that portion of the whole *Godhead* to be understood, which was about to retire into the designation of 'the Son.' The Spirit of God in this passage must be the same *as the* Word. For just as, when John says, 'The Word was made flesh,' we understand the Spirit also in the mention of the Word: so here, too, we acknowledge the Word likewise in the name of the Spirit. For both the Spirit is the substance of the Word, and the Word is the operation of the Spirit, and the Two are One (and the same)' (ch. 26) (Tertullian, 'Against Praxeas', ANF, III, p. 622, emphasis added).

distinction between the designations Logos, Wisdom, and the preexistent Son; however, the Father, Son, and the Holy Spirit subsisting in the undivided divine substance are distinct (chs. 5-8; 14). Third, the Holy Spirit is the agent of the incarnation (chs. 2; 26). Fourth, by way of contrast to Praxeas' assertion that the flesh was the Son born of Mary, implying that deity was transfigured or altered, Tertullian avers two unaltered and uncompounded natures united in one person: Christ was Son of God according to the Spirit and Son of Man according to human nature, body and soul (chs. 21; 27). Tertullian sharply distinguishes these natures (ch. 29),[104] so that the divine nature remains impassible, while the human nature is anointed by the Spirit and suffers on the cross: 'since he says that it was Christ (that is, the Anointed One) that died, he shows us that that which died was the nature which was anointed; in a word the flesh'.[105] Fifth, after the ascension, Christ receives the promise of the Father and sheds forth the Holy Spirit to reveal God, to lead into all truth, and to empower believers (ch. 30).

Contrary to Praxeas, Tertullian's Spirit christological paradigm, thus, affirms a monotheistic view of God that includes distinction of relationships within the unity of the divine essence, so that the Father, Son, and Holy Spirit are distinguished in creative and salvific mission. Also, in teaching the dual natures of Christ, Tertullian asserts, through the agency of the Holy Spirit, the preexistent divine Logos becomes incarnate in human flesh; thus, the Son is not the flesh of Christ.[106] When Tertullian synonymously refers to the Logos and Spirit incarnate in Christ, he does not refer to the

---

Cf. Roy Kearsley, *Tertullian's Theology of Divine Power* (Rutherford Studies in Historical Theology; Carlisle: Paternoster, 1998), pp. 72-74, 121, 138; Grillmeier, *Christian Tradition*, I, pp. 121-22.

[104] Although each nature performs distinct actions, Tertullian also acknowledges a transfer of functions between these natures, a *communicatio idiomatum* (ch. 27). For a discussion of Tertullian's soteriological understanding of Christ's soul, see Maurice F. Wiles, *Working Papers in Doctrine* (London: SCM Press, 1976), pp. 52-53.

[105] Tertullian, 'Against Praxeas', ANF, III, p. 626. Cf. chs. 27–30; McDonnell, *The Baptism of Jesus in the Jordan*, pp. 114-15. In discussing the cry of dereliction from the cross, Tertullian refutes Praxeas' patripassianism: 'if it was the Father who suffered, then to what God was it that He addressed His cry? But this was the voice of flesh and soul, that is to say, of man – not of the Word and Spirit, that is to say, not of God; and it was uttered so as to prove the impassibility of God' (ch. 30). Tertullian, 'Against Praxeas', ANF, III, p. 627.

[106] Dunn, *Tertullian*, p. 36-37.

Holy Spirit, but he attributes divine nature to the Logos who is the Son of God. Distinguishing between the divine and human natures, Tertullian accentuates the Spirit anointing Christ's human nature. Spirit, consequently, is essential to Christ's identity and mission.

It is not certain that Tertullian's Spirit christological views are normative for all of the New Prophecy movement; nonetheless, he does at least represent some part of the movement's theology, and his writings have revealed a mutual opposition with Modalism that casts doubt on the preceding witnesses' assertion that the movement taught a Modalist Monarchian form of Spirit Christology.[107] It is possible, therefore, that the previously examined oracles of Montanus may only depict how the Paraclete, the prophetic Spirit that Christ has bestowed upon the church, operates through believers.[108] In other words, Montanus might have been prophetically speaking, in the first person, in a manner that his opponents either considered unacceptable or were unaccustomed to hearing; he was a vessel of the Paraclete.[109] If this is the case, then, along with Tertullian, the New Prophecy teaches that the Spirit mediates Christ's incarnation, soteriological mission, and is the empowering presence that continues among believers.[110] Tertullian's trinitarian theology, therefore,

---

[107] 'Due allowances must be made for distortion since these available sources stem from their opponents.' Pelikan, *Christian Tradition*, I, p. 97. 'The New Prophecy seemed to acknowledge the same Father and Son as the catholic church. Indeed, any connection between Montanism and the various brands of Monarchianism was only accidental; there was no inherent affinity between the two.' Wright, 'Montanists', p. 16.

[108] Trevett asserts that the functions of the Johannine Paraclete are prophetic functions. Trevett, *Montanism*, p. 66.

[109] 'His adversaries wrongly inferred from the use of the first person for the Holy Spirit in his oracles, that he made himself directly the Paraclete, or, according to Epiphanius, even God the Father.' Schaff, *History*, II, p. 418. Cf. Wright, 'Montanists', p. 19; Robeck, *Prophecy in Carthage*, p. 117. 'They are the fragments of much longer utterances – really introductory formulae only, originally legitimizing the Prophet as the source of the divine message.' Trevett, *Montanism*, p. 80.

[110] Tertullian asserted that the charismata were present among faithful Christians and challenged Marcion to demonstrate the presence of the charismata among his followers (*Marc.* 5.8). According to Robeck, Tertullian did not consider the charismata as a sign of spiritual elitism or spiritual maturity, for the charismata were available to new believers as well. Robeck, *Prophecy in Carthage*, p. 97. In fact, according to David Franklin, spiritual gifts are part of the believers' emulation of Christ: 'This concept of emulating Christ is not reserved for the spiritually elite, but should be the prayer of all Christians'. Franklin, 'Spiritual Gifts', p. 46.

integrates Logos Christology and Spirit Christology in a complementary fashion.[111]

Conclusion

Three renditions of Spirit Christology flow from this cacophony of voices from the margins, elucidating Spirit Christology's fluid nature. First, in congruity with some among the developing central tradition, Tertullian integrates a Spirit christological paradigm of pneumatic mediation and Logos Christology, demonstrating their compatibility, within the parameters of trinitarian theology. Second, Modalist Monarchianism posits a Spirit Christology of pneumatic incarnation. Third, Gnosticism, Ebionism, and Dynamic Monarchianism delineate various paradigms of pneumatic inspiration, offering a new direction in Spirit Christology since it rejects Christ's incarnation.

All three versions agree that the Spirit identifies Christ and anoints the salvific mission, but they differ about what this means. For Tertullian, the mode of incarnation is preexistent Spirit and human nature because the person of the incarnate Logos eternally subsists with the Father and Holy Spirit in one undivided divine substance which is Spirit; the Father anoints Christ's humanity with the Holy Spirit empowering it for salvific mission. Modalist Monarchianism, however, asserts that Father, Son, and Holy Spirit are synonymous designations of the one divine essence, so that the Father as divine Spirit becomes incarnate in human flesh, which is the Son, and fulfills the salvific mission. Gnosticism, Ebionism, and Dynamic Monarchianism congruently reject an incarnational Christology; the Spirit is the impersonal power of deity that descends into Jesus at the Jordan identifying him as the Christ, inspiring, and anointing his life and ministry. They differ, nevertheless, concerning the value of Christ's human nature. Gnosticism devalues human flesh and focuses on the revealing anointing present in Christ. Ebionism and Dynamic Monarchianism extol Jesus' humanity; Jesus ministers as a human the Spirit inspires and anoints.

---

[111] For other Spirit christological references, see Tertullian, *Apol.* 21; *Marc.* 3.15; 5.8; 5.17; *Carn. Chr.* 5; 14; 18; 19.

These three paradigms from the margins – pneumatic mediation, incarnation, and inspiration – will continue to function in a reciprocal relationship with the center of the Christian tradition to depict the methodologies for doing Spirit Christology. Concerning this relationship, two issues are noteworthy. First, the concept of the Spirit anointing Christ will become consequential. Second, the importance of Monarchianism 'lies in the fact that with them began the trinitarian and christological controversies that dominated the history of Christian doctrine in the next two centuries'.[112] As the banks of a great river exists on the margins of the central stream, the stream and its margins form, define, and identify one another, so these cacophony of voices from the margins and the central Christian tradition reciprocally delineate these boundaries of doctrinal development, in which Spirit Christology has played a significant role.

---

[112] Frend, *Christianity*, p. 343. Cf. González, *Christian Thought*, I, pp. 259-60.

5

THE LATER APOLOGISTS

Beginning in the second century, replying in a different context to different issues than the Early Apologists, several writers apologetically and polemically responded to the trinitarian and christological issues raised by the doctrines postulated by various marginal groups and theologians within the central tradition. The Later Apologists usually designates this group of writers.[1]

Irenaeus

Among this group of writers, Irenaeus' discourses are the earliest retorts regarding these issues,[2] and his primary extant works *Against Heresies* and the *Demonstration of the Apostolic Preaching*[3] furnish the

---

[1] According to the historian Eusebius, along with others Justin Martyr and Theophilus of Antioch responded, but their treatises have not survived. For a discussion of the christological problems these writers wrestled with, as well as the importance and dangers of the Logos doctrine they develop, see Grillmeier, *Christian Tradition*, I, pp. 106-13.

[2] Stressing the importance of Irenaeus to christological development, Wilhelm Bousset suggests: 'Irenaeus is actually *the* theologian in the second half of the second Christian century who presents the future formation of things in a way in which no other beside or immediately after him does ... One can actually call him the Schleiermacher of the second century'. Bousset, *Christos*, p. 421.

[3] Although these two treatises are the primary surviving works of Irenaeus, there are fragments and titles that remain of seven other works. For information about Irenaeus's writings, see Quasten, *Patrology*, I, pp. 288-93; Schaff, *History*, II, pp. 752-57.

next references to Spirit Christology.[4] Although the bishop of Lyons engaged various marginal groups, Irenaeus primarily wrote *Against Heresies*, between 180 and 188,[5] to present his view of Christian doctrines and to demonstrate their diversity to Gnosticism.[6] This document consists of five books. Book One expounds the tenets of Valentinian Gnosticism and establishes its affinity with other groups. In Book Two, Irenaeus appeals to common sense and logic to controvert Gnostic doctrines which he expostulates as absurd and contradictory.[7] The last three books argue from Scripture and Christian tradition to refute Gnosticism.[8] Since Gnosticism postulated an opposition between the primal divine source and the creator, its soteriology was radically discrete from its cosmology; therefore, similar to Justin, Irenaeus examines the prophecies and types in the Hebrew Scriptures to demonstrate continuity of divine activity in creation and redemption of one God who exists as Father, Son, and Holy Spirit.[9]

---

[4] Because the Spirit christological references in these documents are so similar, the survey will focus on the texts in *Against Heresies* and only note the references in *Demonstration of the Apostolic Preaching*.

[5] For issues concerning date, provenance, and purpose, see Irenaeus, 'Against Heresies', ANF, I, pp. 310, 312; Schaff, *History*, II, p. 753; Frend, *Christianity*, p. 244. Only fragments of the original Greek version of text have been preserved by Hippolytus, Eusebius, and Epiphanius; however, the complete text is extant in a Latin translation, and an Armenian version contains the last two books of the treatise. Quasten, *Patrology*, I, pp. 290-91. The *Demonstration of the Apostolic Preaching* was written about ten years later.

[6] Robert McQueen Grant, *Irenaeus of Lyons* (ECF; London: Routledge, 1997), pp. 11-28; Denis Minns, *Irenaeus* (Washington, DC: Georgetown University Press, 1994), pp. 10-21; Mark Jeffrey Olson, *Irenaeus, the Valentinian Gnostics, and the Kingdom of God (A.H. Book V): The Debate about 1 Corinthians 15:50* (Lewiston, N.Y.: Mellen Biblical Press, 1992).

[7] Hans Urs von Balthasar has collected the texts that refute Gnosticism under the rubric of incarnation. Irenaeus, *The Scandal of the Incarnation: Irenaeus Against the Heresies, Selected and with an Introduction by Hans Urs von Balthasar* (trans. John Saward; San Francisco: Ignatius Press, 1990), pp. 17-46.

[8] Harnack examines Irenaeus's use of Christian tradition as the apostolic rule of faith, apostolic collection of writings, and apostolic succession. Harnack, *Dogma*, II, pp. 5-10, 27-29, 43-44.

[9] González, *Christian Thought*, I, pp. 158-59; Quasten, *Patrology*, I, pp. 289-90; Minns, *Irenaeus*, pp. 36-53; Kelly, *Doctrines*, pp. 147-49; Seeberg and Hay, *History*, I, pp. 124-25; Maurice F. Wiles, *The Christian Fathers* (New York: Oxford University Press, 1982), p. 27; Grillmeier, *Christian Tradition*, I, pp. 98-99.

Five Spirit christological texts support Irenaeus' argument for continuity. For example, Irenaeus asserted that God created all things by his two hands.

> For with Him were always present the Word and Wisdom, the Son and the Spirit, by whom and in whom, freely and spontaneously, He made all things (*Haer.* 4.20.1).[10]

Irenaeus, furthermore, affirmed that the two hands of God were always present with the Father anterior to creation, identifying the Word as the Son and Wisdom as the Holy Spirit (*Haer.* 4.20.3; *Epid.* 5).[11] So Irenaeus accentuates the unity of God, allowing no distinction between the one eternal deity and the God of creation.

Irenaeus, also, links humanity's creation and redemption; the two hands of God – the Word and Spirit – accomplish these events.

> The Word of the Father and the Spirit of God, having become united with the ancient substance of Adam's formation, rendered man living and perfect, receptive of the perfect Father, in order that as in the natural [Adam] we all were dead, so in the spiritual we may all be made alive. For never at any time did Adam escape the *hands* of God, to whom the Father speaking, said, 'Let Us make man in Our image, after Our likeness.' And for this reason in the last times (*fine*), not by the will of the flesh, nor by the will of man, but by the good pleasure of the Father, His hands formed a living man, in order that Adam might be created [again] after the image and likeness of God (*Haer.* 5.1.3).[12]

According to Irenaeus, the Word and Spirit formed the first Adam who was the natural head of the human race and the second Adam, Jesus Christ, who became the spiritual head of the human race.[13]

---

[10] Cited according to the translation of M. Dods, Irenaeus, 'Against Heresies', ANF, I, pp. 487-88. Grant also provides a translation of this text in Grant, *Irenaeus of Lyons*, p. 150.

[11] For discussions of this relationship, see Iain M. MacKenzie and Irenaeus, *Irenaeus's Demonstration of the Apostolic Preaching: A Theological Commentary and Translation* (trans. J. Armitage Robinson; Aldershot: Ashgate, 2002), pp. 81-89; Eric Francis Osborn, *Irenaeus of Lyons* (Cambridge: Cambridge University Press, 2001), pp. 89-93.

[12] Irenaeus, 'Against Heresies', ANF, I, p. 527.

[13] 'That He must needs be born a man among men; and that the same God forms Him from the womb, that is, that of the Spirit of God he should be born' (*Epid.* 51). Cited according to the translation of J. Armitage Robinson, MacKen-

Known as Irenaeus' theory of recapitulation, this concept effectively conjoins humanity's creation and redemption in Christ. Created in the image and likeness of God, as the head of the human race when Adam fell into sin humanity fell with him; however, through the incarnation, Jesus Christ became the head of a re-created humanity by recapitulating in himself humanity's history, thus, providing salvation and restoring what was lost in the first Adam: the image and likeness of God (*Haer.* 3.18.1; 3.18.7; 5.14.2; 5.21.2; *Epid.* 1).[14] In Irenaeus' theology, then, Christ stands as the basis of continuity between creation and redemption; the image of God, according to which and for which humans were made, became flesh and dwelled among humans.[15]

The remaining Spirit christological texts depict the relationship of the Word and Spirit in Christ's salvific mission. Irenaeus, consequently, answers the query: why was Christ anointed by the Spirit?

> For Christ did not at that time descend upon Jesus, neither was Christ one and Jesus another ... In this respect did the Spirit of God rest upon Him, and anoint Him to preach the Gospel to the lowly ... Therefore did the Spirit of God descend upon Him, [the Spirit] of Him who had promised by the prophets that He

---

zie and Irenaeus, *Demonstration of the Apostolic Preaching*, p. 16. 'Christ's body was made by the Spirit' (*Epid.* 71). Robinson, MacKenzie and Irenaeus, *Demonstration of the Apostolic Preaching*, p. 22, cf. pp. 201-205. Cf. Grillmeier, *Christian Tradition*, I, pp. 101-102.

[14] Cf. Harnack, *Dogma*, II, pp. 271-79; Osborn, *Irenaeus of Lyons*, pp. 97-116; González, *Christian Thought*, I, pp. 161-68; Frend, *Christianity*, pp. 246-48; Quasten, *Patrology*, I, pp. 294-96; Minns, *Irenaeus*, pp. 86-99; J.T. Nielsen, *Adam and Christ in the Theology of Irenaeus of Lyons: An Examination of the Function of the Adam-Christ Typology in the Adversus Haereses of Irenaeus, Against the Background of the Gnosticism of His Time* (Assen: Van Gorcum, 1968); Irenaeus, *The Scandal of the Incarnation*, pp. 53-93; Wiles, *The Christian Fathers*, pp. 57-58. Irenaeus extends the concept of recapitulation to include Eve and Mary: 'For what the virgin Eve had bound fast through unbelief, this did the virgin Mary set free through faith' (*Haer.* 3.22.4). Irenaeus, 'Against Heresies', ANF, I, p. 455.

[15] 'For He made man the image of God; and the image of God is the Son, after whose image man was made: and for this cause He appeared in the end of the times that He might show the image [to be] like unto Himself' (*Epid.* 22). Robinson, MacKenzie and Irenaeus, *Demonstration of the Apostolic Preaching*, p. 7. Cf. Wiles, *Working Papers in Doctrine*, p. 52.

would anoint Him, so that we, receiving from the abundance of His unction, might be saved (*Haer.* 3.9.3).[16]

Here, contrary to Gnosticism's use of anointing, Irenaeus asserted that Christ did not descend upon Jesus at the Jordan; the incarnate Word was Jesus Christ, and deity needed no anointing, so the Spirit anointed Christ's human nature empowering it for salvific mission.

> The Lord thus has redeemed us through His own blood, giving His soul for our souls, and His flesh for our flesh, and has also poured out the Spirit of the Father, for the union and communion of God and man, imparting indeed God to men by means of the Spirit, and, on the other hand attaching man to God by His own incarnation (*Haer.* 5.1.1).[17]

By way of contrast to Gnosticism, Irenaeus accentuates the soteriological role of Christ's human nature, body and soul. Irenaeus, moreover, seems to say that as the Spirit mediates the incarnation of the Word, likewise, the Spirit's agency draws humanity into communion with God and communicates the presence of God in them; furthermore, the incarnation becomes a redemptive event, by elucidating the teleological goal of the image of God in which humans are created. Irenaeus, also, describes how Christians grow into the image of God; the Word nourishes believers along their journey.

> We, being nourished, ... become accustomed to eat and drink the Word of God, may be able to also contain in ourselves the Bread of immortality, which is the Spirit of the Father (*Haer.* 4.38.1).[18]

In fact, Irenaeus asserts that God did not statically create humans in the image of God; rather, God created humans with a dynamic

---

[16] Irenaeus, 'Against Heresies', ANF, I, p. 423. Cf. McDonnell, *The Baptism of Jesus in the Jordan*, pp. 57-60, 116-23; D. Jeffrey Bingham, *Irenaeus' Use of Matthew's Gospel in Adversus Haereses* (Traditio Exegetica Graeca 7; Leuven: Peeters, 1998), pp. 98-126; Osborn, *Irenaeus of Lyons*, p. 133. 'He was named Christ, because through Him the Father anointed and adorned all things; and because on His coming as man He was anointed with the Spirit of God' (*Epid.* 53). 'The oil of anointing is the Spirit, wherewith He has been anointed' (*Epid.* 47). Robinson, MacKenzie and Irenaeus, *Demonstration of the Apostolic Preaching*, pp. 17, 15. Cf. *Epid.* 9.

[17] Irenaeus, 'Against Heresies', ANF, I, p. 527. Cf. Osborn, *Irenaeus of Lyons*, p. 103.

[18] Irenaeus, 'Against Heresies', ANF, I, p. 521.

nature capable of maturing into the image and likeness of God. The fall of humanity interrupted this process, but through Christ's redemptive provisions Christians renew the journey toward the perfect image of God (*Haer.* 4.38.1-4).[19] Evidently, for Irenaeus, the missions of the Word and Spirit relate so closely that they coalesce in the analogy of the Bread of immortality.

Under the rubric of the two hands of God, Irenaeus sets forth a paradigm of Logos Christology and Spirit Christology that complement one another, with a soteriological focus that stresses the unity of God and divine activity in creation, history, and redemption. Contrary to Gnosticism's distinction between the creator and the redeemer, Irenaeus holds them together as the Father and his two hands. Although distinguished by their functions, the Father, Son, and Spirit exist in unity of relationship in divine essence, creation, and redemption (*Haer.* 3.6.2). The two hands of God perform the will of the Father in creation as the Word creates and the Holy Spirit vivifies and adorns creation. The teleological goal of humanity, then, becomes conformity to the image of God as depicted by the Son. The two hands of God, hence, perform the will of the Father in the salvific mission as the Word is incarnated, and Christ is anointed by the Holy Spirit. Christ continues to dwell among his people and anoint them through the Spirit. Irenaeus, therefore, delineates an incarnational Spirit Christology of pneumatic mediation and anointing for ministry.

Hippolytus of Rome

Hippolytus, who supposedly was a disciple of Irenaeus, was a prolific writer and a respected theologian of the Roman church.[20] His voluminous literary production included polemical works, doctrinal treatises, commentaries, chronological treatises, homilies, and a manual for church order.[21] Hippolytus' principal work *Refutation of*

---

[19] Cf. Harnack, *Dogma*, II, pp. 267-71; Osborn, *Irenaeus of Lyons*, pp. 211-31; Minns, *Irenaeus*, pp. 56-80; González, *Christian Thought*, I, pp. 162-64.

[20] According to some scholars, Hippolytus was 'the most important third-century theologian of the Roman Church'. 'Hippolytus', *ODCC*, p. 773. Even Origen, when visiting Rome in 212, listened as Hippolytus preached a sermon. Frend, *Christianity*, p. 374; González, *Christian Thought*, I, p. 229.

[21] Only a few extant texts remain. Some scholars have attributed the loss of these manuscripts to Hippolytus's schismatic positions, and the fact that he wrote

All Heresies (222),[22] reveals his opposition, on theological grounds, to several bishops of the Roman church; for example, it associates Noetus' Modalist Monarchian doctrine with two bishops of Rome (*Haer.* 9.5-7; 10.13): Zephyrinus (198–217) and his successor Callistus (217–22). Since Callistus allegedly agreed with Noetus' view, Hippolytus refused to acknowledge Callistus as bishop which led to a schism in the Roman church.[23]

Hippolytus' polemic *Against the Heresy of One Noetus*, which he probably composed in Rome around 200,[24] examines and refutes Noetus' Modalism,[25] and it furnishes the next Spirit christological references. The document consists of eighteen chapters. Chapters 1–3 provide information about Noetus' doctrine, his excommunication from the church at Smyrna, and founding a school. In the

---

in Greek; as the Roman Church turned more to the use of Latin, these Greek documents fell from use. For overviews of Hippolytus' works and the textual traditions, see Quasten, *Patrology*, II, pp. 165-97; Schaff, *History*, II, 763-74; 'Hippolytus', *ODCC*, p. 774.

[22] Hippolytus polemically addressed the history of Greek philosophy, mystery cults, mythology, astrology, magic, Ebionism, Marcionism, Montanism, Monarchianism, and Gnosticism, and he concluded that philosophy constituted the common link and source of theological errors among these groups. According to W.H.C. Frend, Tertullian and Hippolytus 'continued the work of Irenaeus. Hippolytus and Tertullian took their cue from their great predecessor and met the Gnostics head on. Both denied the possibility of a Christian debt to philosophy. Hippolytus' *Refutation of All Heresies* analyzed each Gnostic system in turn, in order to show how all led back to some Greek philosophical system, and hence were to be rejected'. Frend, *Christianity*, p. 282. 'Hippolytus looked upon philosophy as the source of heresies. Yet he borrowed much more from Greek philosophy than Irenaeus.' Quasten, *Patrology*, II, p. 198. Cf. Schaff, *History*, II, p. 764.

[23] Hippolytus also rejected Callistus' successors. This treatise, therefore, accentuates the value of Hippolytus' theological writings and the theological diversity and tension existing in the church at Rome during the early part of the third century. Gregory Dix and Henry Chadwick (eds.), *The Treatise on the Apostolic Tradition of St. Hippolytus of Rome: Bishop and Martyr* (1992 repr.; Alban: London, 1937), pp. xii-xxxv; Hippolytus and Burton Scott Easton, *The Apostolic Tradition of Hippolytus* (Cambridge: Cambridge University Press, 1934), pp. 16-24; Frend, *Christianity*, pp. 344-46; Schaff, *History*, II, p. 765; 'Hippolytus', *ODCC*, pp. 773-74; González, *Christian Thought*, I, pp. 229-33; Kelly, *Doctrines*, pp. 123-26.

[24] This date is by no means certain. Concerning the document's genre scholars are uncertain whether it is a homily or the end of a polemic. Quasten, *Patrology*, II, p. 180; Schaff, *History*, II, pp. 767-68; Daley, 'One Thing and Another', p. 24. There are some questions concerning authorship as well. Allen Brent, *Hippolytus and the Roman Church in the Third Century: Communities in Tension before the Emergence of a Monarch-Bishop* (VCSup 31; Leiden: E.J. Brill, 1995), pp. 116-27, 206-58, 301-45.

[25] Daley, 'One Thing and Another', pp. 24-26.

remaining chapters, Hippolytus develops his Christology in opposition to Noetus' doctrine.

Because Noetus' monotheistic pneumatic Christology emphasized the unity of the divine essence, which is Spirit, and excluded any possibility of distinction between the Father, Son, and Holy Spirit, so that the Father was born, suffered, and died as Christ (*Noet.* 1),[26] Hippolytus used the Fourth Gospel (Jn 16.28) to support his opposing position.

> In reality the Father's power, which is the Word, came down from heaven, and not the Father himself. For thus He speaks: 'I came from the Father, and am come.' Now what subject is meant in this sentence, 'I came forth from the Father,' but just the Word? And what is it that is begotten of Him, but just the Spirit, that is to say, the Word (*Noet.* 16)?[27]

Contrary to Noetus, Hippolytus unambiguously distinguished between the Father and the Logos: the Logos was incarnated in Christ but not the Father.[28] In point of fact, Hippolytus so emphatically asserts this distinction that he must also carefully deny the implication of ditheism by affirming the unity of divine essence.[29] According to Hippolytus, although triune distinctions exist – Father, Logos, and Holy Spirit – the divine essence remains one in power (*Noet.* 7; 8; 11).[30] So Hippolytus speaks of the one divine essence's unity in

---

[26] Cf. Pelikan, *Christian Tradition*, I, p. 180.

[27] Cited according to J.H. MacMahon's translation in Hippolytus, 'Against the Heresy of One Noetus', ANF, V, p. 229.

[28] 'Over against Noetus, Hippolytus is concerned to demonstrate the distinction in the unity of Father and Logos. That is why the fact of the incarnation is stressed so much. For here is convincing proof that the Father and the Logos are distinct from each other, as the Logos now stands visibly over against the Father as "Son."' Grillmeier, *Christian Tradition*, I, p. 114. Cf. Frend, *Christianity*, pp. 344-45.

[29] 'I shall not indeed speak of two Gods, but of one' (*Noet.* 14). Hippolytus, 'Noetus', ANF, V, p. 228. Cf. Shedd, *Doctrine*, I, pp. 285-87.

[30] 'For the Father indeed is One, but there are two Persons, because there is also the Son; and there is the third, the Holy Spirit' (*Noet.* 14). 'These, therefore, are three. But if he desires to learn how it is shown still that there is one God, let him know that His power is one. As far as regards the power, therefore, God is one' (*Noet.* 8). Hippolytus, 'Noetus', ANF, V, pp. 228, 226. Cf. Kelly, *Doctrines*, p. 111-13; González, *Christian Thought*, I, pp. 232-33; Seeberg and Hay, *History*, I, pp. 127-28. Adolf Harnack argues that, along with Tertullian, Hippolytus' trinitarian concept agrees with Valentinian Gnosticism: 'The only difference is that Tertullian and Hippolytus limit the "economy of God" (οἰκονομία τοῦ θεοῦ) to Father,

terms of power; thus, when Hippolytus identifies the Logos with the Father's power, he acknowledges the Logos' deity: the Logos partakes of the divine essence. Hippolytus' pneumatic Christology, therefore, assumes a monotheistic trinitarian framework that distinguishes the Father and Logos, yet this text appears to identify synonymously the Logos with the Spirit in the incarnation.

So Hippolytus deliberates over the incarnate and pre-incarnate states of the Logos.

> Yet there is the flesh which was presented by the Father's Word as an offering – the flesh that came by the Spirit and the Virgin, (and was) demonstrated to be the perfect Son of God. It is evident, therefore, that He offered Himself to the Father. And before this there was no flesh in heaven. Who, then, was in heaven but the Word un-incarnate, who was dispatched to show that He was upon earth and was also in heaven? For He was Word, He was Spirit, He was Power (*Noet.* 4).[31]

According to Hippolytus, the incarnation depicts 'the mystery of the economy by the Holy Ghost and the Virgin' (*Noet.* 4); the Spirit is the agent of the incarnation, and the virgin transmits flesh to the Logos, so that the perfect Son of God is revealed in the incarnation.[32] Against Noetus, then, Hippolytus seems to imply that the event of incarnation not only distinguishes between the Father and Logos but also between the Logos and the Spirit who mediates the event.[33] Hippolytus clearly uses trinitarian language (*Noet.* 8; 14);

Son, and Holy Ghost, while the Gnostics exceed this number'. Harnack, *Dogma*, II, p. 258. Cf. Grillmeier, *Christian Tradition*, I, pp. 127, 124.

[31] Hippolytus, 'Noetus', ANF, V, p. 225. Cf. *Trad. ap.* 4.4-6.

[32] Hippolytus, accordingly, teaches that Christ's (perfect) sonship begins at the incarnation: 'For neither was the Word, prior to incarnation and when by Himself, yet perfect Son, although He was perfect Word, only-begotten. Nor could the flesh subsist by itself apart from the Word, because it has its subsistence in the Word. Thus, then, one perfect Son of God was manifested' (*Noet.* 15). Hippolytus, 'Noetus', ANF, V, p. 229. 'Hippolytus believed that the title Son could only be used properly of Christ incarnate, the pre-existent Christ could only be so called proleptically and prospectively.' Wiles, *Working Papers in Doctrine*, p. 20. Cf. Grillmeier, *Christian Tradition*, I, pp. 115-17; Kelly, *Doctrines*, p. 112; Quasten, *Patrology*, II, pp. 198-200; Seeberg and Hay, *History*, I, p. 128.

[33] 'We accordingly see the Word incarnate, and we know the Father by Him, and we believe in the Son, (and) we worship the Holy Spirit' (*Noet.* 12). Hippolytus, 'Noetus', ANF, V, p. 228. 'In Hippolytus the Holy Spirit is distinct from the Logos.' Wolfson, *Church Fathers*, I, p. 234.

nonetheless, in the pre-incarnate state, Hippolytus identifies the Logos with Spirit.[34]

Next, Hippolytus examines the relationship of the Logos and Holy Spirit in the incarnation.

> This (Word) was preached by the law and the prophets as destined to come into the world. And even as He was preached then, in the same manner also did He come and manifest Himself, being by the Virgin and the Holy Spirit made a new man; for in that He had the heavenly (nature) of the Father, as the Word and the earthly (nature) as taking to Himself the flesh from the old Adam by the medium of the Virgin, He now, coming forth into the world, was manifested as God in a body, coming forth as a perfect man (*Noet.* 17).[35]

Hippolytus alerts his readers to the agencies of the virgin and the Holy Spirit in the incarnation: the virgin functions as the earthly medium of Christ receiving flesh, and the Holy Spirit functions as the divine medium of the event. Although he seems to be implying a differentiation between the Logos and the Holy Spirit, Hippolytus, nevertheless, does not acknowledge any distinction of function;[36] he accentuates that the manifestation of the Logos in the incarnation

---

[34] Alloys Grillmeier recognizes Hippolytus as supporting a

> form of spirit christology (*pneuma, spiritus* as a designation for the person of the pre-existent Christ) ... Although Hippolytus clearly stresses the trinitarian structure of the deity in comparison with Theophilus (*C. Noet.* 12, 14), he can use *pneuma* specifically of the Son of God: What issued from the Father, if not the Logos? 'What was begotten by him if not the *pneuma*, that is, the Logos?' (*C. Noet.* 16; cf. 4).

Grillmeier, *Christian Tradition*, I, p. 198. Cf. Kelly, *Doctrines*, pp. 144-45.

[35] Hippolytus, 'Noetus', ANF, V, p. 230.

[36] 'The implication being that the supernatural birth was effected by the combination of the Logos and the Holy Spirit.' Wolfson, *Church Fathers*, I, p. 239. Wiles, Working Papers in Doctrine, p. 4, writes:

> The impossibility of finding such a clear-cut threefold division of activity is perhaps most clearly shown by the uncertainty throughout the early period as to what activities in many of the primary spheres of God's self-revelation ought to be attributed to the Son and what to the Spirit. This can be illuminated from the spheres of incarnation, inspiration, and creation. Luke 1.35 had declared explicitly that the conception of Christ was effected by the coming of the Holy Spirit upon the Virgin Mary ... The majority of early writers, however, were led by the logic of their thought to identify Holy Spirit in this context with the Logos.'

correlates with the pre-incarnate prophetic activities of the Logos and Holy Spirit.

> And He gave the law and the prophets; and in giving them, He made them speak by the Holy Ghost, in order that, being gifted with the inspiration of the Father's power, they might declare the Father's council and will. Acting then in these (prophets), the Word spoke of Himself. For already He became His own herald, and showed that the Word would be manifested among men (*Noet.* 11–12).[37]

In these pre-incarnate prophetic functions, Hippolytus makes no distinction between the Logos and Spirit: what can be said of the Logos can be said of the Spirit.[38] This prophetic relationship, consequently, becomes a paradigm for the incarnation. Accordingly, when Hippolytus posits the dual natures of Christ, he uses flesh to connote Christ's human nature and Spirit to denote the divine nature.[39] So Hippolytus seems to support a Spirit Christology of pneumatic incarnation which incorporates Logos Christology.

According to Hippolytus' manual for church order, *The Apostolic Tradition* (215),[40] the Spirit's presence and activity is essential for every facet of church operations, in particular, the offices of bishop (*Trad. ap.* 2.1–3.7), presbyter (*Trad. ap.* 8.1-5), and deacon (*Trad. ap.*

---

[37] Hippolytus, 'Noetus', ANF, V, pp. 227-28.

[38] Wiles, *Working Papers in Doctrine*, p. 7.

[39] According to J.N.D. Kelly, 'Like St. John and Irenaeus, he used "flesh" to connote human nature in its integrity, without raising the question of a rational soul, and referred to the divine element in Christ as "spirit."' Kelly, *Doctrines*, p. 149. Cf. Grillmeier, *Christian Tradition*, I, p. 114.

[40] This document 'has given us the richest source of information that we possess in any form for our knowledge of the constitution and life of the Church in the first three centuries'. Quasten, *Patrology*, II, p. 181. It was probably written in Rome; however, there is some discussion about the authorship and provenance. J.A. Cerrato, 'The Association of the Name Hippolytus with a Church Order Now Known As *The Apostolic Tradition*', *SVTQ* 48.2 (2004), pp. 179-94; Paul F. Bradshaw, 'Who Wrote the Apostolic Tradition: A Response to Alistair Stewart-Sykes', *SVTQ* 48.2 (2004), pp. 195-206. For an overview of these issues as well as the textual tradition, contents, and value of this document, see Hippolytus and Alistair Stewart-Sykes, *On the Apostolic Tradition* (Popular Patristics Series; Crestwood, NY: St. Vladimir's Seminary Press, 2001), pp. 11-52; Dix and Chadwick (eds.), *Apostolic Tradition*, pp. xi-xii, xxxv-lxxxi; Hippolytus and Easton, *The Apostolic Tradition*, pp. 24-32; Quasten, *Patrology*, II, pp. 181-82, 186-194. For an overview of this document among other church manuals, see Hippolytus and Easton, *The Apostolic Tradition*, pp. 1-16.

9.10-12).[41] The prayer which is offered to God during the ordination of a bishop contains the next Spirit christological reference.

> And now pour forth that Power which is from Thee, of 'the princely Spirit' which Thou didst deliver to thy beloved Child Jesus Christ, which He bestowed on Thy holy Apostles who established the Church (*Trad. ap.* 3.3).[42]

Jesus' anointing of the Spirit for mission, accordingly, becomes the paradigm for his followers; bishops receive the authority of the bishopric through the anointing of the Spirit, a pneumatic succession extending through the apostles back to Jesus.[43] The Spirit also empowers the laity by bestowing the charismata.[44] Since the Spirit anoints Christ for his mission, and Christ sends the Spirit who permeates the church as the empowering presence of Christ, here, Hippolytus seems to distinguish the Son and Spirit.[45]

Hippolytus' Spirit Christology seems to depict a paradigm of pneumatic incarnation. Hippolytus clearly uses trinitarian language, yet the distinctions between the Logos and Spirit often blur; he conjoins the functions of the Logos and the Holy Spirit in the salvific mission, and in fluid terminology he uses Logos and Spirit as interchangeable terms to express deity in Christ. Nevertheless, after Christ's resurrection and ascension, a fortiori, Hippolytus distinguishes the empowering presence of the Spirit in the church from Christ who anoints believers with the Spirit. Spirit, accordingly, is essential to Christ's identity and mission.

---

[41] This document provides a portal for viewing the activity of Christ and the Spirit in the third-century Roman church. For an exposition of the Spirit's role in this document, see Burgess, *The Holy Spirit: Ancient Christian Traditions*, pp. 81-86.

[42] Cited according to the translation of Gregory Dix and Henry Chadwick (eds.), *Apostolic Tradition*, pp. 4-5. Cf. Pelikan, *Christian Tradition*, I, p. 161; Hippolytus and Stewart-Sykes, *Apostolic Tradition*, pp. 62-63.

[43] 'And that by the high priestly Spirit he may have authority "to forgive sins" according to Thy command, "to assign lots" according to Thy bidding, to "loose every bond" according to the authority Thou gavest to the Apostles' (*Trad. ap.* 3.5). Dix and Chadwick (eds.), *Apostolic Tradition*, p. 5.

[44] Burgess identifies the gifts of healing (*Trad. ap.* 15), teaching (*Trad. ap.* 35.3), and empowering confessors for persecution (*Trad. ap.* 10.1-2). Burgess, *The Holy Spirit: Ancient Christian Traditions*, pp. 83-84.

[45] 'In Hippolytus the Holy Spirit is distinct from the Logos.' Wolfson, *Church Fathers*, I, p. 234.

Clement of Alexandria

Clement succeeded his mentor Pantaenus as teacher of the catechetical school in Alexandria around 200.[46] Alexandria was an ancient center of political and economic power, education, and a melting pot of diverse cultures and doctrines. Scholars from various parts of the empire came to study at the world-renowned Alexandrian Library. Various cultures, philosophies, and doctrines from the East and West converged in Alexandria: the Philonic tradition, Persian dualism, Babylon astrology, Gnosticism, and Neoplatonism. Although Clement left Alexandria, around 202, to avoid the persecution that occurred during the reign of Septimius Severus, it was in this caldron of eclecticism Clement developed his theology.[47]

Along with several surviving fragments from various texts,[48] there are five extant texts attributed to Clement of Alexandria.[49] Clement's trilogy – *Exhortation to the Greeks*, *Christ the Educator*,

---

[46] Clement, 'Clement of Alexandria: Christ the Educator', in Joseph Roy Deferrari (ed.), FC, XXIII, pp. vi-viii; Piotr Ashwin-Siejkowski, *Clement of Alexandria: A Project of Christian Perfection* (London: T. & T. Clark, 2008), pp. 19-31; Charles Bigg, *The Christian Platonists of Alexandria: Eight lectures Preached before the University of Oxford in the Year 1886 on the Foundation of the Late Rev. John Bampton* (New York: AMS Press, 1970), pp. 44-45; González, *Christian Thought*, I, p. 190; Schaff, *History*, II, p. 782; Quasten, *Patrology*, II, pp. 5-6; Frend, *Christianity*, pp. 282-83. With regard to issues concerning a continuing tradition of an Alexandrian Catechetical School passing from Pantaenus through Clement to Origen, the relationship between school and church, and Philonic influence on the school, see Annewies van den Hoek, 'The "Catechetical" School of Early Christian Alexandria and Its Philonic Heritage', HTR 90 (1997), pp. 59-87.

[47] Bigg, *Christian Platonists*, pp. 1-35, 48-51; González, *Christian Thought*, I, pp. 186-90; Eric Francis Osborn, *Clement of Alexandria* (Cambridge: Cambridge University Press, 2005), pp. 16-27; Ashwin-Siejkowski, *Clement*, pp. 39-144; Clement, 'Christ the Educator', FC, XXIII, p. x; Harnack, *Dogma*, II, p. 323. For the relationship of Clement's theology and Gnosticism, see Pelikan, *Christian Tradition*, I, pp. 95-97.

[48] For information about Clement's works that only survive as fragments, see Quasten, II, *Patrology*, pp. 16-19. Many of these fragments can be found in Clement, 'Fragments', ANF, II, pp. 571-87.

[49] In the homily *Salvation of the Rich*, Clement addresses the issues of wealth and the responsibility of the wealthy. G.W. Butterworth provides an introduction, the Greek text, and an English translation of this text in Clement, *Clement of Alexandria* (trans. George William Butterworth; LCL; London: Heinemann, 1919), pp. 265-367. *Excerpts from Theodotus* demonstrates Clement's interest in Gnosticism; it contains notes from Gnostic writings that Clement apparently gathered for a future project. Quasten, *Patrology*, II, p. 15; González, *Christian Thought*, I, p. 190; Frend, *Christianity*, p. 287.

Miscellanies – are the most important sources of his theology, and they provide the next Spirit christological references. Clement planned to write this trilogy around the three-fold function of the Word, who exhorts, tutors, and teaches (*Paed.* 1.1), so Clement attempted to build his theology with the Logos as its basis.[50] The first text of the trilogy, *Exhortation to the Greeks*, consists of twelve chapters in three movements.[51] First, Clement attempted to convince the reader to accept the Christian faith by exposing the folly, worthlessness, and powerlessness of polytheistic worship (chs. 1–4). Second, Clement affirmed that through the Logos the ancient philosophers, poets, and the Hebrew prophets partook of the truth, but the definitive revelation of truth occurred in Christ (chs. 5–8).[52] Third, humans, therefore, should not neglect God's call, but they should abandon their customs that are contrary to the gospel and receive the redemption in Christ (chs. 9–12).

The second text, *Christ the Educator*, comprises three books.[53] Book one depicts the Logos as the tutor training children (1.5.12.1) how to improve the soul and live a virtuous life (1.1.1.4). Clement

---

[50] González, *Christian Thought*, I, pp. 192-204; Quasten, *Patrology*, II, pp. 20-35.

[51] The Greek version of the text, without a translation, is offered in Clement, *Clementis Alexandrini Protrepticus* (VCSup 34; Leiden: E.J. Brill, 1995). G.W. Butterworth furnishes an introduction, the Greek text, and an English translation of this text in Clement, *Clement of Alexandria*, LCL, pp. 3-263. Clement wrote this document in Alexandria around 189. Clement, 'Christ the Educator', FC, XXIII, p. xi.

[52] The Logos, accordingly, becomes the source of all knowledge of God: inspiring the philosophy of the Greeks, the Hebrew prophets, and giving the Law to the Jews, so that the definitive revelation of God occurs when the Logos is incarnated in Jesus Christ (*Protr.* 11; *Paed.* 1.8.74). According to Charles Bigg, this is Clement's guiding principle. 'The Gospel in his view is not a fresh departure, but the meeting-point of two converging lines of progress, of Hellenism and Judaism. To him all history is one, because all truth is one.' Bigg, *Christian Platonists*, pp. 47-49. According to Frend, 'Christianity was the end to which all current philosophy had been moving'. Frend, *Christianity*, p. 286. 'Philo and his school, however, had already attempted a synthesis between Platonism and Judaism in Alexandria. The same work was taken up by the Gnostics, especially Basilides and Valentinus and their followers in the second century. It was to be brought to fruition in the interests of orthodoxy by Clement and Origen.' Frend, *Christianity*, p. 368. Cf. Osborn, *Clement*, pp. 81-105; Harnack, *Dogma*, II, pp. 328-29; Pelikan, *Christian Tradition*, I, pp. 46-48, 56-57; Olson, *Christian Theology*, pp. 87-88.

[53] The Greek text is given, without translation, in Clement, *Clementis Alexandrini Paedagogus* (VCSup 61; Leiden: E.J. Brill, 2002). Simon Wood supplies a translation of the text in Clement, 'Christ the Educator', FC, XIII. Clement composed this treatise about 190 while he was still in Alexandria. Clement, 'Christ the Educator', FC, XXIII, p. xi.

then deals with the issue of defining children. Contrary to Gnosticism's exclusive claim to perfection and illumination, all redeemed individuals possess the potential for illumination and perfection because they are God's children (1.6.26.1). Moreover, against the Gnostic claim that the God of the Hebrew Scriptures, who educates through fear, is distinct from the God that Christ reveals, who trains through love, Clement asserts the unity of God's revelation. The Logos reconciles divine judgment and love; indeed, if it guards against sin, fear is beneficial to the Christian (1.9.83-84.3). Books Two and Three provide casuistries for every realm of life, so that the Logos leads Christians to live ethically and achieve freedom from the slavery of passions.

Clement failed to fulfill his promise to complete his trilogy with an examination of the function of the Logos as teacher; instead, the third text, *Miscellanies*, combines a series of miscellaneous notes.[54] This text is composed of eight books. Book One, affirms the value of Greek philosophy; the providence of God gave philosophy to the Greeks and the law to the Jews as schoolmasters to bring them to Christ (1.5.28). Book Two stresses the limits of philosophy, which can only prepare for faith, and the primacy of faith in attaining the knowledge of God (2.4.14). The remaining six books present two principal themes: (1) the refutation of false Gnosis, and (2) the delineation of the true Gnosis. According to Clement, true Gnosis is contemplating God in the Logos (4.25.155; 5.3.16; 6.9.78); therefore, Christians can attain the true Gnosis (4.21–23).[55] Although Clement's hermeneutic utilizes the historical or literal meaning of the text, following the Alexandrian exegetical tradition, he favors an allegorical interpretation (*Strom.* 6.15).[56] This spiritual

---

[54] It remains unclear why Clement did not fulfill his promise. For possible explanations, see González, *Christian Thought*, I, pp. 91-92; Quasten, *Patrology*, II, p. 12. Simon Wood suggests that Clement wrote the first four books sometime before 190 and the remaining four books after leaving Alexandria in 202. Clement, 'Christ the Educator', FC, XXIII, p. xii.

[55] For overviews of this trilogy, see Quasten, *Patrology*, II, pp. 6-14; González, *Christian Thought*, I, pp. 191-94; Schaff, *History*, II, pp. 783-85; Frend, *Christianity*, pp. 286-87; Olson, *Christian Theology*, p. 86.

[56] This exegetical method had the advantage of lending a spiritual interpretation to troublesome texts, such as anthropomorphic references to God. Gonzalez holds that this hermeneutic is based on a Platonic concept:

the realties of this world are symbols of eternal truths. Just as things in this world are true, but have their greatest value as signs that point to the world of

sense of the text lends itself to the Logos revealing true Gnosis to the children of God (*Strom.* 1.4.26).[57]

Several Spirit christological references are the object of Clement's allegorical interpretation. One text is part of Clement's explication of how a child of God receives Gnosis and grows into perfection (*Paed.* 1.6);[58] in this process, the Logos becomes everything to the believer: father and mother, educator, and nurse. The specific context allegorically examines Jn 6.55; the Lord's command to eat his flesh and drink his blood indicates the nourishment believers need and the Lord provides in this journey.

> The flesh is a figure of speech for the Holy Spirit, for it is He, in fact, who created the flesh; the blood means the Word, for He has been poured forth as precious blood to give us life; the union of the two is the Lord, nourishment of little ones: the Lord both Spirit and Word, is Spirit become flesh, flesh from heaven made holy (*Paed.* 1.6.43).[59]

According to Clement's interpretation, in the incarnation the Logos and Spirit function in an essential relationship of reciprocity, as blood is necessary to the life of flesh. Clement reiterates this analogy.

> Now, the blood of the Lord is twofold: one is corporeal, redeeming us from corruption; the other is spiritual, and it is with

---

ultimate reality, the historical and literal meaning of the sacred text is true, but that text has its greatest value when it is interpreted as signs or allegories that show the more profound truths of the universe (González, *Christian Thought*, I, pp. 195-96).

Charles Bigg points to Strom. 1.1.11 and 7.9.68 as evidence that the Alexandrines 'regarded Allegorism as having been handed down from Christ and a few chosen Apostles, through a succession, not of Bishops, but of Teachers'. Bigg, *Christian Platonists*, p. 57. For overviews of Clement's allegorical method, see González, *Christian Thought*, I, pp. 194-200; Bigg, *Christian Platonists*, pp. 56-58; Osborn, *Clement*, pp. 75-80, 90, 96.

[57] Cf. Harnack, *Dogma*, II, pp. 324-29; Wolfson, *Church Fathers*, I, pp. 122-27.

[58] This is Clement's version of the concept of theosis (*Paed.* 1.6.26). 'In contrast with the barely believing, uncultivated beginner, inclined to externalities, stands the Christian who beholds the mysteries of God, and who, with heart and understanding, receives God to abiding fellowship.' Seeberg and Hay, *History*, I, p. 142. Cf. Ashwin-Siejkowski, *Clement*, pp. 147-87; Osborn, *Clement*, pp. 144-45; Bigg, *Christian Platonists*, pp. 86-87; Olson, *Christian Theology*, pp. 88-90.

[59] Cited according to the translation of Simon Wood, Clement, 'Christ the Educator', FC, XXIII, p. 41. Cf. Wolfson, *Church Fathers*, I, p. 240.

that we are anointed. To drink the blood of Jesus is to participate in His incorruption. Yet, the Spirit is the strength of the Word in the same way that blood is of the body (Paed. 2.2.19).[60]

In the former text, Clement depicts the flesh of Christ as the Spirit and the blood of the Lord as the Logos. In the latter text, Clement designates the Spirit as blood and the Logos flesh. In other words, in the incarnation, what can be said of the Logos can be said of the Spirit,[61] a pneumatic incarnation. The Logos and Spirit, thus, unite in Christ's mission to provide nourishment necessary to attain perfection.

In fact, this relationship of reciprocity extends to all spheres of activity. By the Spirit the Logos orders the cosmos (*Protr.*1.5.3).[62] The Spirit with the Logos speaks through the prophets (*Protr.* 1.8, 8.79). The Spirit, like a magnet, attracts the virtuous as the Logos rules and presides by providence (*Strom.* 7.2.9).[63] The Logos becomes incarnate in Christ (*Protr.* 11.2), and, as the Lamb of God, dies for humanity (*Paed.* 1.5.24).[64] Christ is begotten of the Spirit,

---

[60] Clement, 'Christ the Educator', FC, XXIII, p. 111.

[61] Osborn, *Clement*, p. 152; Wolfson, *Church Fathers*, I, p. 238; Wiles, *Working Papers in Doctrine*, p. 7.

[62] Clement affirms that distinctions between the Father, Son, and Holy Spirit are manifested in their external relationships (*Paed.* 1.8.71). Cf. Osborn, *Clement*, pp. 132-42; Bigg, *Christian Platonists*, p. 68. A question has lingered whether or not Clement held a two-stage concept of the Logos. This view asserts that the Logos eternally existed in the Father and became a second hypostasis when, before all ages, the Logos generated from the Father as the agent of creation. Harry Wolfson leans toward this view but concedes that Clement may have changed his view to a single stage concept. Wolfson, *Church Fathers*, I, pp. 204-17. M.J. Edwards argues that rather than a two-stage Logos hypothesis Clement supports the concept of the Logos' eternal generation. Edwards' argument has three moves: (1) He argues that during Clement's time the two-stage hypothesis was not a universal datum. (2) He challenges the philological and philosophical basis for supposing that Clement held this view. (3) He attempts to demonstrate that Clement has been misquoted. M.J. Edwards, 'Clement of Alexandria and His Doctrine of the Logos', *VC* 54 (2000), pp. 159-77.

[63] Cf. Osborn, *Clement*, pp. 149-53; Bigg, *Christian Platonists*, pp. 70-71. 'The concept of the Logos would prove the most hopeful means of establishing common ground between Greek and biblical ideas of the universe.' Frend, *Christianity*, p. 369. 'The second function of the Logos, which in John is described simply by the statement that, after the creation of the world, "He was in the world," is attributed by many Fathers also to the Holy Spirit, as, for instance, Clement of Alexandria in his statement that the Holy Spirit is "everywhere"'. Wolfson, *Church Fathers*, I, p. 249. Cf. Pelikan, *Christian Tradition*, I, pp. 188-89.

[64] Since Clement asserted that Jesus was exempt from desires and emotion, he seemed to imply that Jesus' flesh was not completely like other humans (*Strom.*

and the Spirit anoints Christ (*Paed.* 2.8.61), so that all the powers of the Spirit reside in him (*Strom.* 4.25).[65] As the Spirit of Christ, the Spirit inspires believers (*Strom.* 5.13), dwells in believers as in temples (*Strom.* 2.20.117), and empowers them with the charismata (*Strom.* 4.21). It is possible, however, that Clement only recognizes the Holy Spirit as the divine impersonal power of God.[66] If this is the case, then, for Clement, the Holy Spirit functions as the power in the divine acts of the Father and the Logos, so that the power of the Father begets the Logos in the incarnation and functions synonymously with the Logos in the salvific mission.

Clement has integrated a nascent form of Logos Christology with Spirit Christology. Clement built his theology on the basis of the Logos. Clement's Logos concept bridged Greek philosophy and Scripture, coalesced the God of the Hebrew Scriptures and the God revealed in Jesus Christ, and its illumination provided true Gnosis for Christians. Since the roles of the Logos and the Spirit are at times synonymous and always functioning in a complementary fashion, they exist in a dyadic relationship of reciprocity in creation, incarnation, and redemption. What can be said of the Logos can be said of the Spirit.

Origen

The writings of Origen, who at the age of eighteen became Clement's successor to the teaching ministry of the Alexandrian catechet-

---

6.9.71). Cf. Frend, *Christianity*, p. 372. 'His christological statements frequently came to formulations that sound docetic. It seems evident that Clement was not in fact a docetist, but he did blur the distinction between the Logos and the soul in a way that could lead in that direction.' Pelikan, *Christian Tradition*, I, p. 47. Cf. González, *Christian Thought*, I, p. 201; Seeberg and Hay, *History*, I, p. 143; Bigg, *Christian Platonists*, p. 71; Kelly, *Doctrines*, pp. 153-54.

[65] Cf. Osborn, *Clement*, pp. 142-44; Bigg, *Christian Platonists*, pp. 63-64; McDonnell, *The Baptism of Jesus in the Jordan*, pp. 55, 116.

[66] 'Clement is jealous of the slightest approach to Pantheism, and takes occasion more than once to warn his readers, that the Holy Spirit, though said to be breathed into the believer, is present in the soul not as part of God, not in essence, but in power.' Bigg, *Christian Platonists*, pp. 70-71. David Runia affirms that Clement appropriates the Philonic doctrine of the divine powers. 'For Clement experience of the divine power (usually in the singular) leads to knowledge of God (to the extent possible) and intimacy with him through the Son.' David T. Runia, 'Clement of Alexandria and the Philonic Doctrine of the Divine Power(s)', *VC* 58 (2004), pp. 256-76.

ical school (203) and later founded a similar school in Caesarea (232), furnish the next Spirit christological references. Along with Augustine, Origen was one of the most prolific writers of the ancient world. Of the six thousand works Epiphanius (*Pan.* 64.63) credits to Origen, there are references to about eight hundred titles. Though only a portion of these are extant, those that remain demonstrate Origen's range of interest: textual criticism of the Hebrew Scriptures, exegetical works – in the literary forms of scholia, homilies, and commentaries – a systematic treatise, an apology, and several minor works of a practical nature.[67] Several of these texts contain Spirit christological references; nevertheless, attention will focus on the systematic work *On First Principles* because it serves as an exposition of Origen's theology.

Origen composed *On First Principles* in Alexandria, sometime between 220 and 230,[68] as a manual to deal with theological issues discussed in the Alexandrian school, probably, in response to Gnosticism.[69] Unfortunately, only a few Greek fragments of this work have survived, but Rufinus has preserved the entire treatise by translating it into Latin.[70] The work consists of a preface and four

---

[67] For overviews of Origen's works see, Bigg, *Christian Platonists*, pp. 123-34; Jean Daniélou, *Origen* (New York: Sheed and Ward, 1955), pp. x-xv; Henri Crouzel, *Origen* (trans. A.S. Worrall; San Francisco: Harper & Row, 1989), pp. 37-50; Quasten, *Patrology*, II, pp. 43-74; Schaff, *History*, II, pp. 793-96; González, *Christian Thought*, I, pp. 208-10.

[68] Concerning the issues of provenance and date of origin, see Origen and Paul Koetschau, *On First Principles: Being Koetschau's Text of the De Principiis Translated into English* (trans. G.W. Butterworth; New York: Harper & Row, 1966), pp. xxviii-xxxi; Joseph Wilson Trigg, *Origen: The Bible and Philosophy in the Third-century Church* (Atlanta: John Knox Press, 1983), pp. 91-93.

[69] 'Origen was dealing with questions which had been raised and discussed in the School before his time, and which were then admitted to be legitimate subjects for inquiry.' Origen and Koetschau, *On First Principles*, p. xxxi. 'As in *Hexapla* the aim was debate, this time with the Gnostics.' Frend, *Christianity*, p. 376. 'Origen aims his polemic mainly at the trio Basilides-Valentinus-Marcion.' Crouzel, *Origen*, pp. 153-56.

[70] Origen and Koetschau, *On First Principles*, pp. xxxi-lii; Panayiotis Tzamalikos, *Origen: Philosophy of History & Eschatology* (VCSup 85; Leiden: E.J. Brill, 2007), pp. 9-17. Rufinus was a fourth-century admirer of Origen. Because Rufinus freely redacted the text to conform to his view of orthodoxy, caution must be exercised in examining Origen's theology. Therefore, the survey will proceed by noting how the theology and the Spirit christological texts in *First Principles* compare with similar texts found in extant texts that survive in Greek: *Contra Celsus*, *Commentary on Matthew*, and *Commentary on John*. 'The Commentaries of St. John and St. Matthew are of value chiefly as a check on the Latin text of the *De Princi-*

132   Spirit Christology

books. The preface presents the treatise's thesis and an overview of its contents. According to Origen, Jesus Christ is the source of grace and truth, and apostolic teaching has delivered and transmitted the truth of Christ in the church by an orderly succession of apostles (*Princ.* Preface, 1-3). These first principles bequeathed by the apostles elucidated issues concerning the one Triune God, Christology, pneumatology, angelology, eschatology, free will and the fall, the origin of the soul, opposing forces, creation, and the inspiration of Scripture (*Princ.* Preface, 4-10). The following four books, therefore, present Origen's explication of apostolic teaching and his speculation on these issues.

According to Origen's doctrine of God, God is simple Spirit and Mind, incorporeal, immutable, and incomprehensible; therefore, human senses do not perceive God (*Princ.* 1.1.1-9).[71] Accordingly, any anthropomorphic language found in Scripture should be interpreted allegorically rather than literally.[72] Furthermore, the one deity exists in unity of substance as the Triune God: Father, Son, and Holy Spirit (*Princ.* 1.3.8). The Father is the primal source of deity from which the Son is generated and the Holy Spirit proceeds.[73]

---

piis, as Rufinus is always open to the suspicion of having watered his author down when he made his translation.' Daniélou, *Origen*, p. 208. For issues concerning date of origin and provenance of these three documents, see Origen, *Contra Celsum* (trans. Henry Chadwick; Cambridge: Cambridge University Press, 1980), pp. xiv-xv; Origen, 'Commentary on Matthew', ANF, IX, p. 411; Origen, *Commentary on the Gospel According to John: Books 1-10*, FC, LXXX, pp. 4-5; Origen, *Commentary on the Gospel According to John: Books 13-32*, FC, LXXXIX, pp. 4-19.

[71] Cf. Bigg, *Christian Platonists*, pp. 155-61; Harnack, *Dogma*, II, pp. 349-51. Origen's doctrine of God demonstrates the Platonic influence on his theology. Daniélou, *Origen*, pp. 75-98; J. Rebecca Lyman, *Christology and Cosmology: Models of Divine Activity in Origen, Eusebius, and Athanasius* (OTM; Oxford: Clarendon Press, 1993), pp. 47-58; Tzamalikos, *Origen*, pp. 17-18; Seeberg and Hay, *History*, I, pp. 148-49; Pelikan, *Christian Tradition*, I, p. 54.

[72] For Origen, the task of theology consists of deciphering the spiritual meaning in the Scriptures. Following the allegorical tradition of the Alexandrian school, Origen's exegesis posits a three-fold sense of scriptural interpretation: (1) literal, (2) moral, and (3) spiritual (*Princ.* 4.11-13). Harnack, *Dogma*, II, pp. 347-48; Bigg, *Christian Platonists*, pp. 134-51; Crouzel, *Origen*, pp. 61-84; González, *Christian Thought*, I, pp. 211-16; Frend, *Christianity*, pp. 378-79; Tzamalikos, *Origen*, pp. 25-37; Morwenna Ludlow, 'Theology and Allegory: Origen and Gregory of Nyssa on the Unity and Diversity of Scripture', *IJST* 4 (2002), pp. 45-53; R.R. Reno, 'Origen and Spiritual Interpretation', *ProEccl* 15 (2006), pp. 108-26; Pelikan, *Christian Tradition*, I, pp. 110-15; Seeberg and Hay, *History*, I, pp. 147-48.

[73] 'The original goodness must be believed to reside in God the Father, and from him both the Son and the Holy Spirit undoubtedly draw into themselves the

Although the Father generated the Son (*Princ.* 1.2.4), this does not mean there was a time when the Father existed without the Son (*Princ.* 4.28). The Son and Holy Spirit are coeternal with the Father (*Princ.* 1.3.4); nevertheless, the Son and Spirit are subordinate to the Father in this relationship (*Princ.*1.2.13).[74] Since the Father is utterly incomprehensible, the Son and Holy Spirit are intermediaries between the Father and creatures; they reveal the Father, so that through the Logos, who is Christ, the Father becomes comprehensible (*Princ.* 1.2.8; *Cels.* 7.17).[75]

Origen's doctrine of dual creation accentuated the interdependence of the doctrines of the soul's origin, free will and the fall, angelology, anthropology, soteriology, and eschatology. The first creation consisted of pure intellects whose sole purpose was to contemplate the divine image. Because God endowed these intellects with a free will, they chose to turn their attention to multiplicity and fell away from the divine image; thus, they became souls. The creation of the corporeal world constituted the second creation, which

---

nature of that goodness existing in the fount from which the one is born and the other proceeds' (*Princ.*1.2.13). Cited according to the translation of G.W. Butterworth, Origen and Koetschau, *On First Principles*, p. 28. Cf. Frend, *Christianity*, pp. 376-77; González, *Christian Thought*, I, pp. 217-20; Quasten, *Patrology*, II, pp. 76-79; Daniélou, *Origen*, pp. 125-27; Seeberg and Hay, *History*, I, pp. 149-50; Wiles, *Working Papers in Doctrine*, pp. 19-27; Maurice Wiles, 'Eternal Generation', *JTS* 12 (1961), pp. 284-91.

[74] 'It is obvious that we, who maintain that even the sensible world is made by the Creator of all things, hold that the Son is not mightier that the Father, but subordinate. And we say this because we believe him who said, "The Father who sent me is greater than I"' (*Cels.* 8.15). Cited according to the translation of Henry Chadwick, Origen, *Contra Celsum*, p. 463. M. Marcovich supplies the Greek text for this polemic in Origen, *Contra Celsum: Libri VIII* (VCSup 54; Leiden: Brill, 2001). Commenting on Jn 1.1, Origen asserts that θεός with the article represents the Father, who is the source and origin of deity, while θεός without the article is an adjectival designation, denoting deity the Son receives from the Father (*Comm. Jo.* 2.1-20). Cf. Daniélou, *Origen*, pp. 252-54; Crouzel, *Origen*, pp. 181-82. In this Triune relationship, the Holy Spirit receives deity from the Father through the Son and is related to the Son as the Son is to the Father, so that the Holy Spirit participates in the character of Christ as the Spirit of Christ (*Comm. Jo.* 2.76). Cf. Harnack, *Dogma*, II, p. 358. For issues concerning subordination in Origen's theology see, Bigg, *Christian Platonists*, pp. 181-88; Shedd, *Doctrine*, I, pp. 288-304; Seeberg and Hay, *History*, I, pp. 150-51; J. Nigel Rowe, *Origen's Doctrine of Subordination: A Study in Origen's Christology* (New York: Peter Lang, 1987).

[75] 'For all knowledge of the Father, when the Son reveals him, is made known to us through the Holy Spirit' (*Princ.* 1.3.4). Origen and Koetschau, *On First Principles*, p. 32. Cf. Daniélou, *Origen*, pp. 257-59; Grillmeier, *Christian Tradition*, I, pp. 142-43.

provided a place for humans and fallen spirits to undergo trials, allowing them to make use of their freedom to return to unity and harmony with God (*Princ.* 2.3.1-7). In point of fact, Origen's eschatology taught a universal restoration of all things to their original spiritual state, so that all will salvifically return to God, including sinners, demons, and even Satan (*Princ.* 1.6.1-4; 3.6.1-9; *Cels.* 8.72).[76]

For Origen, then, the souls of all rational beings pre-existed before the creation of their corporeal being, including Christ's (*Princ.* 2.8.1-5). God implanted souls into the animals, sun, moon, stars, and angels at their creation; however, humans received souls at their conception in the womb. Moreover, the choices made by the soul's free will – good or evil – in their preexistent state determined which rational creature the soul would be implanted into; consequently, the creature's proclivities toward temptation and sin, during their corporeal existence, were present in the soul from the beginning (*Princ.* 2.9.8).[77] Of course, the preexistent soul of Christ was the only soul that remained pure and in union with the Logos.

Origen's Christology and pneumatology closely relate; accordingly, several Spirit christological texts depict the relationship of the Logos and Spirit in Christ's identity and mission. Concerning the incarnation, Origen asserted that the soul of Christ in its pre-incarnate state mediated between God and human flesh; therefore, Christ's soul provided space for the incarnation and connected the divine Logos with the human body of Christ.[78]

---

[76] This is Origen's doctrine of ἀποκατάστασις. Tzamalikos, *Origen*, pp. 237-356; Crouzel, *Origen*, pp. 257-66; Trigg, *Origen*, pp. 108-15; Harnack, *Dogma*, II, pp. 377-78; Pelikan, *Christian Tradition*, I, pp. 151-52; Frend, *Christianity*, p. 377. Ilaria Ramelli argues that Origen has a dual basis for this doctrine: Scripture and Platonism. Ilaria L.E. Ramelli, 'Christian Soteriology and Christian Platonism: Origen, Gregory of Nyssa, and the Biblical and Philosophical Basis of the Doctrine of Apokatastasis', *VC* 61 (2007), pp. 313-56. Concerning the issue of universalism, see Tom Greggs, 'Exclusivist or Universalist? Origen the 'Wise Steward of the Word' (*CommRom.* v.1.7) and the Issue of Genre', *IJST* 9 (2007), pp. 315-27.

[77] Cf. Crouzel, *Origen*, pp. 205-18; Daniélou, *Origen*, pp. 211-19; Trigg, *Origen*, pp. 103-107; Bigg, *Christian Platonists*, pp. 193-99; Harnack, *Dogma*, II, pp. 361-65; Frend, *Christianity*, p. 377; González, *Christian Thought*, I, pp. 220-22; Quasten, *Patrology*, II, pp. 91-92; Tzamalikos, *Origen*, pp. 48-53; Lyman, *Christology and Cosmology*, pp. 58-69; Seeberg and Hay, *History*, I, p. 151.

[78] 'This soul, then, acting as a medium between God and the flesh (for it was not possible for the nature of God to mingle with a body apart from some medium) there is born, as we have said, the God-man, the medium being that existence to whose nature it was not contrary to assume a body' (*Princ.* 2.6.3). Origen

In these last times he emptied himself and was made man, was made flesh, although he was God; and being made man, he remained what he was, namely God. He took to himself a body like our body, differing in this alone, that it was born of a virgin and of the Holy Spirit (*Princ.* Preface. 4).[79]

So Origen affirms two unconfused natures in Christ; deity remained unaltered and assumed a human body fashioned by the Holy Spirit and the virgin (*Cels.* 1.32; 6.69-73; 6.75-77; *Comm. Matt.* 10.17). In the incarnation, nonetheless, deity and humanity united so intimately in Jesus Christ, the God-man, that the attributes of these natures interchanged (*Princ.* 2.6.3; *Cels.* 1.33).[80] In fact, because of its union with the Logos, it was not possible for Christ's soul to sin (*Princ.* 2.6.5). Thereupon, Jesus Christ lived a sinless life, died as a perfect sacrifice for sin, and was resurrected to redeem humanity (*Princ.* Preface 4; *Comm. Jo.* 1.230-233).[81]

According to Origen, the Spirit is essential to Christ's identity and mission.

---

and Koetschau, *On First Principles*, p. 110. According to Maurice Wiles, Origen's affirmation of Christ's human soul had a two-fold theological purpose: (1) its soteriological significance, and (2) its mediating role in effecting the incarnation. Wiles, *Working Papers in Doctrine*, pp. 54-56. Cf. Lyman, *Christology and Cosmology*, pp. 69-81; Grillmeier, *Christian Tradition*, I, pp. 146-47; Harnack, *Dogma*, II, p. 370; Daniélou, *Origen*, pp. 262-63; Bigg, *Christian Platonists*, pp. 189-90; Kelly, *Doctrines*, pp. 154-58; Wolfson, *Church Fathers*, I, pp. 392-94; Wiles, *The Christian Fathers*, pp. 60-62; Quasten, *Patrology*, II, pp. 79-80; Seeberg and Hay, *History*, I, p. 152.

[79] Origen and Koetschau, *On First Principles*, p. 3. Considering Origen's doctrine of the preexistence of souls, it is reasonable to assume that the subject of kenosis here refers to Christ's soul (*Princ.* 2.6.4). In fact, in his discussion of the descent of souls into bodies, Origen seems to imply this view (*Comm. Jo.* 6.217-221). Cf. Crouzel, *Origen*, pp. 193-94.

[80] Origen, therefore, teaches the doctrine of the communication of properties (*communicatio idiomatum*). Crouzel, *Origen*, pp. 192-94; González, *Christian Thought*, I, pp. 222-23; Quasten, *Patrology*, II, p. 81; Trigg, *Origen*, pp. 100-101; Bigg, *Christian Platonists*, p. 190; Seeberg and Hay, *History*, I, pp. 152-53.

[81] Cf. Crouzel, *Origen*, pp. 194-97; Bigg, *Christian Platonists*, pp. 210-12; Trigg, *Origen*, p. 101. Redemption is a Triune event. The Father and the Son work universally in all things that exist: saints, sinners, animals, and inanimate things. The Holy Spirit's ministry, however, only operates in the redeemed; hence, Origen limits the Spirit's role to sanctification of believers (*Princ.* 1.3.5). Origen viewed redemption from two interdependent positions: (1) redemption as a pedagogical process, (2) Christ's death delivered humanity from the tyranny of evil. Daniélou, *Origen*, pp. 269-75; Seeberg and Hay, *History*, I, pp. 153-55.

Although it is the Father, as leader, who sends the Son, the Holy Spirit joins in sending him in advance, promising to descend to the Son of God at the right time and to cooperate in the salvation of men. And this he has done when he lights upon the Savior in bodily form as a dove after his baptism, and remains and does not pass on. Perhaps he would have passed on among men who cannot constantly bear his glory. Wherefore, in regard to his knowledge of who is the Christ, John indicates that it is not only the descent of the Spirit on Jesus, but in addition to the descent, it is the fact that he abides in him. For it is written that John said: He who sent me to baptize said, He on whom you see the Spirit descending and remaining upon him, he it is who baptizes with the Holy Spirit and with fire (*Comm. Jo.* 2.83-85).[82]

Several conclusions emerge from this text. First, along with the Father, the Holy Spirit had an active role in sending the Son on his salvific mission;[83] hence, the Spirit mediates the incarnation of Christ. Second, the Holy Spirit descends upon Christ like a dove to anoint him for his salvific mission.[84] Third, the abiding presence of the Spirit reveals Christ's identity (*Comm. Jo.* 1.236-239; *Cels.* 6.17, 65; *Comm. Matt.* 14.6; *Princ.* 1.3.4). Fourth, Christ's reception of the Spirit is the prolepsis of believers' Spirit baptism: 'He, therefore, received the Spirit which remained on him that he might be able to baptize those who come to him with that very Spirit which

---

[82] Cited according to the translation of Ronald Heine, Origen, *Commentary on the Gospel According to John: Books 1-10*, p. 116.

[83] Since the Spirit sends the Son, in the incarnation, Origen posits a subordination of the Son to the Spirit. 'He has been sent by the Father and His Spirit, it is possible even there to allege of the Spirit which sent the Christ, that he does not excel him in nature, but that the Savior was made less than him because of the plan of the incarnation of the Son of God which was taking place' (*Comm. Jo.* 2.81). Origen, *Commentary on the Gospel According to John: Books 1-10*, p. 115.

[84] 'God hath anointed thee, thy God with the oil of gladness above thy fellows. As a reward for its love, therefore, it is anointed with the "oil of gladness", that is the soul with the word of God is made Christ; for to be anointed with the oil of gladness means nothing else but to be filled with the Holy Spirit' (*Princ.* 2.6.4). Origen and Koetschau, *On First Principles*, p. 112. 'I think that the miracles performed by Jesus are evidence that the Holy Spirit was seen then in the form of a dove' (*Cels.* 1.46). 'Jesus, in fact, showed himself among the Jews to be "the power of God" by the miracles that he did' (*Cels.* 2.9). Origen, *Contra Celsum*, pp. 42, 74. For other texts about the association of Holy Spirit with Christ's anointing and power see, *Cels.* 1.43, 56; 3.2; 4.5; *Comm. Jo.* 1.191-97. Cf. Grillmeier, *Christian Tradition*, I, p. 140.

remained' (*Comm. Jo.* 6.220).⁸⁵ According to this Spirit christological text, the Spirit identifies Christ and encompasses the entire salvific mission.

The final Spirit christological text of interest concerns how Christ dwells among believers as the Spirit of Christ. Asserting that humans derive the knowledge of grace and truth from Christ's teachings, Origen credits the inspiration of prophetic words and deeds to the Spirit of Christ.

> By the words of Christ we do not mean only those which formed his teaching when he was made man and dwelt in the flesh, since even before that Christ the Word of God was in Moses and the prophets. For without the Word of God how could they have prophesied about Christ? In proof of which we should not find it difficult to show from the divine scriptures how that Moses or the prophets were filled with the [S]pirit of Christ in all their words and deeds (*Princ.* Preface. 1).⁸⁶

This text seems to identify the Spirit of Christ with the Logos; nonetheless, in explicating his premise, Origen unambiguously infers that the Holy Spirit is the Spirit of Christ.⁸⁷ Yet, this does not imply that Origen fails to distinguish between the Holy Spirit and the Logos; Origen denotes the Holy Spirit with the designation Spirit of Christ because the Holy Spirit receives deity from the Father through the Son and participates in the character of Christ

---

⁸⁵ Origen, *Commentary on the Gospel According to John: Books 1-10*, p. 228. Cf. Daniélou, *Origen*, pp. 56-61; Everett Ferguson, 'Baptism according to Origen', *EvQ* 78 (2006), pp. 121-23; McDonnell, *The Baptism of Jesus in the Jordan*, pp. 203-206; McDonnell and Montague, *Christian Initiation*, pp. 144-54.

⁸⁶ Origen and Koetschau, *On First Principles*, p. 1. 'Jesus and his disciples explained the meaning of the Spirit that spoke in the prophets (which was none other than the Spirit of Christ)' (*Cels.* 6.19). Origen, *Contra Celsum*, p. 332.

⁸⁷ 'The apostles delivered this doctrine, that the Holy Spirit is united in honor and dignity with the Father and the Son ... It is, however, certainly taught with the utmost clearness in the Church, that this Spirit inspired each one of the saints, both the prophets and the apostles' (*Princ.* Preface. 4). Origen and Koetschau, *On First Principles*, p. 3. Against Gnosticism, Origen affirms the unity of the God of the Hebrew Scriptures and the New Testament:

> Now just as it is the same God himself and the same Christ himself, so also it is the same Holy Spirit himself who was in the prophets and the apostles, that is, both in those who believed in God before the coming of Christ and in those who have taken refuge in God through Christ (*Princ.* 2.7.1) (Origen and Koetschau, *On First Principles*, p. 116).

(*Comm. Jo.* 2.76). According to Origen, therefore, the Spirit of Christ dwells in prophets, apostles, and saints, allowing them to partake of the character of Christ and receive the charismata.[88]

Origen integrates Logos Christology with Spirit Christology. Although Origen carefully distinguishes between the Logos and Spirit, because the Holy Spirit bears the character of Christ, their missions and activities closely correlate. In their soteriological mission, the Holy Spirit sends the Logos and is the agent of conception in the incarnation. The Logos is the deity in Christ, which is linked to human flesh by the soul, but the Holy Spirit anoints and empowers Christ's activities and mission. Congruently, the Son sends the Holy Spirit as the Spirit of Christ to sanctify, anoint, and empower believers to continue Christ's activities. Origen, thus, posits an incipient Logos incarnational Christology and a Spirit Christology of pneumatic mediation that function complementarily.

Conclusion

Several conclusions can be drawn from the survey of Spirit Christology among the Later Apologists. First, methodologically, in congruity with the foregoing groups of writers, the Spirit Christologies of the Later Apologists continue support for two pneumatic christological paradigms: (1) holding Logos Christology and Spirit Christology compatible, Irenaeus, Clement, and Origen advocate pneumatic mediation, and (2) Hippolytus seemingly upholds pneumatic incarnation. Second, they affirm the importance of Christ's anointing of the Holy Spirit, but their polemical writings unambiguously reject all Spirit christological methods of pneumatic inspiration: Gnostic and Dynamic Monarchianism. Third, Hippolytus favors a certain Spirit christological method of pneumatic incarnation, while rejecting another form; all of these writers categorically repudiate

---

[88] 'This material of the gifts which I mentioned is made effective from God; it is administered by Christ; but it subsists in accordance with the Holy Spirit' (*Comm. Jo.* 2.77). Origen, *Commentary on the Gospel According to John: Books 1-10*, p. 114. 'So also the Spirit of Christ sits upon those, so to speak, who are formed like him. Because the Word of God wished to show this, God is described as promising to the righteous: "I will dwell among them and will walk among them, and I will be their God and they shall be my people' (*Cels.* 8.18). Origen, *Contra Celsum*, p. 465.

the Modalist Monarchian Sprit christological model. Fourth, in juxtaposing their methods with Gnosticism and Modalism the dialogue accentuates certain trinitarian issues. Their polemics focus on carefully distinguishing between the Father and the Son, while maintaining the unity of the one divine essence and the monotheistic unity of divine activity in creation and redemption; this often results, especially in Origen, in the subordination of the Son to the Father. Distinguishing the Spirit from the Father and Son receives some attention in Irenaeus and Origen, but terminology designating the Logos and Spirit in Hippolytus and Clement remain fluid. Fifth, christological issues concerning the dual natures of Christ come forward. The fluidity of christological language allows for identifying Christ's divine nature with Logos or Spirit;[89] flesh usually designates Christ's human nature, but Origen interjects Christ's soul into the discussion. Sixth, these writers disagree concerning the value of philosophy for theology and their hermeneutical method. Although integrating philosophical concepts into their theology, overall Irenaeus and Hippolytus view philosophy as the source of heresies and devalue its use in theology, and they rely more on the literal sense of Scripture. Clement's and Origen's theological method begins, however, with philosophy, and they opt for an analogical interpretation of Scripture.

It appears, therefore, that Spirit Christology has been at the heart of these developing christological and trinitarian doctrines. As the survey continues to trace Spirit Christology through the rest of the Patristic era, these trinitarian and christological issues will become more pronounced and finally delineated; indeed, Spirit Christology will play an integral role in these doctrinal developments.

---

[89] Following this trajectory, other writers provide Spirit christological references. 'The Word and the Son of God is sent ... He enters into a virgin; the Holy Spirit put on flesh' (Cyprian, *Idol.* 11). Cited according to the translation of Roy Deferrari, Cyprian, *Treatises*, FC, XXXVI, p. 357. 'The Holy Spirit of God coming down form heaven chose the holy virgin by means of whose womb He would make His way among us. She, filled completely with the divine Spirit, conceived Him' (Lactantius, *Inst.* 4.12). 'He became both Son of God through the Spirit and Son of Man through the flesh, that is, He is both God and man' (Lactantius, *Inst.* 4.13). Cited according to the translation of Mary Francis McDonald, Lactantius, *The Divine Institutes, Books I-VII*, FC, IVIX, pp. 269, 273. Cf. Dionysius of Alexandria, *Epistle to Dionysius Bishop of Rome*, 1.4; Novatian, *Treatise Concerning the Trinity*, 24; Victorinus of Pettau, *Commentary on the Apocalypse of the Blessed John*, 4.1.

6

EASTERN WRITERS

As Christology developed during the remaining part of the Patristic period, christological discussion primarily focused on three issues. The first problem concerned Christ's identity: how could the church proclaim Christ's deity in a monotheistic framework? The second corollary topic addressed the incarnation of deity: what was this divine nature, how did it relate to human nature, and did Christ have a human soul? The third matter regarded the Holy Spirit: how did the Holy Spirit exist in divine relationship with the Father and Son, and what was the Holy Spirit's relationship to the Son in the salvific mission? As churches wrestled with these issues, they came together in various synods and councils seeking to determine a consensus. The majority of this drama played itself out in the Eastern region of the church.

Arius

Arius' theology supplies the watershed for these christological issues. In 318 a dispute concerning the deity of the Son erupted in Alexandria between Arius, who served as priest, and Alexander, the bishop:[1] contrary to Alexander, Arius held that the Son was not

---

[1] For information about Arius' life and the antecedents to this synod, see Rowan Williams, *Arius: Heresy and Tradition* (Grand Rapids: Eerdmans, Revised edn, 2001), pp. 29-47; R.P.C. Hanson, *The Search for the Christian Doctrine of God: The Arian Controversy, 318-381* (Grand Rapids: Baker Academic, 2005), pp. 3-5, 60-98; Charles Kannengiesser, *Arius and Athanasius: Two Alexandrian Theologians* (Brookfield, VT: Gower, 1991), pp. 391-403; Henry Melvill Gwatkin, *Studies of*

divine by nature, for the Son did not originate from the Father's essence. The same year Alexander convened a synod in Alexandria to settle the matter. Although the synod deposed Arius, he had many influential supporters who sought to vindicate him,[2] so the political, ecclesiastical, and theological issues remained volatile. Emperor Constantine, therefore, seeking peace and unity among the bishops, convoked a council at Nicea (325) to settle this debate, as well as other issues. The Council favored Alexander's position and formulated a creed which affirmed the consubstantial (ὁμοούσιος) nature of the Son with the Father, and Constantine exiled Arius.[3]

Arius protested his deposition and delineated his doctrinal positions through four documents he composed: a *Letter to Eusebius of Nicomedia* (318), a *Letter to Alexander of Alexandria* (320), the *Thalia* (320), and a *Letter to Emperor Constantine* (327).[4] Although these three missives and the song, *Thalia*, are preserved by Arius' detractors,[5] and due consideration must be given to this fact, they seem to provide a valid description of Arius' Christology.[6]

Arianism: Chiefly Referring to the Character and Chronology of the Reaction Which Followed the Council of Nicaea (New York: AMS, 1978), pp. 16-20.

[2] These supporters include Eusebius of Nicomedia, Asterius the Sophist, Athanasius bishop of Anazarbus, Theognis, Paulinus of Tyre, Achilleus, and Eusebius of Caesarea. Hanson, *Christian Doctrine of God*, pp. 27-59. Cf. Theodoret, *Hist. eccl.* 1.4; Gwatkin, *Studies of Arianism*, pp. 32-34.

[3] Hanson, *Christian Doctrine of God*, pp. 152-72; Leo Donald Davis, *The First Seven Ecumenical Councils (325-787): Their History and Theology* (Theology and Life Series 21; Collegeville, MN: Liturgical Press, 1990), pp. 33-75; Gwatkin, *Studies of Arianism*, pp. 38-55.

[4] Immediately after the synod in Alexandria Arius wrote the *Letter to Eusebius of Nicomedia* protesting his ill treatment by Alexander and distinguishing his doctrine from his antagonist's. While in Nicomedia, at the invitation of his friend Eusebius, Arius wrote a *Letter to Alexander of Alexandria* as an exposition of his doctrine, and to make his doctrine known among common people he wrote *Thalia* in a fashion similar to a banquet song. After the Council of Nicea, Arius wrote a *Letter to Constantine* containing a creed he composed intending to prove his orthodoxy. For issues concerning purpose, date, and provenance see Johannes Quasten, *Patrology*, III, pp. 10-13; Hanson, *Christian Doctrine of God*, pp. 5-15; Williams, *Arius*, pp. 48-91.

[5] *Letter to Eusebius of Nicomedia* (Theodoret, *Hist. eccl.* 1.4; Epiphanius, *Pan.* 69.6); *Letter to Alexander of Alexandria* (Athanasius, *Syn.* 16; Epiphanius, *Pan.* 69.7-8); *Thalia* (Athanasius, *Syn.* 15; *C. Ar.* 1.2.5); *Letter to Emperor Constantine* (Socrates, *Hist. eccl.* 1.26; Sozomenus, *Hist. eccl.* 2.27).

[6] Concerning these issues, see Robert C. Gregg (ed.), *Arianism: Historical and Theological Reassessments* (Patristic Monograph Series, 11; Eugene, OR: Wipf and Stock, 2006 repr.; Philadelphia: The Philadelphia Patristic, 1985), pp. 1-78.

Three primary themes depict Arius' Christology. First, in order for the Son to become flesh, the Son cannot be of the same divine essence as the Father. Arius, therefore, posited that the essence of the one true God is eternal, ingenerate, and unbegotten; however, the Son was created by the Father's will out of nothing[7] as the first of God's creatures to be the instrument of creation and to mediate between the one transcendent God and creation. The Holy Spirit, accordingly, was the first creature produced from the Son, so, albeit exalted and perfect, Arian theology placed the Son and Spirit on the side of creatures. Since the Son possessed nothing proper to God's essence, the Father was incomprehensible and ineffable to the Son; furthermore, because the Son only partakes of divine attributes by the Father's will, the Son advanced in divine wisdom as the Father taught him how to frame creation. In fact, whereas the transcendent Father could not encounter creation, for the Son to become flesh it was necessary for the Son to be alterable and capable of advancement in grace. Second, the Son must be capable of suffering. Human weaknesses and limitations applied to Christ's human body and the incarnate Son; Christ had no human soul, so the Son functioned as the rational element in Christ and suffered.[8] Third, as reward for obedience to the Father's will, the Son advanced in grace.[9]

Several Spirit christological references support Arius' *motif* of advancement by participation in grace. Athanasius' writings have preserved reasonably reliable examples. Reviewing the *Thalia*, Athanasius notes Arius' assertion that although called God, the Son possesses an alterable nature like other creatures capable of growth and

---

[7] Although Arius taught this doctrine, his followers abandoned it early on. Gregg (ed.), *Arianism: Historical and Theological Reassessments*, pp. 79-83.

[8] According to Maurice Wiles, after the death of Origen, the idea that the Logos replaces the rational soul in Christ was common in the Alexandrian tradition, so that many of Arius' first opponents as well as supporters held the same belief. Wiles, *Working Papers in Doctrine*, pp. 56-58.

[9] For information about Arius' writings and teachings, see Robert C. Gregg and Dennis Groh, *Early Arianism – A View of Salvation* (London: SCM Press, 1981); Gregg (ed.), *Arianism: Historical and Theological Reassessments*; Williams, *Arius*; Henry Melvill Gwatkin, *The Arian Controversy* (New York: AMS Press, 1979); Maurice F. Wiles, *Archetypal Heresy: Arianism through the Centuries* (Oxford: Clarendon Press, 1996), pp. 1-26; Harnack, *Dogma*, IV, pp. 14-21; Quasten, *Patrology*, III, pp. 10-13; Kelly, *Doctrines*, pp. 226-31; Grillmeier, *Christian Tradition*, I, pp. 19-48; González, *Christian Thought*, I, pp. 262-68; Wiles, *The Christian Fathers*, pp. 37-40; Hanson, *Christian Doctrine of God*, pp. 20-23, 106-22; Seeberg and Hay, *History*, I, pp. 202-205.

change; thus, the Son is not truly God but receives this epithet only by participation in grace (Athanasius, *C. Ar.* 1.2.5-6, 9).[10] Correspondingly, the Son advances in grace by participation in the Spirit (Athanasius, *C. Ar.* 1.5.15-16). In interpreting Phil. 2.9-10, Arius affirms that the Father's exaltation of the Son, after resurrection, proves the Son's need of advancement in grace.

> He received what He had as reward of His purpose, and would not have had it, unless he had needed it, and had His work to show for it, then having gained it from virtue and promotion, with reason had He 'therefore' been called Son and God, without being very Son ... Sons from virtue and grace, have put in place of nature a grace by acquisition, and are something else beside the gift itself; as the men who have received the Spirit by participation (Athanasius, *C. Ar.* 1.11.37).[11]

This text depicts the distinction between Athanasius' and Arius' view of divine sonship; the crux of the debate. On the one hand, Athanasius accentuates the Son's ontological relationship with the Father: the Son is divine by nature. On the other hand, Arius argues that the Son was promoted or adopted into deity as a reward for his salvific work, acquiring this status through participation in the Spirit.[12]

The next Spirit christological texts elucidate the significance of Christ receiving the Spirit. Arius uses Ps. 45.7 as a proof-text to explain Christ's anointing with the Spirit.

---

[10] Also, the Father foreknowing the Son's complete obedience proleptically bestows glory on the Son for a reward for his works (Athanasius, *C. Ar.* 1.2.5).

[11] Cited according to Archibald Robertson's revision of John Henry Newman's translation in Athanasius, 'Four Discourses Against the Arians', NPNF, Second Series, IV, p. 328.

[12] Cf. Athanasius, *C. Ar.* 1.11.38-39; McDonnell, *The Baptism of Jesus in the Jordan*, p. 42.

> Arians located and used an extended sense of 'sonship' in Scriptures by which God was said 'to adopt sons' from among creatures. 'Son' in this sense is a circumlocution for 'believer,' ... Consequently, whatever properties or powers can be claimed for the Son in the scriptures are read in this extended sense, according to which the Son himself gains these by adoption as a believer (Gregg and Groh, *Early Arianism*, p. 9).

Cf. Gregg and Groh, *Early Arianism*, pp. 2-30.

Thou hast loved righteousness, and hated iniquity, therefore God, even Thy God, hath anointed Thee with the oil of gladness above Thy fellows (Athanasius, *C. Ar.* 1.12.46).[13]

Three texts clarify Arius' interpretation. First, Arius' thoughts on the subject are implied in Athanasius' rebuttal: 'He is here "anointed," not that He may become God' (Athanasius, *C. Ar.* 1.12.46).[14] Second, against Arius' position, Athanasius argued that the Spirit descending upon Christ in the Jordan neither promoted the Word nor sanctified the Word (Athanasius, *C. Ar.* 1.12.47).[15] Third, Arius argued that Christ was anointed with the Spirit similar to the Hebrew kings, priests, and prophets but in a greater measure (Athanasius, *C. Ar.* 1.12.47-49).[16] Several conclusions can be drawn from these texts to delineate the significance of Christ receiving the Spirit according to Arius. First, because of his righteousness – obedience to the Father's will – Christ received the Spirit which sanctified him. Second, the Spirit's anointing upon the Son was one of inspiration, differing from the Hebrew prophets in degree but not in kind; he was anointed above his fellows.[17] Third, the anointing of the Spirit was a means of grace to promote the Son to an exalted position of deification. Athanasius, consequently, charges Arius with reviving Paul of Samosata's Christology.[18]

Next, pressing the logic of his Christology to its salvific conclusion, Arius explains Jn 10.30 and Jn 17.11: 'so are the Son and the Father One, and so is the Father in the Son and the Son in the Father, as we too may become one in Him' (Athanasius, *C. Ar.*

---

[13] Athanasius, 'Against the Arians', NPNF, Second Series, IV, p. 333.
[14] Athanasius, 'Against the Arians', NPNF, Second Series, IV, p. 333.
[15] Athanasius, 'Against the Arians', NPNF, Second Series, IV, p. 333.
[16] It is important to note that according to Athanasius, Arius affirms that the Logos also came into saints of former times and was incarnated in Jesus Christ (Athanasius, *C. Ar.* 3.26.30-31; Cf. Athanasius, *Tom.* 7).
[17] 'For the Arians the creaturely nature of Jesus portrayed in the Gospels even meant that he stood in need of God's empowering Holy Spirit. Therefore, they seemed to have insisted that the Son, as other persons, received the Spirit for empowerment in his life of obedience to the Father.' Gregg and Groh, *Early Arianism*, pp. 6, 53.
[18] 'If then they suppose that the Savior was not Lord and King, even before He became man and endured the Cross, but then began to be Lord, let them know that they are openly reviving the statements of the Samosatene' (Athanasius, *C. Ar.* 2.15.13). Athanasius, 'Against the Arians', NPNF, Second Series, IV, p. 355. Cf. Athanasius, *C. Ar.* 3.26.26.

3.25.17).¹⁹ Arius consistently has maintained the unity of the Son and Father has existed in oneness of will, judgment, and doctrine (Athanasius, *C. Ar.* 3.25.10), but, here, Athanasius clearly indicates that Arius claims much more.

> That neither we shall ever be as He, nor is the Word as we; except they shall dare, as commonly, so now to say, that the Son also by participation of the Spirit and by improvement of conduct came to be Himself also in the Father (Athanasius, *C. Ar.* 3.25.24).²⁰

Over Athanasius' objections, Arius affirms that believers will essentially stand in likeness to the Son. So, according to Arius, believers follow the Son's paradigm of advancing in grace toward deification through participation in the Spirit.²¹

Arius' theology presents a Christology of mediation. Standing in a long tradition of Logos theology, Arius affirmed the Logos' place of mediation between the transcendent God and creation. Arius presses the subordinationism of this tradition to three radical conclusions: (1) the Son does not partake of the Father's divine essence; (2) the Son is a creature capable of change; (3) in the ultimate act of mediation the Son functions as the rational element in Christ and suffers. In the soteriological mission, however, the Spirit becomes the mediator to the Son. The Spirit anoints and sanctifies the Son, so that the Son advances in grace, and, after the resurrection, by participation in the Spirit the Son is promoted into deification.²²

---

[19] Athanasius, 'Against the Arians', NPNF, Second Series, IV, p. 403.

[20] Athanasius, 'Against the Arians', NPNF, Second Series, IV, p. 407.

[21] 'Thus hearing that men are called sons, they thought themselves equal to the True Son by nature such. And now again hearing from the Savior, "that they may be one as We are," they deceive themselves, and are arrogant enough to think that they may be such as the Son is in the Father and Father in the Son' (Athanasius, *C. Ar.* 3.25.17). Athanasius, 'Against the Arians', NPNF, Second Series, IV, p. 403. One must remember that neither before nor after the incarnation did Arius consider the Son divine in nature as the Father, so Athanasius may have over-reacted on this point. Probably, Arius is laying out some salvific scheme based on theosis; theosis was a commonly accepted redemptive paradigm during this era, even Athanasius supported a form of theosis. Cf. Gregg and Groh, *Early Arianism*, pp. 50-70.

[22] Eusebius of Caesarea seems to posit a similar position: 'he was not anointed with oil prepared from material substances, but, as befits divinity, with the divine Spirit himself, by participation in the unbegotten deity of the Father' (Eusebius, *Hist. eccl.* 1.3.13). Cited according to the translation of Authur Cushman, Eusebius, 'The Church History of Eusebius', NPNF, Second Series, I, p. 86. Ac-

The Spirit, moreover, mediates grace to believers, anointing and advancing them toward deification. Arius' Logos Christology of mediation, therefore, conjoins with a Spirit christological paradigm of pneumatic inspiration.

Eustathius of Antioch

Among the Eastern writers who opposed Arius' Christology, Eustathius, who played a prominent role at the Council of Nicea,[23] has preserved Spirit christological references in his writings. Eustathius wrote several treatises against Arian doctrines, sometime between succeeding Philogonius as bishop of Antioch and Constantine deposing him, responding to persuasive Arian influence.[24] Only frag-

---

cording to J. Rebecca Lyman, 'Substance Language in Origen and Eusebius', in Robert C. Gregg (ed.), *Arianism: Historical and Theological Reassessments*, p. 261, Eusebius' use of

> the concept of participation coupled with the activity of the Spirit and the reference to prophetic anointing suggest Eusebius' concern to protect the uniqueness of the Father's nature as unbegotten, and describe the Son's divinity as a result of proximity and appointment; he has a special and unique derivation as the one anointed with the full or true oil.

It is worthy to note that in at least four points Eusebius deviated from Arius' theology: (1) that the Father created the Son from non-existence, (2) the limitation of the Son's knowledge, (3) although he affirmed the Son was a creature, he refused to place the Son on the level of other creatures, one among many, and (4) he did not argue from the limitations and weaknesses of the incarnate Son to the inferiority of the Son's divinity. Hanson, *Christian Doctrine of God*, p. 59.

[23] According to Theodoret, Eustathius had the honor to welcome Constantine into the assembly of the bishops, and, he probably gave the inaugural address at the Council (Theodoret, *Hist. eccl.* 1.6); Robert Victor Sellers, *Eustathius of Antioch and His Place in the Early History of Christian Doctrine* (Cambridge: The University Press, 1928), pp. 24-26.

[24] Eustathius became bishop in either late 324 or early 325. There is some debate about the date of Eustathius' deposition, with dates ranging from as early as 326 and as late as 331. For a discussion of the context of this issue, as well as an overview of Eustathius' life and writings, see Sellers, *Eustathius*, pp. 1-59; Henry Chadwick, 'The Fall of Eustathius of Antioch', *JTS* 49 (1948), pp. 27-35; Hanson, *Christian Doctrine of God*; Quasten, *Patrology*, III, pp. 302-304; Kelly McCarthy Spoerl, 'Two Early Nicenes: Eustathius of Antioch and Marcellus of Ancyra', in Peter William Martens (ed.), *In the Shadow of the Incarnation: Essays on Jesus Christ in the Early Church in Honor of Brian E. Daley, S.J.* (Notre Dame: University of Notre Dame Press, 2008), pp. 121-24.

ments of these works remain;[25] nevertheless, among the extant fragments, Spirit christological references are numerous.[26]

Eustathius' writings affirm his intransigence toward Arius' Christology, specifically, Arius' doctrine that the Son suffered in Christ which was supported by two premises: (1) Christ's humanity did not include a human soul; (2) the Son possessed a creaturely nature subject to passions, ignorance, change, and advancement in grace. In several Spirit christological texts, Eustathius remonstrates against this position.

> But that these things are suffered both of soul and body no one disputed; certainly, one must not introduce these things in the divine Spirit, when the divine nature has been bound beyond suffering and trouble (Fragment 7.12-15).[27]

So Eustathius attributes a human soul to Christ that suffers along with the body and cautions the Arians about predicating sufferings to the divine nature which is Spirit since it transcends suffering.[28]

> But if he did not assume a soul, how is he man? So that, not only supposing such things, they superstitiously represent the child of God not only half divine, like the Greeks, but also half human. But they do this so that, having attributed the mutable nature of

---

[25] Regarding Eustathius' writings and exegetical method, see Sellers, *Eustathius*, pp. 60-81. Only one complete tract of Eustathius's writings is extant, *On the Witch of Endor against Origen*. The Greek text along with an English translation and notes are provided by Rowan A. Greer and Margaret Mary Mitchell, *The "Belly-Myther" of Endor: Interpretations of 1 Kingdoms 28 in the Early Church* (SBLWGRW 16; Atlanta: SBL, 2007), pp. 62-158. The Greek text without translation can be found in José H. Declerck (ed.), *Evstathii Antiocheni, Patris Nicaeni, Opera Qvae Svpersvnt Omnia* (CChr 51; Turnhout: Brepols Publishers, 2002), pp. 1-60. Declerck also provides the Greek text of a homily, *Homilia Spuria De Lazaro, Maria et Martha*, which is probably not the work of Eustathius. Declerck (ed.), *Evstathii Antiocheni*, pp. 209-24.

[26] José Declerck provides the most recent edition of these fragments in Declerck (ed.), *Evstathii Antiocheni*, pp. 61-208. The overview will examine these fragments as they are found in this edition and follow Declerck's numbering of the fragments which differs from previous editions.

[27] Cited according to my own translation, Declerck (ed.), *Evstathii Antiocheni*, p. 68. Unless otherwise noted, all translations are my own.

[28] 'In so insisting Eustathius was going against the stream of much contemporary thinking, but he was thereby enabled to give a much clearer and more convincing answer to Arian reasoning than Athanasius was in a position to do. Moreover, he stood in the ancient tradition of Tertullian and Origen.' Wiles, *Working Papers in Doctrine*, p. 59.

> the sufferings to the divine Spirit, they might easily persuade those who are simple, that that which is mutable has not been begotten from the immutable nature (Fragment 19a.20-28).[29]

If Christ did not possess a soul, according to Eustathius, he was not fully human; thus, rejecting the Arian view of Christ's humanity, Eustathius dismisses any idea of Christ having a partial human nature. Against the Arian insistence that the Son, possessing a mutable nature, was not of the same immutable divine nature as the Father, Eustathius debars any idea of a diminished deity dwelling in Christ; Christ's human nature is capable of development and change but not the divine nature.[30] Eustathius, accordingly, identifies two natures in Christ; divine Spirit and humanity, body and soul, united in Christ.[31]

Eustathius, also, challenges Arius' exposition of Pr. 8.22 which places the beginning of the Logos as the first of the Father's creative acts.[32]

> But if the Logos was God first with the Father and we affirm the expression begotten through him, it means that God was initiator of the whole birth but not that God was born of a woman, but he is God by nature, sufficient in himself, infinite, and

---

[29] Declerck (ed.), *Evstathii Antiocheni*, p. 81. Cf. Fragments 19b.1-6; 6.1-14; Kelly, *Doctrines*, p. 283; Hanson, *Christian Doctrine of God*, p. 212; Spoerl, 'Two Early Nicenes', p. 125.

[30] According to Eustathius, Christ's human soul developed physically and morally along with his body, while co-existing in a harmonious and reciprocal relationship with the divine Spirit, and after the resurrection Christ's humanity was exalted as a reward for the progress and virtue of the soul. Sellers, *Eustathius*, pp. 104-109. According to Johannes Quasten, 'Eustathius is the first to attempt a Logos-Man Christology against the predominant Logos-Sarx doctrine. It is in his refutation of the latter theory that he wins a position of importance in the history of dogma'. Quasten, *Patrology*, III, p. 305.

[31] See Fragments 7.12-15; 10.1-5; 17.6-8; 19a.23-25; 19b.1-6; 20.30-36; 28.56-64; 49.1-2; 76.1-5; 77.3-5. For an examination of his Christology, see Sellers, *Eustathius*, pp. 100-20; Grillmeier, *Christian Tradition*, I, pp. 296-301; Kelly, *Doctrines*, pp. 281-84; Spoerl, 'Two Early Nicenes', pp. 130-36; González, *Christian Thought*, I, pp. 138-39.

[32] Theodoret mentions that the writings of Eustathius concerning Pr. 8.22, along with the writings of Athanasius, were used to refute the Arian exposition of this text (Theodoret, *Hist. eccl.* 1.7).

unlimited; but the man was born of a woman, who was united with the Holy Spirit in the virgin womb (Fragment 65a.3-8).[33]

So, Eustathius asserts that the term 'begotten' neither refers to creation of the Logos nor to the incarnation of deity in the virgin. Eustathius, thus, argues that the Logos is eternally begotten from the essence of the Father (Fragments 19.10-14; 17); he is Son of God by nature (Fragments 66.4; 85.2-3).[34] Frequently, Eustathius uses Spirit and Logos synonymously to identify the divine element in Christ. To protect the divine element in Christ from human passions, once again, Eustathius draws a sharp distinction between Christ's dual natures: Christ's human nature is the object of the virgin birth, not the divine Spirit.[35]

Although Eustathius taught Christ's human nature was capable of development and change, Christ's soul of was not capable of committing sin.

> But, indeed, the soul of Christ is immaculate, spotless, and undefiled having conduct wholly without sin. Is not its unity with the divine Spirit much greater, because of the extraordinary purity and righteousness? For these others, holy men, having been born from bodily mixing, having manifested shabby temples, they minutely participate in the fragrance of the Spirit; but the Christ was incarnated begotten only by the Holy Spirit, he has not drawn from participation of the more excellent nature, but in himself dwells the fullness of the Godhead (Fragment 50.20-29).[36]

---

[33] Declerck (ed.), *Evstathii Antiocheni*, p. 136. Cf. Hanson, *Christian Doctrine of God*, p. 232; Spoerl, 'Two Early Nicenes', p. 125; Grillmeier, *Christian Tradition*, I, p. 299. Fragments 65-81 come from a commentary on Pr. 8.22.

[34] For other fragments referring to the Son as God, see Fragments 2.20; 21.21; 50.30; 68.1-2. For fragments referring to the Logos as God, see Fragments 21.19; 32.3; 48.2; 57.1; 83.2.

[35] Sellers, *Eustathius*, pp. 110-15. In Christ dwells a 'God-bearing human soul … which coexists with the divine Spirit' (Fragments 56-58). Declerck (ed.), *Evstathii Antiocheni*, p. 97. According to Eustathius, the Son assumed human nature (Fragment 2.18-20). Cf. Spoerl, 'Two Early Nicenes', pp. 131-32. 'Clearly the spiritual nature is that which united with the Holy Spirit and the soul nature which proportionally mixed soul and body' (Fragment 44.5-7). Declerck (ed.), *Evstathii Antiocheni*, p. 117.

[36] Declerck (ed.), *Evstathii Antiocheni*, p. 122.

Several conclusions can be drawn from these texts. First, the Holy Spirit functioned as the agent of the incarnation. Second, Christ's soul was sinless because of its union with the divine Spirit. The divine Spirit in Christ needed neither sanctification nor advancement in grace; rather, the Spirit sanctified the soul as the Spirit united with it in the virginal conception. Third, Christ differed from other humans who were inspired of the Spirit; the Spirit was incarnated in Christ and the fullness of the Godhead dwelled in him, so Eustathius' position differs from Paul of Samosata's Christology of pneumatic inspiration.[37] Eustathius, accordingly, presents a form of pneumatic incarnation.

Eustathius, also, takes Arius' exegesis of Ps. 45.7-8 to task which posits that Christ's anointing of the Spirit advances the Son in divine grace.

> If indeed the one who anoints, he designates God ... clearly the one who has anointed, who is God by nature begotten from God, and the one who has been graciously anointed, has adorned the selected temple by the Godhead dwelling in it (Fragment 85.2-3).[38]

Eustathius postulates a distinction between the one who anoints and the one who is anointed: God and the temple. The one who is God by nature anoints the temple which the Godhead indwells, adorning it as the temple of God. Against Arius, therefore, Eustathius asserts that the incarnate Son does not receive the anointing; rather, the temple of Christ's humanity graciously receives the anointing.

To refute Arius' teaching that the Son suffered in Christ, Eustathius' Christology delineated Christ's dual natures which he sharply distinguished. In the incarnation, Eustathius carefully asserted that the divine Spirit was not begotten in Mary's womb; rather, the divine Spirit conceived Christ's humanity and united, pneumatically indwelling and coexisting, with the human soul. Christ's full humanity suffered, body and soul, but the divine Spirit

---

[37] Robert Sellers suggests that Eustathius' Christology is an advance on Paul of Samosata's. For a summary of Paul's teaching and the affinities and distinctions of Eustathius' and Paul's Christologies, see Sellers, *Eustathius*, pp. 8-9, 96-98, 114-15.

[38] Declerck (ed.), *Evstathii Antiocheni*, p. 154. Cf. Fragments 2.18-24; 3.1-9; Hanson, *Christian Doctrine of God*, pp. 213-14.

in Christ remained impassible. Eustathius' distinction of natures, moreover, allowed space for the Spirit to anoint Christ's humanity while maintaining the divine nature abode in the temple unaffected. Eustathius, also, maintains a monotheistic view of God that affirms the Father, Son, and Holy Spirit exist in one divine essence which is Spirit, so distinctions among them remain ambiguous.[39] Although Eustathius uses Logos and Son to speak of the divine element in Christ, these terms are synonyms with divine Spirit.[40] Following this reading of these fragments, then, Eustathius presents a monotheistic pneumatic Christology, a paradigm of pneumatic incarnation.

Marcellus of Ancyra

The aftermath of the Council of Nicea provided the occasion and purpose for the writings of Marcellus of Ancyra: *Contra Asterium* and his *Letter to Julius of Rome*.[41] As the bishop of Ancyra, Marcellus attended the Council of Nicea.[42] He supported the creed which the

---

[39] Perhaps this is because Eustathius opts to affirm from the Nicene anathema one ὑπόστασις of deity rather than using the Nicene term ὁμοούσιος (Fragment 88). Cf. Hanson, *Christian Doctrine of God*, p. 213-16; Spoerl, 'Two Early Nicenes', p. 125. For an examination of Eustathius' trinitarian theology, see Sellers, *Eustathius*, pp. 86-99; Spoerl, 'Two Early Nicenes', pp. 124-29. According to R.P.C. Hanson, 'It is not surprising, however, that Eustathius was condemned for Sabellianism. His insistence that there is only one distinct reality (hypostasis) in the Godhead, and his confusion about distinguishing the Father, Son, and Holy Spirit, laid him open to such a charge'. Hanson, *Christian Doctrine of God*, p. 216. Concerning the orthodoxy of Eustathius' view of God Robert Sellers asserts that 'the early Church was fully assured of his orthodoxy, despite all that Eusebius of Caesarea had urged against him'. Sellers, *Eustathius*, p. 83.

[40] Sellers, *Eustathius*, pp. 84-85. Cf. Fragments 72; 74; 75.

[41] Over the last several decades, scholarship has attributed to Marcellus nine writings formerly ascribed to other authors; six of these documents were assigned to the Athanasian corpus of writings. See Joseph T. Lienhard, 'Marcellus of Ancyra in Modern Research', *TS* 43 (1982), pp. 493-503; Joseph T. Lienhard, *Contra Marcellum: Marcellus of Ancyra and Fourth-Century Theology* (Washington: Catholic University of America Press, 1999), pp. 19-27; Hanson, *Christian Doctrine of God*, pp. 221-24. Cf. Quasten, *Patrology*, III, pp. 198-200. Most likely, Joseph Lienhard correctly summarizes the issue, 'Whether the attributions are accepted or not, the associations of these writings with Athanasius' name in the manuscripts shows that what can be taken to be Marcellus's theology had affinities with Athanasius''. Lienhard, *Contra Marcellum*, p. 19. Hence, this survey will concentrate on the writings that more certainly depict Marcellus' thought: the fragments of *Contra Asterium* and his *Letter to Julius of Rome*.

[42] The first site chosen for the council was Ancyra, but for uncertain reasons Constantine moved its location to Nicea. B.H. Logan discusses Marcellus' possi-

Council produced and its condemnation of Arius; consequently, Marcellus' writings delineated his theology in opposition to Arius and those who sympathized with him.[43] To refute a *General Letter* (327) which Asterius the Sophist composed in defense of Eusebius of Nicomedia's doctrinal positions,[44] Marcellus wrote *Contra Asterium* (336) and presented it to Constantine in Constantinople; during the same year, a synod at Constantinople deposed Marcellus. Although after the death of Constantine the bishops deposed through Eusebian influence returned to their sees (337), by 339, Marcellus and Athanasius were again deposed and journeyed to Rome to seek restoration from a synod held by Julius, bishop of Rome (340).[45] While in Rome, before the synod convened, Marcellus wrote his *Letter to Julius of Rome* to clarify his doctrinal stance.[46]

---

ble role in this issue and Marcellus' influence in the decision of the Council of Nicea. B.H. Logan, 'Marcellus of Ancyra and the Councils of AD 325: Antioch, Ancyra, and Nicaea', *JTS* 43 (1992), pp. 428-46. According to R.P.C. Hanson, 'the theology of Eustathius and Marcellus was the theology which triumphed at Nicaea. That creed admits the possibility of only one *ousia* and one *hypostasis*. This was the hallmark of the theology of these two men'. Hanson, *Christian Doctrine of God*, p. 235.

[43] Marcellus names Eusebius of Caesarea, Eusebius of Nicomedia, Paulinus of Tyre, Narcissus of Neronias, and Asterius the Sophist as his opponents in the fragments of *Contra Asterium*. Lienhard, *Contra Marcellum*, pp. 69-103; Markus Vinzent (ed.), *Markell Von Ankyra: Die Fragmente; Der Brief an Julius von Rom* (trans. Markus Vinzent; VCSup 39; Leiden: E.J. Brill, 1997), pp. lxxvi-lxxxi. Cf. Hanson, *Christian Doctrine of God*, pp. 27-59; Sara Parvis, *Marcellus of Ancyra and the Lost Years of the Arian Controversy 325-345* (OECS; Oxford: Oxford University Press, 2006), pp. 38-50. For Eusebius of Caesarea's opposition to Marcellus, see Lienhard, *Contra Marcellum*, pp. 104-35.

[44] Although Eusebius of Nicomedia signed the Nicean Creed, soon after the Council he was exiled for his continued support for Arius' position. Eusebius returned from exile in 327 and gained influence in the imperial court; then, 'he led the struggle against Athanasius securing Athanasius's deposition at the Synod of Tyre (335)'. 'Eusebius, Bishop of Nicomedia', *ODCC*, p. 575. Cf. Gwatkin, *The Arian Controversy*, pp. 36-37.

[45] According to Henry Gwatkin, 'Marcellus even more than Athanasius was the champion of the Nicene party in the period preceding the council of Sardica'. Gwatkin, *Studies of Arianism*, p. 79. For information about Marcellus' life, see Vinzent (ed.), *Markell Von Ankyra*, pp. xiv-xxv; Parvis, *Marcellus of Ancyra*, pp. 118-32, 146-62; Lienhard, 'Modern Research', pp. 486-92; Lienhard, *Contra Marcellum*, pp. 1-9; Hanson, *Christian Doctrine of God*, pp. 217-21; Gwatkin, *The Arian Controversy*, pp. 37-39; Quasten, *Patrology*, III, pp. 197-98; Philip Schaff, *History*, III, pp. 651-52; Davis, *Ecumenical Councils*, p. 76.

[46] Apparently, by this time Marcellus had revised two doctrines he was accused of teaching at his deposition in 336: (1) The only appropriate designation for the pre-incarnate Logos is Logos, so that the cognomen Son applies to the

The letter was well received by Julius, and the synod favored Athanasius and Marcellus, declaring their orthodoxy.[47]

Although the full text of *Contra Asterium* is not extant, Eusebius of Caesarea has preserved several fragments. These fragments were separated from Eusebius' writings and published in 1794, and several revised editions and translations have appeared since then.[48] Markus Vinzent's work, which juxtaposes the Greek text with a German translation, seems to be the most recent edition containing the fragments of *Contra Asterium* and *The Letter to Julius of Rome*; the survey will use this edition and follow its presentation and numbering of the fragments.[49]

In *Contra Asterium*, Marcellus uses Scripture to refute what he considers the principle and most dangerous of Asterius' teachings.

---

incarnate Logos, and (2) Christ's reign will end. Lienhard, *Contra Marcellum*, pp. 136-65. Concerning the first issue, although Marcellus affirms that before the incarnation the Logos had only existed as Logos (Fragments 5; 7), Maurice Wiles has noted that Marcellus, in his *Letter to Julius*, refers to the only-begotten-Son-Logos and concludes that Marcellus has accommodated his terminology to the church's general nomenclature. 'Certainly it seems difficult to see how Marcellus could have remained within orthodox life to the extent that he did, had he been wholly unprepared to acknowledge "Son" as a pre-existent title.' Maurice Wiles, 'Person or Personification? A Patristic Debate about Logos', in L.D. Hurst and N.T. Wright (eds.), *The Glory of Christ in the New Testament: Studies in Christology in Memory of George Bradford Caird* (Oxford: Clarendon Press, 1987), p. 283. Cf. Grillmeier, *Christian Tradition*, I, pp. 279-81. Discussing the second issue, R.P.C. Hanson states, 'Marcellus had originally taught that the Son's kingdom would have an end'. Hanson, *Christian Doctrine of God*, p. 223. After examining the letter written to Julius, Hanson states, 'It is obvious that Marcellus has now made some concessions to the critics of his doctrine'. Hanson, *Christian Doctrine of God*, p. 231.

[47] Of course, this did not settle the issue. At the close of the synod, Julius wrote to the Eastern bishops informing them of the synod's findings, enclosing Marcellus' *Letter to Julius* for good measure. The Eastern bishops responded to Julius and the Roman synod at the Dedication Council of Antioch (341) by rejecting Marcellus' theology. To no avail, the emperor Constans attempted to mend the rift these actions created between the East and West by proposing a council at Sardica (343). Because the Western bishops wanted Athanasius and Marcellus seated in the council and those representing the East held that both men were validly deposed, those from the East withdrew to Philippopolis and convoked their own synod. The Western synod of Sardica exonerated Athanasius of all charges and affirmed Marcellus's orthodoxy, while the Eastern synod at Philippopolis upheld their deposition. For further information about these synods, see Lienhard, *Contra Marcellum*, pp. 166-81; Parvis, *Marcellus of Ancyra*, pp. 179-252; Davis, *Ecumenical Councils*, pp. 84-85; Frend, *Christianity*, pp. 528-31.

[48] For an overview of this process and these works, see Lienhard, *Contra Marcellum*, 9-19, 47-48; Vinzent (ed.), *Markell Von Ankyra*, pp. xcii-cii.

[49] Vinzent (ed.), *Markell Von Ankyra*, pp. 1-129.

Asterius asserted that there were not two first divine principles; therefore, the Father was the ingenerate and unbegotten divine source (Fragments 10; 36; 57; 66; 113). The Son did not originate from the Father's essence but was created by the Father's will; accordingly, the Son is a distinct hypostasis from the Father, inhering in unity and harmony of will (Fragments 74; 75; 125), so that the Son can even be spoken of as a subordinate second God (Fragments 91; 121; 124).[50] Whereas Asterius referred to the Godhead as two essences (δύο οὐσίαι), two events (δύο πράματα), and two powers (δύο δυνάμεις),[51] Marcellus asserted the undivided (ἀδιαίρετος) nature of God (Fragments 48; 92; 97); God is one (μονάς).[52]

Marcellus' *Contra Asterium* contains several Spirit christological texts. Although Marcellus disallowed any talk of the Father creating the Son as a second deity, he did allow for a second economy according to the flesh. When discussing the meaning of Prov. 8.22-25,[53] contrary to Asterius' claim that these texts refer to the creation of the Son, Marcellus asserts that they proleptically point to the incarnation of the Logos in human flesh (Fragment 26).[54] In fact, Marcellus argues that Scripture provides no testimony of a genera-

---

[50] For Asterius, then, 'plurality in the Godhead necessarily implied subordinationism'. Lienhard, *Contra Marcellum*, pp. 48-49.

[51] Fragments 113; 117; 120; 124.

[52] Some scholars have reexamined the fourth-century christological controversies and concluded that the traditional categories designating the opposing sides are inadequate: Arian and Nicene, Alexandrian and Antiochene, Eusebian and Athanasian. David M. Gwynn, *The Eusebians: The Polemic of Athanasius of Alexandria and the Construction of the "Arian Controversy"* (OTM; Oxford: Oxford University Press, 2007); Hanson, *Christian Doctrine of God*, pp. xvii-xxi; Wiles, *Archetypal Heresy*, pp. 1-26; Wiles, *Working Papers in Doctrine*, pp. 28-37. Joseph Lienhard suggests that the conflict was actually between two well established theological traditions: one which posited two hypostases in the Godhead while the other maintained a single hypostasis. Joseph T. Lienhard, 'The "Arian" Controversy: Some Categories Reconsidered', *TS* 48 (1987), pp. 415-37; Lienhard, *Contra Marcellum*, pp. 28-46. Also, the nomenclature for designating the unity and distinction of divine essence lacked any consensus, acerbating the dispute. Hanson, *Christian Doctrine of God*, pp. 181-207; Shedd, *Doctrine*, I, pp. 362-72.

[53] Marcellus devoted Fragments 23-46 to discussing the interpretation of Prov. 8.22-25. For Vinzent's theological discussion of these verses, see Vinzent (ed.), *Markell Von Ankyra*, pp. xl-xlvii.

[54] Cf. Lienhard's discussion of Marcellus's Christology. Lienhard, *Contra Marcellum*, pp. 58-61.

tion of the Logos before the incarnation (Fragments 57-60);[55] hence, Logos properly designates the pre-incarnate existence, but Christ, light, bread, and other christological terms are titles of the Logos made flesh (Fragments 3; 5; 7; 65; 94).[56]

> What, therefore, was this one, who came down, before becoming man? Certainly, somewhere he says: 'Spirit'. For if he (Asterius) wanted to say something from this, the angel would not permit him, who spoke to the virgin: 'The Holy Spirit will come upon you'. But if he will say he is Spirit, listen to the savior saying God is Spirit (Fragment 61).[57]

> We know the economy according to the flesh carries through the man; but we have believed his eternal existence according to the Spirit was united to the Father (Fragment 72).[58]

These texts depict the Logos existing as Spirit before the incarnation, confess the Father's and the Logos' eternal unity of divine essence which is Spirit,[59] affirm the Spirit's mediation of the virginal conception, and confirm that the second economy begins with the incarnation.[60]

---

[55] Vinzent (ed.), *Markell Von Ankyra*, l-li; Hanson, *Christian Doctrine of God*, p. 225; Gwatkin, *The Arian Controversy*, pp. 39-40; Schaff, *History*, III, pp. 652-53.

[56] Lienhard, *Contra Marcellum*, pp. 51-52; Vinzent (ed.), *Markell Von Ankyra*, pp. xxxii-xxxvi; Hanson, *Christian Doctrine of God*, p. 225, 227. Maurice Wiles affirms that this exegetical dispute primarily concerns the interpretation of the Fourth Gospel's prologue. Wiles, 'Person or Personification', pp. 281-89.

[57] Cited according to my own translation, Vinzent (ed.), *Markell Von Ankyra*, p. 54. Unless otherwise noted all translations of the Greek text in Vinzent (ed.), *Markell Von Ankyra* are mine. It appears that this text also depicts Asterius supporting a form of Spirit Christology which more than likely follows the same paradigm as Arius and Eusebius of Caesarea.

[58] Vinzent (ed.), *Markell Von Ankyra*, p. 60.

[59] 'Because the one "pneuma-nature" of God is undivided in Father, Son and Spirit, their unity is guaranteed.' Grillmeier, *Christian Tradition*, I, p. 278. 'The Word as such is pure spirit, and only became the Son of God by becoming the Son of Man.' Gwatkin, *The Arian Controversy*, p. 39. 'Because God himself is Spirit, the savior said: God is Spirit' (Fragment 64). Vinzent (ed.), *Markell Von Ankyra*, p. 54. Cf. Hanson, *Christian Doctrine of God*, p. 224; Kelly, *Doctrines*, p. 240.

[60] Cf. Fragment 62; Grillmeier, *Christian Tradition*, I, pp. 281-88; Kelly, *Doctrines*, pp. 240-41; Gwatkin, *Studies of Arianism*, pp. 83-84; Vinzent (ed.), *Markell Von Ankyra*, p. 54. 'If the second economy is the incarnation of the Word, then the first is presumably the Word's going forth at the time of creation.' Lienhard, *Contra Marcellum*, pp. 58-59.

Against Asterius' tendency to fashion the Son in the image of the Father[61] but separate in hypostasis and power (Fragment 91), Marcellus contends the Logos' eternal existence in the Father to be in power (δυνάμει εἶναι) and any distinction from the Father to be in energy (ἐνεργείᾳ εἶναι; Fragment 70).[62]

> For if one examines the existence of the Spirit alone, the Logos properly is revealed as one and the same in God. But if the addition of the savior's flesh is examined, the deity seems to expand in energy alone, so that properly the Monad is really undivided (Fragment 73).[63]

It appears, therefore, according to Marcellus, Spirit and power are interchangeable designations for the one undivided divine essence, and the energy deity manifests in the second economy implies divine distinctions.[64] These apparent distinctions of divine essence Marcellus attributes to the human flesh of Christ.[65] Even though he speaks in trinitarian language of an expansion into a Trinity of Father, Son, and Holy Spirit (Fragment 48), deity remains undivided in

---

[61] Marcellus refutes Asterius' use of Col. 1.15 and his image of God concept in Fragments 51-56.

[62] According to Lienhard, Marcellus' use of *dynamis* and *energeia* differs from Aristotelian categories of potency and act, for

> such a translation would imply that the existence of the Logos had a beginning. Dynamis, in Marcellus's sense, is already real, as real as the man who can speak. When the man does speak, his energy results from his dynamis ... That is, a man's word is not a distinct being, or a source of activity in itself. It can be distinguished from the man only as an act from the one performing it. Hence dynamis and energeia are best translated 'power' and 'active power' (Lienhard, *Contra Marcellum*, pp. 54-55. Cf. Fragment 87).

[63] Vinzent (ed.), *Markell Von Ankyra*, p. 62.

[64] Vinzent (ed.), *Markell Von Ankyra*, pp. li-lvi; Daley, 'One Thing and Another', pp. 33-35; Pelikan, *Christian Tradition*, I, pp. 207-209.

[65] According to Lienhard, for Marcellus the incarnation is the determinative juncture of salvation history. In Marcellus' nomenclature, flesh (σάρξ) signified Jesus' individual humanity and man (ἄνθρωπος) humanity in general; when the Logos takes on flesh, he takes on humanity, so that the incarnation is itself divine redemptive activity (Fragments 97; 104; 79). Lienhard, *Contra Marcellum*, pp. 62-63. Also, Marcellus' anthropology affirmed that Christ had a human soul (Fragments 126-28). Kathy Spoerl posits that Marcellus was one of the primary proponents of dyophysite Christology which Apollinarius opposed. Kelly McCarthy Spoerl, 'Apollinarian Christology and the Anti-Marcellan Tradition', *JTS* 45 (1994), pp. 545-68. Cf. Daley, 'One Thing and Another', pp. 35-36; Lienhard, *Contra Marcellum*, pp. 62-63.

this expansion of divine energy.⁶⁶ Marcellus, furthermore, asserts that these trinitarian distinctions of divine activity will disappear at the telos of the second economy when according to 1 Cor. 15.24-28 all things will be subject to Christ, and Christ returns the kingdom to the Father (Fragment 104).⁶⁷ So Marcellus affirms the eternal unity of divine essence and power.

Marcellus presents a monotheistic pneumatic Christology which supports a paradigm of pneumatic incarnation. According to Marcellus' theology, God is one undivided essence which is Spirit; any apparent distinctions in deity appear only in the second economy which is thoroughly a pneumatic event. Not allowing for the pre-incarnate existence of the Logos, the divine Spirit becomes incarnate in the second economy. During the second economy, the deity expands into a Trinity. When the economy reaches its teleological goal, the Son delivers the kingdom up to the Father, and God becomes all in all, returning to Spirit the distinctions of the second economy disappear.

---

⁶⁶ See Vinzent (ed.), *Markell Von Ankyra*, pp. xlvii-xlviii; Lienhard, *Contra Marcellum*, pp. 56-58; Hanson, *Christian Doctrine of God*, pp. 225-30. To some fourth century theologians this talk of divine expansion sounded like Sabellianism. Consequently, writings attributed to Athanasius, Basil of Caesarea, and Gregory of Nyssa refer to Marcellus by the code-name Sabellius. See Lienhard, *Contra Marcellum*, pp. 210-40; Joseph T. Lienhard, 'Basil of Caesarea, Marcellus of Ancyra, and "Sabellius"', *CH* 58 (1989), pp. 159-67; R.P.C. Hanson, 'The Source and Significance of the Fourth Oratio Contra Arianos Attributed to Athanasius', *VC* 42 (1988), pp. 257-66. It is worthy to note, however, that Epiphanius stated, 'I myself once asked the blessed Pope Athanasius what his attitude toward Marcellus was. He neither defended him nor showed dislike for him, but only suggested with a smile that he had come close to depravity, but that he considered that he had cleared himself' (*Pan.* 4.1). Cited according to the translation of Philip Amidon, Epiphanius, *Panarion*, p. 284. Cf. Joseph T. Lienhard, 'Did Athanasius Reject Marcellus?', in Michel R. Barnes and Daniel H. Williams (eds.), *Arianism after Arius: Essays on the Development of the Fourth Century Trinitarian Conflicts* (Edinburgh: T. & T. Clark, 1993), pp. 65-80. According to J.N.D. Kelly, 'It is clear that Marcellus was not strictly a Sabellian. Several of his ideas are reminiscent of Irenaeus, Hippolytus and Tertullian and the "economic Trinitarianism" associated with them.' Kelly, *Doctrines*, p. 241. Cf. Grillmeier, *Christian Tradition*, I, pp. 279-80.

⁶⁷ Cf. Fragments 101-103; 106; 109; 111; Vinzent (ed.), *Markell Von Ankyra*, pp. lxiv-lxviii; Lienhard, *Contra Marcellum*, pp. 63-66. According to Joseph Lienhard, 'Christ's kingdom, however, is a partial kingdom. It is partial because God's enemies are not yet under his feet ... Hence Marcellus never said that Christ's kingdom would have an end, but only that the partial kingdom would end; it would not be destroyed but united with the kingdom of God'. Lienhard, *Contra Marcellum*, p. 66. Cf. Grillmeier, *Christian Tradition*, I, pp. 290-96.

Aphrahat the Persian

The next Spirit christological references are found in the writings of Aphrahat, a monk of the monastery of Marthai near Nineveh.[68] His extant works, the 23 *Demonstrations*, are important because they open a portal for viewing early Christian practices and theology in Persia.[69] Aphrahat wrote the *Demonstrations* in three phases: (1) the first 10 in 337, (2) the next 12 in 344, and (3) the twenty-third in 345. Structurally, the first 22 are composed on an acrostic pattern, each with the first letter corresponding with a sequential letter of the Syriac alphabet.[70] The first group of ten presents to his fellow-monks a summary of Christian teaching. The next group of thirteen responds to contextual issues pressing upon the Iranian church;[71] nine of these *Demonstrations* (*Dem.* 11–13; 15–19; 21; and parts of 23) give due regard to the Jewish critique of Christianity: Christians worship a man who was begotten among men and crucified, and they have made Jesus a god although God has no son (*Dem.* 17.1).[72] Aphrahat's retort to the Jewish critique professes Christ's deity (*Dem.* 17.2).

---

[68] For a discussion concerning Aphrahat holding an ecclesiastical office, see John Gwynn's introduction to Aphrahat, 'Demonstrations', NPNF, Second Series, XIII, pp. 157-58.

[69] Aphrahat's writings represent Christianity in its most Semitic form, developing independent of Nicea and Hellenistic influence. See Bogdan Gabriel Bucur, *Angelomorphic Pneumatology: Clement of Alexandria and other Early Christian Witnesses* (VCSup 95; Leiden: E.J. Brill, 2009), p. 159; Friedrich Loofs, *Theophilus von Antiochien Adversus Marcionem und die anderen Theologischen Quellen bei Irenaeus* (TUGAL 46; Leipzig: Hinrichs, 1930), p. 260; Grillmeier, *Christian Tradition*, I, pp. 214-15.

[70] For issues regarding structure, date, and authorship, see 'Aphrahat', *ODCC*, p. 82; Aphrahat, 'Demonstrations', NPNF, Second Series, XIII, p. 152-61; Brian Colless, *The Wisdom of the Pearlers: An Anthology of Syriac Christian Mysticism* (Cistercian Studies Series 216; Kalamazoo, MI: Cistercian Publications, 2008), p. 40.

[71] The Iranian church 'was severely persecuted because of its resistance to the taxes Shapur II levied to pay for his war with Christian Rome'. Jacob Neusner, *Judaism, Christianity, and Zoroastrianism in Talmudic Babylonia* (Studies in Judaism; Lanham, MD: University Press of America, 1986), p. 199.

[72] Because converted Jews were a large part of the Iranian church, the Jewish-Christian dialogue was of primary importance. 'What is striking is the utter absence of anti-Semitism from Aphrahat's thought ... On the contrary, Aphrahat conducts the debate through penetrating criticism, never vilification.' Neusner, *Judaism*, p. 199. Aphrahat provides an apology against the Jewish critique of Christianity and a critique of Judaism. According to Neusner, the central theme of Aphrahat's response is that God has rejected the Jews, and the Christian church has taken their place. For Neusner's comments concerning these issues, see Neusner, *Judaism*, pp. 202-28.

The Spirit christological references primarily concern the Spirit's relationship with Christ in salvific mission. This is seen in the Son's humiliation and exaltation. Though he was God and Son of God, he became a servant, taking on human nature so that humans might partake of his nature (*Dem.* 6.9; 6.10).[73]

> For when Gabriel made announcement to the Blessed Mary who bore Him, the word from on high set out and came, and *the word became flesh and dwelt in us* ... And when He went to His Father, He sent to us His Spirit and said to us: – *I am with you till the world shall end.* For Christ *sitteth at the right hand of His Father*, and Christ *dwelleth among men* ... And though He is divided among many, yet He sits at the right hand of His Father. And He is in us and we are in Him, as He said: – *Ye are in Me and I am in you.* And in another place He said: – *I and My Father are one* (*Dem.* 6.10).[74]

This text draws attention to four important aspects of Christ's soteriological relationship with the Spirit. First, Christ dwelling in Christians was the goal of the Logos' salvific mission of incarnation in human flesh, return to the Father, and the descent of the Spirit. Second, since Aphrahat uses a christological text (Mt. 28.20) instead of a Paraclete text to speak of the sending of the Spirit, the indwelling of Christ and the Spirit are synonymous.[75] Third, although Christ sits at the right hand of the Father, through the Spirit Christ indwells believers. Fourth, Aphrahat expresses the unity of the Father, Son, and Spirit in redemptive mission.[76]

---

[73] In regeneration believers receive the Spirit which is the nature of Christ. When Christians die, their human nature remains in the grave awaiting resurrection while the Spirit returns to Christ. The Spirit, furthermore, is the agent of the resurrection. In the resurrection, the Spirit will conjoin with the saints causing their human nature – body and soul – to be fully conformed to the nature of Christ, which is Spirit (*Dem.* 6.14). Cf. Colless, *Pearlers*, pp. 44-45.

[74] Cited according to the translation of John Gwynn, Aphrahat, 'Demonstrations', NPNF, Second Series, XIII, pp. 369-70. Cf. *Dem.* 1.3; 6.14.

[75] Bucur, *Angelomorphic Pneumatology*, p. 178-79.

[76] 'Jeremiah called men temples and said of God that He dwelt in them. And the Apostle said: – *The Spirit of Christ dwelleth in you.* And our Lord said: – *I and my Father are one*' (*Dem.* 1.5). Aphrahat, 'Demonstrations', NPNF, Second Series, XIII, p. 347. According to Aloys Grillmeier, in Aphrahat's christological language the Syriac word *kyanā* which is used to translate the Greek word essence (οὐσία; φύσις) never means abstract substance. Rather it renders the empirical situation or the manner in which a thing appears to humans. Aphrahat often uses this word in texts that discuss Christ's humility and exaltation. Grillmeier, *Christian Tradition*, I, pp. 216-18. Although Aphrahat uses trinitarian language in his doxo-

If the Son and Father dwell in Christians, the question becomes: how can Christ dwell in many temples and neither be many Christs nor be diminished (*Dem.* 6.11)?[77] Aphrahat uses several impersonal analogies to answer this query. For instance, the sun is fixed in the heavens, yet its rays spread over the earth entering many doors, windows, and homes; thus, the one Christ sits at the right hand of the Father in heaven but dwells in humans on the earth. He also uses analogies of the dust of the earth, sand of the seashore, and water from the ocean to illustrate the fact that when saints 'receive of the Spirit of Christ, Christ will not a whit be diminished' (*Dem.* 5.25).[78] God, accordingly, took the Spirit upon Moses and shared it with the seventy elders of Israel (Num. 11.17) without diminishing the Spirit upon Moses (*Dem.* 6.12; 21.10). Aphrahat, then, recounts the Hebrew prophets receiving the Spirit, correlating it with Christians receiving the Spirit, and comparing their experience of the Spirit with Christ's anointing of the Spirit (*Dem.* 6.12-15).

> By this reflection thou canst comprehend that Christ dwells in faithful men; yet Christ suffers no loss though He is divided among many. For the Prophets received of the Spirit of Christ, each one of them as he was able to bear. And of the Spirit of Christ again there is poured forth to-day upon all flesh, and the sons and the daughters prophesy, the old men and the youths, the men-servants and the hand-maids. Something of Christ is in us, yet Christ is in heaven at the right hand of His Father. And Christ received the Spirit not by measure (*Dem.* 6.12).[79]

---

logical language (*Dem.* 23.61; 23.63), he does not use the terms *tlītāyutā* (τρίας) and *qnomā* (ὑπόστασις). It appears that Aphrahat's starting point is not metaphysical; he is more concerned to express the Spirit's indwelling than to determine unity and distinction of divine essence. See Bucur, *Angelomorphic Pneumatology*, pp. 175, 187. Frederick Loofs concludes that the Holy Spirit is not a distinct hypostasis as found in other patristic writers, but the Spirit operates as the divine power within a binitarian framework. Loofs, *Theophilus*, pp. 273-74, 278.

[77] In *Dem.* 6.11, because Aphrahat's focuses exclusively on God and his Christ, it prompts Friedrich Loofs to note that 'there is no place left for the Spirit'. Loofs, *Theophilus*, p. 260. Aphrahat, nonetheless, depicting God as Father and the Spirit as Mother presents deity as a divine couple (*Dem.* 18.10). See Loofs, *Theophilus*, p. 275; Colless, *Pearlers*, p. 40.

[78] Aphrahat, 'Demonstrations', NPNF, Second Series, XIII, pp. 361-62. Cf. *Dem.* 6.11.

[79] Aphrahat, 'Demonstrations', NPNF, Second Series, XIII, pp. 370-71. Cf. *Dem.* 6.14; 6.15; Bucur, *Angelomorphic Pneumatology*, pp. 180-85.

And Jesus, when about thirty years old, came to the Jordan to be baptized, and received the S/spirit, and went forth to preach (*Dem.* 21.9).[80]

These texts suggest four points regarding Christ's relationship with the Spirit. First, in the pre-incarnate prophetic functions, Aphrahat does not distinguish between the Spirit and Christ; the Hebrew prophets received the Spirit of Christ.[81] Second, when Christians receive the prophetic anointing of the Spirit, they receive the Spirit of Christ. Third, Christ's reception of the Spirit differed in degree from the Hebrew prophets and Christians receiving the Spirit: Christ received the Spirit without measure. Fourth, Aphrahat uses several analogies to depict the Spirit as an impersonal force. It seems, therefore, that Christ can dwell in many because the Spirit, which is identical with the nature of Christ, is an impersonal divine force that indwells believers.[82]

Aphrahat delineates a Christology of pneumatic incarnation and indwelling. Aphrahat's language is ambiguous; he interchangeably uses the terms Christ and Spirit in the preexistent and incarnate states. More than likely, he uses Spirit as a two-fold designation: (1) to designate deity and (2) an impersonal divine power. On this reading, when Aphrahat emphatically asserts the Son's deity, he refers to the pre-incarnate state which is Spirit. Moreover, through a pneumatic incarnation Christ is made flesh. Yet Christ also receives the Spirit at the Jordan; here, Aphrahat distinguishes between Christ and Spirit: Christ is the historical human, and Spirit probably refers to an impersonal divine power. Thereupon, the same Spirit of Christ that indwelt the Hebrew prophets in a limited measure indwelt Christ's humanity in the full measure of this anointing. In his exalted position with the Father, Christ, accordingly, sends this

---

[80] Aphrahat, 'Demonstrations', NPNF, Second Series, XIII, p. 396. Cf. McDonnell, *The Baptism of Jesus in the Jordan*, pp. 143, 191-94.

[81] According to Loofs, in the *Demonstrations*, Spirit refers to Christ's deity prior to the incarnation, and Spirit is distinguished from the Father in the incarnation; furthermore, Loofs insists that Aphrahat only makes a distinction between Spirit and Christ when he speaks of the human Jesus Christ, and Aphrahat ambiguously switches between pre-existing Spirit and the historical Christ. In Loofs' view, then, Aphrahat's Christology bears similarities with Dynamic Monarchianism. Loofs, *Theophilus*, pp. 270-78.

[82] Loofs, *Theophilus*, pp. 257-99.

divine power to indwell and charismatically endow Christians, so that Christ indwells in them as the Spirit of Christ.

Photinus

Photinus, a disciple of Marcellus, began his ministry serving as a deacon in Ancyra and ascended to the status of bishop of Sirmium in 344. Photinus followed Marcellus' monotheistic view of God, but his Christology seemed to deviate toward adoptionism; thus, both in conjunction with Marcellus and separately,[83] beginning with the third council of Antioch (345), a series of councils and synods condemned Photinus' teachings.[84] Although he was a prolific writer, none of Photinus' manuscripts has survived; consequently, the semblance of his teachings reflects in the portrait which his opponents have painted.

According to his opponents, Photinus taught a form of Spirit Christology similar to Ebionism and Paul of Samosata.[85] Photinus' monotheistic view of God affirms that Father, Logos, and Holy Spirit are designations of the one essence of God which is Spirit; accordingly, since Photinus makes no distinction between Logos and Holy Spirit which exist as divine spiritual energies, he denies the Son's preexistence.[86] Although Photinus conceded Christ's virgin

---

[83] The Eastern bishops tended to conjoin Marcellus' and Photinus' teachings, while the West tended to distance Marcellus from Photinus (Sulpitius Severus, *Sacred History*, 2.36). Cf. Lienhard, *Contra Marcellum*, pp. 153-56, 176-80. 'He had indeed the misfortune to propound a doctrine, at the meeting of the Eastern and Western Roman Empire, which both Eastern and Western theologians could agree in condemning.' Hanson, *Christian Doctrine of God*, p. 236.

[84] For information about Photinus' life, see 'Photinus', *ODCC*, p. 1283; Lydia Speller, 'New Light on the Photinians: The Evidence of Ambrosiaster', *JTS* 34 (1983), pp. 99-101; Hanson, *Christian Doctrine of God*, pp. 235-36; Schaff, *History*, III, p. 653; Frend, *Christianity*, p. 532.

[85] Epiphanius, *Pan.* 71.1.1; Hilary, *Trin.* 7.3; Sozomenus, *Hist. eccl.* 4.6. 'It was a doctrine recognizably similar to that of Paul of Samosata and invited instant condemnation from Origenist bishops.' Frend, *Christianity*, p. 532. Cf. Grillmeier, *Christian Tradition*, I, pp. 306-307, 395, 401, 406.

[86] Athanasius, *Syn.* 26; 27; Epiphanius, *Pan.* 71.1.3; Hilary, *Trin.* 1.26; Hilary, *Syn.* 38; Ambrose, *Fid.* 3.8.58; Sozomenus, *Hist. eccl.* 4.6. 'He likewise started with a strict distinction between the notion of Logos and Son, rejected the idea of eternal generation, and made the divine in Christ an impersonal power of God.' Schaff, *History*, III, p. 653. Cf. Speller, 'Photinians', pp. 107-109; Hanson, *Christian Doctrine of God*, p. 238.

birth, Mary's son was a mere human and not divine.[87] Similar to the Hebrew prophets, the Spirit anointed and inspired Christ, yet in distinction to these prophets Christ was a human fully inspired of the divine Spirit, so that after the resurrection Christ became the divine Son of God; Christ began his ministry as a person inspired with deity and became God.[88] Photinus seems, therefore, to have taught a form of Dynamic Monarchianism which supports a Spirit christological paradigm of pneumatic inspiration.

Cyril of Jerusalem

Cyril of Jerusalem's[89] literary legacy has bequeathed to the church four extant documents: *Sermon on the Paralytic*, *Letter to Constantius*, *Procatechesis* and *Catecheses*, and *Mystagogical Catecheses*.[90] The latter two

---

[87] Hilary, *Trin.* 7.7; 8.40; Ambrose, *Fid.* 5.8. 'According to the meager accounts we have, Christ was a mere man, though miraculously born, endowed with special power (δραστικὴ ἐνέργεια) by the Father, and finally accepted as Son.' Grillmeier, *Christian Tradition*, I, p. 296.

[88] Hilary, *Trin.* 2.4; Athanasius, *Syn.* 26. 'Everybody in the ancient world accuses Photinus of reducing Christ to a mere man adopted by God, i.e. the union between *Logos* and man was one of inspiration and moral agreement only.' Hanson, *Christian Doctrine of God*, p. 237. Cf. Speller, 'Photinians', pp. 102-13; Schaff, *History*, III, p. 653.

[89] Cyril succeeded Maximus – who participated in deposing Athanasius at the synod of Tyre (335), but at the council at Serdica (343), Maximus supported Athanasius and Marcellus in opposition to the Eastern bishops – as bishop of Jerusalem (348) amid controversy and confusion. Acacias, a supporter of Arian doctrine, consecrated Cyril to the bishopric; nevertheless, conflict quickly emerged between them which caused Cyril's deposition and three periods of exile (357–59; 360–62; 367–78). Although his theology does not readily fit their doctrinal schema, during his first exile, Cyril found companionship and doctrinal affinity among the Homoiousians, who supported Cyril's restoration at the synod of Seleucia (359). By 378, Cyril and many Homoiousians had migrated into the pro-Nicean camp, and the Council of Constantinople (381) took pains to affirm Cyril's ordination and orthodoxy. For information about Cyril's life, see Quasten, *Patrology*, III, p. 362; Hanson, *Christian Doctrine of God*, pp. 398-401; Jan Willem Drijvers, *Cyril of Jerusalem* (VCSup 72; Leiden: Brill, 2004), pp. 31-49; Alexis James Doval, *Cyril of Jerusalem, Mystagogue: The Authorship of the Mystagogic Catecheses* (North American Patristic Society: Patristic Monograph Series 17; Washington: Catholic University of America Press, 2001), pp. 12-22; Edward Yarnold, *Cyril of Jerusalem* (ECF; London: Routledge, 2000), pp. 3-7; Cyril, 'Catecheses 1–12', FC, LXI, pp. 21-34; William Telfer (ed.), *Cyril of Jerusalem and Nemesius of Emesa* (LCC 4; Philadelphia,: Westminster Press, 1955), pp. 19-36; Schaff, *History*, III, p. 924.

[90] Because of certain internal as well as external issues, Cyrilline authorship of *Mystagogical Catecheses* remains uncertain, John of Jerusalem being the other primary contender for this honor. All things considered, the evidence does not seem to

documents are of interest to this survey. As the names imply, they preserve a series of catechetical homilies depicting the practice of the Jerusalem church during the fourth-century.[91] *Procatechesis* served as an introductory discourse to the eighteen *Catecheses* (350) which were delivered during Lent to prepare candidates for baptism at Easter.[92] These pre-baptismal catecheses dissert the proper mental attitude requisite for baptism: to understand penitence, the meaning of baptism and its effects, the nature of faith, the doctrine of God, Christology, and the resurrection of the dead. Later in life, Cyril developed five *Mystagogical Catecheses* (380–87) to explain the mystery encompassing the rites of initiation – baptism, anointing with chrism, and communion – to the neophytes amid the Octave of Easter.[93]

These documents provide Spirit christological references. One reference is located in a discussion of Christ's identity.[94]

> He has two fathers: one, David, according to the flesh, and one, God the Father, according to the Godhead. As the son of David,

---

disprove Cyrilline authorship. For a comprehensive discussion of the issues and evidence, see Doval, *Mystagogue*. Cf. Yarnold, *Cyril* pp. 24-32; Cyril, 'Catecheses 13–18', FC, LXIV, pp. 143-49; Quasten, *Patrology*, III, pp. 364-66. Of course, these issues also determine the document's date.

[91] Schaff, *History*, III, pp. 924-25; Kelly, *Doctrines*, p. 423; F.L. Cross (ed.), *St. Cyril of Jerusalem's Lectures on the Christian Sacraments: The Procatechesis and the Five Mystagogical Catecheses* (trans. R.W. Church; Crestwood, NY: St. Vladimir's Seminary Press, 1995), xxiv-xxix. For overviews of the context – sacred topography, monuments, and culture – of Cyril's ministry in Jerusalem, see Telfer (ed.), *Cyril of Jerusalem*, pp. 30-63; Drijvers, *Cyril*, pp. 65-96; Doval, *Mystagogue*, pp. 13-57; Yarnold, *Cyril*, pp. 8-21; Dayna S. Kalleres, 'Cultivating True Sight at the Center of the World: Cyril of Jerusalem and the Lenten Catechumenate', *CH* 74 (2005), pp. 431-59.

[92] Actually, Cyril preached these sermons, and someone took notes to produce these manuscripts, 'which means that we have a transcript made by one of his listeners, and not the bishop's own hand'. Quasten, *Patrology*, III, p. 363. For a discussion about Cyril's use of Scripture in these sermons, see Pamela Jackson, 'Cyril of Jerusalem's Use of Scripture in Catechesis', *TS* 52 (1991), pp. 431-50. According to Johannes Quasten, Catecheses 6–18 seem to 'contain an exposition of the successive articles of the Jerusalem Creed, which shows great similarity with the so-called Symbol of the Council of Constantinople in 381'. Quasten, *Patrology*, III, p. 364. Cf. Cyril, 'Catecheses', FC, LXI, pp. 4-6, 60-65.

[93] Quasten, *Patrology*, III, pp. 364-66; Cross (ed.), *Lectures on the Christian Sacraments*, pp. xxi-xxiv.

[94] For overviews of Cyril's theology, see Cyril, 'Catecheses', FC, LXI, pp. 34-60; Yarnold, *Cyril*, pp. 56-64; Doval, *Mystagogue*, pp. 23-25; Cross (ed.), *Lectures on the Christian Sacraments*, pp. xxix-xxxiii.

He is subject to time, and He is palpable and His descent is reckoned; but in His Godhead He is subject neither to time nor place nor genealogical reckoning. For 'who shall declare his generation?' 'God is Spirit'; He who is S/spirit begot spiritually, being incorporeal, by an unsearchable and incomprehensible generation. For the Son Himself says of the Father: 'The Lord said to me, You are my son: this day I have begotten you.' Now 'this day' is not recent, but eternal; 'this day' is timeless, before all ages (*Catecheses*, 11.5).[95]

According to Cyril, on the one hand, Christ possessed a genuine human nature, body and soul,[96] which descended through David's genealogy; according to the flesh, he was the Son of David. On the other hand, the Scriptures that speak of the Father begetting the Son refer to an incomprehensible eternal generation of Spirit begetting Spirit; according to the Spirit, he is the Son of God: 'God is S/spirit, and his generation is spiritual' (*Catecheses*, 11.7).[97] So Christ has two natures: flesh and Spirit.

In other words, for Cyril the divine essence is Spirit. Cyril, thereupon, affirms belief in a triune view of God: 'In One God, the Father Almighty, and in our Lord Jesus Christ, His Only-begotten Son, and in the Holy Spirit, the Paraclete. The word itself and the title of "Spirit" are applied to Them in common in the Holy Scriptures' (*Catecheses*, 17.34).[98] Cyril, accordingly, posits that the designation Spirit can properly refer to the Father, Son, or Holy Spirit as they exist in unity of divine essence which is Spirit.[99] Cyril, nonethe-

---

[95] Cited according to the translation of Leo McCauley, Cyril, 'Catecheses', FC, LXI, p. 213.

[96] Although he often referred to Christ's humanity as flesh, Cyril seemed to affirm a human soul as part of Christ's human nature: 'For upon Christ death came in reality, for His soul was truly separated from His body' (*Mystagogical Catecheses*, 2.7). Cited according to the translation of R.W. Church in Cross (ed.), *Lectures on the Christian Sacraments*, p. 62. Cf. Hanson, *Christian Doctrine of God*, pp. 406-407.

[97] Cyril, 'Catecheses', FC, LXI, p. 214. Cf. *Catecheses*, 11.4, 9, 13; Hanson, *Christian Doctrine of God*, pp. 403-404; Quasten, *Patrology*, III, pp. 369-70.

[98] Cyril, 'Catecheses', FC, LXIV, p. 117.

[99] Cyril distinguishes between the Father, Son, and Holy Spirit. 'Cyril does his best to distinguish the Father, the Son, and the Holy Spirit in the Trinity, without the benefit of a single word to indicate what God is as Three in distinction from what he is as One.' Hanson, *Christian Doctrine of God*, p. 408. Cf. Hanson, *Christian Doctrine of God*, pp. 408-12.

less, affirms genuine trinitarian distinctions in Christ's salvific mission (*Catecheses*, 16.4).[100]

Against the Arian claim that the Spirit's anointing advanced the Son in grace, Cyril asserted that Jesus did not advance to the rank of Lord; he possessed it by nature (*Catecheses*, 10.5).

> The Holy Spirit descended when Christ was baptized to make sure that the dignity of Him who was baptized was not hidden, according to the words of John: 'But he who sent me to baptize with water said to me, He upon whom thou wilt see the Spirit descending, and abiding upon him, he it is who baptizes with the Holy Spirit' ... The first-fruits and the first gifts of the Holy Spirit, who is imparted to the baptized, should be conferred on the manhood of the Savior, who bestows such grace (*Catecheses*, 17.9).[101]

> The Father having appointed Him to be Savior of the whole world, anointed Him with the Holy Ghost ... As He was anointed with the spiritual oil of gladness, the Holy Ghost, who is so called, because He is the author of spiritual gladness, so ye were anointed with ointment, having been made partakers and fellows of Christ (*Mystagogical*, 3.2).[102]

These texts signify three aspects of Christ's reception of the Spirit at the Jordan. First, the Spirit anoints Christ's humanity for his salvific mission.[103] Second, the Spirit reveals Christ's dignity; he is divine, for no ordinary person can fulfill the Father's promise to baptize humans in the Holy Spirit. Third, Christ's reception of the Spirit becomes a paradigm for believers to receive the Spirit.[104] Cyril's

---

[100] Hanson, *Christian Doctrine of God*, pp. 405-406; Quasten, *Patrology*, III, pp. 371-72.

[101] Cyril, 'Catecheses', FC, LXIV, p. 101.

[102] Cross (ed.), *Lectures on the Christian Sacraments*, pp. 64-65.

[103] Using the analogy of the dove, which Noah released form the Ark during the flood, as the hope of salvation and the beginning of a new generation, Cyril states that the Holy Spirit descended 'as the spiritual dove at Christ's baptism, to show that He is the same who by the wood of the Cross saves them that believe' (*Catecheses*, 17.10). Cyril, 'Catecheses', FC, LXIV, p. 102.

[104] 'For Cyril the baptism of Jesus at the Jordan is a rite of identification. The one on whom the Holy Spirit descended as a dove is the one who baptizes in the Holy Spirit. What is given to us is first manifested in the baptism of Jesus.' McDonnell and Montague, *Christian Initiation*, p. 215. Cf. McDonnell, *The Baptism of Jesus in the Jordan*, pp. 123, 218-25.

Spirit Christology, thus, precluded Arianism because Christ's anointing of the Spirit neither advanced the Son in grace nor adopted him as Son of God; he was already the Son of God by nature, spiritually begotten from Spirit as the eternal Son, even when he was conceived by the Spirit in Mary's womb.[105] The Spirit, instead, anointed Christ's humanity.

In the sacramental mysteries of baptism and chrism believers' identification with Christ and receiving the Spirit are the axial themes of these events. In baptism catechumens become identified with Christ during his death, burial, and resurrection; they receive purging of sins, adoption as sons, and the Spirit (*Mystagogical*, 2.6; *Catecheses*, 3.2, 7; 17.35-37).[106] In chrism catechumens become identified with Christ in his anointing of the Spirit.

> Now ye are made Christs, by receiving the emblem of the Holy Ghost; and all things were in a figure wrought in you, because ye are figures of Christ. He also bathed Himself in the river Jordan, and having imparted of the fragrance of His Godhead to the waters, He came up from them; and the Holy Ghost in substance lighted on Him, like resting upon like. In the same manner to you also, after you had come up from the pool of the sacred streams, was given the Unction, the emblem of that wherewith Christ was anointed; and this is the Holy Ghost (*Mystagogical*, 3.1).[107]

This text elucidates two important points. First, the Spirit reposes on Christ in the fullness of being, bearing witness to the Son's deity; the Spirit comes to that which is like in substance, Spirit resting upon Spirit.[108] Second, although Cyril asserts that the Spirit is

---

[105] Robert C. Gregg, 'Cyril of Jerusalem and the Arians', *Arianism: Historical and Theological Reassessments*, pp. 85-109.

[106] Kelly, *Doctrines*, pp. 428-29. 'The occasion of Easter baptism called for frequent references to the Holy Spirit, since baptism is the sacrament of the Spirit.' Burgess, *The Holy Spirit: Ancient Christian Traditions*, p. 106. Cf. Burgess, *The Holy Spirit: Ancient Christian Traditions*, p. 10; Quasten, *Patrology*, III, pp. 372-74.

[107] Cross (ed.), *Lectures on the Christian Sacraments*, pp. 63-64.

[108] Hence, Cyril posits the deity of the Son and Spirit. 'On the subject of the Holy Spirit, Cyril is perhaps more remarkable than on any other point. He describes the Spirit's functions but also comes closer to defining his status than anybody else in the mid-fourth century.' Hanson, *Christian Doctrine of God*, p. 407. Cf. Hanson, *Christian Doctrine of God*, pp. 408, 743; Kelly, *Doctrines*, p. 256; Quasten, *Patrology*, III, pp. 371-72.

salvifically connected to the catechumen's baptism in water, he seems to imply an experience of the Spirit subsequent to baptism. In point of fact, Cyril explicitly avers that believers receive the Spirit – which sanctifies them, empowers them, and verifies the name Christian – at the sacrament of chrism which is subsequent to baptism (*Mystagogical*, 3.3-5).[109]

Cyril's account of Jesus' disciples receiving the Spirit seems to provide further evidence for an experience of the Spirit subsequent to the initial conversion experience. After Christ's death, burial, and resurrection, but before his ascension, Christ breathed on the apostles and said to them 'receive the Spirit' (Jn 20.22) which was proleptic of the grace of the Spirit yet to come (*Catecheses*, 17.12).[110] Then, Jesus ascended into heaven, and on the Day of Pentecost he fulfilled his promise to his disciples.[111]

> He came down to clothe with power and to baptize the Apostles. For the Lord says: 'You shall be baptized with the Holy Spirit not many days hence.' The grace was not partial, but His power in all its fullness. For just as one immersed in the waters in Baptism is completely encompassed by water, so they too were completely baptized by the Spirit (*Catecheses*, 17.14).[112]

It appears from this passage and Cyril's ensuing discussion recounting, in the Book of Acts, the Holy Spirit empowering believers for mission (*Catecheses*, 17.20-32), Cyril refers to this subsequent experience as Spirit baptism; furthermore, contrary to Arian theology this experience does not adopt believers as sons of God, rather, it is an endowment of power. This assumption, however, does not ignore

---

[109] According to J.N.D. Kelly, 'In the fourth and fifth centuries confirmation, or consignation, while closely associated with baptism, was also clearly distinguished from it ... The general theory was that through chrismation, with or without the laying on of hands, the Holy Spirit was bestowed'. Kelly, *Doctrines*, pp. 432-33. Cf. Burgess, *The Holy Spirit: Ancient Christian Traditions*, pp. 11-12.

[110] 'Accept for the time the grace for which you are capable, but look forward to yet more. "But wait here in the city," of Jerusalem, "until you are clothed with power from on high." Receive it in part now; then you will be clad in its fullness' (*Catecheses*, 17.12). Cyril, 'Catecheses', FC, LXIV, p. 104. Cf. McDonnell and Montague, *Christian Initiation*, pp. 215-16.

[111] They were baptized in the Holy Spirit, 'and they began to speak in foreign tongues, even as the Holy Spirit prompted them to speak' (*Catecheses*, 17.15-16). Cyril, 'Catecheses', FC, LXIV, p. 106.

[112] Cyril, 'Catecheses', FC, LXIV, p. 105. For Cyril's discussion of the Pentecost event, see (*Catecheses*, 17.13-19).

catechumens receiving the Spirit in baptism; probably, baptism and chrism represent corollary crisis experiences of the Spirit in the salvific journey.[113]

The lineaments of Cyril's Christology are thoroughly pneumatic. The designation Spirit applies to the Son because the divine essence is Spirit, so that Christ is identified by two natures: Spirit and flesh. The Spirit, moreover, mediates Christ's salvific mission. The Spirit is the agent of the Son's incarnation, anoints Jesus for his salvific mission, reveals and verifies Christ's deity, functions as the presence of Christ among believers, and empowers believers for mission by baptizing them in the Holy Spirit. Cyril, therefore, delineates a Spirit christological paradigm of pneumatic mediation that integrates a Son of God Christology within a trinitarian framework.

Athanasius

Athanasius' life and ministry were shaped by the Council of Nicea and contention with Arian doctrine.[114] Athanasius became entangled in this struggle from its earliest stages. Shortly after the synod in Alexandria which deposed Arius, he was ordained a deacon by Alexander (319). Serving as a secretary, Athanasius accompanied Alexander during the Council of Nicea (325). After Alexander's death, Athanasius succeeded him as bishop of Alexandria (328) and became the staunchest defender of Nicean theology and enemy of Arian doctrine.[115] Against continuing persuasive Arian influence in

---

[113] According to Cyril, when does a believer receive the Spirit? Stanley Burgess, probably, correctly assesses the issue: 'Cyril seems to treat baptism and chrism as components in one and the same vital process'. Burgess, *The Holy Spirit: Ancient Christian Traditions*, p. 112. Cf. Cyril, 'Catecheses', FC, LXIV, pp. 174-80; McDonnell and Montague, *Christian Initiation*, pp. 191-251.

[114] For overviews of Athanasius' life, see Khaled Anatolios, *Athanasius* (ECF; London: Routledge, 2004), pp. 1-39; Alvyn Pettersen, *Athanasius* (Harrisburg, PA: Morehouse, 1995), pp. 1-18; Frend, *Christianity*, pp. 523-43; Hans von Campenhausen, *The Fathers of the Church* (II vols.; Peabody, MA: Hendrickson, The Combined Edition of The Fathers of the Greek Church and The Fathers of the Latin Church edn, 2000), I, pp. 69-83; Schaff, *History*, III, pp. 885-91.

[115] Not all groups that Athanasius classified as Arian considered themselves followers of Arius' doctrines. In point of fact, those who composed the creed of the Dedication Council at Antioch (341) began by disavowing that they were disciples of Arius (Athanasius, *Syn.* 22). For an examination of the attitude of Arians toward Arius, see Hanson, *Christian Doctrine of God*, pp. 123-28. It appears that early on Arian doctrine moved past Arius and developed along two paths: Ho-

the royal house of Constantine, Athanasius was unbending in his position; the shifting political winds brought five periods of exile and restoration.[116]

Although Athanasius' writings primarily focused on refuting Arian doctrine[117] by affirming the Son's consubstantial deity with the Father,[118] he also recognized the Holy Spirit's deity. During his third exile, while taking refuge with monks in the Egyptian desert, Athanasius received an inquiry from Serapion about the Holy Spirit's deity. Athanasius answered by writing four missives, *Letters to Serapion concerning the Holy Spirit* (356–62).[119] In the first letter, he argues

---

moian Arians and Neo-Arians. The Homoian group evolved from Eusebius of Caesarea and included Acacias of Caesarea, Eudoxius, Ulfilas, Valens of Mursa, Ursacius of Singidunum, Germinius of Sirmium, Palladius of Ratiaria, Auxentius of Milan, Auxentius of Durostorum, and Maximinus. The Second Sirmium Creed (357) reflects their theology. Neo-Arians developed later through its primary theologians Aetius and his disciple Eunomius. For an examination and comparison of these two groups and their theologies, see Hanson, *Christian Doctrine of God*, pp. 557-603. Because Athanasius neither distinguishes between Arius and these groups nor their respective theologies, some scholars have been led to question the fundamental issues of the controversy. Khaled Anatolios, *Athanasius: The Coherence of His Thought* (London: Routledge, 1998), pp. 93-96; Wiles, *Working Papers in Doctrine*, pp. 28-49; Maurice Wiles, 'Attitudes to Arius in the Arian Controversy', in Michel R. Barnes and Daniel H. Williams (eds.), *Arianism after Arius: Essays on the Development of the Fourth Century Trinitarian Conflicts* (Edinburgh: T. & T. Clark, 1993), pp. 31-43.

[116] Thomas G. Weinandy, *Athanasius: A Theological Introduction* (Great Theologians Series; Burlington, VT: Ashgate, 2007), pp. 1-7.

[117] The possible exceptions being his early work *Against the Heathen* and *The Incarnation of the Word* which in reality are two parts of a single work. Concerning the theology of these documents, see Weinandy, *Athanasius*, pp. 11-48; Anatolios, *Athanasius: The Coherence of His Thought*, pp. 26-84. For an overview of Athanasius's writings, see Quasten, *Patrology*, III, pp. 22-65; Hanson, *Christian Doctrine of God*, pp. 417-21.

[118] Anatolios, *Athanasius: The Coherence of His Thought*, pp. 85-163; Weinandy, *Athanasius*, pp. 49-80; Anatolios, *Athanasius*, pp. 87-211, 234-42; Harnack, *Dogma*, IV, pp. 26-38; Quasten, *Patrology*, III, pp. 66-79; Seeberg and Hay, *History*, I, pp. 206-12; Kelly, *Doctrines*, pp. 243-47; González, *Christian Thought*, I, pp. 291-302; Marvin D. Jones, *Athanasius' Concept of Eternal Sonship as Revealed in Contra Arianos* (Lewiston, NY: Edwin Mellen Press, 2006); Kannengiesser, *Arius and Athanasius: Two Alexandrian Theologians*.

[119] For issues about date of origin and provenance, see C.R.B. Shapland's notes in Athanasius, *The Letters of Saint Anthanasius Concerning the Holy Spirit* (trans. C.R.B. Shapland; London: Epworth Press, 1951), pp. 16-18; Quasten, *Patrology*, III, p. 57. Concerning the textual tradition of these letters, see C.R.B. Shapland's notes in Athanasius, *Holy Spirit*, pp. 43-49. Athanasius' pneumatology is examined by C.R.B. Shapland in Athanasius, *Holy Spirit*, pp. 34-43. Cf. Hanson, *Christian Doctrine of God*, pp. 749-52; Shedd, *Doctrine*, I, pp. 356-57.

for the full deity of the Son and Holy Spirit by examining the Scriptures in dispute[120] and appealing to the tradition and life of the church. Serapion requested an abridgment of this letter, so the second and third letters represent Athanasius' compliance to his petition. The second letter, consequently, addresses the Son's deity, and the third letter relates the Holy Spirit's deity. The fourth letter depicts various issues concerning the Spirit's deity which Athanasius presented and answered in the first letter but omitted in the third letter. The survey, therefore, will proceed by examining the Spirit christological texts found in the first letter and noting corresponding texts in the other three letters.[121]

Serapion had encountered a group, the Tropici,[122] which had forsaken the Arian view of the Son, accepted the consubstantial divine nature of the Son with the Father, but insisted on the creaturely nature of the Holy Spirit (*Ep. Serap.* 1.1).[123] Athanasius responded by placing the Son and the Spirit in the closest possible relationship.

> How then have they endured so much as to hear the Spirit of the Son called a creature? Because of the oneness of the Word with the Father, they will not have the Son belong to things originated, but rightly regard him as Creator of things made. Why then do they say that the Holy Spirit is a creature, who has the same

---

[120] Against the Tropicists' exegesis of Amos 4.13 which asserts the creaturely nature of the Holy Spirit, Athanasius retorts that they are various meanings of spirit in Scripture, but the Holy Spirit is always carefully distinguished in Scripture by appearing with the definite article (*Ep. Serap.* 1.3-10). Also, the Tropicists' exegesis of 1 Tim. 5.21 argues from this text's silence concerning the Holy Spirit; the Spirit is numbered among the creatures, the angels. Athanasius, however, contends that the Spirit is also carefully distinguished from the angels (*Ep. Serap.* 1.10-14). For a discussion of the Tropicists' favorite Scriptures, see Athanasius, *Holy Spirit*, pp. 30-32.

[121] Spirit christological texts found in other Athanasian documents will be noted as well.

[122] This group was known as the Tropici because of their hermeneutical method of interpreting in a tropical or metaphorical sense any Scripture that did not support their position. See C.R.B. Shapland's notes in Athanasius, *Holy Spirit*, pp. 18-34; Quasten, *Patrology*, III, p. 57. Cf. Hanson's discussion about the Macedonians in Hanson, *Christian Doctrine of God*, pp. 760-72; Harnack, *Dogma*, IV, pp. 112-14.

[123] Cf. *Ep. Serap.* 1.10; 1.17; 1.26-27; Pelikan, *Christian Tradition*, I, p. 212. Khaled Anatolios also provides an introduction and English translation of these letters in Anatolios, *Athanasius*, pp. 212-33.

oneness with the Son as the Son with the Father (*Ep. Serap.* 1.2)?[124]

Athanasius' central argument associates the Spirit with the Son: the Spirit is the Spirit of the Son.[125] The Spirit's deity and unity with the Father, therefore, is understood through the Son, so that whoever denies the Spirit's deity also denies the Son's deity and has not the Father; in other words, the question of the Spirit's deity arises out of the Son's deity.

Another Spirit christological text accentuates the divine activity of the Spirit in the incarnation.

> So too when the Word visited the holy Virgin Mary, the Spirit came to her with him, and the Word in the Spirit, moulded [*sic*] the body and conformed it to himself; desiring to join and present all creation to the Father through himself, and in it to reconcile all things (*Ep. Serap.* 1.31).[126]

According to this text, the Logos became incarnate in Christ 'in the Spirit'. It also depicts the soteriological arguments Athanasius uses to affirm the Spirit's deity. The Logos and Spirit's salvific activity operate in a dyadic relationship: the Logos functions in the Spirit redemptively to reconcile all things to the Father. So the Son and Spirit are neither divided in the incarnation nor the salvific mission; the Father does all things through the Son in the Holy Spirit (*Ep. Serap.* 1.14; 1.28; 1.31; *C. Ar.* 3.15.15). Athanasius' soteriology, therefore, places the incarnation in the pivotal position of history, reconciling all of creation to the Father through the Logos in the Spirit.

Athanasius also discusses the significance of Christ receiving the Spirit.

---

[124] Cited according to C.R.B. Shapland's translation in Athanasius, *Holy Spirit*, p. 62. Cf. Pettersen, *Athanasius*, pp. 144-46. Unless otherwise noted, references will be cited from Shapland's translation.

[125] Cf. *Ep. Serap.* 1.20; 3.1; Shapland's introduction to Athanasius, *Holy Spirit*, pp. 35-37; Weinandy, *Athanasius*, pp. 110-17; Hanson, *Christian Doctrine of God*, p. 424; Pelikan, *Christian Tradition*, I, p. 214. 'If the Spirit is thus portrayed in scripture as "belonging" to the Son and as connecting creation to God, and as rendering present the Son's activity, then the Spirit must also be God.' Anatolios, *Athanasius: The Coherence of His Thought*, p. 114.

[126] Athanasius, *Holy Spirit*, pp. 145-46. Cf. *Ep. Serap.* 3.6.

When our Lord was baptized in human fashion because of the flesh he was wearing, the Holy Spirit is said to have descended upon him' (*Ep. Serap.* 1.6).[127]

It is very plain that the Spirit's descent on Him in Jordan was a descent upon us, because of His bearing our body. And it did not take place for promotion to the Word, but again for our sanctification, that we might share His anointing ... And when he received the Spirit, we it was who by Him were made recipients of It' (*C. Ar.* 1.12.47).[128]

Since the Son is divine by nature, against the Arian position, receiving the Spirit adds nothing to the Son's deity; rather, the Spirit anoints Christ's flesh.[129] Christ, moreover, received the Spirit so that believers may receive the Spirit, become sanctified, and share his anointing. Athanasius, hence, affirms that 'when the Lord came and renewed all things by his grace', the prophetic Scriptures were fulfilled that believers would receive the Holy Spirit and their spirits be recreated and renewed (*Ep. Serap.* 1.9).[130] According to Athanasius, then, the Holy Spirit's descent upon Christ, at the Jordan, signifies that humans become redemptively joined to God by receiving the Spirit through the Logos.

---

[127] Athanasius, *Holy Spirit*, pp. 72-73.
[128] Cited according to Archibald Robertson's revision of John Henry Newman's translation, Athanasius, 'Against the Arians', NPNF, Second Series, IV, p. 333. See also Anatolios, *Athanasius: The Coherence of His Thought*, p. 158:

> It is Christ's reception of grace – more specifically, Christ's human reception of the Holy Spirit on our behalf – that is seen as the ultimate 'securing' of grace for humanity. In fact, Athanasius says categorically that our own reception of the Spirit, on which hangs our salvation and deification, is impossible except as derivative of Christ's human reception of it in the incarnation.

For Athanasius, Christ's receiving and giving of the Spirit was 'the supreme instance of grace'. Anatolios, *Athanasius: The Coherence of His Thought*, pp. 155-60. Cf. Weinandy, *Athanasius*, pp. 106-107; Hanson, *Christian Doctrine of God*, pp. 450-51; Pelikan, *Christian Tradition*, I, p. 213.
[129] There remains a question concerning whether or not Athanasius affirms a human soul in Christ. Grillmeier, *Christian Tradition*, I, pp. 308-28; Wiles, *Working Papers in Doctrine*, pp. 58-61, 64; Maurice Wiles, 'The Nature of the Early Debate about Christ's Human Soul', *JEH* 16 (1965), pp. 139-51; Quasten, *Patrology*, III, pp. 73-75; González, *Christian Thought*, I, p. 300; Weinandy, *Athanasius*, pp. 81-82; Anatolios, *Athanasius: The Coherence of His Thought*, pp. 138-61; Khaled Anatolios, 'The Soteriological Significance of Christ's Humanity in St. Athanasius', *SVTQ* 40 (1996), pp. 265-68.
[130] Athanasius, *Holy Spirit*, p. 81.

According to Athanasius, only deity can accomplish this reconciliation and renewal (*C. Ar.* 2.15.18). Athanasius, consequently, rejects the Tropicists' argument that if the Holy Spirit proceeds from the Father, then, the Spirit is a Son and the Logos' brother, and if the Spirit proceeds from the Son, the Spirit is a grandson of the Father (*Ep. Serap.* 1.15-16; 4.1; 4.2).[131]

> For if they thought correctly of the Word, they would think soundly of the Spirit also, who proceeds from the Father, and belonging to the Son, is from him given to the disciples and all who believe in him (*Ep. Serap.* 1.2).[132]

This text depicts the procession of the Spirit from the Father and from the Son,[133] but it does not delineate divine genealogy in a human sense; rather, it affirms that the Father, Son, and Spirit partake of the same divine nature, and it elucidates how believers receive the Spirit: from the Father and Son (*Ep. Serap.* 1.20; 3.2).[134]

The soteriological purpose of believers receiving the Spirit is union with deity and deification.[135] The Spirit christological emphasis here is thick; when the Spirit is in believers, the Son dwells in them (*Ep. Serap.* 1.20). When believers are anointed by the Spirit, the fragrance of the one who anoints accompanies the anointing, so that believers become the fragrance of Christ. The Spirit, furthermore,

---

[131] Athanasius argues that Scripture never confuses the designations Father, Son, and Spirit so the Tropicists do not have Scriptural basis for drawing these suppositions (*Ep. Serap.* 1.16; 4.4; 4.6). According to Athanasius, inventing names leads to Sabellianism and using the analogy of human generation can lead to paganism (*Ep. Serap.* 4.5-6).

[132] Athanasius, *Holy Spirit*, pp. 64-65.

[133] For a discussion about the procession of the Spirit, see Athanasius, *Holy Spirit*, pp. 40-43.

[134] Of course, believers understand the mystery of this perichoretic relationship through revelation. The Father is light and the Son his radiance; the Spirit is seen in the Son, and when believers are enlightened by the Spirit, it is Christ who enlightens them (*Ep. Serap.* 1.19).

[135] Concerning Athanasius' doctrine of deification, see Athanasius, *Holy Spirit*, pp. 37-39; Weinandy, *Athanasius*, pp. 96-100; Anatolios, *Athanasius: The Coherence of His Thought*, pp. 149-54; Hanson, *Christian Doctrine of God*, pp. 456-57; Seeberg and Hay, *History*, I, pp. 212-15; Kelly, *Doctrines*, p. 243. 'Deification is not then the changing of our human nature into something other than it is, that is, into another kind of being. Rather, deification for Athanasius is the making of humankind into what it was meant to be from the very beginning, that is, the prefect image of the Word who is the prefect image of the Father.' Weinandy, *Athanasius*, p. 99.

bearing the form of Christ, seals believers and forms Christ in them (*Ep. Serap.* 1.23; 3.3).

> Being thus sealed, we are duly made, as Peter put it, 'sharers in the divine nature'; and thus all creation partakes of the Word in the Spirit. Further it is through the Spirit that we are all said to be partakers of God. For it says: 'Know ye not that ye are a temple of God and that the Spirit of God dwells in you' (*Ep. Serap.* 1.23-24)?[136]

This text depicts the goal of creation and redemption: that all creation will partake of the divine nature through the Logos in the Spirit. In point of fact, Athanasius, appealing to church tradition, contends that the activity of the Son and Spirit is indivisible: there is nothing that is not originated and actuated through the Word in the Spirit (*Ep. Serap.* 1.31; 1.33; 3.5; 4.3).[137] Since believers begin the process of deification when they receive the Spirit, by receiving the Spirit, they receive the Son who gives the Spirit and the Father who is in the Word (*Ep. Serap.* 1.30; 3.6; 4.4; *C. Ar.* 3.25.24; *Syn.* 50).[138] The Spirit, therefore, cannot be a creature; only God can deify creatures.

Athanasius posits a monotheistic view of God set in a trinitarian framework that integrates Logos Christology and Spirit Christology. In Christ's identity and salvific mission the Logos and Spirit function in a perichoretic relationship; the activity of the Logos and Spirit are indivisible. The virgin birth of Christ was accomplished by the Logos in the Spirit. At the Jordan, Christ's flesh received the Spirit for believers' sanctification and anointing. After his death, resurrection, and ascension, the Son gives the Spirit to believers; the Spirit dwells in believers, as the Spirit of the Son, initiating their journey toward theosis. The Spirit, therefore, mediates the Son's mission, so that the Son does all things in the Spirit. Athanasius'

---

[136] Athanasius, *Holy Spirit*, pp. 124-26. Cf. *C. Ar.* 1.12.46-47; Athanasius, *Holy Spirit*, p. 40.

[137] Probably, this tradition stems from Irenaeus. Anatolios, *Athanasius: The Coherence of His Thought*, pp. 18-25. Cf. Athanasius, *Holy Spirit*, p. 143.

[138] 'In partaking of the Spirit, we partake of the Son, and in partaking of the Son, we partake of the Father. This model of immediate participation in the whole Trinity through the mediation of the Son and Spirit stands self-consciously in contrast to the model of "exclusive" hierarchic participation, in which creation partakes only in the Son, while only the Son partakes of the Father.' Anatolios, *Athanasius: The Coherence of His Thought*, p. 115. Cf. Weinandy, *Athanasius*, p. 111.

Spirit Christology, therefore, supports a paradigm of pneumatic mediation.

Apollinarius of Laodicea

The writings of Apollinarius, bishop of Laodicea (361), supply the next Spirit Christological references. Apollinarius was a notable teacher; even Jerome attended his lectures at Antioch in 374. He was also a prolific writer, standing shoulder to shoulder with his friends Athanasius and Basil of Caesarea in opposition to Arian doctrine, producing works in a variety of genres: poetry, scriptural commentaries, apologetical and polemical works, and dogmatic treatises. Toward the end of his life, his christological writings – which opposed Arian Christology, Marcellus of Ancyra, and Diodore of Tarsus – aroused opposition, even among former companions, and were condemned by synods in Rome (374–80) and by the Council of Constantinople (381).[139] Most of his extensive writings have survived in fragmentary form, along with several complete works preserved pseudonymously under more amicable and authoritative names.[140]

---

[139] Athanasius, Basil of Caesarea, Gregory of Nazianzus, Gregory of Nyssa, Diodore of Tarsus, and Theodore of Mopsuestia wrote in opposition to Apollinarius' mutilation of Christ's human nature which stripped the incarnation and redemption of its meaning. Quasten, *Patrology*, III, pp. 381-83. Regarding his life, see Charles E. Raven, *Apollinarianism: An Essay on the Christology of the Early Church* (Cambridge: Cambridge University Press, 1923), pp. 126-31, 142-52; Frend, *Christianity*, p. 634; Quasten, *Patrology*, III, p. 377; Schaff, *History*, III, pp. 709-10.

[140] Apollinarius' followers preserved seven documents by attributing them to orthodox writers: (1) one document was attributed to Gregory of Thaumaturgus, *A Detailed Confession of Faith*; (2) three documents were attributed to Athanasius, *Quod unus sit Christus, De incarnatione Dei Verbi*, and a *Profession of Faith* addressed to the Emperor Jovian; and (3) three documents were attributed to Pope Julius (337–52), *De unione corporis et divinitatis in Christo, De fide et incarnatione*, and a letter addressed to a presbyter Dionysius. Another document, *Proof of the Incarnation of God according to the Image of Man*, can be partially reconstructed from Gregory of Nyssa's attack against it in his *Antirrheticus*. *Recapitulatio*, also, can be reconstructed from a pseudo-Athanasian source. Finally, several early historians have preserved many Apollinarian fragments: Socrates, Sozomenus, Rufinus, and Theodoret. Hans Lietzmann has collected into one text the surviving Apollinarian documents and fragments. Hans Lietzmann, *Apollinaris von Laodicea und seine Schule: Texte und Untersuchungen* (Hildesheim: Georg Olms, 1970 repr.; Tübingen: J.C.B. Mohr [Paul Siebeck], 1904). The dates for his writings range from 360–80. For overviews of Apollinarius' writings, see Lietzmann, *Apollinaris*, pp. 129-63; 'Apollinarius and

Apollinarius' discussion of the Scriptural contrast between flesh and spirit holds the central place in his Christology. In his earlier works, Apollinarius' anthropology postulates that human nature is composed of two incomplete parts, a rational soul and body, which constitute a single nature and is signified by one name: flesh (*Union*, 5).[141] In several Spirit christological texts, however, Spirit in Christ denotes deity.

Divine Spirit is united to flesh (*Recapitulatio*, 16.4-5).[142]

The Logos became flesh, and the last Adam became a life-giving Spirit (*Union*, 2).[143]

But (he says) he is God because of the Spirit which is incarnated but human because of the flesh assumed by God (Fragment 19).[144]

By these means (he says) the prophetic word signifies that he is consubstantial with God not according to the flesh but according to the Spirit which is united with the flesh (Fragment 41).[145]

These texts educe three points about deity incarnate in Christ. First, Spirit is used interchangeably with Logos to express deity in Christ. Second, divine Spirit is consubstantial in divine essence with God. Third, Spirit is incarnated; it unites with flesh. So Christ is composed of an incarnate divine nature and human nature: Spirit and flesh.

Apollinarius' spirit-flesh paradigm, moreover, avers the unity of these natures. In opposition to those who sharply distinguish between the divine and human natures in Christ,[146] Apollinarius promulgates their unity.

Apollinarianism', *ODCC*, p. 86; Quasten, *Patrology*, III, pp. 377-81; Raven, *Apollinarianism*, pp. 131-33, 139-42, 152-76.

[141] Regarding the philosophical and theological context of anthropology in the fourth and fifth centuries, see Richard A. Norris, *Manhood and Christ: A Study in the Christology of Theodore of Mopsuestia* (Oxford: Clarendon Press, 1963), pp. 1-78.

[142] Cited according to my own translation, Lietzmann, *Apollinaris*, p. 244. Cf. Raven, *Apollinarianism*, pp. 185-88; Pelikan, *Christian Tradition*, I, p. 248.

[143] Cited according to my own translation, Lietzmann, *Apollinaris*, p. 186. Cf. Fragment 29.

[144] Cited according to my own translation, Lietzmann, *Apollinaris*, p. 209.

[145] Cited according to my own translation, Lietzmann, *Apollinaris*, p. 213.

[146] For example, Eustathius of Antioch and Diodore of Tarsus followed this christological trajectory. According to Apollinarius, they have introduced a divi-

178   Spirit Christology

It is inconceivable that the same person should be both God and an entire man. Rather, he exists in the singleness of an incarnate nature which is commingled [with flesh] (Fragment 9.26-28).[147]

So the God who became human, the Lord and ruler of all that comes to be, may have come of a woman, yet he is Lord. He may have been formed after the fashion of slaves, yet he is Spirit. He may be proclaimed as flesh because of his union with the flesh, yet according to the apostle he is not a human being; and though he is preached as human by the same apostle, yet he calls the whole Christ invisible God transformed by a visible body, uncreated God made manifest in a garment. He emptied himself after the fashion of a slave, but in his divine essence he is unemptied and unaltered and undiminished (for no alteration can affect the divine nature), neither is he decreased or increased (*Union*, 6).[148]

Thus he is both coessential with God in the invisible Spirit (the flesh being comprehended in the title because it has been united to that which is coessential with God), and again coessential with men (the Godhead being comprehended with the body because it has been united to what is coessential with us) (Union, 8).[149]

These texts accentuate three Apollinarian christological premises. First, the uniting of divine Spirit with flesh did not alter the Spirit's divine essence. Second, there was a genuine incarnation of deity in

---

sion in the nature of the one Lord. The summary of Apollinarius' retort to this position is Jn 1.14: only through a genuine incarnation of deity can humans be redeemed. Raven, *Apollinarianism*, pp. 179-81. Cf. Wiles, *Working Papers in Doctrine*, pp. 61-62; Kelly, *Doctrines*, p. 290; Frend, *Christianity*, p. 634; Quasten, *Patrology*, III, p. 381. For a discussion of Apollinarius' opposition to Arianism and Marcellus of Ancyra, see Spoerl, 'Apollinarian Christology and the Anti-Marcellan Tradition', pp. 545-68.

[147] Cited according to the translation of Richard A. Norris, *The Christological Controversy* (Sources of Early Christian Thought; Philadelphia: Fortress Press, 1980), p. 108. Cf. Raven, *Apollinarianism*, pp. 181-85; Grillmeier, *Christian Tradition*, I, pp. 330-33.

[148] Cited according to the translation of Richard Norris, *The Christological Controversy*, p. 104. Cf. Robert Victor Sellers, *Two Ancient Christologies: A Study in the Christological Thought of the Schools of Alexandria and Antioch in the Early History of Christian Doctrine* (London: SPCK, 1954), p. 51.

[149] Cited according to the translation of Richard Norris, *The Christological Controversy*, p. 105.

human flesh and *communicatio idiomatum*.[150] Third, divine nature replaces the rational human nature; Christ is not a human being, for in Christ flesh refers to the human body. So the divine Spirit commingles with flesh in Christ to form a single incarnate divine nature.[151]

To explain how Christ is constructed of a composite union of Spirit and flesh,[152] in his later writings,[153] Apollinarius draws from 1 Thess. 5.23 to discuss the human constitution: humans are composed of spirit, soul, and body (Fragment 89). According to Apollinarius' anthropology, the soul, which humans and animals have in common, is irrational, impersonal, and passive. Rational faculties and personality, however, are attributed to the human spirit (Fragment 22; 28).

So Christ, having God as his spirit – that is, his intellect – together with soul and body, is rightly called 'the human being from heaven' (Fragment 25).[154]

---

[150] According to Charles Raven, the kenosis of deity taking on the form of a servant in the incarnation depicts divine self-limitation. Raven, *Apollinarianism*, pp. 202-208. Furthermore, Raven posits Christ's kenosis or self-limitation in the incarnation allows the conditions of human existence to be taken up into deity: the flesh by union in Christ receives the qualities of deity. The kenosis is the union, and the union is a communication of divine and human attributes. Raven, *Apollinarianism*, pp. 209-11. Cf. Norris, *The Christological Controversy*, pp. 22-23; Grillmeier, *Christian Tradition*, I, pp. 333-40; Sellers, *Two Ancient Christologies*, pp. 51-52.

[151] Raven suggests that 'he adopts "commixture" (σύγκρασις) as a fitting description for the method of Incarnation instead of the familiar "indwelling" (ἐνοίκησις) which he criticized'. Raven, *Apollinarianism*, p. 204. If the deity and a human personality coexisted in Christ, Apollinarius believed this would equate incarnation with a unique degree of prophetic inspiration (Fragment 83). Cf. Norris, *Manhood and Christ*, pp. 112-13.

[152] Fragments, 111; 149. Cf. Norris, *Manhood and Christ*, pp. 104-106; Sellers, *Two Ancient Christologies*, pp. 52-57.

[153] There has been some discussion about Apollinarius' earlier and later writings depicting two distinct concepts of the person of Christ. Lietzmann, *Apollinaris*, pp. 5-6. Rather than distinct christological theories, more than likely, this can be explained by a shift in emphasis: the earlier works stress the unity of Christ's person, and the later works accentuate the soteriological significance of πνεῦμα and νοῦς. Concerning these issues and the unity of Apollinarius' teaching, see Norris, *Manhood and Christ*, pp. 81-94; Raven, *Apollinarianism*, pp. 169-76.

[154] Cited according to the translation of Richard Norris, *The Christological Controversy*, p. 108. There is some discussion concerning the 'human being from heaven' statement that it depicts the Logos as the archetype of humanity. Probably, this statement denotes the distinction between Christ and ordinary humans. For

In the incarnation, therefore, divine Spirit came to occupy the place of the human spirit in Christ, the rational intellect, so that the Logos became incarnate intellect joined to flesh and irrational soul; accordingly, divine Spirit governs, informs, and guides Christ's flesh (Fragments 69–72).[155]

The divine Spirit became incarnate intellect joined to flesh for soteriological reasons. According to Apollinarius, if a human intellect existed in Christ, salvation would not be possible. This is because the root of sin lies in the flesh; the human intellect is mutable and consents to the promptings of the flesh which fights against the spirit and resists the intellect. For redemption to occur, then, an immutable intellect, which is neither affected by sin nor dominated by the flesh, must become incarnate in flesh and destroy sin in the flesh (Fragment 74; 22; 76).[156]

> The Godhead was not named 'Jesus' before his birth from a virgin; neither did it receive the chrism of the Holy Spirit, because the Word of God is the giver of the Spirit, not the one who is sanctified by the Spirit (*Union*, 9).[157]

Deity in Christ was not anointed by the Spirit; rather, the divine Spirit in the incarnation united with the flesh and sanctified it for its soteriological mission (*Union*, 13). Humans, thus, are redeemed as they are divinized by receiving the Holy Spirit and participating in Christ (*Faith*, 32; Fragment, 76; 116; 128).[158]

Arian Christology had broached the issue of how an immutable deity could unite with a mutable humanity. Apollinarius' Christology answers this conundrum by denying a mutable human intellect in Christ: the divine Spirit is incarnated as immutable intellect in human flesh. Against those Christologies which respond to the Arian

---

an examination of this issue, see Norris, *Manhood and Christ*, pp. 98-101; Raven, *Apollinarianism*, pp. 185-89.

[155] Harnack, *Dogma*, IV, pp. 149-57; Kelly, *Doctrines*, pp. 292-95; González, *Christian Thought*, I, pp. 346-48; Raven, *Apollinarianism*, pp. 198-202; Quasten, *Patrology*, III, pp. 382-83; Norris, *The Christological Controversy*, pp. 21-22; Sellers, *Two Ancient Christologies*, pp. 60; Schaff, *History*, III, pp. 710-12; Seeberg and Hay, *History*, I, pp. 244-47; Shedd, *Doctrine*, I, pp. 394-95.

[156] Norris, *Manhood and Christ*, pp. 112-19; Frend, *Christianity*, pp. 634-35; Kelly, *Doctrines*, p. 291; Sellers, *Two Ancient Christologies*, pp. 61-62.

[157] Cited according to the translation of, Richard Norris, *The Christological Controversy*, p. 105.

[158] Norris, *Manhood and Christ*, pp. 119-22.

challenge by positing complete dual natures in Christ, divine and human, Apollinarius constates a single incarnate divine nature which commingles with flesh in a genuine *communicatio idiomatum* between Spirit and flesh. Apollinarius synonymously refers to this incarnate nature, which is consubstantial with God, as Logos and Spirit. Apollinarius' Spirit Christology, therefore, supports a paradigm of pneumatic incarnation which integrates with Logos Christology.

The Cappadocian Fathers

The region of Cappadocia produced three eminent theologians collectively known as the Cappadocian Fathers: Basil of Caesarea, his brother Gregory of Nyssa, and his friend Gregory of Nazianzus. Although Basil and Gregory of Nazianzus received philosophical training in Athens, the Cappadocian Fathers had inherited an Alexandrian theological tradition extending from Gregory Thaumaturgus back to Origen.[159] This legacy allowed them to use the language of contemporary philosophy and Hellenistic culture to discuss the Hebrew concepts of the gospel.[160] The Cappadocians, nevertheless, in certain ways carefully distinguished themselves from Platonism, and they modified Alexandrian doctrine.[161] As a group, the Cappa-

---

[159] Gregory Thaumaturgus was a missionary to Cappadocia. It seems that Basil's grandmother was a convert of Gregory Thaumaturgus which caused Basil and his brothers to hold him in high esteem. Anthony Meredith, *The Cappadocians* (Crestwood, NY: St. Vladimir's Seminary Press, 1995), pp. 2-3. Since Basil accompanied Basil of Ancyra to the synod of Constantinople (359), R.P.C. Hanson has noted that Basil of Ancyra had some influence on Basil of Caesarea. Hanson, *Christian Doctrine of God*, p. 680.

[160] Stephen M. Hildebrand, *The Trinitarian Theology of Basil of Caesarea: A Synthesis of Greek Thought and Biblical Truth* (Washington: Catholic University of America Press, 2007), pp. 30-149; Frederick W. Norris and Gregory, *Faith Gives Fullness to Reasoning: The Five Theological Orations of Gregory Nazianzen* (trans. Lionel Wickham and Frederick Williams; VCSup 13; Leiden: E.J. Brill, 1990), pp. 17-39; Brian Daley, *Gregory of Nazianzus* (ECF; London: Routledge, 2006), pp. 34-41; Lucian Turcescu, *Gregory of Nyssa and the Concept of Divine Persons* (AARAS; Oxford: Oxford University Press, 2005), pp. 25-46.

[161] Regarding the Cappadocian Fathers' cultural context and theological background, see Meredith, *The Cappadocians*, pp. 1-17; Hanson, *Christian Doctrine of God*, pp. 676-79; Anthony Meredith and Gregory, *Gregory of Nyssa* (ECF; London: Routledge, 1999), pp. 6-15.

docian Fathers became a predominate force, and individually each figure achieved the status of a major theologian.[162]

The Cappadocian Fathers significantly impacted the theological discussion of the latter part of the fourth century, especially at the Council of Constantinople (381),[163] in at least four ways. First, their influence largely contributed to resolving the debate concerning the Son's deity and consubstantial nature with the Father while maintaining their distinction.[164] Second, they clarified the equivocal nomenclature used to designate deity.[165] Third, they contributed to

---

[162] Basil succeeded Eusebius as bishop of Caesarea around 370. For overviews of his life, see Philip Rousseau, *Basil of Caesarea* (TTCH 20; Berkeley: University of California Press, 1994); Meredith, *The Cappadocians*, pp. 20-24; Hildebrand, *Trinitarian Theology*, pp. 18-29; Hanson, *Christian Doctrine of God*, pp. 679-86; Quasten, *Patrology*, III, pp. 204-207. Basil consecrated Gregory of Nazianzus as bishop of Sasima in 371, but when his father, the bishop of Nazianzus, died in 374, Gregory took over the administration of the diocese; then, in 380 he assumed the bishopric of Constantinople. Gregory resigned this post during the Council of Constantinople (381) and returned to Nazianzus. For overviews of his life, see Christopher A. Beeley, *Gregory of Nazianzus on the Trinity and the Knowledge of God: In Your Light We Shall See Light* (OSHT; Oxford: Oxford University Press, 2008), pp. 3-16, 34-62; Daley, *Gregory of Nazianzus*, pp. 3-26; Norris and Gregory, *Faith Gives Fullness to Reasoning*, pp. 1-12; Gregory of Nazianzus, 'Prolegomena', NPNF, Second Series, VII, pp. 187-200; Meredith, *The Cappadocians*, pp. 39-42; Hanson, *Christian Doctrine of God*, pp. 699-707; Quasten, *Patrology*, III, pp. 236-38. Basil consecrated his brother Gregory bishop of Nyssa in 371. For overviews of his life, see Meredith and Gregory, *Gregory of Nyssa*, pp. 1-6; 'Prolegomena', NPNF, Second Series, V, pp. 1-8; Meredith, *The Cappadocians*, pp. 52-54; Quasten, *Patrology*, III, pp. 254-55; Hanson, *Christian Doctrine of God*, pp. 715-16.

[163] Davis, *Ecumenical Councils*, pp. 108-29. For a discussion of fourth-century doctrinal issues, see Beeley, *Trinity and the Knowledge of God*, pp. 16-34.

[164] Meredith, *The Cappadocians*, pp. 102-10; Daley, *Gregory of Nazianzus*, pp. 41-50; Hanson, *Christian Doctrine of God*, pp. 688-99, 711-14, 719-23, 730-31, 734-37; Beeley, *Trinity and the Knowledge of God*, pp. 187-233; Norris and Gregory, *Faith Gives Fullness to Reasoning*, pp. 39-47; Turcescu, *Concept of Divine Persons*, pp. 47-107; Pelikan, *Christian Tradition*, I, pp. 218-24; Kelly, *Doctrines*, pp. 263-68; Quasten, *Patrology*, III, pp. 249-50, 285-87; Boris Bobrinskoy, 'The Indwelling of the Spirit in Christ: "Pneumatic Christology" in the Cappadocian Fathers', *SVTQ* 28.01 (2001), pp. 54-59.

[165] This was Basil's great contribution to the debate, and the two Gregorys followed his lead. Basil distinguished between two terms that were commonly used synonymously: οὐσία and ὑπόστασις. He designated οὐσία as divine essence and ὑπόστασις as mode of being or person, so that God is one divine ousia existing as three hypostases in divine relationship as Father, Son, and Holy Spirit (Basil, *Letters*, 214.3-4; 210.5). Meredith, *The Cappadocians*, pp. 102-105; Hanson, *Christian Doctrine of God*, pp. 690-92, 707-708, 723, 731, 734-37; Daley, *Gregory of Nazianzus*, pp. 45-50; Turcescu, *Concept of Divine Persons*, pp. 47-60; Quasten, *Patrology*, III, pp. 228-29; Bobrinskoy, 'Pneumatic Christology', p. 54. The clarification of these terms contributed to the vindication and acceptance of the Nicene

trinitarian doctrine by affirming the Holy Spirit's deity along with the Father and Son.[166] Fourth, regarding Christ's person, they posited dual natures in one person; Christ was fully divine and fully human.[167] Although differing in certain points individually, the Cappadocians seem to present similar trinitarian and christological doctrines; therefore, the survey will proceed by narrowing the focus to the Spirit christological references preserved in Basil's writings, spe-

---

homoousios position and the victory of the Cappadocian position at the Council of Constantinople (381); the Father, Son, and Holy Spirit are consubstantial in divine essence. Adolf Harnack, however, posited that the Cappadocians held this trinitarian consubstantiality in the homoiousios position: the divine unity is a matter of likeness. Harnack, *Dogma*, IV, pp. 80-89. Of course, several scholars disagree with Harnack. See Quasten, *Patrology*, III, p. 230; González, *Christian Thought*, I, pp. 323-25.

[166] Primarily they were reacting to the Pneumatomachian denial of the Holy Spirit's deity and positing a creaturely nature for the Spirit. In discussing the nature of the Spirit, Basil avoided applying the concept of consubstantial to the Holy Spirit; rather, he affirmed the Spirit's equality of honor with the Father and the Son. Gregory of Nazianzus and Gregory of Nyssa, nonetheless, offer a more pronounced insistence on the Holy Spirit's deity. Hanson, *Christian Doctrine of God*, pp. 772-90; Pelikan, *Christian Tradition*, I, pp. 211-18; Quasten, *Patrology*, III, pp. 231-33; Kelly, *Doctrines*, pp. 258-63; Meredith, *The Cappadocians*, pp. 105-106; Beeley, *Trinity and the Knowledge of God*, pp. 153-86; Turcescu, *Concept of Divine Persons*, pp. 109-14; Bobrinskoy, 'Pneumatic Christology', p. 59.

[167] Rather than emphasizing the unity of person, Basil's Christology was more concerned to distinguish two natures in Christ as a means of protecting deity in Christ from suffering; nonetheless, the two Gregorys stood against the Apollinarian christological paradigm for soteriological reasons. If Christ did not possess a full human nature, humanity was not redeemed: 'for that which He has assumed He has healed' (Gregory of Nazianzus, *Letters*, 101). Cited according to the translation of Charles Browne and James Swallow, Gregory of Nazianzus, 'Select Letters', NPNF, Second Series, VII, p. 440. Cf. Grillmeier, *Christian Tradition*, I, pp. 367-77; Beeley, *Trinity and the Knowledge of God*, pp. 115-51; Norris and Gregory, *Faith Gives Fullness to Reasoning*, pp. 47-53; Meredith, *The Cappadocians*, pp. 110-14; Hanson, *Christian Doctrine of God*, pp. 731-34. According to Beeley and Norris, in Gregory of Nazianzus' Christology, these dual natures, however, seem to commingle as one single subject of existence. Christopher A. Beeley, 'Gregory of Nazianzus on the Unity of Christ', in Peter William Martens (ed.), *In the Shadow of the Incarnation: Essays on Jesus Christ in the Early Church in Honor of Brian E. Daley, S.J* (Notre Dame: University of Notre Dame Press, 2008), pp. 97-120; Beeley, *Trinity and the Knowledge of God*, pp. 128-43; Norris and Gregory, *Faith Gives Fullness to Reasoning*, pp. 167, 172-76. Cf. Quasten, *Patrology*, III, pp. 251-52; Kelly, *Doctrines*, pp. 295-97. Gregory of Nyssa's Christology, however, sharply distinguishes between the two natures in Christ but carefully affirms one person; then, after the resurrection, the human nature like a drop of vinegar falling into the sea is absorbed into the divine. Kelly, *Doctrines*, pp. 298-300; Quasten, *Patrology*, III, p. 288.

cifically those found in *On the Holy Spirit* (375), and noting the texts found in the two Gregorys' writings.[168]

Basil wrote *On the Holy Spirit* (375) to answer criticism of the doxology he used in public worship which gave equal honor to the Holy Spirit along with the Father and the Son: Glory to the Father with the Son with the Holy Spirit (Basil, *DSS*, 1.3).[169] Basil, consequently, begins defending his doxology by demonstrating that although the Father, Son, and Holy Spirit are distinct, common terms are used to describe their divine operations;[170] it is through these functions humans gain knowledge of God.

> 'God is a S/spirit, and they that worship Him must worship Him in spirit and truth,' as it is written 'in light shall we see light,' namely by the illumination of the Spirit, 'the true light which lighteth every man that cometh into the world.' It results that in

---

[168] The survey will also note references in other writings of Basil. Basil was a prolific writer bequeathing to the church doctrinal, ascetic, pedagogic, and liturgical writings, as well as a multitude of homilies and letters. Owing to the high esteem given Basil in antiquity, many writings were also pseudonymously attributed to him. For overviews of Basil's writings, see St. Basil, 'On the Spirit', NPNF, Second Series, VIII, pp. xxxii-lxxvii; Quasten, *Patrology*, III, pp. 208-27; Hanson, *Christian Doctrine of God*, pp. 686-87. Regarding Gregory of Nazianzus' writings, see Quasten, *Patrology*, III, pp. 239-47; Norris and Gregory, *Faith Gives Fullness to Reasoning*, pp. 12-17; Nazianzus, 'Prolegomena', NPNF, Second Series, VII, pp. 200-202; Meredith, *The Cappadocians*, pp. 42-49; Hanson, *Christian Doctrine of God*, pp. 707-708; Daley, *Gregory of Nazianzus*, pp. 26-34. Concerning Gregory of Nyssa's writings, see Quasten, *Patrology*, III, pp. 255-82; Hanson, *Christian Doctrine of God*, pp. 716-19; Meredith, *The Cappadocians*, pp. 54-97.

[169] The most common doxology was 'Glory to the Father through the Son in the Holy Spirit'. Basil seems to be opposing Arian and Pneumatomachian subordination of the Son and Spirit. Cf. Basil, *DSS*, 6.13, 15. According to David Anderson, 'Arianizing elements felt that by fighting against the doctrine of the Holy Spirit's divinity (thus earning for themselves the name *Pneumatomachoi*, or fighters against the Spirit) they would succeed in undermining Nicene orthodoxy. But St. Basil realized that by writing a book affirming the equality of the Spirit with the Father and the Son, he could make a water-tight case for orthodoxy'. Basil, *On the Holy Spirit* (trans. David Anderson; Crestwood, NY: St. Vladimir's Seminary Press, 1980), p. 9. Cf. Norris and Gregory, *Faith Gives Fullness to Reasoning*, pp. 39-71.

[170] See Basil, *DSS*, chs. 4; 5; Gregory of Nazianzus, *Oration*, 30.18-21; Gregory of Nyssa, *Against Eunomius*, 2.14. Cf. Norris and Gregory, *Faith Gives Fullness to Reasoning*, pp. 178-82; Meredith, *The Cappadocians*, pp. 30-32. According to Basil, in using such terms as 'through whom' and 'of whom' to depict these operations, 'these are the words of a writer not laying down a rule, but carefully distinguishing the hypostases' (*DSS*, 5.7). Cited according to the translation of Broomfield Jackson, Basil, 'On the Spirit', NPNF, VIII, pp. 5. Unless otherwise noted, citations form Basil's *DSS* will come from this source.

Himself He shows the glory of the Only begotten, and on true worshippers He in Himself bestows the knowledge of God. Thus the way of the knowledge of God lies from One Spirit through One Son to the One Father, and conversely the natural Goodness and the inherent Holiness and the royal Dignity extend from the Father through the Only-begotten to the Spirit (Basil, *DSS*, 18.47).[171]

From this text five important points emerge. First, the essence of God is Spirit.[172] Second, Basil's quotation of Jn 1.9 places the illumination of the Spirit in close proximity with the Logos. Third, true worship is in the Spirit. Fourth, through an ascending grace – in the Spirit, through the Son, to the Father – true worshippers gain knowledge of God. Fifth, through a descending grace – from the Father, through the Son, by the Spirit – salvation extends to humans.[173] Against those who assert that the Spirit should not be glorified, Basil constates the Spirit's equal honor with the Father and Son in salvific mission and trinitarian relationships (Basil, *DSS*, 19.48-50; 17.43).

Regarding the economy of salvation, the Spirit receives equal honor because Christ's salvific mission has been accomplished in the Spirit. Basil builds his trinitarian theology on the concept of monarchy;[174] therefore, in the descending movement of grace, the Father sends the Son through the Spirit.

---

[171] Basil, 'On the Spirit', NPNF, Second Series, VIII, p. 29. Cf. Gregory of Nazianzus, *Oration*, 31.3; 31.12; 31.28; Gregory of Nyssa, *Against Eunomius*, 1.36; Gregory of Nyssa, *On the Holy Spirit*, NPNF, Second Series, V, p. 324.

[172] Cf. Basil, *DSS*, 9.22; 21.52; Gregory of Nazianzus, *Oration*, 31.12; Gregory of Nyssa, *Against Eunomius*, 4.6; 5.2. Against Eunomius' assertion that, in the phrase 'Now the Lord is the Spirit' (2 Cor. 3.17), the word Lord refers to God's essence and not to the Son, Gregory of Nyssa argues: 'If the essence of the Son is called "Spirit," and God also is Spirit, (for so the Gospel tells us), clearly the essence of the Father is called "Spirit" also. But if it is their peculiar argument that things which are introduced by different names are different also in nature, the conclusion surely is, that things which are named alike are not alien one from the other in nature either. Since then, according to their account, the essence of the Father and that of the Son are both called "Spirit" hereby is clearly proved the absence of any difference in essence' (*Against Eunomius*, 7.1). Gregory of Nyssa, 'Against Eunomius', NPNF, Second Series, V, p. 193.

[173] Boris Bobrinskoy provides a helpful discussion about the importance of this dual movement of trinitarian grace in Bobrinskoy, 'Pneumatic Christology', pp. 49-65.

[174] See Basil, *DSS*, 18.44-47; Gregory of Nazianzus, *Oration*, 31.14. 'But Monarchy is that which we hold in honor. It is, however, a Monarchy that is not lim-

> When we speak of the dispensations made for man by our great God and Savior Jesus Christ, who will gainsay their having been accomplished through the grace of the Spirit? ... Or on the other hand the things done in the dispensation of the coming of our Lord in the flesh – all is through the Spirit. In the first place he was made an unction, and being inseparably present was with the very flesh of the Lord, according to that which is written, 'Upon whom thou shalt see the Spirit descending and remaining on Him, the same is' 'my beloved Son;' and 'Jesus of Nazareth' whom 'God anointed with the Holy Ghost.' After this every operation was wrought with the co-operation of the Spirit (Basil, *DSS*, 16.39).[175]

This text affirms two things. First, the Spirit has operated throughout history to accomplish God's plan.[176] Second, the Spirit mediated the Christ event. For example, the Spirit was the agent of Christ's incarnation,[177] and the descent of the Spirit testified to Christ's deity;[178] also, the Spirit anointed Christ's humanity for his salvific mis-

---

ited to one Person' (Gregory of Nazianzus, *Oration*, 29.2). Cited according to the translation of Charles Browne and James Swallow, Gregory of Nazianzus, 'Select Orations', NPNF, Second Series, VII, p. 301. Cf. Beeley, *Trinity and the Knowledge of God*, pp. 201-17; Norris and Gregory, *Faith Gives Fullness to Reasoning*, pp. 133-35.

[175] Basil, 'On the Spirit', NPNF, Second Series, VIII, p. 25. Cf. Gregory of Nazianzus, *Oration*, 31.29; Gregory of Nyssa, *Against Eunomius*, 2.2; Gregory of Nyssa, *On the Holy Spirit*, NPNF, Second Series, V, p. 321; Gregory of Nyssa, *On Not Three Gods: To Ablabius*, NPNF, Second Series, V, pp. 334-35. Cf. Norris and Gregory, *Faith Gives Fullness to Reasoning*, p. 209.

[176] Gregory of Nazianzus advocates a form of progressive revelation to account for the Holy Spirit's deity becoming an issue at this time (*Oration*, 31.25-29). Cf. Norris and Gregory, *Faith Gives Fullness to Reasoning*, pp. 205-209.

[177] 'That which is conceived in her, says the angel, "is of the Holy Ghost", and the Lord says "that which is born of the Spirit is spirit"' (Basil, *DSS*, 5.9). Basil, 'On the Spirit', NPNF, Second Series, VIII, p. 7. 'Is it Christ's advent? The Spirit is forerunner. Is there the incarnate presence? The Spirit is inseparable' (Basil, *DSS*, 19.49). Basil, 'On the Spirit', NPNF, Second Series, VIII, p. 31. Cf. Gregory of Nazianzus, *Oration*, 30.21; Gregory of Nyssa, *Against Eunomius*, 4.1.

[178] Cf. Basil, *DSS*, 12.28; 14.31; 15.35-36; Gregory of Nazianzus, *Oration*, 39.16. 'For the naming of Christ is the confession of the whole, showing forth as it does the God who gave, the Son who received, and the Spirit who is, the unction. So we have learned from Peter, in the Acts, of "Jesus of Nazareth whom God anointed with the Holy Ghost;" and in Isaiah, "The Spirit of the Lord is upon me, because the Lord hath anointed me;" and the Psalmist, "Therefore God, even thy God, hath anointed thee with the oil of gladness above thy fellows." Scripture, however, in the case of baptism, sometimes plainly mentions the

sion, so that every operation was accomplished with the Spirit: overcoming temptation in the wilderness, exorcisms, miracles, the resurrection, believers receiving remission of sins, and believers receiving the Spirit.[179]

Basil's Christology and pneumatology seem, therefore, to conjoin in a complementary fashion in salvific mission; in point of fact, Basil affirms that the same language Scripture uses to speak of the Son also speaks of the Spirit.[180] Wherefore, in the descending movement of grace, the Spirit dwells among believers as the Spirit of Christ sanctifying and anointing them.[181]

> The Spirit is frequently spoken of as the *place* of them that are being sanctified ... This is the special place and peculiar place of true worship; for it is said 'Take heed to thyself that thou offer not thy burnt offerings in every place ... but in the place the Lord thy God shall choose.' Now what is a spiritual burnt offering? 'The sacrifice of praise.' And in what place do we offer it? In the Holy Spirit. Where have we learnt this? From the Lord himself in the words 'The true worshippers shall worship the Father in spirit and in truth.' This place Jacob saw and said 'The Lord is in this place.' It follows that the Spirit is verily the place of saints and the saint is the proper place for the Spirit, offering himself as he does for the indwelling of God, and called God's Temple (Basil, *DSS*, 26.62).[182]

Spirit alone' (Basil, *DSS*, 12.28). Basil, 'On the Spirit', NPNF, Second Series, VIII, p. 18.

[179] See Basil, *DSS*, 16.39-40; 19.49. Cf. Basil's Homily on Ps. 44, Basil, *Exegetical Homilies*, FC, XLVI, 17.8, p. 289; Gregory of Nazianzus, *Oration*, 31.29; 41.5; 41.11; 30.21; Gregory of Nyssa, *Against Eunomius*, 2.2; McDonnell, *The Baptism of Jesus in the Jordan*, pp.68, 129-30.

[180] See Basil, *DSS*, 22.53; 21.52; 17.43; 18.46; 19.48. Cf. Gregory of Nyssa, *Against Eunomius*, 2.14. According to Basil, when the apostle Paul affirms that Christ speaks in him, it is the Spirit speaking mysteries (Basil, *DSS*, 26.62). 'The Holy Spirit is found at once in closest union; not subsequent in existence to the Son, as if the Son could be thought of as ever having been without the Spirit' (Gregory of Nyssa, *Against Eunomius*, 1.26). Nyssa, 'Against Eunomius', NPNF, Second Series, V, p. 70.

[181] 'He is moreover styled "Spirit of Christ," as being by nature closely related to Him. Wherefore, "If any man have not the Spirit of Christ, he is none of His"' (Basil, *DSS*, 18.46). Basil, 'On the Spirit', NPNF, Second Series, VIII, p. 29.

[182] Basil, 'On the Spirit', NPNF, Second Series, VIII, p. 39.

Here, Basil uses a spatial image to depict three salvific activities of the Spirit as the Spirit of Christ. First, the Spirit consecrates the place of sanctification in the believer's heart. Second, the Spirit is the place of true worship. Third, the Spirit becomes the place of the saint, and reciprocally the saint becomes the proper place of the Spirit because the believer becomes the dwelling place of God, the temple of God. So in this descending incarnational Christology which extends salvation – from the Father, through the Son, and by the Holy Spirit – to humans, the Spirit fulfills the salvific mission. Pentecost, then, becomes the purpose and goal of the incarnation.[183]

In the ascending movement of grace, the Spirit joins humans to the Son and through the Son to the Father, so that the knowledge of God ascends in this manner.

> The 'worship in the Spirit' suggests the idea of the operation of our intelligence being carried on in light ... Thus fitly and consistently do we behold the 'Brightness of the glory' of God by means of illumination of the Spirit, and by means of the 'Express Image' we are led up to Him of whom He is the Express Image and Seal, graven to the like (Basil, *DSS*, 26.64).[184]

This text suggests two things. First, worship in the Spirit positions and opens the human mind to divine illumination. Second, the Spirit initiates divine revelation. The Spirit, thus, becomes the indispensable prism through which humans can contemplate the divine Word, who is the image of the Father.

Cappadocian Christology is thoroughly pneumatic, and it directly opposes Apollinarian Christology. In the descending movement of grace, the Father sends the Son, and the Son becomes incarnate in the virgin's womb by the Spirit. Christ, then, is composed of dual natures, divine and human, in a single person. At the Jordan, the Spirit anoints Christ's human nature, so that the Son and Spirit function in perichoretic relationship to consummate the salvific mission; the Son and Spirit co-operate to accomplish all operations. After Christ's ascension, the Spirit returns at Pentecost as the Spirit

---

[183] Bobrinskoy, 'Pneumatic Christology', p. 55.
[184] Basil, 'On the Spirit', NPNF, Second Series, VIII, p. 40. Cf. Basil, *Letter*, 226.3; Gregory of Nyssa, *Against Eunomius*, 1.36; Gregory of Nyssa, *On the Holy Spirit*, NPNF, Second Series, V, p. 319.

of Christ to sanctify, empower, and indwell believers. The saint, accordingly, as the temple of God becomes the place of the Spirit, and the Spirit becomes the place of the saint: the place of worship and knowledge of God. In the ascending movement of grace, true worship ascends in the Spirit through the Son to the Father. In the Spirit worshippers' minds are illuminated and gain knowledge of the triune God. Whether descending to accomplish salvation or ascending in worship and knowledge of God, both *motifs* occur by and in the Spirit,[185] so the Spirit mediates Christ's identity and salvific mission. The Cappadocians, therefore, have constructed a Spirit Christology of pneumatic mediation set within a trinitarian structure that integrates Logos Christology.

Nestorius

Nestorius' teaching represents the consummate development of the Antiochian Syrian christological tradition extending from Eustathius of Antioch.[186] While serving as a presbyter in Antioch, Nestorius achieved acclaim as a preacher and exegete of Scripture which incited Theodosius II to appoint him bishop of Constantinople in 428. Unlike his only predecessor from this Syrian tradition to attain this

---

[185] Bobrinskoy, 'Pneumatic Christology', p. 56; Hildebrand, *Trinitarian Theology*, pp. 160-87; Meredith, *The Cappadocians*, pp. 33-35; Beeley, *Trinity and the Knowledge of God*, pp. 174-80.

[186] This trajectory is usually called the Antiochene tradition, but I have chosen to refer to it as the Antiochian Syrian tradition because a Greek tradition, through Malchion and the school of Lucian, also descended in Antioch as well. The Antiochian Syrian school of thought descended through Flavian of Antioch and Diodore of Tarsus. Diodore taught Theodore of Mopsuestia and John Chrysostom; then, those indebted to the teaching of Theodore were Andrew of Samosata, Nestorius, and Theodoret of Cyrus. Henceforth, when I refer to the Syrian christological tradition, I am accrediting this trajectory. Quasten, *Patrology*, III, pp. 397-98, 401, 424-25, 514; Sellers, *Two Ancient Christologies*, pp. 107-108; J.F. Bethune-Baker, *An Introduction to the Early History of Christian Doctrine: To the Time of the Council of Chalcedon* (London: Methuen, 11 edn, 1954), pp. 255-60. James Franklin Bethune-Baker, *Nestorius and his Teaching: A Fresh Examination of the Evidence* (Cambridge: Cambridge University Press, 1908), pp. 2-4; Schaff, *History*, III, pp. 715-16. Friedrich Loofs, however, for chronological reasons does not think that Nestorius was a pupil of Theodore. Friedrich Loofs, *Nestorius and His Place in the History of Christian Doctrine* (Cambridge: Cambridge University Press, 1914), p. 36. Since these theologians are similar in thought, the survey will examine Nestorius' doctrine and Spirit christological references and note the corresponding passages in the writings of other Antiochenes.

prestigious position, John Chrysostom (398–404), who shied away from using the Constantinople pulpit to preach this school's doctrine, Nestorius boldly and frequently expounded its christological tradition.[187] Nestorius, accordingly, sharply distinguished between Christ's divine and human natures which ultimately led to Nestorius' critique of using *Theotokos* as an epithet for Mary. Forthwith, Cyril of Alexandria took umbrage at Nestorius' remarks.[188] The upshot of the ensuing controversy was Nestorius' deposition at the Council of Ephesus (431) and ultimately the demise of the Syrian christological influence.[189]

A copious writer, Nestorius produced sermons, letters, and treatises.[190] Because Theodosius II in 435 commanded the destruction of Nestorius' writings, most of them perished in flames; nevertheless, some works have survived. Friedrich Loofs in 1905 gathered and edited the known extant fragments of these works; among the

---

[187] Chrysostom focused on reforming municipal and clerical corruption, but Nestorius attacked Arians, Pneumatomachians, Novatians, Quartodecimans, and anything he considered contrary to sound doctrine. Chrysostom also suffered deposition at the Synod of Oak (403). Two points are noteworthy. First, Chrysostom in 402 presided over a synod in Constantinople to examine charges brought against the bishop of Alexandria, Theophilus, by the monks of the Nitrian desert. Theophilus turned the tables on Chrysostom by fabricating 29 charges against Chrysostom and successfully deposed Chrysostom at the Synod of Oak. Second, Theophilus was succeeded by his nephew Cyril of Alexandria. These points are noteworthy because a similar situation developed between Cyril and Nestorius. Quasten, *Patrology*, III, pp. 100-101, 116-18, 426-28.

[188] Actually, the dispute probably did not begin over doctrinal issues. According to Henry Chadwick, four Alexandrians complained to Theodosius II about the way their bishop, Cyril, had treated them. Consequently, the emperor commissioned Nestorius, who served as bishop of Constantinople, to investigate these charges; therefore, Cyril sent agents to Constantinople to stir up the *Theotokos* issue to avert attention from him. Chadwick, furthermore, suggested that the doctrines of the Eucharist and atonement were more likely concerns that Cyril had with Antiochene Christology. Henry Chadwick, 'Eucharist and Christology in the Nestorian Controversy', *JTS* 2 (1951), pp. 145-64. Cf. Bethune-Baker, *Nestorius*, pp. 6-21; Loofs, *Nestorius*, pp. 18-22.

[189] Davis, *Ecumenical Councils*, pp. 134-68; 'The Third Ecumenical Council of Ephesus', NPNF, Second Series, XIV, pp. 191-242; Bethune-Baker, *Christian Doctrine*, pp. 262-74; Schaff, *History*, III, pp. 716-29; Seeberg and Hay, *History* I, pp. 261-66. According to Robert Sellers, 'the downfall of the Antiochene school is to be regarded as on to the tragedies in the history of the Early Church'. Sellers, *Two Ancient Christologies*, p. 108.

[190] For overviews of Nestorius' writings, see Quasten, *Patrology*, III, pp. 515-19; Loofs, *Nestorius*, pp. 1-6; Bethune-Baker, *Nestorius*, pp. 22-26.

fifteen letters he lists, ten are virtually complete.[191] Also, an entire treatise preserved in a Syriac translation, the *Bazaar of Heracleides*, was discovered in 1895.[192] After the Council of Chalcedon (451), to ensure its publication Nestorius pseudonymously wrote this treatise in the form of a dialogue between the author and an Egyptian named Sophronius.[193]

The content of the *Bazaar of Heracleides* consists primarily of doctrinal and historical emphases which shade off into one another.[194] The doctrinal attention is two-fold. First, it consists of attacking the christological views of the Jews, Manichaeans, Paul of Samosata, Photinus, Arians, Apollinarius, and Cyril of Alexandria. Second, Nestorius defends his Christology which divides into two parts: denying the charge that he teaches two Sons in Christ and setting forth his own views. The arguments of the historical sections are two-fold. First, Nestorius criticizes his deposition at Ephesus and describes how Cyril through bribery and violence gained episcopal and imperial support for the verdict. Second, Nestorius contends that since his views correspond to that of Flavian of Constantinople and Pope Leo I, the Council of Chalcedon vindicates his Christolo-

---

[191] Friedrich Loofs, *Nestoriana: die Fragmente des Nestorius gesammelt, untersucht und herausgegeben* (Halle: Max Niemeyer, 1905).

[192] For discussions of the discovery and publication of this document, see Nestorius, *The Bazaar of Heracleides* (trans. Godfrey Rolles Driver and Leonard Hodgson; Eugene, OR: Wipf and Stock, 2002 repr.; Oxford: Oxford University Press, 1925), pp. ix-xvi; Bethune-Baker, *Nestorius*, pp. 27-41; Loofs, *Nestorius*, pp. 6-12; Quasten, *Patrology*, III, p. 516.

[193] The provenance is probably from Nestorius' place of exile in Egypt, and the date can safely be placed in 451 or 452. Nestorius, *The Bazaar of Heracleides*, p. x. There is some controversy concerning the authorship, date, and provenance of the first 125 pages of the *Bazaar of Heracleides*. On the one hand, Luise Abramowski denies Nestorius' authorship of these pages in question; she attributes authorship to a devoted disciple of Nestorius writing in the monastery of Acoimetai at Constantinople sometime between 523–33. Luise Abramowski, *Untersuchungen zum Liber Heraclidis des Nestorius* (Louvain: CSChO 242, 1963). On the other hand, Robert Chesnut argues against Abranowski's conclusions and provides plausible explanations for his position which affirms Nestorius as the author and suggesting that the date for this section of the document may be as early as 437–38. Robert Chesnut, 'The Two Prosopa in Nestorius' Bazaar of Heracleides', *JTS* 29 (1978), pp. 392-98.

[194] In Nestorius, *The Bazaar of Heracleides*, the doctrinal material can be found on pages 7-95; 143-264; 294-328. The historical sections are found on pages 96-142; 265-93; 329-80.

gy.[195] The survey will focus on this treatise and note the corresponding texts of interest and Spirit christological passages among the extant fragments and letters.

In order to give Nestorius a fair hearing, it will be helpful to clear the ground by examining three terms central to his Christology: ousia, hypostasis, and prosopon. First, for Nestorius, an ousia (nature) can exist either incomplete or complete. Through a natural composition two incomplete natures can commingle and form a new nature; for example, the incomplete natures of soul and body unite to form a complete human nature. Second, Nestorius employs the term hypostasis to designate a complete nature. Third, prosopon depicts the distinguishing properties that complete a nature, so that it is identified as a hypostasis; each hypostasis is recognized and characterized by its prosopon. So according to Nestorius, in Christ two prosopa, human and divine, exist in prosopic union, but their union neither produces a new hypostasis nor mixes the hypostases. Nestorius, thus, rejects Cyril's natural or hypostatic union of one incarnate divine nature in Christ, which for Nestorius smacks of Apollinarianism, and charges Cyril with confusing Christ's dual natures and mutilating the human nature.[196]

This is the basis of Nestorius' critique of applying the title *Theotokos* to Mary. In addressing this issue Nestorius refers to Mt. 1.20

---

[195] An examination of the *Bazaar of Heracleides* has led some scholars to a revision of the common consensus regarding Nestorius' Christology. For a comparison of Nestorius' christological views with Flavian and Pope Leo, see Bethune-Baker, *Nestorius*, pp. 189-96. 'From all this it seems clear that Nestorius is hardly deserving of the title "Nestorian", and that this is a legitimate conclusion is borne out by statements of his which show that for him Jesus Christ is very God incarnate.' Sellers, *Two Ancient Christologies*, pp. 164-66. For an examination of the question was Nestorius a Nestorian, see Carl E. Braaten, 'Modern Interpretations of Nestorius', *CH* 32 (1963), pp. 251-67. Friedrich Loofs maintains that Nestorius' Christology can be reconciled with Pope Leo's letter and the Chalcedonian definition, and he argues that the Syrian tradition Nestorius represents shares a similar tradition with the Western tradition which Tertullian represents. Nonetheless, Loofs has agreed that the Cyrillian revised and influenced christological definition held by the Second Council of Constantinople (553) has effectively excluded the views of this Syrian tradition. Loofs, *Nestorius*, pp. 51-70. Cf. Harnack, *Dogma*, IV, pp. 180-90; Kelly, *Doctrines*, pp. 310-17.

[196] Nestorius, *The Bazaar of Heracleides*, pp. 9, 14-18, 24-28, 33-43, 80, 84-86, 154-66, 177-79, 227-46, 294, 300-301, 303-304, 310, 314, 325-35, 402-10. Cf. Nestorius, Fragment 300; Fragment 306; González, *Christian Thought*, I, pp. 360-64; Chesnut, 'Two Prosopa', pp. 399-409; Bethune-Baker, *Nestorius*, pp. 47-54, 148-88; Sellers, *Two Ancient Christologies*, pp. 146-51, 156-62, 186-88.

and the central Scripture in Cyril's doctrine of incarnation, Jn 1.14.[197]

> The Fathers said in their laying down of the Faith not that he was born of the Holy Spirit and the Virgin Mary, but that he was made flesh, in order that they might not say that the Holy Spirit was Father or that which was created [was] Son, but rather that he was made flesh by the Holy Spirit and of the Virgin Mary, in order that they might attach 'became' to the flesh, because he was made flesh … I say that the flesh came into being of the Virgin Mary [and] appertained not unto God the Word; for I confess him neither made nor come into being nor created.[198]

This text elucidates three cogent points regarding Nestorius' view of the activity of the Spirit and the Spirit's relationship with the Son in the incarnation. First, Nestorius attests the Holy Spirit's agency in the incarnation, but he carefully rejects any notion that the Holy Spirit is the divine Son's Father.[199] Second, Nestorius stresses that God the Logos was not born of Mary. Third, the phrase 'became flesh' in Jn 1.14 means that Christ's human nature came into being by the Holy Spirit in Mary's womb. In other words, since Nestorius acknowledges that the Son exists in eternal triune relationship with the Father and Holy Spirit, he rejects any christological language alluding to the Son coming into being during the incarnation; Mary is not the mother of God the Son.[200]

---

[197] In contrast, Phil. 2.5-11 occupies the central place in Nestorius' Christology. Nestorius, *The Bazaar of Heracleides*, pp. 166-70; Sellers, *Two Ancient Christologies*, pp. 117-18; Pelikan, *Christian Tradition*, I, pp. 255-56.

[198] Cited according to the translation of G.R. Driver and Leonard Hodgson, Nestorius, *The Bazaar of Heracleides*, pp. 198-99.

[199] Cf. Fragment 271; Fragments. 262–64; Nestorius, *The Bazaar of Heracleides*, pp. 387, 389-91.

[200] Nestorius, *The Bazaar of Heracleides*, pp. 242-44; Nestorius, Fragment 264. Cf. Bethune-Baker, *Nestorius*, pp. 55-68. According to Theodore of Mopsuestia,

> When they ask whether Mary is a man's mother or God's mother, we must say, 'Both,' the one by the nature of the thing, the other in virtue of relation. Mary was a man's mother by nature, since what was in her womb was a man, just as it was also a man who came forth from her womb. But she is God's mother, since God was in the man who was fashioned – not circumscribed in him by nature but existing in him according to the dispensation of his will. Therefore, it is right to say both, but not in the same sense. God the Logos did not, like the man, begin to exist when he was in the womb, for he existed before every creature. Therefore, it is right to say both, and each in an appropriate sense (Theodore, *On the Incarnation*, 12.11).

This sharp distinction of two prosopa eventually led to the accusation that Nestorius taught two Sons existed in Christ;[201] nonetheless, Nestorius steadfastly denied this charge.[202] Instead, Nestorius teaches one Son in Christ because deity has voluntarily united – in will, operation, and revelation – with human nature, so that the Logos indwells the humanity.[203]

> In Christ – all the [properties] of God the Word whose nature is impassible and is immortal and eternal, and all the [properties] of the humanity, which are / a nature mortal and passible and created, and those of the union and of the incarnation since the womb and since the incarnation – are referred to one *prosopon*, to the common *prosopon* of our Lord Jesus Christ ... For until his

---

Cited according to the translation of Richard Norris, *The Christological Controversy*, pp. 121-22. It seems that Martin Luther after objectively examining Nestorius' Christology decided that Nestorius had been misrepresented. According to Luther, Nestorius did not teach two sons, but one Christ; also, he rightly taught that the Son was eternally begotten of the Father and man was born of Mary: Mary did not bear the Godhead. See Loofs, *Nestorius*, pp. 9-10. Regarding Nestorius' affirmation of the Trinity, see Nestorius, *The Bazaar of Heracleides*, pp. 14, 25, 37, 160, 234-35.

[201] Nestorius, *The Bazaar of Heracleides*, pp. 152-53. Cf. Sellers, *Two Ancient Christologies*, pp. 190-200.

[202] Nestorius, *The Bazaar of Heracleides*, pp. 47-50, 146, 160, 189-91, 196, 209-10, 215, 227, 237-38, 295-302, 314, 317. Cf. Nestorius, Fragments 297; 302; Bethune-Baker, *Nestorius*, pp. 82-100; Sellers, *Two Ancient Christologies*, pp. 162-66.

[203] Nestorius, *The Bazaar of Heracleides*, pp. 23, 37, 53-62, 81, 89, 156-59, 163-64, 172, 179, 181-82, 207, 218-19, 227, 231-33, 245-48, 260-61; Nestorius, Fragment 256. Cf. Theodore of Mopsuestia, *On the Incarnation*, 7.2; 7.3; 7.4; John Chrysostom, *Hom. Matt.* 4.6; Sellers, *Two Ancient Christologies*, pp. 151-52, 155-56; Loofs, *Nestorius*, pp. 40-49.

> There was born of the Virgin Mary a man, the Son of God, since this humanity was the Son of God by union with the Son and not by nature? For by the union God the Word made these [properties] of the flesh his own, not that the divinity was born in the birth of the flesh, nor again that the flesh was born naturally in the birth of the divinity, but [that] by the union with the flesh God is called flesh and the flesh by union with the Son, God the Word, is called Son (Nestorius, *The Bazaar of Heracleides*, p. 191).

In this sense, then, Nestorius can concede the term *Theotokos* to Mary. He does not reject applying *Theotokos* to Mary, but he wants the term to be properly understood: Mary did not give birth to God, but because God can properly be applied to the temple, Mary can be called *Theotokos*. Nestorius, however, prefers the term *Christotokos*. Sellers, *Two Ancient Christologies*, pp. 171-75. 'Nestorius found it possible to reconcile himself to Theotokos, not only because there was a sense in which he could accept its orthodoxy, but perhaps also because its position in Christian worship was so firmly established as to be unassailable.' Pelikan, *Christian Tradition*, I, pp. 242, 252-53.

incarnation, they taught us everything in terms of God the Word and after he was made flesh they speak of this union which [proceeded] from the Holy Spirit and the Virgin Mary.[204]

According to this text, in the christological union which issues from the Holy Spirit and Mary the properties of each prosopon is attributed to a common prosopon, Jesus Christ. This union does not occur to complete either nature, as the soul and body complete human nature; rather, each prosopon shares commonly in the one prosopon.

> And for this reason the divinity also on account of the union is named Christ after the humanity which was anointed, and there exists / of two natures, of divinity and of humanity, Christ, one Son, one Lord; through the union of the divinity and of the humanity the same is Son and Lord and God.[205]

Two noteworthy points arise from this text. First, because of the prosopic union, divine and human designations are common to the one prosopon: Jesus, Christ, Son, Lord, and God. Second, the Holy Spirit anointed Christ's human nature, not the divine nature.[206]

Nestorius' ability to distinguish between Christ's human and divine natures enabled him to allow for the unique growth, development, and anointing of Christ's human nature.[207] Not that Nestorius

---

[204] Nestorius, *The Bazaar of Heracleides*, p. 171. Cf. Nestorius, *The Bazaar of Heracleides*, pp. 207-12, 313-14, 319-24. According to Nestorius, the Logos retained impassibility and the human nature was passible and capable of suffering. Pelikan, *Christian Tradition*, I, pp. 231-32.

[205] Nestorius, *The Bazaar of Heracleides*, p. 301. Cf. Nestorius, *The Bazaar of Heracleides*, p. 58; Theodore of Mopsuestia, *On the Incarnation*, 5.1.

[206] This anointing of the Spirit that Christ received at the Jordan event revealed the deity of Christ. Nestorius, *The Bazaar of Heracleides*, pp. 51, 65. Cf. John Chrysostom, *Hom. Jo.* 17.2-3; 78.2; *Hom. Matt.* 11.6; 12.2.

[207] Albeit there was a natural physical and psychological development, because of its prosopic union with deity, the human prosopon uniquely advanced in moral development, wisdom, and other attributes beyond other humans. Nestorius, *The Bazaar of Heracleides*, pp. 200-202, 243. Cf. Pelikan, *Christian Tradition*, I, pp. 251, 253-54.

> For he had union with the Logos straightway from the beginning when he was formed in his mother's womb. And when he arrived at maturity, when there comes a natural birth in human persons a judgment as to what is good and what is not (rather even before this age), he demonstrated a much quicker and more acute power of judgment in this regard than others ... And it was suitable that he should have something beyond the ordinary in his human qualities, because he was not born according to the common nature of human

taught that Jesus was a mere human anointed by the Spirit, like the Hebrew prophets; he unambiguously rejected this proposition.[208] Nonetheless, even though Cyril ascribed Christ's miracles to the Holy Spirit's activity, in his ninth anathema against Nestorius at the Council of Ephesus, he leveled this charge. Nestorius responded with his own counter anathema.

> If anyone says that the form of a servant is of like nature with the Holy Ghost, and not rather that it owes its union with the Word which has existed since the conception, to his mediation, by which it works miraculous healings among men, and possesses the power of expelling demons; let him be anathema.[209]

---

beings, of a man and a woman, but was fashioned by the divine energy of the Spirit (Theodore of Mopsuestia, *On the Incarnation*, 7.3).

Norris, *The Christological Controversy*, pp. 117-18. Cf. Chrysostom, *Hom. Heb.* 5.1-2. For an examination of Theodore's Christology, see Francis Aloysius Sullivan, *The Christology of Theodore of Mopsuestia* (Romae: Apud Aedes Universitatis Gregoriana, 1956), pp. 197-288; Norris, *Manhood and Christ*, pp. 123-288.

[208] Nestorius, *The Bazaar of Heracleides*, pp. 51-53, 64-65, 213-204. Cf. Bethune-Baker, *Nestorius*, pp. 126-27; Cyril's seventh anathema against Nestorius, 'Ephesus', NPNF, Second Series, XIV, pp. 213-14; Nestorius, *The Bazaar of Heracleides*, pp. 43-47. 'He was counted worthy of higher gifts than the rest of humanity as the special endowment of the union became his. Thus he was the first to be found worthy of the indwelling of the Spirit in a degree surpassing the rest of humanity' (Theodore of Mopsuestia, *On the Incarnation*, 7.6). Norris, *The Christological Controversy*, pp. 119-20. Cf. Chrysostom, *Hom. Heb.* 3.2; 15.4; Chrysostom, *Hom. Jo.*, 30.2; McDonnell, *The Baptism of Jesus in the Jordan*, pp. 39, 70-71, 213-15, 225-27; McDonnell and Montague, *Christian Initiation*, pp. 259-82.

[209] Cited according to the translation of Henry R. Percival, 'Ephesus', NPNF, Second Series, XIV, p. 215. Cf. Chrysostom, *Hom. Jo.* 5.1. This is Nestorius' counter anathema to Cyril's ninth anathema against Nestorius which states,

> If any man shall say that the one Lord Jesus Christ was glorified by the Holy Ghost, so that he used through him a power not his own and from him received power against unclean spirits and power to work miracles before men and shall not rather confess that it was his own Spirit through which he worked these divine signs; let him be anathema ('Ephesus', NPNF, Second Series, XIV, pp. 214-15).

Nestorius indicates that Cyril often misquoted him. Nestorius, *The Bazaar of Heracleides*, pp. 295-309. Those from the Syrian tradition charged Cyril with contradicting himself; at times Cyril said that Christ worked miracles by the Holy Spirit, and at other times he denied the Spirit's agency in these miracles. For example, in his letter to Nestorius Cyril states, 'For as man he was anointed with us, although it is he himself who gives the Spirit ... he used the Holy Spirit to show forth his own divinity in his mighty works'. 'Ephesus', NPNF, Second Series, XIV, pp. 202, 204. Theodoret of Cyrus countered Cyril's anathema in favor of Nestorius' position. 'Ephesus', NPNF, Second Series, XIV, pp. 215-16. Cf. Bethune-Baker,

Several conclusions can be gleaned from this text. First, Nestorius avows the reality of Christ's human nature which he refers to as the form of a servant; although in union with deity, it remains genuinely human and unconfused with the divine nature.[210] Second, the Holy Spirit is the agent of the human nature's conception, and the Spirit mediates the union of the two prosopa in Jesus Christ. Third, the Spirit anoints Christ's humanity to heal the sick and exorcise demons.[211] Since Cyril's dispute with Nestorius focused on the issues of the christological union and the anointing of the Spirit, Spirit christological issues were central to this controversy.

The pneumatological basis for this Syrian christological line of development is evident in Nestorius' teachings regarding Christ's incarnation and anointing. In the incarnation the Holy Spirit conceives, forms, and unites Christ's human nature to God the Son in Mary's womb. Nestorius, however, firmly attests that neither is the Holy Spirit the Son's Father, nor is Mary the mother of God; the Father, Son, and Holy Spirit already exist in consubstantial triune unity.[212] In Christ, although remaining distinct, each prosopon shares commonly with the other in the prosopic union. The Holy Spirit mediates this voluntary union of two complete natures, so that this indwelling of deity in humanity is aptly called Christ. Because Nestorius preserves the distinction of natures, he allows space for the human nature to receive the anointing of the Spirit. Nestorius' Spirit Christology, therefore, delineates a paradigm of pneumatic mediation which integrates with a Son of God Christology.

Christian Doctrine, pp. 265-66. Speaking about John Cassian's role in interpreting Nestorius' Christology for Leo the Archdeacon of Roman, Aloys Grillmeier states,

> The whole complex of the biblical-messianic spirit-christology is something which he will not recognize as such. He will not concede that Jesus as a man needs to be filled with the Holy Spirit, because in this way Christ is represented as weak and in need of help ... Through fear of teaching two persons, he assigns to the divinity of Jesus everything that falls within the sphere of the biblical-messianic grace of the Spirit. In so doing Cassian draws a very empty picture of the humanity of Jesus (Grillmeier, *Christian Tradition*, I, pp. 470-71).

[210] The natures are united not mixed. Nestorius, Fragments 314; 289; 394. Cf. Theodore of Mopsuestia, *On the Incarnation*, 5.1; 7.7; Chrysostom, *Hom. Phil.* 7; Chrysostom, *Hom. Jo.* 11.2; Pelikan, *Christian Tradition*, I, pp. 254-55.

[211] Cf. Chrysostom, *Hom. Act.* 1.

[212] Cf. Chrysostom, *Hom. Jo.* 52.3; 54.2; 75.2; 78.1.

Furthermore, Nestorius and Cyril represent diverse models of the christological union.

Conclusion

Several conclusions can be drawn from the foregoing discussion. Methodologically, three pneumatic christological paradigms emerge among these writers: (1) pneumatic inspiration, (2) pneumatic mediation, and (3) pneumatic incarnation. The Spirit christological method of pneumatic inspiration continues through Photinus: Jesus was a human uniquely anointed by the Spirit. Although the proponents of pneumatic incarnation congruently employ Logos and Spirit as synonymous designations to identify the divine element incarnate in Christ, some distinction subsists among them. Apollinarius explicitly expresses triune distinctions yet refers to the mode of incarnation as a union of divine Spirit and flesh. Eustathius, likewise, recognizes trinitarian designations but fails to clarify them. Marcellus, however, allows for only economic trinitarian distinctions during the salvific mission of the second economy, while Aphrahat seems to present his Spirit Christology in a ditheistic framework. The exponents of pneumatic mediation unequivocally agreed concerning the Logos becoming incarnate in Christ, but diversity arose among them regarding the Logos' deity and the Spirit's role in Christ's mission. Arius denied the Logos' deity, so through pneumatic inspiration during the salvific mission the Spirit's anointing advanced Christ in grace and deified him. Cyril of Jerusalem, Athanasius, the Cappadocian Fathers, and Nestorius, conversely, attested to trinitarian distinctions existing in the one divine essence which is Spirit, the divine Logos becoming incarnate in Christ, and the reciprocal relationship of the Son and Spirit in salvific mission, affirming the compatibility of their paradigm of Spirit Christology with Logos Christology.

Advocates of pneumatic incarnation and mediation paradigms, fundamentally, concur regarding at least three issues. First, acknowledging Arius as an aberration among them, they unanimously oppose Arian theology. Second, they reject Photinus' model of pneumatic inspiration. Third, these writers designate the divine essence Spirit and identify Christ's divine nature as Spirit.

Spirit Christology was central to the issues debated at the Councils of Nicea and Constantinople I. Spirit Christology, therefore, acted as a catalyst in the development of Christian doctrine; indeed, significant doctrinal developments occurred in Christian theology's task of proclaiming Christ's deity in a monotheistic framework, especially in nomenclature. Arius was the impetus of this development. Against Arius and his supporters, the Council of Nicea decreed the Son's consubstantial (ὁμοούσιος) nature with the Father. The controversy, nevertheless, raged for many more years because of the equivocal nature of the language; common terms were used to express Christ's deity, but their meaning remained ambivalent, serving only to augment the discussion. The Cappadocian Fathers contributed to the debate by clarifying and distinguishing between the terms ousia (οὐσία) and hypostasis (ὑπόστασις) which had been used synonymously. Accordingly, they designated ousia as divine essence and hypostasis as mode of being or person, so that God is one divine ousia existing as three divine hypostases in divine relationship as Father, Son, and Holy Spirit. The clarification of these terms contributed to the triumph of the Nicene homoousios theology and the Cappadocian position at the Council of Constantinople (381). With this development in nomenclature, Christ's deity can be proclaimed within a monotheistic framework: the Father, Son, and Holy Spirit are consubstantial in divine essence, which is Spirit.

Two consequent doctrinal issues emanated from these discussions of Christ's person: (1) deity's relationship with human nature, and (2) the Spirit anointing Christ. Regarding the first matter, four patterns of thought emerged. First, Photinus asserted that Christ possessed a human soul, but deity was not incarnated in Christ; Christ was a uniquely born human adopted by God into deity. Second, Arius and Apollinarius denied that Christ possessed a human soul; instead, they both agreed that the divine Logos functioned as the rational element in Christ, so that the Logos suffered in Christ. The diversity between Arius and Apollinarius regarded Christ's divine nature. Whereas Arius repudiated the Logos' divine nature, Apollinarius asserted one incarnate divine nature in Christ. Third, Eustathius, Marcellus, Aphrahat, Cyril of Jerusalem, and Nestorius, advocated the union of two distinct natures in Christ, divine and human; the human nature consisting of a body and a rational soul.

This distinction of divine and human natures allowed the immutable deity to indwell Christ's humanity, as in a temple, and not to suffer; the human nature was subject to change and suffering. Fourth, Athanasius, and the Cappadocian Fathers accentuated the unity of Christ's incarnate nature: the Logos became flesh. Some dissimilarity, however, inhered among them. Although Athanasius did not concentrate attention on Christ's soul, the Cappadocians for soteriological purposes professed the distinction of divine and human natures: what was not assumed was not healed. Of course, the latter two patterns stood together in opposing the former models.

Concerning the Spirit anointing Christ, two basic methods emerged. First, Eustathius, Marcellus, Aphrahat, Cyril of Jerusalem, and Nestorius advocated a union of deity and humanity that distinctly preserved the human rational element, so that the Holy Spirit anointed Christ's human nature: soul and body.[213] Second, Athanasius and the Cappadocians maintained that the Logos became flesh, the human soul being assumed into the Logos. Since the Logos functioned as the rational element in Christ, and, the Logos and Spirit being inseparably united, the Spirit is the Spirit of the Son, the Spirit anointed Christ's flesh.[214] At various times skirmishes occurred between these christological heritages; great contention, however, erupted between them when Cyril of Alexandria began to beat Nestorius with the *Theotokos* cudgel. The ensuing conflict between these traditions played itself out through the christological councils of the fifth and sixth centuries.

---

[213] Adamantius (*Dialogue* 5.11) and Diodore of Tarsus supported this form of Spirit Christology. For an examination of primary texts and Diodore's Christology, see Sullivan, *Theodore*, pp. 172-96. Of course, Photinus' view was unacceptable to the proponents of this method.

[214] Ephrem the Syrian supported this form of Spirit Christology (Ephrem, *Hymns on the Faith*, 10.17; 40.3; *Hymns for the Feast of the Epiphany*, 3.1; *Hymns on Virginity*, 4.8). Apollinarius and Arius also fit into this group. Apollinarius carried this method to an extreme conclusion; therefore, he was rejected by the moderate proponents of this method. Of course, Arius' extreme form of Logos Christology was also unacceptable to the proponents of this method.

7

WESTERN WRITERS

Although some variations existed, Spirit Christology appeared more structured and settled among Western writers of the church than in the East, owing to the christological legacy they inherited from Tertullian.[1] According to Tertullian, the Logos eternally existed with the Father and Holy Spirit, a distinct person in relationship but one in substance (*Prax.* 2) which is Spirit; therefore, being divine Spirit, the Logos became incarnated in Mary's womb (*Prax.* 7), receiving flesh from her by mediation of the Holy Spirit (*Prax.* 26). Regarding Christ's human nature, Tertullian affirmed a genuine and complete human nature, body and soul, in the one person of Christ (*Prax.* 21; 27; *Carn. Chr.* 1; 5; 9); in fact, Christ's human soul was a salvific necessity for humanity's redemption (*Carn. Chr.* 10–13). Tertullian's distinction of natures in Christ, also, allowed space for the Spirit to anoint Christ's human nature (*Prax.* 29). Following Tertullian, then, Western Spirit Christology was structured around a paradigm of pneumatic mediation.

---

[1] According to J.N.D. Kelly, the Christology of the West follows Tertullian:

In general they reproduce the framework of ideas, and even the formulae, inherited from Tertullian. If they seem to lack the speculative interest of the East, this is to some extent explained by the remarkable success with which Tertullian's theory held both the aspects which reflection was showing to be necessary to a sound Christololgy in balance (Kelly, *Doctrines*, p. 334).

Cf. Kelly, *Doctrines*, pp. 150-52; González, *Christian Thought*, I, pp. 326-27.

Hilary of Poitiers

The writings of Hilary, who was elected bishop of Poitiers around 350, seemed to bridge the West and East.[2] With the approval of Constantius, a synod convened at Béziers (356) to settle a dispute between Hilary, who supported Athanasius and the Nicene position, and his Arian adversaries;[3] the synod's decision to send Hilary into exile at Phrygia was a defining moment in Hilary's theological development. In Eastern exile Hilary learned the Greek language, grasped the complexities of the Arian controversy, and found friendship among the Homoiousians. In fact, Hilary was among the ranks of the Homoiousians at Seleucia (359) and accompanied them to Constantinople to present to Constantius the results of the synod.[4] So while Hilary's theological foundations lay in the Latin West, he became well acquainted with the issues of Eastern theology and convinced of two doctrinal positions: (1) orthodox Christology required distance from both Arius' position and Sabellianism, and (2) the Nicean Homoousios position and the Homoiousian response were concordant solutions to the Arian argument.[5]

---

[2] Hilary's writings consist of doctrinal works, historical works, exegetical works, and hymns. For overviews of Hilary's writings, see Quasten, *Patrology*, IV, pp. 39-54; Hanson, *Christian Doctrine of God*, pp. 468-71.

[3] In 350 Constans was killed in an insurrection led by Magnentius. Constantius decisively defeated Magnentius in battle at Mursa in 351. Valens who was bishop of Mursa announced to Constantius the victory, claiming that an angel had given this good news to him in a vision; thus, Constantius received this as a sign of divine favor, and his allegiance to Valens and his Arian proclivities were formed. In 350 the war ended with Magnentius' suicide leaving Constantius as the sole ruler of the Roman world. Since Valens' loyalty to Constantius had previously been demonstrated, and Constantius suspected Athanasius of being friendly with Magnentius, Constantius naturally took Valens' side against Athanasius as well as any who supported him. Frend, *Christianity*, pp. 533-37. Cf. Mark Weedman, *The Trinitarian Theology of Hilary of Poitiers* (VCSup 89; Leiden: E.J. Brill, 2007), pp. 44-49; Carl L. Beckwith, *Hilary of Poitiers on the Trinity: From De fide to De Trinitate* (OECS; Oxford: Oxford University Press, 2008), pp. 30-53.

[4] For information about Hilary's life, see Hanson, *Christian Doctrine of God*, pp. 459-68; Quasten, *Patrology*, IV, pp. 36-38; Hilary, *The Trinity*, FC, XXV, pp. v-vii; Hilary, 'On the Trinity', NPNF, Second Series, IX, pp. i-lvii; Schaff, *History*, III, pp. 959-61; Weedman, *Trinitarian Theology*, pp. 3-22; Beckwith, *Trinity*, pp. 6-11.

[5] This is evident in Hilary's work *De Synodis* (359) which he wrote in preparation for the dual councils of Ariminum and Seleucia. This work consists of two sections: (1) historical, and (2) theological. The first section recounts and assesses several previous councils and creeds: the Sirmium Creed (357) and the 12 anathemas against it produced by the synod of Ancyra (358), the meaning and similarity of the words essence and substance, the Dedication Creed of Antioch (341),

Hilary integrated these positions into his doctrinal work *The Trinity* which consisted of 12 books.[6] Book one introduces the reader to the document's structure and the author's purpose for writing: refuting Arian and Sabellian doctrines.[7] The remaining books of the treatise naturally fall into three sections. Books 2–3 take up the issue of the Son's divine status in relation to the Father, affirming the eternal generation of the Son from the Father and the triune nature of God. Books 4–7 present Arius' profession of faith, which he sent to Alexander of Alexandria, and offer a rebuttal from Scripture.[8] Books 8–12 examine various Arian arguments, which assert the Son's subordination to the Father, and attempt to confute them. The document concludes by attesting to the triune role of the Holy Spirit (*Trin.* 12.55–57).[9]

Hilary uses several Spirit christological texts to support his argument. For instance, Hilary addresses the Arian assertion that the Son possesses a creaturely nature inferior to the Father.

---

the Creed produced by the synod of Philippopolis (343), and the formula drawn up at Sirmium (351) against Photinus. In the theological section, he discusses the possible meanings of the word ὁμοούσιος. Then, appealing to the Western bishops, he sought to prove that, properly understood, ὁμοιούσιος leads to ὁμοούσιος. For an examination of Hilary's *De Synodis* in light of Basil of Ancyra's influence on Hilary, see Weedman, *Trinitarian Theology*, pp. 93-115.

[6] Hilary probably wrote this document during his exile in Phrygia around 356–60. A question remains, however, about the date and provenance of the first three books. It is possible that Hilary began composing these books as a single document known as *De Fide* before he went into exile and finished it in exile before he wrote *De Synodis* (353–59). Concerning these issues, see Beckwith, *Trinity*, pp. 71-150; Quasten, *Patrology*, IV, pp. 39-40; Hilary, *The Trinity*, FC, XXV, pp. vii-viii; Hanson, *Christian Doctrine of God*, p. 471; Weedman, *Trinitarian Theology*, pp. 80-86.

[7] This work was explicitly written for the purpose of refuting Arian and Sabellian doctrines (*Trin.* 1.16–19; 2.4–23). Cf. Hilary, *The Trinity*, FC, XXV, pp. viii-xv. According to Justo González, these twelve books 'clearly reflect the influences that he received during his exile in the East. His discussion of the Trinity has no great originality, and its importance lies rather in having offered to the Latin-speaking world a treatise that summarized the issues at stake in the Arian controversy and the arguments in favor of the Nicene faith'. González, *Christian Thought*, I, p. 327.

[8] Hilary presents Arius' profession of faith in 4.3–21 and repeats it in 6.1–22. Philippians ch. 2 plays an important role in Hilary's exegesis. For an analysis of Hilary's hermeneutic, see Weedman, *Trinitarian Theology*, pp. 119-35.

[9] Hilary, 'Trinity', NPNF, Second Series, IX, pp. 32-39; Quasten, *Patrology*, IV, pp. 39-43.

> He is, therefore, the perfect Son of the perfect Father, the only-begotten offspring of the unbegotten God, who has received everything from Him who possesses everything. He is God from God, Spirit from Spirit (*Trin*. 3.4).[10]
>
> Since God is a Spirit, there is no doubt that the one born from Him has nothing in Him that is different from or alien to Him from whom He has been born (*Trin*. 7.14).[11]

According to these texts, the Son is not a creation of God; rather, the Son is begotten from the Father: God begotten from God.[12] The Son, thus, is neither inferior nor alien to the Father because the Son possesses the same divine nature as the Father;[13] apparently, Spirit signifies the divine nature. In point of fact, when confronting the Arian proof-text (Pr. 8.22) used to argue for the Son's creation, Hilary maintained that the text upheld the Son's immutable nature as Spirit begotten from Spirit (*Trin*. 12.1–8);[14] consequently, in Hilary's Christology, Spirit emerges as a synonym for the divine substance, denoting unity within the Godhead, against the Arian attempt to diminish the Son's deity.[15]

---

[10] Cited according to the translation of Stephen McKenna, Hilary, *The Trinity*, FC, XXV, p. 67. Unless otherwise noted, translations for this document come from this source. Cf. *Matt*. 4.14; Weedman, *Trinitarian Theology*, pp. 27-28; Hanson, *Christian Doctrine of God*, pp. 479-80, 484, 490-92.

[11] Hilary, *The Trinity*, FC, XXV, p. 238.

[12] Hilary confirmed the Son's eternal generation from the Father (*Trin*. 3.3; 6.35; 7.27; 9.57; 10.6; 12.14; 12.21).

[13] *Trin*. 3.23; 7.11. Cf. Quasten, *Patrology*, IV, pp. 55-59. 'His doctrine of the incarnation is fully incorporated into the great framework of his trinitarian doctrine. For him, the incarnation is a revelation of the threefold God, and especially the Sonship in God.' Grillmeier, *Christian Tradition*, I, p. 395. Cf. Hanson, *Christian Doctrine of God*, pp. 476-77; Hilary, 'Trinity', NPNF, Second Series, IX, pp. lxiv-lxvi.

[14] Hilary, *The Trinity*, FC, XXV, p. 506, writes:

> His whole nature points out the attribute of the birth of His Only-begotten through the power of His unchangeable nature. For Him who is born as the Spirit from the Spirit, although He is born from the nature of the Spirit whereby He is Spirit, there is no other cause of that which is born except it come from the causes that are perfect and unchangeable cause (*Trin*. 12.8).

Cf. Weedman, *Trinitarian Theology*, pp. 180-95; Hilary, 'Trinity', NPNF, Second Series, IX, pp. lxvi-lxvii.

[15] '*Spiritus*, used to designate the divine substance, has a long tradition in Western theology. It appeared in contexts with a strong emphasis on the unity of the Godhead ... In Christology it became a common correlative to indicate the divine element in Christ.' Paul C. Burns, *The Christology in Hilary of Poitiers' Commen-*

Against the Sabellian claim that no distinction exists between Father and Son, Hilary attests the divine relations: Fatherhood cannot be separated from the Father; Sonship cannot be separated from the Son; gift cannot be separated from the Holy Spirit (*Trin.* 2.4–23).[16] For example, the inherent relation of Father and Son distinguishes between the one who begets and the one begotten. Furthermore, distinctions of relations are seen in the sending of the Paraclete: the Paraclete proceeds from the Father, but the Son sends the Paraclete from the Father (*Trin.* 8.19–20). Hilary, nevertheless, uses Spirit as a designation for both Father and Son; he concedes this designation can cause confusion (*Trin.* 8.21; 8.27).

> Certain people remain in ignorance and doubt because they see this third one, that is, the one called the Holy Spirit, often referred to as the Father and the Son. In this there is nothing contradictory, since, whether we speak of the Father or the Son, each is a S/spirit and each is holy (*Trin.* 2.30).[17]

> I am well aware that the Son of God is signified in the Spirit of God in such a manner as to make us realize that God the Father is revealed in Him, that the expression 'Spirit of God,' may serve to designate either one ... These words seem to refer clearly either to the Father or the Son, yet they manifest the power of the nature (*Trin.* 8.23).[18]

Some conclusions can be gleaned from these texts. First, when Hilary uses Spirit interchangeably to signify Father and Son, he endeavors to maintain distinction between Father and Son while accentuating their unity of divine nature which is Spirit.[19] Second, in the incarnation the Son manifests the likeness of divine nature with

---

tary on Matthew (Studia Ephemeridis Augustinianum 16; Roma: Institutum Patristicum Augustinianum, 1981), p. 70. Cf. Burns, *Christology*, pp. 69-72.

[16] Quasten, *Patrology*, IV, pp. 58-59. For a discussion of Hilary's rejection of Sabellianism, see Weedman, *Trinitarian Theology*, pp. 25-43.

[17] Hilary, *The Trinity*, FC, XXV, p. 59. Cf. *Trin.* 2.31–32.

[18] Hilary, *The Trinity*, FC, XXV, pp. 292-93.

[19] For discussions of Hilary's pneumatology, see Hanson, *Christian Doctrine of God*, pp. 502-506; Quasten, *Patrology*, IV, pp. 59-60; Schaff, *History*, III, p. 664. According to Hanson, 'Hilary certainly believed in the mutual indwelling of the Father and the Son, but he would only have said "in the Spirit" in the sense that spirit is what constitutes God anyway'. Hanson, *Christian Doctrine of God*, p. 504.

the Father (*Trin.* 8.24–25), so that Christ can say, 'I and the Father are one' (Jn 10.30);[20] they are Spirit.

Denying a human soul existed in Christ, Arius attributed ignorance, weakness, and suffering to the Logos incarnated in Christ; antithetically, Hilary posited a doctrine of two complete natures in Christ. Guided by Phil. 2.6-7, Hilary posited that Christ was in the form of God and in the form of a servant (*Trin.* 9.14; 9.38; 10.7; 11.6).[21]

> Christ Jesus is the true God as well as the true man. And it is equally dangerous to deny that Christ Jesus is God the Spirit as it is to deny that He is flesh of our body ... He Himself, by reason of the two natures that are united in Him, is the same person in both natures, but in such a manner that He is not wanting in anything that belongs to either, so that He does not cease to be God by His birth as a man, and again, He is man even while He remains God (*Trin.* 9.3).[22]

According to this text, within the one person of Christ genuine deity and genuine human nature existed without diminishing either nature. The form of God referred to the divine Spirit incarnated in Christ,[23] whereas the form of a servant referred to the human nature the divine Son assumed; moreover, the actions attributed to one nature are communicated to the other nature because of their union in the one person of Christ, a *communicatio idiomatum*.

> What was it that wept in Him? Was it God the Word or the soul of His body? Although tears are a bodily function, a certain sorrow of the soul uses the body as its servant and brings them

---

[20] *Trin.* 7.5; 7.31; 5.4. Cf. Hanson, *Christian Doctrine of God*, p. 479.

[21] 'The key to understanding Hilary's Christology is to recognize the weight he gives to Philippians 2.6-7.' Weedman, *Trinitarian Theology*, p. 157. Cf. Weedman, *Trinitarian Theology*, pp. 158-66.

[22] Hilary, *The Trinity*, FC, XXV, p. 324. Cf. *Trin.* 2.24; 2.26; Hanson, *Christian Doctrine of God*, pp. 477-78; Hilary, 'Trinity', NPNF, Second Series, IX, pp. lxix-lxxix; Pelikan, *Christian Tradition*, I, pp. 256-57; Seeberg and Hay, *History*, I, p. 255-56.

[23] Cf. *Trin.* 11.13; 11.17. 'For by this *"in forms Dei esse"* he expresses what the Antiochenes, especially Nestorius and Theodoret, and even Alexandrians like Didymus, understand by *"prosopon"* in its relationship to *"physis"*: an emanation, a manner of appearance, a visible representation of a nature, of a being.' Grillmeier, *Christian Tradition*, I, p. 396.

forth as if they were sweat ... But, God the Word is not subject to pain, nor the Spirit to tears (*Trin.* 10.55).[24]

Contrary to the Arian position, affirming Christ's humanity included body and soul, Hilary attributes suffering to Christ's human nature; however, he does not attribute pain to the divine Spirit.[25]

Hilary also challenged the Arian interpretation of Ps. 45.7 which insisted that Christ's anointing above his fellows advanced him in grace and adopted him into deity.

> The anointing did not procure any advantage for that blessed and incorrupt birth that abides in the nature of God, but for the mystery of the body and for the sanctification of the manhood which He took upon Himself ... And there is no difficulty in regard to the manner in which He was anointed by the Spirit and by the power of God, since at that moment when He comes up from Jordan the voice of God the Father is heard: 'Thou art my Son, this day have I begotten thee,' in order that the anointing of the spiritual power might be recognized through this testimony of the flesh that was sanctified in Him (*Trin.* 11.18).[26]

> And certainly it was not necessary for God, who is the Spirit and the power of God, to be anointed by the Spirit and power of God. Hence, God is anointed by His God above His fellows ... And since God is anointed by His God, then everything pertain-

---

[24] Hilary, *The Trinity*, FC, XXV, pp. 442-43. Cf. *Trin.* 10.9–49; 10.56–71; Hanson, *Christian Doctrine of God*, pp. 495-96; Grillmeier, *Christian Tradition*, I, pp. 395-98; Weedman, *Trinitarian Theology*, pp. 166-73.

[25] 'According to the *communicatio*, God suffered, but that should not be understood to mean that the substance or essence of God is corruptible and passible.' Carl L. Beckwith, 'Suffering Without Pain: The Scandal of Hilary of Poitiers' Christology', in Peter William Martens (ed.), *In the Shadow of the Incarnation: Essays on Jesus Christ in the Early Church in Honor of Brian E. Daley, S.J* (Notre Dame: University of Notre Dame Press, 2008), p. 83. Cf. Kelly, *Doctrines*, pp. 334-35. Through the years, several scholars have thought they discerned the specter of Docetism among Hilary's christological writings. Hilary, 'Trinity', NPNF, Second Series, IX, pp. lxxvi-lxxvii; Hanson, *Christian Doctrine of God*, pp. 501-502. Carl Beckwith surveys this issue, and by focusing on *Trin.* Books 9 and 10, he concludes that 'when we read Hilary's comments on Christ's suffering in the context of his discussion of the incarnation and human soul in Christ and when we observe his indebtedness to a Stoic moral psychology, it is apparent that he is neither "nakedly Docetic" nor does he sail close to the cliffs of Docetism'. Beckwith, 'Suffering Without Pain', p. 91.

[26] Hilary, *The Trinity*, FC, XXV, pp. 474-75.

ing to a slave that He received in the mystery of the flesh is anointed (*Trin.* 11.19).[27]

Hilary, then, rejected the idea that the divine Son incarnated in Christ was anointed by the Spirit and advanced in grace because the Son was eternally begotten from the Father; God, who is Spirit, does not need the Spirit's anointing. Hilary, accordingly, repudiated any suggestion that Christ was merely a human prophetically inspired by the Spirit.[28] Nevertheless, Hilary's distinction of natures in Christ allowed for the Spirit anointing the human nature for redemptive mission.[29] Wherefore, when Scripture declares that God is anointed by his God, this acknowledges the singularity of Christ's person and his dual natures. At the Jordan, then, the Spirit fully descends and abides upon Christ, but the declaration from heaven of Christ's sonship is not the Father's adoption of Christ; rather, it reveals Christ's divine sonship and signifies the anointing of power and sanctification of Christ's human nature for all humanity.

According to Hilary, Christ's reception of the Spirit at the Jordan becomes paradigmatic of believers' water baptism and Spirit baptism. At baptism believers receive the Spirit and are adopted as sons of God; nonetheless, Hilary seems to indicate that Christians can also receive a subsequent Spirit baptism. He emphasized that at Pentecost those disciples gathered in Jerusalem in obedience to Christ's command to await the fulfillment of the Father's promise were baptized in the Holy Spirit and received the charisms of the

---

[27] Hilary, *The Trinity*, FC, XXV, pp. 475-77. Cf. Hanson, *Christian Doctrine of God*, p. 494.

[28] *Trin.* 10.22; 10.50–51.

[29] Discussing Hilary's text in *On Matthew*, 2.5 concerning Jesus' baptism, Killian McDonnell rightly states, 'Jesus of course, had no sin, and therefore no need of baptism. Nonetheless because he was human, and precisely to fulfill "the mysteries of human salvation," Jesus went down into the Jordan, sanctifying the human person through his incarnation and baptism'. Kilian McDonnell, McDonnell and Montague, *Christian Initiation*, p. 174. 'That He might receive the nature of our flesh from the Virgin when He became man, and through this commingling and fellowship the body of the entire human race might be sanctified in Him' (*Trin.* 2.24). Hilary, *The Trinity*, p. 55. Hilary also advocated that Christ's flesh was assumed into deity by the Spirit in Christ's exaltation (*Trin.* 11.9; 11.39–40; *Syn.* 48). Cf. McDonnell, *The Baptism of Jesus in the Jordan*, pp. 44-45; Grillmeier, *Christian Tradition*, I, pp. 398-400; Burns, *Christology*, pp. 111-12; Weedman, *Trinitarian Theology*, pp. 174-79.

Spirit (*Trin.* 8.30).[30] Hilary, then, moves into an extensive discussion of the charismata listed in 1 Corinthians 12 (*Trin.* 8.29-34).[31]

> These various gifts are bestowed by the Spirit and in the Spirit (for to be given through the Spirit is not the same as to be given in the Spirit), because this bestowal of the gift which is obtained in the Spirit is, nevertheless, granted through the Spirit (*Trin.* 8.31).[32]

So Hilary conjoins the impartation of chrisms to Spirit baptism. Charisms, accordingly, are bestowed by the agency of God the Spirit; the Son sends the Holy Spirit from the Father, so that the charisms are received in the Spirit; believers receive the Spirit.

Hilary's Spirit Christology is a paradigm of pneumatic mediation set within a trinitarian framework; Christ's identity is signified and the entire redemptive mission fulfilled by the Spirit and in the Spirit. Hilary uses Spirit synonymously as a designation for the Father, Son, and Holy Spirit, thus, designating the divine substance as Spirit and denoting the unity of divine nature. The Holy Spirit mediates the incarnation as the form of God and the form of a servant unite in Mary's womb. The one Christ consists of two natures: (1) divine Son which is Spirit and (2) human which is body and soul. Hilary distinguishes between the divine and human natures, so that the human nature is capable of suffering while the Spirit remains immutable. Also, Hilary allows space for Christ's human nature to receive the Spirit; Christ is anointed by the Spirit and fulfills the redemptive mission in the power of the Spirit. At Pentecost Christ sends the promise of the Father, and the disciples are baptized by the Spirit and in the Spirit. Hilary, consequently, sets forth a Spirit christolog-

---

[30] According to Killian McDonnell, 'Hilary gives the impression that the imparting of the Spirit is distinct from and following baptism when he writes of "the sacraments of baptism and of the Spirit"' in *On Matthew*, 4.27, yet he concludes that 'the latter imparting of the Spirit is still within the same rite'. McDonnell and Montague, *Christian Initiation*, pp. 175-76.

[31] Hilary recounts Paul's list of chrisms in 1 Corinthians 12 four times in this document: *Trin.* 2.34; 8.29; 8.30; 8.33. A partial discussion is given twice: *Trin.* 8.33; 8.34. Cf. McDonnell and Montague, *Christian Initiation*, pp. 177-81. 'No evidence can be found in the text to support the supposition that Hilary was purposing something new and unheard of. The impression is given that Hilary was handing on something important and traditional.' McDonnell and Montague, *Christian Initiation*, pp. 180-81.

[32] Hilary, *The Trinity*, FC, XXV, p. 299.

ical paradigm of pneumatic mediation that integrates Logos Christology.

Marius Victorinus

Marius Victorinus' writings furnish the next Spirit christological references. Born in Africa (280–85), Victorinus came to Rome around 350 to teach rhetoric; his teaching received such high acclaim that a statue was erected in the Forum to honor him. Victorinus converted to Christianity in 355 and immediately began to defend his new faith. So Victorinus' copious literary production easily divides according to these two stages of his life.[33] In the pre-Christian stage, Victorinus produced philosophical commentaries on the writings of Aristotle and Cicero, and he translated the writings of Aristotle, Porphyry, and Plotinus. During the Christian stage, Victorinus generated theological works and commentaries; actually, Victorinus was the first Christian to write Latin commentaries on the Pauline Epistles and systematic metaphysical treatises on the Trinity.[34]

Of particular interest to this survey are 12 theological works, collectively known as *Theological Treatises on the Trinity*. In the first three documents, written in form of epistles (357–58) and evoked by the Second Sirmium Creed (357),[35] Victorinus placed the Arian view on

---

[33] For overviews of Victorinus' life and writings see, 'Victorinus Afer, Caius (or Fabius) Marius', *ODCC*, p. 1694; Quasten, *Patrology*, IV, pp. 69-76; Hanson, *Christian Doctrine of God*, pp. 531-34. Cf. Mary Clark's introduction to Marius Victorinus, *Theological Treatises on the Trinity*, FC, LXIX, pp. 3-37.

[34] Apparently, Victorinus had a significant influence on Latin theology. According to Mary Clark,

> By translating the 'books of the Platonists,' which came into Augustine's hands around 386, Victorinus helped Augustine to understand, to some extent, spiritual reality and the nature of evil, thereby removing an intellectual block to his believing what the God of Scripture was teaching … It can be suggested that through Augustine Boethius, Cassiodorus, Bede, Alcuin, Isidore of Seville, Europe became a new forum for Victorinus … If the scholastic method means the harmonizing of reason and faith for their common benefit, Victorinus is an early example of this method. As the first Latin writer to compose a systematic metaphysical treatise on the Trinity, he is the precursor of the medieval theologians; he is also the first Latin commentator on the Epistles of St. Paul (Victorinus, *Theological Treatises*, FC, LXIX, p. 5).

Cf. Hanson, *Christian Doctrine of God*, pp. 531-32.

[35] For an examination of Victorinus' reaction to the Sirmium Creed, see Weedman, *Trinitarian Theology*, pp. 63-73.

the lips of an imaginary figure named Candidus in order to oppose Arian opinions.[36] Victorinus composed the next five treatises to refute Arianism and the Homoiousians: *Against Arius* 1a (359), *Against Arius* 1b (359), *Against Arius* 2 (360), *Against Arius* 3 (361), and *Against Arius* 4 (362). The ninth treatise demonstrated *The Necessity of Accepting the Homoousion* (363) position as the best expression of Christian dogma. The remaining three treatises were hymns written in adoration to the Trinity (358–59).[37]

Before proceeding to examine these treatises, a word about the vocabulary Victorinus uses may be helpful.[38] In his apophatic theology, God is absolutely transcendent; God is anterior to every classification and category, even being (*Ad. Ar.* 1b.49; 3.11; 4.19). God, therefore, is non-being because God transcends being (*Ad. Cand.* 2-13; *Ad. Ar.* 4.23). Nevertheless, God is not an abstract entity since God is: 'For his "to be" is his substance, but not that substance known to us; but to himself, because he is "To Be" itself, is not from substance but is substance itself, the parent of all substances, giving himself "to be" from himself, first substance, universal substance, substance from substance' (*Ad. Ar.* 2.1).[39] Victorinus, thus, uses substance (*substantia*) to refer to the essence or nature of God which primarily designates the 'to be' (*esse*) of God. According to Victorinus, the Scriptural God has the ability to act, and act corresponds to form, so using the principle of predominance (the predominant form distinguishes the reality) the Father is distinguished by 'to be' (*esse*), the Son by 'to live' (*vivere*), and the Holy Spirit by 'to

---

[36] The first and third of this set of three treatises were constructed as letters from Candidus to Victorinus, and the second treatise represented Victorinus' refutation of Candidus' first correspondence: *Candidus* 1, *Against Candidus*, and *Candidus* 2.

[37] Regarding issues about the purpose, date, provenance, structure and content of these treatises, see Victorinus, *Theological Treatises*, FC, LXIX, pp. 18-37; Hanson, *Christian Doctrine of God*, pp. 532-34; Quasten, *Patrology*, IV, pp. 71-73. Victorinus composed these treatises using Neo-Platonic conceptual structures which also form the basis for his metaphysical principles. Victorinus, *Theological Treatises*, FC, LXIX, pp. 38-40; Quasten, *Patrology*, IV, pp. 76-77.

[38] According to Mark Weedman, 'Victorinus' philosophical vocabulary does depart from that of his Latin predecessors'. Weedman, *Trinitarian Theology*, p. 63.

[39] Cited according to the translation of Mary Clark, Victorinus, *Theological Treatises*, FC, LXIX, p. 196. Unless otherwise noted, all citations will come from this source. Cf. Hanson, *Christian Doctrine of God*, pp. 534-36; Kelly, *Doctrines*, p. 270; Quasten, *Patrology*, IV, pp. 76-77. It seems that this preexistent existence of God is Spirit (*Ad. Ar.* 1b.50).

understand' (*intelligere*).⁴⁰ Dovetailing with these designations are their manifestations in salvific operations. So he employed the word existence (*existentia*) to indicate *esse* determined by form; accordingly, God is one substance and three existences. Victorinus, consequently, uses subsistence (*subsistentia*) to denote and distinguish these existences. Victorinus, furthermore, affirms that every form implies 'to be' so these divine existences are consubstantial (*homoousios*); God is one (*Ad. Ar.* 1b.54; 3.7).⁴¹

Spirit christological texts permeate these treatises, even when Victorinus discusses divine substance and consubstantiality.

> If God is Spirit and Jesus is Spirit and the Holy Spirit is Spirit, the three are from one substance. Therefore the three are *homoousion* (consubstantial) (*Ad. Ar.* 1a.12).⁴²

> Therefore there is only one substance because there is the same Spirit, but the same in three; therefore, they are *homoousion* (consubstantial). Whence, the substance is not similar because it is the same Spirit (*Ad. Ar.* 1a.17).⁴³

> All three are therefore *homoousia* (consubstantial) with respect to action and *homoousia* (consubstantial) with respect to substance, because all three are Spirit (*Ad. Ar.* 1a.18).⁴⁴

> For the Spirit is one substance. The Spirit is 'to be' itself. But 'to be' itself is both life and 'to understand.' These three are in each one, and for that reason there is one divinity, the totality is one, God is one, because the Father, the Son, and the Holy Spirit are one; with difference appearing only through power and action, because God in power and in a hidden movement moves all things and directs all things as in silence, whereas the *Logos*, Son which is also Holy Spirit, expresses himself through the Word to produce all things, according to life and according to under-

---

⁴⁰ Victorinus, *Theological Treatises*, pp. 14-15. Cf. *Ad. Ar.* 1b.52. Victorinus also uses the trinitarian paradigm of 'to be', 'life', and 'knowledge' (*Ad. Ar.* 3.9). Cf. Hanson, *Christian Doctrine of God*, p. 554; Kelly, *Doctrines*, p. 271.

⁴¹ Victorinus, *Theological Treatises*, FC, LXIX, pp. 10-18, 40-42; Quasten, *Patrology*, IV, pp. 76-78.

⁴² Victorinus, *Theological Treatises*, FC, LXIX, pp. 103-104. Cf. *Ad. Ar.* 1a.16; Weedman, *Trinitarian Theology*, pp. 70-72.

⁴³ Victorinus, *Theological Treatises*, FC, LXIX, p. 113. Cf. *Ad. Ar.* 2.10.

⁴⁴ Victorinus, *Theological Treatises*, FC, LXIX, p. 115.

standing, serving as foundation for the 'to be' of all things (*Ad. Ar.* 1b.59).[45]

So against the Arian insistence on the creaturely nature of the Son and Holy Spirit and their inferiority to the Father, Victorinus asserts that the Father, Son, and Holy Spirit exist in one consubstantial substance;[46] the divine substance is Spirit (*Ad. Ar.* 1b.55). Victorinus, here, attempts to remove the basis of the Homoiousian argument. The distinct trinitarian existences do not partake of similar substance, but the same substance.[47] The triune God is also consubstantial in power and act; here, distinctions appear both internally and externally, so that substance becomes known by its act (*Ad. Ar.* 4.19-20). Internally, God passes from rest to movement in an act of self-generation without dividing (*Ad. Ar.* 3.17; *Ad. Ar.* 1a.31): it is the essence of the Father to repose, the Son to act, and the Holy Spirit to know or understand (*Ad. Ar.* 4.21-29).[48] Externally, God becomes the foundation of all being as the Father expresses himself through the creative Logos: a dyadic union of Son and Spirit, life and understanding.[49] The Father, Son, and Holy Spirit, then, are consubstantial in substance, power, and act. God is Spirit forms the basis of Victorinus' concept of consubstantiality.

The Son and Holy Spirit, thereupon, simultaneously proceed salvifically, in a dyad of life and intelligence.[50]

---

[45] Victorinus, *Theological Treatises*, FC, LXIX, p. 186. Cf. *Ad. Ar.* 2.7; 3.1-2; 3.6; 4.4-5; 4.9-10; Hanson, *Christian Doctrine of God*, pp. 550-56.

[46] Victorinus also refutes the Arian assertion that the Son was created from nothing (*Ad. Cand.* 17-30).

[47] Cf. *Ad. Ar.* 1a.21-22; *Ad. Ar.* 1a.28-32; Hanson, *Christian Doctrine of God*, p. 547; Weedman, *Trinitarian Theology*, pp. 65-66.

[48] 'This passage from rest to motion must be understood as a purely logical, not chronological, succession (*Ad. Ar.* 1.31), inasmuch as being is endowed with an interior movement' (*Ad. Ar.* 4.8). Quasten, *Patrology*, IV, p. 77; Hanson, *Christian Doctrine of God*, pp. 637-46; Quasten, *Patrology*, IV, pp. 77-78.

[49] Victorinus also presents the triune God existing as two dyadic unions: (1) Father and Son (*Ad. Ar.* 3.7; 3.17) and (2) Son and Holy Spirit (*Ad. Ar.* 3.8; 3.9; 3.18). Cf. Quasten, *Patrology*, IV, p. 79.

[50] 'First of all, the Father and Son are identical; the Son and the Holy Spirit are identical ... Indeed, "to be" is both life and knowledge, identical and *sunōnuma* (synonyms). They are therefore begotten at the same time' (*Ad. Ar.* 1b.54). Victorinus, *Theological Treatises*, FC, LXIX, p. 179. Cf. Quasten, *Patrology*, IV, p. 79. 'Thus the Homoians are wrong when they claim that the generation of the Son excludes any knowledge of the Son's substance, because the Son himself has revealed the Father to us.' Weedman, *Trinitarian Theology*, p. 69.

> It is necessary therefore to believe in the Son of God so that life may be in us, that life which is both true and eternal life. For if we shall have faith in Christ of Nazareth, who took flesh from Mary, we shall have faith in the Son of God who was the Spirit and has been made Spirit incarnate (*Ad. Ar.* 1b.53).[51]

> These two, the Logos and the Holy Spirit, in one sole movement 'came' in order that Mary might conceive so that there might be constituted flesh from flesh, the temple and the dwelling of God (*Ad. Ar.* 1b.58).[52]

Several conclusions can be drawn from these texts. First, faith in Christ is essential for salvation. Second, Victorinus does not allow for two Christs: faith in Jesus Christ is faith in the divine Son of God. Third, Christ's virgin birth produced human flesh as a temple of deity. Fourth, Victorinus makes no distinction between the Son and the Spirit in Christ's identity and mission; what can be said of one can be said of the other, for they function in dyadic unity. The Son was the Spirit incarnate, a pneumatic incarnation.[53]

Victorinus, consequently, affirms the dual natures of Christ; the divine nature is Spirit, and the human nature is flesh which includes body and soul.[54]

> Therefore, according to the flesh the Savior has suffered, but according to the Spirit which he was before he was in the flesh, he is without suffering. Whence, our teaching differs from that of the Patripassians (*Ad. Ar.* 1a.44).[55]

Hence, against Arian presuppositions, Victorinus denied that the Son suffered in Christ and attested to Christ's assumption of a human soul and its suffering. Also, contrasting his view with Modalism's belief, that the Father suffered in Christ, Victorinus

---

[51] Victorinus, *Theological Treatises*, FC, LXIX, p. 178. Cf. *Ad. Ar.* 4.6-7; *Ad. Ar.* 1a.17.

[52] Victorinus, *Theological Treatises*, FC, LXIX, p. 185.

[53] 'Christ himself who is the Son of the Father is also himself the Holy Spirit' (*Ad. Ar.* 1a.8). Victorinus, *Theological Treatises*, FC, LXIX, p. 99. Cf. *Ad. Ar.* 1b.51; 4.11; 4.18.

[54] 'For it is clear that he also had a soul, since the same Savior said: "My soul is sorrowful even unto death"' (*Ad. Ar.* 3.3). Victorinus, *Theological Treatises*, FC, LXIX, p. 225. Cf. *Ad. Ar.* 3.11-12; 4.7; Hanson, *Christian Doctrine of God*, pp. 548-50; Grillmeier, *Christian Tradition*, I, pp. 406-407.

[55] Victorinus, *Theological Treatises*, FC, LXIX, p. 162.

maintained that the divine nature, which is Spirit, remained impassible.[56]

During the salvific sojourn to the cross, Victorinus verifies that Jesus manifests the Spirit, but after the death, resurrection, and ascension, Christ returns as the promised Paraclete sanctifying and infusing knowledge to believers, for it is the proper act of the Holy Spirit to testify of Christ (*Ad. Ar.* 3.14–16).

> From all this it is shown that the Holy Spirit is somehow identical to Jesus, although they are different through the proper movement of their action, because the former teaches understanding, and the latter gives life (*Ad. Ar.* 4.18).[57]

According to Victorinus, both Christ and the Spirit function in the role of a Paraclete.[58] Even though their proper salvific missions of either infusing life or understanding distinguish between Christ and the Spirit, they remain identical. Christ manifests the Spirit in his flesh, and the Spirit manifests Christ among believers.

Victorinus bequeathed to the Latin tradition a Spirit Christology of pneumatic incarnation framed in trinitarian thought. The basis for his trinitarian theology is that the existences – Father, Son, and Holy Spirit – consubstantially share one divine substance which is Spirit. The only distinctions appear as substantial acts; thus, Victorinus arranges his trinitarian thought into substantial relationships, so that the designation Spirit appropriately applies to the Father, Son, or Holy Spirit. The Son and Spirit proceed on their salvific mission in a dyadic union; whatever can be said of one can be said of the other. Christ's dual natures are composed of flesh and Spirit, so that in the flesh Christ manifests the Spirit. Victorinus, however, distinguished Christ's divine and human natures; the human nature suffered while the Spirit remained impassible. After Christ's ascension and exaltation, the Spirit returns and manifests Christ; the Spirit becomes the presence of Christ among believers. Victorinus' Christology of the Spirit's and the Son's dyadic union, identity, and

---

[56] Cf. *Ad. Ar.* 2.1; Hanson, *Christian Doctrine of God*, p. 554; Quasten, *Patrology*, IV, p. 79.
[57] Victorinus, *Theological Treatises*, p. 277. Cf. *Ad. Ar.* 4.17; Hanson, *Christian Doctrine of God*, p. 554.
[58] Cf. *Ad. Ar.* 1a.12.

mission, thus, presents a Spirit Christology that brackets Logos Christology.

Ambrose of Milan

Now, attention turns to Ambrose of Milan whose ministry and writings carried significant political influence.[59] Ambrose was born into a family with considerable political prestige.[60] After his father's death, Ambrose and his family moved to Rome (353) where he studied rhetoric and law. His skill as a lawyer led to his appointment as prefect of Sirmium (368), and in 370 he was commissioned as consul of Liguria and Aemilia. When Auxentius the Arian bishop of Milan died and conflict ensued between supporters of Nicene doctrine and Arians concerning a successor, exercising his authority as consul, Ambrose intervened to restore peace. During the process of choosing a successor, the multitude with one voice acclaimed Ambrose their choice. Although only a catechumen, within eight days of his election Ambrose was baptized, progressed through the various ecclesiastical qualifications, and was consecrated bishop of Milan (374). After the emperor Valentinian died (375), his youthful

---

[59] Recognized as one of the four doctors of the Latin Church, Ambrose's ministry and writings contributed to ideas and practices that continued in the Western Church through the Middle Ages, ended a polytheistic revival among Roman aristocracy, helped defeat Arianism in the West, and asserted the autonomy and superiority of the church over the state. For an examination of Ambrose's influence regarding church and state relations, see Frend, *Christianity*, pp. 618-26. For a comprehensive analysis of his political influence, see Neil B. McLynn, *Ambrose of Milan: Church and Court in a Christian Capital* (Berkeley: University of California Press, 1994). Regarding his struggle with Arianism, see Daniel H. Williams, *Ambrose of Milan and the End of the Nicene – Arian Conflicts* (OECS; Oxford: Clarendon Press, 1995).

[60] Ambrose's father, who bore the same name, served as prefect of Gaul. Ambrose's genealogy also included Christian martyrs. Ambrose died in 397; however, with dates ranging from 337 to 340, the date of Ambrose's birth remains uncertain. For overviews of his life and ministry, see Boniface Ramsey, *Ambrose* (ECF; London: Routledge, 1997), pp. 1-54; McLynn, *Ambrose* pp. 1-52; Ambrose, *Theological and Dogmatic Works*, FC, XLIV, pp. vii-xxii; Ambrose, 'Select Works And Letters', in NPNF, Second Series, X, pp. xv-xvii; Quasten, *Patrology*, IV, pp. 144-52; Schaff, *History*, III, pp. 961-67. Sometime around 412–13 or perhaps 422, at the urging of Augustine, a deacon, Paulinus of Milan who knew Ambrose personally wrote *The Life of Saint Ambrose*. An English translation of this document can be found in Ramsey, *Ambrose*, pp. 195-218.

successor Gratian formed a close relationship with Ambrose, adding imperial weight to Ambrose's ministry.

This survey will focus on three of Ambrose's dogmatic works replete with Spirit christological references: *On the Christian Faith*, *On the Holy Spirit*, and *The Sacrament of the Incarnation of Our Lord*.[61] Ambrose penned *On the Christian Faith* in response to Gratian's request for instruction in the faith against Arian doctrine, completing the first two books between 377–78 and the last three books around 380. *On the Holy Spirit* (381) continued Gratian's instruction, affirming the Holy Spirit's deity and place in the Trinity. *The Sacrament of the Incarnation of Our Lord* (382) was occasioned when two Arian chamberlains of the emperor challenged Ambrose to debate certain issues raised in a sermon he had preached on the incarnation.

In writing these treatises, Ambrose freely imbibed from the theological wells of Athanasius, Basil of Caesarea, Didymus of Alexandria, and Hilary of Poitiers, synthesizing their works and thought into his own,[62] so his Spirit Christology does not differ much from his sources. Against the Arian argument that the begotten Son is not consubstantial with the unbegotten Father, Ambrose argues the Son is eternally from the Father (*Fid*. 4.9.97-116). Although the Father, Son, and Holy Spirit are distinct, they have a common divine substance.[63] For Ambrose this divine substance is Spirit: the Father is Spirit; the Son is Spirit; the Holy Spirit is Spirit (*Spir*. 1.9.105-106).

The Son and Spirit function in a reciprocal salvific relationship and mission. In Christ's virgin birth 'the birth from the Virgin was,

---

[61] Ambrose was a copious writer in a variety of genres including exegetical, ascetical, moral, and doctrinal works, along with sermons, letters, and hymns. Regarding information about his writings, see Quasten, *Patrology*, IV, pp. 152-80; Ambrose, 'Select Works And Letters', NPNF, Second Series, X, pp. xvii-xxii; Ramsey, *Ambrose*, pp. 55-68.

[62] *Fid*. 4.8.92; *Incarn*. 8.84; 9.89-102. According to Justo González, Ambrose does not 'have anything new to contribute to trinitarian doctrine. He defended the Nicene faith mostly as a very able church leader and a preacher. But when Emperor Gratian asked him to compose a treatise on the Holy Spirit, Ambrose simply took Basil's work on the same subject and produced a free version and slight adaptation of it'. González, *Christian Thought*, I, pp. 327-28. Cf. Quasten, *Patrology*, IV, pp. 169-70.

[63] Cf. Hanson, *Christian Doctrine of God*, pp. 670-71; Kelly, *Doctrines*, p. 269.

then, the work of the Spirit' (*Spir.* 2.5.38)[64] to bring salvation to lost humanity, for 'both the Father and the Spirit sent the Son' (*Spir.* 3.1.8).[65] Common designations, thus, accentuate the unity of the Son's and the Holy Spirit's salvific relationship and missions: Christ, Lord, and Paraclete.

> That which is the Name of the Son is also that of the Holy Spirit, when the Son also called Paraclete, as is the Holy Spirit. And therefore does the Lord Jesus say in the Gospel: 'I will ask My Father, and He shall give you another Paraclete, to be with you for ever, even the Spirit of Truth.' And He said well 'another,' that you might not suppose that the Son is also the Spirit, for oneness is of the Name, not a Sabellian confusion of the Son and of the Spirit. So, then, the Son is one Paraclete, the Holy Spirit another Paraclete ... As there is oneness of name, so too, there is oneness of power, for where the Paraclete Spirit is, there is also the Son ... Therefore the Son and Spirit are one (*Spir.* 1.13.156-58).[66]

The Son and Spirit, therefore, share common names and are one in relationship, power, function, and mission; what can be said of one can be said of the other, and what the Son does the Spirit does. Nonetheless, to avoid the charge of Sabellianism Ambrose carefully distinguishes the Son from the Holy Spirit.

Against the Arian recalcitrant insistence that Christ lacked a human soul, Ambrose asserted that in the incarnation the divine Son assumed a complete human nature: body and rational human soul. Any Scripture, consequently, that implies subordination, ignorance, growth and maturity, weakness, or suffering Ambrose attributes to Christ's human nature, not to the divine nature.[67] So Ambrose sharply distinguishes between Christ's dual natures. Ambrose, nevertheless, attests to the perichoretic unity of Christ; there is only one

---

[64] Cited according to the translation of H. De Romestin, Ambrose, 'On The Holy Spirit', NPNF, Second Series, X, p. 119. Cf. *Spir.* 3.11.79; *Fid.* 4.4.45; Pelikan, *Christian Tradition*, I, pp. 289-90.
[65] Ambrose, 'Holy Spirit', NPNF, Second Series, X, p. 136. Cf. *Fid.* 2.9.75.
[66] Ambrose, 'Holy Spirit', NPNF, Second Series, X, p. 111. Cf. *Spir.* 1.3.44; 1.13.132-59; 2.1.17-18; 3.14.101-103.
[67] *Fid.* 2.7.56; 5.14.171; 5.15.182-87; *Incarn.* 5.35-45; 7.63-69; 7.72-77; 9.103-16. Cf. Hanson, *Christian Doctrine of God*, pp. 672-75; Grillmeier, *Christian Tradition*, I, pp. 404-405; Kelly, *Doctrines*, p. 336; Pelikan, *Christian Tradition*, I, pp. 245, 257.

Christ, so that it can properly be said: the Lord of glory was crucified (*Fid.* 2.7.56, 58).[68]

Ambrose also challenged the Arian claim that Christ's anointing above his fellows, according to Ps. 45.7, depicted Christ's growth in grace, virtue, and merit toward deification (*Spir.* 1.9.100-101).

> Upon the Lord Jesus, when He was in the form of man, the Spirit abode, as it is written: 'Upon Whom thou shall see the Spirit descending from heaven, and abiding upon Him, He it is Who baptizeth with the Holy Spirit' (*Spir.* 1.8.93).[69]

> Can we, then, wonder if the Spirit sent both the prophets and the apostles, since Christ said: 'The Spirit of the Lord is upon Me'? And rightly did He say 'upon Me,' because He was speaking as the Son of Man. For as the Son of Man He was anointed and sent to preach the Gospel (*Spir.* 3.1.2).[70]

> And he said fittingly, 'abiding upon Him,' because the Spirit inspired a saying or acted upon the prophets as often as He would, but abode always in Christ. Nor, again, let it move you that he said 'upon Him,' for he was speaking of the Son of Man, because he was baptized as the Son of Man. For the Spirit is not upon Christ, according to the Godhead, but in Christ; for, as the Father is in the Son, and the Son in the Father, so the Spirit of God and the Spirit of Christ is both in the Father and in the Son (*Spir.* 3.1.5-6).[71]

Several conclusions can be drawn from these texts. First, Christ's anointing differed from the anointing which the Hebrew prophets experienced; the Spirit inspired and acted upon the prophets, but the Spirit abode in its fullness with Christ. Second, Christ's reception of the Spirit and the Spirit's abiding presence revealed Christ's deity: the one who baptizes with the Spirit.[72] Third, regarding the Spirit's abiding presence in these texts, Ambrose uses the words 'upon' and 'in' to distinguish between Christ's divine and human natures; the Spirit abides 'upon' the human nature and 'in' the

---

[68] Kelly, *Doctrines*, pp. 335-36.
[69] Ambrose, 'Holy Spirit', NPNF, Second Series, X, pp. 105-106.
[70] Ambrose, 'Holy Spirit', NPNF, Second Series, X, p. 135.
[71] Ambrose, 'Holy Spirit', NPNF, Second Series, X, p. 136.
[72] Ambrose teaches that believers can be baptized in water and in the Spirit (*Spir.* 1.6.76-80).

divine nature. Although the Spirit commissions, empowers, and sends apostles and prophets, and, likewise, the Spirit anoints and sends Christ on his salvific mission, this refers to Christ's human nature receiving the anointing of the Spirit; the Spirit abides 'upon' the Son of Man. Christ's divine nature has no need of the Spirit's anointing; accordingly, the Spirit abides 'in' Christ, elucidating the Spirit's perichoretic relationship with the divine Son in salvific mission: 'neither can Christ be without the Spirit, nor the Spirit without Christ, for the unity of the divine nature cannot be divided' (*Spir.* 3.7.44).[73] Hence, humans participate in sonship by grace, but the Christ possesses sonship by nature (*Fid.* 4.4.38).

Ambrose constructs his Spirit Christology of pneumatic mediation within a trinitarian framework. Ambrose depicts the Father, Son, and Holy Spirit consubstantially partaking of one divine substance which is Spirit; consequently, the Son whose divine nature is Spirit becomes incarnate in Christ. The Holy Spirit is the agent of Christ's virgin birth; Christ is flesh and Spirit, so that within the one Christ two natures exist: divine and human. The Holy Spirit anoints Christ's human nature and reposes in the divine nature, so that the Son and Holy Spirit exist in a perichoretic relationship in salvific mission; accordingly, they are one in name, power, and function: what is said of one is said of the other. Ambrose's Spirit Christology, therefore, integrates Logos Christology.

Augustine

Augustine's writings and theology developed along his spiritual journey into truth and his involvement in doctrinal controversies.[74] Although his mother had taught him the Christian faith, his study of the Hebrew Scriptures did not satisfy his inquiring mind, so he

---

[73] Ambrose, 'Holy Spirit', NPNF, Second Series, X, p. 141.
[74] For biographies of Augustine's life and introductions to his theology, see Gerald Bonner, *St Augustine of Hippo: Life and Controversies* (London: SCM Press, 1963); Peter Robert Lamont Brown, *Augustine of Hippo: A Biography* (London: Faber, 1967); Jacques Chabannes, *St. Augustine* (trans. Julie Kernan; Garden City, NY: Doubleday, 1962); Serge Lancel, *Saint Augustine* (trans. Antonia Nevill; London: SCM Press, 2002); Schaff, *History*, III, pp. 988-1002; Philip Schaff, 'Prolegomena: St. Augustin's Life and Work', NPNF, First Series, I, pp. 1-25.

turned to the Manichaeans for answers.[75] Nevertheless, Manichean teachers never fully satisfied Augustine; consequently, he lost confidence in Manichaean doctrine. As his quest for truth continued, Augustine taught rhetoric at Carthage (375–83), Rome (384), and Milan (384–86). While at Milan, he became acquainted with Neo-Platonist writings and the sermons of Ambrose, the bishop of Milan. Contrary to the Manichaeans, Neo-Platonism offered Augustine a method of affirming God's incorporeal nature and explaining evil's existence without recourse to dualism; moreover, Ambrose's allegorical interpretation of the Hebrew Scriptures dispensed with many problems that vexed Augustine. These two powerful influences, therefore, intellectually cleared the way for Augustine's dramatic conversion (386),[76] finding fulfillment in his quest for truth in the Christian faith.

In 395 Augustine was consecrated bishop of Hippo, and his episcopal duties soon brought him into doctrinal conflict with three groups: the Manicheans, the Donatists, and the Pelagians. Augustine's involvement in these controversies occasioned numerous works[77] that significantly impacted Christian theology in its view of God and the presence of evil, trinitarian theology, ecclesiology, and soteriology. Since Spirit christological references are scattered

---

[75] For Augustine, the Manicheans proffered a more enlightened system, which they claimed was exclusively rational and scientific, and an acceptable solution to the problem of reconciling the goodness and love of God with the existence of evil by rejecting the concept of one eternal divine principle and asserting the existence of two principles: one evil and one good. Regarding Augustine's involvement with the Manicheans, see Justo L. González, *Christian Thought*, II, pp. 17-20; Frend, *Christianity*, pp. 661-63; Quasten, *Patrology*, IV, pp. 345-46.

[76] Augustine's conversion was also emotionally influenced by the testimony of the great rhetorician Marius Victorinus' conversion to Christianity and the testimony of two men who were converted after reading the *Life of Saint Anthony*; these testimonies brought an overwhelming sense of guilt and conviction of sin to Augustine. González, *Christian Thought*, II, pp. 21-22. Cf. Frend, *Christianity*, pp. 663-66; Quasten, *Patrology*, IV, pp. 346-47.

[77] Augustine's writings concerning the Manichaeans and Donatists can be found in Augustine, 'The Writings against the Manichaeans and against the Donatists', NPNF, First Series, IV. Regarding his Pelagian writings, see Augustine, 'The Anti-Pelagian Writings', NPNF, First Series, V. For the theological issues involved in these controversies and Augustine's response, see Bonner, *Augustine*, pp. 36-393. Cf. Frend, *Christianity*, pp. 666-80; González, *Christian Thought*, II, pp. 34-55; Pelikan, *Christian Tradition*, I, pp. 300-301, 308-18; Quasten, *Patrology*, IV, pp. 348-50. For an overview of his writings, see Quasten, *Patrology*, IV, pp. 355-403; Schaff, *History*, III, pp. 1003-16.

among his writings, this survey will narrow the focus to four documents: (1) *The Trinity*, (2) *Tractates on the Gospel of John*, (3) *Enchiridion on Faith, Hope, and Love*, and (4) *The Predestination of the Saints*.[78]

According to Augustine, the Father, Son, and Holy Spirit are a unity of one divine substance in indivisible equality (*Trin.* 1.4.7), yet they are distinct in relations (*Trin.* 1.5.8). To illustrate the distinct trinitarian relations and unity of substance, Augustine uses a psychological analogy of the human mind's functions of memory, understanding, and will.[79] Augustine, also, finds a trinitarian analogy in human love: the one who loves, that which is loved, and love.[80] Augustine, moreover, uses the Johannine designation 'God is Spirit' (Jn 4.24).

> The Trinity cannot in the same way be called the Father, except perhaps metaphorically, in respect of the creature, on account of the adoption of sons ... Neither can the Trinity in any wise be called the Son, but it can be called, in its entirety, the Holy Spirit, according to what is written, 'God is a Spirit;' because both the

---

[78] *The Trinity* consisted of 15 books which were published in two stages. Books 1–12 were published without Augustine's knowledge between 399–412; Augustine published the final 15 book edition in 420. The document's structure moves through four stages: (1) books 1–4 present a biblical exposition of the Trinity; (2) books 5–8 defend trinitarian doctrine; (3) books 9–14 seek to expose the trinitarian image in humans; (4) book 15 summarizes Augustine's exposition and defense of the Trinity and offers his conclusions. *Tractates on the Gospel of John* is a commentary on the Fourth Gospel consisting of 124 pastoral sermons. The date of composition remains uncertain: Tractates 1–54 (411–14) and Tractates 55–124 (416–20). *Enchiridion on Faith, Hope, and Love* represents a manual of Christian doctrine which Augustine produced around 421 at the request of Laurentius to address certain theological issues. Augustine unpacks the lineaments of Christian doctrine through a discussion of the virtues of faith, hope, and love. *The Predestination of the Saints* was written to Prosper and Hilary (428–29) in response to Pelagian views being advocated in Marseilles. Here, Augustine insists that salvific faith and predestination are gifts of God's grace and refutes the idea of salvation attained with human free will and merits.

[79] 'Since, then, these three, memory, understanding, will, are not three lives, but one life; it follows certainly that neither are they three substances, but one substance (*Trin.* 10.11.18). Cited according to the translation of Arthur Haddan, Augustine, 'On the Holy Trinity', NPNF, First Series, III, p. 142. Cf. *Trin.* 10.11.17; 10.10.13; 11.1.1–11.18; 14.6.8–8.11; 4.21.30; Kelly, *Doctrines*, pp. 271-79; González, *Christian Thought*, II, pp. 329-30; 233-34; Quasten, *Patrology*, IV, pp. 427-29; Harnack, *Dogma*, IV, pp. 129-30; Schaff, *History*, III, pp. 684-86; Seeberg and Hay, *History*, I, pp. 238-41. Here, Augustine is probably following Marius Victorinus' exposition of the soul as an image of an intellectual triad reflecting deity (Victorinus, *Ad. Ar.* 1b.61).

[80] *Trin.* 9.2.2; 9.3.3; 9.4.4; 10.3.5–4.6. Cf. González, *Christian Thought*, I, p. 332.

> Father is a S/spirit and the Son is a S/spirit, and the Father is holy and the Son is holy. Therefore, since the Father, the Son and the Holy Spirit are one God, and certainly God is holy, and God is S/spirit, the Trinity can be called also the Holy Spirit. But yet that Holy Spirit, who is not the Trinity, but is understood as in the Trinity, is spoken of in His proper name of the Holy Spirit relatively, since He is referred both to the Father and to the Son, because the Holy Spirit is the Spirit both of the Father and of the Son ... In order, therefore, that the communion of both may be signified from a name that is suitable to both, the Holy Spirit is called the gift of both (*Trin.* 5.11.12).[81]

So Augustine demonstrates that some things that are spoken of the trinitarian relations are not applicable to the divine substance; neither Father nor Son is a proper name for the Trinity. Holy Spirit, nevertheless, is a proper designation for the Trinity because God is Spirit. Gift, however, is an acceptable designation for the Holy Spirit who exists in trinitarian relationship as the communion of the Father and Son because the Holy Spirit is the Spirit of the Father and Son and proceeds as the gift of both.[82]

The concept of the Holy Spirit as gift and anointing is central to Augustine's Christology.

> The Lord Jesus Christ Himself not only gave the Holy Spirit as God, but also received it as man, and therefore He is said to be full of grace, and of the Holy Spirit. And in the Acts of the Apostles it is more plainly written of Him, 'Because God anointed Him with the Holy Spirit.' Certainly not with visible oil but with the gift of grace which is signified by the visible ointment wherewith the Church anoints the baptized. And Christ was certainly not then anointed with the Holy Spirit, when as a dove,

---

[81] Augustine, 'Trinity', NPNF, First Series, III, p. 93.

[82] The Holy Spirit is the bond of love in trinitarian relations (*Trin.* 15.17.27; 15.18.32–19.37). 'Therefore the Holy Spirit, whatever it is, is something common to both the Father and Son. But what is common itself is consubstantial and co-eternal; and if it may fitly be called friendship, let it be so called; but it is more aptly called love' (*Trin.* 6.5.7). Augustine, 'Trinity', NPNF, First Series, III, p. 100. Cf. Joseph T. Lienhard, 'The Glue Itself Is Charity: Ps. 62.9 in Augustine's Thought', in Joseph T. Lienhard, Earl C. Muller, and Roland J. Teske (eds.), *Augustine: Presbyter Factus Sum* (New York: Peter Lang, 1993), pp. 375-84; Kelly, *Doctrines*, pp. 275-76; Quasten, *Patrology*, IV, pp. 428-29; Harnack, *Dogma*, IV, pp. 131-33; Schaff, *History*, III, pp. 686-89.

descended upon Him at His baptism. For at that time He deigned to prefigure His body, i.e. His Church, in which especially the baptized receive the Holy Spirit. But he is to be understood to have been then anointed with that mystical and invisible unction, when the Word of God was made flesh (*Trin.* 15.26.46).[83]

When John the Baptist said, 'For God giveth not the Spirit by measure,' he was speaking exclusively of the Son of God, who received not the Spirit by measure; for in Him dwelleth all the fullness of the Godhead. And no more is it independently of the grace of the Spirit that the Mediator between God and men is the man Christ Jesus: for with his own lips He tells us that the prophetical utterance had been fulfilled in Himself: 'The Spirit of the Lord is upon me; because He hath anointed me, and hath sent me to preach the gospel to the poor.' For his being the Only-begotten, the equal of the Father, is not of grace, but of nature; but the assumption of the human nature into the personal unity of the Only-begotten is not of nature, but of grace ... But to others He is given by measure (*Tract. Ev. Jo.* 74.3).[84]

Several conclusions can be gleaned from these texts. First, at Pentecost, Christ as God gives the Spirit, so that the Holy Spirit as the promise of the Father proceeds from the Father and the Son;[85] the Spirit is the gift of both. Second, Augustine affirms Christ's dual natures, divine and human. Third, the Father anoints Christ's human nature with the Holy Spirit, and the Father and the Spirit send the Son on his salvific mission.[86] Fourth, Christ did not receive the Spirit's anointing in a limited measure, as others had received, but in its fullness. Fifth, Christ was not anointed with the Holy Spirit at the Jordan; rather, the anointing of the Sprit occurred during the incarnation, when as an act of grace, the divine Son assumed human nature. Sixth, Christ's reception of the Spirit at the Jordan was pro-

---

[83] Augustine, 'Trinity', NPNF, First Series, III, p. 224.
[84] Cited according to the translation of John Gibb and James Innes, Augustine, 'Homilies on the Gospel of John', NPNF, First Series, VII, p. 334.
[85] Cf. *Trin.* 4.20.28.
[86] Cf. *Trin.* 1.11.22; 2.5.8.

leptic of believers' receiving the Spirit at their baptism.[87] So, according to Augustine, the Holy Spirit functions with Christ in salvific mission as gift of grace and anointing.

How does the Holy Spirit relate as gift and anointing to Christ's identity and mission?

> The meaning of the Word made flesh, is not that the divine nature was changed into flesh, but that the divine nature assumed our flesh ... Wherefore Christ Jesus, the Son of God, is both God and man; God before all worlds; man in our world: God because the Word of God (for 'the Word was God'); and man, because in His one person the Word was joined with a body and a rational soul ... For when He was the only Son of God, not by grace, but by nature, that He might be also full of grace, He became the Son of man; and He himself unites both natures in His own identity, and both natures constitute one Christ (*Enchir.* 34; 35).[88]

Augustine acknowledges the Logos' divine preexistence and denies any change in deity in the incarnation; instead, the Logos assumed human nature: body and rational soul. Augustine, also, sharply distinguishes between Christ's divine and human natures: the Son is divine by nature, and through the Spirit Christ's human nature is united to deity by grace. In point of fact, Augustine attributes all scriptural references to Christ's subordination, ignorance, and suffering to the human nature, while he assigns Christ's miracles to the divine nature (*Trin.* 1.11.22–12.27).[89] Augustine, however, carefully

---

[87] J. Patout Burns, 'Christ and the Holy Spirit in Augustine's Theology of Baptism', in Joanne McWilliam (ed.), *Augustine: From Rhetor to Theologian* (Waterloo, ON: Wilfrid Laurier University Press, 1992), pp. 161-71.

[88] Augustine, 'The Enchiridion', NPNF, First Series, III, p. 249.

[89] Kelly, *Doctrines*, pp. 336-37; Quasten, *Patrology*, IV, pp. 430-31; González, *Christian Thought*, I, p. 337; Seeberg and Hay, *History*, I, pp. 259-60. According to Grillmeier, in Augustine's Christology 'there occurs a comparatively comprehensive formula whose affinity to the most moderate Antiochene theology is striking'. Grillmeier, *Christian Tradition*, I, pp. 407-13. There has been some discussion regarding the dynamics of grace in Augustine's view of the christological union; in fact, some scholars argue that Augustine's Christology bears striking similarities, even dependence, with Syrian Christology, particularly Theodore of Mopsuestia's. Harnack, *Dogma*, V, pp. 125-34; Eugene TeSelle, *Augustine the Theologian* (London: Burns & Oates, 1970), pp. 146-56; J. McWilliam Dewart, 'The Influence of Theodore of Mopsuestia on Augustine's Letter 187', *Augustinian Studies* 10 (1979), pp. 113-32. According to David Maxwell, during the The-

attests that distinction of natures does not imply two Sons. How do these distinct natures unite, forming the identity of the one Christ?

> Was it not by the act and assumption of the Word that that man, from the time He began to be, began to be the only Son of God? Did not that woman, full of grace, conceive the only Son of God? Was He not born the only Son of God, of the Holy Spirit and the Virgin Mary, – not of the lust of the flesh, but by God's peculiar gift? ... Therefore in Him who is our Head let there appear to be the very fountain of grace, whence, according to the measure of every man, He diffuses Himself through all His members. It is by that grace that every man from the beginning of his faith becomes a Christian, by which grace that one man from his beginning became Christ. Of the same Spirit also the former is born again of which the latter was born. By the same Spirit is effected in us the remission of sins, by which Spirit it was effected that He should have no sin (*Praed.* 30; 31).[90]

According to Augustine, The Father bestowing the Holy Spirit as the anointing and the gift of grace to Christ's human nature effected the incarnation, uniting the Logos with human nature, and the human nature's sinlessness. Here, Augustine's Spirit Christology integrates Logos Christology.[91] Salvifically, moreover, the same gift of

---

opaschite Controversy, a group of monks from Scythia came to Constantinople to gain approval from the emperor for their Theopaschite formula (519) which advocated a Monophysite position: 'One of the Trinity was crucified in the flesh'. These Scythian monks used Cyril of Alexandria's christological writings and Augustine's writings for their doctrine of grace. Maxwell asks the question: since these monks had Augustine's christological writings in their possession, why did they choose not to use them? Maxwell concludes that Augustine's Christology must have sounded too similar to Nestorius' for them. David R. Maxwell, 'What Was "Wrong" with Augustine? The Sixth-Century Reception (or Lack Thereof) of Augustine's Christology', in Peter William Martens (ed.), *In the Shadow of the Incarnation: Essays on Jesus Christ in the Early Church in Honor of Brian E. Daley, S.J* (Notre Dame: University of Notre Dame Press, 2008), pp. 212-27. John McGuckin has examined the evidence and concludes that Augustine's view of the christological union is not attributable to Syrian influence; rather, it stands in a long tradition of Latin Christology. John Anthony McGuckin, 'Did Augustine's Christology Depend on Theodore of Mopsuestia?', *HeyJ* 31 (1990), pp. 39-52.

[90] Augustine, 'On the Predestination of the Saints', NPNF, First Series, V, pp. 512-13.

[91] According to David Coffey, Augustine's Spirit Christology is 'in no way incompatible with Logos Christology, that indeed as *requiring* a Logos Christology'. Coffey, 'Spirit Christology and the Trinity', p. 323.

grace that has effected the incarnation, now, regenerates believers and dwells among them as the presence of Christ. So the Holy Spirit as the anointing and gift of grace effect the incarnation of the Son and the salvific mission.

Augustine's Spirit Christology supports a paradigm of pneumatic mediation within a trinitarian framework. According to Augustine, God is Trinity. The Father begets the Son, and the Holy Spirit is the communion of the Father and Son and proceeds as the gift of both. The Father bestows the Spirit as the gift of grace and anointing to Christ's human nature effecting the incarnation and the salvific mission; thus, the Spirit unites the human nature to the divine Son; the Logos is made flesh. Augustine, accordingly, distinguishes between the Spirit-anointed human nature and the divine Son which constitute the identity of the one Christ. Augustine, therefore, posits a Spirit Christology which integrates Logos Christology without any diminishing of Christ's deity.

Conclusion

These Western writers' Spirit christological paradigms essentially agree; they present models of pneumatic mediation within a trinitarian framework, yet they remain fluid enough to enclose a form of pneumatic incarnation and to integrate Logos Christology. All acknowledge the consubstantial divine unity of the Father, Son, and Holy Spirit, and Spirit is a common designation for the divine substance. Although, in the sense that the Son partakes of the divine substance which is Spirit, Christ's virgin birth may be spoken of as a pneumatic incarnation, these writers unambiguously affirm the distinct trinitarian relation of the Holy Spirit; the Logos was made flesh, not the Holy Spirit. All recognize that Son and Holy Spirit function in a perichoretic relationship in salvific mission, so that the Spirit effects the incarnation, and since Pentecost, Christ salvifically dwells among believers through the Spirit and empowers them. All sharply distinguish between Christ's divine and human natures, so that ignorance, subordination, and suffering is attributed to the human nature, while strictly maintaining the unity of the one Christ; there are not two Sons. All affirm that the Spirit effects the incarnation and mediates the unity of these natures. All grant that Christ's human nature was anointed by the Spirit; however, ambiguity arises among them concerning this issue. Hilary and Ambrose allow for an anointing of the human nature through Christ's reception of the Spirit at the Jordan, but Victorinus and Augustine seem to place this anointing exclusively in the incarnation. Of course, the issues of Christ's dual natures and the anointing of the Spirit will come to a head in the christological councils of the fifth and sixth centuries as East and West convene to discuss Christ's identity and mission.

8

SETTING THE BOUNDARIES

The Council of Constantinople (381) defined, clarified, and limited language concerning the Godhead, so that terms acquired common meanings, facilitating dialogue concerning the divine mystery; however, christological terms remained fluid; often the same terms designating Christ's identity carried different import, causing confusion and controversy. It was the task of the christological councils of the fifth and sixth centuries to delineate the limits of articulating the identity and mission of Christ within the boundaries of orthodox Christology. This survey now presses forward by examining the role of Spirit Christology in the controversies that generated these boundaries and its place within these circumscribed bounds.

The Council of Ephesus (431)

The main characters in the controversy which occasioned the third ecumenical council were Cyril[1] representing the Alexandrian tradi-

---

[1] At the age of 25, Cyril was ordained Lector of the church (403) by his uncle Theophilus, the bishop of Alexandria. He accompanied Theophilus to the synod of Oak that deposed John Chrysostom (403). After succeeding his uncle Theophilus as bishop of Alexandria (412), Cyril set about with a heavy hand to rid his diocese of the vestiges of heresies and polytheism, and to restore the strained relationships between his see and Rome and Constantinople owing to Chrysostom's deposition. By the time he came into conflict with Nestorius, Cyril had 25 years of experience of ecclesiastical politics at its highest level; he was a consummate politician. For information about Cyril's life and role in the controversy, see John Anthony McGuckin, *St. Cyril of Alexandria: The Christological Controversy: Its History, Theology, and Texts* (VCSup 23; Leiden: E.J. Brill, 1994), pp. 1-20; Susan

tion and Nestorius[2] representing the Syrian Antiochene tradition. These traditions focused on the same christological concerns: the relationship of Christ's deity to the Godhead, the christological union of deity and humanity in Christ, and Christ's salvific mission. Nonetheless, their hermeneutical and theological starting points dramatically diverged. The Alexandrian tradition had inherited the Platonic philosophical legacy and an allegorical exegesis of Scripture. Their Christology emphasized Christ's deity and accentuated the unity of Christ's natures. Conversely, it appears that the Syrian tradition operated in either the Stoic or Aristotelian philosophical conventions and stressed a literal interpretation of Scripture. Christologically, they asserted Christ's true deity and true humanity and sharply distinguished between these natures.[3]

Wessel, *Cyril of Alexandria and the Nestorian Controversy: The Making of a Saint and of a Heretic* (OECS; Oxford: Oxford University Press, 2004), pp. 15-73; Norman Russell, *Cyril of Alexandria* (ECF; London: Routledge, 2000), pp. 3-11; Cyril, *On the Unity of Christ* (trans. John Anthony McGuckin; Crestwood, NY: St. Vladimir's Seminary Press, 1995), pp. 9-32; Quasten, *Patrology*, III, pp. 116-17; Schaff, *History*, III, pp. 942-49.

[2] Nestorius ascended to the episcopal throne of Constantinople (428) amid factional disputes, arguably, securing his consecration to the bishopric because of his tremendous preaching ability and on the recommendation of his friend John bishop of Antioch. Immediately, Nestorius enacted various reforms intended to consolidate the religious views and practices in his diocese which, rather than lessening the tensions, aggravated the disputes between the monks, the local hierarchs, and the imperial court. For example, Nestorius' attempt to reign in certain ministries implemented by the monks only succeeded in turning them against Nestorius. Prior to Nestorius' arrival in Constantinople, Pulcheria, the emperor's sister, had enjoyed the eucharistic privilege given the reigning emperor in the liturgy. Nestorius, however, refused her this privilege. Also, in devotion to the Virgin Mary and as a sign of her own consecrated virginity, Pulcheria had given the church a beautiful garment to lie on the holy altar; Nestorius promptly removed this robe, offending Pulcheria's honor and incurring her ire. Although Pulcheria continued to oppose Nestorius throughout the controversy, he seemed to retain the favor of Theodosius II until the end of the controversy. This information and an overview of Nestorius' life can be found in McGuckin, *Cyril of Alexandria*, pp. 20-27; Russell, *Cyril of Alexandria*, pp. 31-33; Cyril, *On the Unity of Christ*, p. 17; Quasten, *Patrology*, III, p. 514.

[3] Stephen W. Need, *Truly Divine and Truly Human: The Story of Christ and the Seven Ecumenical Councils* (London: SPCK, 2008), pp. 17-39; Sellers, *Two Ancient Christologies*, pp. 1-201; John Meyendorff, *Christ in Eastern Christian Thought* (Crestwood, NY: St. Vladimir's Seminary Press, 1975), pp. 15-19; Williston Walker, *A History of the Christian Church* (New York: Charles Scribner's Sons, 1918), pp. 144-45; González, *Christian Thought*, I, pp. 337-49; J.F. Bethune-Baker, *An Introduction to the Early History of Christian Doctrine: To the Time of the Council of Chalcedon* (London: Methuen, 8 edn, 1949), pp. 255-60; Davis, *Ecumenical Councils*, pp. 136-39; Har-

Christological vocabulary also caused semantic confusion between Cyril and Nestorius. Three basic terms were available to express the christological union during the fifth century: physis, hypostasis, and prosopon.[4] Nestorius chose prosopon. For Nestorius, a hypostasis is a complete nature, and every hypostasis has its prosopon, the sum of its distinguishing characteristics (idiomata) by which it is made known to others. In the one Christ two prosopa, divine and human, exist in prosopic union neither mixing the hypostasis nor producing a new hypostasis, externally manifesting a single concrete reality.[5] Although Cyril opted primarily to use hypostasis, he frequently employed physis (nature) and hypostasis synonymously. For Cyril, in the incarnation the Logos took human nature to himself, making it his own, in hypostatic union. Cyril, accordingly, posited that the divine and human in Christ existed in hypostatic union with one center of subjectivity which was the Logos; there was one incarnate nature of the divine Logos in Christ.[6] With this much fluidity of meaning in christological terms,

---

nack, *Dogma*, IV, pp. 165-74; 142-48; Gerald O'Collins, *Christology: A Biblical, Historical, and Systematic Study of Jesus* (Oxford: Oxford University Press, 2nd edn, 2009), p. 188; Russell, *Cyril of Alexandria*, pp. 41-45; Wessel, *Nestorian Controversy*, pp. 1-4, 113-37; Quasten, *Patrology*, III, p. 135; Daley, 'One Thing and Another', pp. 36-38. Some scholars have argued that the primary concern of the christological debates was the impassibility of God. Cf. John J. O'Keefe, 'Impassible Suffering? Divine Passion and Fifth-Century Christology', *TS* 58 (1997), pp. 39-60; Geoffrey D. Dunn, 'Divine Impassibility and Christology in the Christmas Homilies of Leo the Great', *TS* 62 (2001), pp. 71-85.

[4] For a discussion of these terms, see Sellers, *Two Ancient Christologies*, pp. 46-50; McGuckin, *Cyril of Alexandria*, pp. 138-51; Meyendorff, *Christ in Eastern Christian Thought*, pp. 19-22; Russell, *Cyril of Alexandria*, pp. 39-40; Grillmeier, *Christian Tradition*, I, pp. 459-60; Need, *Truly Divine and Truly Human*, p. 87; Daley, 'One Thing and Another', pp. 38-42; O'Collins, *Christology*, pp. 182-89.

[5] For an overview of Nestorius' Christology, see McGuckin, *Cyril of Alexandria*, pp. 126-74; Sellers, *Two Ancient Christologies*, pp. 128-30, 146-66; Grillmeier, *Christian Tradition*, I, pp. 457-63; Chesnut, 'Two Prosopa', pp. 392-409; González, *Christian Thought*, I, pp. 358-64; Kelly, *Doctrines*, pp. 312-17; O'Collins, *Christology*, pp. 190-91; Walker, *History*, pp. 145-46; Frend, *Christianity*, p. 754.

[6] Cyril was attempting to solve the Apollinarian impasse in the Alexandrian tradition: how can the existence of a human soul in Christ be reconciled with a single subject Christology? According to J.N.D. Kelly, to depict this union Apollinarius used '*hypostasis*, being the first to introduce it into the vocabulary of Christology; it connotes for him a self-determining reality'. Kelly, *Doctrines*, p. 293. Although Apollinarius was considered a heretic and his critics often charged him with Apollinarianism, Cyril responded that everything Apollinarius said was not heretical; in fact, Cyril regarded Apollinarius' formula for a single subject in Christ

conflict was inevitable.⁷

In 429, Nestorius preached a series of sermons regarding proper faith in Christ, which ignited the ensuing controversy, beginning with why applying the designation *Theotokos* to Mary was not appropriate. It meant that the Logos, who was eternally begotten from the Father, was born a second time of a woman, and it confused the natures so that Christ was divine but not human; consequently, it was tinctured with Apollinarianism, deprecating human salvation. For Nestorius, *Christotokos* was a better designation because it indicated that the Logos eternally existed with the Father, and Mary did not give birth to God; rather, deity united with a complete human nature in her womb, so that she bore the Christ.⁸ Thus, instead of Mary being the dwelling place of God, Christ's humanity became the temple of God.⁹ Since *Theotokos* had become a marker of faith

---

as correct: 'we confess moreover that there is one incarnate nature of the Son' (*Letter to Eulogius*, 1). Cited according to the translation of John Anthony McGuckin, *Cyril of Alexandria*, p. 349.

> As far as Cyril was concerned, even if Apollinaris' overall scheme had been a failure, his fundamental insights that the church's faith demanded a confession of a single subject in the incarnate Lord, and also his fidelity to the Alexandrian tradition (at least in his desire to safeguard a dynamic soteriology) were both absolutely and uncontrovertibly right (McGuckin, *Cyril of Alexandria*, p. 183).

Cf. Grillmeier, *Christian Tradition*, I, pp. 452, 457, 473-83; González, *Christian Thought*, I, pp. 365-66; O'Collins, *Christology*, pp. 191; Davis, *Ecumenical Councils*, p. 153; Need, *Truly Divine and Truly Human*, p. 87. Regarding Cyril's Christology, see Sellers, *Two Ancient Christologies*, pp. 80-106; Kelly, *Doctrines*, pp. 317-23; Quasten, *Patrology*, III, pp. 136-40; McGuckin, *Cyril of Alexandria*, pp. 175-226; Harnack, *Dogma*, IV, pp. 174-80; Cyril, *On the Unity of Christ*, pp. 32-47; Frend, *Christianity*, pp. 753-54; Wiles, *Working Papers in Doctrine*, pp. 63-65; Walker, *History*, p. 146.

⁷ 'It would seem that Nestorius regularly uses ὑπόστασις as practically equivalent to οὐσία, and in Trinitarian doctrine would himself speak of three πρόσωπα in one ὑπόστασις (or οὐσία). But Cyril has the later usage in which the two are distinguished, and so speaks of three ὑπόστασις in one οὐσια. Nestorius evidently appreciates this difference of terminology in Trinitarian doctrine, and tries to find in it a clue to the understanding of Cyril's Christology, asking whether after all Cyril always means by ὑπόστασις what he himself calls πρόσωπον.' Nestorius, *The Bazaar of Heracleides*, p. 156, n. 2. Cf. Grillmeier, *Christian Tradition*, I, p. 458.

⁸ See Nestorius' *First Sermon against the Theotokos* in Norris, *The Christological Controversy*, pp. 123-31. Cf. Sellers, *Two Ancient Christologies*, pp. 172-73, 177; Kelly, *Doctrines*, 310-11; González, *Christian Thought*, I, p. 354; Grillmeier, *Christian Tradition*, I, p. 451; Frend, *Christianity*, p. 755; O'Collins, *Christology*, p. 191.

⁹ According to C. Clark Carlton, Nestorius was reacting against Marian devotion as found in Marian hymnography which conjoined two themes: (1) Mary as the temple or dwelling place of God, and (2) Mary as a sacrificial offering to God.

for Marian devotion, Nestorius enraged many of the laity, monks, and clergy of his diocese; it appeared to them that Nestorius was attacking Mary's honor and Christ's deity.[10]

Nestorius published these sermons and sent them to other areas, including Egypt and Rome, producing seven consequent actions. First, it initiated an acrimonious literary exchange between Cyril and Nestorius, refuting one another's christological positions;[11] politically, Cyril's letters implied that Rome supported him and was upset with Nestorius, while Nestorius' rejoinders threatened ecclesiastical action against Cyril.[12] Second, Nestorius sent a letter to Celestine,

---

C. Clark Carlton, 'The Temple that Held God: Byzantine Marian Hymnography and the Christ of Nestorius', *SVTQ* 50 (2006), pp. 99-125.

We can easily see why Nestorius reacted so strongly to Proclus' sermon (and to the title *Theotokos* in general). By referring to the Virgin as the temple of God – not merely the temple of Christ's humanity – Proclus had essentially co-opted the role that Christ's humanity played in the drama of salvation and assigned it to Mary. It is the Virgin who represents a true 'union of wills' between God and man. It is the Virgin, not the man Jesus, who is prepared by the Holy Spirit to be the dwelling-place of God; the Virgin, not the man Jesus, who provides God with flesh; the Virgin, not the man Jesus, who is the 'sinless temple' offered to God on behalf of the human race (Carlton, 'The Temple that Held God', p. 121).

[10] Need, *Truly Divine and Truly Human*, pp. 81-86, McGuckin, *Cyril of Alexandria*, pp. 27-32; Bethune-Baker, *Christian Doctrine*, pp. 260-62; Davis, *Ecumenical Councils*, pp. 140-41; Harnack, *Dogma*, IV, pp. 180-82; Russell, *Cyril of Alexandria*, pp. 33-35; Cyril, *On the Unity of Christ*, pp. 17-19; Quasten, *Patrology*, III, p. 514; Walker, *History*, pp. 146-47. According to Grillmeier, 'a central feature of the faith and preaching of the church had been attacked in the sight and hearing of simple believers and their bishops. Matters were the more serious because *Theotokos* was a key word for faith in the incarnation'. Grillmeier, *Christian Tradition*, I, p. 448. For a Pentecostal response to Marian devotion, stemming from the modern ecumenical discussion between Pentecostals and Roman Catholics, see Jerry L. Sandidge, 'A Pentecostal Response to Roman Catholic Teaching on Mary', *Pneuma*, Fall (1982), pp. 33-42.

[11] Davis, *Ecumenical Councils*, p. 141; McGuckin, *Cyril of Alexandria*, p. 33; Bethune-Baker, *Christian Doctrine*, pp. 262-63; Wessel, *Nestorian Controversy*, pp. 76-82; Need, *Truly Divine and Truly Human*, p. 86; Russell, *Cyril of Alexandria*, p. 35; Kelly, *Doctrines*, pp. 323-24.

[12] Since the Council of Constantinople (381) had elevated Constantinople to the primary see in the East, which essentially made Constantinople the supreme ecclesiastical court of appeal in the East, Nestorius began hearing the appeals of Alexandrian clerics deposed by Cyril, and he began reviewing the cases of Pelagians exiled by Western synods, living in Constantinople. It is noteworthy that against Apollinarianism Diodore 'had resolutely defended the full divinity and humanity of Christ and had been singled out in Theodosius I's letter ratifying the Council of Constantinople of 381 as an orthodox model for other bishops'. Davis, *Ecumenical Councils*, pp. 141-43; McGuckin, *Cyril of Alexandria*, pp. 34-37; Rus-

bishop of Rome, depicting Cyril's engagement in the *Theotokos* dispute as an attempt to avoid an ecclesiastical trial.[13] Third, Cyril compiled a dossier containing excerpts from Nestorius' writings, had the dossier translated into Latin, and sent it along with a *Letter to Pope Celestine* (430) to Rome asking for Celestine's response.[14] Fourth, Celestine convoked a synod in Rome (August 430) to address the matter. The Roman synodical verdict condemned Nestorius' writings, requiring Nestorius to abjure his teachings and to make a profession of faith concordant with Rome and Alexandria before he could be restored to communion; consequently, Celestine appointed Cyril his delegate to execute the directive. Fifth, Celestine communicated this edict directly to the prominent Eastern bishops.[15] Sixth, Cyril convened a synod of Egyptian bishops (Nov. 430)

---

sell, *Cyril of Alexandria*, pp. 35-36; González, *Christian Thought*, I, pp. 353-54; Frend, *Christianity*, p. 755.

[13] Wessel, *Nestorian Controversy*, pp. 107-109. Celestine gave John Cassian the task of translating Nestorius' letters into Latin. Cassian's translation depicted Nestorius as supporting the Pelagian position, placing the death nail in Nestorius' arguments as far as Rome was concerned. McGuckin, *Cyril of Alexandria*, p. 42. Grillmeier and Bernard Green suggest that Cassian inaccurately interpreted these writings by aligning Nestorius with Pelagius and Leporius, who taught a form of adoptionism before Augustine rehabilitated him, so that Nestorius' Christology sounded to Celestine as a mix of Pelagianism and adoptionism. Grillmeier also depicts Cassian as interpreting the Spirit christological issues in a negative light. Grillmeier, *Christian Tradition*, I, pp. 464-72; Bernard Green, *The Soteriology of Leo the Great* (OTM; Oxford: Oxford University Press, 2008), pp. 22-37.

[14] The dossier also contained Cyril's *Second Letter to Nestorius* (Feb. 430), Nestorius' recent reply to Cyril's second letter, and some texts from Athanasius and Gregory of Nazianzus. The letter to Celestine recounted Dorotheus' sermon, the unrest in Egypt among the monks, and Cyril's correspondences with Nestorius. McGuckin, *Cyril of Alexandria*, pp. 37-38; Russell, *Cyril of Alexandria*, pp. 36-38; Cyril, *On the Unity of Christ*, pp. 19-23; Wessel, *Nestorian Controversy*, pp. 105-107. Davis, *Ecumenical Councils*, p. 148; Kelly, *Doctrines*, p. 324. In the spring of 430, Cyril wrote *Five Tomes against Nestorius* which set forth the issues in the debate and sent it to Rome, so Celestine was well acquainted with the issues, from Cyril's point of view, when the dossier arrived during the summer. The *Five Tomes* along with an English translation can be found in Russell, *Cyril of Alexandria*, pp. 130-74. Cyril also sent a letter, *De Recta Fide*, to the emperor and a separate treatise, *Ad Reginas*, to the empresses Eudoxia and Pulcheria, presenting the issues and positing his position. Cyril's separate appeal to the women of the royal household angered the emperor and helped Nestorius. McGuckin, *Cyril of Alexandria*, pp. 39-40. For an overview of Cyril's writings against Nestorius, see Quasten, *Patrology*, III, pp. 126-29.

[15] Davis, *Ecumenical Councils*, p. 148; McGuckin, *Cyril of Alexandria*, pp. 42-43; Wessel, *Nestorian Controversy*, pp. 110-11; Russell, *Cyril of Alexandria*, p. 38; Grillmeier, *Christian Tradition*, I, p. 472; Harnack, *Dogma*, IV, pp. 182-86; González,

which affirmed the Roman decree. Since the edict omitted any christological construal, Cyril filled this void by writing and attaching to the Roman decree his *Third Letter to Nestorius* and *Twelve Anathemas* (430) which represented Cyril's christological position and refuted the premises of Nestorius' Christology. Cyril made it clear; to be restored to communion with Rome and Alexandria Nestorius must accept the anathemas' christological propositions. Seventh, Cyril dispatched four bishops to Constantinople, demanding Nestorius' recantation and acceptance of the anathemas, but Nestorius refused their directive.[16]

Emperor Theodosius II, nevertheless, had previously decided (Nov. 430) to convoke an ecumenical council in Ephesus, 7 June 431.[17] The emperor desiring to settle the dispute through theological discussion instructed his imperial representative, Candidian, to debar the council convening until all the parties were present. Nevertheless, when the Antiochene delegation, headed by John of Antioch, delayed its arrival, Cyril took control and opened the council

---

Christian Thought, I, pp. 354-55; Walker, *History*, pp. 147-48. According to Harnack, Celestine

> in interfering on behalf of Cyril disowned his western view and in the most frivolous fashion condemned Nestorius without having considered his teaching. That he did both things may be easily shown. In his letter to the Pope Nestorius laid before the latter the formula "utraque natura quae per conjunctionem summam et inconfusam in una persona unigeniti adoratur" ('the two natures which, perfectly joined together and without confusion, are adorned in the one person of the only-begotten'). *This was the Western formula, and Coelestin himself held no other view* (Harnack, *Dogma*, IV, p. 183).

[16] Davis, *Ecumenical Councils*, pp. 148-53; Bethune-Baker, *Christian Doctrine*, pp. 263-66; McGuckin, *Cyril of Alexandria*, pp. 44-47; Russell, *Cyril of Alexandria*, pp. 38-39; González, *Christian Thought*, I, p. 355; Kelly, *Doctrines*, pp. 324-25; Frend, *Christianity*, pp. 757-58. Nestorius, however, conceded that the title *Theotokos* could be applied to Mary if it was properly defined. Nestorius probably consented to the use of Theotokos at the advice of John of Antioch and Theodoret of Cyrus. Paul B. Clayton, *The Christology of Theodoret of Cyrus: Antiochene Christology from the Council of Ephesus (431) to the Council of Chalcedon (451)* (OECS; Oxford: Oxford University Press, 2007), p. 15.

[17] Wessel, *Nestorian Controversy*, pp. 138-46; González, *Christian Thought*, I, pp. 354-55; Schaff, *History*, III, pp. 722-24. Pulcheria seems to be behind this choice of venue, sending her own message to Nestorius. The greatest shrine to Mary in existence was located in Ephesus, and the council convened in the great basilica dedicated to Mary. McGuckin, *Cyril of Alexandria*, pp. 47, 60-61; Cyril, *On the Unity of Christ*, p. 23.

(22 June).[18] The council proceeded by reading the Nicene Creed and Cyril's *Second Letter to Nestorius* (430); the council judged Cyril's letter to express the Nicene faith. Then, they read Rome's and Alexandria's synodical decrees, including Cyril's *Third Letter to Nestorius* and the *Twelve Anathemas*.[19] Since Nestorius was not present to defend himself, the council asked if there were any evidence, in his own words, of Nestorius christological teaching. Cyril gladly offered into evidence Nestorius' writings contained in his dossier. The council, subsequently, drew up a formal declaration denouncing Nestorius' Christology; the bishops in attendance signed it and sent a notice of deposition to Nestorius.[20]

The matter, however, was far from being settled; groups from both sides had not yet arrived. Candidian, therefore, annulled the proceedings, refused to allow the bishops to leave the city, and sent a report to the emperor. John of Antioch finally arrived (26 June) with the Syrian delegation, and immediately they convened their own council, known as the conciliabulum, declaring Cyril's council indecorous. After studying Cyril's third letter and the 12 anathemas, the Antiochenes inferred that Cyril advocated Apollinarian Christology; consequently, they charged Cyril with canonical impropriety for illegally opening the council and teaching Apollinarian doctrine. The conciliabulum concluded by excommunicating Cyril, Memnon the bishop of Ephesus, and the other bishops in agreement with

---

[18] Russell, *Cyril of Alexandria*, pp. 46-48; Cyril, *On the Unity of Christ*, pp. 23-24; González, *Christian Thought*, I, p. 356; Schaff, *History*, III, p. 724; Wessel, *Nestorian Controversy*, p. 147. There was some confusion regarding which bishop should preside at the council. Ordinarily, as bishop of Constantinople Nestorius would hold the primary position, but Cyril and his delegation did not recognize the right of the emperor to set aside the Roman and Alexandrian synods, so Cyril claimed the right as bishop of Alexandria and Celestine's representative. Albeit, Theodoret of Cyrus, the primary theologian chosen to defend Syrian Christology, and other supporters of Nestorius were present in Ephesus, they refused to attend because the main body of the Syrian delegates had not arrived. McGuckin, *Cyril of Alexandria*, pp. 65-74.

[19] The anathemas were viewed with some suspicion, so Cyril's *Third Letter to Nestorius* and the *Twelve Anathemas* were not received in the same manner as Cyril's *Second Letter to Nestorius*.

[20] McGuckin, *Cyril of Alexandria*, pp. 75-90; Grillmeier, *Christian Tradition*, I, pp. 484-87; Wessel, *Nestorian Controversy*, pp. 147-61; Russell, *Cyril of Alexandria*, pp. 48-50; Davis, *Ecumenical Councils*, pp. 153-56; Bethune-Baker, *Christian Doctrine*, pp. 267-72; Harnack, *Dogma*, IV, pp. 186-89; Kelly, *Doctrines*, p. 327; Schaff, *History*, III, pp. 724-25; Cyril, *On the Unity of Christ*, p. 25; Frend, *Christianity*, pp. 758-60; O'Collins, *Christology*, pp. 192-94.

Cyril.²¹ When the papal legates arrived in Ephesus (10 July), Cyril convoked a second session of the Council, and the next day during a third session, the legates approved the former actions of Cyril's Council and subscribed to Nestorius' deposition.²²

Theodosius II surprised everyone by ratifying both Cyril's and John's councils, deposing Nestorius, Cyril, and Memnon. He also called for a small number of delegates from both sides to a synod at Chalcedon to debate the issues.²³ The Antiochene Syrian delegation, forthwith, drew up a confession of faith and delivered it to the emperor.²⁴ Meanwhile, Cyril used the riches of Alexandria to bribe court officials to influence imperial opinion, so the meeting at Chalcedon turned against the Syrians.²⁵ Finally, in August Theodosius II closed the Council of Ephesus. Though Theodosius II cautiously accepted the Syrian position as orthodox, Cyril's position seemed to triumph. The Council restored Cyril and Memnon to their sees, upheld Nestorius' deposition, confirmed Cyril's position as orthodox,

---

²¹ McGuckin, *Cyril of Alexandria*, pp. 90-98; Wessel, *Nestorian Controversy*, pp. 168-73; Russell, *Cyril of Alexandria*, p. 50; Cyril, *On the Unity of Christ*, p. 25; Need, *Truly Divine and Truly Human*, p. 90; Davis, *Ecumenical Councils*, p. 156; Quasten, *Patrology*, III, p. 118; González, *Christian Thought*, I, p. 356; Schaff, *History*, III, p. 725; Frend, *Christianity*, p. 760.

²² 'The papal legates – two Italian bishops and the priest Philip – arrived with instructions not to enter into the debates but to act as judges and to defer in all things to Cyril.' Davis, *Ecumenical Councils*, pp. 156-57. Cf. Wessel, *Nestorian Controversy*, pp. 173-75; Cyril, *On the Unity of Christ*, pp. 25-26; Russell, *Cyril of Alexandria*, p. 51; Schaff, *History*, III, p. 726; Frend, *Christianity*, pp. 760-61. In the fourth and fifth sessions of Cyril's Council, the conciliabulum's decisions were set aside and John of Antioch was reprimanded. Davis, *Ecumenical Councils*, pp. 157-58.

²³ Wessel, *Nestorian Controversy*, pp. 256-61; Russell, *Cyril of Alexandria*, p. 51; Cyril, *On the Unity of Christ*, pp. 26-27; González, *Christian Thought*, I, pp. 356-57; Schaff, *History*, III, p. 726. The debate was primarily between Theodoret of Cyrus, representing the Syrian position, and Acacius of Melitene, representing Cyril's position, and centered on the 12 anathemas. Davis, *Ecumenical Councils*, p. 159.

²⁴ This confession of faith is essentially the same confession of faith that Cyril accepted as orthodox in the Formula of Union.

²⁵ One gets this sense from reading the letter which Theodoret wrote during this time. There are two reoccurring themes that suggest this: (1) Theodoret complained that the bishops deposed by the conciliabulum were allowed to perform priestly duties and celebrate the Eucharist, and (2) the Syrians were neither allowed to enter the churches at Chalcedon nor to celebrate the Eucharist. Theodoret, 'Letters', 163–70, NPNF, Second Series, III, pp. 336-44. Cf. Clayton, *Theodoret of Cyrus*, pp. 154-57.

ratified *Theotokos* as a proper title for Mary, and accepted hypostasis as the proper term for speaking of the christological union.[26]

Several Spirit christological texts emerged in the writings during the controversy that occasioned the Council of Ephesus. When Nestorius' sermons arrived in Egypt, they caused quite a stir among the monks, so Cyril composed a *Letter to the Monks of Egypt* (429) refuting Nestorius' teaching. For Cyril, Nestorius' rejection of *Theotokos* carried several implications: it repudiated Christ's deity (*Monks*, 7-9); Jesus was a God-bearing man in the line of inspired prophets (*Monks*, 19-20); no real union of natures existed, so Nestorius advocated two sons (*Monks*, 13-14);[27] therefore, it undermined the incarnation and attenuated human salvation (*Monks*, 26). Cyril, accordingly, reacts to Nestorius' supposal that the name Christ signifies the anointing of the Spirit (*Monks*, 10-11).

> In their ignorance they have wronged the nature of the Only Begotten and have perverted the mystery of the economy with flesh. For if it is the Word who is anointed with the Holy Spirit then they confess, like it or not, that the Word existed in former times (when he had not yet been anointed) as wholly lacking in holiness, and was non-participant in this gift which was later bestowed on him. But anything that is lacking in holiness is changeable by nature and cannot be considered as altogether sinless or beyond the capability of transgression (*Monks*, 15).[28]

Here, Cyril attacks Nestorius' distinction of natures in Christ which allows for an anointing of the human nature through Christ's reception of the Spirit at the Jordan. Since Cyril posits one incarnate nature in Christ, any anointing of the Spirit subsequent to the incarna-

---

[26] McGuckin, *Cyril of Alexandria*, pp. 98-107; Wessel, *Nestorian Controversy*, pp. 261-63; Davis, *Ecumenical Councils*, pp. 158-59; Cyril, *On the Unity of Christ*, pp. 27-28; Frend, *Christianity*, p. 761. Of course, this neither represents the full proceedings nor all the rulings of the Council of Ephesus. For more complete information about these matters, see 'Ephesus', NPNF, Second Series, XIV, pp. 191-242; Peter L'Huillier, *The Church of the Ancient Councils: The Disciplinary Work of the First Four Ecumenical Councils* (Crestwood, NY: St. Vladimir's Seminary Press, 1995), pp. 143-74.

[27] Cf. Cyril's *Twelve Anathemas* 5.

[28] Cited according to the translation of John Anthony McGuckin, *Cyril of Alexandria*, pp. 253-54. Cf. Cyril of Alexandria, *Letters*, FC, LXXVI, p. 24. For similar Spirit christological texts in this letter, see *Monks*, 11, 16. Cf. Cyril, *On the Unity of Christ*, pp. 65-67.

tion denies the Logos' deity: it indicates a deficiency of holiness by denying the Logos' immutable and sinless nature; thus, salvation is compromised.[29] The Spirit christological issue of the Spirit's anointing and its relation to Christ's identity and mission, therefore, was an integral part of the controversy.[30]

Cyril's *Third Letter to Nestorius* and *Twelve Anathemas* (Nov. 430) were read during the council. After reciting the Nicene Creed, Cyril asserts that the reference to 'one Son of God' in this document exactly depicts his doctrine of hypostatic union (*Ep. Nestorius* 3.3-4). Cyril, hence, refuses to speak of deity assuming or dwelling in human nature because it implies two Christs, a God-bearing man (*Ep. Nestorius* 3.4-6).[31] Cyril, accordingly, rejects Nestorius' practice of dividing the sayings of the Lord in the gospels between those that apply to the human and to the divine nature as if they are two hypostases or prosopa;[32] instead, he attributes all the sayings in the gospels to one prosopon, and to the one incarnate hypostasis of the Word (*Ep. Nestorius* 3.8). The Spirit christological issue, then, arises in connection with the Spirit's anointing.

> When he says of the Spirit: 'And he shall glorify me' (Jn 16.14), if we want to think correctly we will not say that the One Christ and Son received glory from the Holy Spirit as if he stood in need of glory from another; for his own Spirit is neither greater than him nor above him. But since he used his own Spirit in great miracles for the manifestation of his own Godhead, this is why he says that he is glorified by him (*Ep. Nestorius* 3.10).[33]

---

[29] Conversely, Cyril argues that the Logos did not assume a body as an instrument; rather, the Logos became flesh for the salvation of the world. If the Logos is God by nature, *Theotokos* is an appropriate title for Mary (*Monks*, 21-27).

[30] The Syrians staunchly denied teaching that Christ was only a human inspired by the Spirit, a Spirit Christology of inspiration. Sellers, *Two Ancient Christologies*, pp. 177-79.

[31] Cf. Cyril's *Twelve Anathemas* 5.

[32] Cf. Cyril's *Twelve Anathemas* 4. Theodoret retorts that Cyril's hypostatic union in the second anathema mixes and confuses Christ's nature similar to Apollinarius, and in the fourth anathema Cyril does not allow any dividing of the sayings in the gospels, so that passions are applied to deity. Theodoret, however, defends from Scripture the division of sayings and asserts that he does not divide Christ but affirms that two natures are united without confusion in one Christ (*Letter* 151).

[33] Cited according to the translation of John Anthony McGuckin, *Cyril of Alexandria*, p. 272. The Greek text without translation can be found in T. Herbert

> If anyone says that the One Jesus Christ was glorified by the Spirit, using the power that came through him as if it were foreign to himself, and receiving from him the power to work against unclean spirits and to accomplish divine signs for men, and does not rather say that the Spirit is his very own, through whom he also worked the divine signs, let him be anathema (*Twelve Anathemas* 9).[34]

Several conclusions can be drawn from these texts regarding Cyril's understanding of the Spirit's anointing in relation to Christ. First, the eternal divine Son and Holy Spirit existed in consubstantial unity and glory; the Spirit is the Spirit of the Son. Second, in the incarnation the Logos united with human nature in one incarnate hypostasis, so deity did not need anointing. Third, Christ worked miracles and exorcisms through the Spirit; nevertheless, this power was not alien to Christ: it was his Spirit and power. So contrary to Nestorius, the Spirit's anointing did not empower Christ's human nature to perform miracles.

Because Cyril's anathemas collectively threatened Syrian Christology, John of Antioch turned to Theodoret of Cyrus,[35] requesting a rebuttal.[36] Theodoret, subsequently, wrote a *Refutation of the Twelve Anathemas of Cyril of Alexandria against Nestorius* (early 431) which presented the Syrian christological view, defended Nestorius, labeled Cyril's Christology Apollinarian, and controverted each anathema.[37] While refuting two anathemas in this document, Theodoret directly addressed Spirit christological issues. Regarding Cyr-

---

Bindley and F.W. Green (eds.), *The Oecumenical Documents of the Faith* (Westport, CT: Greenwood Press, 1980), pp. 108-15.

[34] Cited according to the translation of John Anthony McGuckin, *Cyril of Alexandria*, p. 274. The Greek text without translation along with an English translation of Theodoret's refutation of the anathemas can be found in Bindley and Green (eds.), *Oecumenical Documents*, pp. 125-37.

[35] For information about Theodoret's life, see Clayton, *Theodoret of Cyrus*, pp. 7-14; Quasten, *Patrology*, III, pp. 537-38.

[36] Regarding Theodoret's place in the Antiochene Syrian tradition, see Clayton, *Theodoret of Cyrus*, pp. 53-74.

[37] Clayton, *Theodoret of Cyrus*, pp. 141-53; Grillmeier, *Christian Tradition*, I, pp. 488-89; Kelly, *Doctrines*, pp. 325-26; Frend, *Christianity*, p. 758. Theodoret had also written *On the Holy and Vivifying Trinity* and *On the Incarnation of the Lord* during 430. The latter shares the same perspective as his *Refutation of the Anathemas*. Quasten, *Patrology*, III, pp. 546-47. For overviews of Theodoret's writings, see Quasten, *Patrology*, III, pp. 538-53; Clayton, *Theodoret of Cyrus*, pp. 3-7.

il's first anathema, Theodoret challenged Cyril's anathematization of anyone not agreeing with his position on *Theotokos*.

> Wherefore also we style that holy Virgin θεοτόκος, not because she gave birth in natural manner to God, but to man united to the God that had fashioned Him. Moreover if He that was fashioned in the Virgin's womb was not man but God the Word Who is before all ages, then God the Word is a creature of the Holy Ghost. For that which was conceived in her, says Gabriel, is of the Holy Ghost.[38]

Theodoret argued that the central question was: who was conceived by the Holy Spirit in the virgin's womb? For Theodoret, it was absurd to reply that the Logos was conceived in Mary's womb; this would make the Logos a product of the Spirit. Theodoret, instead, posited that by the grace of the Holy Spirit Christ's human nature was conceived and united to the divine Logos; the form of God assumed the form of man.[39] Theodoret, therefore, allows the use of *Theotokos* properly defined, while maintaining the distinction of natures in Christ.

Concerning Cyril's ninth anathema, Theodoret disputed Cyril's condemnation of anyone affirming the Spirit's anointing empowered Christ to perform miracles and exorcisms.

---

[38] Cited according to the translation of Bloomfield Jackson, Theodoret, 'The Counter-Statements of Theodoret', NPNF, Second Series, III, p. 26. Cf. Bindley and Green (eds.), *Oecumenical Documents*, p. 125; Theodoret, 'Letter 151', NPNF, Second Series, III, pp. 329-32; Clayton, *Theodoret of Cyrus*, pp. 142-43; Sellers, *Two Ancient Christologies*, pp. 173-74; Grillmeier, *Christian Tradition*, I, pp. 493-94.

[39] Theodoret is working from the trinitarian language of the Cappadocian Fathers: one ousia and three hypostases. The Cappadocians also used the terms prosopon and hypostasis interchangeably but preferred hypostasis to avoid implications of Sabellianism. Theodoret also used hypostasis and prosopon synonymously but opted to use prosopon to express the christological union. Clayton, *Theodoret of Cyrus*, pp. 84-88, 91-93, 104; Grillmeier, *Christian Tradition*, I, pp. 489-93; Daley, 'One Thing and Another', p. 39. According to Clayton,

> Gregory's solution of how to unite two distinct *physeis* in the one Son is not that of Theodoret, but the fundamental metaphysical assumptions of the Cappadocians and Theodoret's Antiochene tradition are the same ... The Cappadocian-Antiochene apologetic against Apollinarian one *physis* Christology, in any case, is rooted in attributing to the Christ two real natures: the divinity of the Logos, and a full, real humanity (Clayton, *Theodoret of Cyrus*, p. 88).

The Lord Himself after reading the passage 'The S/spirit of the Lord is upon me because He hath anointed me,' said to the Jews, 'This day is this scripture fulfilled in your ears.' And to those who said that He was casting out devils by Beelzebub, He replied that He was casting them out by the Spirit of God. But we maintain that it was not God the Word, of one substance and co-eternal with the Father, that was formed by the Holy Ghost and anointed, but the human nature which was assumed by Him at the end of days. We shall confess that the Spirit of the Son was His own if he spoke of it as of the same nature and proceeding from the Father, and shall accept the expression as consistent with true piety. But if he speaks of the Spirit as being of the Son, as having its origin through the Son we shall reject this statement as blasphemous and impious.[40]

Theodoret makes several assertions. First, Cyril has anathematized the prophets, the apostles, the angel Gabriel, and even the Lord himself, for they all testify of the Spirit anointing Christ.[41] Second, the Logos, who eternally existed in consubstantial unity with the Father, was neither formed in Mary's womb nor anointed by the Holy Spirit; rather, it was Christ's human nature. Third, Theodoret avers that the Holy Spirit proceeds from the Father. Fourth, if Cyril implies, by attesting that the Spirit is the Spirit of the Son, the Holy Spirit's origin is in the Son, then, he holds an inappropriate view of

---

[40] Theodoret, 'Counter-Statements', NPNF, Second Series, III, p. 30. Cf. Bindley and Green (eds.), *Oecumenical Documents*, p. 133; Bethune-Baker, *Christian Doctrine*, p. 216; Clayton, *Theodoret of Cyrus*, p. 151. According to Theodoret, anathema 9 depicts the fruit of Cyril's Apollinarianism. Theodoret, 'Letter 151', NPNF, Second Series, III, p. 326

[41] Theodoret uses the following Scriptures to validate his assertion: Isa. 11.1-2; 42.1; Mt. 1.18; Acts 10.38; Jn 1.33; Lk. 1.34-35; Mt. 1.20; Lk. 4.17, 21; Mt. 12.28. Theodoret, furthermore, makes a case for Christ being the anointed Messiah in the temptations in the wilderness and in his role as the anointed priest in Heb. 1.9; 2.14-18 which addresses Cyril's *Twelve Anathemas* 10. *The Incarnation of the Lord*, J.P. Migne (ed.), *PG*, 75, cols. 1437-38; 1455-60. Cf. Clayton, *Theodoret of Cyrus*, pp. 120-29. Theodoret also avows that Syrian Christology is the same as the great fathers of the East and West: Ignatius of Antioch, Eustathius of Antioch, Meletius of Antioch, Flavian of Constantinople, Ephraim the Syrian, Cyprian of Carthage, Damasus of Rome, Ambrose of Milan, Athanasius of Alexandria, Gregory of Nazianzus, John Chrysostom, Atticus of Constantinople, Basil of Caesarea, Gregory of Nyssa, Amphilochius of Iconium, Polycarp of Smyrna, Irenaeus of Lyons, Methodius of Patara, and Hippolytus of Rome. Theodoret, 'Letter 151', NPNF, Second Series, III, p. 332.

trinitarian relations and a sacrilegious doctrine of the Spirit. Theodoret, hence, suggests that Cyril's denial of the Spirit anointing Christ's human nature hinges on a defective pneumatology.

Theodoret constructs his Spirit Christology with the lineaments of pneumatic mediation and indwelling which defines Christ's identity and mission. He carefully acknowledges the triune nature of God and the distinction of hypostases: Father, Son, and Holy Spirit. The Holy Spirit mediates the incarnation by forming Christ's human nature, so that by the grace of the Spirit the Logos unites with the human temple for the salvation of humanity. At the Jordan, Christ's human nature receives the Spirit's anointing, empowering it to perform miracles and identifying the Christ. Theodoret, therefore, defends a Spirit christological paradigm that integrates Logos Christology.

The conciliabulum's analysis of the twelve anathemas caused concern among Cyril's supporters, so to quiet their incertitude, while under house-arrest in Ephesus awaiting Theodosius' decision, Cyril composed an *Explanation of the Twelve Anathemas* (431). Cyril, thus, attempted to explain his position regarding the Spirit's anointing apropos of Christ's identity and mission.

> We say that he is the Word of God the Father, but when he became a man like us he was also called apostle, and anointed along with us according to the human condition.[42]

> But he is also called Christ since as man he is anointed along with us as the Psalmist says: 'You have loved righteousness and hated iniquity and so God, your God, has anointed you with the oil of gladness above your fellows' (Ps. 44.8 *sic*). Even though he himself is the dispenser of the Holy Spirit (Jn 3.34) ... nevertheless he is said to have been anointed economically and spiritually as man when the Spirit descended upon him. This was so that the Spirit might once again abide among us whom of old he had abandoned because of Adam's transgression. And this is why the

---

[42] This is the explanation of anathema 2 (*Explanation* 9). Cited according to the translation of John Anthony McGuckin, *Cyril of Alexandria*, p. 285. Cf. Theodoret, 'Counter-Statements', NPNF, Second Series, III, pp. 26-27; Clayton, *Theodoret of Cyrus*, pp. 13-45.

Only Begotten Word of God himself, as he becomes flesh, is called Christ.[43]

When the Only Begotten Word of God became man, he remained, even so, God, having absolutely all that the Father has with the exception of being the Father. He had as his very own the Holy Spirit which is from him and within him essentially and so he brought about signs, and even when he became man he remained God and accomplished miracles in his very own power through the Spirit.[44]

Several implications emerge from these texts. First, Cyril acknowledged that Christ's humanity was anointed similar to other humans: according to the human condition. Second, Christ's humanity was anointed for the economy of salvation, so that the Spirit could be redemptively restored to fallen humanity. Third, the Logos eternally existed consubstantially with the Father and Holy Spirit; the hypostatic union neither diminished the incarnate Logos' deity nor the Logos' perichoretic union with the Father and Holy Spirit. Fourth, the Spirit did not anoint Christ's humanity subsequent to the incarnation; the Logos performed miracles through his own power. These texts, thereupon, suggest that Cyril concedes a place for the anointing of the Spirit in Christ's salvific mission and places it in the incarnation, so that Christ's reception of the Spirit at Jordan serves only as a redemptive symbol; the hypostatic union is the anointing of Christ's humanity.[45]

---

[43] This is the explanation of anathema 7 (*Explanation* 21). Cited according to the translation of John Anthony McGuckin, *Cyril of Alexandria*, p. 289. Cf. Theodoret, 'Counter-Statements', NPNF, Second Series, III, p. 29; Clayton, *Theodoret of Cyrus*, pp. 148-49. Cyril has cited the quotation from Ps. 44.8; the correct reference is Ps. 45.7.

[44] This is the explanation of anathema 9 (*Explanation* 25). Cited according to the translation of John Anthony McGuckin, *Cyril of Alexandria*, pp. 290-91. The *Twelve Anathemas* and the *Explanation of the Twelve Anathemas* can also be found with an English translation in Russell, *Cyril of Alexandria*, pp. 175-89.

[45] Some of Cyril's earlier work prior to the controversy seems to bear out this conclusion; for example, his examination of Isa. 61.1-3, regarding the phrase 'The Spirit of the Lord is upon me, therefore he anointed me,' places this anointing in the incarnation:

> How, then, did he come to be sanctified? Existing as both God and man, he gives the Spirit to creation in a divine way, but receives it from God the Father in the human way. This reception we call the anointing. Thus he clearly establishes the cause of the Incarnation. For saying that it was from the Fa-

When the Council of Ephesus closed, it appeared that Cyril had won the day; nevertheless, for the Syrians all was not lost. Theodosius II had refused to condemn Syrian Christology; instead, he pressured both sides to reach an agreement and reconciliation. Both sides, however, required certain conditions of peace. Cyril mandated that the Syrians must condemn Nestorius and his teachings, and the Syrians imperiously demanded that Cyril retract his 12 anathemas. Nevertheless, both sides soon began to give ground under imperial exigency.[46] John of Antioch, accordingly, through Paul of Emesa, sent an amicable rejoinder to Cyril (433), which included the Syrian profession of faith submitted to the emperor at Chalcedon during the Council of Ephesus, asking for some clarifications. Cyril then wrote to John (433) delineating a formula for peace. On his part, Cyril accepted the Syrian confession of faith; it had fully convinced Cyril 'that the division between the churches came about altogether

---

ther, he felt obliged to add, 'Therefore he anointed me, he sent me to announce good news to the poor, to heal the broken hearted, to announce release to the captives, to give sight to the blind, and to call for these a day of retribution' (Cyril, *Commentary on Isaiah* 5.5, Migne [ed.], *PG*, 70, cols. 1349-52. Cited according to the translation of David Coffey, 'Spirit Christology', p. 320).

Daniel Keating points out that Cyril acknowledges Christ redemptively receiving the Spirit for humanity, in a representative way as the second Adam, so that Christ's baptism becomes a revelation of the re-acquisition of the Spirit and sanctification of the human race, but he places the anointing and sanctification of human nature in the incarnation. Daniel Keating, 'The Baptism of Jesus in Cyril of Alexandria: The Re-creation of the Human Race', *ProEccl* 8 (1999), pp. 201-22. In his conclusion, Keating rightly recognizes the weakness of Cyril's Christology on this point:

I would suggest one deficiency, however, in Cyril's exegesis of Jesus' baptism, due in large part to the *representative* emphasis in his interpretation. He does not accord to the descent of the Spirit any significant role for Jesus himself in his earthly career as Messiah. Cyril appears so intent on defending the Son's possession of the Spirit essentially and eternally, that he can allow only a representative or exemplary interpretation of the baptism (Keating, 'The Baptism of Jesus', p. 218).

[46] At the emperor's request Acacius of Beroea, wrote a letter (432), setting out the Syrian's conditions of peace, and sent it along with the letter from the emperor to Cyril. Cyril quickly responded in a letter to Acacius (432), denying that he espoused Apollinarian doctrine, explaining his single subject Christology, and giving ground on his 12 anathemas, attesting that he wrote the anathemas to defeat Nestorius' teachings, so if the Syrians will condemn Nestorius' teachings, there will be peace. Quasten, *Patrology*, III, pp. 118, 537; Davis, *Ecumenical Councils*, p. 160; McGuckin, *Cyril of Alexandria*, pp. 108-10; Russell, *Cyril of Alexandria*, pp. 52-53; Wessel, *Nestorian Controversy*, pp. 264-65; Frend, *Christianity*, p. 761.

needlessly and groundlessly,[47] and both the Alexandrian and the Syrian christological traditions agreed with Scripture and the apostolic tradition.[48] Although Cyril did not require the Syrians to affirm his 12 anathemas, he was unbending on the *Theotokos* issue and the condemnation of Nestorius and his teachings. On John's part, he relented in his demand that Cyril reject his 12 anathemas and agreed to Cyril's requirements: he affirmed Mary as *Theotokos*, condemned Nestorius, and Nestorius' teachings that conflicted with apostolic faith.[49]

Although Cyril gained a great victory at the Council of Ephesus, the Formula of Reunion originated from the pen of Theodoret of Cyrus.[50]

> We confess that Our Lord Jesus Christ, the Only Begotten Son of God, is perfect God and perfect Man, of a rational soul and body. He is born of the Father before the ages according to the

---

[47] *Letter to John of Antioch*, 3; 6. Cited according to the translation of John Anthony McGuckin, *Cyril of Alexandria*, pp. 344-45.

[48] McGuckin, *Cyril of Alexandria*, pp. 111-14; Davis, *Ecumenical Councils*, pp. 160-63; Clayton, *Theodoret of Cyrus*, pp. 157-66; Russell, *Cyril of Alexandria*, pp. 53-55; Grillmeier, *Christian Tradition*, I, pp. 497-98; O'Collins, *Christology*, pp. 194-95; Wessel, *Nestorian Controversy*, pp. 267-70; González, *Christian Thought*, I, p. 357; Harnack, *Dogma*, IV, p. 189.

[49] For some Syrians, John had betrayed their cause and remained obstinate until imperial pressure convinced them to comply. McGuckin, *Cyril of Alexandria*, pp. 113-17; Clayton, *Theodoret of Cyrus*, p. 18; Russell, *Cyril of Alexandria*, p. 56; Wessel, *Nestorian Controversy*, pp. 272, 274; González, *Christian Thought*, I, pp. 357-58; Walker, *History*, pp. 148-49. Although Theodoret reluctantly accepted the conditions of peace, he refused to condemn Nestorius until he was forced to do so at the Council of Chalcedon.

[50] Clayton, *Theodoret of Cyrus*, pp. 18, 161-62. Cf. Grillmeier, *Christian Tradition*, I, p. 491; Kelly, *Doctrines*, pp. 327-28; Chadwick, 'Eucharist and Christology', p. 147, n. 2. There are few variations, if any, with this confession of faith and the ones that Theodoret had previously put forth. For example, the confession in Theodoret, 'Letter 151', NPNF, Second Series, III, p. 326. There remains an ongoing discussion regarding Theodoret's Christology remaining consistent throughout his writings. There are three trains of thought regarding this issue: (1) beginning with his early writings before the Council of Ephesus and continuing to the time of the Council of Chalcedon, Theodoret did not deviate from teaching two centers of subjectivity in Christ; (2) a change in vocabulary occurred in Theodoret's christological writings after Ephesus; (3) Theodoret's and Cyril's christological models are essentially congruent, but their nomenclature was incongruous, so they needed to agree on common terms and meanings. For an overview of this discussion, see Clayton, *Theodoret of Cyrus*, pp. 33-52. Theodoret in a Letter to Leo (449), bishop of Rome, insisted that had he never changed his christological doctrine. Theodoret, 'Letter 113', NPNF, Second Series, III, p. 294.

Godhead, and the same one in these last days for us and for our salvation was born of the virgin Mary according to the manhood. The same one is consubstantial with the Father according to the Godhead, and consubstantial with us according to the manhood, for there was a union of the two natures, and this is why we confess One Christ, One Son, One Lord. According to this understanding of the unconfused union we confess that the holy virgin is the Mother of God, because God was made flesh and became man, and from the very moment of conception he united to himself the temple that was taken from her. As for the evangelical and apostolic sayings about the Lord, we are aware that theologians take some as common, as referring to one prosopon, but distinguish others as referring to two natures; that they interpret the God-befitting ones in accordance with the Godhead of the Christ, and the humble ones in accordance with the manhood.[51]

Here, several important points emerge. First, Cyril does not object to speaking of the union of two distinct natures, divine and human, in the incarnate Christ. Second, Cyril does not protest using the term prosopon to designate this union. Third, neither does Cyril demur at the Syrian insistence that deity united and dwelt in the temple of Christ's humanity, nor does he charge them with teaching two sons. Fourth, Cyril accepts the Syrian explication of how they apply the title *Theotokos* to Mary. Fifth, Cyril does not challenge the Syrians dividing the sayings of the gospels about Christ, applying some Scriptures to the deeds of the human nature and other Scriptures to the actions of deity. Cyril, therefore, either for the sake of peace concedes much to the Syrians, or Cyril and the Syrians have always held the same christological doctrines but have misunderstood one another's nomenclature.[52] Whichever conclusion is accurate remains unclear.

---

[51] Cyril's, *Letter to John of Antioch*, p. 5. Cited according to the translation of John Anthony McGuckin, *Cyril of Alexandria*, pp. 344-45. Cyril includes this confession by copying it from John's *Letter to Cyril* (433). Alexandria, *Letters*, 38, FC, LXXVI, pp. 145-46. Cf. Davis, *Ecumenical Councils*, pp. 161-62; Grillmeier, *Christian Tradition*, I, 498-99; Kelly, *Doctrines*, pp. 328-29; Wessel, *Nestorian Controversy*, p. 270; Schaff, *History*, III, p. 727; Frend, *Christianity*, pp. 761-62.

[52] Sellers, *Two Ancient Christologies*, pp. 179-80, 189-201; Grillmeier, *Christian Tradition*, I, pp. 495, 499-501; Kelly, *Doctrines*, pp. 329-30. Among Cyril's supporters, some thought he had capitulated to the Syrians. According to Cyril, it was a

At stake in this controversy were the proper boundaries of speaking in an orthodox manner about the christological union and the Holy Spirit's relationship to Christ's identity and mission, and the survival of Spirit Christology. Spirit christological issues were integral to the primary documents which emerged prior to and considered during the Council of Ephesus.[53] The Syrian tradition, distinguishing the divine and human natures, pointed to the Holy Spirit as the agent of grace for the conception and formation of Christ's humanity and the anointing of Christ's human nature for salvific mission. Cyril, conversely, would have none of it; for him, the Syrian trajectory depicted Christ as just another God-bearing man inspired of the Spirit. Cyril, accordingly, posited that the Logos hypostatically united with human nature, so the Holy Spirit did not through an act of grace conceive Christ in Mary's womb; rather, the Logos took unto himself human nature. Although Scripture and tradition testify to the Holy Spirit anointing Christ, according to Cyril, since the Spirit is the Spirit of the Son, the anointing transpires in the hypostatic union, forming one incarnate nature of the Logos. Cyril essentially advocated the supremacy of his Logos christological paradigm, circumscribing its bounds so as to exclude any form of Spirit Christology. Nevertheless, under imperial exigency, both sides moved their vocabulary about the christological union toward the center, reaching a compromise in the Formula of Reun-

---

matter of working out the vocabulary. Cyril, therefore, wrote letters defending his acceptance of two natures in Christ because the Syrians charged him with Apollinarianism:

> this is why we gave way to them: not to divide the one Son into two, God forbid, but only in so far as to confess that there occurred neither confusion nor mixing ... They only tried to distinguish the terms. They make the distinction in such as way as to say that there are some terms appropriate to the Godhead, and some to the manhood, and some which are referred in common as being appropriate both to the Godhead and the manhood, except they are attributed to one and the same person. This is not what Nestorius does' (*Letter to Eulogius*, 2; 3; cited according to the translation of John Anthony McGuckin, *Cyril of Alexandria*, pp. 350-51).

Cf. Cyril, *On the Unity of Christ*, pp. 28-29; Russell, *Cyril of Alexandria*, pp. 55-56; Wessel, *Nestorian Controversy*, pp. 275-78; Frend, *Christianity*, p. 762. Theodoret's writings, nonetheless, indicated that he thought Cyril had reversed his position (*Letters*, 171-78).

[53] In point of fact, among these documents, deliberations regarding Spirit christological issues address seven of Cyril's twelve anathemas (*Anathemas* 1; 2; 4; 5; 7; 9; 10).

ion, therewith brokering an uneasy peace, for the time being, and bringing the parties into agreement apropos of speaking about Christ's identity and mission after a fashion not eliding Spirit Christology.

The Council of Chalcedon (451)

As most of the principal leaders passed from the scene, through death, the solicitous peace they brokered did not continue. Sixtus III succeeded Celestine (432), and after him Leo ascended to the papal throne (440) in Rome. Eagerly submitting to Theodoret of Cyrus' tutelage, Domnus supervened (441) his uncle John as bishop of Antioch. Dioscorus replaced Cyril in the episcopal see of Alexandria (444). Following Proclus (434–46), Flavian was consecrated bishop of Constantinople (446). Along with these bishops, Eutyches, an archimandrite and revered leader in the monastic world, and his godson Chrysaphius, who wielded great influence with the emperor, were the primary characters in the controversy that occasioned the fourth ecumenical council.[54] The line of battle was drawn along their acceptance or rejection of the Formula of Reunion.

Leo represented the Western christological tradition, descending from Tertullian through Ambrose and Augustine,[55] which had consistently affirmed the union of two complete and distinct natures, divine and human, in Christ. The divine nature remained transcendent and unaltered, while the human nature was subject to growth, change, passions, and sufferings. Yet they attested to the inseparable unity of these two natures, each with distinct properties, in one person (*una persona*).[56] Leo, furthermore, stood in the lineage of

---

[54] Davis, *Ecumenical Councils*, pp. 164-70; Schaff, *History*, III, pp. 734-36; Need, *Truly Divine and Truly Human*, pp. 94-95; Grillmeier, *Christian Tradition*, I, pp. 520-23; Kelly, *Doctrines*, pp. 330-31; Frend, *Christianity*, pp. 762-64; Walker, *History*, pp. 149-50; González, *Christian Thought*, I, p. 369; Harnack, *Dogma*, IV, pp. 190-95.

[55] Robert Victor Sellers, *The Council of Chalcedon: A Historical and Doctrinal Survey* (London: SPCK, 1953), pp. 182-203; Green, *Leo the Great*, pp. 45-51; Kelly, *Doctrines*, pp. 334-37; Susan Wessel, *Leo the Great and the Spiritual Rebuilding of a Universal Rome* (VCSup 93; Leiden: E.J. Brill, 2008), pp. 209-11, 219-46.

[56] See Tertullian, *Prax.* 27; *Carn. Chr.* 5; 18; *Apol.* 21. Cf. Hilary, *Trin.* 9.4; 9.14; 9.38; 10.7; 10.55; 11.6; 11.18; 11.19; Ambrose, *Spir.* 1.9.107; 3.22.168; *Fid.* 1.4.32; 2.7.56; 2.7.58; 2.8.62; 2.8.64; *Incarn.* 5.35; 6.47-48; 7.67-68; Augustine, *Tract. Ev. Jo.*

Western Spirit Christology.[57]

Probably, the best indication that Leo supports a form of Spirit Christology is his letter to the bishops in Sicily (447), regarding the proper time to baptize during the liturgical year. After affirming the Holy Spirit's agency in the incarnation of the Logos and recounting the events of Christ's childhood, Leo ties these events to Christ's baptism.

> What doubt was left about the divinity of the Lord Jesus Christ when, at His baptism, the Holy Spirit in the form of a dove came down upon Him and remained, as the voice of the Father from heaven was heard saying: 'Thou art my beloved Son, in thee I am well pleased' (*Letter* 16).[58]

Subsequently, he redemptively conjoins baptism to Christ's death, resurrection, ascension, and Pentecost, concluding that Easter and Pentecost are the proper days to baptize because Pentecost is the sequel and completion of the Paschal feast.

> The very Son of God, the Only-begotten, wished that there be no distinction between Himself and the Holy Spirit, either in what the faithful believed about them or in the power of their works, since there is no difference in their nature ... And so, since Christ is truth and the Holy Spirit is the Spirit of truth and

---

78.3; 74.3; *Trin.* 1.11.22–12.27; 4.30; 15.26.46 *Enchir.* 34; 35; 36; 40, *Letter* 137.2.8–3.12.

> The almost symmetrical juxtaposition of the two natures in Christ and their firm anchorage in the one person give Leo his certainty in the use of the *communicatio idiomatum* or exchange of predicates. This is possible because of his concept of person is not so suspect as that of the Antiochenes and of Nestorius in particular. With the Latin tradition behind him, Leo already had *de facto* the true Chalcedonian content of the word 'person' (Grillmeier, *Christian Tradition*, I, p. 536).

Cf. Grillmeier, *Christian Tradition*, I, pp. 530-39; Green, *Leo the Great*, pp. 48-52; Kelly, *Doctrines*, pp. 337-38.

[57] For overviews of Leo's life and writings, see Green, *Leo the Great*; Schaff, *History*, III, pp. 314-22; Leo, *Letters*, FC, XXXIV, pp. 5-11; Leo, *Sermons*, FC, XCIII, pp. 3-17; Wessel, *Leo the Great*, pp. 34-51; Quasten, *Patrology*, IV, pp. 589-98. For the development of Leo's Christology during the debates, see Philip L. Barclift, 'The Shifting Tones of Pope Leo the Great's Christological Vocabulary', *CH* 66 (1997), pp. 221-39.

[58] Cited according to the translation of Edmund Hunt, Leo, *Letters*, FC, XXXIV, p. 70. Cf. Green, *Leo the Great*, pp. 192-93.

the title 'Advocate' is proper to both, there is no difference in the feast where there is but one mystery (*Letter* 16).[59]

It appears that Leo follows Augustine's view of Christ's relationship with the Spirit. For example, he coalesces the incarnation with Christ's reception of the Spirit at the Jordan, so that the Spirit's anointing, the grace which affects the incarnation, reveals Christ's human and divine natures at Christ's baptism. For Leo, both natures are requisite for redemption; thus, Christ's baptism becomes proleptic of his redemptive acts and believers' appropriation of them in baptism. Leo affirms the consubstantial divine nature of the Son and Spirit and acknowledges their coinherence in power, acts, and name,[60] so that Pentecost completes Easter; Christ dwells in believers and empowers them through the Spirit.[61] Leo's soteriology, therefore, integrates Logos Christology and Spirit Christology. So Leo found the Formula of Reunion amicable with his theology.[62]

Flavian and Theodoret, likewise, agreed with the Formula's premises; however, Dioscorus perceived the Formula of Reunion as a Nestorian document, which he emphatically rejected. According to Dioscorus, Cyril had conceded too much, so he awaited an opportunity to challenge the Formula's Christology. Finding an ally in Eutyches, it was not difficult for Dioscorus to stir up contention between Eutyches and the Formula's supporters. Emboldened by Dioscorus' support and the favor he enjoyed in the imperial court, Eutyches rejected the Formula's statement that Christ's human nature was consubstantial with other humans, and he advocated that there were two natures before the incarnation and one nature after the union.[63]

---

[59] Cited according to the translation of Edmund Hunt, Leo, *Letters*, FC, XXXIV, p. 73.

[60] 'So he imagines the union in Christ as a *circumincessio* of the two natures.' Grillmeier, *Christian Tradition*, I, p. 537. Cf. Grillmeier, *Christian Tradition*, I, pp. 534-36.

[61] Cf. Leo, *Sermons* 22.2; 23.2; 25.2; 26.3; 27.6; 66.2, 4; 76.2,7, 8; Green, *Leo the Great*, pp. 167, 171, 192-93; Augustine, *Praed.* 30; 31; Hilary, *Trin.* 8.29-34; Victorinus, *Ad. Ar.* 1b.53; 1b.58; 3.14–16; 4.18; Ambrose, *Spir.* 1.13.156-58; 3.1.5-6; 3.1.8; 3.7.44; David Charles Robinson, 'Informed Worship and Empowered Mission: The Integration of Liturgy, Doctrine, and Praxis in Leo the Great's Sermons on Ascension and Pentecost', *Worship* 83 (2009), pp. 524-40.

[62] Quasten, *Patrology*, IV, pp. 600-11.

[63] Sellers, *Chalcedon*, pp. 30-36; McGuckin, *Cyril of Alexandria*, pp. 228-30; Davis, *Ecumenical Councils*, pp. 170-71; Kelly, *Doctrines*, p. 331; Schaff, *History*, III, pp.

Eutyches' confession of faith, opposing the Formula of Reunion, produced six consequent events. First, Theodoret of Cyrus wrote his most definitive christological treatise, *Eranistes* (447), to defend the doctrine of two natures in Christ against Eutyches' confusion of these natures. Second, Dioscorus convinced the emperor to publish an anti-Nestorian edict against Theodoret's activities, which Domnus fully supported; accordingly, Theodosius II ordered Theodoret to desist from disturbing the peace and to remain in Cyrus, so Dioscorus had effectively restricted the Syrian's most able theologian. Third, during a synod at Constantinople (448), known as the Home Synod, over which Flavian presided, Eusebius of Dorylaeum charged Eutyches with heresy; the synod ended with Eutyches' deposition.[64] Fourth, Eutyches, Flavian, and the emperor wrote to Leo asking for his opinion. After due correspondence and consideration, Leo responded with his *Tome to Flavian*, stating his christological position, refuting Eutyches' confession, and upholding the Formula of Reunion.[65] Fifth, Dioscorus rejected the synod's

---

736-37; Need, *Truly Divine and Truly Human*, p. 95; Meyendorff, *Christ in Eastern Christian Thought*, p. 23; Harnack, *Dogma*, IV, pp. 195-97; Walker, *History*, p. 150.

> Eutyches however had based his understanding exclusively on Cyril's earlier writings, failing to take into account consideration the letters Cyril wrote after the council met at Ephesus. These more recent letters supported the view that Christ was 'from two natures' after the incarnation. Reluctant to subscribe to the Formula, Eutyches offered only qualified acceptance: he was willing to confess that Christ was 'from two natures' before the union, but that Christ was only 'one nature after the union' (Wessel, *Nestorian Controversy*, p. 280).

[64] Regarding the proceedings of the synod, see Grillmeier, *Christian Tradition*, I, pp. 523-26. Cf. Kelly, *Doctrines*, pp. 332-34; Bethune-Baker, *Christian Doctrine*, pp. 281-82; Schaff, *History*, III, pp. 737-38; Frend, *Christianity*, pp. 764-66; Harnack, *Dogma*, IV, pp. 200-201.

[65] Regarding the correspondences leading up to the Council of Ephesus (449), see Leo's *Letters*, 20–38. The letter known as Leo's Tome is *Letter* 28. The purpose and origin of Leo's *Tome*

> was not to speculate on the mystery but to declare once more the Rule of Faith as it had been handed down from the beginning in its Western form. Hence the Tome is not an original work: it does little more than reproduce the teaching and even the phraseology of Irenaeus, Tertullian, and Cyprian, as developed by Athanasius, Hilary, and St. Augustine (Bindley and Green [eds.], *Oecumenical Documents*, p. 162).

For the provenance, date, occasion, and purpose, along with an overview and examination the content of Leo's *Tome*, see Green, *Leo the Great*, pp. 209-25; Sellers, *Chalcedon*, pp. 228-53; Bindley and Green (eds.), *Oecumenical Documents*, pp. 159-67; Bethune-Baker, *Christian Doctrine*, pp. 288-92; Meyendorff, *Christ in Eastern Christian Thought*, pp. 24-25; Harnack, *Dogma*, IV, pp. 201-202.

decision and offered communion to Eutyches.⁶⁶ Sixth, the emperor convened the second Council of Ephesus (449) to settle the quarrel.

Leaving no doubt which side he favored, the emperor appointed Dioscorus to preside over the council, forbade Theodoret's attendance, and excluded the participation of any bishops who condemned Eutyches at Constantinople. Although the papal legates twice asked for Leo's *Tome* to be read, Dioscorus deferred its reading. The council, instead, read Eutyches' confession of faith and accepted it as orthodox, along with Cyril's *Twelve Anathemas*. Several of Theodoret's anti-Cyrillian writings were read and used against him. From the beginning, the outcome of the council was assured: Eutyches was vindicated; Dioscorus and Eutyches' Christology reigned supreme in the East; Flavian, Eusebius of Dorylaeum, Ibas of Edessa, Domnus, and Theodoret were deposed.⁶⁷

Several documents containing Spirit christological references were involved in the controversy. Theodoret's *Eranistes*, *Commentary on Psalms* 45, letter to the Syrian monks, *Defense of Diodore of Tarsus and Theodore of Mopsuestia*, and Cyril's *Twelve Anathemas*. The first two writings helped occasion this council whereas the last three writings were read and discussed during the Second Council of Ephesus.

Eranistes delineates Theodoret's christological premises by way of contrast to Eutyches' Christology. The work consists of five parts: a prologue, three dialogues, and an epilogue. In the prologue Theodoret links the name Eranistes with the actions of a beggar, collecting scraps of clothing from various heresies to stitch together the garment of heresy. Eranistes, thus, represents Theodoret's heretical opponent in the three dialogues with Orthodox, the voice of Theodoret. Dialogue one discusses the immutability of the Logos: the Logos took flesh but was not changed into flesh. Dialogue two presents the case for two unmixed natures in Christ. Dialogue three

---

⁶⁶ Sellers, *Chalcedon*, pp. 36-71; González, *Christian Thought*, I, pp. 370-73; Davis, *Ecumenical Councils*, pp. 171-74; Green, *Leo the Great*, pp. 202-203; Need, *Truly Divine and Truly Human*, pp. 95-98.

⁶⁷ For overviews of the proceedings, see Sellers, *Chalcedon*, pp. 78-87; Bethune-Baker, *Christian Doctrine*, pp. 282-84; Davis, *Ecumenical Councils*, pp. 177-80; McGuckin, *Cyril of Alexandria*, pp. 231-32; Schaff, *History*, III, pp. 738-40; González, *Christian Thought*, I, pp. 375-76; Grillmeier, *Christian Tradition*, I, pp. 526-28; Pelikan, *Christian Tradition*, I, pp. 262-63; Need, *Truly Divine and Truly Human*, pp. 96-98; Frend, *Christianity*, pp. 766-69; Wessel, *Nestorian Controversy*, pp. 281-86; O'Collins, *Christology*, p. 195; Meyendorff, *Christ in Eastern Christian Thought*, p. 23; Harnack, *Dogma*, IV, pp. 207-10; Walker, *History*, pp. 150-51.

examines the impassibility of the divine nature, while attributing suffering to the human nature. Theodoret ends each dialogue with extensive patristic quotations to validate his position's place in tradition.[68] The epilogue recapitulates the preceding arguments in 40 syllogisms.[69]

There are several Spirit christological references in *Eranistes*; however, most of these occur in quotations of earlier works, which this survey has already examined, so attention will focus on three texts in dialogue one. First, in discussing the difference between divine substance and hypostasis, Theodoret affirms that 'we understand the divine substance to indicate the Holy Trinity; but the hypostasis denotes any person, as the Father, Son and the Holy Ghost'.[70]

> [Scripture] calls both the Father and the Son 'Spirit,' signifying by this term the incorporeal illimitable character of the divine nature. The Holy Scripture only calls the hypostasis of the Spirit 'Holy Ghost.'[71]

Second, to posit that the Logos does not change into flesh in the incarnation, Theodoret turns to Heb. 10.5.

> He did not say, 'You changed me into a body,' but, 'You formed a body for me.' He reveals that the body was formed by the Spirit, in keeping with the words of the angel who says, 'Do not be afraid to take Mary your wife; for what was begotten in her is from the Holy Spirit.'[72]

---

[68] Theodoret quotes 238 passages from 88 different sources. It is possible that these quotations are taken from the florilegium Theodoret composed to use against Cyril at the Council of Ephesus (431). Quasten, *Patrology*, III, p. 574. Cf. Clayton, *Theodoret of Cyrus*, pp. 218-20.

[69] For overviews of *Eranistes*, including provenance, date, occasion, and purpose see Clayton, *Theodoret of Cyrus*, pp. 215-63; Theodoret, *Eranistes*, FC, CVI, pp. 2-21.

[70] Cited according to the translation of Bloomfield Jackson, Theodoret, 'Eranistes', NPNF, Second Series, III, p. 162. Cf. Clayton, *Theodoret of Cyrus*, pp. 220-24.

[71] Cited according to the translation of Bloomfield Jackson, Theodoret, 'Eranistes', NPNF, Second Series, III, p. 162. Cf. Clayton, *Theodoret of Cyrus*, pp. 225-27.

[72] Cited according to the translation of Gerard Ettlinger, Theodoret, *Eranistes*, FC, CVI, p. 49.

Third, when discussing to whom the prophecy of Isa. 11.1-3 applies, regarding the root of Jesse receiving the gifts of the Spirit, Theodoret argues for Christ.

> No one would apply these words to a mere human being, since the gifts of the Spirit are given in different ways even to the very holy people ... But here the prophet has said that the one born from the root of Jesse has all the powers of the Spirit.[73]

Several conclusions emerge from these texts. First, Theodoret's trinitarian vocabulary follows that of the Cappadocians. There is one divine substance which is Spirit and three hypostases: Father, Son, and Holy Spirit. Second, Theodoret maintains the distinction of divine and human natures in the incarnation. Third, the Holy Spirit is the agent of the incarnation, forming Christ's human body and uniting it to the Logos. Fourth, Christ's anointing of the Spirit differed from the Hebrew prophets who only received certain gifts of the Spirit; Christ's human nature was endowed with all the gifts of the Spirit. Theodoret, therefore, still maintained a Spirit christological paradigm that integrated Logos Christology.

Bearing striking similarities with *Eranistes*, Theodoret's *Commentary on Psalms* 45 (about 447) was directed against Eutyches' Christology.[74] His comments on Ps. 45.7 addressed the issue of the Spirit anointing Christ.

> Thus he was also anointed in the all-holy Spirit, not as God but as a human being: as God he was of one being with the Spirit, whereas as a human being he receives the gifts of the Spirit like a kind of anointing.[75]

Again, Theodoret attests to the distinction of natures in Christ. The divine nature is Spirit and does not need the anointing, but the human nature is anointed by the Spirit and empowered with the gifts of the Spirit.

---

[73] Cited according to the translation of Gerard Ettlinger, Theodoret, *Eranistes*, FC, CVI, p. 55.

[74] For an overview of Theodoret's *Commentary on the Psalms*, including provenance, date, occasion, and purpose see, Theodoret, *Commentary on the Psalms: Psalms 1–72*, FC, CI, pp. 2-36; Quasten, *Patrology*, III, p. 540. Regarding Theodoret's Christology of the Psalms, see Theodoret, *Psalms*, FC, CI, pp. 25-28.

[75] Theodoret, *Commentary of Psalms*, 45.6. Cited according to the translation of Robert Hill, Theodoret, *Psalms*, FC, CI, p. 263. Cf. Kelly, *Doctrines*, pp. 325-26.

Since most monks aligned themselves with Cyril, Theodoret's letter to the Syrian monks (431) attempted to win them over to Dyophysite Christology.[76] He directed the thrust of his argument against Cyril's anathemas, correlating them with various heresies; specifically, he challenged anathemas one, two, three, four, and nine. Similar to his *Refutation of the Twelve Anathemas*, regarding Cyril's rejection of the Spirit anointing Christ's human nature in anathema 9, Theodoret charges Cyril with a distorted view of the Trinity and a deficient pneumatology.[77]

Meanwhile, a revival of interest in Theodore of Mopsuestia's writings emerged in Armenia, which elicited demands for their condemnation from Cyril and Proclus (437). John of Antioch quickly responded by putting his theological cards on the table: he had been willing to condemn Nestorius for the sake of peace, but he would neither condemn his heritage nor a deceased person's theology that died in communion with the church.[78] Before Cyril and Proclus relented in their demands and agreed to maintain the peace, Theodoret of Cyrus had already penned his *Defense of Diodore of Tarsus and Theodore of Mopsuestia* (438).[79] Theodoret defended Theodore's Christology by appealing to the long tradition of Spirit Christology in the East and West.

> What has he said beyond those ancient doctors? For each and every one of them openly and clearly taught that the human nature was visited and assumed and anointed by the Holy Spirit (*Fragment* 15).[80]

---

[76] For an overview of this letter, see Quasten, *Patrology*, III, pp. 552-53.

[77] 'Furthermore he blasphemes against the Holy Ghost, denying that It proceeds from the Father, in accordance with the word of the Lord, but maintaining that It has Its origin of the Son' (*Letter* 151). Cited according to the translation of Bloomfield Jackson, Theodoret, 'Letters', NPNF, Second Series, III, p. 326. Cf. Clayton, *Theodoret of Cyrus*, pp. 136-41.

[78] Davis, *Ecumenical Councils,* pp. 164-65; Sellers, *Chalcedon*, pp. 26-30; Grillmeier, *Christian Tradition*, I, pp. 520-23.

[79] Only fragments of this text remain which were used against Theodoret at the Council of Ephesus (449) and the Second Council of Constantinople (553). Quasten, *Patrology*, III, pp. 549-50. For the provenance, date, purpose, occasion, and an examination of these fragments, see Clayton, *Theodoret of Cyrus*, pp. 207-13.

[80] Cited according to the translation of Paul Clayton, *Theodoret of Cyrus*, p. 212. Cf. Clayton, *Theodoret of Cyrus*, pp. 207-208, n. 100.

So Theodoret affirmed Theodore's view of the Spirit's role in Christ's identity and mission: the Holy Spirit conceived the human nature, united it to the Logos, and anointed it for salvific mission.

Spirit Christology, therefore, through the writings of Theodoret of Cyrus and Cyril's twelve anathemas played an integral role in the Second Council of Ephesus.[81] Juxtaposing Theodoret's writings with Cyril's anathemas, Dioscorus and his supporters vindicated Cyril's writings and condemned Theodoret's. Dioscorus' and Eutyches' Logos christological paradigm had ascended to supremacy, affirming two natures before the incarnation and only one after the union and denying the consubstantiality of Christ's human nature with other humans. Spirit Christology, furthermore, was no longer permitted a seat at the theological table.

What should have been an ecumenical meeting of the three great branches of christological thought – Alexandrian, Syrian, and Latin – failed to happen at the Second Council of Ephesus. Neither was Leo's *Tome* read nor was the Syrian case presented; consequently, when Leo received a report of the council's proceedings, he dubbed it the Robber Synod (*Latrocinium*)[82] and began a vigorous campaign to overturn the council's decisions, writing to various bishops, monks, politicians, and the imperial family. The emperor, nonetheless, ratified the council and supported its decisions. The situation changed, however, when Theodosius II suddenly died (July 450). Pulcheria immediately seized power, ordered Chrysaphius executed, married the senator Marcian, and had Eutyches confined to a monastery.[83] The political winds had shifted and the vane pointed in the direction of restoring what was purloined in the Second Council of Ephesus.

Pulcheria and Marcian, hence, decided to bring these three streams of christological traditions together again at the fourth

---

[81] Because the Spirit christological texts in Cyril's anathemas have previously been examined, there is no need to repeat them here.

[82] Leo, *Letters*, FC, XXXIV, p. 169. For Leo's role in overturning the Robber Synod, see Wessel, *Leo the Great*, pp. 259-83; Schaff, *History*, III, pp. 740-41.

[83] Davis, *Ecumenical Councils*, pp. 179-88; González, *Christian Thought*, I, pp. 376-78; Green, *Leo the Great*, pp. 204-205; Need, *Truly Divine and Truly Human*, pp. 95-98; Kelly, *Doctrines*, pp. 338-39; Schaff, *History*, III, pp. 741-42; Frend, *Christianity*, pp. 769-70; Bethune-Baker, *Christian Doctrine*, p. 284; McGuckin, *Cyril of Alexandria*, p. 233; Harnack, *Dogma*, IV, pp. 212-15; Walker, *History*, p. 151.

ecumenical council.⁸⁴ The Council of Chalcedon (451) proceeded by reading the acts of Ephesus (449) and the Home Synod (448), Cyril's *Letter to John of Antioch*,⁸⁵ the Nicene Creed, the Creed of Constantinople, Cyril's *Second Letter to Nestorius*, and Leo's *Tome to Flavian*. The council acted by deposing Dioscorus and the recalcitrant bishops who participated in the *Latrocinium* and upholding Eutyches' condemnation. The requirements for remaining in communion were tightly drawn: Dioscorus' deposition and Eutyches' condemnation must be affirmed and Leo's *Tome* accepted. Along with Domnus of Antioch and Ibas of Edessa, Theodoret was restored after reluctantly condemning Nestorius. The imperial commissioners formed an ecumenical committee, with representatives from the three major traditions, to construct a doctrinal statement.⁸⁶

The committee's deliberations produced a christological statement, the Definition of the Council of Chalcedon. The Definition begins by expressing a desire for peace through teaching common doctrine. Next, it confirms the Creeds of Nicea (325) and Constantinople (381), the Council of Ephesus (431), Cyril's *Second Letter to Nestorius*, Cyril's *Letter to John of Antioch*, and Leo's *Tome to Flavian*. It condemns the christological concepts of dividing Christ into two sons, a passible nature of deity in Christ, mixing or confusing Christ's dual natures, a heavenly origin of the form of a servant, or two natures before the incarnation and only one after the union. Then, the Definition proper follows.⁸⁷

---

⁸⁴ Political maneuvering to exclude rival parties did not succeed. For example, before the council convened, Dioscorus attempted to excommunicate Leo; also, the papal legates sought to have Dioscorus excluded. Bethune-Baker, *Christian Doctrine*, pp. 284-85.

⁸⁵ This letter included the Formula of Reunion.

⁸⁶ Davis, *Ecumenical Councils*, pp. 180-85; Bethune-Baker, *Christian Doctrine*, pp. 285-86; Need, *Truly Divine and Truly Human*, pp. 98-100; González, *Christian Thought*, I, pp. 377-79; Grillmeier, *Christian Tradition*, I, pp. 541-43; Harnack, *Dogma*, IV, pp. 215-19; Bindley and Green (eds.), *Oecumenical Documents*, pp. 183-88; Schaff, *History*, III, pp. 742-44; Frend, *Christianity*, pp. 770-73; Kelly, *Doctrines*, p. 339; McGuckin, *Cyril of Alexandria*, pp. 233-36; Wessel, *Nestorian Controversy*, pp. 287-95; O'Collins, *Christology*, p. 196. For an examination of the background, proceedings, and the canons ratified at the Council of Chalcedon, see L'Huillier, *Ancient Councils*, pp. 181-301.

⁸⁷ Sellers, *Chalcedon*, pp. 207-10, 221-25; Kelly, *Doctrines*, p. 339; Bethune-Baker, *Christian Doctrine*, pp. 286-87; McGuckin, *Cyril of Alexandria*, pp. 236-37; Walker, *History*, p. 151.

Following, then, the holy Fathers, we all unanimously teach that our Lord Jesus Christ is to us One and the same Son, the Self-same Perfect in Godhead, the Self-same Perfect in Manhood; truly God and truly Man; the Self-same of a rational soul and body; consubstantial with the Father according to the Godhead, the Self-same consubstantial with us according to the Manhood; like us in all things, sin apart; before the ages begotten of the Father as to the Godhead, but in the last days, the Self-same, for us and for our salvation (born) of Mary the Virgin Theotokos as to the Manhood; One and the Same Christ, Son, Lord, Only-begotten; acknowledged in Two Natures unconfusedly, unchangeably, indivisibly, inseparably; the difference of the Natures being in no way removed because of the Union, but rather the property of each Nature being preserved, and (both) concurring into One Prosopon and One Hypostasis; not as though He were parted or divided into Two Prosopa, but One and the Self-same Son and Only-begotten God, Word, Lord, Jesus Christ; even as from the beginning the prophets have taught concerning Him, and as the Lord Jesus Christ Himself hath taught us, and as the Symbol of the Fathers hath handed down to us.[88]

The framers of the Definition carefully crafted the language so that it agreed with christological tradition. The phrase the 'one and the same Son' expresses the soteriological truth all three traditions profess: (1) the only begotten Son who eternally exists with the Father has become incarnate in Jesus Christ and born of Mary for our salvation; (2) it acknowledges that Christ has been revealed to us in two natures. In other words, the Definition circumscribes orthodox

---

[88] Cited according to the translation of Herbert Bindley, *Oecumenical Documents*, pp. 234-35. Cf. 'The Fourth Ecumenical Council: The Council of Chalcedon', NPNF, Second Series, XIV, pp. 264-65; Sellers, *Chalcedon*, pp. 210-11; Grillmeier, *Christian Tradition*, I, p. 544; McGuckin, *Cyril of Alexandria*, p. 237; González, *Christian Thought*, I, p. 379; Davis, *Ecumenical Councils*, p. 186; Need, *Truly Divine and Truly Human*, p. 100; Kelly, *Doctrines*, pp. 339-40; Schaff, *History*, III, pp. 744-46; Bethune-Baker, *Christian Doctrine*, p. 287; Frend, *Christianity*, p. 771; Pelikan, *Christian Tradition*, I, pp. 263-64; Meyendorff, *Christ in Eastern Christian Thought*, pp. 25-26; O'Collins, *Christology*, p. 196; Walker, *History*, pp. 151-52; Harnack, *Dogma*, IV, pp. 219-25. The Greek text of the Definition can be found in Bindley and Green (eds.), *Oecumenical Documents*, p. 193. Greek and Latin versions can be found in Philip Schaff (ed.), *The Creeds of Christendom* (3 vols.; Grand Rapids: Baker Book House, 2007 repr.; New York: Harper & Row, Sixth edn, 1931), II, pp. 62-63.

boundaries for speaking about the mystery of Christ: Christ's divine nature is consubstantial (ὁμοούσιον) with the Father; Christ's human nature, consisting of body and rational soul, is consubstantial (ὁμοούσιον) with other humans; Christ's two natures are distinct but indivisible and inseparable; they are united but not confused or changeable; there are not two persons in Christ, but two natures (ἐν δύο φύσεσιν), retaining their properties after the incarnation, concurring (συντρεχούσης)[89] in one person; prosopon (πρόσωπον) and hypostasis (ὑπόστασιν) carry the same meaning, depicting the union of natures in the one person of Christ.[90] The Definition, thus, attempts to clarify the vocabulary used to express the christological union. Both prosopon and hypostasis synonymously mean person, while physis designates nature, so nature cannot be used interchangeably with person.[91] The christological union, therefore, is a personal union.

---

[89] The word συντρέχω carries the meaning to come together, coincide, agree, and concur which depicts two distinct natures coming together in one person, aptly depicting the *communicatio idiomatum*. Henry George Liddell and Robert Scott, 'συντρέχω', *An Intermediate Greek-English Lexicon, Founded upon the Seventh Edition of Liddell and Scott's Greek-English Lexicon* (Oxford: Oxford University Press repr.; New York: Harper & Brothers, 1889), p. 178. Cf. Bethune-Baker, *Christian Doctrine*, pp. 293-94.

[90] Sellers, *Chalcedon*, pp. 211-21; Grillmeier, *Christian Tradition*, I, pp. 544-54; Schaff, *History*, III, pp. 747-58; Davis, *Ecumenical Councils*, pp. 186-88; Pelikan, *Christian Tradition*, I, pp. 264-66; McGuckin, *Cyril of Alexandria*, pp. 237-40; Need, *Truly Divine and Truly Human*, pp. 100-103; Bindley and Green (eds.), *Oecumenical Documents*, pp. 186-87; Kelly, *Doctrines*, pp. 340-42.

[91] Meyendorff, *Christ in Eastern Christian Thought*, pp. 24, 28, writes:

> The solution was found in a recourse to Western Christology, and this meant a terminological innovation – the distinction between nature and hypostasis. Such a distinction had not been admitted until then by the East, Antioch or Alexandria: it was Chalcedon's essential and original contribution to Christology ... After Chalcedon, the distinction provided theologians with the proper terms to designate both the unity and the duality in Christ.

Cf. O'Collins, *Christology*, pp. 197-98:

> In confessing that the unity of Christ exists on the level of person and the duality on that of his natures the Council of Chalcedon proved a lasting success in regulating language about Christ. Its terminology of 'one person in two natures' became normative down to the twentieth century ... In its historical context, the teaching of Chalcedon effected a brilliant synthesis between the Alexandrians, who highlighted Christ's unity, and the Antiochenes, who championed the duality of Christ's distinct natures. The subject who acts is one (divine) person; in what he does he reveals the two natures through which he acts.

The Council of Chalcedon was an ecumenical attempt at bringing the three great christological traditions together to define the orthodox bounds of speaking about Christ's identity and mission. Moderates from the Alexandrian and Syrian traditions accepted the Formula of Reunion's Christology; nevertheless, the fragile peace it brokered was shattered with the death of its principals. Understanding and articulating the christological union and its soteriological significance were the issues that fueled the fire of ensuing controversy. Driven by Spirit christological impetus, the Formula of Reunion, Theodoret of Cyrus' writings, and Cyril's *Third Letter to Nestorius* and *Twelve Anathemas* became the literary points of contention between those advocating two natures in Christ after the incarnation and those who argued for only one after the union. So Spirit Christology played an integral role in the controversy that occasioned the Council of Chalcedon. Chalcedon produced a statement of the christological union that excluded improper interpretations, attempted to settle the semantic confusion of terms, and delineated the limits of speaking about the christological union. To remain in the boundaries of orthodoxy, then, Spirit Christology became narrowed to only one paradigm, pneumatic mediation; Spirit Christology must integrate with Logos Christology.

The Council of Constantinople II (553)

The decisions of Chalcedon, however, did not settle the christological issues, so the dispute continued between the supporters of Chalcedon's Dyophysite position and the Monophysite stance of its detractors.[92] The Monophysites took exception to Chalcedon on at

---

[92] Such able leaders as Leontius of Byzantium and Ephraim of Antioch represented the defenders of Chalcedon, while Timothy Aelurus, Philoxenus of Mabbug, and Severus of Antioch capably typified Monophysite objections to Chalcedon. The supporters of Chalcedon were divided between those who followed the classical Syrian teaching and those who upheld two natures after the incarnation, marked with Origenism influence, within a Cyrillian construct. Ephraim of Antioch represented the former school of thought and Leontius of Byzantium the latter. Sellers, *Chalcedon*, pp. 308-23. The enhypostasis theory which became the standard formula to depict the christological union was brought to fruition by Leontius of Byzantium. Sellers, *Chalcedon*, pp. 315-19; Meyendorff, *Christ in Eastern Christian Thought*, pp. 61-68; González, *Christian Thought*, II, pp. 96-98; Harnack, *Dogma*, IV, pp. 232-35; Frend, *Christianity*, pp. 849-50; Walker, *History*, p. 155-56.

least four points. First, they declared that Chalcedon confirmed Nestorian doctrine; for example, Theodoret of Cyrus and Ibas of Edessa were restored along with their writings. Second, Chalcedon failed to use Cyril's christological formulas: (1) one incarnate nature of the divine Logos, (2) the hypostatic union, and (3) the confession out of two natures. Third, they were convinced that Chalcedon did not adhere to christological tradition and had altered the faith: it affirmed two natures after the union. According to the Monophysites, Leo's *Tome* dissolved the hypostatic union and replaced it with a conjunction of deity and humanity, so the acceptance of Leo's *Tome* validated this charge. Fourth, Chalcedon's attempt to clarify christological vocabulary contained an inherent contradiction: each hypostasis denotes a nature, but Chalcedon posits two natures in the one hypostasis of Christ, pointing antithetically to two persons.[93] The Monophysites, accordingly, called for the nullification of Chalcedon, adoption of the Cyrillian christological formulas, condemnation of Leo's *Tome*, and the anathematization of certain Syrian writers. The Chalcedonian defenders countered by attempting to demonstrate that Cyril's acceptance of the Formula of Reunion and his later writings agreed with the Definition of Chalcedon. After the death of emperor Marcian (457), the political environment supported Monophysite dominance,[94] but the political

---

[93] John Meyendorff surmises, 'The distinction established at Chalcedon between the terms φύσις and ὑπόστασις was too new and revolutionary in the theology of the incarnation not to bring about divergent interpretations and misunderstandings'. Meyendorff, *Christ in Eastern Christian Thought*, p. 29. Cf. O'Collins, *Christology*, p. 199.

[94] For instance, Emperor Zeno, willing to placate the Monophysites, sponsored Acacius, bishop of Constantinople to compose the *Henoticon* (482) as an instrument of reconciliation between the factions. The *Henoticon* affirmed the Nicene faith as confirmed at Constantinople (381) and supervened at Ephesus (431); also, it accepted Cyril's *Twelve Anathemas*, condemned Nestorius and Eutyches, but it ignored the 'two natures' issue, Leo's *Tome*, and made a vague disavowal of Chalcedon. Pope Felix III reacted by excommunicating Acacius, producing the 'Acacian Schism' between Rome and Constantinople (484–519). Sellers, *Chalcedon*, pp. 274-83; Grillmeier, *Christian Tradition*, II, pp. 38-52, 229-34; González, *Christian Thought*, II, pp. 76-81; Need, *Truly Divine and Truly Human*, pp. 111-12; Davis, *Ecumenical Councils*, pp. 201-204; Pelikan, *Christian Tradition*, I, pp. 274-75; Harnack, *Dogma*, IV, pp. 226-30; Meyendorff, *Christ in Eastern Christian Thought*, p. 34; Schaff, *History*, III, p. 765; Walker, *History*, p. 154; 'Henoticon', *ODCC*, p. 750. Peace was restored between Rome and Constantinople (519) after Justin became emperor. His nephew Justinian conciliated this peace by agreeing to Rome's demands by accepting the decisions of Chalcedon and Leo's *Tome*

winds shifted in favor of Chalcedon with the coronation of Justin (518); furthermore, his successor Justinian (527) was determined to unite the Christian faith, as defined at Chalcedon. The disparity between these groups regarding christological issues and the political situation occasioned the fifth ecumenical council.[95]

Justinian, therefore, convened Constantinople II to affirm Chalcedon, demonstrate Cyrillian concurrence with Chalcedon's definition, and find a resolution to the Three Chapters controversy which concerned the condemnation of certain Syrian writings: Theodore of Mopsuestia's, Theodoret of Cyrus' anti-Cyrillian writings, and a letter written by Ibas of Edessa to Maris the Persian.[96] The council proceeded by reading Pope Vigilius' condemnation of the Three Chapters, confessing the faith of the previous four ecumenical councils, examining the Three Chapters, and considering the propriety of anathematizing the person and works of someone who died in communion with the church. The council found precedence

---

and condemning Acacius who authored the *Henoticon*. Sellers, *Chalcedon*, pp. 302-303.

[95] Sellers, *Chalcedon*, pp. 254-301; Davis, *Ecumenical Councils*, pp. 194-240; Need, *Truly Divine and Truly Human*, pp. 109-18; Green, *Leo the Great*, pp. 230-46; Harnack, *Dogma*, IV, pp. 230-41; Schaff, *History*, III, pp. 762-67; Meyendorff, *Christ in Eastern Christian Thought*, pp. 29-46; McGuckin, *Cyril of Alexandria*, pp. 240-41; Frend, *Christianity*, pp. 837-40, 848-50; Walker, *History*, pp. 153-54; O'Collins, *Christology*, p. 199; Bethune-Baker, *Christian Doctrine*, p. 292.

[96] In 509 the Monophysites led by Philoxenus demanded not only the condemnation of Nestorius but all they believed had taught the doctrine of two sons in Christ, so the writings of Theodore of Mopsuestia, Diodore of Tarsus, Theodoret of Cyrus, and Ibas of Edessa were condemned. After holding several meetings with the defenders of Chalcedon and the Monophysites, pursing his goal of unification, Justinian decided that the best route to rapprochement was by appeasing the Monophysites, so he published an edict (543) condemning the writings of Theodore of Mopsuestia, the anti-Cyrillian writings of Theodoret of Cyrus, and a letter written by Ibas of Edessa to Maris the Persian; thus began, the Three Chapters controversy. With some coercion, most of the East accepted the emperor's edict. Pope Vigilius wrote *Judicatum* (548), agreeing with the edict and affirming Chalcedon, but he vacillated in his support of the Three Chapters condemnation after the document raised the ire of many in the West. In fact, it became evident to Justinian from the reaction to the edict in the West and the lack of support among some in the East that another ecumenical council was necessary to unify the Christian faith. Sellers, *Chalcedon*, pp. 323-25; Meyendorff, *Christ in Eastern Christian Thought*, pp. 80-81; Davis, *Ecumenical Councils*, pp. 215, 234-37; Harnack, *Dogma*, IV, pp. 241-49; González, *Christian Thought*, II, pp. 83-87; Schaff, *History*, III, pp. 768-70; Pelikan, *Christian Tradition*, I, pp. 275-77; Need, *Truly Divine and Truly Human*, pp. 117-18; Frend, *Christianity*, pp. 850-53; Walker, *History*, pp. 156-57; Grillmeier, *Christian Tradition*, II, pp. 61-62.

among the bishops of Rome and Augustine for anathematizing the writings of deceased heretics, clearing the ground for the condemnation of the Three Chapters. The council concluded by reading its Sentence against the Three Chapters and the 14 anathemas the bishops appended to the Sentence.[97]

These anathemas confirm Chalcedon's christological definition contrary to the Three Chapters (*Anathemas* 5; 6; 14); also, to elucidate that Chalcedon's confession of faith implicitly contains Cyril's christological formulas, they integrate Cyrillian terminology. For example, the anathemas correlate Cyril's 'hypostatic union' with Chalcedon's 'one hypostasis', signifying the unconfused and undivided christological union (*Anathemas* 4; 5; 7; 8; 13). Furthermore, this hypostatic union, according to Cyril's terminology, has taken place 'out of two natures' (*Anathema* 8); the divine nature is eternally begotten and consubstantial with the Father, and the human nature is consubstantial with other humans and born of Mary (*Anathemas* 8; 2; 6); indeed, one of the Trinity was incarnated and crucified in the flesh (*Anathema* 10),[98] so that hypostatic union expresses the Cyrillian formula 'one incarnate nature of the divine Logos' (*Anathema* 8).[99] The council, also, retains Chalcedon's premise that Christ has been revealed 'in two natures,' with each unmixed nature unchangeably retaining it properties (*Anathema* 7), so in the one person of

---

[97] 'The Fifth Ecumenical Council: The Second Council of Constantinople', NPNF, Second Series, XIV, pp. 302-11; Sellers, *Chalcedon*, pp. 325-29; Davis, *Ecumenical Councils*, pp. 237-44; Meyendorff, *Christ in Eastern Christian Thought*, pp. 82-85; Need, *Truly Divine and Truly Human*, pp. 118-20; Pelikan, *Christian Tradition*, I, pp. 277, 337-38, 340-41; Schaff, *History*, III, pp. 351-52, 770-72. The council also condemned Origen's cosmology, anthropology, and Christology as professed by Evagrius Ponticus; accordingly, the council appended to the Statement 15 anathemas against Origen. 'Constantinople II', NPNF, Second Series, XIV, pp. 316-17. Cf. Meyendorff, *Christ in Eastern Christian Thought*, pp. 47-68; Walker, *History*, p. 157. By linking treatises in the Nag Hammadi Library with Origenism and Shenoute's writings, the founder of Coptic theological literature, which refuted Gnostic proclivities among Coptic monks, Grillmeier has noted that Origenism not associated with Evagrius Ponticus existed among the Copts. Grillmeier, *Christian Tradition*, II, pp. 167-214.

[98] This expresses the formula occasioned by the Theopaschite controversy. Meyendorff, *Christ in Eastern Christian Thought*, pp. 34-37; González, *Christian Thought*, II, pp. 82-83; Frend, *Christianity*, pp. 841-43; Harnack, *Dogma*, IV, pp. 230-32.

[99] For an examination of this phrase found in Apollinarius, Cyril, Eutyches, and this council, see V.C. Samuel, 'One Incarnate Nature of God the Word', GOTR 10 (1964-65), pp. 37-53.

Christ two natures exist after the union: divine and human, which includes body and rational soul (*Anathemas* 7; 4). Following Cyrillian logic, however, these undivided and unconfused natures are recognized through intellectual analysis alone (*Anathemas* 7). The council, thus, distinguishes the natures but does not divide the person: the properties of the two natures are properties of one person (*Anathemas* 3; 5; 7; 9).[100] To avoid implying two sons or persons in Christ, the council employs Cyril's christological formulas expressing the christological union; therefore, the council interpreted the Definition of Chalcedon through Cyrillian terms.[101]

The Spirit christological issue apropos of the Spirit anointing Christ arises among these anathemas. The council accuses Theodore of Mopsuestia of positing two persons in Christ; accordingly, Christ is a human capable of experiencing sufferings, temptations, and progress which culminates in Christ's reception of the Spirit.[102]

> Theodore of Mopsuestia, who has said that the Word of God is one person, but that another person is Christ ... as a mere man was baptized in the name of the Father, and of the Son, and of the Holy Ghost, and obtained by this baptism the grace of the Holy Spirit, and became worthy of Sonship (*Anathema* 12).[103]

Following Cyrillian logic, which exclusively confines the anointing of the Spirit to the incarnation event, the council does not allow for

---

[100] 'Constantinople II', NPNF, Second Series, XIV, pp. 312-14; Sellers, *Chalcedon*, pp. 329-41; Davis, *Ecumenical Councils*, pp. 244-45; Need, *Truly Divine and Truly Human*, p. 120; O'Collins, *Christology*, pp. 199-200.

[101] According to John Meyendorff, 'the theopaschite formulas used by Cyril had to be either accepted or rejected; and if they were accepted, a christological vocabulary had to be constructed that would remain Chalcedonian while integrating Cyril's basic soteriological intuition, of which theopaschism was the key element'. Meyendorff, *Christ in Eastern Christian Thought*, p. 70. Cf. Harnack, *Dogma*, IV, pp. 249-51; Meyendorff, *Christ in Eastern Christian Thought*, pp. 69-80; McGuckin, *Cyril of Alexandria*, pp. 241-43. Gerald O'Collins concludes: 'The Second Council of Constantinople (553) was to interpret Chalcedon in a way that represented a return to the Alexandrian triumph at Ephesus'. O'Collins, *Christology*, pp. 198-99.

[102] Theodore did teach that two unmixed natures united in Christ: (1) an impassible divine nature and (2) a passible human nature uniquely capable of natural and psychological development beyond other humans, for he was not born by normal human procreation but fashioned by the divine energy of the Spirit (Theodore, *On the Incarnation*, 7.3).

[103] Cited according to the translation of Henry Percival, 'Constantinople II', NPNF, Second Series, XIV, p. 315.

Christ's reception of the Spirit at the Jordan since the Logos is divine and has no need for the anointing of the Spirit;[104] accordingly, if Christ's human nature receives the Spirit, it would imply another person alongside the Logos who the Spirit sanctifies and elevates into divine sonship.[105] Of course, Theodoret of Cyrus opposed Cyril on this very point. Theodoret's anti-Cyrillian tractates, which included his debate with Cyril regarding Christ's relationship with the Spirit,[106] were censured at the *Latrocinium*, but after denouncing Nestorius at Chalcedon, Theodoret and these writings were restored. Although the previous ecumenical councils had not received Cyril's *Third Letter to Nestorius* and *Twelve Anathemas* as a standard of orthodoxy, Constantinople II used them to measure and to condemn Theodoret's anti-Cyrillian treatises, along with their Spirit christological emphases (*Anathema* 13).[107] Constantinople II in ef-

---

[104] According to Grillmeier, Cyril restricts the anointing to the incarnation:

the anointment is spoken of openly for those who comprehend that he was anointed at his incarnation and is thus named [i.e., as the anointed One] (cf. Acts 10.38). Thus in order not to jeopardize the unity of the one Christ through the doctrine of the anointment, Cyril wants nothing to stand between the assuming Logos and the assumed humanity: no messianic gifts, no 'created grace', but only the 'uncreated grace' that the *Logos* is for the united humanity. Therefore the anointment is accomplished exclusively in the incarnation of the Son. Only the incarnation makes it possible to speak of the anointment at all ... For Cyril joins Logos and humanity so closely together in the incarnate One that there is no longer any place for a lasting impartation of grace by the Spirit to inhere in the humanity as such. The 'Logos' as such lays claim to the term *anointment* for itself (Grillmeier, *Christian Tradition*, II, pp. 342-43).

Unfortunately Cyril fails to leave room here for a christological pneumatology. The messianic status of Jesus, which must also be possible in a Logos Christology, can no longer experience an enlightening substantiation. The pneumatic equipping of the human being Jesus, so important an element of the image of Christ, must necessarily come up short (Grillmeier, *Christian Tradition*, II, p. 356).

[105] Theodore's distinction between the divine and human natures allowed for the human nature to receive the Spirit's anointing at the Jordan event in a degree surpassing all other humans, not as an act of adoption but empowerment (Theodore, *On the Incarnation*, 5.1; 7.6).

[106] The council, however, neither condemned *Eranistes* nor his *Commentary on the Psalms*. Like Cyril after the Formula of Reunion, by the time of these writings, Theodoret's language had matured and moved more toward the center between the Alexandrian and Syrian christological nomenclatures.

[107] See the translation of Henry Percival, 'Constantinople II', NPNF, Second Series, XIV, p. 315:

fect, following Cyrillian analyticity, restricted discussion about the Spirit anointing Christ to the incarnation.

Whereas Chalcedon circumscribed the boundaries for speaking about Christ's identity and mission and limited the Spirit christological paradigms that fit within the boundaries of orthodox Christology, the Council of Constantinople II gave precedence to Cyrillian interpretation; consequently, this form of Logos Christology ascended to dominance, effectively displacing Spirit Christology. Actually, in order to gain this consensus and reject any position contrary to Cyrillian Christology, this council unjustly condemned the writings of two theologians – Theodore of Mopsuestia and Theodoret of Cyrus – who had died in good standing with the church. Henceforth, except in a few cases, proponents of Logos Christology will maintain a truculent disposition toward Spirit Christology.

Conclusion

These christological councils endeavored to establish the proper boundaries of speaking in an orthodox manner about the christological union, and the Holy Spirit's relationship to Christ's identity and mission, and the survival of Spirit Christology. Actually, these three facets of Christology dovetailed; therefore, Spirit Christology was *integral* to these controversies. In fact, during the Council of Ephesus, seven of Cyril's anathemas directly addressed Spirit christological issues. The ascendency of Cyril's dominant form of Logos Christology almost placed the death nail in the heart of the Syrian Antiochene Spirit christological tradition, yet the Formula of Reunion breathed new life into it.

When the Council of Chalcedon convened, Spirit christological issues were once again debated, resulting in the christological defini-

---

If anyone defend the impious writings of Theodoret, directed against the true faith and against the first holy Synod of Ephesus and against St. Cyril and his XII Anathemas, and [defends] that which he has written in defence of the impious Theodore and Nestorius ... and if anyone does not anathematize these impious writings and those who have held or who hold these sentiments, and all those who have written contrary to the true faith or against St. Cyril and his XII Chapters, and who die in their impiety: let them be anathema.

Since the Spirit christological references in these tractates previously have been examined, there is no need to go over the same ground at this time.

tion which circumscribed the boundaries of orthodox Christology and limited the Spirit christological models within its bounds exclusively to the paradigm of pneumatic mediation. The Definition of Chalcedon, juxtaposing the two natures in hypostatic union, provided for an anagogic christological framework, making it possible for Spirit Christology to advance from Jesus' humanity, recognizing and affirming the anointing of the Spirit in Christ's life and ministry, into the depths of the divine person, while identifying the Logos as the single subjectivity of the two natures.[108]

The Council of Constantinople II, however, interpreted the Definition of Chalcedon through Cyrillian terms, effectively displacing Spirit Christology with a dominant form of Logos Christology which confined the christological focal point of the Spirit's agency and anointing to the incarnation. With the axial christological focus on the Logos, the scope of the Spirit's role in the identity and mission of Christ diminishes, and the christological emphasis on the human nature insipidly fades from view. Though Spirit Christology's nature is inherently fluid, integrating with this restrictive form of Logos Christology presents an arduous task.

---

[108] Grillmeier, *Christian Tradition*, I, p. 552, writes:

> But whereas the *mia physis* formula can only express a 'katagogic' christology, the Chalcedonian form is also capable of providing a basis for an 'anagogic' christology. In other words, it is possible to advance from the human reality of Jesus into the depths of the divine person. At the same time, Chalcedon leaves no doubt that that [*sic*] the one Logos is the subject of both the human and divine predicates.

Leo, who was instrumental in forming the Definition of Chalcedon, grasped the concept of anagogic union and adopted the word persona to depict it. Green, *Leo the Great*, p. 51. According to Grillmeier,

> The Chalcedonian unity of person in the distinction of natures provides the dogmatic basis for the preservation of the divine transcendence, which must always be a feature of the Christian concept of God. But it also shows the possibility of a complete immanence of God in our history, an immanence on which the biblical doctrine of the economy of salvation rests (Grillmeier, *Christian Tradition*, I, p. 553).

9

SUMMARY/CONCLUSION TO PART ONE

As this examination of Spirit Christology in this era concludes, the survey will assess its purposes: to trace Spirit Christology's presence, or lack thereof, and to identify the Spirit christological paradigms and their relationships with doctrinal development in the Christian tradition.

This inquiry has demonstrated that Spirit Christology has played an integral role in the development of Christian doctrine; indeed, Spirit christological issues were central to the debates in the first five ecumenical councils. The form of pneumatic Christology a writer or group proposed delineated their positions in these debates: some stood in congruity with the developing christological and trinitarian doctrines while others did not. In point of fact, among the Patristic writers who delineate a form of Spirit Christology, Spirit seems to be the decisive christological concept. How these writers formulate their Spirit christological paradigms discloses their view of God and Christ's relationship with the Spirit, which is the key to understanding Christ's identity and mission. This survey has identified three primary methods, emerging during this epoch, for constructing Spirit Christology: pneumatic inspiration, incarnation, and mediation.

The Spirit christological paradigm of pneumatic inspiration depicts a non-incarnational view. This survey's historical analysis has demonstrated that this form of Spirit Christology was common among the Gnostics, Ebionites, and Dynamic Monarchians. These groups concurred that at the Jordan the Spirit, the impersonal power of deity, descended into Jesus, anointing his life and ministry and identifying him as the Christ. They differed, however, on at least two points. First, Gnosticism devalued Christ's flesh, emphasizing instead the salvific gnosis available through the Spirit, but Ebionism and Dynamic Monarchianism accentuated Jesus' human nature as the prophetically inspired messianic bearer of the Spirit. Second, although Gnostic Christology demonstrated affinities with Logos Christology, these were incongruent Christologies because of Gnosticism's polytheistic bent, whereas Ebionism and Dynamic Monarchianism unequivocally opposed Logos Christology as antithetical to monotheism. This method of pneumatic Christology, consequently, was incompatible and incapable of developing alongside the Logos Christology that appeared and unfolded in the central christological tradition.

The Spirit christological paradigms of pneumatic incarnation and meditation delineate incarnational views. Because of the fluidity of terminology, some overlap exists between these models. They concur that God is one undivided divine substance which is Spirit, so the mode of incarnation is the union of preexistent Spirit and flesh; also, Christ's humanity originated in the virginal conception and was anointed for salvific mission by the Spirit. Although these writers used trinitarian terms, often they failed to distinguish adequately between triune relationships, struggling to present Christ's deity while maintaining a monotheistic view of God, so that Spirit synonymously referred to Father, Son, and Holy Spirit; in a paradigm of pneumatic incarnation, then, the incarnate divine Spirit may refer to Holy Spirit, Logos, or for Modalist Monarchianism the Father.[1] Nevertheless, with the trinitarian definition and clarification of terms accepted at the Council of Constantinople (381), Spirit as the subject of incarnation became circumscribed to either the Holy Spirit or the divine essence in Modalism. Paradigms of pneumatic incarnation, henceforth, became clearly demarcated from models of pneumatic mediation and incompatible with the developing Logos christological tradition.

---

[1] Certain forms of pneumatic incarnation integrated nascent forms of Logos Christology and developed into paradigms of pneumatic mediation with trinitarian distinctions. For example, the trajectory of Eustathius' Christology culminated in Nestorius' and Theodoret of Cyrus' trinitarian theology, and Basil of Ancyra found its apogee in Basil of Caesarea.

Spirit christological paradigms of pneumatic mediation demonstrate compatibility with Logos Christology. Even as early as Ignatius this form of Spirit Christology integrated an incipient form of Logos Christology, acknowledging the distinction between the Father and the preexistent Logos and identifying the incarnation as a union of Spirit and flesh. Spirit designates the divine nature because the one undivided substance of God is Spirit, existing in triune relations as Father, Son, and Holy Spirit; therefore, the Logos, who became incarnated in Christ, pre-existed as Spirit. According to the paradigm of pneumatic mediation, the Spirit functioned as the agent of Christ's virgin birth, by an act of grace forming Christ's human nature and uniting it to the Logos.[2] This model, moreover, sharply distinguished between Christ's divine nature and human nature, consisting of body and rational soul, allowing the Spirit to anoint and dynamically empower Christ's human nature for salvific mission. This model developed along with Logos Christology through Justin Martyr, Tertullian, Irenaeus, Clement of Alexandria, Origen, Cyril of Jerusalem, Athanasius, the Cappadocian Fathers, Ambrose, Hilary, Augustine, Nestorius, and Theodoret of Cyrus.[3] This form of Spirit Christology, therefore, not only exhibited compatibility with Logos Christology, it integrated Logos Christology, delineating an incarnational pneumatic Christology set within a trinitarian framework.

The question remains: what led to the replacement of Spirit Christology by Logos Christology? The answer has pointed to the christological councils of the fifth and sixth centuries. Although Spirit Christology enjoyed strong support in the Latin West and the Syrian tradition, the Council of Ephesus (431), accepting Cyril of Alexandria's christological formula, severely challenged its christological validity but did not vanquish it. Cyril of Alexandria's christological formula opposed distinguishing Christ's deity and humanity, the Spirit effecting the incarnation by grace, and the Spirit subsequently anointing Christ. According to Cyril, Christ was one incar-

---

[2] Early on Spirit, Logos, and Holy Spirit were synonymous appellations, but after the Council of Constantinople (381), reference to the Spirit's mediation explicitly meant the Holy Spirit.

[3] Of course, Arius supported a form of pneumatic mediation, but Arian Christology with its diminished view of the Logos' deity was not accepted among the proponents of this paradigm.

nate divine nature and did not need a subsequent anointing; since the Spirit is the Spirit of the Son, and the Son assumed human flesh, the incarnation is the anointing of the human nature. The Council of Chalcedon's christological definition circumscribed the boundaries of orthodox Christology, limiting the Spirit christological models within its bounds exclusively to the paradigm of pneumatic mediation. The Council of Constantinople II, however, interpreted the Definition of Chalcedon through Cyrillian terms, effectively displacing Spirit Christology with a dominant form of Logos Christology which restricted the christological focus to the Logos.

PART TWO

SPIRIT CHRISTOLOGY FROM THE FIFTH
ECUMENICAL COUNCIL TO THE RISE OF
PENTECOSTALISM

10

EASTERN WRITERS

The fifth ecumenical council did little to attenuate the christological debate; the West strongly objected to the decisions, deepening the rift between East and West,[1] and the East divided along factional lines supporting Monophysite and Dyophysite Christologies.[2] The debate's focus, however, shifted to Christ's will and energy (activity or operation) and iconoclastic issues, giving rise to the sixth and seventh ecumenical councils.

The Council of Constantinople III (680)

The Monophysites, of course, advocated one will (Monothelitism) and energy (Monenergism) in Christ against those arguing for two wills and energies. Though he died before the sixth ecumenical

---

[1] Besides the christological issues, at least five theological issues caused conflict during this period of time, leading to the final break between East and West: (1) papal authority and how it was derived, (2) the Western defence of the filioque doctrine, (3) the East's rejection of the West's doctrine of purgatory, (4) the East denying the propriety of the Western practice of using azymic (unleavened) bread in the Eucharist, and (5) disagreement over what effected the sacramental miracle of changing the bread and wine into the body and blood of the Lord. Regarding the last issue, the West asserted that the proper repetition of the words of institution affected the miracle, but Eastern theology attributed it to the invocation of the Holy Spirit in the epiclesis. Pelikan, *Christian Tradition*, II, pp. 146-98, 270-80. Cf. Schaff, *History*, IV, pp. 306-25.

[2] The Dyophysite groups were those of the Byzantine and East Syrian traditions, while the Monophysite groups were those of the Alexandrian, Coptic, West Syrian (Jacobite), Armenian, and Ethiopian traditions. Davis, *Ecumenical Councils*, pp. 247-53; González, *Christian Thought*, II, pp. 100-105; Pelikan, *Christian Tradition*, II, pp. 37-49; Walker, *History*, pp. 157-59; O'Collins, *Christology*, p. 200.

council convened, Maximus the Confessor's christological formula carried the day, posthumously, earning him the sobriquet the father of Byzantine theology.[3] Appealing to the Eastern tradition's normative consensus,[4] Constantinople III settled this dispute in harmony with Chalcedon's christological definition: Christ has two natures, two wills, and two energies existing in hypostatic union.[5] Since the East's doctrine of deification was central to this debate, stressing the incarnation's redemptive significance and the Holy Spirit's soteriological activity in believers, the Spirit's role in Christ's salvific mission was intrinsic to the debate.

---

[3] 'In fact, Maximus can be called the real father of Byzantine theology. Only through his system, in which the valid traditions of the past found their legitimate place, were the ideas of Origen, Evagrius, the Cappadocians, Cyril, and Pseudo-Dionysius preserved in Eastern Christianity.' Meyendorff, *Christ in Eastern Christian Thought*, pp. 131-32. Cf. Meyendorff, *Christ in Eastern Christian Thought*, pp. 131-51; Pelikan, *Christian Tradition*, II, pp. 62-90; O'Collins, *Christology*, pp. 200-201; González, *Christian Thought*, II, pp. 98-100. For examinations of Maximus' life, writings, and Christology, see Andrew Louth, *Maximus the Confessor* (ECF; London: Routledge, 1996); Demetrios Bathrellos, *The Byzantine Christ: Person, Nature, and Will in the Christology of Saint Maximus the Confessor* (OECS; Oxford: Oxford University Press, 2004); Torstein Tollefsen, *The Christocentric Cosmology of St. Maximus the Confessor* (OECS; Oxford: Oxford University Press, 2008); Ian A. McFarland, 'Developing an Apophatic Christocentrism: Lessons from Maximus the Confessor', *ThTo* 60 (2003), pp. 200-14; Ian A. McFarland, 'Fleshing out Christ: Maximus the Confessor's Christology in Anthropological Perspective', *SVTQ* 49 (2005), pp. 417-36; González, *Christian Thought*, II, pp. 98-100; Schaff, *History*, IV, pp. 623-26.

[4] From the previous controversies emerged a consensus in the East for testing the orthodoxy of christological doctrine: it must be in accord with the apostolic witness of Scripture, the Patristic Fathers, and the ecumenical councils. Any Spirit christological paradigm seeking recognition, therefore, must meet this criterion. Pelikan, *Christian Tradition*, II, pp. 16-30.

[5] Davis, *Ecumenical Councils*, pp. 258-87; Need, *Truly Divine and Truly Human*, pp. 120-28; Schaff, *History*, IV, pp. 490-500; González, *Christian Thought*, II, pp. 88-91; Walker, *History*, pp. 160-62; Kenneth Scott Latourette, *A History of Christianity* (2vols.; New York: Harper & Row, Rev. edn, 1975), I, pp. 284-85; Paul Verghese, 'The Monothelete Controversy: A Historical Survey', *GOTR* 13 (1968), pp. 196-211. For overviews of contemporary interest in Christ's two wills, see Ivor J. Davidson, '"Not My Will but Yours Be Done": The Ontological Dynamics of Incarnational Intention', *IJST* 7 (2005), pp.178-204; Thomas Watts, 'Two Wills in Christ? Contemporary Objections Considered in the Light of a Critical Examination of Maximus the Confessor's *Disputation with Pyrrhus*', *WTJ* 71 (2009), pp. 455-87.

The Council of Nicea II (787)

Though the iconoclastic controversy[6] (725–842) primarily addressed the propriety of Christians using images in worship, christological issues permeated this debate. Those who espoused banning images, the iconoclasts, appealed to the Scriptural prohibition against idolatry: God is transcendent and un-circumscribable. From numerous Patristic texts, they argued that an image is homoousios with the essence of the archetype it depicts; thus, a corporeal image divides Christ's natures, for an image only portrays Christ's humanity.[7] Following John of Damascus' theology, those defending the use of images, the iconophiles, subtly distinguished between veneration and worship; an icon is an object of veneration (προσκυνέω) while worship (λατρεύω) belongs to God alone.[8] They insisted, furthermore, that the incarnation has made a crucial difference; deity has united with human flesh, so icons representing Christ express faith in the

---

[6] This controversy emerged during the reigns of 2 emperors who supported iconoclasm: Leo III (717–41), Constantine V (741–75). Three main components provide the context for the iconoclasm movement to emerge: (1) military confrontation and debate with Islam regarding images, (2) the heritage of paganism in religious culture, and (3) Hellenic spiritualism. For a discussion of these elements underlying the controversy, see John Meyendorff, *Byzantine Theology: Historical Trends and Doctrinal Themes* (New York: Fordham University Press, 1974), pp. 42-44; John Meyendorff, *Christ in Eastern Christian Thought*, pp. 174-75; González, *Christian Thought*, II, pp. 196-98; Harnack, *Dogma*, IV, pp. 317-29; Latourette, *History*, I, pp. 292-97. Regarding the issues involved in the controversy, see Patrick Henry, 'What Was the Iconoclastic Controversy About?', *CH* 45 (1976), pp. 16-31; Joseph Bossakov, 'The Iconoclastic Controversy: Historical Perspectives', *GOTR* 38 (1993), pp. 215-30; Blagoy Tschiflianov, 'The Iconoclastic Controversy: A Theological Perspective', *GOTR* 38 (1993), pp. 231-64; Theodore Sideris, 'Theological Position of the Iconophiles during the Iconoclastic Controversy', *SVTQ* 17 (1973), pp. 210-26.

[7] Pelikan, *Christian Tradition*, II, pp. 91-117; Meyendorff, *Christ in Eastern Christian Thought*, pp. 173-77; Davis, *Ecumenical Councils*, pp. 290-305; Need, *Truly Divine and Truly Human*, pp. 129-33.

[8] St. John of Damascus, *Three Treatises on the Divine Images* (trans. Andrew Louth; Press PPS; Crestwood: St. Vladimir's Seminary Press, 2003). For expositions of John of Damascus' context, life, and teachings, see Andrew Louth, *St. John Damascene: Tradition and Originality in Byzantine Theology* (OECS; New York: Oxford University Press, 2002); Meyendorff, *Christ in Eastern Christian Thought*, pp. 153-72; Need, *Truly Divine and Truly Human*, pp. 133-38; Meyendorff, *Byzantine Theology*, pp. 45-46; González, *Christian Thought*, II, pp. 199-204; Schaff, *History*, IV, pp. 448-63, 626-36; Latourette, *History*, I, pp. 291-92; Walker, *History*, pp. 163-64; Majorie O'Rouke Boyle, 'Christ the ΕΙΚΩΝ in the Apologies for Holy Icons of John of Damascus', *GOTR* 15 (1970), pp. 175-86.

Word becoming flesh.⁹ Accordingly, repudiating the appropriateness of icons in worship, essentially, disavows the incarnation. Affirming the Chalcedonian Definition, the seventh ecumenical council, Nicaea II, sanctioned the use of images in Christian worship. As the iconoclastic debate continued after this council,¹⁰ Nicephorus and Theodore the Studite¹¹ in opposition to the iconoclasts attested to the reality of Christ's full and individual human nature, reaffirming the Syrian Antiochene contribution to Christology.¹² The iconoclastic controversy, therefore, avers the importance of the hypostatic union of Christ's divine and human natures.

Central to these debates, Eastern theology's *leitmotiv* doctrine of deification accentuated the functions of Christ and the Spirit in soteriology; thus, Eastern Christology contained a robust pneumatological emphasis which became evident in the Byzantine mystical theological tradition.

Byzantine Mystical Theological Tradition

Epistemologically, this tradition employs an apophatic method which conjoins with personal religious experience: God cannot be known in essence but can be known from the effects of God's energies. So in this tradition, religious experience becomes an epistemological principle in theology; actually, it is a spirituality of experience that expresses a doctrinal attitude of life and worship. Its an-

---

⁹ Essentially, the problem of the hypostatic union was implicit in this quarrel, with the iconoclasts representing the Monophysite position, and their opponents delineating the Chalcedonian Definition's position. Meyendorff, *Christ in Eastern Christian Thought*, pp. 175-89.

¹⁰ The next phase of the debate occurred during the reigns of three iconoclastic emperors Leo V (813–20), Michael II (820–29), and Theophilus (829–42).

¹¹ Meyendorff, *Christ in Eastern Christian Thought*, pp. 185-92; Meyendorff, *Byzantine Theology*, pp. 56-58; Schaff, *History*, IV, pp. 464-65. In his polemic against the iconoclasts, Theodore the Studite came close to espousing a form of Spirit Christology: 'the veneration of Christ in the image belongs to the discussion of the economy. Although Christ is Spirit because He is God, yet He is also flesh because He is man' (*On the Holy Icons* 3.C.15). Cited according to the translation of Catharine Roth, Theodore the Studite, *On the Holy Icons* (trans. Catharine P. Roth; Crestwood, NY: St. Vladimir's Seminary Press, 1981), p. 108. Cf. *On the Holy Icons* 3.A.3; 2.41.

¹² In fact, according to John Meyendorff, 'the orthodox polemic against iconoclasm insisted first on the fullness of the human nature in Christ, thus largely recovering the christological tradition of Antioch'. Meyendorff, *Christ in Eastern Christian Thought*, p. 185.

thropology denies the transmission of guilt through conception and birth; rather, the fall produced death, corruption, and loss of the Spirit. Salvifically, in the incarnation, the Logos assumed human nature, anointing it with the Spirit thus becoming the archetype of humanity's deification, and cosmically joined with creation, initiating creation into its journey toward theosis. The Spirit, moreover, draws humanity and creation into deifying union with God in Christ, so that humans participate in the divine energy and become susceptible to the vision of the divine light. Pneumatology, consequently, imbues the anthropology, soteriology, ecclesiology, and Christology of this mystical tradition.[13] From the eleventh through the fourteenth centuries, the Byzantine mystical tradition developed a method of theologizing, Hesychasm, which formulated doctrinal implications from their practices of devotion and prayer.[14]

Symeon the New Theologian

The writings of Symeon the New Theologian[15] stand in the lineage of mystic spirituality and theology, extending back to Macarius,

---

[13] For presentations of Eastern mystical theology, see Vladimir Lossky, *The Mystical Theology of the Eastern Church* (trans. Members of the Fellowship of St. Alban and St. Sergius; Crestwood, NY: St Vladimir's Seminary Press, 1976 repr.; London: J. Clarke, 1957); Vladimir Lossky, *In the Image and Likeness of God* (Crestwood, NY: St. Vladimir's Seminary Press, 1985); John Meyendorff, *St. Gregory Palamas and Orthodox Spirituality* (trans. Fiske Adele; Crestwood, NY: St. Vladimir's Seminary Press, 1974), pp. 1-42.

[14] Pelikan, *Christian Tradition*, II, pp. 252-54; Lossky, *Mystical Theology*, pp. 209-16; Meyendorff, *Byzantine Theology*, pp. 76-77, 108-109; Meyendorff, *Orthodox Spirituality*, pp. 52-69; Gregory Palamas, *The Triads* (trans. Nicholas Gendle; CWS; New York: Paulist Press, 1983), pp. 1-5; Latourette, *History*, I, pp. 570-71.

> The hesychast tradition took different forms down through the centuries, but it remained unified in its fundamental inspiration: in Christ (ἐν Χριστῷ) man recovers his original destiny, re-adapts his existence to the divine model, rediscovers the true *freedom* that slavery to Satan made him lose, and makes use of that freedom, with the collaboration (σύνεργεία) of the Holy Spirit, in order to know and love God (Meyendorff, *Christ in Eastern Christian Thought*, pp. 127-28).

The Hesychasts placed great importance on unceasingly repeating the Jesus Prayer in order to attain the union of the mind and heart, so that prayer became a prayer of the heart, which potentially prepared for the vision of divine light. Meyendorff, *Orthodox Spirituality*, pp. 25-33; 'Hesychasm', *ODCC*, pp. 763-64. The Jesus Prayer was practiced with the head bowed, eyes fixed on the heart, and breathing controlled in rhythm with the words of the prayer: 'Lord Jesus Christ, Son of God, have mercy upon me'. 'Jesus Prayer', *ODCC*, pp. 875.

[15] It is possible that the sobriquet 'New Theologian' was not a complement; usually, theological innovation among the Byzantines brought suspicion of here-

which often opposed the rise of humanism in the East and the hierarchical tendency to institutionalize the Spirit in the sacramental system;[16] in fact, Symeon functioned in prophetic authority proclaiming the Christian faith as a dynamic experience of the Spirit of Christ.[17] Two central themes, hence, run congruently throughout

---

sy. But more than likely, this designation being attributed to Symeon was a great honor, for only two other people had this title added to their names: John the Evangelist and Gregory of Nazianzus. Symeon, *On the Mystical Life: The Ethical Discourses* (trans. Alexander Golitzin; 3 vols.; Crestwood, NY: St. Vladimir's Seminary Press, 1995), III, pp. 7-11. 'The term "theologian" is to be understood here, as with most Greek Fathers, not in the sense of a theologian working our new dogmas, but as one who has reached the heights of contemplation. The adjective "New" would mean a re-newer of the apostolic life which had been in large part forgotten, as Symeon himself states.' Basil Krivocheine, *In the Light of Christ: Saint Symeon the New Theologian (949-1022) Life-Spirituality-Doctrine* (trans. Anthony P. Gythiel; Crestwood, NY: St. Vladimir's Seminary Press, 1986), pp. 62-63. Symeon's theology seemed to agree with the Eastern consensus. See Hilarion Alfeyev, *St. Symeon the New Theologian and Orthodox Tradition* (OECS; Oxford: Oxford University Press, 2000).

[16] Meyendorff, *Byzantine Theology*, pp. 54-73; Pelikan, *Christian Tradition*, II, pp. 242-60. Cf. Lossky, *Mystical Theology*, pp. 23-43, 156-73; Lossky, *Likeness of God*, pp. 31-43, 97-110. 'The whole life of Symeon illustrates the conflict between Prophet and Priest, between the Experience and the Institution.' Meyendorff, *Orthodox Spirituality*, p. 48. Cf. Meyendorff, *Orthodox Spirituality*, pp. 44-51.

[17] The prophetic authority he claimed and his insistence on the life in the Spirit soon caused conflict between Symeon and ecclesiastical officials, namely, Stephen who served as chancellor in the patriarchate. This dispute was an episode 'in the longstanding conflict between pneumatic monarchism and hierarchical authority'. Symeon, *The Practical and Theological Chapters and the Three Theological Discourses* (trans. Paul McGuckin; CSS 41; Kalamazoo, MI: Cistercian Publications, 1982), p. 18. Cf. Symeon, *On the Mystical Life: The Ethical Discourses*, III, pp. 38-53; Meyendorff, *Byzantine Theology*, p. 74. After having served as abbot for 25 years (980–1005), Symeon was compelled to retire from the monastery of St. Mamas and exiled to Chrysopolis (1009). Within a year the exile was lifted, but Symeon decided to remain in voluntary exile while gathering a monastic community. Symeon's final vindication came with his canonization by the Byzantine Church (1054). According to John Meyendorff, by canonizing Symeon, 'Byzantine Christianity has recognized that, in the Church, the Spirit alone is the ultimate criterion of truth and the only final authority'. Meyendorff, *Byzantine Theology*, p. 75. For overviews of Symeon's life and ministry, see Krivocheine, *In the Light of Christ*, pp. 15-63 Symeon, *On the Mystical Life: The Ethical Discourses*, III, pp. 13-38; Alfeyev, *Orthodox Tradition*, pp. 13-42; Symeon, *The Discourses* (trans. C.J. deCatanzaro; CWS; New York: Paulist Press, 1980), pp. 1-12; Symeon, *Theological Chapters*, pp. 11-27; Symeon, *The Sin of Adam and Our Redemption: Seven Homilies* (trans. Nicetas Stethatos; OTT 2; Platina, CA: Saint Herman of Alaska Brotherhood, 1979), pp. 9-29; Stanley M. Burgess, *The Holy Spirit: Eastern Christian Traditions* (Peabody, MA: Hendrickson, 1989), pp. 53-55.

Symeon's primary writings:[18] (1) the direct conscious experience of God is the heart of the Gospel and the Christian faith; (2) the Gospel is continually renewed in the Holy Spirit, so the same charismata of the Spirit evident in the lives of the apostles are available for contemporary Christians.[19] According to Symeon, in water baptism believers receive the Spirit and are joined to God in Christ; nevertheless, although all have not received it, a subsequent experience of Spirit baptism is available to Christians, which is the portal to the charismata, greater consciousness of the indwelling divine life, and participation in God's deifying energy. Hesychasm, therefore, advocated a dynamic experience of God's energies through the Spirit.

---

[18] The *Catechetical Discourses* were teachings preached to the monks at St. Mamas (980–98). The *Catechetical Discourses* accent two main characteristics: (1) the praxis and virtues needed to attain the true state of contemplation, and (2) the operation of the Holy Spirit effecting mystical union with the Trinity. Consisting of his discourses written in poetic form, composing the *Hymns of Divine Love* extended throughout Symeon's adult life; presumably, he finished writing and editing them at Chrysopolis (1009–22). Likewise, there is no accurate date for the *Practical and Theological Chapters*; the nature of the texts suggests that they were composed over Symeon's long career. The *Chapters* instruct the monks in attaining the state of *apatheia*, the gift of infused knowledge, and a conscious experience of God. Probably, the *Three Theological Discourses* were written during Symeon's conflict with Stephen (1000–1009). The *Theological Discourses* defend trinitarian doctrine and affirm the necessity of the Spirit in attaining theological truth. Though the date of origin and provenance of the *Ethical Discourses* remain uncertain Symeon often uses sharp language to castigate his opponents, so these texts reflect the controversy either between Symeon and his antagonists while he was either at St. Mamas (1003–1009) or living in voluntary exile (1010–22). The *Ethical Discourses* depict the church as the body of Christ, examines the Eucharist, discuss the experience of the Holy Spirit and the meaning of true knowledge, and discept the traditional virtues of the mystical life. For discussions about these documents context, date, provenance, structure, and content, see Symeon, *The Discourses*, pp. 13-36; Symeon, *Theological Chapters*, pp. 27-30; Symeon, *On the Mystical Life: The Ethical Discourses*, I, pp. 7-11; Burgess, *The Holy Spirit: Eastern Christian Traditions*, pp. 55-56.

[19] Krivocheine, *In the Light of Christ*, pp. 141-48; Symeon, *On the Mystical Life: The Ethical Discourses* I.1, pp. 11-13, 33, 54-59, 72; I.2, pp. 111-15; I.3, pp. 122-23, 128-29, 137-39; I.10, pp. 146, 153-58; II.4, pp. 15, 24-25; II.5, pp. 44-62; II.6, pp. 67-70; II.7, pp. 91-94; II.9, pp. 112-15, 120-27; II.11, p. 152; II.12, p. 161; II.13, pp. 166-69; Symeon, *The Sin of Adam*, pp. 37, 52-53, 60, 70; Symeon, *Theological Chapters*, pp. 34, 42, 50, 63-64, 84, 99, 135-38; Symeon, *The Discourses*, pp. 52-53, 80, 110-30, 154, 180-200, 264, 336-37, 342, 349, 353. Cf. Burgess, *The Holy Spirit: Eastern Christian Traditions*, pp. 58-62; González, *Christian Thought*, II, pp. 209-10. For a contemporary Pentecostal assessment, see Olga Zaprometova, 'Experiencing the Holy Spirit: A Pentecostal Reading of the Early Church Fathers Part 2: Isaac of Nineveh and Simeon the New Theologian', *JEPTA* 30 (2010), pp. 1-19

Gregory Palamas

The writings of Gregory Palamas[20] continued and defended this tradition during the Hesychast controversy.[21] This dispute originated when Barlaam the Calabrian attacked the hesychastic repetition of the Jesus Prayer and their claim to a direct experience of God. Barlaam insisted that God is unknowable because of the finite nature of humanity; thus, God is only known through indirect revelation: Scripture and inference from nature.[22] According to Barlaam, if Christians directly experience God, they participate in the essence of God, making them divine by nature. Barlaam, consequently, accused the Hesychasts of teaching Messalian doctrine: those purified by continual prayer and the dynamic experience of the Spirit receive a vision of the trinitarian essence.[23] Palamas responded by writing his *Triads* (1338–41), seeking to preserve the hesychastic doctrine of salvation as deification without implying that Christians become God by nature. To accomplish this task, Palamas distinguished be-

---

[20] Gregory Palamas was born (1296) in Constantinople. He joined a monastery on Mt. Athos (1316) and later moved to Thessalonica, where Palamas encountered the Bogomils (a group speaking from the margins of the christological discussion which will be examined in due course). Palamas returned to Mt. Athos in 1331 and began his spiritual writings. Later, he became abbot of the monastery of Esphigmenou (1335–36). For overviews of Palamas' life, see John Meyendorff's introduction to Palamas, *The Triads*, pp. 5-10; Burgess, *The Holy Spirit: Eastern Christian Traditions*, p. 69; Meyendorff, *Orthodox Spirituality*, pp. 71-80.

[21] Burgess, *The Holy Spirit: Eastern Christian Traditions*, pp. 15-16; Lossky, *Likeness of God*, pp. 45-52; González, *Christian Thought*, II, pp. 295-96; Meyendorff, *Orthodox Spirituality*, pp. 88-101. The controversy ended with the condemnation of Barlaam's position and the vindication of Palamas' hesychastic theology in 1341, 1347, and 1351. Palamas' ultimate vindication came with his posthumous canonization in 1368.

[22] Palamas, *The Triads*, 1.1.1–2.2.20. According to Gonzalez,

> The one point at which the question of relations with the West took an original turn was the Hesychastic or Palamite controversy, for here Western scholasticism clashed with Eastern mysticism ... These teachings drew the ridicule of Barlaam, a Calabrian monk who was well versed in Aristotelianism and Western scholasticism (González, *Christian Thought*, II, p. 295).

Cf. Meyendorff, *Orthodox Spirituality*, pp. 81-85; Palamas, *The Triads*, pp. 6, 10-22.

[23] Palamas, *The Triads*, 2.3.8–68. The Messalians were also known as the Euchites, the praying people. Regarding Messalian doctrine, see Burgess, *The Holy Spirit: Eastern Christian Traditions*, pp. 213-15; Meyendorff, *Orthodox Spirituality*, pp. 85-90; 'Messalians', *ODCC*, p. 1075. According to Burgess, 'While such accusations clearly were unfounded, because of Palamas' dedication to church traditions – many of which the dualistic heresies rejected – it could not be denied that the hesychasts did share with the Messalians an emphasis on knowledge of God by direct experience'. Burgess, *The Holy Spirit: Eastern Christian Traditions*, p. 70.

tween divine ousia, hypostasis, and energies in actions of grace. First, humans cannot know or participate in the divine ousia; this knowledge belongs to the Father, Son, and Holy Spirit. Second, although possession and exercise of the divine energies are common to the divine hypostases, the energies are not the hypostases; rather, the energies are the hypostases' actions of divine grace to humanity and creation. Third, through the Spirit's deifying grace humans participate in the divine energies, but not in the transcendent divine essence.[24] Palamas, therefore, worked out the vertex of the christological doctrine of divine actions affirmed in the sixth ecumenical council.[25]

Nicholas Cabasilas

Opposition against Gregory Palamas' teaching persisted for some time in the East, as well as in the West, so Nicholas Cabasilas picked up the ecumenical mantle to reconcile hesychastic doctrine with traditional patristic sacramental theology.[26] Continuing the

---

[24] Palamas, *The Triads*, 3.1.9–3.3.15. According to Palamas, 'The deifying gift of the Spirit thus cannot be equated with the superessential essence of God' (*Triads*, 3.1.34). Cited according to the translation of Nicholas Gendle, Palamas, *The Triads*, p. 89. Cf. Burgess, *The Holy Spirit: Eastern Christian Traditions*, pp. 70-72; Pelikan, *Christian Tradition*, II, pp. 261-70; Meyendorff, *Byzantine Theology*, pp. 76-78; Meyendorff, *Eastern Christian Thought*, pp. 202-207; Lossky, *Mystical Theology*, pp. 69-90, 222-26; Lossky, *Likeness of God*, pp. 52-69; Meyendorff, *Orthodox Spirituality*, pp. 102-24. Cf. John Meyendorff, 'The Doctrine of Grace in St. Gregory Palamas', *SVTQ* 2 (1954), pp. 17-26; Alexis Torrance, 'Precedents for Palamas' Essence-Energies Theology in the Cappadocian Fathers', *VC* 63 (2009), pp. 47-70; Thomas L. Anastos, 'Gregory Palamas' Radicalization of the Essence, Energies, and Hypostasis Model of God', *SVTQ* 38 (1993), pp. 335-49; Edmund M. Hussey, 'Persons: Energy Structure in the Theology of St. Gregory Palamas', *SVTQ* 18 (1974), pp. 22-43.

[25] According to Jaroslav Pelikan,

> The systematic justification for this view of the relation between the participable and the imparticipable in God was a combination of the doctrine of divine actions (ἐνέργειαι), as worked out in the christological controversies, with the doctrine of divine essence (οὐσία), as worked out in the trinitarian controversies. The various distinctions formulated during the controversies with Monenergism were helpful to Palamas and his disciples. Out of the Monenergist controversies had come the teaching that the divine action was eternal and uncreated and yet was distinct from the divine ousia. It was no more than a corollary of this teaching to maintain that the ousia of God was incommunicable, but that the actions of God were communicable (Pelikan, *Christian Tradition*, II, p. 269).

[26] Regarding information about his life, see Boris Bobrinskoy's introduction to Nicolas Cabasilas, *Life in Christ* (trans. Margaret I. Lisney; Worthing: Church-

mystical tradition of affirming that God is light and by the Spirit humans are deified and participate in the light through the grace of the divine energies, Nicholas' writing *The Life of Christ* (1354–87) insists that this life in Christ is attained only through the sacraments of the church.[27] According to Nicholas, believers receive the Spirit in water baptism,[28] yet in the mystery of chrismation the Paraclete comes and imparts to Christians the energies of the Holy Spirit and the charismata.[29] So although Nicholas does not teach an experience of the Spirit outside the institutional sacramental system, he abides within the rich integration of Christology and pneumatology.[30]

In the mystical theological tradition Logos Christology continued to dominant; probably, the reason for the scarcity of Spirit Christology was the dominance of the Cyrillian christological model, even among the Hesychasts.[31] Nevertheless, because Eastern theology's doctrine of deification emphasized the role of Christ and the Spirit in soteriology, their Christology contained a robust pneumatological accent. This pneumatological integration affirmed

---

man Publishing, 1989), pp. 9-10, 18-21; Meyendorff, *Byzantine Theology*, p. 107; Burgess, *The Holy Spirit: Eastern Christian Traditions*, pp. 74-75; Meyendorff, *Orthodox Spirituality*, pp. 127-31. According to Boris Bobrinskoy, 'The dimension of hesychasm with its experience of the vision of the light of Tabor and of pure prayer must be integrated into the spiritual and catholic tradition of Orthodoxy. If it remains apart from this it becomes sterile and bears no fruit.' Cabasilas, *Life in Christ*, p. 19.

[27] For issues concerning the date of origin and provenance as well as the cultural and theological contexts, see Cabasilas, *Life in Christ*, pp. 10-13. Concerning Cabasilas' sacramental mysticism and its relation to hesychasm, see Cabasilas, *Life in Christ*, pp. 21-39.

[28] Cabasilas, *Life in Christ*, 1.1–2.22.

[29] Cabasilas, *Life in Christ*, 3.1-7. According to Cabasilas, the Eucharist completes the other sacramental mysteries. Cabasilas, *Life in Christ*, 4.1-20. Cf. Burgess, *The Holy Spirit: Eastern Christian Traditions*, pp. 75-77; Meyendorff, *Byzantine Theology*, pp. 107-109, 191-95; Meyendorff, *Christ in Eastern Christian Thought*, p. 207; Meyendorff, *Orthodox Spirituality*, pp. 131-36.

[30] Burgess, *The Holy Spirit: Eastern Christian Traditions*, p. 77, writes:

> In this he clearly moves away from Symeon the New Theologian's teaching that there is a special experience of the Spirit of God outside the established sacramental system, namely, the baptism of the Holy Spirit. Both men emphasize the work of the divine Spirit in the perfection of mankind. They differ only on the means of obtaining such grace. Once again in the history of the church, the tension between the prophetic element and the established order is apparent.

[31] Damascus, *Divine Images*, 1.4, p. 22; Symeon, *On the Mystical Life: The Ethical Discourses*, 1, p. 54; 2, pp. 111-13; 13, pp. 166-68; Palamas, *The Triads*, 3.1.34, p. 89; Cabasilas, *Life in Christ*, 3.2, p. 104.

the Christian faith as a dynamic experience of the Spirit in Christ: through the Spirit believers are joined to Christ, become acutely aware of the divine indwelling, and participate in the grace of the Spirit's deifying energies. Although this theological context seemingly provided an environment from which models of Spirit Christology could emerge, this did not happen; instead, there appeared a mystical pneumatic theology, in which the Spirit permeates all doctrines and Christian experience.

The Fall of Constantinople (1453)

The fall of Constantinople to the Ottoman Turks produced several crucial results. First, it brought an end to the Byzantine Empire. Although the Byzantine state capitulated and no longer existed, the patriarchate survived; the patriarch being appointed by the Muslim ruler served more or less as a liaison between the Sultan and the subordinated Christian population. Accordingly, development of Christian theology in Muslim ruled areas was restrained.[32] Second, augmenting the rise of the Protestant Reformation, the influx of Eastern immigrants into the West – bringing with them Greek literature, language, and scholars – contributed to the intellectual climate created by the Renaissance and humanism in the West.[33] Third, Russia attributed the calamity to divine judgment; Constantinople had slipped into apostasy. With a sense of divine providence, Russia viewed itself as inheriting the Byzantine legacy; consequently, Russia dubbed itself the 'Third Rome,' the sole preserver of orthodox doctrine.[34] Fourth, successfully resisting Muslim encroachment,

---

[32] Elizabeth A. Zachariadou, 'The Great Church in Captivity, 1453–1586', *CHC*, V, pp. 169-86; Timothy Ware, *The Orthodox Church* (London: Penguin Group, 1964), pp. 96-111; Justo L. González, *Christian Thought*, III, pp. 411-16, 425-27.

[33] The Council at Florence (1438–39) provided opportunity for this kind of interaction between the Eastern tradition and humanists in Italy. For example, George Gemistos Plethon, a scholar representing the Eastern delegation, depicted the Eastern position in relation to Aquinas' theology; consequently, he was invited by the Italian humanists to lecture on the distinction between Plato and Aristotle. So the process of transmitting Byzantine's classical heritage to the West actually began during this ecumenical meeting, and the fall of Constantinople augmented it. Michael Angold, 'Byzantium and the West, 1204–1453', *CHC*, V, pp. 73-78. Cf. González, *Christian Thought*, III, pp. 21-23.

[34] Russia pointed to the Council of Florence asserting that Constantinople had apostatized when it conceded the Orthodox position to the West by agreeing

286 Spirit Christology

the kingdom of Ethiopia became an enisled form of Christianity amid the encompassing power of Islam.[35] So by mid-fifteenth century, Islam had conquered most of Eastern Christendom and sequestered what remained of the Christian East.[36]

The Ethiopian Tradition

Spirit Christology in Ethiopia should be understood in light of the development of Christology in the Ethiopian Christian tradition[37]

---

to reconciliation on Latin terms. In fact, when Russia's representative, Isidore, returned to Moscow (1441), he was promptly sent to prison. The idea of Russia inheriting the Byzantine legacy was assisted by Ivan III marrying Sophia, the niece of the last Byzantine emperor, and assuming the title 'Tsar' (an adaptation of 'Creaser'). Ware, *The Orthodox Church*, pp. 80-81, 112-19; Pelikan, *Christian Tradition*, II, pp. 295-98; Serge Bolshakoff, *Russian Nonconformity: The Story of "Unofficial" Religion in Russia* (Philadelphia: Westminster Press, 1950), pp. 19-20, 46-57; A.P. Dobroklonsky, *Rukovodstvo Po Istorii Russkoi Tserkvi* (Material for the History of the Church 25; Moscow: Society of Friends of Church History, 2001 repr.; Moscow: Moscow University Press, 1893), pp. 102-22, 149-55, 194-204, 280-88; Stella Rock, 'Russian Piety and Orthodox Culture, 13380–1589', *CHC*, V, pp. 271-72; I.M. Kontzevitch, *The Acquisition of the Holy Spirit in Ancient Russia* (trans. Olga Koshansky; The Acquisition of the Holy Spirit in Russia Series; Platina, CA: St. Herman of Alaska Brotherhood, 1988), pp. 249-53; Albert F. Heard, *The Russian Church and Russian Dissent: Comprising Orthodoxy, Dissent, and Erratic Sects* (New York: Harper & Brothers, 1887), pp. 12-38. It appears that dialogue between the East and Protestants produced a patriarch, Cyril Lucaris, with Protestant proclivities, if not actually Calvinist ones. Cyril became patriarch of Alexandria in 1602 and Constantinople in 1620. George A. Hadjiantoniou, *Protestant Patriarch: The Life of Cyril Lucaris, 1572–1638, Patriarch of Constantinople* (Richmond: John Knox Press, 1961). Cf. Paschalis M. Kitromilides, 'Orthodoxy and the West: Reformation to Enlightenment', *CHC*, V, pp. 188-202; González, *Christian Thought*, III, 412-14; Ware, *The Orthodox Church*, pp. 106-108.

[35] Donald Crummey, 'Church and Nation: The Ethiopian Orthodox Täwahedo Church', *CHC*, V, p. 459.

[36] It is worth noting that Russian Christianity theologically and spiritually trifurcated: (1) the intuitional state-church, the Russian Orthodox Church, which according to its critics had become desiccate of any emotional, intellectual, and spiritual vitality; (2) the hesychastic tradition, with its rich pneumatologically imbued theology; (3) a number of Russian dissident sects, protesting the liturgical practices and spirituality of the Russian Orthodox Church. It is among this last group that Spirit Christology is found in Russia. Since these groups were persecuted by the Russian central tradition, these groups will be included in a section, among other voices, which speak from the margins.

[37] As Ethiopian Christianity developed in isolation, it accommodated several aspects of Hebrew rituals and culture, as well as contextualizing into its theology and rituals some of the practices, beliefs, symbols and gods of the indigenous African primal religions. For information about these issues, see Calvin E. Shenk, 'Reverse Contextualization: Jesuit Encounter with the Ethiopian Orthodox

formed by the confluence of three powerful influences: the king, bishop and priests, and monastic piety. Christianity became the official state religion during the reign of king Ezana (350–56).[38] Athanasius of Alexandria ordained and consecrated (356) the first bishop of Ethiopia, Frumentius; subsequently, bishops of Ethiopia received their elevation to the bishopric from Alexandria, and they were Egyptians. Ethiopia, thus, depended on Alexandria for its ecclesiastical tradition; however, as the head of the church, the King had the power to accept or reject whomever the Alexandrian patriarch sent.[39] The monastic lineage stemmed from the 'Nine Saints': Monophysite dissenters who took refuge in Ethiopia in the aftermath of the Council of Chalcedon.[40] The Ethiopian royal Solomon-

---

Church', *Direction* 28 (1999), pp. 88-91; Calvin E. Shenk, 'The Ethiopian Orthodox Church: A Study in Indigenization', *Missiology* 16 (1988), pp. 259-65; Sergew Hable Selassie, 'The Establishment of the Ethiopian Church', in Sergew Hable Sellassie (ed.), *The Church of Ethiopia: A Panorama of History and Spiritual Life* (Addis Ababa: Ethiopian Orthodox Church, 1970), pp. 1-2.

[38] The Ethiopian Christian tradition points to its foundation in the first century preaching of the apostle Matthew and the 'Ethiopian Eunuch' (34), who was converted to the Christian faith and baptized by Philip (Acts 8.26-39). Actually, Ethiopians trace their worship of the true God back to the covenant God made with Noah. This worship later disappeared among them and was restored when the Ethiopian Queen Makeda visited Solomon; a royal son was produced from the conjugal visit, King Menelik, and later he brought the Ark of the Covenant to Ethiopia where it remains in St. Mary of Zion Church in Axum. Archbishop Yesehaq, 'The Ethiopian Church and Its Living Heritage', *Journal of the Interdenominational Theological Center* 16 (1988–89), pp. 84-87. More than likely, Ethiopian Christianity originated when the Ethiopian king, Ezana, and his court converted to Christianity (350). S. Munro-Hay, 'Christianity, History of Christianity', in S. Uhlig (ed.), *Encyclopedia Æthiopica* (Wiesbaden: Harrassowitz Verlag, 2003), I, pp. 717-18; Wondmagegnehu Aymro and Joachim Motovu (eds.), *The Ethiopian Orthodox Church* (Addis Ababa: Ethiopian Orthodox Mission, 1970), pp. 1-4; Selassie, 'The Establishment of the Ethiopian Church', pp. 2-6; Bruce Manning Metzger, *The Early Versions of the New Testament: Their Origin, Transmission, and Limitations* (Oxford: Clarendon Press, 1977), pp. 215-21.

[39] Teklehaymanot Ayele, *The Ethiopian Church and Its Christological Doctrine* (trans. Teklehaymanot Ayele; Addis Ababa: Graphics Printers, Revised English edn, 1982), pp. 29-39. This was originally published as Teklehaymanot Ayele, *La Dottrina Della Chiesa Etiopica Dissidente Sull'unione Ipostatica* (Roma: Pont. Institutum Orientalium Studiorum, 1956). Cf. Christine Chaillot, *The Ethiopian Orthodox Tewahedo Church Tradition: A Brief Introduction to Its Life and Spirituality* (Paris: Inter-Orthodox Dialogue, 2002), pp. 26-28; Harry Middleton Hyatt, *The Church of Abyssinia* (The Oriental Research Series 4; London: Luzac, 1928), pp. 29-31; Selassie, 'The Establishment of the Ethiopian Church', p. 9.

[40] The Nine Saints arrived in Ethiopia around 480.

ic tradition has maintained the ancient connection between the queen of Sheba and Solomon, king of Israel, as the basis for the royal legacy of Ethiopian rulers standing in the tradition of messianic kings. Since Israel rejected Christ as the messianic king and savior, Ethiopian Christianity claimed to be the true heirs of the messianic people of God.[41] In this context, the Spirit anointing Jesus as the messiah became extremely significant; from their Christology flowed their understanding of orthodoxy. Following Cyril of Alexandria's formulation of the incarnation being the anointing, their christological tradition – known as *Täwahedo*, meaning union – stressed the unique union of deity and humanity in Christ: Christ is

---

As their names indicate, they came from different parts of the Eastern Roman Empire, such as Constantinople and Syria. They were all adherents of the same doctrine, however. It seems that they left the countries of their origin because of religious differences; they were anti-Chalcedonians, and thus were persecuted by the Roman Emperor, who was an ardent supporter of the Chalcedonian doctrine (Selassie, 'The Establishment of the Ethiopian Church', p. 7).

Cf. Selassie, 'The Establishment of the Ethiopian Church', pp. 7-8; J.L. Bandrés and U. Zanetti, 'Christology', *Encyclopedia Æthiopica*, I, pp. 728-29; Munro-Hay, 'History of Christianity', *Encyclopedia Æthiopica*, I, pp. 718-19; Burgess, *The Holy Spirit: Eastern Christian Traditions*, p. 163; Crummey, 'Church and Nation', *CHC*, V, pp. 457-61; Metzger, *The Early Versions of the New Testament*, p. 221; Leonardo Cohen, 'Visions and Dreams: An Avenue of Ethiopians' Conversion to Catholicism at the Beginning of the Seventeenth Century', *Journal of Religion in Africa* 39 (2009), p. 5; Donald Crummey, *Priests and Politicians: Protestant and Catholic Missions in Orthodox Ethiopia, 1830–1868* (Oxford Studies in African Affairs; Oxford: Clarendon Press, 1972), p. 15; Hyatt, *The Church of Abyssinia*, pp. 31-32. Teklehaymanot Ayele challenges this historical narrative. According to him, the 'Nine Saints' were actually Catholic missionaries; the Ethiopian Church was in fellowship with Rome; and the Ethiopians neither reject Chalcedon nor accepted the Monophysite position until a much later date, the seventh century. Ayele, *Christological Doctrine*, pp. 40-48. His work was not well received by Ethiopian scholars, and several of them reacted polemically against it. Uqbit Tesfazghi, *Current Christological Positions of Ethiopian Orthodox Theologians* (Orientalia Christiana Analecta 196; Rome: Pont. Institutum Studiorum Orientalium, 1973), pp. 14-17, 87-108. Regarding the history and influence of monasticism in Ethiopia, see Hyatt, *The Church of Abyssinia*, pp. 65-73.

[41] Grillmeier, *Christian Tradition*, II, pp. 336-41; González, *Christian Thought*, II, pp. 300-301. This Solomonic tradition was restored in 1270. Munro-Hay, 'History of Christianity', *Encyclopedia Æthiopica*, I, pp. 720-21; Crummey, 'Church and Nation', *CHC*, V, pp. 467-76; Cohen, 'Visions and Dreams', pp. 5-6; Aymro and Motovu (eds.), *The Ethiopian Orthodox Church*, pp. 5-6; Taddesse Tamrat, 'Revival of the Church', in Sergew Hable Selassie (ed.), *The Church of Ethiopia: A Panorama of History and Spiritual Life* (Addis Ababa: Ethiopian Orthodox Church, 1970), pp. 17-20.

one person with one nature. The Ethiopian tradition, thus, received its christological trajectory from three sources: Alexandria, the Nine Saints, and the messianic concept of anointing.[42]

This tradition's understanding of anointing in relation to the christological union remained virtually unchallenged until the sixteenth century. At the request of the Ethiopian king, Portuguese soldiers intervened in Ethiopia (1541) to help defeat a Muslim invasion; subsequently, Jesuit missionaries from Portugal arrived (1557), attempting to unite the Ethiopian Church with Rome. Their Dyophysite teaching laid the basis for christological controversy to erupt in Ethiopia. King ZäDengel (1603–1604) was sympathetic to the Jesuit teachings; then, his successor, king Suseneyos (1607–32), accepted the Catholic faith (1612).[43] As Suseneyos attempted reforms aimed at bringing Ethiopia into conformity with Catholic faith, a bloody rebellion soon followed, and Suseneyos abdicated the throne to his son Fäsiladas (1632–67); Fäsiladas restored *Täwahedo* orthodoxy and expelled the missionaries from Ethiopia (1633).[44] The expulsion of the Jesuits, however, did not end the

---

[42] Grillmeier, *Christian Tradition*, II, pp. 341-45; Crummey, 'Church and Nation', *CHC*, V, p. 459. The 'Nine Saints' were probably Monophysites, and 'Cyrillian Christology continued, more or less unchallenged, to be the unique teaching of the Ethiopian Church until the 17th century'. Bandrés and Zanetti, 'Christology', *Encyclopedia Æthiopica*, I, p. 729. It also appears that the Monophysite patriarch of Alexandria, Peter III (Mongos), consecrated the bishop of Ethiopia in 448. 'Later, records from the history of the Patriarchs of Alexandria attest to the sending of Egyptian monks as metropolitans of Ethiopia, all of them Monophysites deriving from the Coptic Church.' Munro-Hay, 'History of Christianity', *Encyclopedia Æthiopica*, I, p. 719. Again, Teklehaymanot Ayele challenges this traditional perspective. According to him, the Ethiopians were misinformed about the Council of Chalcedon and rejected it on spurious testimony; actually, the Ethiopians entirely agree with the Chalcedonian definition, and the lack of agreement stems from linguistic confusion. Ayele, *Christological Doctrine*, pp. 54-74.

[43] The most tactful and successful Jesuit missionary was Pero Paez. Regarding Pero Paez's role in the conversion of King Susneos and the christological controversy, see Ayele, *Christological Doctrine*, pp. 79-82, 93-97; Shenk, 'Reverse Contextualization', pp. 94-96; Tesfazghi, *Christological Positions*, pp. 58-64; Hyatt, *The Church of Abyssinia*, pp. 38-40, 100-101.

[44] Tesfazghi, *Christological Positions*, pp. 49-71. Cf. Crummey, 'Church and Nation', *CHC*, V, pp. 462-64, 476-78; Munro-Hay, 'History of Christianity', *Encyclopedia Æthiopica*, I, pp. 721-23; Bandrés and Zanetti, 'Christology', *Encyclopedia Æthiopica*, I, p. 730; Shenk, 'Reverse Contextualization', pp. 96-99; Cohen, 'Visions and Dreams', pp. 6-20; Ayele, *Christological Doctrine*, pp. 75-83; Hyatt, *The Church of Abyssinia*, pp. 34-41; Aymro and Motovu (eds.), *The Ethiopian Orthodox Church*, pp. 6-7; Crummey, *Priests and Politicians*, pp. 18-20; Chaillot,

christological debate; it continued as an internal debate among Ethiopians until the synod of Berru-Meda (1878) settled the matter.[45]

It appears that the first internal dispute regarding the Spirit anointing Christ occurred (1612–13) during the reign of Emperor Suseneyos between three groups of Ethiopian monks with distinct christological views: the *Karra*, *Qebat*, and *Sägga*.[46] The central question asked: was an incarnated divine person of the Trinity anointed with the Spirit? King Suseneyos ruled in favor of the *Qebat's* position: the 'Unction of Our Lord and Saviour Jesus Christ is the grace of the Holy Spirit given to his humanity at the time of the union of humanity and divinity'.[47] Suseneyos, therefore, decided in favor of the *Qebat* against the traditional *Täwahedo* view supported by the *Karra* and opened the door for the *Sägga* to contribute to the debate.[48]

Tewahedo Church Tradition, pp. 31-33; Tamrat, 'Persecution and Religious Controversies', pp. 28-30.

[45] Tesfazghi, *Christological Positions*, pp. 72-86; Crummey, 'Church and Nation', *CHC*, V, pp. 479-82; Selassie, 'The Period of Reorganization', pp. 32-34. Owing to its emphasis on the relation of the Spirit's anointing to the christological union, this christological controversy became known as the 'Unction' disputes.

[46] The *Karra* (knife), meaning to cut away the Spirit, represented the traditional Ethiopian christological view that the incarnation is the anointing. The *Qebat* (unction) emphasized the agency of the Spirit's anointing in the incarnation. The *Sägga* (grace) accentuated the anointing as the gracious activity of the Spirit.

[47] Cited according to the translation of Getatchew Haile, *The Faith of the Unctionists in the Ethiopian Church* (trans. Haile Getatchew; CSCO, Scriptores Æthiopici 92; Leuven: Peeters, 1990), p. vii. Cf. Ayele, *Christological Doctrine*, pp. 97-98; Tesfazghi, *Christological Positions*, pp. 63-64. This is the topic sentence from a lengthy citation which is contained on pages vii-viii of this text. According to Getatchew Haile,

> The doctors of the church were aware, of course, that *Krestos* 'Christ' means *Mäsih* 'Messiah' of 'the Anointed'. But they seem, until the days of Emperor Suseneyos (who was converted to Catholicism), to be content (without questioning) with Cyril's interpretation of the name and the cause of his unction, *Krestos behil qehil* 'Christ means the anointed' and *bäzä-täsäba täqäba* 'Because he was incarnated he was anointed,' respectively ... For a diehard *Täwahedo* (Monophysite) Church of Ethiopia, some of whose members, indeed, show, judging from the literature, a tendency towards Eutychism, the decree of the emperor must have struck like lightning (Haile, *The Faith of the Unctionists*, pp. viii-ix).

[48] See the introduction by Getatchew Haile, *The Faith of the Unctionists*, pp. ix-xiii; Getatchew Haile, 'Materials on the Theology of Qebat or Unction', in G. Goldenberg (ed.), *Ethiopian Studies: Proceedings of the Sixth International Conference, Tel-*

This inquiry will focus on two primary documents involved in this debate which delineated the positions of these three groups: *The Faith of the Unctionists in the Ethiopian Church* and *A Treatise on the Theology of the Qebat in Old Amharic.*[49] *The Faith of the Unctionists in the Ethiopian Church* recounts the decisions of an ecclesiastical council at Aringo (1647) which Fäsiladas had convened to debate the christological issues and attempt a settlement.[50] It is composed of six parts and a conclusion. The first two parts present Scriptural proofs affirming trinitarian doctrine and rejecting the doctrines of Sabellius, Arius, Macedonius, Nestorius, and Pope Leo.[51] Parts three, four, and five examine Scripture and excerpts from respected Church

Aviv, 14–17 April 1980 (Rotterdam: A.A. Balkema, 1986), pp. 205-208. Cf. Ayele, *Christological Doctrine*, pp. 97-117; Crummey, *Priests and Politicians*, pp. 20-27.

[49] *A Letter of Metropolitan Mareqos on the Theology of Qebat* is also important because it was written by Abunä *Mareqos*, defending *Qebat* Christology during the reign of Emperor Tewofelos (1708–11) who supported the *Karra* position. For information regarding, date, provenance, authorship, and context, see Haile, 'Materials on the Theology of Qebat or Unction', pp. 229-30. Haile includes the un-translated Ethiopic text and an English translation. Haile, 'Materials on the Theology of Qebat or Unction', pp. 231-32. This letter's Christology agrees with the other two sources; to avoid repetition the Spirit christological references in it will be noted. For information concerning the available sources, see Haile, 'Materials on the Theology of Qebat or Unction', pp. 205-208. Also, for information about sources that antedate the Unction disputes yet contribute to the discussion, see Getatchew Haile, 'Religious Controversies and the Growth of Ethiopic Literature in the Fourteenth and Fifteenth Centuries', *Oriens Christianus* 65 (1981), pp. 102-36.

[50] The un-translated Ethiopic version of the text is found in Getatchew Haile (ed.), *The Faith of the Unctionists in the Ethiopian Church* (Corpus Scriptorum Christianorum Orientalium, Scriptores Æthiopici 91; Leuven: Peeters, 1990). Dr. Getatchew Haile directed me via email correspondence to his English translation of this text, Getatchew Haile, *The Faith of the Unctionists*, (CSCO, Scriptores Æthiopici 92; Leuven: Peeters, 1990). For the documents from which Haile bases his translation, as well as his textual criticism of these documents, see Haile, *The Faith of the Unctionists*, pp. xiii-xv.

[51] Haile, *The Faith of the Unctionists*, 1-2, pp. 1-12. Interestingly, Leo is portrayed as a ravening wolf, and Dioscorus is exalted as a hero of the faith. Haile, *The Faith of the Unctionists*, 2, pp. 7-12; Ayele, *Christological Doctrine*, pp. 54-62, 83-84. For a current assessment of the contemporary position, see Aymro and Motovu (eds.), *The Ethiopian Orthodox Church*, pp. 96-101; V.C. Samuel, 'The Faith of the Church', in Sergew Hable Selassie (ed.), *The Church of Ethiopia: A Panorama of History and Spiritual Life* (Addis Ababa: Ethiopian Orthodox Church, 1970), pp. 43-54. For overviews of the Spirit's presence and importance in Ethiopic worship, see Habtemichael Kidane, 'The Holy Spirit in the Ethiopian Orthodox Church Täwahedo Tradition', in Teresa Berger and Bryan D. Spinks (eds.), *The Spirit in Worship, Worship in the Spirit* (Collegeville, MN: Liturgical Press, 2009), pp. 179-205.

Fathers, which elucidate the agency of the Spirit's anointing in Christ's life and ministry.[52] Part six juxtaposes the three groups' positions regarding the Spirit's anointing in relation to Christology.[53] In the conclusion the council's edict favors the *Qebat*.[54]

Although this document essentially is a *Qebat* confession of faith, it accurately depicts the faith of all groups involved in the dispute.

> There are some who say, 'The Only-Begotten Son is not anointed on his own behalf by God his Father. And the anointing of the Holy Spirit is nothing for him. Is he, indeed, inferior to the Father and divested of the Holy Spirit? Rather, he is anointed to give us, who believe in his name, (power) to become children of God by grace.'[55]

Here, the *Karra* position is stated. First, incarnated deity had no need for the anointing of the Spirit. Second, if Christ received the Spirit's anointing, it would imply the Son's subordination and lack

---

[52] Haile, *The Faith of the Unctionists*, 3-5, pp. 12-24. The dispute largely focused on interpretations of Scripture speaking of the Spirit anointing the Servant of Yahweh in application to Christ: Isa. 61.1; Pss. 2.2; 44.8; Dan. 9.25; Mt. 3.16; Lk. 4.18; Acts 4.27; 10.38; Heb. 1.9. Tesfazghi, *Christological Positions*, p. 72; Ayele, *Christological Doctrine*, pp. 91-93. For an analysis of the Ethiopian hermeneutical tradition, see Roger W. Cowley, *Ethiopian Biblical Interpretation: A Study in Exegetical Tradition and Hermeneutics* (University of Cambridge Oriental Publications 38; Cambridge: Cambridge University Press, 1988). It should be noted that according to Ethiopic tradition the Nine Saints translated the entire Bible into the Ethiopic language. Selassie, 'The Establishment of the Ethiopian Church', p. 8; Cf. Metzger, *The Early Versions of the New Testament*, pp. 222-23. According to Sergew Selassie,

> Since they were familiar with both Syriac and Greek, they used a Syrio-Greek text for this purpose. Most probably each of the Nine Saints translated one portion of the Bible. This is why the Ethiopic version reveals considerable differences in style from one Book to another. The Ethiopic version is one of the earliest Bible translations, and as such it is of great importance in textual criticism and in establishing the original text (Selassie, 'The Establishment of the Ethiopian Church', p. 8).

Hyatt rejects the idea that the Nine Saints translated the Bible into Ethiopic; rather, it occurred over a long period of translation and revision. Hyatt, *The Church of Abyssinia*, pp. 79-81. For a thorough analysis of NT Ethiopic manuscripts and editions of the Ethiopic NT, see Metzger, *The Early Versions of the New Testament*, pp. 223-56.

[53] Haile, *The Faith of the Unctionists*, 6.1-6, pp. 24-31. Clearly, the imperial influence which the *Qebat* garnered with Suseneyos continued under the reign of Fäsiladas.

[54] Haile, *The Faith of the Unctionists*, pp. 31-32.

[55] Haile, *The Faith of the Unctionists*, 6, pp. 24-25.

of consubstantial nature with the Father. Third, the Son became incarnated, salvifically anointed, to redeem humanity. So, for the *Karra* the anointing and the divine Son's assumption of human nature are synonymous; there is no place for the Spirit's agency or grace in this act.[56]

Regarding the *Sägga's* viewpoint, the Spirit's anointing was essential to Christ's redemptive mission. God created Adam and made him a son of grace – as well as a king, priest, and prophet – through the Holy Spirit, and in the fall Adam lost these relationships of grace with God.

> In the latter days, when the Son became man, he was anointed for himself according to the dispensation of the humanity; and through it he became [Son], king, priest and prophet by grace.[57]

The *Sägga*, therefore, asserted two distinct natures in Christ: divine and human. By an act of grace the Spirit anointed Christ's human nature as archetypical humanity restoring it to sonship, kingship, and priesthood. So, the Spirit's anointing was essential to Christ's identity and salvific mission, so that redeemed humans could participate in these relationships of grace.

The *Qebat* supported their position with the premise that the Spirit's anointing constituted Christ the natural Son, king, and high priest.[58]

> That the Word was anointed on his own behalf is known from his name, for Christ means anointed; he is not called (so) for an-

---

[56] Tesfazghi, *Christological Positions*, p. 73, writes:
> If this unction of the Holy Spirit concerns the humanity of Jesus Christ, as it truly does, who after the Incarnation was a true man, and if that one human nature was not absorbed and destroyed but distinct from the divine nature, these biblical passages as understood thus are contrary to monophysitism. In order not to have to admit that the unction refers to the manhood of the Word, the Monophysitizers gave to the word 'unction' the meaning of 'union' ... So they deny that the Holy Spirit is the unction, but affirm that the Son Himself is the anointing, the anointed, and the unction.

[57] Haile, *The Faith of the Unctionists*, 6, p. 25.

[58] This premise is stated and explicated in Haile, *The Faith of the Unctionists*, 6.1-6, pp. 26-31. For example, 'Furthermore, that through it [his anointment] he became natural Son is known from the words of God the Father who said in the Second Book of Kings, "I will be for him his Father and he will be for me my son." This text is not about his prior birth but about that which was going to happen later at his incarnation'. Haile, *The Faith of the Unctionists*, 6.1, p. 27.

other matter that does not pertain to him. Furthermore, the name Christ leads (us) to three names, which are: Father, the Anointer; Son, the Anointed; and Holy Spirit, the Ointment. Formerly the Father was called the Father because he begat the Son of his nature [*bahreyenna*]; the Son was called Son because he was born from him; and the Holy Spirit was called Holy Spirit because he was the Spirit of the Father and the Son. Later, because of the incarnation of the Son, the Father is called the Anointer of the Son, and the Son the Anointed, and the Holy Spirit the Ointment.[59]

Here, the *Qebat* stated their interpretation of Cyril of Alexandria's teaching of the Spirit's anointing in relation to Christology.[60] First, the *Qebat* affirmed traditional trinitarian doctrine. Second, the incarnation was a perichoretic divine act, revealing each triune person functioning in a distinct role: the Father as the anointer, the Son as the anointed, and the Spirit as the anointing. Third, an integral aspect of the incarnation, the Spirit's anointing made Christ a natural son, king, priest, and prophet. The Spirit accomplished this by con-

---

[59] Haile, *The Faith of the Unctionists*, 6.6, p. 31. Cf. Haile, *The Faith of the Unctionists*, 1, p. 3; (*A Letter of Metropolitan Mareqos*), Haile, 'Materials on the Theology of Qebat or Unction', p. 232.

[60] They examine Cyril's position in Haile, *The Faith of the Unctionists*, 6.5, pp. 30-31. More than likely, they derived this interpretation of Cyril's view from the Jesuits since in his labors to convert King Suseneyos Pero 'Paez used Ethiopian materials such as *Haimanot Abew* (Faith of Our Fathers) which were considered authoritative by Ethiopians. Though the material was Monophysite in tenor, it contained passages that were in harmony with Catholic teaching and enabled Paez to support his position'. Shenk, 'Reverse Contextualization', p. 95. There were two primary extra-biblical christological documents which Ethiopians considered authoritative: *Qerellos* and *Haymanotä abäw*. The *Qerellos* (Cyril) was an anti-Nestorian document, compiled subsequent to the Council of Ephesus and prior to the Council of Chalcedon. The Nine Saints translated the *Qerellos* from Greek into Ethiopic. Selassie, 'The Establishment of the Ethiopian Church', p. 8. This document derived its authority and name from the Cyrillian works it contained. The *Haymanotä abäw* also was a rich source of Cyrillian influence, 'which became the foundation, along with the Bible, of all subsequent Christological debate, thus replacing to a large extent the use of the ancient *Qerellos*'. Bandrés and Zanetti, 'Christology', *Encyclopedia Æthiopica*, I, p. 728. For the Cyrillian authority attached to these documents, see Bandrés and Zanetti, 'Christology', *Encyclopedia Æthiopica*, I, pp. 728-30. For a comprehensive overview of Ethiopian christological commentaries, see Cowley, *Ethiopian Biblical Interpretation*, pp. 267-369. It should be noted that *Haimanot Abew* and *Haymanotä abäw* are the same documents but with different spelling. This is the case with many names, such as Susneos and Suseneyos, and the designations for various groups and places.

ceiving Christ's human nature and uniting it with deity in the incarnation.

A Treatise on the Theology of the Qebat in Old Amharic was composed during the seventeenth-century to distinguish the theology of the *Qebat* from the *Karra* and the *Sägga*, probably, in response to a treatise of the *Karra* known as *Haymanot lämmiyyäkkäs*.[61] The document progresses in phases. First, certain personal and theological queries are posed and answered from the perspective of the *Qebat*.[62] Second, terms common to the debate are defined.[63] Third, the doctrine of the Trinity is discussed and affirmed.[64] Fourth, the Christology of the *Qebat* is depicted in opposition to the *Karra* and the *Sägga*.[65] Fifth, the document closes with a discussion about human nature in the resurrection.[66]

The central questions concern the Spirit's anointing in the incarnation and christological union.

> How is the incarnation of the Son? Normally when a man is born, a perfect man is born when the seed from the father is joined to the blood of the mother. But he was not (conceived) in this manner. (The Holy Spirit) created soul from her soul and flesh from her flesh and united (the person of the Word with it) when St. Gabriel said to Our Lady Mary, The Holy Spirit will come upon you and power of the Highest will overshadow you.[67]

---

[61] The author and exact date is unknown. For issues regarding date, provenance, context, and text critical issues, see Haile, 'Materials on the Theology of Qebat or Unction', pp. 208-209, 232-40. Getatchew Haile provides an English translation of the text in Haile, 'Materials on the Theology of Qebat or Unction', pp. 220-29. The un-translated Ethiopic text is presented in Haile, 'Materials on the Theology of Qebat or Unction', pp. 210-20.

[62] (*Treatise*, 1-10), Haile, 'Materials on the Theology of Qebat or Unction', pp. 220-21.

[63] (*Treatise*, 11-23), Haile, 'Materials on the Theology of Qebat or Unction', pp. 221-22. Cf. Tesfazghi, *Christological Positions*, pp. 21-48.

[64] (*Treatise*, 24-39), Haile, 'Materials on the Theology of Qebat or Unction', pp. 222-23.

[65] (*Treatise*, 40-62), Haile, 'Materials on the Theology of Qebat or Unction', pp. 224-28.

[66] (*Treatise*, 63-67), Haile, 'Materials on the Theology of Qebat or Unction', p. 229.

[67] (*Treatise*, 43), Cited according to the translation of Getatchew Haile, 'Materials on the Theology of Qebat or Unction', p. 224. Unless otherwise noted, English translations will come from this source.

> Why did he need the Holy Spirit to create for him? Could he not have created (his flesh) and be incarnated? Creating was, certainly, not impossible for him. But we say about the Father, 'He generated his Son for us;' we say about the Son, 'He is born for us.' What would we say about what the Holy Spirit did for us if he had not, having created the flesh, made (the Son) incarnate? Our faith as well as our love could not have been steadfast in the Holy Trinity.[68]

According to the *Qebat*, the Spirit created a complete human nature, body and soul, from Mary, and united it to the divine Son; furthermore, the incarnation was a triune event, and the appropriate role of the Holy Spirit was to create the human nature and function as the agent of unity in the christological union.

After reviewing the *Täwahedo* view of the christological union, one nature and one person, the *Qebat* juxtaposes their opinion with the *Karra*.

> When the Holy Spirit created the body and made him incarnated, what did he (himself) become to God the Word? His father, God the Father, anointed him; he was anointed; and the Holy Spirit became the ointment. But the heretics say, 'The Holy Spirit did not become ointment but the union of divinity with flesh is (itself) the ointment.' We, however, say, 'The Father is the anointer; the Son is the anointed; (and) the Holy Spirit the ointment.'[69]

This text elucidates the similarity and contrast between the *Qebat* and *Karra*. Both parties agree that although Christ is composed of humanity and deity, the christological union posits only one nature in one person. They disagree regarding how this union occurs. According to the *Karra*, the divine Son assumed human nature into the divine nature, so that this act of union constitutes the anointing apart from any agency of the Spirit. The *Qebat*, nonetheless, argues that the Spirit's anointing is the agent of union.

Next, in order to refute the *Sägga*, the treatise discusses the meaning of the anointing.

---

[68] (*Treatise*, 45), Haile, 'Materials on the Theology of Qebat or Unction', pp. 224-25.

[69] (*Treatise*, 52), Haile, 'Materials on the Theology of Qebat or Unction', p. 226.

What does ointment mean? Indwelling. When she said, '*Be it unto me according to thy word,*' his original life, the Holy Spirit, dwelt in the womb of his mother. When the heretics are asked: 'What did the Holy Spirit who dwelt in his body become to him?' They say, 'He made him, too, Son by grace when he dwelt in him in the womb (of his mother) as he makes us child(ren) by grace when he dwells in us at baptism.' But we say about him, 'He became a natural Son' as David said, '*Therefore God, your God, has anointed you with the oil of gladness above your fellows.*'[70]

Several conclusions emerge from this text. First, the meaning of the anointing is indwelling. Second, the Spirit's indwelling, for the *Qebat*, signifies the natural sonship of Christ. Third, according to the *Sägga*, by grace, the Spirit's anointing, indwelled Mary's womb, conceiving and giving birth to Christ, so that Christ was a son by grace.

These three groups, then, maintained disparate views regarding the Spirit's role in constituting the incarnation, christological union, and Christ's sonship. The *Qebat* advocated the natural sonship of Christ and a two birth view: one from the Father and one from the virgin. The Spirit's anointing affected the incarnation, the second birth, and functioned as the agent of the christological union, while remaining within the parameters of the Ethiopian tradition: one nature in one person. The *Sägga* recognized three births: one eternal birth from the Father and two by the grace of the Spirit's anointing. Though they upheld the birth from Mary, they also asserted another birth at the Jordan: Christ's human nature received the Spirit's anointing enduing him with messianic gifts and divinizing the human nature. So, Christ became the Son of God by the Spirit's gracious anointing during the incarnation and Christ's reception of the Spirit at his the Jordan. The third group rejected the *Qebat's* and the *Sägga's* christological premises regarding the Spirit's anointing; instead, they asserted that in the incarnation Christ's humanity was assumed into the divine person and nature of the Son. There was no need for the Spirit's anointing; the christological union was the unction. This group, consequently, bore the designation *Karra*, meaning knife, because their opponents alleged they had cut off the

---

[70] (*Treatise*, 54), Haile, 'Materials on the Theology of Qebat or Unction', p. 226. Cf. (*Treatise*, 55), Haile, 'Materials on the Theology of Qebat or Unction', p. 227; (*A Letter of Metropolitan Mareqos*), Haile, 'Materials on the Theology of Qebat or Unction', p. 232.

298   Spirit Christology

Spirit.[71] When the synod of Berru-Meda (1878) finally settled the disputes, the *Sägga* and *Qebat* positions were condemned and the *Karra* doctrine established as orthodox.[72]

Spirit christological issues pervaded these controversies in the Ethiopian Church, challenging their understanding of the Holy Spirit's relation to Christ's life and mission. Arguably, two models of Spirit christological paradigms of pneumatic mediation came to light, once again denoting the fluidity of Spirit Christology. First, with the *Qebat* a Spirit Christology of pneumatic mediation emerged which integrated with Logos Christology, bearing striking similarities with its counterpart in the Western Spirit christological tradition: in the incarnation the Spirit mediated the conception of the human nature and the christological union of the divine and human natures. Yet this model is distinct from the Western version because it does not maintain two natures in the christological union: there is one nature and one person. Second, according to *Sägga* Christology, the Holy Spirit mediated the incarnation, the christological union, and the divine filiation of Christ's human nature by Christ's reception of the Spirit at the Jordan. *Sägga* Christology, therefore, supported a paradigm of pneumatic mediation which integrated with Logos Christology.

Conclusion

Eastern writers provided a pneumatologically rich environment for the emergence of Spirit Christology, yet it needed an impetus to stimulate its reappearance. Given the fact that pneumatology had permeated Eastern theology, once the influence of Byzantine's dominate form of Logos Christology was hindered in Ethiopia an

---

[71] Tesfazghi, *Christological Positions*, pp. 74-82; Haile, 'Materials on the Theology of Qebat or Unction', pp. 205-208. Cf. Grillmeier, *Christian Tradition*, II, pp. 347-62; Burgess, *The Holy Spirit: Eastern Christian Traditions*, p. 165; Hyatt, *The Church of Abyssinia*, pp. 102-107; Crummey, 'Church and Nation', *CHC*, V, pp. 478-79; Bandrés and Zanetti, 'Christology', *Encyclopedia Æthiopica*, I, p. 730; Munro-Hay, 'History of Christianity', *Encyclopedia Æthiopica*, I, p. 722. For literary works supporting these various groups, see Ayele, *Christological Doctrine*, pp. 121-33.

[72] Tesfazghi, *Christological Positions*, pp. 83-86; Crummey, 'Church and Nation', *CHC*, V, pp. 479-82; Selassie, 'The Period of Reorganization', pp. 32-34; Bandrés and Zanetti, 'Christology', *Encyclopedia Æthiopica*, I, p. 731; Munro-Hay, 'History of Christianity', *Encyclopedia Æthiopica*, I, p. 223.

evolution of christological thought was not long in coming, allowing for the emanation of Spirit Christology. In Ethiopia's isolation as a Christian kingdom amid encompassing Muslim domination, Spirit Christology issued forth from Western influence which advocated two natures in Christ, dilating the horizons of the commonly held Logos christological view of the Spirit's anointing. From the ensuing christological controversy which focused on the Spirit's anointing in Christ's identity and redemptive mission, two diverse Spirit christological paradigms of pneumatic mediation emerged. One paradigm set the anointing in the incarnation, so that the Spirit mediated the conception of Christ's human nature and its union with the divine nature. The other model recognized the incarnation of the divine Son in human flesh, but also posited that the Spirit's anointing mediated the adoption of Christ's human nature into divine filiation. Both models, therefore, accentuated the Spirit's anointing in relation to Christ's human nature, so it is reasonable to infer that this was the catalyst of its emanation.

This chapter, therefore, has depicted the environment which supports the appearance of Spirit Christology, and it has distinguished between a pneumatically permeated Logos Christology and Spirit Christology. Spirit Christology emerged in a pneumatically permeated environment; however, this was not sufficient to produce Spirit Christology. A pneumatologically permeated Logos Christology can delineate the Spirit's presence and power in the life of believers, including a doctrine of Spirit baptism; nevertheless, this in itself does not comprise a genuine Spirit Christology. A Spirit christological paradigm must depict how the Spirit's anointing genuinely relates to Christ's humanity in his life and mission, so that the believer's experience and relationship with the Spirit is based on Christ's experience of the Spirit.

11

WESTERN WRITERS

During the ecumenical councils of the fifth and sixth centuries, the relation of the Spirit's anointing to Christ's life and ministry was the central Spirit christological issue in these controversies. The Council of Constantinople II had displaced Spirit Christology by integrating Cyrillian nomenclature with Chalcedon's christological definition. For Cyril, the anointing was the incarnation; the Logos hypostatically assumed human nature and anointed it. Notwithstanding many objections to the council's decisions in the West, it should be noted that in the Western Spirit christological tradition beginning with Augustine the focal point of the Spirit's anointing was moving to the incarnation, so that the Jordan event testified to the fullness of anointing resting on Christ's entire life and ministry and typified believers receiving the Spirit at their baptism. Although the distinction between Cyril and Augustine on this point was slight, the implications for Christology were enormous. On the one hand, Cyril rejected the possibility of any grace or anointing mediating between deity and humanity in Christ.[1] On the other hand, Augustine posited that the Spirit anointing Christ's human nature in the incarnation was an act of grace, forming the human nature and uniting it to the Logos. Considering Western Spirit Christology's development peaked with Augustine and his pervasive influence, if Spirit Christology existed in the Medieval Period, it probably resembled his paradigm.

---

[1] Grillmeier, *Christian Tradition*, II, pp. 342-43.

The Venerable Bede

Among the Western writers of the Medieval Period, the writings of Bede furnish the first Spirit christological texts. At the age of seven, Bede entered monastic life as an oblate under the tutelage of Benedict Biscop and received his education at the twin cloisters of St. Peter and St. Paul at Wearmouth and Jarrow in Northumbria, which housed a great library that aided Bede throughout his literary career. Ordained a deacon at age nineteen and a priest eleven years later (702), henceforth, Bede consecrated the rest of his life to teaching and writing.[2] His literary ingenuity propagated an environment of intellectual productivity in northern England known as the Northumbrian Renaissance, which portended and, through Bede's disciples, influenced the Carolingian Renaissance.[3] A prolific writer, Bede produced educational treatises, exegetical works, homilies, hagiography, poems, letters, and histories.[4]

Spirit christological references are scattered among his exegetical works and homilies, specifically, his commentary on Acts and homilies on the Gospels.[5] At the request of Acca, bishop of Hexham in

---

[2] For information about Bede's life and context, see George Hardin Brown, *Bede the Venerable* (Twayne's English Authors Series; 443; Boston: Twayne, 1987), pp. 1-23; Benedicta Ward, *The Venerable Bede* (Outstanding Christian Thinkers; Harrisburg, PA: Morehouse, 1990), pp. 1-39; Schaff, *History*, IV, pp. 670-73; Stanley M. Burgess, *The Holy Spirit: Medieval Roman Catholic and Reformation Traditions* (Peabody, MA: Hendrickson 1997), pp. 21-22.

[3] According to González, 'The tradition that Bede and his fellow workers represented was the connecting link between antiquity and the theological and philosophical awakening that took place in the Carolingian empire'. González, *Christian Thought*, II, pp. 107-108. Regarding Bede's influence and legacy, see Brown, *Bede*, pp. 97-103; Ward, *Bede*, pp. 134-45; Bede, *The Venerable Bede Commentary on the Acts of the Apostles* (trans. Lawrence T. Martin; CSS; 117; Kalamazoo, MI: Cistercian, 1989), pp. xv-xvii.

[4] Although his contemporaries primarily recognized Bede as an exegete, among modern readers, he has become known as a historian because of his most famous work the *Ecclesiastical History of the English People*. For overviews of Bede's writings, see Brown, *Bede*, pp. 24-96; Ward, *Bede*, pp. 41-132; Schaff, *History*, IV, pp. 673-77; Burgess, *The Holy Spirit: Medieval Roman Catholic and Reformation Traditions*, p. 22.

[5] The survey will focus on the texts in his Acts commentary and note any corollary texts in the homilies. The Homilies were probably written in the 720's. For issues about date of origin, provenance, occasion, and purpose, see Bede, *Homilies on the Gospels* (trans. Lawrence T. Martin and David Hurst; CSS; 110–11; 2 vols.; Kalamazoo, MI: Cistercian, 1991), I, pp. xi-xxiii; Brown, *Bede*, pp. 62-65; Ward, *Bede*, pp. 62-65.

Northumbria, Bede wrote his *Commentary on the Acts of the Apostles* (709)[6] and sent it to him. Bede's eclectic hermeneutical method applied whatever exegetical techniques and instruments fit the task at hand.[7] He freely employed text critical analysis, addressed historical issues, explicated the literal sense of the text, and interspersed allegorical interpretation in his comments. Though not commenting on all verses, Bede' analysis sequentially followed the narrative.

The first Spirit christological text sits within the context of the historical and prophetic fulfillment of Pentecost. In the first chapter, Bede accentuated Jesus' deeds, teachings, and continuation with his disciples forty days after the resurrection instructing them through the Holy Spirit. Jesus, therein, promised they would be baptized in the Holy Spirit (Acts 1.1-5).[8] In chapter two, after reflecting on the signification of the number 50, the fire at Sinai, Christ's resurrection, and his ascension to the Father, Bede attached their meaning to the visible and audible signs of the Spirit descending on the Day of Pentecost, fulfilling the promise of baptizing the disciples in the Spirit (Acts 2.1-33a).[9]

> And having received from the Father the promise of the Holy Spirit, he has poured forth this Spirit, whom you see and hear. [Whom] you see in the tongues of fire; [whom] you hear in our discourse. Indeed, by saying that *He received from the Father the promise of the Holy Spirit and he poured* [the Spirit] *forth, both natures of*

---

[6] This commentary is among Bede's earliest works written from the Northumbrian cloister. Concerning issues about the date of origin and provenance, see Bede, *Acts of the Apostles*, p. xviii; Brown, *Bede*, pp. 57-58; Ward, *Bede*, p. 58. For the commentary's occasion and purpose, see Bede's introduction. Bede, *Acts of the Apostles*, p. 3. 'Twenty years later, Bede sent Acca another tract on Acts: this was his *Retractation on the Book of Acts*. His increasing mastery of Greek and access to Greek manuscripts had shown him errors in his first treatise; he therefore made a second and revised edition.' Ward, *Bede*, p. 59. Cf. Bede, *Acts of the Apostles*, pp. xxiii-xxiv; Brown, *Bede*, p. 59.

[7] Regarding Bede's hermeneutical method and literary style, see; Brown, *Bede*, pp. 42-51; Ward, *Bede*, pp. 41-50; Bede, *Acts of the Apostles*, pp. xviii-xxvii; Arthur G. Holder, 'Bede and the Tradition of Patristic Exegesis', *ATR* 72 (1990), 399-411.

[8] In Acts 1.5, Bede affirms that the disciples had already been baptized in water, or else Christ would not have washed their feet. Bede, *Acts of the Apostles*, pp. 10-11.

[9] One important point of fulfillment, according to Bede, was that the manifestation of glossolalia indicated the recovering of the unity of languages which was fragmented at Babylon (Acts 2.4-11). Bede, *Acts of the Apostles*, pp. 29-31.

> *Christ are manifested, for he received* [the Spirit] *as a man, and poured* [him] *forth as God* (Acts 2.33b).[10]

Several conclusions arise from this text and context. First, on the Day of Pentecost, the disciples were baptized in the Holy Spirit, fulfilling the Father's promise.[11] Second, the Spirit descending on the disciples validated Christ's deity; only God can send the Spirit. Third, following Augustine, Bede distinguished between Christ's divine and human natures; the human nature received the Spirit. Because Christ had received the Spirit, thereupon, the disciples received Spirit baptism.

The healing of a lame man through the name of Jesus Christ provides the context for the next Spirit christological text (Acts, chs. 3–4). When the Sadducees confronted the disciples, concerning this miracle and the disciples preaching the resurrection of the dead through Christ, Peter, filled with the Holy Spirit, preached that the man received healing through the name of Jesus Christ; furthermore, Jesus Christ is the only redemptive name given to humanity (Acts 4.1-26).

> *For Christ took his name from chrism, that is, from anointing.* It is accordingly said, *Therefore God, your God, has anointed you with the oil of gladness,* that is, with the Holy Spirit (Acts 4.27).[12]

---

[10] Cited according to the translation of Martin Lawrence, Bede, *Acts of the Apostles*, p. 35. Lawrence places the direct quotations which Bede draws from his sources in italics: Augustine, *Trin.* 15.16.46. Carefully documenting and giving credit to his sources through marginal source marks, Bede's analysis freely drew from his predecessors. He extensively drew from Arator, a Roman author who wrote a commentary on Acts, as well as Ambrose, Augustine, Jerome, Hilary, Isidore, and Gregory. For his sources, see Bede, *Acts of the Apostles*, pp. xxvii-xxxi, 3-6.

[11] 'Now the giving of charismatic gifts in the Spirit is properly called the "baptism" of the Spirit, as he himself bore witness.' Cited according to the translation of Martin Lawrence and David Hurst, Bede, *Homilies on the Gospels*, I, 1, p. 7. 'He pledged that power would come down upon them from on high, because already they possessed the Holy Spirit before, yet they received him more fully once he ascended into heaven.' Cited according to the translation of Martin Lawrence and David Hurst, Bede, *Homilies on the Gospels*, II, 15, p. 138. Cf. Bede, *Homilies on the Gospels*, II, 15, p. 144; Burgess, *The Holy Spirit: Medieval Roman Catholic and Reformation Traditions*, pp. 22-24; Jaroslav Pelikan, *Christian Tradition*, III, p. 26.

[12] Cited according to the translation of Martin Lawrence, Bede, *Acts of the Apostles*, p. 51. Here, Bede quotes from Augustine, *The City of God*, 16.38 and Ps. 45.7.

According to Bede, the name Christ is a redemptive name meaning anointing, depicting the Spirit's relationship in Christ's life and salvific mission. In other words, the Spirit anointed Christ so that believers may salvifically receive the Spirit.[13]

Peter's sermon and the Gentiles' subsequent Spirit baptism at Cornelius' house supply the context for the next Spirit christological text (Acts 10.34-48). Peter again expounded the soteriological value of Christ's name: Jesus is the Christ, Lord of all, sent to reconcile the world to God, announced by John, and anointed by the Spirit (Acts 10.34-37).

> How God anointed him with the Holy Spirit and with power. Another text says: *Inasmuch as God anointed him*. John preached Jesus inasmuch as God anointed him with the Holy Spirit at the time when he said, *He will baptize you in the Holy Spirit*; and again, *I saw the Spirit descending as a dove upon him*. Jesus was anointed *not with oil, but with the gift of grace, which is signified by the visible oil with which the church anoints those who are baptized. Yet, Christ was not anointed with the Holy Spirit at the time when it descended as a dove upon him at his baptism, for at that time he condescended to prefigure his body, that is, his church, in which the baptized principally receive the Holy Spirit. Rather he must be understood to have been anointed with a mystical and invisible anointing when the Word of God was made flesh, that is, when human nature, without any preceding merits from good works, was joined to the Word of God in the womb of the Virgin, so as to become one person with him. Because of this we confess that he was born of the Holy Spirit and the virgin Mary* (Acts 10.38a).[14]

Several observations emerge from this text. First, except for a few words, Bede's comments are direct quotations from his sources: Mt.

---

[13] See the translation of Martin Lawrence and David Hurst, Bede, *Homilies on the Gospels*, I, 5, p. 50, who write:

> Jesus is the name of the Son who was born of a virgin, and, as the angel explained, [this name] signified that he would save his people from their sins ... From this anointing, that is, the chrism, he himself is called 'Christ,' and those who share this anointing, that is, spiritual grace, are called 'Christians.'

Cf. Bede, *Homilies on the Gospels*, I, 11, pp. 107-108.

[14] Cited according to the translation of Martin Lawrence, Bede, *Acts of the Apostles*, p. 102. 'Bede summarizes in a masterful way the soteriological and theological implications of a Spirit Christology in an authentic Trinitarian framework.' Veli-Matti Kärkkäinen (ed.), *Holy Spirit and Salvation: The Sources of Christian Theology* (Louisville, KY: Westminster/John Knox Press, 2010), p. 138.

3.11; Jn 1.32; Augustine, *Trin.* 15.26.46. Second, into his analysis of the Spirit anointing Christ in Acts 10.38, he integrates two Gospels' accounts of the Spirit descending upon Christ at the Jordan event and the Father's promise that Christ will baptize believers with the Holy Spirit. Third, Bede's interpretation of God anointing Christ with the Holy Spirit depends on Augustine's concept of the Spirit being the gift of grace to Christ's human nature.[15] Consequently, Bede denies that the Holy Spirit anointed Christ during the Jordan event; rather, the Holy Spirit as the anointing and the gift of grace to Christ's human nature effected the incarnation in Mary's womb,[16] uniting the Logos with human nature. During the Jordan event, therefore, the Spirit descended upon Christ to prefigure believers receiving the Spirit at their baptism in the redemptive name of Jesus Christ.[17]

According to Bede, the Holy Spirit functions as gift of grace and anointing throughout Christ's entire life and ministry. The Spirit's anointing conceives and joins human nature to the Logos in Mary's womb. The Spirit, henceforth, rests in the fullness of anointing on Christ's human nature; thus, he bears the redemptive name, the Christ. So, as a human Christ received the Spirit, and as God he salvifically gives the Spirit to believers; accordingly, in the Spirit Bede redemptively conjoins Christ's incarnation, life, ministry, death, resurrection, and ascension with Pentecost. Bede's Spirit Christology, therefore, supports a paradigm of pneumatic meditation which integrates Logos Christology within a trinitarian framework.

---

[15] For an examination of Augustine's Spirit Christology, v.s. pp. 220-27.

[16] Cf. Bede, *Homilies on the Gospels*, I, 3, p. 24; I, 12, p. 116; I, 15, p. 153; II, 20, p. 203; II, 23, p. 238.

[17] According to Bede, the rule of faith demands that believers are baptized in the name of the Trinity, but in the Book of Acts believers are baptized in the name of Jesus Christ, so he resolves this problem by affirming that baptism in the name of Jesus Christ implies the trinitarian name. '*Through the unity of the name the mystery is completed. If you say "Christ," you have designated at the same time God the Father, by whom the Son was anointed, and the Son who was himself anointed, and the Spirit with whom he was anointed*' (Acts 10.48). Cited according to the translation of Martin Lawrence, Bede, *Acts of the Apostles*, p. 103. Here, Bede is quoting Ambrose, *Spir.* 1.3.43-45. For an examination of Ambrose's Spirit Christology, v.s. pp. 217-22.

Elipandus

Elipandus, archbishop of Toledo (754–802), led a group of Spanish theologians that taught a form of adoptionism. Since Muslims had conquered Toledo by 712 and most of the Iberian Peninsula by 718, Elipandus avoided direct condemnation and successfully retained his see and doctrine.[18] Those living under the rule of Charlemagne, who followed the teaching of Elipandus' strongest supporter Felix of Urgel, nonetheless, suffered repeated condemnation for teaching that during the Jordan event Christ's human nature was adopted into the status of Son of God.[19]

A few of Elipandus' writings have survived. The survey will focus on Elipandus' profession of faith, *Symbolus Fidei Elipandianae* (785),[20] preserved in a polemical writing of Elipandus' primary antagonist in Spain: Beatus of Liebana's *Two Books against Elipandus* (785).[21] The structure of Elipandus' creed consists of two parts. In

---

[18] Regarding the issues of Muslim conquest, rule, and influence in Spain during this controversy, see Roger Collins, *Early Medieval Spain: Unity in Diversity, 400-1000* (New York: St. Martin's Press, 1983), pp. 146-82, 212-13; Roger Collins, *Early Medieval Europe, 300-1000* (New York: St. Martin's Press, 1991), pp. 204-208; González, *Christian Thought*, II, p. 109.

[19] Felix defended Elipandus' Christology and was condemned at three councils called by Charlemagne: Regensburg (792), Frankfurt (795), and Aachen (799). Papal admonitions and condemnations also proceeded from Hadrian I (785) and Leo III (798). Felix's primary antagonist was Alcuin, the cultural adviser to Charlemagne and organizer of the palace school and library. For the political and theological context of this struggle, see John C. Cavadini, *The Last Christology of the West: Adoptionism in Spain and Gaul, 785-820* (Middle Ages Series; Philadelphia: University of Pennsylvania Press, 1993), pp. 1-7, 71-73; Collins, *Early Medieval Spain*, pp. 210-11; Collins, *Early Medieval Europe*, pp. 281-86; Eleanor Shipley Duckett, *Alcuin, Friend of Charlemagne: His World and His Work* (New York: Macmillan, 1951), pp. 3-171; Pelikan, *Christian Tradition*, III, p. 52; Schaff, *History*, IV, pp. 513-17; Harnack, *Dogma*, V, pp. 287-89; Latourette, *History*, I, pp. 359-60; Walker, *History*, pp. 207-208. Regarding Felix's and Alcuin's writings in this dispute, see Duckett, *Alcuin*, pp. 178-90, 233-42; Cavadini, *The Last Christology of the West*, pp. 73-102, 107-27; Harnack, *Dogma*, V, pp. 289-91. Alcuin's polemic *Against the Adoptionist Heresy of Felix* can be found in an English translation in Edward Peters, *Heresy and Authority in Medieval Europe: Documents in Translation* (Philadelphia: University of Pennsylvania Press, 1980), pp. 53-56.

[20] For the document's purpose, occasion, date, context, and provenance see Cavadini, *The Last Christology of the West*, pp. 27-28. His other writings include *Letter to Migetius* (782), *Letter to Fidelis* (785), *Letter to the Bishops of Frankland* (792), *Letter to Charlemagne* (792), *Letter to Alcuin* (798), *Letter to Felix of Urgel* (798).

[21] Elipandus' *Symbolus Fidei Elipandianae* is found in Latin, without translation, in Beatus and Etherius, *Beati Liebanensis et Eterii Oxomensis Adversus Elipandum Libri Duo* (Corpus Christianorum. Continuatio Mediaevalis 59; Turnholti: Brepols,

the first section, Elipandus explicates his faith in the triune doctrine of God: the Father, Son, and Holy Spirit exist in one nature and essence of deity. Arguing from various analogies, Elipandus demonstrates distinction in triune unity and that giving several appellations to the same thing does not require multiplication of substances.[22] The second section presents Elipandus' christological confession. According to Elipandus, the Word, who eternally existed with the Father, emptied himself of his divinity and was made human to redeem the world. Elipandus sharply distinguishes between Christ's divine and human natures: whereas the divine nature is Son of God by generation and nature, the human nature is Son of God by adoption and grace.[23] Since Elipandus' creed contains no allusion to the adoptionism controversy and considering its trinitarian emphasis, more than likely, it stands as a riposte against the trinitarian errors of Migetius.[24]

Elipandus' creed contains a Spirit christological text located in a discussion regarding the redemptive significance of Christ's human nature experiencing adoption, which he extrapolates from Phil. 2.6-8. It allows saints salvific conformity to the Son of God according to grace: with the Adopted One they become adoptive ones, with the Advocate they become advocates, with Christ they become

---

1984), 1025-90, pp. 27-29. Bengt Löfstedt edits this work and provides an introduction in German, discussing issues concerning manuscripts, previous editions, authorship, and the text's nomenclature see Beatus and Etherius, *Adversus Elipandum*, pp. v-xxi. For an examination of Beatus' work, see Cavadini, *The Last Christology of the West*, pp. 45-70. Cf. González, *Christian Thought*, II, pp. 110-11; Collins, *Early Medieval Spain*, pp. 245-46.

[22] 'Symbolus Fidei', in Beatus and Etherius, *Adversus Elipandum*, 1025-64, pp. 27-28. Cf. Cavadini, *The Last Christology of the West*, p. 28.

[23] 'Symbolus Fidei', in Beatus and Etherius, *Adversus Elipandum*, 1065-91, pp. 28-29. Cf. Cavadini, *The Last Christology of the West*, pp. 28-31; Pelikan, *Christian Tradition*, III, pp. 53-59; Harnack, *Dogma*, V, pp. 283-84; Schaff, *History*, IV, pp. 518-21. Most scholars charge Elipandus with teaching two persons in Christ, a type of Nestorianism. González, *Christian Thought*, II, pp. 111-12. John Cavadini challenges this conclusion by arguing that this inference is deduced by analyzing 'Elipandus' adoptionism on premises other than his own'. Cavadini, *The Last Christology of the West*, pp. 38-44.

[24] According to Elipandus, Migetius claimed that three corporeal persons exist in deity: David is the person of the Father; the human Jesus who was made from the seed of David according to the flesh is the person of the Son; Paul is the person of the Holy Spirit. Cavadini, *The Last Christology of the West*, pp. 10-23; González, *Christian Thought*, II, pp. 109-10; Pelikan, *Christian Tradition*, III, pp. 58-59; Collins, *Early Medieval Spain*, pp. 209-10.

christs, with he who is the little one they become little ones, and with the Servant they become servants.²⁵

> I believe also that among the selfsame gifts of grace of the Holy Spirit is the adopting Holy Spirit, in whom we cry out Abba Father, in which Spirit I do not deny that the Christ-man is adopted.²⁶

Elipandus believed in the resurrection saints shall be like the Son, not in his divinity, but in the flesh of his humanity which he received from the virgin.²⁷ Several conclusions emerge from this text and its context. First, Elipandus carefully rejects any notion of the adoption of Christ's divine nature. Second, conforming saints to Christ is the redemptive telos. Third, the Holy Spirit functions as the gift of grace to Christ's human nature, adopting it into Sonship. Elipandus, therefore, affirms that the Holy Spirit adopting Christ's humanity as Son of God becomes paradigmatic of the saints' adoption as sons according to grace. In point of fact, these christological inferences are the gist of Beatus' polemic against Elipandus. Charging Elipandus with exegetical impropriety, Beatus contends that Paul never said, as Elipandus does, that we are adoptive ones and he is adoptive; we are christs and he is Christ; we are little ones and he is the little one; he is a servant among servants.²⁸ Beatus, hence, rejects any suggestion of adoption.

Since, according to Elipandus, Christ's reception of the Holy Spirit was the event of adoption, Beatus' dispute with Elipandus essentially became a Spirit christological question: when did Christ receive the Holy Spirit as the gift of adopting grace? According to Beatus, Elipandus pointed to the Jordan event; consequently,

---

²⁵ 'Symbolus Fidei', in Beatus and Etherius, *Adversus Elipandum*, 1083-85, p. 29. Cf. Cavadini, *The Last Christology of the West*, pp. 31-38.

²⁶ Cited according to my own translation, with the assistance of Dr. Terry L. Cross, 'Symbolus Fidei', in Beatus and Etherius, *Adversus Elipandum*, 1086-88, p. 29. Cf. Cavadini, *The Last Christology of the West*, pp. 32, 153, n. 65.

²⁷ 'Symbolus Fidei', in Beatus and Etherius, *Adversus Elipandum*, 1089-91, p. 29. Cf. Cavadini, *The Last Christology of the West*, p. 31.

²⁸ 'Symbolus Fidei', in Beatus and Etherius, *Adversus Elipandum*, 1310-14, p. 35. Cf. Cavadini, *The Last Christology of the West*, pp. 59-61. Elipandus claims that his interpretation of Phil. 2.7 correlates with Augustine, Hilary, Ambrose, Jerome, Leo, Fulgentius, Isidore, Ildefonsus, Julian, and the Creeds of Toledo. Cavadini, *The Last Christology of the West*, pp. 33-38, 43, 51; Harnack, *Dogma*, V, pp. 278-87; Pelikan, *Christian Tradition*, III, pp. 55, 63-66; Collins, *Early Medieval Spain*, pp. 211-12; Schaff, *History*, IV, pp. 517-18.

Beatus asserted that it was absurd to believe that Jesus, at thirty years of age, came to John's baptism to receive the Holy Spirit.[29] Contrary to Elipandus' position, Beatus attested to Christ being full of the Spirit previous to the Jordan event because the Spirit had conceived and anointed Christ in the virgin's womb.[30] For Beatus, then, Elipandus' Christology was culpable of denigrating Christ's uniqueness: Jesus is not an adoptive son; rather, he is the proper and true son of God, so he is not one god among gods, or one lord among lords, or one christ among christs.[31] So Christ's experience of the Spirit and his filiation to the Father is unique.

Elipandus' Christology differed from other forms of adoptionism. Elipandus never implied that Christ was a mere human adopted by the Spirit into deity; instead, he affirmed triune distinctions in the one essence of deity and avouched that the divine Son assumed human nature in the incarnation. Elipandus, nevertheless, sharply distinguished between Christ's divine and human natures, allowing for the Holy Spirit to anoint and adopt Christ's human nature into filiation as a paradigm of the Spirit redemptively anointing, adopting into filiation, and conforming saints to Christ. The Holy Spirit, thus, mediates the filiation of human nature in Christ's life and ministry. Elipandus' Christology, therefore, supports a paradigm of pneumatic mediation which integrates with Logos Christology.

Bonaventure

Bonaventure received his early education at a Franciscan friary in the small town of his birth and rearing, Bagnoregio.[32] When he was

---

[29] 'Symbolus Fidei', in Beatus and Etherius, *Adversus Elipandum*, 307-309, p. 8. Cf. Cavadini, *The Last Christology of the West*, p. 67.

[30] 'Symbolus Fidei', in Beatus and Etherius, *Adversus Elipandum*, 310-15, p. 9. Beatus is following Augustine in this assertion, but it is unclear whether or not he supports Spirit Christology.

[31] 'Symbolus Fidei', in Beatus and Etherius, *Adversus Elipandum*, 316-18, p. 9. Cf. Cavadini, *The Last Christology of the West*, pp. 63-68.

[32] Though it remains uncertain whether or not Bonaventure ever met Francis of Assisi, it is possible that Francis visited Bagnoregio, for Bonaventure testified that through Francis' prayer he received healing from a serious illness during his childhood. For overviews of Bonaventure's life, see Christopher M. Cullen, *Bonaventure* (Great Medieval Thinkers; Oxford: Oxford University Press, 2006), pp. 3-14; Bonaventure and Ewert H. Cousins, *Bonaventure* (CWS; New York: Paulist Press, 1978), pp. 2-8; Bonaventure, *Saint Bonaventure's Disputed Questions on the Knowledge of Christ* (trans. Zachary Hayes; Works of St. Bonaventure 4; 2005 repr.;

seventeen, Bonaventure began his studies at the University of Paris (1234), and after joining the Franciscan mendicant order (1243), he inaugurated his teaching and prolific writing career in Paris.[33] During this time, using scholastic methods, Bonaventure published numerous treatises, biblical commentaries, and a summary of his theology. In 1257, amid a time of unrest and schism, Bonaventure became minister general of the Franciscans;[34] his leadership and writings, thus, earned him the sobriquet the second founder of the Franciscan order. Bonaventure, thenceforth, focused on authoring spiritual writings, reflecting Franciscan devotion to and mystical contemplation of Christ's humanity and passion: the portal through which the believer's soul enters its journey into union with God and

---

St. Bonaventure, NY: Franciscan Institute Publications, 1992), pp. 40-41; Burgess, *The Holy Spirit: Medieval Roman Catholic and Reformation Traditions*, p. 70; Jacques Guy Bougerol, *Introduction to the Works of Bonaventure* (trans. José de Vinck; Paterson, NJ: St. Anthony Guild Press, 1964), pp. 3-10, 18-20; Zachary Hayes, *Bonaventure: Mystical Writings* (The Crossroad Spiritual Legacy Series; New York: Crossroad, 1999), pp. 15, 18-21; González, *Christian Thought*, II, pp. 249-50; Walker, *History*, pp. 270-71; Latourette, *History*, I, pp. 507-508.

[33] Bonaventure's writings were published in three phases corresponding to three epochs of his life. First, during his teaching at Paris (1243–57) he published his *Commentary on the Sentences* of Peter Lombard, several biblical commentaries, and three sets of disputed questions: *On Evangelical Perfection*, *On Christ's Knowledge*, and *On the Mystery of the Trinity*. He also published a summary of his theology, *Breviloquium*, and the treatise *On the Reduction of the Arts to Theology*. Second, his spiritual writings as minister general of the Franciscans (1257–67) include *The Soul's Journey into God*, *The Tree of Life*, *The Triple Way*, *Soliloquy on the Four Spiritual Exercises*, *On the Government of the Soul*, *On the Five Feasts of the Child Jesus*, and *The Life of St. Francis* (*Legenda maior*). Third, during his time of responding to controversy (1269–73), he published *Defense of the Poor* and three series of university lectures or sermons: *On the Ten Commandments*, *On the Seven Gifts of the Holy Spirit*, and on *The Six Days of Creation*. Regarding Bonaventure's writings, see Bonaventure and Cousins, *Bonaventure*, pp. 8-48; Cullen, *Bonaventure*, pp. 15-20; Bougerol, *Introduction* pp. 94-162; Bonaventure, *Knowledge of Christ*, pp. 41-44; Burgess, *The Holy Spirit: Medieval Roman Catholic and Reformation Traditions*, p. 71; Hayes, *Bonaventure: Mystical Writings*, pp. 16-18; González, *Christian Thought*, II, pp. 252-54; Seeberg and Hay, *History*, II, p. 100.

[34] González, *Christian Thought*, II, pp. 231-32, writes:

While John of Parma was Minister General of the order (1247–57), the rigorist party grew, and also infiltrated by the eschatological ideas of Joachim of Fiore. The year 1260, of great importance in Joachimist expectations, was drawing near, and some of the strict Franciscans came to identify themselves with what Joachim had called the 'church of the Holy Spirit' ... It was in the midst of this situation that John of Parma was succeeded by Bonaventure.

Cf. Walker, *History*, p. 261; Latourette, *History*, I, p. 434.

mystical ecstasy.³⁵ In 1269, responding to attacks on the mendicant orders, Bonaventure initiated three series of university lectures against a heterodox form of Aristotelianism taught among the faculty of the University of Paris. The lectures prematurely ended when Pope Gregory X elevated Bonaventure to the cardinalate and Bishop of Albans (1273), and he commenced assisting Gregory X in the preparation of the Second Council of Lyons (1274). Although Bonaventure's influence carried much weight during the council's discussions, he died before the council ended. Overall, Bonaventure's writings were grounded in Augustine and drew from Anselm, Bernard of Clairvaux, Richard of St. Victor, and Aristotle, as well as integrating the Greek spirituality of Pseudo-Dionysius with the Franciscan devotion to Christ's humanity and passion, producing a spiritual synthesis: 'Bonaventure achieved for spirituality what Thomas did for theology'.³⁶

Several of Bonaventure's writings contain Spirit christological references; this survey will focus on the texts found in his *Commentary on the Gospel of Luke*³⁷ which he wrote early in his teaching career in Paris (1248–50).³⁸ Hermeneutically, Bonaventure gives primacy to

---

³⁵ For the similarities between Gregory Palamas' and Bonaventure's mystical theology, see Russel Murray, 'Mirror of Experience: Palamas and Bonaventure on the Experience of God – A Contribution to Orthodox-Roman Catholic Dialogue', *JES* 44 (2009), pp. 432-60.

³⁶ Bonaventure and Cousins, *Bonaventure*, p. 2. Cf. Burgess, *The Holy Spirit: Medieval Roman Catholic and Reformation Traditions*, p. 71. Bonaventure was canonized a saint in 1482 and honored as doctor of the church in 1588 and has borne the moniker the Seraphic Doctor. Concerning Bonaventure's influence, see Cullen, *Bonaventure*, pp. 20-23; Bonaventure and Cousins, *Bonaventure*, pp. 1-2; Hayes, *Bonaventure: Mystical Writings*, pp. 145-50; Seeberg and Hay, *History*, II, p. 98.

³⁷ Spirit christological texts are also found in the *Disputed Questions on the Knowledge of Christ* (1254) and *The Tree of Life* (1259–67). These texts will be noted in due course of the discussion. For the date of origin, provenance, historical context, structure, and content of the *Disputed Questions on the Knowledge of Christ*, see Zachary Hayes' introduction, Bonaventure, *Knowledge of Christ*, pp. 21-44. For the date of origin, provenance, historical context, structure, and content of *The Tree of Life*, see Ewert Cousins' introduction, Bonaventure, 'The Tree of Life', *Bonaventure* (trans. Ewert H. Cousins; New York: Paulist Press, 1978), pp. 8-11, 16-18, 34-37.

³⁸ For a discussion of date of origin, provenance, and context, see Robert Karris' introduction, Bonaventure, *St. Bonaventure's Commentary on the Gospel of Luke: Chapters 1–8* (trans. Robert J. Karris; Works of St. Bonaventure 8; St. Bonaventure, NY: Franciscan Institute Publications, 2001), pp. vi-vii.

the literal sense of the text[39] and grounds his interpretation in tradition by copiously citing from Scripture and his predecessors: Augustine, Jerome, Ambrose, Gregory the Great, Bernard of Clairvaux, Bede, and the *Glossa Ordinaria*.[40] Bonaventure introduces the Gospel of Luke by quoting Lk. 4.18 (Preface, 1). According to Bonaventure, this text implies that the anointing of the Spirit is a requisite experience for any teacher of Scripture (Preface, 2-15).[41] Moreover, Lk. 4.18 depicts Christ's entire life and ministry as uniquely anointed by the Spirit – Christ as mediator, preacher, restorer, and conqueror – which corresponds to Bonaventure structuring the commentary into four chapter divisions: Christ as (1) mediator focuses on the mystery of the incarnation Luke 1–3, (2) preacher concerns Christ's magisterial preaching Luke 4–21, (3) restorer deals with the medicine of the passion Luke 22–23, and (4) conqueror proclaims the triumph of the resurrection Luke 24 (Preface, 17-23).[42]

By granting Lk. 4.18 a privileged position in his commentary, Bonaventure gives pride of place to the Spirit's anointing in Christ's life and ministry; it is the hermeneutical key to the Gospel of Luke.

> *The Spirit of the Lord is upon me*, etc. Here the text notes *the fittingness of the testimony*. For it gives expression to four notes of excellence which were in our Savior. For he is *mediator, teacher, restorer,*

---

[39] See Robert Karris' introduction, Bonaventure, *Gospel of Luke*, pp. viii-x; Bougerol, *Introduction*, pp. 90-94.

[40] The *Glossa Ordinaria* (ordinary interpretation). 'The "gloss" or commentary on the Latin Vulgate ... became a significant medieval resource for interpreting Scripture. The glosses added to biblical texts were drawn from patristic writers. More than 3,000 manuscripts with such glosses exist.' Donald K. McKim, *Westminster Dictionary of Theological Terms* (Louisville: Westminster / John Knox Press, 1996), p. 114. Regarding his sources, see Robert Karris' introduction, Bonaventure, *Gospel of Luke*, pp. xi-xxii. Cf. Bougerol, *Introduction*, pp. 23-48, 85-90; Hayes, *Bonaventure: Mystical Writings*, pp. 21-26; González, *Christian Thought*, II, pp. 250.

[41] 'Now the teacher of evangelical scripture must be *anointed* with divine grace, *instituted* by genuine obedience, and *inflamed* by fraternal love. – He must be *anointed* by divine grace. And this is meant when it says: *The Spirit of the Lord is upon me, because he has anointed me*.' Cited according to the translation of Robert Karris, Bonaventure, *Gospel of Luke*, Preface, 3, pp. 2-3. 'Little importance should be given to inquiry, but much to unction ... little importance should be given to words and to writing, but all to the gift of God, that is, the Holy Spirit.' Cited according to the translation of Ewert Cousins, Bonaventure, 'The Tree of Life', 7.5, p. 113.

[42] Cf. Robert Karris' introduction, Bonaventure, *Gospel of Luke*, pp. xxxviii-xliv.

and *rewarder*. And these four are brought out in Jesus' sermon which follows.

First, then, it is indicated that he is *mediator through the mystery of the incarnation* when it says: *The Spirit of the Lord is upon me*, because *he has anointed me*. Me points here to the person of Christ in his assumed nature, upon which the Holy Spirit has come to rest, according to what Isaiah 11.2 says: 'And the Spirit of the Lord will rest upon him.' And John 1.33 has: 'He upon whom you see the Spirit descending and remaining, he it is who baptizes with the Holy Spirit.' And therefore, it is said in Acts 10.34, 37-38: 'Peter said ... you know what took place throughout Judea; for he began in Galilee after the baptism preached by John; how God anointed Jesus of Nazareth with the Holy Spirit,' etc ... And note that the human nature in Christ was conceived by the power of the Holy Spirit and united by his grace to the divine nature. And on account of these two it says that the Spirit of the Lord *is upon him* and *anointed him* (Lk. 4.18).[43]

Now the text introduces *the plenitude of the grace* in Christ when it says: *Now Jesus, full of the Holy Spirit, returned from Jordan*, not because he had been first filled with the Spirit there, but because now his fullness of the Holy Spirit first began to be apparent, overflowing to others according to what John 1.14, 16 has: 'And we have seen his glory ... Of his fullness we have all received' (Lk. 4.1).[44]

Several conclusions emerge from these texts. First, similar to Augustine, the Spirit's anointing as gift of grace conceives the human nature and unites it to the divine nature.[45] Second, Bonaventure

---

[43] Cited according to the translation of Robert Karris, Bonaventure, *Gospel of Luke*, 2.4.36, p. 320. Cf. Bonaventure, *Gospel of Luke*, Preface, 18, p. 10. For Bonaventure's application of Lk. 4.18 to Christ as teacher, restorer, and rewarder, see Bonaventure, *Gospel of Luke*, 2.4.37-46, pp. 321-29. The italics in the text are Karris' emphasis.

[44] Cited according to the translation of Robert Karris, Bonaventure, *Gospel of Luke*, 2.4.2, p. 292.

[45] See the translation of Ewert Cousins, Bonaventure, 'The Tree of Life', 1.3, p. 127, who writes:

> The Archangel Gabriel was sent to the Virgin. When she gave her consent to him, the Holy Spirit came upon her like a divine fire inflaming her soul and sanctifying her flesh in perfect purity. But the *power of the Most High overshadowed* her (Luke 1.35) so that she could endure such fire. By the action of that

sharply distinguishes between Christ's divine nature and human nature: the Spirit anoints and rests on the assumed human nature.[46]

> power, instantly his body was formed, his soul created, and at once both were united to the divinity in the Person of the Son, so that the same Person was God and man, with the properties of each nature maintained.

Veli-Matti Kärkkäinen examines this text and concludes: 'Bonaventure anchors his doctrine of the Trinity in salvation history and develops a biblical Spirit Christology'. Kärkkäinen (ed.), *Holy Spirit and Salvation*, pp. 131-32. Cf. Cullen, *Bonaventure*, pp. 142-44; Seeberg and Hay, *History*, II, p. 110. Bonaventure, *Knowledge of Christ*, pp. 45-194. 'Therefore, though God is a man and a man is God because of the union of person and hypostasis, nonetheless the operations of each nature are to be maintained unconfused, even though they are predicated mutually because of the communication of idioms.' Cited according to the translation of Zachary Hayes, Bonaventure, *Knowledge of Christ*, 6, conclusion, p. 170.

[46] This sharp distinction between the human and divine natures is clearly evident as Bonaventure discusses the question of Christ' human knowledge: is the knowledge of deity in Christ's created human soul limited or does it partake of uncreated divine wisdom? Methodologically, Bonaventure proceeds by presenting the question which is followed by thesis statements, antithetical statements, and reaching a conclusion.

> The third chapter of John says: 'It is not by measure that God gives the Spirit'; and the *Glossa* says: 'While God measures for human beings, there is no measure in God with respect to the Son. But, as God generates the Son totally from the totality of the divine being, so God gives the whole of the Spirit to the incarnate Son, not partially and in pieces but completely and universally.' But the measure of the gift of the Spirit is the measure of the knowledge of truth. Therefore, if the soul of Christ receives the Spirit without measure, it knows God without measure. But this means nothing other than to comprehend the divine wisdom itself (Cited according to the translation of Zachary Hayes, Bonaventure, *Knowledge of Christ*, 6.1, p. 161).

In this thesis statement Bonaventure seems to advocate that the Spirit mediates the divine wisdom, to which the Logos is eternally privy, to Christ's human nature. Bonaventure's counter argument to this text agrees that the Spirit given to Christ without measure refers to the grace of union of two natures in one person; however, Christ's humanity remains finite and limited, so Christ's human soul does not fully comprehend divine wisdom. Bonaventure, *Knowledge of Christ*, 6.1-4, p. 172.

> Again, although the soul of Christ is united with the essence of the Word, still it is not present to as many things as the Word itself is. But, the same sort of relation that exists between the two essences is found between the two sorts of knowledge. Therefore, the soul of Christ never knows all those things which the Word itself knows (Cited according to the translation of Zachary Hayes, Bonaventure, *Knowledge of Christ*, 7.8, p. 185).

Cf. Zachary Hayes analysis of question six, Bonaventure, *Knowledge of Christ*, pp. 62-64; Cullen, *Bonaventure*, pp. 78-86. Nevertheless, Bonaventure affirms that Christ's humanity is mystically open to an ecstatic knowledge, so that it is transcendently drawn beyond itself toward the infinite. Bonaventure, *Knowledge of Christ*, 7, conclusion, pp. 186-88. For Bonaventure, then, the Spirit mediates the union of natures in Christ, and although it is possible that the Spirit's anointing

Third, Bonaventure conjoins the Scriptures speaking about the incarnation, Jordan event, and Christ's salvific mission, so that they coalesce into one event of the Spirit anointing Christ; the Spirit anointed Christ's entire life and ministry. Fourth, Christ was not anointed during the Jordan event. Fifth, the Spirit uniquely anointed Christ: Christ's human nature received the plenitude of the Spirit; other humans receive a partial anointing.[47] Sixth, After Christ returned from the Jordan, the Spirit's anointing manifested clearly Christ's identity and mission: he is the one who baptizes with the Holy Spirit.[48] These Spirit christological texts, therefore, elucidate the central role of the Spirit's anointing in Christ's life and mission.

Pneumatology permeates Bonaventure's Christology. Christ is the salvific mediator between God and humans because the Spirit's anointing as the gift of grace effected the incarnation, conceiving the human nature and joining it to deity. Faithful to the Western Spirit christological tradition, Bonaventure distinguishes the divine and human natures, allowing the Holy Spirit as an act of grace to anoint the human nature. Since this anointing occurred at the time of conception, the Spirit anointed Christ's entire life and mission as mediator, preacher, restorer, and conqueror. Bonaventure's Spirit Christology, consequently, supports a paradigm of pneumatic mediation which integrates with Logos Christology.

Conclusion

Although scarce, Spirit Christology did survive in the West during this epoch; moreover, the relation of the Spirit's anointing to

---

draws Christ's human soul into an ecstatic illumination of divine wisdom, it is unclear whether or not this is the case.

[47] See the translation of Robert Karris, Bonaventure, *Gospel of Luke*, 1.3.53, pp. 270-71, who writes:

> *The Holy Spirit descended upon him in bodily form as a dove.* John 1.33 has: 'He upon whom you will see the Spirit descending and abiding upon him, he it is who baptizes with the Holy Spirit.' – Now the Holy Spirit descends upon him in the form of a *dove* because of its signification ... Thus, the Holy Spirit appeared to Christ in *full animal form*, but to his disciples in *tongues*, so that it may be signified that the Holy Spirit was in Christ with complete plenitude, but only partially in the others. Therefore, it is said in John 3.34: 'Not by measure does God give the Spirit' (Lk. 3.22).

[48] Cf. Bonaventure's depiction of Jesus as giver of the Spirit on the Day of Pentecost, Bonaventure, 'The Tree of Life', 10.39, pp. 163-64.

Christ's life and ministry remained the central issue among those advocating pneumatic Christology, disclosing agreements and distinctions. All proponents of Spirit Christology examined in this era concurred that the Spirit anointed Christ's human nature, not the divine nature, but they differed concerning when this anointing occurred and what it affected. Adhering to Augustine's view, Bede's and Bonaventure's opinions dovetailed: the Spirit's anointing as gift of grace formed Christ's human nature in Mary's womb and joined it to deity, so that the Spirit anointed Christ's entire life and ministry. The Spirit did not anoint Christ during the Jordan event; rather the Spirit descended typologically, testifying to the fullness of the Spirit resting upon Christ and revealing his divine nature, the one who baptizes in the Holy Spirit. Elipandus, also, acknowledged the incarnation of the divine Logos in Christ; nevertheless, his belief regarding the anointing differed from Bede's and Bonaventure's: the Spirit anointed Christ during the Jordan event, adopting Christ's human nature into filiation with the Father. Elipandus, however, was no ordinary adoptionist; he agreed with Bede and Bonaventure regarding trinitarian theology, the incarnation of deity in Christ, and the Spirit's role in mediating Christ's salvific mission. These Medieval theologians' Spirit Christologies, therefore, supported diverse paradigms of pneumatic mediation which integrated with Logos Christology, and as such structured in trinitarian theology.

12

PROTESTANT WRITERS

The Protestant reformation opened a stream of liturgical, ecclesiastical, conciliar, historical, biblical, and doctrinal criticism which could not be stemmed and produced an environment amicable to a resurgence of Spirit Christology: (1) Scripture received special emphasis and was linked with pneumatology; (2) pneumatology gained a hearing in christological discussions; and (3) the ancient christological issues debated in the ecumenical councils resurfaced.[1] Nevertheless, neither did Spirit Christology explicitly appear among the Magisterial Reformers nor the Radical Reformers. This conclusion sounds a bit odd since one would expect to find Spirit Christology among the Radical Reformers; indeed, the Anabaptists and the spiritualists placed significant emphasis on the Spirit's activity in the life of believers. Their Christologies however, stood solidly on the foundation of Logos Christology, but not a Spirit Christology; moreover, the rationalists, such as the Socinians, rejected both Logos and Spirit Christologies.[2]

Although appearing only sporadically, Spirit Christology is found among various Protestant writings. For reasons which will become obvious as this inquiry progresses into the age of Enlightenment –

---

[1] Gary D. Badcock, *Light of Truth and Fire of Love: A Theology of the Holy Spirit* (Grand Rapids: Eerdmans, 1997), pp. 86-108.
[2] Stanley Burgess, succinctly sets forth the distinctions among these groups regarding these issues. 'Most Evangelical Rationalists tended toward anti-Trinitarianism, and therefore gave little attention to the concept of the Holy Spirit. In contrast, the person and work of the divine Third Person was central to the theologies of both Anabaptists and Spiritualists.' Burgess, *The Holy Spirit: Medieval Roman Catholic and Reformation Traditions*, p. 202.

with its historical, philosophical, and scientific challenges to Christian thought[3] – it will be expedient to assort the various groups, movements, and writers into two classifications: (1) the Protestant tradition of conservative self-criticism which struggled to revive and continue reforms within Protestantism while preserving classical Christian doctrine, and (2) the Protestant tradition of liberal self-criticism which sought to reinterpret Christian doctrine in light of the shifting modern enlightened scientific world-view.

The Protestant Tradition of Conservative Self-Criticism

This tradition's critical nature of seeking reform and revival was evident during the seventeenth century, as the Arminians endeavored to amend Reformed theology,[4] the Pietist movement attempted to ameliorate Lutheranism,[5] and Puritans ventured a Calvinist revision of the Church of England.[6] Among Puritan writings, struggling with issues of reformation and the encroachment of enlightenment rationalism denying traditional christological doctrine, Spirit christo-

---

[3] According to Immanuel Kant, 'Enlightenment is man's release from self-incurred tutelage. Tutelage is man's inability to make use of his understanding without direction from another ... Have courage to use your own reason! – that is the motto of the enlightenment'. Immanuel Kant, *Foundations of the Metaphysics of Morals: What Is Enlightenment? And a Passage from the Metaphysics of Morals* (Chicago: University of Chicago Press, 1950), p. 286. The Enlightenment exalted autonomous human reason and conscience as the fundamental judge of truth, not biblical or ecclesiastical authority. Nature was also elevated to a position of authority: truth is both reasonable and natural, for truth is grounded in the nature of things. The Enlightenment; furthermore, placed great hope in human nature and reason to improve and advance the plight of humanity. Accordingly, there was increased toleration for other religions and varied beliefs; in fact, Christianity was depicted as a religion of superstition, the cause of intolerance and much bloodshed. James C. Livingston, *Modern Christian Thought: The Enlightenment and the Nineteenth Century* (2 vols.; Upper Saddle River, NJ: Prentice Hall, 2nd edn, 1997), I, pp. 5-13. Cf. Stanley Grenz and Roger E. Olson, *20th Century Theology: God & the World in a Transitional Age* (Downers Grove: InterVarsity Press, 1992), pp. 15-18; Olson, *Christian Theology*, pp. 538-42; Jaroslav Pelikan, *Christian Tradition*, V, pp. 60-61. Christologically, this meant a general rejection of Christ's divine nature, miracles, death as atonement for sin, and resurrection. Alister E. McGrath, *The Making of Modern German Christology, 1750–1990* (Eugene, OR: Wipf and Stock, 2005 repr.; London: Inter-Varsity Press, 2nd edn, 1994), pp. 14-28.

[4] Olson, *Christian Theology*, pp. 454-72; Pelikan, *Christian Tradition*, V, pp. 30, 37-38, 45, 139-40.

[5] Olson, *Christian Theology*, pp. 473-92; Pelikan, *Christian Tradition*, V, pp. 53-54; Walker, *History*, pp. 495-507, 501-507.

[6] Olson, *Christian Theology*, pp. 493-504.

logical references appeared. For example, Spirit Christology permeates the sermons of the Puritan pastor Richard Sibbes; the ensuing christological debate, in England, between the Socinians and Puritans has bequeathed several Spirit christological references in the writings of John Owen.

Richard Sibbes

Richard Sibbes was a Puritan educator and preacher with a significant amount of influence.[7] Puritan efforts at reforming the Church of England and controversy over Calvinistic doctrine permeated the environment of Sibbes' time; in fact, during the reign of Charles I (1625–49), Puritans experienced severe persecution (1629–40).[8] Rather than advocating separation from the Church of England, Sibbes maintained a position of reform while remaining in the church; hence, Sibbes' sermons and writings reflected his position as a moderate Puritan reformer. Preferring reformation of human hearts, Sibbes' sermons and writings were primarily pastoral in nature. He was a doctor of the soul, drawing his patients' affections

---

[7] Richard Sibbes (1577–1635) was admitted as a fellow at St. John's College, Cambridge, subsequent to earning his BA (1599) and MA (1602) degrees at St. John's. During 1605, Sibbes experienced conversion, and in 1608 he was ordained as a deacon and priest, initiating his preaching career as minister of Thurston and preaching during chapel at St. John's. By 1610, he had earned his BD degree and a growing reputation as a preacher, giving him the opportunity to hold the influential position of lecturer at Holy Trinity Church, Cambridge (1610–16). In 1617, Sibbes became the preacher at Gray's Inn, London, which also provided him with a significant amount of influence. While continuing to preach at Gray's Inn, Sibbes was elected senior fellow at St. Johns (1619), Master of Catherine Hall, and vicar of Holy Trinity (1626). For overviews of Sibbes' life and context, see Mark Dever, *Richard Sibbes: Puritanism and Calvinism in Late Elizabethan and Early Stuart England* (Macon, GA: Mercer University Press, 2000), pp. 9-95; Alexander Balloch Grosart, 'Memoir of Richard Sibbes', in Alexander Balloch Grosart (ed.), *Works of Richard Sibbes* (7 vols.; 1973 repr.; Edinburgh: Banner of Truth Trust, 1862–64), I, pp. xxiv-cxxxi; Erroll Hulse, *Who Are the Puritans?: And What Do They Preach?* (Darlington, England: Evangelical Press, 2000), pp. 83-84.

[8] Archbishop William Laud, a trusted royal advisor to the king, influenced Charles I to persecute all non-conformists. Hulse, *Puritans*, pp. 48-51. Regarding Sibbes' dealings with Laud, see Grosart, 'Memoir of Richard Sibbes', *Works*, I, pp. lvii-lxxxi; Dever, *Sibbes*, pp. 42-48, 77-79. During this time, many Puritans migrated to New England in America, including some of Sibbes' disciples; for example, John Cotton. Dever, *Sibbes*, 40-41; Hulse, *Puritans*, pp. 83.

and wills to Christ by preaching to their hearts and inviting and acknowledging the Spirit's agency.[9]

Sibbes' writings are replete with Spirit christological references; this inquiry will focus on the sermon the *Description of Christ* which is an exposition of Mt. 12.18-19.[10] *Description of Christ* originally was designated by Sibbes as the introductory sermon to the treatise *The Bruised Reed and Smoking Flax* (1630),[11] and it was later published posthumously in a collection of sermons entitled *Beams of Divine Light* (1639). In the sermon's introduction, Sibbes accentuates three purposes for Isaiah's messianic prophecy (Isa. 42.1-2) which are fulfilled in Jesus Christ: (1) to turn the peoples' hearts from idolatry to the genuine worship of God, (2) to accentuate the fulfillment of the messianic promise in Jesus Christ, and (3) to turn human hearts from secularism and elevate the soul by beholding Christ. The sermon progresses through four main points drawn from the text.[12] The Spirit christological texts are primarily found in the sermon's first two sections.[13]

The sermon's first point renders a description of Christ as the beloved servant of God: 'Behold, my servant whom I have chosen, my beloved with whom my soul is well pleased' (v. 18). First, Sibbes depicts Christ as the chosen servant of the Lord apropos of his humanity: God became man to redeem humanity. According to

---

[9] For examinations of Sibbes' theology and preaching, see Dever, *Sibbes*, pp. 97-210; John R. Knott, *The Sword of the Spirit: Puritan Responses to the Bible* (Chicago: University of Chicago Press, 1980), pp. 42-61. Concerning Sibbes' anthropology and emphasis on human affections, see Dever, *Sibbes*, pp. 135-60. It is possible that Sibbes' attention to affections adumbrated Jonathan Edwards' ministry. Hulse, *Puritans*, pp. 84.

[10] Other Spirit christological references in Sibbes' works will be noted as they relate to the references in this document.

[11] The sermon's title page provides this information. Sibbes, 'Description of Christ', *Works*, I, p. 2. Grosart has arranged it so that it now immediately precedes *The Bruised Reed and Smoking Flax*. Sibbes probably preached this sermon at Gray's Inn.

[12] The introduction is located in Sibbes, 'Description of Christ', *Works*, I, pp. 3-5.

[13] The last two sections of the sermon lack any Spirit christological references, so they will not be examined; however, for contextual reasons the sermon's last two points are worthy of inclusion. The sermon's third point investigates Christ's preaching ministry: 'he shall proclaim justice to the Gentiles' (v. 18). The fourth point contemplates Christ's amicable nature and peaceable demeanor in fulfilling his salvific mission: 'He will not wrangle or cry aloud, nor will any one hear his voice in the streets' (v. 19).

Sibbes, Christ's human nature could neither merit nor choose its union with deity, so the election of Christ's human nature was entirely by grace: 'the knitting together of the human nature of Christ to his divine, it is called the grace of union'.[14] Next, Sibbes discusses in what sense Christ is called the beloved of God. Although Christ is one person, he ascribes beloved-ness to both natures. Sibbes quotes Mt. 3.17, affirming that during the Jordan event God acknowledged Christ as the beloved, denoting Christ's filial relationship with God. The Father has eternally loved the only begotten Son, who exists in consubstantial divine essence with the Father, so, in his divine nature Christ is beloved of the Father. The Father also loves Christ as a human.

> And as man he loves him, for as man he was the most excellent creature in the world, he was conceived, fashioned, and framed in his mother's womb by the Holy Ghost. It is said, Heb. 10.5, God gave him a body. God the Father by the Holy Ghost fashioned and framed and fitted him with a body, therefore God must needs love his own workmanship. Again there is nothing in him displeasing to God, there is no sin found in his life any way, therefore as man he was pleasing to God.[15]

> The same Spirit when Christ took our nature, that sanctified that blessed mass whereof he was made, when there was a union between him and the second person, the same Spirit sanctifies our souls and bodies.[16]

God, therefore, loves Christ's human nature because it is the workmanship of the Father by the agency of the Spirit. The Spirit, accordingly, mediated the formation of Christ's humanity, its sanctification, and the grace of union of the divine and human natures.[17]

The second point examines Christ's qualification for his salvific mission: 'I will put my Spirit upon him' (v. 18).

---

[14] Sibbes, 'Description of Christ', *Works*, I, p. 10. Cf. Sibbes, 'Description of Christ', *Works*, I, pp. 5-11.
[15] Sibbes, 'Description of Christ', *Works*, I, p. 11.
[16] Sibbes, 'Description of Christ', *Works*, I, p. 14.
[17] 'There was a fullness of the Spirit poured out upon Christ *in the union of the human nature with the divine*. Union and unction went together. There was anointing of the Spirit, together with the union of the Spirit.' Sibbes, 'The Excellency of the Gospel above the Law', *Works*, IV, p. 207; Sibbes, 'Miracle of Miracles', *Works*, VII, p. 119; Sibbes, 'Commentary on 2 Corinthians Ch. 1', *Works*, III, pp. 442-43.

> Now there were divers degrees of Christ receiving the Spirit at several times ... The Holy Ghost did sanctify that blessed mass whereof his body was framed in the womb of the virgin, he was quickened in the womb in his conception by the Holy Ghost, and he was graced by the Holy Ghost, and led by the Spirit in all things before his baptism. But afterward, when he came to set upon his office, to be the prophet and priest and king of his church, that great office of saving mankind ... then God poured upon him a special portion of the Spirit, answerable to that great calling ... This was accomplished when Christ, at his baptism, entered upon his office. God put his Spirit upon him, to set him apart, to ordain him, and to qualify him with abundance of grace for the work.[18]

According to Sibbes, Christ received infusions of the Spirit at various occasions, yet he carefully asserted that Christ was full of the Spirit in congruity with his human development and task at hand. During the Jordan event, the Spirit commissioned and inaugurated Christ into his salvific mission, endowing the beloved servant with gifts of the Spirit to accomplish his ministry;[19] the anointing of the Spirit qualified and empowered Christ to function as prophet, priest, and king. The Spirit, therefore, imbued Christ's entire life and mission.

Sibbes, then, turns to answer certain objections concerning his premise that the Spirit anointed Christ for salvific mission: if Christ is God and now sends the Spirit upon believers, why did he receive the Spirit's anointing?

> I answer, Christ is both God and man. Christ as God, gives the Spirit to his human nature; so he communicates his Spirit. The Spirit is his Spirit as well as the Father's. The Spirit proceeds from them both. Christ, as man, receives the Spirit. God the Fa-

---

[18] Sibbes, 'Description of Christ', *Works*, I, p. 15. 'Now Christ was to be a prophet, a priest, and a king. Therefore he was to be anointed with the Spirit, to enable him to these three offices.' Sibbes, 'Description of Christ', *Works*, I, pp. 15-16. 'There was a more full manifestation of the Spirit *in his baptism*. When the Spirit fell on him in the shape of a dove, then he received the Spirit. He was to enter into the ministry of the gospel.' Sibbes, 'Excellency of the Gospel', *Works*, IV, p. 207; Sibbes, 'A Fountain Sealed', *Works*, V, p. 433.

[19] 'For there are these three things especially meant by putting the Spirit upon him, separation or setting apart, and ordaining, and enriching with the gifts of the Spirit.' Sibbes, 'Description of Christ', *Works*, I, p. 15.

ther and the Son put the Spirit upon the manhood of Christ; so Christ both gives and receives the Spirit in diverse respects. As God, he gives and sends the Spirit. The spiration and breathing of the Spirit is from him as well as from the Father, but as man he received the Spirit. And this is the reason for it: next under the Father, Son, and Holy Ghost, Christ the Mediator, was to be the spring and original of all comfort and good. Therefore, Christ's nature must not only be sanctified and ordained by the Spirit; but he must receive the Spirit to enrich it, for whatsoever is wrought in the creature is by the Spirit. Whatsoever Christ did as man, he did by the Spirit. Christ's human nature, therefore, must be sanctified, and have the Spirit put upon it. God the Father, the first person in Trinity, and God the Son, the second, they work not immediately, but by the Holy Ghost, the third person. Therefore, whatsoever is wrought upon the creature, it comes from the Holy Ghost immediately ... We have not the Holy Ghost immediately from God, but we have his as sanctifying Christ first, and then us; and whatsoever the Holy Ghost doth in us, he doth the same in Christ first, and he doth it in us because in Christ ... The Holy Ghost fetcheth all from Christ in his working and comfort, and he makes Christ the pattern of all; for whatsoever is in Christ, the Holy Ghost, which is the Spirit of Christ, works in us as it is in Christ. Therefore, in John 1.13 [*sic*], it is said, 'of his fullness we receive grace for grace' – that is, grace answerable to his grace.[20]

Several noteworthy conclusions emerge from this text. First, the sending of the Spirit upon Christ's humanity demonstrates the perichoretic nature of triune relations; the Spirit is the Spirit of the Father and Son, and the Father and Son send the Spirit. Second, the Spirit anointing Christ depicts Christ's dual natures; as God, he sends the Spirit upon the human nature, and the human nature re-

---

[20] Sibbes, 'Description of Christ', *Works*, I, pp. 17-18. Cf. Sibbes, 'Description of Christ', *Works*, I, pp. 19-26. Veli-Matti Kärkkäinen aptly states, 'The implication of this Spirit Christology for us is that whatever the Father is doing in the life of the Son through the Spirit is being given to us in Christ through the Spirit'. Kärkkäinen (ed.), *Holy Spirit and Salvation*, p. 193. Cf. Sibbes, 'Excellency of the Gospel', *Works*, IV, p. 208. Sibbes incorrectly attributed this quotation to Jn 1.13; actually, the correct reference is Jn 1.16.

ceives the Spirit.[21] Third, the Spirit empowered all the deeds of Christ's human nature. Fourth, the Spirit's agency immediately affects humans, and the Spirit mediates God's presence to creatures; Christ functioning in the salvific role of mediator[22] receives the Spirit's anointing and bestows it upon believers. Christ, thereupon, now dwells among believers and empowers them through his Spirit, the Spirit of Christ.[23]

Sibbes' Spirit Christology supports a form of pneumatic mediation set within a trinitarian structure. Although Sibbes accentuates the *perichoresis* of the Father, Son, and Holy Spirit in essence and external operations, the Spirit is seen mediating the divine dance in the incarnation event: the Spirit forms and sanctifies Christ's human nature and functions as the grace of union of Christ's divine and human natures. The Spirit mediates Christ's life; the Spirit continues to infuse Christ's human nature with grace according to its development and context. The Spirit mediates Christ's salvific mission;

---

[21] This agrees with Sibbes' exposition of 2 Cor. 3.17-18:

> Now the Lord is that Spirit: and where the Spirit of the Lord is, there is liberty ... He sets down what Christ is by what he doth; Christ is 'that Spirit,' because he gives the Spirit ... *First*, He was 'that Spirit,' as *having the Holy Ghost in himself as man*. The Holy Ghost filled the human nature and made it spiritual. The Spirit is all in all in the human nature of Christ; and whatsoever he doth, he doth, as it were, being full of the Spirit, in himself. He gives the Spirit as God, and receives it as man' (Sibbes, 'Excellency of the Gospel', *Works*, IV, pp. 205-206).

[22] It appears that Sibbes was aware of the Socinian polemic against Christ's atoning death paying a debt of satisfaction and answered their objections: 'Some heretics that would shake the foundation of our faith, will grant Christ to be a *Mediator* to intercede for us, and a *Redeemer* to set us at liberty from slavery, &c., but *not* to be a *surety* to pay our debt, by way of satisfaction to God for us'. Sibbes, 'Christ's Sufferings for Man's Sin', *Works*, I, p. 357. Cf. Sibbes, 'Excellency of the Gospel', *Works*, IV, pp. 209-10; Sibbes, 'Purchased by His Humiliation', *Works*, V, p. 329.

[23] Sibbes, 'Description of Christ', *Works*, I, p. 22, writes:

> As we partake of his name, so we must also of his anointing. Thereupon we are called Christians, because we partake of the anointing and Spirit of Christ, and if we have the Spirit of Christ, it will work the same in us as it did in Christ ... The Spirit of Christ is a Spirit of power and strength. It will enable us to perform duties above nature, to overcome ourselves and injuries, it will make us to want and to abound, it will make us to live and to die, as it enabled Christ to do things that another man could not do.

Cf. Sibbes, 'The Art of Contentment', *Works*, V, pp. 182-83; Sibbes, 'A Fountain Sealed', *Works*, V, pp. 412-13, 486-87; Sibbes, 'Miracle of Miracles', *Works*, VII, pp. 110-11.

during the Jordan event, the Spirit's anointing commissions, inaugurates, and qualifies Christ for his ministry. In fact, what Christ did in his humanity he did by the Spirit, becoming a paradigm for believers' reception of the Spirit and Spirit empowered ministry. Sibbes, thus, integrates Logos Christology with his Spirit Christology of pneumatic mediation.

John Owen

John Owen was a Puritan pastor, statesman, and theologian. While serving as vicar at Coggeshall (1647), Owen gained the honor of preaching before Parliament and the House of Commons, which captured the attention of Oliver Cromwell. Through Cromwell's influence, the House of Commons appointed Owen dean of Christ's Church (1651), Oxford, and later vice-chancellor of the university (1652–57); also, for an ephemeral time he served in Parliament (1654).[24] Owen, accordingly, preached at many state functions, providing this Puritan pastor and statesman with an enormous amount of influence.

Owen, consequently, became one of the most eminent voices of Puritan theology, producing voluminous amounts of doctrinal, practical, and polemical publications.[25] With the introduction of Socinianism into England and prominence afforded Socinian doctrine in John Biddle's writings, controversy erupted. The Council of State forthwith commissioned Owen to refute Socinian doctrine; Owen responded by writing *Vindiciae Evangelicae* (1655). *Vindiciae* controverts three sources of Socinian thought: Biddle's *Two-Fold Catechism*, the *Racovian Catechism*, and certain exegetical annotations of Hugo Grotius. Owen structured the document so that it seriatim confuted

---

[24] John Owen (1616–83), after having received his education at Queen's College, Oxford, earning his BA (1632) and Master's degrees (1635), began his pastoral ministry in the parish of Fordham in Essex (1642). Later, he accepted the position of vicar at Coggeshall (1647). For information about Owen's life, see Andrew Thomson, 'Life of Owen', in William H. Goold (ed.), *The Works of John Owen* (16 vols.; London: Banner of Truth Trust, 1965), I, pp. xix-cxxii; Robert W. Oliver, 'John Owen: His Life and Times', in Robert W. Oliver (ed.), *John Owen: The Man and His Theology: Papers Read at the Conference of the John Owen Centre for Theological Study, September 2000* (Darlington: Evangelical Press, 2002), pp. 9-39; 'Owen, John', *ODCC*, p. 1203.

[25] Carl R. Trueman, 'John Owen as a Theologian', in Robert W. Oliver (ed.), *John Owen the Man and His Theology: Papers Read at the Conference of the John Owen Centre for Theological Study, September 2000* (Darlington: Evangelical Press, 2002), pp. 41-64.

Socinian doctrine by affirming trinitarian doctrine, Christ's deity, the hypostatic union of Christ's divine and human natures, the doctrine of original sin, Christ's substitutionary death in atonement for sins, election and predestination, and justification by grace through faith.[26] Several of Owen's doctrinal works oppose Socinian views; especially, Πνευματολογια and Χηριστολογια.[27] The former treatise sets forth a form of Spirit Christology.

Πνευματολογια is Owen's encyclopedic work regarding the Holy Spirit's deity, person, mission, operations, and effects. Πνευματολογια consists of several sequential publications[28] with one uniform design, uniting in one monograph, and it is structurally presented as five books. The context and occasion which prompted Owen to write this treatise was the growing contempt for the Holy Spirit among believers.[29] Owen, therefore, in book one takes aim at the Socinian rationalistic denial of the Spirit's deity; arguing from

---

[26] John Owen, 'Vindiciae Evangelicae, or the Mystery of the Gospel Vindicated and Socinianism Examined', *Works*, XII, pp. 1-590; Alan Spence, *Incarnation and Inspiration: John Owen and the Coherence of Christology* (London: T. & T. Clark, 2007), pp. 91-101, 141-42; Thomson, 'Life of Owen', *Works*, I, lxii-lxiv; Richard Daniels, *The Christology of John Owen* (Grand Rapids: Reformation Heritage Books, 2004), p. 33-34, 61; Sinclair B. Ferguson, 'John Owen and the Doctrine of the Person of Christ', in Robert W. Oliver (ed.), *John Owen: The Man and His Theology: Papers Read at the Conference of the John Owen Centre for Theological Study, September 2000* (Darlington: Evangelical Press, 2002), pp. 72, 74; Carl R. Trueman, 'John Owen's Dissertation on Divine Justice: An Exercise in Christocentric Scholasticism', *CTJ* 33 (1998), pp. 87-103.

[27] Χηριστολογια (1679) was Owen's most comprehensive christological treatise and was primarily directed against the opponents of the christological foundation of the church: Roman Catholics, Socinians, Arianism, Quakers, and Spiritualists. John Owen, 'Christologia, or a Declaration of the Glorious Mystery of the Person of Christ—God and Man', *Works*, I, pp. 1-272; Thomson, 'Life of Owen', *Works*, I, pp. xcix-c; Ferguson, 'Person of Christ', pp. 77-97; Daniels, *Christology*, pp. 66-71. For an overview of the theological context of Owen's christological writings, see Daniels, *Christology*, pp. 22-48.

[28] The work consists of six publications: *Owen on the Holy Spirit* (1674); *The Reason of Faith* (1677); *The Causes, Ways, and means of Understanding the Mind of God* (1678); *The Work of the Holy Spirit in Prayer* (1682); and *On the Work of the Holy as a Comforter* and *The Holy Spirit as the Author of Spiritual Gifts* were published posthumous (1693). John Owen, 'Pneumatologia, or a Discourse Concerning the Holy Spirit', *Works*, III, p. 2.

[29] According to Owen, it had become 'a matter of reproach and scorn for anyone to make mention of his grace, or to profess an interest in that work of his'. Owen, 'Pneumatologia', Preface, *Works*, III, p. 8. Cf. John Owen, *The Holy Spirit: His Gifts and Power* (2007 repr.; Fearn, Scotland: Christian Focus Publications, 2004), p. 32; Geoffrey F. Nuttall, *The Holy Spirit in Puritan Faith and Experience* (Chicago: University of Chicago Press, 1992), pp. 72-73.

Scripture and the writings of the ancient fathers,[30] he asserts the Spirit's deity, personhood, and divine operations (Πνευματολογια, 1.3).[31] Book two examines the Spirit's operations in the Hebrew Scriptures in preparation for the new creation, and he elucidates the Holy Spirit's agency in Christ as the head of the new creation. The last three books, respectively, explicate the Spirit's instrumentality in regeneration, sanctification, and the necessity of holiness in believers.[32]

The Spirit christological texts are located in Owen's dispute with the Socinians concerning the operations of the Holy Spirit in Christ's human nature. Although the Socinians conceded that Christ was conceived by the Holy Spirit, they argued this was not an incarnation of deity; neither the Holy Spirit nor Christ was divine. Christ was a human in a unique relationship with the Spirit, the impersonal presence and power of God available to all humans; he was called Son of God because of this relationship and the decree of God, but he did not preexist as the divine Son.[33] Therefore, mocking those holding incarnational and trinitarian views, the Socinians assert: if Christ's human nature exists in hypostatic union with the divine Son, there is no need for the operations of the Spirit in Christ's

---

[30] Regarding Owen's view of scriptural authority, theological method, and sources of theology, see Daniels, *Christology*, pp. 78-93. Cf. Barry H. Howson, 'The Puritan Hermeneutics of John Owen: A Recommendation', *WTJ* 63 (2001), pp. 351-76.

[31] Cf. Owen, *Holy Spirit*, pp. 39-54. After examining the promises regarding spiritual gifts, Owen also warns the Spirituals of their scriptural excesses; furthermore, he puts the Quakers on guard concerning their mystical teaching of the inner light, that it is inconsistent with the Spirit's claims (Πνευματολογια, 1.1; Preface, *Works*, III, pp. 2-3). Cf. Owen, *Holy Spirit*, pp. 39-54; Spence, *Incarnation and Inspiration*, pp. 43-50; Nuttall, *The Holy Spirit*, pp. 28-31; Michael A.G. Haykin, 'John Owen and the Challenges of the Quakers', in Robert W. Oliver (ed.), *John Owen: The Man and His Theology: Papers Read at the Conference of the John Owen Centre for Theological Study, September 2000* (Darlington: Evangelical Press, 2002), pp. 131-49; David J. McKinley, 'John Owen's View of Illumination: An Alternative to the Fuller-Erickson Dialogue', *BSac* 154 (1997), pp. 96-102.

[32] Regarding the document's date, occasion, purpose, and structure, see Owen, 'Pneumatologia', *Works*, III, pp. 2-14; Owen, *Holy Spirit*, pp. 29-38.

[33] Faustus Socinus, 'Epitome of a Colloquium Held in Raków in the Year 1601', in George Huntston Williams (ed.) *The Polish Brethren: Documentation of the History and Thought of Unitarianism in the Polish-Lithuanian Commonwealth and in the Diaspora, 1601–85* (trans. George Huntston Williams; 2 vols.; Missoula, MT: Scholars Press, 1980), pp. 90-95. For an examination of Owen's defense of Christ's deity, see Daniels, *Christology*, pp. 117-45.

human nature because the divine person of the Son can perform all requisite operations (Πνευματολογια, 2.3).

In rebuttal, Owen begins by affirming that the one substance of God, the principium of all divine operations, is undivided, so the external operations of God are indivisible, yet owing to the subsistent relations of the Father, Son, and Holy Spirit, distinct operations are ascribed to them in the incarnation (Πνευματολογια, 2.3).[34]

> The *framing, forming, and miraculous conception of the body of Christ in the womb of the blessed Virgin* was the peculiar and especial work of the Holy Ghost. This work; I acknowledge, in respect of *designation*, and the authoritative disposal of things, is ascribed to the Father ... As to *voluntary assumption*, it is ascribed to the Son himself ... he took upon him a body and soul, and entire human nature ... But the immediate divine *efficiency* in this matter was the peculiar work of the Holy Ghost.[35]

> This act of the Holy Ghost, in *forming the body of Christ*, differs from the act of the Son in *assuming* the human nature into personal union with himself: for this act of the Son was not a creating act ... but it was an ineffable act of love and wisdom, taking the nature so formed by the Holy Ghost, so prepared for him, to be his own in the instant of its formation ... It hence follows that the conception of Christ in the *womb*, being the effect of a *creating act*, was not accomplished *successively* and in the process of time, but it was perfected in an *instant*.[36]

So, Owen attested to triune operations in the incarnation. Owen, moreover, carefully repudiated any suggestion that Christ can be called the Spirit's Son;[37] the Son exists in an eternal filial relationship with the Father who sent the Son. Creating and assuming constitute distinct acts; nevertheless, disallowing any separation in time, Owen

---

[34] Cf. Spence, *Incarnation and Inspiration*, pp. 124-29. For an overview of Owen's trinitarian doctrine, see Daniels, *Christology*, pp. 94-115.

[35] Owen, 'Pneumatologia', *Works*, III, 2.3, pp. 162-63. Cf. Owen, *Holy Spirit*, pp. 115-17; Spence, *Incarnation and Inspiration*, pp. 55-56, 129-31; Ferguson, 'Person of Christ', pp. 88-91; Daniels, *Christology*, pp. 267-73.

[36] Owen, 'Pneumatologia', *Works*, III, 2.3, p. 165. Cf. Owen, *Holy Spirit*, pp. 117-19; Spence, *Incarnation and Inspiration*, pp. 54-56.

[37] 'The Lord Jesus Christ could not on this account, no, not with respect unto his human nature only, be said to be the *Son of the Holy Ghost*.' Owen, 'Pneumatologia', *Works*, III, 2.3, p. 164.

posited that, in the same instant of conception, the Holy Spirit created the human nature, and the Son assumed the human body and soul into hypostatic union with himself. Against the Socinians, therefore, Owen asserts the Holy Spirit's deity, Christ's divine nature, the hypostatic union, and the Spirit's distinct operation in Christ's human nature apart from the divine Son. In this external trinitarian operation, the incarnation, the Spirit was the immediate efficient cause.

Owen, then, addresses the issues of Christ's bodily substance and his sinlessness.[38]

> The human nature of Christ being thus formed in the womb by a *creating act* of the Holy Spirit, was in the instant of conception *sanctified*, and filled with grace according to the measure of its receptivity ... And this work of sanctification, or the original infusion of all grace into the human nature of Christ, was the immediate work of the Holy Spirit; which was necessary unto him: for let the natural faculties of the soul, the mind, will, and affections, be created pure, innocent, undefiled.[39]

Several conclusions can be drawn out of these texts. First, Christ possessed a true human nature, body and soul, which the Holy Spirit formed from Mary's substance. Second, Owen attributes Christ's sinlessness to the Spirit's direct operation, in the original infusion of grace sanctifying Christ's human nature in the instance of concept

---

[38] In the creation of Christ's human body the Holy Spirit functions as the active efficient cause operating on Mary's passive humanity, forming Christ's body from her substance: 'such was this act of the Holy Ghost in forming the body of our Lord Jesus Christ; for although it was effected by an act of infinite creating power, yet it was formed or made of the substance of the blessed Virgin'. Owen, 'Pneumatologia', *Works*, III, 2.3, p. 164.

[39] Owen, 'Pneumatologia', *Works*, III, 2.4, p. 168.

> From this miraculous creation of the *body of Christ*, by the immediate power of the Holy Ghost, did it become a *meet habitation* for his holy soul, every way ready and complying with all actings of grace and virtue ... But the body of Christ being formed pure and exact by the Holy Ghost, there was no disposition or tendency in his constitution to the least deviation from perfect holiness (Owen, 'Pneumatologia', *Works*, III, 2.3, p. 167).

Cf. Owen, *Holy Spirit*, p. 120; John Owen, 'Communion with God the Father, Son, and Holy Ghost, Each Person Distinctly, in Love, Grace, and Consolation', *Works*, II, pp. 63-66; John Owen, *Communion with the Triune God* (Wheaton, IL: Crossway Books, 2007), pp. 164-67; Spence, *Incarnation and Inspiration*, p. 56; Daniels, *Christology*, pp. 286-88.

tion; the Spirit is the agent of Christ's sinless humanity. Third, the Spirit completely filled Christ's human nature with grace according to its receptivity, indicating a greater capacity for receiving grace as Christ's humanity grew and developed.

Owen, next, attempts to answer the Socinian criticism regarding the need of the Spirit's operation in Christ's human nature if it exists in hypostatic union with deity.

> His divine nature was not unto him in the place of a soul, nor did immediately operate the things which he performed, as some of old vainly imagined; but being a perfect man, his rational soul was in him the immediate principle of all his moral operations, even as ours are in us. Now, in the improvement and exercise of these faculties and powers of his soul, he had and made a progress after the manner of other men; for he was made like unto us 'in all things,' yet without sin. In their increase, enlargement, and exercise, there was required a progression in grace also ... And this growth in grace and wisdom was the peculiar work of the Holy Spirit; for as the faculties of his mind were enlarged by degrees and strengthened, so the Holy Spirit filled them up with grace for actual obedience.[40]

In answering the Socinian query, Owen, therefore, distinguishes between Christ's divine nature and human nature in the one person of Christ. Neither did the divine nature supplant Christ's rational human soul, nor were the operations of deity intrinsically communicated to the human nature; they were voluntary.[41] Owen, consequently, affirmed that Christ possessed a true human nature subject

---

[40] Owen, 'Pneumatologia', *Works*, III, 2.4, pp. 169-70. Cf. Owen, *Holy Spirit*, p. 121; Owen, 'Communion with God', *Works*, II, 2.3, Digression 1, pp. 66-68; Owen, *Communion with the Triune God*, pp. 167-82; Spence, *Incarnation and Inspiration*, p. 57; Daniels, *Christology*, pp. 295-97.

[41] Owen, 'Pneumatologia', *Works*, III, 2.3, p. 161, writes:

> That all the actings of God in the *person of the Son* towards the human nature were *voluntary*, and did not necessarily ensue on the union mentioned; for there was no transfusion of the properties of one nature into the other, nor real physical communication of divine essential excellencies unto the humanity.

Cf. Owen, 'Communion with God', *Works*, II, 2.2, pp. 51-52; Owen, *Communion with the Triune God*, pp. 148-49 Owen's most comprehensive discussion of the hypostatic union is found in Owen, 'Christologia', *Works*, I, 18, pp. 223-35. Cf. Daniels, *Christology*, pp. 273-86.

to passion, temptation, and ignorance, so the human nature needed the Spirit's infusion of grace. Christ's humanity, furthermore, was capable of growth in rational faculties and experientially learning obedience through the things he suffered like any other human; accordingly, as the human nature progressively developed, it needed the Spirit's immediate infusion of grace.[42]

In point of fact, the Spirit's grace was requisite for Christ's human nature to execute its role in the salvific mission. According to Owen, Christ sparingly exercised the office of king, and performed the role of priest only at the cross, but his entire life and ministry was given to discharging the prophetic office (Πνευματολογια, 2.4).

> The Holy Spirit, in a peculiar manner, anointed him with all those *extraordinary powers and gifts* which were necessary for the exercise and discharging of his office on the earth ... Hereunto was he fitted by this unction of the Spirit. And here, also, is a distinction between the 'Spirit that was upon him,' and his being 'anointed to preach,' which contains the communication of the gifts of that Spirit unto him ... And this collation of extraordinary gifts for the discharge of his prophetical office was at his baptism ... The fullness of gifts for his work he received not until the time of his baptism, and, therefore, before that he gave not himself up wholly unto his public ministry.[43]

> It was in an especial manner by the power of the Holy Spirit he wrought those great and *miraculous works* whereby his ministry was attested unto and confirmed.[44]

---

[42] Owen, 'Pneumatologia', *Works*, III, 2.4, p. 170, writes:

> He 'learned obedience by the things he suffered,' Heb. 5.8. In the representation, then, of things anew to the human nature of Christ, the wisdom and knowledge of it was *objectively* increased, and in new trials and temptations he *experimentally* learned the new exercise of grace. And this was the constant work of the Holy Spirit in the human nature of Christ.'

Cf. Owen, *Holy Spirit*, pp. 121-22. It should be noted that Puritans, including Owen, give place for experience in their exposition. Nuttall, *The Holy Spirit*, pp. 7-8.

[43] Owen, 'Pneumatologia', *Works*, III, 2.4, pp. 171-72. Cf. Owen, *Holy Spirit*, p. 123; Spence, *Incarnation and Inspiration*, p. 57; Daniels, *Christology*, pp. 298-99.

[44] Owen, 'Pneumatologia', *Works*, III, 2.4, p. 174. Cf. Owen, *Holy Spirit*, p. 124; Spence, *Incarnation and Inspiration*, p. 57; Daniels, *Christology*, pp. 299-300.

> Now, all the voluntary communications of the divine nature unto the human were, as we have showed, by the Holy Spirit.[45]

Several important inferences can be drawn from these texts regarding the Spirit's anointing. First, Owen's distinction between Christ's human and divine natures allowed space for the human nature to receive the Spirit's anointing. Second, the Spirit anointing Christ's human nature during the Jordan event was a significant turning point in Christ's life: it commissioned and initiated him into public ministry. Third, Owen discriminated between the Spirit's antecedent sanctifying infusion of grace and the Spirit's anointing which the human nature received during the Jordan event; it was an endowment of spiritual gifts and power for prophetic ministry.[46] Fourth, the Spirit's anointing empowered Christ's human nature to work miracles, confirming Christ's ministry.[47] Fifth, Owen insisted the Holy Spirit mediated these voluntary communications of divine properties from Christ's divine nature to the human nature. So, the Spirit supported Christ's entire ministry: through the Spirit Christ offered himself as a sacrifice; the Spirit preserved Christ's corpse from corruption in death, resurrected Christ, and glorified Christ's human nature; after Christ's ascension, the Spirit has salvifically returned to bear witness unto Christ, reveal Christ, serve as the vicar of Christ on earth, and to regenerate and anoint believers.[48]

---

[45] Owen, 'Pneumatologia', *Works*, III, 2.4, p. 175. Cf. Owen, *Holy Spirit*, p. 124.

[46] 'Our Lord Jesus Christ, as the foundation of his church, was anointed with all the gifts and graces of the Spirit in their perfection.' Owen, 'Pneumatologia', *Works*, III, 1.5, p. 123. Cf. Owen, *Holy Spirit*, p. 91.

[47] Owen, 'Pneumatologia', *Works*, III, 2.1, p. 145, writes:

> Now, these were all the *immediate effects* of the divine power of the Holy Ghost. He is the sole author of all real miraculous operations ... Now, it is said expressly that our Lord Jesus Christ wrought miracles (for instance, the casting out of devils from persons possessed) by the Holy Ghost; and if their immediate production were by him in the human nature of Jesus Christ, personally united unto the Son of God, how much more must it be granted that it was he alone by whose power they were wrought in those who had no such relation unto the divine nature!

Cf. Owen, *Holy Spirit*, pp. 103-104.

[48] For information about these assertions, see Owen, 'Pneumatologia', *Works*, III, 2.4–3.1, pp. 174-228. Cf. Owen, *Holy Spirit*, pp. 123-60, 366-75; Owen, 'Communion with God', *Works*, II, 2.3, Digression 1, pp. 68-69; Owen, *Communion with the Triune God*, pp. 170-82; Spence, *Incarnation and Inspiration*, pp. 57-59.

Like Sibbes and certain other Puritan theologians, Owen posited a Spirit christological paradigm of pneumatic mediation which enclosed an incarnational Logos Christology set within a trinitarian framework.[49] The Socinians were strict monotheists desiring to return to the apostolic age before layers of tradition and superstition – the ecumenical councils that had decreed the incarnation, trinitarian doctrine, and the hypostatic union of divine and human natures normative standards of orthodoxy – had buried the christological truth that Christ was a human existing in a unique relationship with the impersonal power of God, the Holy Spirit. In order to refute Socinian Christology and its implications for triune doctrine and soteriology, Owen retrieved a Spirit christological paradigm of pneumatic mediation, antecedently existing within the Spirit christological traditions of both East and West, congruously fitting within the circumscribed boundaries of Chalcedon's christological confession.[50]

---

[49] For similar Spirit christological texts among other Puritan theologians, see Thomas Goodwin, 'Christ the Mediator', *The Works of Thomas Goodwin* (14 vols.; Grand Rapids: Reformation Heritage Books, 2006 repr.: James Nichol, 1861-1866), V, 2.7, pp. 59-60; Thomas Goodwin, 'The Work of the Holy Ghost in Our Salvation', *The Works of Thomas Goodwin*, VI, 1.3, pp. 11-13; Jonathan Edwards, 'A History of the Work of Redemption ', in John F. Wilson (ed.), *Works of Jonathan Edwards* (23 vols.; New Haven: Yale University Press, 1989), IX, 7, pp. 204-205, 210-11; IX, 8, p. 221; IX, 14, p. 297; IX, 15, pp. 315-18; IX, 20, p. 375.

[50] As the title of Alan Spence's book indicates, his thesis is that Owen's Christology reaches a synthesis of the two disparate christological paradigms of inspiration and incarnation. Spence, *Incarnation and Inspiration*, pp. 1-16, 138-54. By a Christology of inspiration Spence means 'the interpretation of Christ as a person in whom God has acted graciously through his Spirit, comforting and strengthening him in his spiritual life, equipping and empowering him in his mission'. Spence, *Incarnation and Inspiration*, p. 4. Instead of identifying this as a form of Spirit Christology, Spence provides a cursory overview of Spirit Christology – including Ignatius, Second Clement, and Justin Martyr – and distinguishes Spirit Christology from his concept of Christology of inspiration, concluding that Spirit 'christologies, although using the word "Spirit" are clearly incarnational, and show no awareness of Jesus' dependence in his life and ministry on God's empowering through his Spirit'. Spence has failed to see the fluid nature of Spirit Christology which provides paradigms of pneumatic incarnation, pneumatic mediation, as well as pneumatic inspiration; also, he has failed to see the historical development of Spirit Christology. For Spence's assessment of the coherence between Owen's Christology and Chalcedon, see Spence, *Incarnation and Inspiration*, pp. 144-49.

The Protestant Tradition of Liberal Self-Criticism

This tradition originated in the ethos of Enlightenment rationalism and seemed to flow from the emergence of Cartesianism in continental Europe and Deism among the Anglicans in England during the late seventeenth century. Deism, essentially, endeavored to establish a natural religion based on human reason and universally held axiomatic religious notions.[51] Methodologically, they selectively pared away any doctrine which did not agree with their schema of natural religion, reducing Christianity to just a few doctrines which divinely sanction morality; accordingly, the doctrines of the Trinity, divine revelation, and incarnation were considered unreasonable among Deists.[52]

Indubitably, the most censorious trimming of christological doctrine came from the knife of Germany's most eminent Deist, Hermann Samuel Reimarus.[53] According to Reimarus' historical analy-

---

[51] Deist theology begins with the presupposition, 'Nothing should be accepted as true by an intelligent being, such as man, unless it is grounded in the nature of things and is in harmony with right reason'. Samuel Gring Hefelbower, *The Relation of John Locke to English Deism* (Chicago: The University of Chicago Press, 1918), p. 117. Cf. Grenz and Olson, *20th Century Theology*, pp. 18-23; Olson, *Christian Theology*, pp. 519-23; González, *Christian Thought*, III, pp. 335-36. For similarities and distinctions between the Socinians and the Deists, see Gerard Reedy, 'Socinians, John Toland, and the Anglican Rationalists', *HTR* 70 (1977), pp. 285-304; Walker, *History*, pp. 494-95.

[52] The precursors to English Deism were Lord Herbert of Cherbury (*De Veritate*, 1624), John Tillotson, and John Locke (*An Essay Concerning Human Understanding*, 1690). It is important to note that these precursors prepared the ground for Deism, but they still retained a place for divine revelation to explain and affirm those Christian doctrines which were beyond reason and the nature of things. John Toland's (*Christianity Not Mysterious*, 1696) and Matthew Tindal's (*Christianity as Old as the Creation*, 1730) writings, however, do represent this description of English Deism, and Voltaire's writings depict French Deism (*Sermon of the Fifty*, 1751). For overviews of their writings and teachings, see Livingston, *Modern Christian Thought*, I, pp. 14-28; Olson, *Christian Theology*, pp. 519-32; González, *Christian Thought*, III, pp. 332-37; 'Deism', *ODCC*, p. 465. For an overview of the religious context as it relates to the Enlightenment and rationalism, see Claude Welch, *Protestant Thought in the Nineteenth Century* (2 vols.; New Haven: Yale University Press, 1972), I, pp. 30-41; Karl Barth, *Protestant Thought: From Rousseau to Ritschl; Being the Translation of Eleven Chapters of Die Protestantische Theologie Im 19. Jahrhundert* (trans. Brian Cozens; New York: Simon and Schuster, 1969), pp. 11-57; Walker, *History*, pp. 483-94, 524-29.

[53] Hermann Reimarus (1694–1768) was educated at the University of Jena, where he studied theology, philosophy, and ancient languages (1714–16). After graduating, he taught philosophy at Wittemberg (1716–23). While studying abroad in England and Holland, he became acquainted with Deism (1720–21).

sis:[54] (1) Jesus failed in his messianic mission and died in disillusionment and defeat;[55] (2) Christ's resurrection was a hoax perpetuated by his disciples to shift Jewish messianic expectations to a revised gospel of Jesus' redemptive suffering, resurrection, ascension, and immanent return to establish the Kingdom of God;[56] (3) The delay of the Parousia, subsequently, forced further theological revi-

---

Subsequently, he served as Rector at Wismar (1723–27), and, in 1727, Reimarus became professor of Hebrew and oriental languages at Hamburg, where he spent the rest of his academic career. For overviews of Reimarus' life and context, see H.S. Reimarus, *Fragments from Reimarus: Consisting of Brief Critical Remarks on the Object of Jesus and His Disciples as Seen in the New Testament* (trans. G.E. Lessing; London: Williams and Norgate, 1879), pp. 1-4; Robert B. Strimple, *The Modern Search for the Real Jesus: An Introductory Survey of the Historical Roots of Gospels Criticism* (Philipsburg, NJ: P&R Publishing, 1995), p. 16.

[54] In his *Wolffenbüttel Fragments* (1774–78), precisely, the seventh fragment, *On the Intentions of Jesus and His Disciples*, Reimarus explicates Christian origins and focuses on Christology. Reimarus composed the original 4,000 page manuscript, entitled *An Apology for the Rational Worshippers of God*, between 1744 and 1767, but, because it was so controversial, he refused to have it published during his life time. On the condition that the author's name would remain anonymous, Reimarus' daughter granted Lessing permission to publish it, so Lessing issued only fragments of the immense manuscript. Reimarus, *Fragments*, pp. 4-6; Livingston, *Modern Christian Thought*, I, p. 30; 'Reimarus, Hermann Samuel', *ODCC*, p. 1378; Walker, *History*, pp. 526-27.

[55] Reimarus, *Fragments*, pp. 9-28; Albert Schweitzer, *The Quest of the Historical Jesus: A Critical Study of Its Progress from Reimarus to Wrede* (trans. W. Montgomery; New York: MacMillan, 1948), pp. 16-18. Reimarus placed Jesus' ministry in the context of Jewish messianic eschatology, which implied a political redemption, consisting of a prophetic Messiah delivering Israel from foreign subjugation. According to Albert Schweitzer, 'His work is perhaps the most splendid achievement in the whole course of the historical investigation of the life of Jesus, for he was the first to grasp the fact that the world of thought in which Jesus moved was essentially eschatological'. Schweitzer, *The Quest of the Historical Jesus*, p. 23.

[56] Reimarus, *Fragments*, pp. 28-47. Schweitzer's critique of Reimarus asserts that Reimarus made a mistake in assuming

> that the eschatology was earthly and political in character ... He recognized that two systems of Messianic expectation were present side by side in Late Judaism. He endeavored to bring them into mutual relations in order to represent the actual movement of the history. In so doing he made the mistake of placing them in consecutive order, ascribing to Jesus the political Son-of-David conception, and to the Apostles, after His death, the apocalyptic system based on Daniel, instead of superimposing one upon the other in such a way that the Messianic King might coincide with the Son of Man, and the ancient prophetic conception might be inscribed within the circumference of the Daniel-descended apocalyptic, and raised along with it to the supersensuous plane (Schweitzer, *The Quest of the Historical Jesus*, pp. 23-24).

sions by the early Christian community.⁵⁷ Reimarus, therefore, posited a distinction between the reality of the historical person of the human Jesus and the fabrication of apostolic memory depicting him as the incarnate divine Son of God.⁵⁸ Subsequently, numerous and various attempts to reconstruct the life of Jesus followed.⁵⁹

By the end of the eighteenth century, Enlightenment rationalism caused much disillusionment, giving rise to two movements critical of rationalism: empiricism and romanticism. Whereas rationalism, epistemologically, denigrates experience and asserts that innate ideas, which structure knowledge of the world, are present in the human mind and accessible to reason, empiricism insists on the precedence of experience over innate knowledge: the human mind is a blank slate on which only experience writes, for humans gain knowledge of the world through observation and reflection.⁶⁰ Ro-

---

⁵⁷ Reimarus, *Fragments*, pp. 48-68. Schweitzer, *The Quest of the Historical Jesus*, pp. 18-22; Livingston, *Modern Christian Thought*, I, pp. 30-31; Strimple, *The Modern Search for the Real Jesus*, pp. 17-19.

⁵⁸ Reimarus, *Fragments*, pp. 69-119. Cf. McGrath, *German Christology*, pp. 33-35; Hans W. Frei, *The Eclipse of Biblical Narrative: A Study in Eighteenth and Nineteenth Century Hermeneutics* (New Haven: Yale University Press, 1974), pp. 114-16, 261; Pelikan, *Christian Tradition*, V, pp. 29, 94-94, 112-14, 225-26.

⁵⁹ For overviews of the quest for the historical Jesus, see Schweitzer, *The Quest of the Historical Jesus*; Warren S. Kissinger, *The Lives of Jesus: A History and Bibliography* (Garland Reference Library of the Humanities; New York: Garland, 1985); Craig A. Evans, *Life of Jesus Research: An Annotated Bibliography* (NTTS 13; Leiden: E.J. Brill, 1989); Carl E. Braaten and Roy A. Harrisville, *The Historical Jesus and the Kerygmatic Christ: Essays on the New Quest of the Historical Jesus* (New York: Abingdon Press, 1964); N.T. Wright, 'Jesus, Quest for the Historical ', *ABD*, III, pp. 796-802; McGrath, *German Christology*, pp. 27-28; 'Historical Jesus, Quest of The', *ODCC*, p. 775.

⁶⁰ Responding to this epistemological discussion in his *Critique of Pure Reason* (1781), Immanuel Kant asserted that the mind is not a passive receptor, but a priori cognitive categories function as grids to organize and interpret sensory experiences, so that reason and experience operate in a dynamic reciprocal synthesis producing understanding. Livingston, *Modern Christian Thought*, I, pp. 18-21, 49-60; González, *Christian Thought*, III, pp. 318-41; Frederick C. Copleston, *A History of Philosophy* (9 vols.; New York: Doubleday, Image Books edn, 1994), V, pp. 67-142, 258-341; VI, pp. 211-34; Welch, *Protestant Thought*, I, pp. 42-48; John Elbert Wilson, *Introduction to Modern Theology: Trajectories in the German Tradition* (Louisville: Westminster / John Knox Press, 2007), pp. 27-31; McGrath, *German Christology*, pp. 36-38; Barth, *Protestant Thought*, pp. 150-59; Grenz and Olson, *20th Century Theology*, pp. 25-28; Walker, *History*, pp. 529-31; Frei, *The Eclipse of Biblical Narrative*, pp. 283, 323; Pelikan, *Christian Tradition*, V, p. 117; Immanuel Kant, 'The Critique of Pure Reason', GBWW, XXXIX, pp. 1-250. Of course, metaphysical truths, such as God's existence, are not matters of experience and must be known another way. Kant, accordingly, in his *Critique of Practical Reason* (1788)

manticism, however, proposed a much broader and diversified experience than either rationalism or empiricism offered. Contending that reason could not penetrate into all spheres of reality, it appealed to human imagination and allowed space for mystery in religion; moreover, an infinite Spirit immanently and dynamically worked in all things, so Romanticism affirmed a 'feeling' or 'sentiment' (*das Gefühl*) which prompted in an individual an awareness of their own subjectivity and oriented them toward communion with this divine Spirit.[61]

Friedrich Schleiermacher

Friedrich Schleiermacher was a prominent proponent of Romanticism.[62] In his publication *On Religion: Speeches to its Cultured Despisers*

---

posited that knowledge of God's existence is a postulate of moral reason drawn from certain a priori moral propositions. Immanuel Kant, 'The Critique of Practical Reason', GBWW, XXXIX, p. 345. Cf. Kant, 'The Critique of Pratical Reason', GBWW, XXXIX, pp. 289-361; Livingston, *Modern Christian Thought*, I, pp. 60-64; González, *Christian Thought*, III, pp. 342-44; Wilson, *Modern Theology*, pp. 31-37; Barth, *Protestant Thought*, pp. 159-96; Grenz and Olson, *20th Century Theology*, pp. 28-31; Walker, *History*, p. 531; Pelikan, *Christian Tradition*, V, p. 118. True theology, then, is moral theology; the human moral conscience, knowledge of God, and moral duty imply one another and coalesce in Kant.

[61] Livingston, *Modern Christian Thought*, I, pp. 83-93; Welch, *Protestant Thought*, I, pp. 52-55; McGrath, *German Christology*, pp. 38-41. Representatives of Romanticism include Friedrich Schlegel, Novalis, and Samuel Taylor Coleridge.

[62] Friedrich Schleiermacher (1768–1834) was born in Breslau, in contemporary times it is Wroclaw in southern Poland. After being placed by his parents in a Moravian school at Niesky (1783), his mother died and his father's duties as chaplain in the Prussian army kept him away from his son, so Friedrich and his sister were essentially reared in the communal atmosphere of the Moravians during his adolescence years. Schleiermacher began his theological training at the Moravian theological seminary at Barby (1785–87); then, he furthered his education at Halle (1787–90) where he intensely studied Kant's philosophy. After working as a tutor (1790–94), Schleiermacher served as assistant pastor of a Reformed congregation at Landsberg in Brandenburg (1794–96). He moved to Berlin (1796) to become chaplain at its principle hospital; here, he became acquainted with the leaders of the German movement of Romanticism. Finally, he served as professor at Halle (1804–1809), lecturing on philosophy, systematic theology, ethics, NT exegesis, and hermeneutics. After Napoleon took Jena in 1806, he returned to Berlin (1807), where he married and became minister at Trinity Church (1809). Later, he was appointed to the chair of theology and the first dean of the theological faculty of the University of Berlin (1810) and Rector of the University (1815). For overviews of Schleiermacher's life and context, see Friedrich Schleiermacher and Keith Clements, *Friedrich Schleiermacher: Pioneer of Modern Theology* (The Making of Modern Theology; Minneapolis: Fortress Press, 1991 repr.; London: Collins, 1987), pp. 7-34; Terrence N. Tice, *Schleiermacher* (Abingdon Pillars of Theology; Nashville: Abingdon, 2006), pp. 1-17; Stephen

(1799), Schleiermacher argued that the essence of piety is neither rational nor moral.[63] Furthermore, the essence of the Christian religion was not a system of dogmas or creeds; rather, the starting point of theology was *das Gefühl*: the immediate self-consciousness and absolute dependence on the infinite God, given in a world of relatedness.[64]

Schleiermacher explicates what this means in relation to Christology in his systematic theology of Christian doctrine, *The Christian Faith* (1821–22).[65] The lineaments of Schleiermacher's systematic

---

Sykes, *Friedrich Schleiermacher* (Richmond, VA: John Knox Press, 1971), pp. 1-15; Martin Redeker, *Schleiermacher: Life and Thought* (trans. John Wallhausser; Philadelphia: Fortress Press, 1973), pp. 6-100, 187-213; Livingston, *Modern Christian Thought*, I, pp. 93-94; Grenz and Olson, *20th Century Theology*, pp. 40-43; McGrath, *German Christology*, p. 41; Catherine L. Kelsey, *Thinking About Christ with Schleiermacher* (Louisville: Westminster John Knox Press, 2003), pp. 23-29; Olson, *Christian Theology*, pp. 542-43; Walker, *History*, pp. 532-33. For overviews and examinations of his theology, see Karl Barth, *The Theology of Schleiermacher: Lectures at Göttingen, Winter Wemester of 1923/24* (trans. Geoffrey W. Bromiley; Grand Rapids: Eerdmans, 1982); Barth, *Protestant Thought*, pp. 306-54; Sykes, *Friedrich Schleiermacher*, pp. 16-51; Tice, *Schleiermacher*, pp. 32-46; Redeker, *Schleiermacher*, pp. 100-74; Walker, *History*, pp. 533-34.

[63] Welch, *Protestant Thought*, I, pp. 62-64. For a discussion of Schleiermacher's hermeneutic of understanding, see Richard E. Palmer, *Hermeneutics: Interpretation Theory in Schleiermacher, Dilthey, Heidegger, and Gadamer* (Northwestern University Studies in Phenomenology & Existential Philosophy; Evanston: Northwestern University Press, 1969), pp. 84-97; Frei, *The Eclipse of Biblical Narrative*, pp. 290-324; Redeker, *Schleiermacher*, pp. 174-80; Wilson, *Modern Theology*, pp. 85-87; González, *Christian Thought*, III, pp. 348-49.

[64] 'The contemplation of the pious is the immediate consciousness of the universal existence of all finite things, in and through the Infinite, and of all temporal things in and through the Eternal ... True religion is sense and taste for the Infinite.' Cited according to the translation of John Oman, Friedrich Schleiermacher, *On Religion: Speeches to Its Cultured Despisers* (trans. John Oman; Louisville, KY: Westminster/John Knox Press, translated from 3rd German edn, 1994), pp. 36, 39. Cf. Schleiermacher, *On Religion*, pp. 1-21, 26-101, 147-80; Schleiermacher and Clements, *Friedrich Schleiermacher*, pp. 36-40, 66-99; Livingston, *Modern Christian Thought*, I, pp. 94-100; Welch, *Protestant Thought*, I, pp. 64-68; McGrath, *German Christology*, p. 41; Copleston, *A History of Philosophy*, VII, pp. 151-58; Wilson, *Modern Theology*, pp. 46-48; Badcock, *Light of Truth and Fire of Love*, pp. 112-13; Grenz and Olson, *20th Century Theology*, pp. 43-46; Pelikan, *Christian Tradition*, V, pp. 172-74; Olson, *Christian Theology*, pp. 543-44.

[65] Schleiermacher also delineates his christological concepts in *The Life of Christ* (1832); however, the focus will be on *The Christian Faith*, and appropriate references from *The Life of Christ* will be noted. Schleiermacher produced numerous sermons, letters, and theological works, including his *Brief Outline of the Study of Theology* (1810) and *Christmas Eve: Dialogue on the Incarnation* (1826). For overviews of his writings, see Schleiermacher and Clements, *Friedrich Schleiermacher* and Jack

theology arise from the foundation of piety, and he structures *The Christian Faith* according to various levels of human self-consciousness.[66] Religious self-consciousness and feeling of dependence tends toward communion with others; this innate human need for fellowship has accounted for various religions, of which monotheism is the purest form of religion.[67] Schleiermacher, hence, delineates an unambiguous distinction between Christianity and other religions: Christ's redemptive life and mission is the central premise of Christianity.[68] Christianity, thus, is uniquely a community of redemptive fellowship.[69] Schleiermacher's theology, consequently, is christocentric: everything centers around and stems from the person and work of Christ.

Regarding the person of Christ, Schleiermacher attempts to reconstruct the doctrine of two natures in Christ. Schleiermacher asserts that the idea of two natures in one person is untenable and cannot be proved by the New Testament; furthermore, interjecting the triune doctrine of distinction in unity of essence does not clarify

---

Verheyden's introduction to Friedrich Schleiermacher, *The Life of Jesus* (Lives of Jesus Series; Philadelphia: Fortress Press, Gilmour, Jack C. edn, 1975), pp. xi-lx.

[66] 'The self-identical essence of piety is this: the consciousness of being absolutely dependent, or, which is the same thing, of being in relation with God.' Cited according to the translation of H.R. Mackintosh and J.S. Stweart, Friedrich Schleiermacher, *The Christian Faith* (trans. H.R. Mackintosh and J.S. Stweart; Berkeley, CA: Apocryphile Press, 2011), p. 12. Cf. Welch, *Protestant Thought*, I, pp. 68-73; Veli-Matti Kärkkäinen, *Pneumatology: The Holy Spirit in Ecumenical, International, and Contextual Perspective* (Grand Rapids: Baker Academic, 2002), pp. 62-63; Badcock, *Light of Truth and Fire of Love*, pp. 113-14; González, *Christian Thought*, III, pp. 350-55; Wilson, *Modern Theology*, pp. 87-89; Olson, *Christian Theology*, pp. 544-45.

[67] Schleiermacher, *The Christian Faith*, pp. 26-52. Cf. Schleiermacher and Clements, *Friedrich Schleiermacher*, pp. 40-42, 99-107; Welch, *Protestant Thought*, I, pp. 73-76; McGrath, *German Christology*, pp. 41-42; González, *Christian Thought*, III, p. 351.

[68] 'Christianity is a monotheistic faith, belonging to the teleological type of religion, and is essentially distinguished from other such faiths by the fact that in it everything is related to the redemption accomplished by Jesus of Nazareth.' Schleiermacher, *The Christian Faith*, p. 52. Cf. Schleiermacher and Clements, *Friedrich Schleiermacher*, pp. 40-42, 108-15; McGrath, *German Christology*, pp. 42-43; Schweitzer, *The Quest of the Historical Jesus*, pp. 64-67; Kelsey, *Thinking About Christ with Schleiermacher*, pp. 14-15, 31-36; Wilson, *Modern Theology*, pp. 90-91.

[69] 'There is no other way of obtaining participation in the Christian communion than through faith in Jesus as the Redeemer.' Schleiermacher, *The Christian Faith*, p. 68. Cf. Schleiermacher and Clements, *Friedrich Schleiermacher*, pp. 115-23; Welch, *Protestant Thought*, I, pp. 73-85; Kelsey, *Thinking About Christ with Schleiermacher*, pp. 16-18.

christological concepts, but muddies the waters, so he seeks to establish christological doctrine independent of triune doctrine, as well as the doctrine of Christ's virgin birth.[70] Yet Schleiermacher does advocate a doctrine of the incarnation. Whereas innate in human nature is the potential of taking the divine into itself,[71] an impeccable and powerful God-consciousness was in Christ from his conception.

> That divine influence upon the human nature is at one and the same time the incarnation of God in human consciousness and the formation of the human nature into the personality of Christ.[72]

> The Redeemer, then, is like all men in virtue of the identity of human nature, but distinguished from them all by the constant potency of His God-consciousness, which was a veritable existence of God in Him.[73]

So, Schleiermacher rejects the creedal formulation of two natures in Christ; instead, he avers one nature in one person.[74] Since human nature has been constituted to contain and allow for the development of God-consciousness within it, God-consciousness, deity,

---

[70] Schleiermacher, *The Life of Jesus*, pp. 389-424. Cf. Schleiermacher, *The Life of Jesus*, pp. 81-87; McGrath, *German Christology*, pp. 44-47; Veli-Matti Kärkkäinen, *Christology: A Global Introduction* (Grand Rapids: Baker Academic, 2003), p. 94; González, *Christian Thought*, III, pp. 355-56; Kärkkäinen, *Pneumatology*, p. 63; Olson, *Christian Theology*, p. 546; Pelikan, *Christian Tradition*, V, pp. 198, 300; Grenz and Olson, *20th Century Theology*, p. 49. According to Livingston, Schleiermacher 'did not consider the Trinity as immediately given in the Christian consciousness'. Livingston, *Modern Christian Thought*, I, p. 101. Although his thought on the subject is ambiguous, in discussing the Trinity and the doctrine of God, Schleiermacher seems to accept a modified form of Sabellianism. Schleiermacher, *The Christian Faith*, pp. 399, 750.

[71] So, according to Schleiermacher, even if the 'implanting therein of the divine element must be purely a divine and therefore an eternal act, nevertheless the temporal appearance of this act in one particular Person must at the same time be regarded as an action of human nature, grounded in its original constitution'. Schleiermacher, *The Christian Faith*, p. 64.

[72] Schleiermacher, *The Christian Faith*, p. 402. Cf. Badcock, *Light of Truth and Fire of Love*, pp. 115-17; Kelsey, *Thinking About Christ with Schleiermacher*, pp. 75-78.

[73] Schleiermacher, *The Christian Faith*, p. 385. Cf. Badcock, *Light of Truth and Fire of Love*, pp. 114-15; Kelsey, *Thinking About Christ with Schleiermacher*, pp. 69-75.

[74] Lori Pearson argues that Schleiermacher's Christology actually contains aspects of both types of pre-Chalcedonian Christologies, Antiochene and Alexandrian, bringing then into a synthesis. Lori Pearson, 'Schleiermacher and the Christologies Behind Chalcedon', *HTR* 96 (2003), pp. 349-67.

progressively became incarnate in Christ's human nature, forming his human personality, so that Christ completed the telos of human nature.

Regarding Christ's work, Schleiermacher's soteriology integrates Christology and pneumatology. Schleiermacher acknowledges that Jesus as the last Adam stands in complete solidarity with humans and therefore able salvifically to evoke God-consciousness in those who have faith in him.[75]

> The Redeemer assumes believers into the power of His God-consciousness, and this is His redemptive activity.[76]

> The Holy Spirit is the union of the Divine Essence with human nature in the form of the common Spirit animating the life in common of believers.[77]

> In Christ there was present nothing less than the Divine Essence, which also indwells the Christian Church as its common Spirit.[78]

Here, Schleiermacher identifies the divine essence indwelling Christ with the Holy Spirit; actually, he makes no distinction between God-consciousness, divine essence, and Holy Spirit. The Holy Spirit, consequently, is the 'common Spirit' that communicates the new communal life in Christ.[79] Hence, as the Spirit mediated God-

---

[75] Schleiermacher, however, carefully distinguishes between Jesus' unique God-consciousness and the general God-consciousness among people. God-consciousness dominated in Christ, determining every moment and accounted for his essential sinlessness and perfection, but humans in general are beset with sensuous desires at every point. Schleiermacher, *The Christian Faith*, pp. 377-89, 413-17. Cf. Schleiermacher and Clements, *Friedrich Schleiermacher*, pp. 53-56, 209-21; Schleiermacher, *The Life of Jesus*, pp. 87-122; González, *Christian Thought*, III, pp. 356-58.

[76] Schleiermacher, *The Life of Jesus*, p. 425. Cf. Schleiermacher and Clements, *Friedrich Schleiermacher*, p. 57, 221-27; Livingston, *Modern Christian Thought*, I, pp. 101-103; Kärkkäinen, *Christology*, p. 94.

[77] Schleiermacher, *The Christian Faith*, p. 569.

[78] Schleiermacher, *The Christian Faith*, p. 738.

[79] According to Schleiermacher, the Spirit is 'common' because it is derived from the same source, Christ. Schleiermacher, *The Christian Faith*, pp. 560-69. Cf. Kelsey, *Thinking About Christ with Schleiermacher*, pp. 99-101. 'The Redeemer assumes the believers into the fellowship of His unclouded blessedness, and this is His reconciling activity.' Schleiermacher, *The Christian Faith*, p. 431. Cf. Schleiermacher and Clements, *Friedrich Schleiermacher*, pp. 227-34; Livingston, *Modern Christian Thought*, I, pp. 104-105; González, *Christian Thought*, III, pp. 358-

consciousness in Christ, the presence of deity, likewise, it is pneumatically communicated to believers.

Schleiermacher's Christology bears similar characteristics with Spirit Christology; however, it is a bit ambiguous whether or not it supports a form of Spirit Christology. This is because Schleiermacher's anthropology and pneumatology seem to coalesce.[80] Perhaps,

---

60; Kevin W. Hector, 'The Mediation of Christ's Normative Spirit: A Constructive Reading of Schleiermacher's Pneumatology', *Modern Theology* 24 (2008), pp. 1-10. Schleiermacher's attempt to revise christological creeds essentially places redemption and reconciliation in union with Christ, while avoiding the use of ransom and penal satisfaction atonement theories. Schleiermacher, *The Christian Faith*, pp. 431-75. Cf. Schleiermacher and Clements, *Friedrich Schleiermacher*, p. 57. For Schleiermacher's explication of how God-consciousness redemptively plays out in the individual soul, see Schleiermacher, *The Christian Faith*, pp. 476-524.

[80] Schleiermacher, *The Christian Faith*, p. 65, writes:

> For the highest goal that is set for these workings of redemption is always a human state which not only would obtain the fullest recognition from the common human reason, but in which also it is impossible always to distinguish, even in the same individual, between what is effected by the divine Spirit and what is effected by the human reason. Inasmuch, then, as the reason is completely one with the divine Spirit, the divine Spirit can be itself conceived as the highest enhancement of the human reason, so that the difference between the two is made to disappear.

Karl Barth acknowledges that Schleiermacher places Christ and the Spirit at the center of his theology, but he questions whether or not Schleiermacher posits the deity of the Spirit: 'the Reformers posited the divinity of the Spirit, and whether, if this was not the case, the *divinity* of the Spirit which seemingly formed the center of his theology was really the *divinity* of the Holy Spirit'. Barth, *Protestant Thought*, p. 343. Barth, thus, critiques Schleiermacher for collapsing the Holy Spirit into human religious consciousness. Barth, *Protestant Thought*, pp. 352-53. In concluding his reflections on Schleiermacher's theology, Barth reiterated that in Schleiermacher pneumatology became anthropology and confessed that he dreamed of

> the possibility of a theology of the third article, in other words, a theology predominately and decisively of the Holy Spirit. Everything which needs to be said, considered, and believed about God the Father and God the Son in an understanding of the first and second articles might be shown and illuminated in its foundations through God the Holy Spirit, the *vinculum pacis inter Patrem et Filium* ... Might not even the christology which dominates everything be illuminated on this basis (*conceptus de Spiritu Sancto!*) ... I would like to reckon with the possibility of a theology of the Holy Spirit, a theology of which Schleiermacher was scarcely conscious, but which might actually have been the legitimate concern dominating his theological activity (Barth, *The Theology of Schleiermacher*, p. 278).

According to Gary Badcock, Barth's critique of the liberal tradition's pneumatology, at least in the case of Schleiermacher and Ritschl, got it wrong. Badcock, *Light of Truth and Fire of Love*, p. 118.

by taking Schleiermacher on his own terms and proceeding with pneumatological sensitivity, a determination can be made regarding Spirit Christology. First, Schleiermacher uses the phrases God-consciousness, divine essence, and Holy Spirit interchangeably. Second, Schleiermacher lays aside the metaphysical issues concerning deity. Although he acknowledges the divine presence in Christ as Spirit or Holy Spirit, Schleiermacher does not speak of Spirit in terms of trinitarian doctrine: Spirit indicates divine essence and presence. Third, the Spirit or God-consciousness gradually develops and is incarnated in Christ's human nature. Fourth, the Holy Spirit is the common Spirit between Christ and believers, which forms the redemptive community and imparts God-consciousness or the divine presence to believers. Fifth, the divine presence of the Spirit in Christ and in believers is distinguished: in Christ the Spirit is particular and full, but in believers the Spirit is communal and ecclesial, derived from Christ, and limited. Though continuity exists between divine Spirit and human spirit in Schleiermacher's writings, the Spirit's presence in Christ differs in degree from the derived presence in the church and the universal innate potential for God-consciousness among all humans. Therefore, the lineaments of a modalist form of Spirit Christology seem to emerge in Schleiermacher's theology: a Spirit christological paradigm of pneumatic inspiration.[81]

Gottfried Thomasius

Gottfried Thomasius (1802–75) studied at various universities between 1821 and 1825: Erlangen, Halle, and Berlin. During his time at Berlin, he came under the influence of Hegel and Schleiermacher. So Thomasius' concept of history was affected by Hegel, and Schleiermacher carried much weight in his theology. After spending seventeen years in pastoral ministry at Nürnberg, Thomasius became professor of theology at Erlangen (1842 –75),[82] where he was

---

[81] Although it may be possible to classify this as paradigm of pneumatic incarnation, because Schleiermacher posits a progressive incarnation of the Spirit in Christ, basically developing by degrees, and the distinction of the Spirit's presence in Christ and the ecclesial community as one of degree, a paradigm of pneumatic inspiration seems a better classification.

[82] For information about Thomasius' life, see Claude Welch (ed.), *God and Incarnation in Mid-Nineteenth Century German Theology* (trans. Claude Welch; A Library of Protestant Thought; New York: Oxford University Press, 1965), p. 10, n. 15.

a central figure in the *kenotic* controversy, representing the christological position known as the Erlangen school.[83] As the name implied, this controversy arose over differing interpretations of Phil. 2.6-8, regarding the divine humiliation or *kenosis* in the incarnation. Thomasius opted for developing a concept of *kenosis* which delineated the idea of the divine self-limitation of deity, a laying aside of relative divine attributes and privileges of deity, in the incarnation.[84] Thomasius, therefore, attempted to construct a Christology that accentuated Christ's human nature while validating the divine nature.[85]

---

[83] Characteristically, Erlangen theology sought to integrate faithfulness to Lutheran confessions with contemporary scholarship, Schleiermacher's theology, and biblical theology. Welch (ed.), *God and Incarnation*, pp. 3-11. Cf. Bruce L. McCormick, 'Karl Barth's Christology as a Resource for a Reformed Version of Kenoticism', *IJSTheo* 8 (2006), pp. 244-45.

[84] Gottfried Thomasius, 'Christ's Person and Work; Part II: The Person of the Mediator', in Claude Welch (ed.), *God and Incarnation in Mid-Nineteenth Century German Theology* (trans. Claude Welch; New York: Oxford University Press, 1965), pp. 67-74.

> Thomasius sought to preserve the Godness of God in the midst of this sort of metaphysical self-emptying by means of a distinction between 'immanent' and 'relative' divine attributes. The 'immanent' attributes are those things that are essential to God as God, things which God 'has' in and for himself without respect to the existence of the world, things like truth, holiness and love. The 'relative' attributes are called relative because they presuppose the existence of the world; that is, they describe God only in his relation to the world. Thomasius was thinking here above all of omnipotence, omniscience and omnipresence. The crucial point is this: 'relative' attributes could be surrendered by God the Logos without detriment to that which he is 'immanently' or essentially as God (McCormick, 'Kenoticism', p. 246).

Thus, Thomasius' view of kenosis should be distinguished from the views held in the earlier kenotic controversy represented by theologians at the universities at Giessen and Tübingen during the seventeenth century. Here, representatives of both positions agreed that Christ retained the divine attributes during the period from incarnation to ascension, but they disagreed regarding how to explain the apparent lack of manifestation of these attributes. On the one hand, the Tübingen theologians asserted that Christ secretly used his divine power. On the other hand, the Giessen theologians affirmed that Christ simply abstained from using the divine attributes. McGrath, *German Christology*, pp. 79-80.

[85] During the nineteenth century, the developments of Hegelian philosophy and historical inquiry regarding the historical Jesus challenged the traditional two-natures Christology. Welch (ed.), *God and Incarnation*, pp. 9-10. According to Bruce McCormick, 'In the face of these developments, it was Gottfried Thomasius, especially, who sought to find a way to preserve the two-natures Christology without raising a principled objection to "life of Jesus" research. He accomplished this with a new form of kenoticism'. McCormick, 'Kenoticism', p. 245.

Thomasius set forth his mature christological views in his treatise *Christ's Person and Work* (1852–61), consisting of three parts.[86] Part one posits the centrality of Christ by depicting the doctrines of God, anthropology, sin, and soteriology as presuppositions of Christology; essentially, he avers that Christology is the content of Christian faith. In part two, Thomasius fleshes out his Christology, and in part three he deduces the consequences of Christ's redemptive work.[87] The focus here will narrow to the second part of this monograph which contains several Spirit christological references. Part two consists of an introduction and three sections: (1) the incarnation, (2) the person of the God-man, and (3) the divine-human states of the mediator. Thomasius, then, closes part two with an appendix which discusses the christological differences between him and one of his opponents in this controversy, Issak August Dorner.[88]

Thomasius laid the basis for the incarnation in the eternal will of the triune God, in the pre-temporal decree of redemption. Affirming traditional trinitarian doctrine, Thomasius carefully pointed out that although the incarnation was a triune act in unity of operation, only the eternal Son was incarnated in human flesh. So, the incarnation correlates with the universal form of divine revelation: from the Father, through the Son, and in the Spirit.[89]

> It is the Father who sends the Son, the Son who appears in the flesh according to the Father's will, the Holy Spirit who mediates the union of the Son with humanity.[90]

The incarnation, therefore, is a trinitarian event in which the Holy Spirit mediates the union of the eternal Son with human flesh.

---

[86] Thomasius had already broached his *kenotic* theory in his two-part essay *Beiträge zur kirchlichen Christologie* (*Contributions to Ecclesiastical Christology*, 1845). Welch (ed.), *God and Incarnation*, pp. 26-29. Cf. 'Kenotic Theories', *ODCC*, p. 923.

[87] Regarding introductory information and an overview of the treatise, see Welch (ed.), *God and Incarnation*, pp. 25-30. Cf. McGrath, *German Christology*, p. 78.

[88] Welch includes sections of Dorner's *System of Christian Doctrine* which appropriately represent his christological position in opposition to Thomasius, see Welch (ed.), *God and Incarnation*, pp. 181-284.

[89] Concerning Thomasius discussion about how his *kenotic* Christology relates to trinitarian theology. Thomasius, 'Christ's Person and Work', pp. 81-86.

[90] Cited according to the translation of Claude Welch, Thomasius, 'Christ's Person and Work', p. 39.

Thomasius, then, accentuates the importance of maintaining a proper view of this union. Two extremes must be avoided. On the one hand, the Son did not unite with an existing human person and gradually transform it into deity; Christ was not a deified human. On the other hand, annulling the distinction of natures by deity assuming human nature must be avoided; this was Thomasius' central concern.[91] According to Thomasius, the assumption of human nature does not adequately express the concept of incarnation; it is also the self-limitation of the Son. The incarnation, conceptually, encompasses two acts of the Son in one event: assuming human nature and divesting of deity.[92]

Christ's self-consciousness grew and developed like other humans; moreover, God-consciousness and an awareness of his redemptive vocation unfolded from this personal union of divine and human natures.[93]

> This development is mediated by the same principle that conditions in general the development of the new (redeemed) humanity, and both from the outside by direction throughout the whole of life and by its immanence in the heart wakens the spiritual life-bud in the depth and opens it into bloom – *i.e.* by the Holy Spirit.[94]

> The Holy Spirit first governs formatively in the depth of his natural and personal life and then imparts himself to him in peculiar fullness for his vocation; the Spirit shows him the temporal moments of the divine will of salvation and mediates to his human nature the ability to carry out that will.[95]

> By virtue of his unity with the Father, he beholds the Father's eternal thoughts; and so he speaks of them as one who has learned them not through outward revelation but from his own immediate intuition. For even if it happens that these divine thoughts come only gradually to consciousness for him through the mediation of the Holy Spirit, this is still only a development

---

[91] Thomasius, 'Christ's Person and Work', pp. 42-46.
[92] Thomasius, 'Christ's Person and Work', pp. 46-56.
[93] Regarding Thomasius' exposition of the development of consciousness in Christ, see Thomasius, 'Christ's Person and Work', pp. 65-74.
[94] Thomasius, 'Christ's Person and Work', p. 65.
[95] Thomasius, 'Christ's Person and Work', p. 66.

of what is contained in the depths of his own being; it arises for him in the form of human knowing.[96]

Humiliation is at the same time *divesting*, continuous divesting of the divine mode of being and activity which he renounced in becoming flesh ... He was no omnipotent man. Even the miracles which he performed prove nothing to the contrary, for these are the works which the Father gives him; he does not do them out of his own capability, but in the power and at the behest of him who sent him; they belong to the works of vocation, for which his humanity is anointed with the Holy Spirit.[97]

Several observations emerge from these Spirit christological texts. First, similar to Schleiermacher, the Spirit mediated God-consciousness to Christ; the Spirit took what was already in the depths of his being and brokered its revelation to him in the form of human understanding. Second, from the act of incarnation Christ's human nature and self-consciousness developed under the agency of the Spirit, so that the Spirit directed and assisted Christ in doing the divine will. Third, distinction between the divine and human natures was maintained to the extent that the Spirit anointed the human nature. Fourth, Christ neither performed miracles through his own power nor did they prove his deity; instead, the Spirit's anointing produced these miracles, empowering Christ to fulfill his salvific vocation.

The Holy Spirit holds a central place in Thomasius' *kenotic* Christology. Advocating a traditional orthodox form of trinitarian theology, Thomasius attests that the Spirit functions as the agent of the christological union, mediating the divine Son's assumption of human nature. Since the incarnation also includes the divesting of divine attributes, the Spirit brokers God-consciousness, divine knowledge, divine will, and empowerment in Christ's human nature. Thomasius' Spirit Christology, consequently, delineates a Spirit christological paradigm of pneumatic meditation, structured on trinitarian theology, which integrates a subordinate form of Logos Christology; it is subordinate because although the eternal Son retained all the essential immanent attributes of deity, in the incarna-

---

[96] Thomasius, 'Christ's Person and Work', pp. 69-70.
[97] Thomasius, 'Christ's Person and Work', p. 70.

tion the Son voluntarily endured a denudation of economic attributes appropriate to Christ's salvific mission.

Hermann Gunkel

Criticism of the Protestant liberal tradition's anthropocentric view regarding the Holy Spirit emerged in the early work of Hermann Gunkel,[98] *The Influence of the Holy Spirit* (1888), which, among other pneumatological questions, revisited issues with a Spirit christological bent.[99] In at least three points Gunkel's pneumatological inquiry criticizes the liberal anthropocentric view of Spirit. First, Gunkel distinguishes between the divine Spirit and human spirit. Among the early Christian communities, pneumatic activity was not natural,

---

[98] Hermann Gunkel (1862–1932) was born in Springe and reared in Lüneburg. After studying theology in Göttingen (1881–85), he taught at various locations – Göttingen (1888–90), Halle (1890–94), and Berlin (1894–1907) – before serving as Professor of Old Testament Theology at Giessen (1907–20) and Halle (Halle 1920–27). Gunkel was a prominent leader in the *Religionsgeschichtliche Schule* (History of Religion School), flourishing from 1880–1920, which extensively integrated data from the comparative study of religions in its interpretation of Scripture; also, the *Religionsgeschichtliche Schule* presented a major challenge to Ritschlian theology's life of Jesus movement. McGrath, *German Christology*, pp. 99-102. Gunkel, also, pioneered *Formgeschichte* (Form Criticism) which attempted, by scrutinizing the structural forms of isolated scriptural pericope, to uncloak its origin and formation in oral tradition and *Sitz im Leben* (setting in life; the phrase Gunkel originally coined was *Sitz im Volksleben*, setting in the life of the people). Hendrikus Boers, 'Religionsgeschichtliche Schule', *DBI*, II, pp. 383-87; Martin J. Buss, 'Form Criticism, Hebrew Bible', *DBI*, I, pp. 406-13; Livingston and Fiorenza, *Modern Christian Thought*, II, pp. 13-17. Gunkel developed this method in his commentary on Genesis (1901) and employed it in his commentary on the Psalms (1925–26). Gunkel authored several works focusing on the Hebrew Scriptures. For overviews of his life, context, and writings, see J.J. Scullion, 'Gunkel, Johannes Heinrich Hermann', *DBI*, I, pp. 472-73; 'Gunkel, Hermann', *ODCC*, p. 722.

[99] Gunkel's stated purpose of this work 'was to ascertain the symptoms by which an "effect" of the Spirit was recognized, and in face of the modernizings of exegetes who, without historical reflection and influenced by rationalism, know nothing of the "effects" of the πνεῦμα and render "Spirit" a pure abstraction'. Cited according to the translation of Roy Harrisville and Philip Quanbeck, Hermann Gunkel, *The Influence of the Holy Spirit: The Popular View of the Apostolic Age and the Teaching of the Apostle Paul* (trans. Roy A. Harrisville and Philip A. Quanbeck; Philadelphia: Fortress Press, 1979), p. 2. Although he includes certain activities of the Spirit in the Hebrew Scriptures, after examining the historical sources, Gunkel narrows the focus to the Synoptic Gospels, Acts, 1 Corinthians, and the Apocalypse to determine the early Christian communities' and the Pauline view of the Spirit's activity. Gunkel, *The Influence of the Holy Spirit*, pp. 11-15. For an examination of Gunkel's analysis of the divine Spirit in Israelite, Jewish, and early Christian literature, see John R. Levison, *Filled with the Spirit* (Grand Rapids: Eerdmans, 2009).

rational, moral, nor ethical; rather, early Christians only experienced the Spirit as a transcendent divine intervention into their lives, producing supernatural effects.[100] In fact, according to Gunkel, the Spirit's activity often had no divine purpose,[101] other than giving evidence to the Spirit's presence, influence, and possession of an individual.[102] For the early church and Pauline theology, the divine Spirit was neither a projection of human reason nor the human spirit; it was a transcendent power and supernatural influence that seized believers.[103]

Second, Gunkel distinguished between the divine Spirit and the community Spirit: the Holy Spirit is not the product of the community; instead, the exalted Christ mediates the Spirit to believers.[104] Although faith is a gift, it differs from the divine Spirit: faith is the prerequisite for receiving the Spirit.[105] Also, the Spirit's presence

---

[100] The divine Spirit's and the human spirit's activity and effects were therefore clearly demarcated. Gunkel, *The Influence of the Holy Spirit*, pp. 15-30, 79-81, 97-102, 106. Cf. Levison, *Filled with the Spirit*, pp. 279-83.

[101] According to Gunkel, 'All these examples support our thesis that the consciousness of a special divine purpose did not belong to the symptoms of an activity of the Spirit'. Gunkel, *The Influence of the Holy Spirit*, pp. 25-26.

[102] 'If we intend to understand the view of the Spirit cherished by the apostolic age, then we must begin from the Spirit's most striking and characteristic activity, that of glossolalia ... The symptoms of the presence of the divine Spirit were most clearly and conspicuously present in glossolalia.' Gunkel, *The Influence of the Holy Spirit*, pp. 30-31. For Gunkel's discussion of the importance of glossolalia, as well as gifts of the Spirit, see Gunkel, *The Influence of the Holy Spirit*, pp. 25-26, 30-38, 66-67. Cf. Levison, *Filled with the Spirit*, pp. 336-47.

[103] Gunkel, *The Influence of the Holy Spirit*, p. 32, writes:

> It is the mysterious and the overwhelming in human life which is derived from the Spirit of God. Hence the apostolic age recognizes certain phenomena that manifest a power that 'fills' a person, that is, which so completely possesses a person that he often becomes its all but unwilling instrument. They are occurrences that seem to defy every explanation by natural powers inherent in man; and precisely because they cannot be derived from the world or from human nature, they are regarded as being of divine origin, as activities of the Spirit.

Cf. Gunkel, *The Influence of the Holy Spirit*, pp. 59-66, 75.

[104] Gunkel, *The Influence of the Holy Spirit*, p. 41, explains:

> The Spirit of God given the community and manifested in signs and wonders is not to be identified with the community spirit of the earliest Christians. A community spirit is both the presupposition and product of fellowship. But the Holy Spirit is neither begotten nor transmitted by human beings.

Cf. Gunkel, *The Influence of the Holy Spirit*, pp. 40-42.

[105] 'The reception of the Spirit is thus God's witness to the existence of faith (Acts 15.8ff; 11.17). Faith, then, is not derived from the Spirit but is held to be

and influence differs in degrees among believers; hence, some Christians manifest the charismata, while others do not.[106] Manifestations of the charismata, furthermore, have an eschatological significance for the community and its mission: they portend the kingdom of God.[107] The kingdom of God, then, comes as transcendent manifestations of the Spirit in divine power, opposing the powers of the age, not in human acts of social ministry ameliorating culture and society.[108] Gunkel, thereby, distinguishes between the communal human spirit and the divine Spirit: the Spirit is a supernatural endowment to believers already in communal fellowship and the charismata function as signs of the numinous in-breaking of the kingdom of God.

Third, by closely associating Christ and divine Spirit, Gunkel asserts that the Spirit is more than an abstract concept or principle.[109] According to Gunkel, Paul often equated the Spirit with Christ.[110]

---

the prerequisite for receiving the Spirit.' Gunkel, *The Influence of the Holy Spirit*, p. 17. Cf. Gunkel, *The Influence of the Holy Spirit*, pp. 91, 106.

[106] Gunkel, *The Influence of the Holy Spirit*, pp. 42-44.

> But the idea that the Spirit is actually given to all members of the Christian community cannot have been the firm, unshakeable component of Christian conviction and daily experience, as it was for Paul. Otherwise, use of the term πνευματικός for glossolalia, which inclined one to assign the Spirit only to certain Christians, would be absolutely inexplicable. But even where we encounter the conviction that all Christians have the Spirit, the idea of varying degrees in the apportionment of the Spirit is not ruled out. On the contrary, this idea inheres in the nature of things. The Spirit is given to individuals in varying strengths (Gunkel, *The Influence of the Holy Spirit*, p. 42).

[107] 'Thus for Paul the present possession of the Spirit and the future possession of the kingdom are so mutually related that they can be interchanged.' Gunkel, *The Influence of the Holy Spirit*, p. 82. Cf. Gunkel, *The Influence of the Holy Spirit*, pp. 81-85.

[108] Gunkel, *The Influence of the Holy Spirit*, pp. 71-74. This is an obvious critique of Ritschlian theology.

[109] During the Jordan event the Spirit visibly appeared and anointed Jesus: 'This is a true indication of the fact that the Spirit in the early Christian era was more than a concept, an abstraction'. Gunkel, *The Influence of the Holy Spirit*, pp. 65-66. Cf. Gunkel, *The Influence of the Holy Spirit*, pp. 40-41, 75, 114.

[110] Gunkel, *The Influence of the Holy Spirit*, pp. 40-41. Gunkel affirms that the presence of the Spirit among believers evokes remembrance of the historical Jesus as a bearer of the Spirit, preserving Christianity's historical character. 'It was rather the infinitely powerful impression of the historical Jesus which prevented Christendom from forfeiting its historical character. In this respect the remembrance of Jesus paralyzed the pneumatic phenomenon of the apostolic age and it still survives after more than a thousand years.' Gunkel, *The Influence of the Holy Spirit*, p. 74.

> In some passages Paul simply identifies the Spirit with Christ (1 Cor. 15.45; see 6.17; 2 Cor. 3.17). According to these passages the Spirit does not simply come through Christ; rather, Christ is himself the Spirit.[111]

So, Paul uses christological terms to explicate his pneumatology. Considering Paul's salvific experience, when Christ appeared to Paul in divine glory, this should not cause surprise: 'Paul's first pneumatic experience was an experience of the Christ'.[112] Nevertheless, at other times, Gunkel ambiguously distinguishes between Christ and the Spirit.

> Accordingly, the teaching concerning the πνεῦμα and the teaching concerning Χριστός are parallel. What each has to say differs from the other merely by the fact that in the one the supernatural is derived from a divine power; in the other, it is derived from a divine person who has this power in himself.[113]

Here, the distinction is between the person of Christ and power of the Spirit, but this alterity only extends so far: believers' mystical experience and union with Christ, being 'in Christ', is a pneumatic experience. Gunkel, thus, posited that Paul's and the early Christians' experience of the Spirit was not an abstraction; rather, it was a mystical pneumatic experience of the risen Christ.

Gunkel's pneumatological inquiry, therefore, contains an implicit Spirit Christology in need of explication. For example, he broaches the question of the Spirit's presence and influence in Christ's life but does not pursue it; also, he explores the Spirit's influence in Christ's mission and links it to believers' union with Christ and the presence of the charismata.[114] What Gunkel did achieve was to re-

---

[111] Gunkel, *The Influence of the Holy Spirit*, p. 113.

A noteworthy parallel to our apostle's teaching concerning the πνεῦμα is his doctrine of Christ. In other passages, all sorts of activities of the πνεῦμα appear as the activities of Christ himself. This is why in what was stated above we could occasionally use expressions concerning Christ to explain the teaching concerning the Spirit (Gunkel, *The Influence of the Holy Spirit*, p. 111).

[112] Gunkel, *The Influence of the Holy Spirit*, p. 114.
[113] Gunkel, *The Influence of the Holy Spirit*, p. 115.
[114] In Gunkel's own words, 'It would be particularly fruitful to investigate the pneumatic aspect in the person of the Lord. Actually, my book dealt with many pneumatic experiences, but of course not in total or in sufficient depth'. Gunkel, *The Influence of the Holy Spirit*, p. 2.

trieve a biblical notion of the Spirit in contrast to the coeval anthropocentric pneumatology, to break up the fallow pneumatological ground of the nineteenth-century Protestant liberal tradition, and to establish a trajectory of Pauline or Christ-mysticism. In this trajectory of Christ-mysticism the risen Christ is identified with divine Spirit which is evident in the writings of Adolf Deissmann (1866–1937), Wilhelm Bousset (1865–1920), and Albert Schweitzer (1875–1965).[115]

Conclusion

Although scarce, Spirit Christology continued in a limited and diverse fashion among both liberal and conservative Protestant traditions. Both Protestant traditions emphasized Christ's true humanity and recognized the Spirit's activity; however, the fluid nature of Spirit Christology was apparent, as both traditions differed regarding Christ's deity and produced distinct paradigms of pneumatic Christology.

Several commonalities existed among the Spirit Christologists of the conservative tradition: Richard Sibbes and John Owen. First, each proponent of Spirit Christology followed the Protestant emphasis on Scripture; they based their understanding of God, Christology, and pneumatology on a historical-grammatical hermeneutic. Second, they affirmed a trinitarian view of God. The incarnation was a perichoretic divine act, each divine person with its proper activity: the Father sent the Son, the Son was incarnated, and the Holy Spirit functioning in the grace of union formed and united Christ's human nature to the Son. Third, their emphasis on holiness or sanctification attested to the Holy Spirit's mediation of sinlessness, divine power, and divine attributes to Christ's human nature. The Spirit sanctified Christ's humanity, forming it in Mary's womb. As Christ's humanity grew, the Spirit sanctified it according to its measure of development. At the Jordan event, the Spirit anointed, commissioned, and empowered Christ's human nature for its salvific mission. Though the Son could have communicated divine

---

[115] Cf. Adolf Deissmann, *Paul: A Study in Social and Religious History* (trans. William E. Wilson; Harper Torchbooks 15; New York: Harper & Brothers, Harper Torchbook edn, 1957), Deissmann, *The Religion of Jesus and the Faith of Paul*, Bousset, *Kyrios Christos*; Schweitzer, *The Mysticism of Paul the Apostle*.

attributes to Christ's human nature, the Godhead determined that the Spirit's mediation was proper to this activity. These Spirit Christologists, therefore, posited Spirit christological paradigms of pneumatic mediation.

The liberal tradition's proclivity was to fuse pneumatology into anthropology; nevertheless, their historical emphasis on Jesus' humanity posited a human Christ with an affinity for the inspiration of the divine Spirit. Friedrich Schleiermacher laid the conceptual framework for a monotheistic Christology of pneumatic inspiration, based on the concept of God as Spirit. For Schleiermacher, the Spirit inspires God-consciousness in Christ, which is indwelling deity; likewise, functioning as the common Spirit, the Spirit of Christ redemptively inspires God-consciousness in believers, forming the community of faith. So, in Schleiermacher's christological construction, Christ enjoys the divine presence or God-consciousness in its fullness, whereas believers participate in a lesser degree of the universal potential for God-consciousness. Arguably, Schleiermacher laid the groundwork in the liberal tradition for a Spirit christological paradigm of pneumatic inspiration.[116]

Somewhat of an aberration among the theologians of the liberal tradition, Gottfried Thomasius, reacting to the liberal tradition's proclivity to ignore, if not reject, Christ's deity, attempted to fashion a Christology which attested to Christ's deity while limiting its divine attributes. Thomasius, also, endeavored to maintain the dominant position of Christ's humanity held in the liberal tradition and its relationship to the Spirit, so that the Spirit mediated to Christ God-consciousness, divine attributes, and empowered the salvific mission. Thomasius, therefore, constructed a Spirit Christology of pneumatic mediation which subordinated and integrated a form of Logos Christology.

Recognizing the transcendent nature of Spirit and its power, Hermann Gunkel's biblical elucidation of the Spirit's inspiration freed the Holy Spirit from the anthropocentric shackles in which the liberal tradition had restrained the Spirit. Gunkel and those who followed his trajectory of affirming a Pauline Christ-mysticism, being 'in Christ' – Adolf Deissmann, Wilhelm Bousset, and Albert

---

[116] This conceptual framework for a theology of God as Spirit laid on the foundation of a Spirit christological paradigm of pneumatic inspiration is picked up and elaborated in the modern discussion by G.W.H. Lampe.

Schweitzer – synonymously identified the Spirit's anointing and presence as Christ in and among believers. The Protestant liberal tradition's Christology and spirit theology, therefore, produced a human Jesus and an environment for the emergence of a Spirit Christology of pneumatic inspiration, latently, awaiting its appearance and fruition in the modern discussion.

13

VOICES FROM THE MARGINS

The earlier voices speaking from the margins of christological development did not fare well in the ecumenical councils. Modalist Monarchianism was repudiated early on; during the councils, whether or not the designation fit, often Sabellianism was used calumniously to attenuate an opponent's position. Likewise, the rejection of Dynamic Monarchianism became attached to the name of Paul of Samosata, so the sobriquet Samosatene was maliciously bestowed upon those who strongly emphasized Christ's human nature. Arian Christology was censured at Nicea (325) and soundly defeated at Constantinople (381). Montanism continued under heavy persecution until its death-knell sounded with Emperor Justinian's legal codes (529), denying them any standing in the empire and promulgating their forced conversion; disappearing as a movement, its adherents integrated into other groups.

Although also condemned, Gnosticism's resilience and fluidity allowed its lineaments to continue among certain Christian groups with dualist affinities: the Messalians, Paulicians, and Bogomils in the East, and the Cathars in the West.[1] Although some distinctions

---

[1] The Messalians originated in Mesopotamia around 360, were condemned at the Council of Ephesus (431), and continued well into the seventh century. The origination of the Paulicians remains obscure; probably the sect began near Samosata (641–68). The Bogomils originated in the Balkans during the 8th century. Influenced by the Bogomils the Cathars appeared in Germany around 1140 and spread through Europe; in France they were known as Albigenses and Patarenes in Italy. For the history of these groups, see 'Messalians; Paulicians; Bogomils; Cathari; Albigenses; Patarenes', *ODCC*, pp. 1075-76; 1243; 219-20; 301; 35; 1230; Steven Runciman, *The Medieval Manichee: A Study of the Christian Dualist Heresy*

existed among these groups, doctrinal commonality inhered regarding certain theological positions. First, they held a dualistic view of God and evil; an evil entity produced creation, not the gracious and good God. Second, anthropologically, they viewed the corporeal nature of humanity as a prison detaining the light of divinity indwelling humans. Third, they maintained a docetic Christology, Christ brought the salvific message, not redemption through fleshly sacrifice and resurrection. Fourth, they rejected Marian devotion and abhorred any reference to Mary as *Theotokos*. Fifth, they were decidedly anti-sacramentalists, as well as repudiating prayer to the saints, veneration of relics, and the sign of the cross. Sixth, though most employed some form of structure, they generally detested the hierarchical composition of the mainstream church. Seventh, pneumatology permeated their theology; in nearly all of these groups the *spiritual ones* among them, *the elect*, had received the true baptism, in the Spirit. Eighth, they argued that the church had lost its way, and they alone represented the true apostolic tradition.[2] Although the Paulicians were generally identified among these groups, the Paulicians in Armenia, especially those known as the Thonraki, held a different christological position than their docetic Paulician neighbors and Byzantine cousins.[3]

(1969 repr.; Cambridge: Cambridge University Press, 4 edn, 1960); Dimitri Obolensky, *The Bogomils: A Study in Balkan Neo-Manichaeism* (2004 repr.; Cambridge: Cambridge University Press, pbk. edn, 1948); Malcolm Lambert, *The Cathars* (Malden, MA: Blackwell Publishers, 1998); Yuri Stoyanov, *The Other God: Dualist Religions from Antiquity to the Cathar Heresy* (Yale Nota Bene; New Haven: Yale University Press, 2000); Malcolm Lambert, *Medieval Heresy: Popular Movements from Bogomil to Hus* (New York: Holmes & Meier Publishers, 1977); Walker, *History*, pp. 235, 249; González, *Christian Thought*, II, p. 192; Schaff, *History*, IV, pp. 573-76; Latourette, *History*, I, pp. 453, 576.

[2] Regarding the theology of these groups, see Runciman, *Medieval Manichee*, pp. 21-25, 51-53, 73-79, 147-62; Obolensky, *Bogomils*, pp. 111-267; Lambert, *The Cathars*, pp. 29-34, 73-77, 196-209, 250-55; Burgess, *The Holy Spirit: Eastern Christian Traditions*, pp. 213-23; Burgess, *The Holy Spirit: Medieval Roman Catholic and Reformation Traditions*, pp. 134-39; Pelikan, *Christian Tradition*, II, pp. 216-27; Pelikan, *Christian Tradition*, III, pp. 237-42; Schaff, *History*, IV, pp. 576-78; Walker, *History*, pp. 249-51; Latourette, *History*, I, pp. 299-300, 454-55, 577; González, *Christian Thought*, II, p. 193.

[3] Burgess, *The Holy Spirit: Eastern Christian Traditions*, p. 216, writes:

Byzantine Paulicians appeared more Marcionist than their Armenian brothers. They distinguished between the good God of the New Testament and an evil God of the Old Testament who created the world. Because they rejected all of creation as evil, especially flesh, they taught against the incarnation and

Armenian Paulicians

Normally, when one begins an inquiry into the Christology of a sect branded as heretics, research depends on hearing the echo of their voice through their opponents' writings because the sect's primary documents lie in the ashes of past millennia. However, this is not the case for the Armenian Paulicians since Fredrick Conybeare's discovery of *The Key of Truth* during a trip to Armenia (1891). Conybeare's subsequent translation and publication of this manuscript (1898) has allowed a primary hearing of the ancient movement's voice.[4] According Conybeare, Smbat Bagratuni, the founder of the Thonraki, probably wrote *The Key of Truth* during a ninth century revival of Adoptionism in Armenia, as a manual recording their rituals and passing on a hidden tradition as old as the apostles.[5]

---

were decidedly docetic. In contrast, the Armenian Paulicians were adoptionist (stressing the humanity of Jesus) rather than docetic (which denied his humanity).

There is some discussion concerning the identification of the Thonraki with Armenian Paulicians. Fredrick Conybeare argues that the Thonraki are Paulicians, while Steven Runciman and Dimitri Obolensky make a distinction between them. See Conybeare's introduction, *The Key of Truth: A Manual of the Paulician Church of Armenia*, (trans. F.C. Conybeare; Oxford: Clarendon Press, 1898), pp. v-vi; Runciman, *Medieval Manichee*, pp. 51-59; Obolensky, *Bogomils*, pp. 41-53. Conybeare's thesis seems to carry more weight; after all, Paulician doctrine could have varied in different locations. Since they often existed in the same regions as the Messalians, Gnosticism could have influenced Paulician doctrine in these areas. In the eleventh century there were clearly two branches of Paulicians: 'the Adoptionist wing lying on the Armenian side, the dualists in the Balkans'. Lambert, *Medieval Heresy*, p. 33.

[4] The moniker Paulician seems to have been attached to this group for two possible reasons. One possibility stems from their respect for the apostle Paul. This group named their churches after places where Paul had established churches, and their leaders often took the names of Paul's disciples and co-workers. The other possibility traces their origin back to Paul of Samosata; they had preserved Paul's legacy and tradition. Since this group advocated an adoptionist Christology, the latter possibility is more than likely correct. Also it is important to note that the 'ic' or 'ik', depending on which form of spelling is used, was a derisive term added into the sobriquet Paulician, meaning the son or follower of the wretched Paul. Conybeare's introduction, *The Key of Truth*, pp. cv-vi, cxxxix-cxxx; Runciman, *Medieval Manichee*, pp. 46-59; Obolensky, *Bogomils*, pp. 54-57; Lambert, *Medieval Heresy*, pp. 10-11. Conybeare traces out the history of Adoptionist doctrine and compares it to *The Key of Truth*. Conybeare's introduction, *The Key of Truth*, pp. viii-x, lxxxvi-civ.

[5] '*The Key of Truth* contains the baptismal service and ordinal of the Adoptionist Church, almost in the form in which Theodotus of Rome may have celebrated those rites.' Conybeare's introduction, *The Key of Truth*, p. vi. Because some mate-

Loosely structured, *The Key of Truth* begins with an introduction,[6] and the body of text flows through a schema addressing several theological issues: Christ's baptism, their claim to be the true apostolic church, the genuine sacraments, the rite of election, the virgin Mary, Christology, and a catechism for Christians.

Their *leitmotiv* doctrine regarded Christ's reception of the Spirit during the Jordan event.[7]

> First was our Lord Jesus Christ baptized by the command of the heavenly Father, when thirty years old, as St. Luke has declared his years ... So then it was in the season of his maturity that he received baptism; then it was that he received authority, received the high-priesthood, received the kingdom, and the office of chief shepherd. Moreover, he was then chosen, then he won lordship ... Then he became the foundation of our faith; then he became Savior of us sinners; then he was filled with the Godhead; then he was sealed, then anointed; then was he called by the voice, then he became the loved one, then he came to be guarded by angels, then to be the lamb without blemish. Furthermore, he then put on that primal raiment of light, which Adam lost in the garden. Then accordingly it was that he was invited by the Spirit of God to converse with the heavenly Father; yea, then also was he ordained king of beings in heaven and on earth and under the earth; and all else [besides] all this in due order the Father gave to his only born Son; – even as he himself, being appointed our mediator and intercessor, saith to his holy,

---

rial in this manuscript is older than other parts, Conybeare suggests that some of it existed as early as the seventh century, but its completed form came through Smbat no later than 850. For issues regarding this document's authorship, date, provenance, purpose, and cultural context, see Conybeare's introduction, *The Key of Truth*, pp. vi-ix, xxix-xxxii, cxvii-cxx.

[6] The document begins and ends with the date and location it was last copied: 'The Book called the Key of Truth. It was written in the era of the Savior 1782, but of the Armenians 1230; and in the province of Taron'. Cited according to the translation of Fredrick Conybeare, *The Key of Truth*, p. 71. Cf. *The Key of Truth*, p. 124. Conybeare provides a copy of the Armenian text in *The Key of Truth*, pp. 1-65.

[7] In point of fact, the writer in the introduction asserts that this is the central theme of the document: '*Concerning the holy baptism of our Lord Jesus Christ, which hath been handed down for the sake of those who believe and repent*'. Cited according to the translation of Fredrick Conybeare, *The Key of Truth*, p. 72. Unless otherwise indicated, all citations from this document are according to the translation of Fredrick Conybeare.

universal, and apostolic church, Mt. 28.18: And Jesus came and spoke unto them and said: 'There hath been given unto me all authority in heaven and on earth. As the Father sent me, so do I send you,' and what follows. Thus also the Lord, having learned from the Father, proceeded to teach us to perform holy baptism and all his other commands at an age of full growth (*or lit.* in a completed or mature season), and at no other time.[8]

What can be the coming upon him of the Holy Spirit? What can be all this greatness, and all this authority in heaven and on earth?[9]

Blessed art thou, Spirit of the heavenly Father ... and coming, didst give unto our Lord Jesus Christ authority over all flesh; and did make him king and head of beings in heaven and in earth and under the earth.[10]

Several conclusions emerge from these texts regarding this movement's theology: (1) they were proponents of Adoptionist Christology; (2) soteriologically, they emphasized the redemptive significance of Christ's human nature; (3) they considered themselves the rightful heirs of Christ's authority, and they performed their rituals and sacraments according to the paradigm of Christ's baptism.[11] These aspects of their theological tenets deserve a closer examination.

First, this movement's Adoptionist Christology attributed a prominent role to the Spirit in Christ's life and identity. Though by the Spirit Mary conceived Jesus as a virgin, neither was Mary *Theotokos* nor did she remain a virgin.[12] So Jesus was born a new human without original sin – the second Adam – but in no wise was he di-

---

[8] *The Key of Truth*, ch. 2, pp. 74-75.
[9] *The Key of Truth*, ch. 4, p. 80.
[10] *The Key of Truth*, ch. 21, p. 100.
[11] For summaries of the Paulicians doctrinal tenets, see Conybeare's introduction, *The Key of Truth*, pp. xxxiii-xl, lxxvi-lxxxi. For a comparison of Armenian Paulician doctrines and the history of Adoptionist doctrines, see Conybeare's introduction, *The Key of Truth*, lxxxvi-civ.
[12] *The Key of Truth*, pp. 113-14. Note that this reference does not contain a chapter number; this is because some material is missing from the document, as well as some chapter numbers. Regarding this missing material, see Conybeare's introduction, *The Key of Truth*, p. xxix.

vine.¹³ Having fulfilled all righteousness, at the mature age of thirty years, Jesus was baptized. During the Jordan event, Jesus received the grace of the Spirit's anointing, giving birth to Jesus as the Son of God;¹⁴ moreover, the Spirit's anointing identified him as the *elect one*, chosen and adopted by God into deification to receive authority and lordship in heaven and earth.¹⁵

Second, soteriologically, the Spirit's anointing commissioned and empowered Jesus as the Christ – the anointed one, Messiah, mediator, intercessor, and Savior – for his salvific mission; accordingly, the Father, appointed Christ as high-priest, the lamb without blemish, and the chief shepherd. Receiving the raiment of light – the Spirit – lost through Adam's transgression, Christ now redemptively restores the Spirit to those who have believed in him. This movement, hence, stressed the redemptive significance of Christ's Spirit anointed human nature: 'by man came death and by man salvation'.¹⁶

Third, according to this movement, Christ receiving the Spirit at the Jordan event served as the foundation of the apostolic faith, and they avowed that Christ bequeathed this legacy of authority to them.¹⁷ Among this group, there existed only one rank of ecclesiastical authority, the *elect*; as such Christ's authority of binding and loosing, given by the Spirit, passed from Jesus through the apostles

---

[13] *The Key of Truth*, ch. 4, p. 79; ch. 20, p. 94; ch. 22, p. 108; catechism, p. 119. Regarding the relation of Jesus' virginal conception and sinlessness, see Conybeare's introduction, *The Key of Truth*, pp. clxxxvi-clxxxviii.

[14] According to this group, the Jordan event was Christ's real nativity; therefore, they continued to celebrate the nativity and Jesus' baptism on the same day, 6 January. According to Conybeare, this is why the fish is a symbol of Christ. See Conybeare's introduction, *The Key of Truth*, pp. vii-viii, lxxxi, cxli-cxliv, clii-cliii.

[15] It appears that the deification process continued into the wilderness temptation: 'When therefore he had pleased his increate and loved Father, at once the Spirit led him on to the mountain of temptation and admitted him into the mystery of Godship'. *The Key of Truth*, ch. 5, p. 80.

[16] *The Key of Truth*, ch. 22, p. 108. There is neither any indication of Docetism nor denial of Christ's passion, which stands in stark contrast with the other forms of Paulician theology, as well as the Messalians, Bogomils, and Cathars. Cf. Conybeare's introduction, *The Key of Truth*, pp. xliv-xlv, cv, cxxx-cxliv.

[17] They argued this point in opposition to those who considered themselves orthodox. *The Key of Truth*, chs. 1–19, pp. 72-93. Cf. Conybeare's introduction, *The Key of Truth*, pp. clxiv-clxviii. It is noteworthy that the Armenian Paulicians rejected the veneration of images and relics, crosses, springs, incense, the intercession of the saints, and the doctrine of purgatory. *The Key of Truth*, ch. 15, p. 86; catechism, pp. 120-22.

to them.[18] This group, consequently, based their rite of initiation into the *elect* on Christ's election, namely, by the Spirit.[19] After having been thoroughly vetted, the candidate for election appeared before the *elect*, and the ritual proceeded with the candidate confessing their readiness and desire to become one of the *elect*, prayer given to God, certain Scriptures read – Mt. 1.1-16; Acts 6.1-8; Acts 1.1-5; Mt. 3.1-17; Acts 13.1-6 – then the candidate received the name of Peter and the authority of binding and loosing,[20] followed by the reading of Mt. 18.18; Jn 20.23; Lk. 2.1-13; Mt. 2.1-13; thereupon, the elders prayed for the candidate to receive the promise of the Spirit according to Acts 1.4-5.

> Now therefore, forasmuch as this man, who hath been baptized in thy holy name, and hath been elected by the Holy Spirit of thy Father, doth now earnestly await thy faithful promise [which said]: 'Ye shall abide in the city of Jerusalem, until ye be clothed with power from on high.' Now therefore, falling on our faces at thy feet with ardent love, with bitter tears, we beseech, entreat, and beg thee, send into him the grace of thy Father ... And bestow on him thy Spirit, which thou didst receive from the Father in the river Jordan.[21]

The ritual concluded with the bishop blowing three times in the face of the person and reading Lk. 1.26-38; Acts 2.1-21; Jn 20.19-23; Heb. 13.17-21. A few observations emerge from this text and its context. First, this movement's doctrines and rituals were firmly rooted in biblical theology. Second, their assertion of apostolic authority was predicated on a genuine pneumatic succession. Third, apparently, they attested to an experience of the Spirit subsequent to their baptism as a believer in water.[22] Consisting of more than a

---

[18] *The Key of Truth*, ch. 22, pp. 105-106, 108. Cf. Conybeare's introduction, *The Key of Truth*, pp. cxxii-cxxiv.

[19] The regulations regarding candidates for election and the rite of election are preserved in *The Key of Truth*, ch. 22, pp. 101-12. Although the elect was a single grade of ecclesiastical order, in the rite of election certain ones among them functioned with various ecclesial titles: priest, elder, bishop, doctor, president, or apostle. *The Key of Truth*, ch. 22, p. 105.

[20] The acceptance and amicable use of Peter's name, also, demonstrates this group's distinction with other coeval marginal groups. See Conybeare's introduction, *The Key of Truth*, p. cxxx.

[21] *The Key of Truth*, ch. 22, p. 109.

[22] *The Key of Truth*, ch. 3, pp. 76-77; ch. 16, pp. 86-87; catechism, p. 119.

symbolic ritual, initiation into the *elect* was a dynamic experience of the Spirit, in which the *elect* became anointed christs.[23] Jesus' reception of the Spirit and election, therefore, became paradigmatic of initiation into the elect and receiving apostolic authority; thus, only the *elect* were qualified to perform the rituals and sacraments.[24]

This movement' christological lineage probably extends back to Paul of Samosata. Like Paul, *The Key of Truth* depicts Jesus as a sinless human born of Mary, the new Adam; nevertheless, it never implies an incarnation. In obedience to the Father, Jesus as a human fulfilled the requirements of righteousness. The Jordan event, however, signified the pivotal point of Jesus' life and mission, receiving the Spirit Jesus was joined to God and entered the process of deification: the Son born of the Spirit and adopted by the Father. *The Key of Truth*, thereupon, stresses the redemptive value of Christ's humanity and the Spirit's anointing, so that the Jordan event becomes paradigmatic of believers receiving the Spirit; likewise, they become christs: humans anointed and empowered by the Spirit. Christ, therefore, was a human uniquely born, anointed, and inspired by the Spirit in his life and salvific mission. *The Key of Truth*, ergo, delineates a non-incarnational Spirit christological paradigm of pneumatic inspiration.

---

[23] See Conybeare's introduction, *The Key of Truth*, pp. li-lvi.

[24] The Armenian Paulicians were not anti-sacramentalists; they advocated three genuine sacraments requisite to salvation: repentance, baptism, and the body and blood of Christ. They never recruited people for baptism, but they baptized only those who personally and earnestly requested it with tears. *The Key of Truth*, ch. 3, p. 77; ch. 18, p. 91; ch. 19, p. 92; ch. 21, p. 96. In fact, this group alleged that the orthodox churches had allowed the sacrament of baptism to become perverted, so their regulations and candidates for baptism differed significantly. The catechumens for baptism must be of a mature age, so that they can cognitively understand, discern, and repent of sin; consequently, repentance and faith must precede baptism. They, thus, rejected the practice of infant baptism because infants lack original and operative sin, so they have no need of baptism. *The Key of Truth*, chs. 1–3, pp. 72-77; ch. 16, p. 88; ch. 18, p. 92; ch. 21, p. 96; catechism, pp. 117-18. Cf. Conybeare's introduction, *The Key of Truth*, p. cxl. It is unclear whether this group taught the literal presence of the Lord in the Eucharist, or the bread and wine served as symbols; at times, they spoke of the Eucharist in both ways. For an exposition on the Eucharist, see *The Key of Truth*, catechism, pp. 123-24. According to Conybeare, it was a symbolic meal. See Conybeare's introduction, *The Key of Truth*, pp. xlvii, clxii-clxiv. Another interesting fact is that this group required their bishops to marry and to be a father of a family. See Conybeare's introduction, *The Key of Truth*, pp. cxxiii, cxliv.

Russian Nonconformists: Khlysty and Skoptsy

With the fall of Constantinople, Russia viewed itself as picking up the mantle of the Byzantine heritage, becoming the 'Third Rome' and preserver of the true orthodox faith. During this transitional epoch, some monastics remonstrated against state interventions into ecclesiastical affairs;[25] primarily, Russian nonconformity challenged the secularization of the church, clerical support, and social injustices.[26] Certain councils and liturgical reforms exacerbated the volatile cultural and ecclesiastical environment. National church councils, which condemned a sect known as the Judaizers, conven-

---

[25] With the changing political, ecclesiastical, and spiritual situation in Russia, monasticism bifurcated into two main branches, espousing distinct views regarding Russian spirituality and church-state relations. One branch stemming from St. Cyril of White Lake was given to seclusion and the pneumatically permeated hesychast spirituality, while the other branch flowed from cenobite monasteries aligned with the ecclesiastical and political conventions of Moscow, and they avidly supported the 'Third Rome' theory. Kontzevitch, *The Acquisition of the Holy Spirit*, pp. 191-206, 212-15. Cf. Dobroklonsky, *Russkoi Tserkvi*, pp. 240-44; Louis Bouyer, *Orthodox Spirituality and Protestant and Anglican Spirituality* (trans. Barbara Wall; HCS; 3 vols.; London: Burns & Oates, 1968), III, pp. 19-26; Rock, 'Russian Piety', *CHC*, V, pp. 262-63; Latourette, *History*, I, pp. 616-18. So, in Russia at least one branch continued the mystical spirituality and pneumatically permeated theology which had descended from Marcarius and Palamas. This lineage of Eastern mystical theology was carried forward through such notable proponents as Seraphim of Sarov (1759–1833). Regarding Seraphim's life, teaching, and influence, see Valentine Zander, *St. Seraphim of Sarov* (trans. Gabriel Anne; Crestwood, NY: St. Vladimir's Seminary Press, 1975); Burgess, *The Holy Spirit: Eastern Christian Traditions*, pp. 79-83; Bouyer, *Orthodox Spirituality*, HCS, III, pp. 48-53; Kontzevitch, *The Acquisition of the Holy Spirit*, pp. 169-71. For information about Russian monasticism, see Kontzevitch, *The Acquisition of the Holy Spirit*, pp. 147-292; Dobroklonsky, *Russkoi Tserkvi*, pp. 81-88, 240-69, 419-21; Bouyer, *Orthodox Spirituality*, HCS, III, pp. 5-19; Rock, 'Russian Piety', *CHC*, V, pp. 266-71; Latourette, *History*, I, pp. 615-16.

[26] Bolshakoff, *Russian Nonconformity*, pp. 13-22; Dobroklonsky, *Russkoi Tserkvi*, pp. 136-55, 289-303; Kontzevitch, *The Acquisition of the Holy Spirit*, pp. 186-87, 249-53; F.C. Conybeare, *Russian Dissenters* (HTS 10; Cambridge: Harvard University Press, 1921), pp. 13-41. Of course some dissent groups preceded this time; for example, the Stringolniks in the fourteenth century had protested against charging a fee for ordination to the priesthood, considering this simony. Since the Stringolniks considered the clergy's ordination invalid, they believed it was blasphemous to receive the sacraments from them. This movement was persecuted and although their leaders were executed in Novgorod (1375), the sect survived. Vladimir Anderson, *Staroobriadchestvo I Sektantstvo* (St. Petersburg: Gubinsky, 1909), pp. 15-22; Dobroklonsky, *Russkoi Tserkvi*, pp. 186-87; Bolshakoff, *Russian Nonconformity*, pp. 29-31; Rock, 'Russian Piety', *CHC*, V, p. 259; González, *Christian Thought*, II, pp. 296-98; Latourette, *History*, I, pp. 618-19.

ing in 1490 and in 1504, occasioned disputes between monastic communities.[27] Hence, when Nikon ascended to the patriarchal throne (1652) and instituted liturgical reforms aimed at reconciling with the Greeks, controversy ensued.[28] To settle the matter a council was convoked (1667); the councilor edict deposed Nikon but upheld his reforms and excommunicated his opponents, provoking the Great Russian Schism and giving rise to the nonconformist groups the Raskolniks (Old Believers), which believed that the Antichrist now ruled the 'Third Rome' and its priesthood had become heretical.[29] Raskolnik nonconformity took various forms and descriptive designations: the Priestists, Priestless, Shore Dwellers, Theodosians, Philippians, Wanderers, and Saviorites.[30]

---

[27] Rejecting the doctrines of the Trinity, Christ's deity, incarnation, sacraments, veneration of saints, church festivals, and stressing observance of the Torah, the Judaizers attempted to synthesize Christianity and Judaism. When the second council assembled, the two aforementioned monastic streams disputed two issues: the severity of punishment meted out to the Judaizers and monastic real-estate ownership. On the one hand, devoted to hesychastic spirituality, the Nonpossessors led by Nilus of Sora advocated leniency toward the Judaizers and denied the right of monasteries to own land. On the other hand, the Possessors led by Joseph of Volokolamsk upheld the imperial death sentence for Judaizers, and he not only advocated monastic possession of property but also had built a wealthy community, becoming a nursery from which bishops emerged. Anderson, *Staroobriadchestvo I Sektantstvo*, pp. 23-41; Dobroklonsky, *Russkoi Tserkvi*, pp. 188-91, 245-50; Kontzevitch, *The Acquisition of the Holy Spirit*, pp. 188, 206-15; Ware, *The Orthodox Church*, pp. 114-19; Bolshakoff, *Russian Nonconformity*, pp. 31-45; Rock, 'Russian Piety', *CHC*, V, pp. 259-60; Bouyer, *Orthodox Spirituality*, HCS, III, pp. 26-29; González, *Christian Thought*, II, pp. 299; Latourette, *History*, I, pp. 618-19.

[28] For information about Nikon, his reforms, and the context of the controversy see Anderson, *Staroobriadchestvo I Sektantstvo*, pp. 57-67; Dobroklonsky, *Russkoi Tserkvi*, pp. 327-44; Conybeare, *Russian Dissenters*, pp. 41-59; Heard, *Russian Dissent*, pp. 39-107; González, *Christian Thought*, III, pp. 416-21. For an overview of the historical context and issues involved, see Lawrence Barriger, 'The Legacy of Constantinople in the Russian Liturgical Tradition', *GOTR* 33 (1988), pp. 387-416.

[29] This was no small division; in fact, the nonconformist numbered in the millions. Anderson, *Staroobriadchestvo I Sektantstvo*, pp. 68-126; Bolshakoff, *Russian Nonconformity*, pp. 46-57; Ware, *The Orthodox Church*, pp. 119-25; Kontzevitch, *The Acquisition of the Holy Spirit*, pp. 252-53; Bouyer, *Orthodox Spirituality*, HCS, III, pp. 30-32; Conybeare, *Russian Dissenters*, pp. 59-68, 79-99; Heard, *Russian Dissent*, pp. 179-219; González, *Christian Thought*, III, pp. 421-22.

[30] For example, a question arose regarding the validity of the ordination to the priesthood of anyone aligning with the Russian state church and those it had ordained after the schism. All the bishops remained faithful to the Russian church, but many of the priests ordained before Nikon's reforms abdicated and joined the nonconformists, administering the sacraments to the true believers. At some

It was in this context of protest against the institutional state-church that Spirit Christology emerged. Emanating from the central tradition onto the margins of theological and ecclesiastical discussion, Spirit Christology was present among certain nonconforming sects, whose Christology resembled and was probably influenced by Armenian Paulicians, which emphasized the indwelling of the divine Spirit: the *Khlysty* and *Skoptsy*.[31]

Although distinct in certain ways, the *Skoptsy* appear to hold the same Spirit christological ideas as the *Khlysty*. Given the fact the *Skoptsy's* christological views seem to stem from the *Khlysty*, the focus will narrow to the *Khlysty*, and the *Skoptsy* references will be noted along the way. Whereas the *Khlysty* left scant writings, mostly existing in songs – which were well known, preserved, and documented among historians of Russian dissidents – the inquiry will depend on several secondary sources for information regarding their Christology.

The *Khlysty*, likely, originated (1631) through a peasant, Danila Philippov, who proclaimed himself God.[32] According to *Khlysty* leg-

---

point, all the authentically ordained priests would eventually die out, leaving the true believers without a priesthood or access to the sacraments since there were no bishops to ordain a new generation of priests. Among the nonconformists, two schools of thought prevailed. The Priestless (*Bezpopovtsy*) asserted that when the last true priest died, the priesthood and sacraments would vanish from the earth. The Priestists (*Popovtsy*), however, took a more moderate view; those ordained in the Russian church could dispense valid sacraments after they had abjured their heresy. Except for the Priestists, all of the aforementioned groups come under the umbrella of the Priestless sects. Bolshakoff, *Russian Nonconformity*, pp. 58-82. Cf. Conybeare, *Russian Dissenters*, pp. 101-258; Anderson, *Staroobriadchestvo I Sektantstvo*, pp. 127-288; Heard, *Russian Dissent*, pp. 219-49.

[31] The Molokan-Jumpers could also be classified as Russian Nonconformists; nevertheless, since the Molokan-Jumpers have a direct connection to the Azusa Street Revival, and their theology is very similar to early Pentecostal theology, an examination of this group's writings will be presented later in the chapter entitled Proto-Pentecostals.

[32] According to what is known about Danila Philippov's life, he was born to peasant parents and deserted his military obligations; he was literate, had accumulated Old-believer texts, and was acknowledged as a teacher. Other than this information, not much is known about Philippov's life before he experienced his epiphany. Konrad Grass, *Die Russischen Sekten* (2 vols.; Leipzig: J.C. Hinrichs, 1905–14), I, pp. 7-8; Conybeare, *Russian Dissenters*, p. 357. The *Khlysty* tradition, possibly, goes back as far as the fourteenth century. During the time of muscovite Grand Prince Dmitry Donskoi (1363–89) a man named Awerjan holding similar claims as a *Khlysty* Christ was slain in battle, and a tribute to him was preserved in a *Khlysty* song. Another person, Ivan Jemeljan, claimed the attributes of a *Khlysty* Christ in Moscow, suffered martyrdom for his faith (1538–84) which was also

end, Philippov experienced an epiphany on the mountain, Gorodno, in the province of Vladimir: the angelic hosts descended with the Lord God Sabaoth himself who took possession of Philippov, so that God was incarnated in him.[33] The *Khlysty* have commemorated this event in several prophetic songs. One such song begins by recounting the diminishing of Christian faith, disunity, and lack of spirituality in Russia, so concerned believers were led by God to this mountain to pray for a revival and manifestation of the Spirit. As they raised their hands and voices toward heaven in supplication, God answered them from behind a bright cloud.

> Listen, my faithful! I, God, will come down to you from heaven to earth; I will choose a most pure flesh and wrap myself in it; I will be a man according to the flesh but God according to the Spirit.[34]

---

commemorated in a song. Nevertheless, the *Khlysty* point to the deification of Danila Philippov as the beginning of their group. Grass, *Die Russischen Sekten*, I, pp. 1-6. Concerning *Khlysty* history from the 18th into the 20th century, see Grass, *Die Russischen Sekten*, I, pp. 101-252; Konstantin Kutepov, *Sekty Khlystov I Skoptsov* (Kazan: Imperial University, 1882), pp. 39-96; Anderson, *Staroobriadchestvo I Sektantstvo*, pp. 289-314; Dobroklonsky, *Russkoi Tserkvi*, pp. 376-77. The founder and Christ of the *Skoptsy* was Andrei Ivanov who became known as Kondrati Selivanov after he was proclaimed Christ among the *Khlysty* (1770). Selivanov found the restrictions regarding sex too lenient among the *Khlysty*, so he castrated himself with a hot iron and began teaching that this was the true manner of salvation, found only among the group he founded, the *Skoptsy*. Later on, he was arrested, given a life sentence for what the government considered sedition, and sent to Siberia; while there he began to pass himself off as a member of the royal family, Peter III. After the emperor brought him to St. Petersburg, he continued this masquerade, which allowed him to integrate the titles of Tsar and Christ in himself. Since daddy was a popular term to refer to the Tsar, Selivanov referred to himself not only as the risen Christ and savior but also as daddy. Konrad Grass, *Die Geheime Heilige Schrift Der Skopzen* (trans. Konrad Grass; Leipzig: J.C. Hinrichs, 1904), pp. 3-4. Regarding *Skoptsy* history extending to 1909, see Grass, *Die Russischen Sekten*, II, pp. 1-586. Cf. Kutepov, *Sekty Khlystov I Skoptsov*, pp. 97-268; Anderson, *Staroobriadchestvo I Sektantstvo*, pp. 315-61; Conybeare, *Russian Dissenters*, pp. 363-67; Bolshakoff, *Russian Nonconformity*, pp. 92-94. Much history is also contained in Selivanov's autobiographical letters, recounting his suffering. See Konrad Grass' German translation, Grass, *Die Geheime Heilige Schrift Der Skopzen*.

[33] Grass, *Die Russischen Sekten*, I, pp. 6-11; Kutepov, *Sekty Khlystov I Skoptsov*, p. 38. For a full account of the *Khlysty* legend, see Grass, *Die Russischen Sekten*, I, pp. 1-39. For an assessment of the historical creditability of the legend, see Grass, *Die Russischen Sekten*, I, pp. 39-101.

[34] Cited according to my own translation, Grass, *Die Russischen Sekten*, I, pp. 8-9. Cf. Kutepov, *Sekty Khlystov I Skoptsov*, p. 273.

Danila Philippov, therefore, became the answer to this prayer for a manifestation of God among them.

> He went up the mountain Gorodno, and this is where, among the angels, archangels, seraphim, and other heavenly hosts, the Lord Sabaoth himself descended from heaven. The powers of heaven ascended back to heaven, but the Lord Sabaoth remained on earth in human form, incarnated in Danila Philippov. Since that time, Danila Philippov became a living god and ... his followers became known as the People of God.[35]

So, *Khlysty* legend delineated the incarnation of God, the Lord of Hosts, in Danila Philippov as the origination of their sect.

According to the *Khlysty*, this was an incarnation of the Spirit. Philippov, subsequently, began to teach that neither the old doctrinal books of the Orthodox Church nor the new liturgical books produced by patriarch Nikon's liturgical reforms possessed any value for Christian spirituality;[36] rather, only the teaching of the Lord himself – Philippov, who is the Holy Spirit in human flesh – is necessary for salvation.[37] Spirit Christology, consequently, permeated *Khlysty* teaching.

---

[35] Cited according to my own translation, Kutepov, *Sekty Khlystov I Skoptsov*, p. 272.

> At the request of those people, God, the Lord of Hosts, descended on fiery clouds in a chariot of fire, surrounded by angels, archangels, cherubim, and seraphim, and the whole celestial power descended. When the heavenly powers ascended again to heaven, the most-high God was visible only in the form of Danila Philippov, the most pure flesh which the Lord of Hosts had accepted. Thus, Danila became the 'living God' (Cited according to my own translation, Grass, *Die Russischen Sekten*, I, pp. 9-10).

[36] This group's existence antedates the Nikon reforms which they soundly rejected. Grass, *Die Russischen Sekten*, I, pp. 366-67; Kutepov, *Sekty Khlystov I Skoptsov*, p. 274.

[37] As a symbol of his authority and the worthlessness of the documents, he threw Orthodoxy's sacred books into the Volga River. When Nikon heard of this activity, Philippov was arrested and incarcerated. According to *Khlysty* legend, God plagued the land with a dense mist until Philippov was released from bondage, whereupon, it dissipated. Subsequently, he reiterated his demand for his followers to eschew the doctrines of the Orthodox Church, which were interpolated with human tradition; instead, the People of God should adhere to his teachings which were the divine revelations of the Holy Spirit. Philippov, then, fashioned his most important oral teachings in written form as 12 commandments, reminiscent of God giving the commandments to Moses. These commandments prohibited intoxication, marriage, profanity, invocations of the devil, attending weddings, stealing, and revealing their secrets; they extoled evangelism and hospitali-

In point of fact, Spirit Christology is the integrative *motif* of *Khlysty* doctrine. As the number of disciples increased, Philippov appointed his spiritual son, Ivan Suslov, as the chief prophet of the movement: he was anointed by the Spirit and became an incarnate Christ, the Son of God.[38] Thus, began a pneumatic succession of Christs among this group;[39] the teaching of multiple incarnations was the *Khlysty's* central doctrine.[40] According to *Khlysty* Christology, Jesus Christ was a human born by natural means, and the virgin birth meant that Mary brought up Jesus in the true faith.[41] After being found morally pure and having faithfully kept all the statutes of the Hebrew Law and prophets, consequently, Jesus became the ultimate incarnate Christ, Son of God, when the Spirit descended into him during the Jordan event.[42] Hence, incarnation and becoming

---

ty. However, here, the focus must rest on the first, second, and twelfth commandments. The first accentuated Philippov's deity; the second asserted the exclusiveness of his teaching; the twelfth mandated faith in and obedience to the Holy Spirit; of course, Philippov was the Holy Spirit in human flesh. Grass, *Die Russischen Sekten*, I, pp. 13-16; Kutepov, *Sekty Khlystov I Skoptsov*, pp. 271-72. Cf. Conybeare, *Russian Dissenters*, p. 358.

[38] Grass, *Die Russischen Sekten*, I, p. 255; Kutepov, *Sekty Khlystov I Skoptsov*, pp. 272-74; Conybeare, *Russian Dissenters*, pp. 342, 357-59; Bolshakoff, *Russian Nonconformity*, pp. 84-84.

[39] Grass, *Die Russischen Sekten*, I, pp. 16-39. The image of pneumatic succession is drawn from the Spirit which was upon Moses being passed on to the 70 elders of Israel (Num. 11.25). During the 18th century, the Russian state began a severe persecution designed to eradicate the group. Grass, *Die Russischen Sekten*, I, pp. 111-45; Bolshakoff, *Russian Nonconformity*, pp. 83-84; Heard, *Russian Dissent*, pp. 253-57; Conybeare, *Russian Dissenters*, pp. 359-61.

[40] The Trinity, according to the *Khlysty*, exists not as three hypostases in one ousia; rather, the Trinity depicts the three-fold immanent manifestation of divine power in humanity and the world. Grass, *Die Russischen Sekten*, I, pp. 252-54; Kutepov, *Sekty Khlystov I Skoptsov*, pp. 278, 282, 288-89. For overviews of *Khlysty* doctrine, see Grass, *Die Russischen Sekten*, I, pp. 252-366; Kutepov, *Sekty Khlystov I Skoptsov*, pp. 269-344; Dobroklonsky, *Russkoi Tserkvi*, pp. 673-76; Bolshakoff, *Russian Nonconformity*, pp. 87-91. Selivanov held the same doctrine of multiple incarnations, yet his doctrine of castration differentiated the *Skoptsy* from the other groups which held similar Christologies. For examinations of *Skoptsy* doctrine, see Grass, *Die Russischen Sekten*, II, pp. 587-788; Kutepov, *Sekty Khlystov I Skoptsov*, pp. 345-449; Dobroklonsky, *Russkoi Tserkvi*, pp. 677-80. Regarding their creed, a copy can be found in Anderson, *Staroobriadchestvo I Sektantstvo*, pp. 325-39.

[41] Grass, *Die Russischen Sekten*, I, p. 256. Accordingly, the resurrection and ascension of Jesus and Philippov were spiritual, while their bodies remained in the grave. Grass, *Die Russischen Sekten*, I, pp. 256-57; Kutepov, *Sekty Khlystov I Skoptsov*, pp. 275-76.

[42] Kutepov, *Sekty Khlystov I Skoptsov*, pp. 282-83; Grass, *Die Russischen Sekten*, I, p. 256.

Son of God denoted the full possession of the Spirit.[43] Jesus, furthermore, was not the first incarnation of deity; the Hebrew prophets and patriarchs were Christs, possessed of the Spirit.[44] Consequently, the *Khlysty* believed that Jesus Christ was an incarnation of the divine Spirit,[45] and this incarnation was available to all believers who followed his moral example and received the Spirit. So, albeit in different degrees, according to their fullness of the Spirit, all *Khlysty* potentially could become Christs.[46] Since Philippov was the incarnation of the Lord of Hosts, he differed in degree to any previous Christs, including Jesus; whereas Jesus had brought the old revelation, Philippov was filled with the greatest possible endowment of the Spirit and brought the new revelation of God.[47] The *Khlysty*, therefore, predicated their doctrine of multiple incarnations on a Spirit christological model of pneumatic incarnation.

The *Khlysty*, accordingly, laid the lineaments for a pneumatic ecclesiology, which was evident in their leadership, worship, prophetic speech, and sacraments. The leader of each group of *Khlysty* was a human possessed of the Spirit, an incarnate Christ and prophet; standing alongside this Christ was a female counterpart: the *Theotokos*, the spiritual wife of the Christ.[48] The impetus of their

---

[43] 'The incarnation of God in Jesus of Nazareth is therefore understood as the complete fulfillment of Jesus with the Spirit of God, and accordingly, then all later incarnations).' Cited according to my own translation, Grass, *Die Russischen Sekten*, I, p. 257. Cf. Kutepov, *Sekty Khlystov I Skoptsov*, pp. 275, 283-86.

[44] Grass, *Die Russischen Sekten*, I, pp. 255-56.

[45] This is why the *Khlysty* used the designations Christ and Holy Spirit interchangeably, as if they are names for the same person. Grass, *Die Russischen Sekten*, I, p. 257, n. 2.

[46] Kutepov, *Sekty Khlystov I Skoptsov*, pp. 274-306. Cf. Grass, *Die Russischen Sekten*, I, pp. 253-56; Conybeare, *Russian Dissenters*, pp. 339-41. 'Now every person on their own can achieve the highest moral perfection (may even become God), and the *Khlysty* see an example ... in the history of the life and work of the Lord Jesus Christ.' Cited according to my own translation, Kutepov, *Sekty Khlystov I Skoptsov*, p. 269. 'The *Khlysty's* moral system revolves mainly around the question of the relationship of humanity to God and how the incarnation is affected.' Cited according to my own translation, Kutepov, *Sekty Khlystov I Skoptsov*, p. 274. Regarding how the *Khlysty* moral doctrine integrates with their Christology and soteriology, see Kutepov, *Sekty Khlystov I Skoptsov*, pp. 306-22.

[47] Grass, *Die Russischen Sekten*, I, pp. 257-58, 260.

[48] For a woman to be qualified to become a Mother of God, she must possess the Spirit in great quantity. Grass, *Die Russischen Sekten*, I, pp. 258-59. It has been suggested that all adherents of the *Khlysty* had spiritual marriages. Kutepov, *Sekty Khlystov I Skoptsov*, pp. 83-84, 292-306; Conybeare, *Russian Dissenters*, pp. 351-54; Bolshakoff, *Russian Nonconformity*, pp. 87-88; Heard, *Russian Dissent*, pp. 257, 260-

secret worship,⁴⁹ which was held at night in an undisclosed location and known as the mysteries, was to induce the presence and an experience of the divine Spirit.⁵⁰ The participants – adorned in white apparel and waving handkerchiefs in the air, symbolizing the wings of the angels present among them⁵¹ – began to sing hymns which the Spirit had prophetically bequeathed to them.⁵² While continuing their singing, the group joined hands and began a circular dance, the *Radenija*,⁵³ which, according to the *Khlysty*, provided the primary access to union with the Spirit.⁵⁴ As individuals received the Spirit, their response was clearly demarcated from the normal worship and dance: they began to jump, run, whirl, fall in ecstasy, enter a trance, prophesy, or manifest glossolalia.⁵⁵ Several of the participants, thus,

---

61. The *Skoptsy* also maintained a female prophetess in each congregation, *Theotokos*, along with the Christ. Grass, *Die Russischen Sekten*, II, pp. 587-90.

⁴⁹ According to Serge Bolshakoff, 'When outsiders were present, the services progressed in a devout and puritanical way and were hardly distinguishable from the usual Protestant services. The preachers stressed the vanity of life and the pressing need for true conversion'. Bolshakoff, *Russian Nonconformity*, p. 90. It is unclear whether or not Protestantism influenced the *Khlysty*. Regarding possible influences on *Khlysty* origination, see Grass, *Die Russischen Sekten*, I, pp. 588-648.

⁵⁰ There is no difference between the *Khlysty* and the *Skoptsy*. Kutepov, *Sekty Khlystov I Skoptsov*, pp. 465-82. Cf. Grass, *Die Russischen Sekten*, I, pp. 366-410; Grass, *Die Russischen Sekten*, II, pp. 809-13; Bolshakoff, *Russian Nonconformity*, p. 90; Conybeare, *Russian Dissenters*, pp. 367-68.

⁵¹ There is no difference between the *Khlysty* and the *Skoptsy*. Kutepov, *Sekty Khlystov I Skoptsov*, pp. 482-86. Cf. Grass, *Die Russischen Sekten*, I, pp. 381-83; Grass, *Die Russischen Sekten*, II, pp. 813-18.

⁵² There is no difference between the *Khlysty* and the *Skoptsy*. Kutepov, *Sekty Khlystov I Skoptsov*, pp. 270-71, 486-90, 525-31. Cf. Grass, *Die Russischen Sekten*, I, pp. 270-71, 403-405; Grass, *Die Russischen Sekten*, II, pp. 818-26; Conybeare, *Russian Dissenters*, pp. 344-46, 351. For an examination of their use of these songs, see Grass, *Die Russischen Sekten*, I, pp. 402-10.

⁵³ For a complete discussion about this dance, see Grass, *Die Russischen Sekten*, I, pp. 381-402.

⁵⁴ The *Khlysty* insisted that this was the same method employed by David in the Hebrew Scriptures and the apostles on the day of Pentecost to entice the descent of the Spirit. Grass, *Die Russischen Sekten*, I, pp. 267-69. They also practiced the hesychastic Jesus prayer as another means of invoking an outpouring of the Spirit. Grass, *Die Russischen Sekten*, I, pp. 265, 406.

⁵⁵ There is no difference between the *Khlysty* and the *Skoptsy*. Kutepov, *Sekty Khlystov I Skoptsov*, pp. 490-525. Cf. Grass, *Die Russischen Sekten*, I, pp. 272-84; Grass, *Die Russischen Sekten*, II, pp. 826-35; Conybeare, *Russian Dissenters*, pp. 346-51; Bolshakoff, *Russian Nonconformity*, pp. 90-91. It is interesting to note, according to eyewitness reports, that when the Spirit descended upon senior adults who were hardly able to walk, they often were enabled to dance or run very swiftly. Grass, *Die Russischen Sekten*, I, p. 272. For a complete description of these experiences, see Grass, *Die Russischen Sekten*, I, pp. 264-304.

manifested prophetic speech and pneumatic language. Primarily, the *Khlysty* recognized two signs of the Spirit's language: (1) speaking in rhythm and rhyme and (2) glossolalia.[56] Essentially, these manifestations of the Spirit demonstrated the person's participation in one of the *Khlysty's* two chief sacraments: Spirit baptism.[57] The *Khlysty* replaced water baptism with Spirit baptism, which initiated them into Christhood.[58] As Jesus Christ received the Spirit during the Jordan event, likewise, the *Khlysty* Christs must be baptized in the Spirit. The *Khlysty*, therefore, structured their ecclesiology and Christology on a foundation of charismatic experience.

Pneumatology imbued *Khlysty* Christology. Jesus Christ was born a human, by natural means, and during the Jordan event the divine Spirit became incarnated in Jesus: the Spirit indwelt and possessed him, constituting him Christ and Son of God. On this rendering of incarnation, Jesus Christ became the archetype of what believers could become, so the *Khlystys* accentuated experiences of the divine

---

[56] The speaking in rhythm and rhyme under the inspiration of the Spirit as well as glossolalia and interpretation of tongues produced the *Khlysty's* songs and poems. Grass, *Die Russischen Sekten*, I, pp. 282-84. For their use among the *Skoptsy*, see Grass, *Die Russischen Sekten*, II, pp. 608-45. Members of the group would begin to sing in the Spirit, and someone would record the verses, so that the group would faithfully remember and use these spiritual songs to induce the presence of the Spirit in their worship. These hymns of the Spirit were compiled in a book known as the *Dove Book* and supposedly given more authority than Scripture among the group. Grass, *Die Russischen Sekten*, I, pp. 13-14, 284, 298-304; Grass, *Die Russischen Sekten*, II, pp. 749, 767-69; Bolshakoff, *Russian Nonconformity*, pp. 83-87; Heard, *Russian Dissent*, pp. 257-60.

[57] The other chief sacrament is suffering: as Jesus Christ received the Spirit and suffered at the hands of evil humans, so must the *Khlysty* Christs be baptized in the Spirit and enter the messianic sufferings, which often arose from persecution by the Russian government. When a person is 'in the Spirit', they believed that person was impervious to pain. Grass, *Die Russischen Sekten*, I, pp. 258-59. This sect originally went by the moniker 'Christ-believers', but a corruption of the word rendered it *Khlysty*, meaning whips or flagellants, which the *Khlysty* considered a sobriquet of honor. Conybeare, *Russian Dissenters*, pp. 340, 346. Herein lies the chief distinction between the *Khlysty* and the *Skoptsy*. The *Skoptsy* agreed with the *Khlysty* regarding Jesus' Spirit baptism and the need for believers to be baptized in the Spirit, yet the *Skoptsy* also included fire or castration: baptism in Spirit and fire. They maintained that during the Jordan event Jesus was castrated, probably by John the Baptist, and received the Spirit. Grass, *Die Russischen Sekten*, II, pp. 645-56, 840-41. Cf. Conybeare, *Russian Dissenters*, pp. 367-68; Bolshakoff, *Russian Nonconformity*, pp. 94-95.

[58] Also, instead of wine the *Khlysty* used water in the Eucharist. Kutepov, *Sekty Khlystov I Skoptsov*, pp. 570-73; Grass, *Die Russischen Sekten*, I, pp. 410-17; Grass, *Die Russischen Sekten*, II, pp. 835-44; Conybeare, *Russian Dissenters*, pp. 355-56.

Spirit, especially, Spirit baptism. Among the *Khlystys*, there was no indication of the incarnation of the preexistent Logos, but they affirmed an incarnation of the divine Spirit. More precisely, this incarnation of the Spirit actually referred to the Spirit anointing, indwelling, and inspiring Christ, so that Christ became Son of God by the Spirit's anointing, similar to a Dynamic Monarchian view. On the basis of this interpretation, the *Khlysty* and the *Skoptsy* appear to delineate a Spirit christological paradigm of pneumatic inspiration.

Conclusion

These marginal groups have much in common. They viewed the state-church as spiritually desiccate, having erred from the apostolic faith, and influenced by the spirit of antichrist. They, also, rejected the sacramentalism and creedalism of the institutional church, which prompted them to seek a renewal of what they considered to be true apostolic doctrine, sacramental practice, and ecclesiology. This was most evident in their Christology, from which other doctrines were formed. These groups advocated a form of Spirit Christology in which Jesus became Christ when he received Spirit baptism at the Jordan, and this experience was paradigmatic of believers' receiving Spirit baptism and entering Christhood; furthermore, Spirit baptism was the genuine sacramental form of apostolic baptism. Arguably, these groups taught Spirit christological paradigms of pneumatic inspiration, yet the manner in which they present them varies.

Seemingly, the greatest distinction between them concerns the doctrine of incarnation. The Paulicians present a non-incarnational Spirit Christology. Christ was a unique human, the new Adam, born of Mary, but this does not imply the incarnation of deity in Jesus. When Jesus received the Spirit during the Jordan event, he was adopted by God as the Christ and began the process of deification; his entire ministry was conducted through the anointing and inspiration of the Spirit. The *Khlystys*, however, taught a doctrine of incarnation which significantly varied from the traditional Orthodox doctrine of incarnation. According to the *Khlystys*, when Jesus received the fullness of the Spirit in Spirit baptism, at the Jordan, deity was incarnated in him; he entered Christhood. This experience was not unique to Jesus; rather, the OT prophets had received the same experience of the Spirit, just not in the same degree as Jesus. In fact, the supreme example of Spirit fullness or incarnation of deity in a human was not Jesus; this honor belonged to Philippov. Nevertheless, the potential for entering Christhood, through receiving the fullness of the Spirit, exists for every follower of Philippov. Though the *Khlystys'* Christology advocates a form of incarnation, essentially, it is a Spirit christological form of pneumatic inspiration. So, the issue of incarnation is only an apparent distinction; actually, all these groups support Spirit christological paradigms of pneumatic inspiration.

14

SUMMARY/CONCLUSION TO PART TWO

As the second part of this inquiry draws to a close, it is time to assess its purposes: to trace Spirit Christology's presence, or lack thereof, and to identify the Spirit christological paradigms and their relationships with doctrinal development in the Christian tradition.

Although most inquiries into Spirit Christology focus on the early Patristic Period and then move to the modern Spirit christological discussion, while scarcely acknowledging the existence of Spirit Christology in the intervening period, the second part of this inquiry has tracked Spirit Christology's existence in the writings of the three major branches of Christianity and certain voices on the margins and identified the Spirit christological paradigms supported by these writers. Albeit Spirit Christology only occurred sporadically during this epoch, it was present during this epoch.

Spirit Christology is not limited to one particular model; rather, it is very fluid in nature and transcends rigid boundaries. Nevertheless, this inquiry has identified the diverse characteristics of Spirit Christology so that three paradigms have emerged: pneumatic inspiration, pneumatic incarnation, and pneumatic mediation. The first part of this inquiry has demonstrated these three paradigms were present in the early church and instrumental in the development of christological and trinitarian doctrine. In the second part of this inquiry, with the exceptions of Bede and Bonaventure, Spirit Christology either emerged among writers or groups embroiled in christological debate, such as Elipandus and the Ethiopian tradition, or among those seeking doctrinal reform and critiquing the desiccation of the institutional church: Protestants and certain voices from the margins.

Pneumatic inspiration stands alone as a non-incarnational form of Spirit Christology. According to this model, Christ was a human anointed with the impersonal power of the Spirit; the messianic bearer of the Spirit, but Jesus was in no wise divine. In part one, this form of Christology was common among the Ebionites, various Gnostics, and Dynamic Monarchianism. In part two this paradigm was common to certain marginal groups such as the *Paulicians*, *Skoptsy* and the *Khlysty*, as well as the Liberal Protestant tradition.

Pneumatic incarnation held that the one divine essence of deity, which is Spirit, was incarnated in Jesus Christ. The adherents to this model denied triune doctrine and maintained a strict monotheistic view of God; thus, the designation Modalist Monarchianism became attached to them in part one.[1]

Pneumatic mediation delineates the agency of the Spirit in every facet of Christ's life and mission. It recognizes triune doctrine, so that the eternal Son was incarnated in Christ, yet in the grace of union, the Spirit conceived the human nature in Mary's womb and joined it to the divine nature. This paradigm allows space for the Spirit to function as the agent anointing, commissioning, and empowering Christ's human nature for ministry. This model developed in part one through Justin Martyr, Tertullian, Irenaeus, Clement of Alexandria, Origen, Cyril of Jerusalem, Athanasius, the Cappadocian Fathers, Ambrose, Hilary, Augustine, Nestorius, and Theodoret of Cyrus. In part two, pneumatic mediation continued in a limited sense in the Catholic and Ethiopian traditions, as well as among Protestants such as the Puritans.

Regarding the paradigm of pneumatic mediation, it should be noted, two distinct models emerged in part one. One model stemming from Augustine taught that the incarnation was the anointing of the Spirit, so Christ remained anointed for his entire ministry, and all subsequent experiences of the Spirit, such as the Jordan event, were merely typological. The other model affirmed Christ's subsequent experiences of the Spirit as genuine experiences in Christ's life and ministry; the Spirit anointing Jesus' humanity,

---

[1] During this epoch, this paradigm emerged among Oneness Pentecostals; an examination of their Spirit Christology will appear in Part Three.

therefore, is vital to this christological construct. The two-fold division of this paradigm continued in part two; the former model appeared among Catholic writers and the latter model emerged in Protestant writings, specifically, Puritan sermons.[2]

Moreover, this inquiry has identified the environment which supports the appearance of Spirit Christology and distinguished between a pneumatically permeated Logos Christology and Spirit Christology. Spirit Christology emerged in an environment which focused on pneumatology and the humanity of Jesus Christ; any hint of Docetism was completely rejected. Pneumatological emphases, however, were not sufficient to produce Spirit Christology. A pneumatologically permeated Logos Christology can delineate the Spirit's presence and power in the life of believers flowing from the ascended Christ, including a doctrine of Spirit baptism, but this in itself does not constitute a genuine Spirit Christology. To fall within the boundaries of Spirit Christology, a paradigm must acknowledge and depict how the Spirit relates to Christ's humanity in his life and mission, so that the believer's experience and relationship with the Spirit is based on Christ's experience of the Spirit. This two-fold focus on pneumatology and Christ's humanity were important catalysts in the emergence of the modern discussion of Spirit Christology.

---

[2] This paradigm also appears among proto-Pentecostal writers, Holiness writers, and in early Pentecostal periodical literature in Part Three.

PART THREE

THE RISE OF PENTECOSTALISM

15

PROTO-PENTECOSTALS

Consisting of two parts, this chapter directs attention to the early part of the nineteenth-century when the Spirit was poured out in Pentecostal-like fashion on various groups, in diverse geographical locations, which experienced Spirit baptism and the charismata antecedent to the global Pentecostal revival beginning in the early twentieth-century, and their theologies were remarkably similar to early Pentecostal theology, thus the designation proto-Pentecostals. The first part examines Spirit Christology among the writings of the Molokan-Jumpers; noteworthily, this group has a direct historical connection with the Azusa Street Revival. The second part surveys the writings of Edward Irving.

Molokan-Jumpers (*Pryguny*)

The *Pryguny* belonged to the Russian sectarian branch of believers, which accepted the designation Spiritual Christians, protesting the apostasy and spiritual desiccation of the Russian Orthodox Church: the Doukhobors and Molokans.[1] The *Pryguny* originated from bifur-

---

[1] According to Daniel Shubin, 'Siluan Kolesnikov was the harbinger of Spiritual Christianity in Russia, and spread the philosophy that led to the formation of what would become known as the Dukhabor in the next generation'. Daniel H. Shubin, *A History of Russian Christianity* (4 vols.; New York: Algora Publishing, 2005), III, p. 61. Kolesnikov organized and led a group (1732–75) known as the *Ikonobortzi* (Iconoclasts): they rejected the use of icons in worship and the sacraments of the institutional church. They trusted in the inner revelation of the Spirit, and under the Spirit's inspiration they would jump, dance, and prophesy. Kolesnikov's successor to group leadership (1775–90), Ilarion Pobirokin, taught that

cations of the Spiritual Christians; presumably, the Molokans parted ways from the Doukhobors with regard to the authority of the canonical Scriptures (1823).[2] The Doukhobors gave preeminence to their oral tradition and an inward intrinsic divine illumination above that of Scripture.[3] Conversely, the Molokans affirmed the prestige

---

the enlightenment of the Word-God dwelt in the soul of every person; accordingly, rejecting Jesus Christ's deity, he taught that the Word dwelled in Jesus constituting him Christ and son of God, so the inner divine Word dwells in all righteous people, so that they become Christs or sons of God. Under the leadership of a disciple of Ilarion Pobirokin, Saveli Kapustin, the movement developed in the Doukhobor sect (1790–85). Shubin, *Russian Christianity*, III, pp. 60-62. Furthermore, the Doukhobors dismissed the orthodox triune doctrine of God. Using a psychological analogy of deity, they posited an immanent God in the human memory, understanding, and will, so that each Doukhobor is an incarnation of the Trinity. Christologically, they debarred the orthodox notion of incarnation: Christ was possessed of the divine Logos and wisdom, and he personified piety and purity, but he was son of God like any other human has the ability to be son of God, but in a greater degree. The Doukhobors rejected the state church, sacraments including marriage, taking oaths, military service, Orthodox rituals and fasts, the idea of heaven and hell, the doctrine of the resurrection, and the veneration of icons; since the image of God is in human beings, they venerated those in whom God dwells by kissing and bowing to them. They also taught the preexistence and transmigration of the human soul. The earliest Doukhobor confession of faith was presented in 1791 to Kakhavski, the Governor-General of Ekaterinoslav Province. The name Doukhobor connotes a Spirit wrestler. Their antagonists associated the name with the 4th century Pneumatomachoi who fought against the Spirit; yet the Dukhobors insisted it denoted that they were champions of the Spirit. Regarding Dukhobor history and doctrine, see Anderson, *Staroobriadchestvo I Sektantstvo*, pp. 371-99; Alexander M. Evalenko, *The Message of the Doukhobors: A Statement of True Facts by 'Christians of the Universal Brotherhood' and by Prominent Champions of Their Cause* (New York: International Library Publishing Company, 1913); Shubin, *Russian Christianity*, III, pp. 62-69, 140-48; Conybeare, *Russian Dissenters*, pp. 263-87; Aurelio Palmieri, 'The Russian Doukhobors and Their Religious Teachings', *HTR* 8 (1915), pp. 62-81; Bolshakoff, *Russian Nonconformity*, pp. 97-105; Dobroklonsky, *Russkoi Tserkvi*, pp. 681-85; J. Eugene Clay, 'The Woman Clothed in the Sun: Pacifism and Apocalyptic Discourse among Russian Spiritual Christian Molokan-Jumpers', *CH* 80 (2011), pp. 109-10.

[2] Daniel Shubin asserts that the Molokans antedate the Doukhobors and had existed independently, and the only parting of the ways was when Semeon Matveich Uklein, the son-in-law of the leader of the Doukhobors, separated from the Doukhobors over the issue of Biblical authority; accordingly, Uklein joined the Molokans because they advocated Scriptural authority. Nevertheless, it is certain that after joining the Molokans and rising to a position of leadership, Uklein organized the Molokan movement, giving it a definite structure and systematizing a rational and comprehensible theology, integrating Molokan ideas with Doukhobor and Judaizers' Hebrew concepts. Shubin, *Russian Christianity*, III, pp. 72-80.

[3] Handing down their oral tradition and doctrines were known as the 'Living Book', which they contrasted with the dead letter of Scripture. Children were taught this 'Living Book' between the ages of 6 and 15, at which time the soul

of Scriptural authority, while acknowledging the validity of inward enlightenment. According to the Molokans, Scripture is the primary source of doctrine and of moral perfection. Hermeneutically, they were prone to interpret allegorically passages about Christ and his miracles.[4] A revival and powerful outpouring of the Holy Spirit (1833) – with manifestations of glossolalia, miracles, prophecy, trances, and dancing in the Spirit – occasioned a parting of the ways among the Molokans. Those who repudiated the new demonstrations of the Spirit continued to be known simply as Molokans or Constant Molokans; those who accepted the experience were dubbed the *Pryguny* (Jumpers) by their antagonists, signifying their common response to the Spirit.[5]

The various writings of the *Pryguny* were compiled in a book, *Spirit and Life – Book of the Sun*.[6] Subsequent to the editor's comments the book consists of seven sections and an appendix. Section 1 provides an historical overview of the group's inception, the outpouring of the Spirit, the life and teachings of their founders, and the severe persecution heaped upon them by the Russian clergy and

---

entered the child. Conybeare, *Russian Dissenters*, pp. 273, 275; Palmieri, 'Russian Doukhobors', pp. 73-74; Shubin, *Russian Christianity*, III, pp. 65-66; Bolshakoff, *Russian Nonconformity*, p. 105.

[4] The name Molokan means milk-drinker which was attached to this group because its adherents did not keep the fasts of the Orthodox Church and often drank milk on these days. For overviews of Molokan history and doctrine, see Anderson, *Staroobriadchestvo I Sektantstvo*, pp. 400-29; Dobroklonsky, *Russkoi Tserkvi*, pp. 685-90; Conybeare, *Russian Dissenters*, pp. 289-326; Shubin, *Russian Christianity*, III, pp. 70-80, 131-40; Bolshakoff, *Russian Nonconformity*, pp. 105-12; Clay, 'The Woman Clothed in the Sun', pp. 110-11; Pauline V. Young, *The Pilgrims of Russian-Town* (Chicago: University of Chicago Press, 1932), pp. 54-57, 61-69.

[5] Clay, 'The Woman Clothed in the Sun', pp. 110-15; Bolshakoff, *Russian Nonconformity*, pp. 109-10; Shubin, *Russian Christianity*, III, pp. 132-35.

[6] This work was first published as handwritten manuscripts (1915) titled *Morning Star* and *Spirit and Life*; however, the initial common name was *Book of the Sun*. It was printed in type in an expanded edition which included several of Rudometkin's writings that were not accessible during the first publication (1928); this inquiry will work from a 1983 reprint of the text. The purpose of this work is to inform the younger generation of *Pryguny* in America of their spiritual heritage. See the editors' notes and preface, Ivan Gureivich Samarin and Daniel H. Shubin (eds.), *Spirit and Life–Book of the Sun: Divine Discourses of the Preceptors and the Martyrs for the Word of God, the Faith of Jesus, and the Holy Spirit, of the Religion of the Spiritual Christian Molokan-Jumpers, Including a History of the Religion* (trans. John W. Volkov; 1983 repr.; USA: Daniel H. Shubin, 1928), pp. 3-8.

state.⁷ Sections 2-4 preserve the writings of the sect's founders: Lukian Petrovich Sokolov (2 letters), David Yesseyevich (3 books), and Maxim Gavrilovich Rudometkin (14 books).⁸ Section 5 is comprised of Efim Gerasimovich Klubnikin's prophetic articles and drawings.⁹ Section 6 supplies posterity with Rudometkin's prayer book and liturgy.¹⁰ Section 7 recounts the group's journey into refuge in obedience to Klubnikin's prophecy.¹¹ The appendix contains various prophetic writings and drawings.¹² Since Spirit christological references permeate the book, and considering that Rudometkin was their most eminent leader, actually being crowned king of spirits,¹³ the focus of this inquiry will narrow to Rudometkin's writings.

---

⁷ Samarin and Shubin (eds.), *Spirit and Life*, pp. 11-64. The text seems to agree with Shubin's premise that the Molokans existed independently of the Doukhobors, and it also suggests that a certain unnamed Protestant doctor from England influenced their understanding of Scripture. Samarin and Shubin (eds.), *Spirit and Life*, p. 23.

⁸ Samarin and Shubin (eds.), *Spirit and Life*, pp. 65-631. It should be noted that Feodor Osipovich Bulgakov (1809–76), who was a prophet and leader of the *Pryguny*, took the messianic name David son of Jesse (David Yesseyevich). From his cell in monastic prison, which was a seven foot deep hole in the ground covered with a piece of wood, Yesseyevich wrote his *Book of Zion* to depict the role of the *Pryguny* in the immanent return of Jesus Christ and to explicate the Scriptural and prophetic distinction between the Constant Molokans and the *Pryguny*. According to Yesseyevich, Armageddon and the return of Christ was at hand. The beast and false prophet – the tsarist regime and Russian clergy – would persecute the woman clothed in the sun, but the destruction of the beast system was certain and soon (Rev. 12.1-17). Interestingly, he identified the *Pryguny* with the 144,000 who were sealed with the Holy Spirit (Rev. 7.4-8); accordingly, he identified the Constant Molokans with the great multitude from every nation clothed in white apparel (Rev. 7.9). He prophesies, therefore, that the woman's child whom she will bring forth will be a great prophet that will arise from among the *Pryguny*. David Yesseyevich, 'Book of Zion', in Ivan Gureivich Samarin and Daniel H. Shubin (eds.), *Spirit and Life*, pp. 81-91. Cf. Clay, 'The Woman Clothed in the Sun', pp. 114-21; Shubin, *Russian Christianity*, III, pp. 135-37. Yesseyevich wrote his *Book of Zion* (1833–76) while in prison in Tavria (the Crimea) and Georgia (the Transcaucasus).

⁹ Samarin and Shubin (eds.), *Spirit and Life*, pp. 632-706.
¹⁰ Samarin and Shubin (eds.), *Spirit and Life*, pp. 707-43.
¹¹ Samarin and Shubin (eds.), *Spirit and Life*, pp. 745-58.
¹² Samarin and Shubin (eds.), *Spirit and Life*, pp. 759-68.
¹³ Maxim Rudometkin (1832–77) was born in Algasovo village in Tambov province. Along with his family, at the age of 8, he left the institutional church, joining the Zionites, a designation for the *Pryguny* stemming from the teaching of David Yesseyevich. After being deported to Armenia (1842), these *Pryguny* established a village named Nikitino. Rudometkin began to preach the faith of the *Pryguny* at an early age, gaining respect and notoriety among his peers. Obeying

To elucidate how the Spirit relates to Christ's identity and mission in Rudometkin's writings, this inquiry will proceed by delineating his concepts of God, creation, the fall, and redemption. Regarding the essence of deity, God is Spirit existing as Father, Son, and Holy Spirit.[14] According to Rudometkin, God revealed to him in a vision the inner life and emanation of deity.[15] The Father, existing alone, began to think about a companion, so he spoke, and the Word quickened through himself an image of himself, and this emanation of the divine Word became equated with the Son and was named Alfeyil. The Holy Spirit is the mutual Spirit or divine power that emanates from the Father and Son.[16] Unambiguously, Rudometkin does not recapitulate an orthodox form of trinitarian doctrine; instead, he posits a monarchial triune view, with the Son and Spirit existing in subordinate roles: 'We, His true worshippers, faithfully acknowledge Him (God) always and forever: that the Father, the Word and the Holy Spirit are personally one in the deity,

---

the Spirit, Rudometkin called a fast and invited the elders of the neighboring villages to participate. After fasting three days and during a time of worship, another mighty outpouring of the Holy Spirit and revival was initiated at Nikitino (1853), in which glossolalia and mighty signs and wonders were manifested among them. It was as if God had especially anointed Rudometkin with the Spirit; in fact, during the initial outpouring of the Spirit, while thunder reverberated, a bright light shined, and a choir of angels sang above his house, Rudometkin was bestowed the honor of being called the king of spirits and leader of Zion. Attaining messianic status as the major leader and inspired prophet in the movement, Rudometkin was arrested and brutally treated in a monastic prison (1858–77). While he was in prison, he wrote his 14 prophetic books which are contained in *Spirit and Life*. Samarin and Shubin (eds.), *Spirit and Life*, pp. 50-52; Clay, 'The Woman Clothed in the Sun', pp. 121-22.

[14] Maxim Gavrilovich Rudometkin, 'Divinely-Inspired Discourses of Maxim Gavrilovich Rudometkin, King of Spirits and Leader of the People of Zion, the Spiritual Christian Molokan Jumpers', in Ivan Gureivich Samarin and Daniel H. Shubin (eds.), *Spirit and Life*, 2.2.2, p. 207; 3.6.8, p. 237.

[15] According to the translation of John Volkov, Rudometkin, 'Discourses', 1.2.1-2, p. 170,

> In this [prayer] I in the Spirit constantly and everywhere brought unto God the fragrant sacrifice [of salvation], with a song of victory over those who offend me. This therein opened the eyes of my heart, so I was quickly able to see this mysterious matter: how and from where the God of gods Himself first emanated, and likewise all the spirits eternally subject to Him.

[16] Rudometkin, 'Discourses', 1.4.6–6.5, pp. 172-75. It is interesting to note that Rudometkin posits a form of dualism regarding the emanation of this mutual Spirit: it divides into light and darkness, good and evil, and is constantly in conflict with one another under the authority of Alfeyil (the Son) and Lebeyil (the devil). Rudometkin, 'Discourses', 1.4.6-8, p. 172.

but in power and authority are not equal'.[17] Rudometkin, nonetheless, draws the closest possible relationship between the Son and Spirit in creation: the Father created by His Word and established everything with the Spirit of his lips.[18] God placed the primal humans, Adam and Eve, whom he created in paradise, where the tree of life aromatically permeated the garden; metaphorically speaking, the aroma of the tree of life is the Holy Spirit who gives eternal life. When Adam and Eve fell through the enticement of the serpent, they no longer could partake of the tree of life nor experience its fragrance; in other words, they lost eternal life: the experience of the Spirit.[19] Therein lies the obligation of Christ's redemptive mission: to restore eternal life to humanity through the presence of the Spirit.

To explore the role of the Spirit in Christ's soteriological mission, it is expedient to examine a confession of faith Rudometkin presents.[20] The foundational tenet of *Pryguny* faith is a Spirit christological statement.

---

[17] Cited according to the translation of John Volkov, Rudometkin, 'Discourses', 11.11.1, p. 538.

> For we believe that God the Father is everywhere without beginning and without end, and eternally has no director above Him, higher than Himself. And He is the creator of all His creatures. For He Himself desired and gave birth to all, of which He speaks to the Son, 'I gave birth to You before the dawn.' And all that followed was created by Him, as by His (God's) Word. This is His omnipotent, secret enthroned Word eternally acting as the ambassador of God in heaven and on earth, and truly always maintains obedience unto the Father, and also has most of it over Himself. Of this He Himself speaks, 'The Father is greater than I.'

Cited according to the translation of John Volkov, Rudometkin, 'Discourses', 11.11.2-5, pp. 538-39.

[18] Rudometkin, 'Discourses', 1.12.2, p. 182; 6.6.4-8, pp. 336-37; 7.1.2-4, p. 374; 7.8.15-17, p. 384. 'For the Word and the Holy Spirit forever emanate in power from the Father of all worlds and universes, under the name of the seven Spirits of God, straight to us upon earth. They always travel personally about the world in this Spirit of God as kings and priests.' Rudometkin, 'Discourses', 7.2.7-8, pp. 376-77. Rudometkin uses this power of the spoken word to validate his authority and fulfillment of his prophecies. Cited according to the translation of John Volkov, Rudometkin, 'Discourses', 14.1.14-15, p. 589.

[19] It seems that the devil was not allowed to enter paradise, so recognizing the desire the serpent had for Eve, the devil taught the serpent how to seduce Eve, while Adam was away doing business for God; therefore, original sin was the serpent implanting his seed within Eve. When Adam returned, his conjugal visit resulted in his fall as well. Rudometkin, 'Discourses', 1.12.7–16.6, pp. 182-87. Cf. Rudometkin, 'Discourses', 2.6.13–10.3, pp. 213-18.

[20] Rudometkin, 'Discourses', 5.9.1–14.37, pp. 303-18.

All of us believe that Jesus Christ is the Son of God, born of the virgin Mary, conceived of the Holy Spirit by the Word of the kiss of the Angel Gabriel. All of us believe that at the time of His manifest bodily washing by water in the river Jordan at the age of thirty, and the descent upon Him of the Holy Spirit appearing like a dove, He was exalted by the voice of His Father from heaven, Who said to Him, 'This is My beloved Son, with Whom I am well pleased.'[21]

And it is certain this occurred in the thirtieth year and not on the twelfth day, and for no other reason but to publicly announce Himself: To present Himself in this wash by water to all the people of Israel, and to give concerning Himself a new spiritual sign, that He is in truth the Son of God and the sacrificial Lamb offered to take away the sins of the world, and yet not with the water of the river Jordan, but with the living blood and water continually flowing from the heavenly city or the palace of the King, The Lord Almighty. And so today and always, He Himself generously baptizes and cleanses all of us together who come to Him in full faith, directly with this invisible, living water and blood of His, that is, the Holy Spirit, fire, and the fan of purging for the eternal division.[22]

Several observations arise from this text. First, Rudometkin acknowledges Christ's deity.[23] Second, he affirms the Spirit's agency in the incarnation.[24] Third, at his baptism in the Jordan, along with Christ's flesh, the Spirit anointed the incarnate Son, depicting the Son's eternal subordination and obedience to the Father.[25] Fourth,

---

[21] Cited according to the translation of John Volkov, Rudometkin, 'Discourses', 5.9.1-2, p. 303.

[22] Cited according to the translation of John Volkov, Rudometkin, 'Discourses', 5.12.4-8, pp. 307-308.

[23] 'Jesus Christ is Himself the Word of God, Creator of all the ages and the Giver of the strict law. He, the selfsame, is the Holy One in Israel and the Lord Sabaoth in [*sic*] His name.' Cited according to the translation of John Volkov, Rudometkin, 'Discourses', 5.12.1, p. 307. Rudometkin states that the Son, Alfeyil, is Jesus Christ. Rudometkin, 'Discourses', 1.17.2, p. 187.

[24] 'His second birth is the Lord from heaven. This signifies he was born by way of the Spirit.' Cited according to the translation of John Volkov, Rudometkin, 'Discourses', 3.24.7, p. 259.

[25] But the Son learned by obedience, for He says, 'I am in the Father, and the Father is in Me; and I am among you until the end of the age by the Spirit of the Father.' It is this Spirit that eternally and always promotes Him in every

this anointing of the Spirit identified Jesus Christ as the Son of God. Fifth, the Spirit descending upon Christ as the sacrificial Lamb of God[26] was a spiritual sign, attesting to the fallacy of baptismal regeneration, affirming the weighty nature of Spirit baptism: it was a salvific necessity and a sign of division excluding nonbelievers. From these observations, one may infer that the Spirit's anointing was integral to Christ's salvific mission; receiving the Spirit was a salvific necessity and the goal of the redemptive movement; Spirit baptism holds an intrinsic position in Rudometkin's theology.

These inferences must be understood in light of Rudometkin's pneumatic Christology conjoining with ecclesiology and eschatology. Rudometkin rejects the Russian Orthodox Church's concept of church. The true church is not a physical institution, but it is a spiritual entity where the Spirit dwells in believers as temples of God.[27]

> And it is the selfsame woman of the Apocalypse, clothed in the sun. The sun is the true Christ, and His radiance upon her is the Holy Spirit, sent to her under the division of the ten gifts, to each member according to his strength.[28]

> This is why I feel today that the tree of life, and the image of its standing in the heart of the Paradise of God, universally signifies the immortality of every man who always lives upon earth in the Spirit of truth ... And the Paradise of God and its beauty is the gathering of holy people, or in other words, the woman clothed in Christ and the radiant Spirit of His truth.[29]

> Heed that you drink always the water from the fountain of life. And shun the strange fountains of water, for their water is always bitter and forever deadly, and always flowing willfully

---

place with the power of the authority of God his Father. For we see that He died by the flesh, but was enlivened by the Spirit; for the Spirit is the freedom for a man in truth.
Cited according to the translation of John Volkov, Rudometkin, 'Discourses', 11.11.6-8, p. 539.

[26] Christ has consummated the sign of the Hebrew Passover: 'Christ our Passover has been sacrificed. Moreover, in the Holy Spirit He offered Himself unblemished as a sacrifice to God'. Rudometkin, 'Discourses', 1.32.6, p. 200. Cf. Rudometkin, 'Discourses', 1.34.1-10, pp. 202-203; 5.14.26, p. 316.

[27] Rudometkin, 'Discourses', 5.13.38-39, p. 313. For the confession of faith regarding the church, see Rudometkin, 'Discourses', 5.13.38-46, pp. 313-14.

[28] Rudometkin, 'Discourses', 5.13.40, p. 313.

[29] Rudometkin, 'Discourses', 2.10.1, 5, p. 218.

straight from the mouths of the ancient serpent having seven branching heads, which is his false teaching, which in the past was released by him through the ecumenical councils and like a mighty river upon the woman, in order to drown her in it at the time. O, woman vested in Christ and His Spirit of the radiance of the new, fiery tongues! Are you not presently hidden from the face of that seven-headed ecumenical council and its demonic false papal teaching?[30]

So, Rudometkin figuratively depicted the true church as the woman clothed in the sun: the spiritual bride of Christ.[31] Pneumatically constituted, the true church basking in the fiery radiance of new tongues and illumination of the charismata partakes of the fruit of immortality from the tree of life, and it is the locus of the restored paradise of God where the aroma of the tree of life, which is the Spirit, permeates its atmosphere.[32] The moon beneath the woman's feet represents the old written law, and the crown of twelve stars upon her head depicts the new apostolic spiritual gospel. The woman's birth pains, as she travails to bring forth her son, portray the dragon's persecution of the woman (Rev. 12.1-5).[33] The seven crowns which the dragon dons reveal its identity: the dragon is the

---

[30] Rudometkin, 'Discourses', 7.15.2-5, pp. 400-401.

[31] 'The newly-promised Israel, always living by the law of the faith of our Lord Jesus Christ and the covenant of the love of flaming union: [His] wife clothed in the sun.' Cited according to the translation of John Volkov, Rudometkin, 'Discourses', 13.1.10, p. 575. Cf. Rudometkin, 'Discourses', 1.32.3, p. 200; 2.2.5-6, p. 208; 2.5.1, p. 211; 2.11.1-13; 3.7.5-13, p. 239; 6.9.2-12, pp. 341-42.

[32] I have included all of my inscrutable mysteries of the newly-coming age, and a revelation of the Spirit of Mount Zion in new fiery tongues. Which today the sinistral cannot yet learn with the exception of only ourselves, the sons and daughters of God, the newly-promised Israel of the newly-sealed members of the woman clothed in the sun. All of them everywhere possess the vivid sign of the seal of the living God, in the Spirit the new fiery tongues and His diverse miracle-working activity, each one according to his ability in the body of the church.

Rudometkin, 'Discourses', 5.1.1-3, p. 293. 'This Spirit would have filled the nostrils of all of you with the fragrance of the aroma of the new Paradise and the power of the Spirit of the new age, approaching age, speaking the truth in new, fiery tongues.' Cited according to the translation of John Volkov, Rudometkin, 'Discourses', 12.4.7, p. 560. Cf. Rudometkin, 'Discourses', 1.12.7-14, pp. 182-83; 4.3.14-15, p. 273.

[33] Rudometkin, 'Discourses', 5.13.41-45, p. 313. Cf. Rudometkin, 'Discourses', 3.18.1-26, pp. 249-52; 5.17.3-4, p. 321.

institutional state-church coronated with the tiaras of its seven ecumenical councils.³⁴ Rudometkin, the king of spirits, will fulfill the prophecy concerning the woman's son, who shall come forth to defeat her enemies and rule with a rod of iron.³⁵ According to Rudometkin's pneumatic ecclesiology and eschatology, then, the *Pryguny* composing the true church of pneumatic believers, standing under the sign of glossolalia and in contradistinction to the institutional church of the seven ecumenical councils, will rule and reign with Christ.³⁶

Because God is Spirit, the *Pryguny* worship God in Spirit;³⁷ they reject the liturgy, rituals, fasts, and sacraments of the institutional-state church, replacing them with their own spiritual versions.³⁸ Regarding water baptism, the *Pryguny* recognized this as a proleptic ritual, practiced by Jews and John the Baptist, pointing to Spirit baptism which Christ received and has now bequeathed to the

---

³⁴ Rudometkin, 'Discourses', 1.33.1-10, pp. 201-202; 3.18.21–19.1-20, pp. 251-54; 3.22.2-3, p. 256; 4.6.4-11, pp. 277-78; 4.9.7-11, pp. 281-82; 4.9.12-19, pp. 282-83; 4.12.4-12, pp. 288-89; 5.2.10-13, p. 295; 5.6.6, p. 299; 5.15.1–18.20, pp. 318-25; 6.12.1–10, pp. 345-48. Rudometkin posits that early on the institutional-church had repressed the Spirit's activity: 'by the end of the third century the new pathways of the Spirit of truth were lost, and therein all the commandments of love, the law of Christ, were manifestly trampled down'. Cited according to the translation of John Volkov, Rudometkin, 'Discourses', 8.3.5, p. 419.

³⁵ Rudometkin, 'Discourses', 1.35.1-9, pp. 203-204; 3.16.5-6, p. 248; 3.18.11, p. 250; 3.25.1-9, pp. 261-62; 4.1.14, p. 248; 4.2.3-23, pp. 269-71; 4.3.13, p. 273; 4.4.1-2, p. 274; 4.14.15, p. 292; 6.1.4-5, pp. 232-33; 7.13.8, p. 399; 7.28.1, p. 415; 9.25.1-7, p. 476; 12.7.3, p. 564. Rudometkin prophesied that the Lord would return to earth in the southern part of the Transcaucasus near Mount Ararat and rule from there during his millennial reign, so Rudometkin encouraged the migration of the *Pryguny* to this area. Rudometkin, 'Discourses', 10.7.1-8, pp. 496-97.

³⁶ Rudometkin, 'Discourses', 5.3.1-6, pp. 296-97; 8.22.10, p. 442; 9.30.1, p. 482.

³⁷ Rudometkin, 'Discourses', 3.5.7-9, p. 235; 3.26.1-2, p. 262; 4.5.3, p. 276; 11.22.8, p. 549.

³⁸ We all everywhere sanctify with the Word of God, prayer and the sprinkling of the invisible essence – the Holy Spirit, and not with tangible river water or the blood of a sacrificed natural lamb, which was set down for us as an example by the olden law. Today this is replaced everywhere by the spiritual, not the physical. For Jesus Christ, who is Himself the sacrificed true Lamb of God, born of the Holy Spirit, by way of His own Spirit established all of this for us, in order that everyone who believes on Him should live spiritually, and not physically, so that all of us might resurrect in this Holy Spirit of His on the last day.

Cited according to the translation of John Volkov, Rudometkin, 'Discourses', 5.14.23-27, pp. 316-17. Cf. Rudometkin, 'Discourses', 5.13.1–14.21, pp. 309-16.

church.³⁹ In point of fact, Rudometkin asserts that the foundation of the church rests on Christ and the Pentecostal experience of Spirit baptism;⁴⁰ therefore, all who have received Spirit baptism have become prophets and sons of God.⁴¹ Hence, anyone who preaches or teaches among the *Pryguny* must have received Spirit baptism.⁴²

> This baptism must abide among all adherents, the small and the great of us alike. Wherein each one baptized must have the *spiritual sign* upon him, which is *speech of the Spirit* in *new, fiery tongues*. This is a flail in the hand of the Lord, with which He will manifestly purge His threshing-floor: the wheat to the granary, the straw to the fire.⁴³

---

[39] Rudometkin, 'Discourses', 5.9.1–12.17, pp. 303-309.

[40] Rudometkin, 'Discourses', 5.2.1-2, p. 294.

[41] 'For the Kingdom of God is of the steadfast and those everywhere standing firmly upon the foundation of the testimony of Jesus, which is the Spirit of prophecy, for all those who speak according to their strength with the Apostolic tongues, in the new, promised Spirit.' Cited according to the translation of John Volkov, Rudometkin, 'Discourses', 14.9.5, p. 605. According to Rudometkin, God has always led his people with anointed prophets, so when Christ came, he came as an anointed king, yet he was anointed in a greater degree than his predecessor for he was the incarnation of divine Word and Wisdom. Rudometkin, 'Discourses', 8.1.1-14, pp. 416-17. Rudometkin records Uklein praying, asking God to reveal himself as he did to Abraham, and God responded: 'Proper is your request to Me; according to your word I shall always appear unto you as a man – a prophetic individual in the Spirit'. Cited according to the translation of John Volkov, Rudometkin, 'Discourses', 9.11.6, p. 460. Cf. Rudometkin, 'Discourses', 8.23.8-14, p. 443; 9.15.4, p. 465.

[42] And therein we entreat Him concerning the gift of the descent upon us of the Holy Spirit, under the sign of fiery, new tongues ... All of us in this Holy Spirit of His have no need that we be taught by a man or two, but we learn from the one active Spirit of Our God and His Lamb, which everywhere admonishes us unto all truth, all the small and great, of both sexes alike, on the fields and at home. None of us today have any need for any teacher or preacher who himself was not baptized from above by the Holy Spirit and fire. For today all of us everywhere are baptized after the manner of the holy Apostles and all like unto them, all of whom then spoke by way of the Spirit in new, fiery tongues.

Rudometkin, 'Discourses', 5.9.8-10, pp. 304-305. Cf. Rudometkin, 'Discourses', 6.7.4-12, pp. 338-39.

[43] (italics added by the author) Cited according to the translation of John Volkov, Rudometkin, 'Discourses', 2.15.1-2, p. 222.

So, according to Rudometkin, water baptism has no contemporary significance for the *Pryguny*,[44] but Spirit baptism is essential to their faith: the basis of this experience rests on Christ's experience of the Spirit; it identifies them as the true church; it is the instrument which separates the chaff from the wheat;[45] the external sign of Spirit baptism is glossolalia.[46]

The *Pryguny* built their theology on a Spirit christological foundation. Although their doctrine of God is a non-council form of theology, the *Pryguny* speak in trinitarian terms: Father, Son, and Holy Spirit. Arguably, their explication of deity, regarding Christ's salvific mission, delineates a primitive monarchial concept of economic Trinity. The Son or divine Word and the Holy Spirit emanate from the divine essence in relationships subordinate to the Father, and they are sent from the Father with distinct economic missions: the Son is incarnated in Christ and receives the Spirit, whereas the Spirit mediates the incarnation and anoints Christ. Since the soteriological necessity of humanity is the restoration of eternal life through the Spirit, Christ's experience of the Spirit's descent at the Jordan becomes the archetype of believers receiving the Spirit: Spirit baptism. For the *Pryguny* Spirit baptism is a definite experience of identification – determining the boundaries of Christ's spiritual bride, the woman clothed in the sun – with a definitive external sign: glossolalia. Thus, the *Pryguny* view their doctrines of soteriology, eschatology, and ecclesiological order and practices through a Spirit christological prism, a paradigm of pneumatic mediation which integrates with a primitive form of Logos Christology.

Noteworthy is the stress the *Pryguny* lays on the experience of Pentecost – Spirit baptism – being a foundational doctrine in which the church is constructed: the Spirit cleanses, identifies, and empowers the mission of this eschatological community. With these characteristics along with the determinative external sign of glossolalia, the *Pryguny* bear remarkable similarities with early classical Pentecostals. Difficulty arises, however, if one attempts to fit their doc-

---

[44] Cf. Rudometkin, 'Discourses', 2.15.4–16.1, pp. 222-23; 2.18.8, p. 227.
[45] Cf. Rudometkin, 'Discourses', 5.14.28-33, 37, pp. 317-18; 6.20.20, p. 359; 8.7.7–8.2, p. 425; 8.16.1, p. 435; 10.1.9-12, p. 491; 11.36.12, p. 554.
[46] Concerning glossolalia as the external sign of Spirit baptism, see Rudometkin, 'Discourses', 2.16.1, 10-11, pp. 223-24; 2.18.16, p. 227; 4.10.6, p. 283; 5.20.1-13, pp. 326-27; 6.7.1-2, pp. 337-38; 8.7.13, p. 425; 9.20,3-6, p. 471; 12.4.7, p. 560; 14.9.1, 5, p. 605; 14.14.1, p. 613; 14.17.8, p. 618; 14.18.9, p. 619.

Proto-Pentecostals 391

trine of God neatly into an early Pentecostal schema, either trinitarian or Oneness; this observation reiterates the fluid nature of Spirit Christology. Nevertheless, attention should be given to the fact that a group of *Pryguny* migrated to Los Angeles, California (1905),[47] and some of them participated in the Azusa Street revival (1906).[48]

---

[47] They migrated to America in obedience to the prophetic word of Efim Gerasimovich Klubnikin to journey into refuge in order to survive the coming war. Efim Gerasimovich Klubnikin, 'Articles and Plans of Efim Gerasimovich Klubnikin', in Ivan Gureivich Samarin and Daniel H. Shubin (eds.), *Spirit and Life*, 1.1–5.9, pp. 635-38; 22.1-5. pp. 651-52. The record of their migration is preserved in 'The Journey into Refuge from the Transcaucasus and Transcaspia to America', in Ivan Gureivich Samarin and Daniel H. Shubin (eds.), *Spirit and Life*, pp. 744-58. Cf. Clay, 'The Woman Clothed in the Sun', pp. 123-38. For an examination of *Pryguny* migration and enculturation into the ethos of American urban society in Los Angeles, see Young, *Pilgrims*.

[48] Concerning the *Pryguny* connection with the Azusa Street revival, Stanley Burgess provides a brief historical overview of Molokan history, including the migration to Los Angeles. Although Burgess does not cite any source, he asserts: 'There they became involved in the famous Azusa Street Revival in 1906'. Stanley M. Burgess, *Christian Peoples of the Spirit: A Documentary History of Pentecostal Spirituality from the Early Church to the Present* (New York: New York University Press, 2011), p. 214. For Burgess' historical account and several excerpts from the *Spirit and Life* which he includes in this monograph, see Burgess, *Christian Peoples of the Spirit*, pp. 213-20. Daniel Shubin makes an interesting statement regarding the *Pryguny* migrating to America and their connection with early Pentecostals: 'A small community of Molokan Jumpers was formed toward the close of the 19th century. Many of them followed the Molokans to America at about the same time. The best-known of them is the Shakarian family, although they prefer to use the term Pentecostal'. Shubin, *Russian Christianity*, III, pp. 137-38. Demos Shakarian was prominent in the Pentecostal/Charismatic movement as founder of the Full Gospel Business Men's Fellowship International. Regarding sources making the connection between Demos Shakarian's grandparents and father as part of the *Pryguny* migration to Los Angeles and their involvement in the Azusa Street Revival, see Demos Shakarian, John L. Sherrill, and Elizabeth Sherrill, *The Happiest People on Earth: The Long-Awaited Personal Story of Demos Shakarian* (Old Tappan, NJ: Chosen Books: Distributed by F.H. Revell Company, 1975); Vinson Synan, *Under His Banner* (Costa Mesa, CA: Gift Publications, 1992); Matthew William Tallman, *Demos Shakarian: The Life, Legacy, and Vision of a Full Gospel Business Man* (The Asbury Theological Seminary Series in World Christian Revitalization Movements in Pentecostal/Charismatic Studies; Lexington, KY.: Emeth Press, 2010). In its coverage of the revival, the Los Angeles Times acknowledged the presence of the *Pryguny* among the worshippers of the Azusa Street Revival: 'Before the meeting closed the picturesque "Priguni" outrivaled the wildest orgies of the Azusa Street revelers'. *Los Angeles Times*, October 9, 1906, p. 17; cited by Matthew Tallman, *Demos Shakarian*, p. 47, n. 147.

Edward Irving

The writings of Edward Irving, a Scottish-Presbyterian pastor, contain several Spirit christological references.[49] Irving initiated his pastoral ministry in a struggling Scottish congregation of 50 members, the Caledonian Chapel, in London (1822). Irving's prowess as a preacher was quickly recognized and accepted by the London elite, as well as the city's poor, so that, within three months, crowds exceeding the structure's seating capacity packed into the church.[50] Plans immediately began for building a larger facility to accommodate the crowds; thus, after completing the edifice, the congregation relocated to the National Scot Church at Regent Square (1827).[51] During his early ministry at the Caledonian Chapel, Irving's ser-

---

[49] At age 13, Edward Irving (1792–1834) entered the University of Edinburgh and graduated four years later (1805–1809). While furthering his education in theological studies part-time (1810–15), Irving supported himself by teaching at Haddington and Kirkcaldy. Although he passed his theological examinations and was licensed to preach in the Church of Scotland by the Kirkcaldy Presbytery (1815), Irving was unsuccessful in obtaining a pastorate. In 1819, one of Scotland's most eminent pastors, Dr. Thomas Chalmers hired Irving as his assistant pastor at St. Johns, Glasgow; while faithfully serving in this position, Irving was offered a pastorate, so his home Presbytery of Annan ordained him, and he began serving as pastor of the Caledonian Chapel in London (1822). For information about Irving's early life, formation, and context in Scotland, see Arnold Dallimore, *The Life of Edward Irving: Fore-Runner of the Charismatic Movement* (Edinburgh: Banner of Truth Trust, 1983), pp. 3-28; David W. Dorries, *Edward Irving's Incarnational Christology* (Fairfax, VA: Xulon, 2002), pp. 23-25; William S. Merricks, *Edward Irving: The Forgotten Giant* (East Peoria, IL: Scribe's Chamber Publications, 1983), pp. 1-36; Andrew Landale Drummond, *Edward Irving and His Circle* (London: J. Clarke & Co., 1937), pp. 13-43; Henry Charles Whitley, *Blinded Eagle: An Introduction to the Life and Teaching of Edward Irving* (London: SCM Press, 1955), pp. 9-18; Liam Upton, '"Our Mother and Our Country": The Integration of Religious and National Identity in the Thought of Edward Irving', in Robert Pope (ed.), *Religion and National Identity: Wales and Scotland C. 1700–2000* (Cardiff: University of Wales Press, 2001), pp. 242-51.

[50] Concerning his ministry at the Caledonian Chapel, see Dallimore, *The Life of Edward Irving*, pp. 31-74; Merricks, *Edward Irving*, pp. 37-143; Drummond, *Edward Irving and His Circle*, pp. 44-102; Dorries, *Incarnational Christology*, pp. 23-25; Whitley, *Blinded Eagle*, pp. 18-20.

[51] According to A.L. Drummond, 'Even before Irving descended upon London, the question had been raised whether it might not be practical to erect a kind of national "Cathedral" to represent the Church of Scotland in the metropolis. There were a hundred thousand Scotsmen with their descendants living in London'. Drummond, *Edward Irving and His Circle*, p. 102. Cf. Upton, "Our Mother and Our Country", pp. 255-56.

mons bore the imprint of Puritan influence;[52] yet, Irving's thinking was soon influenced by the philosophy of Samuel Taylor Coleridge,[53] and the millenarian apocalyptic views of Henry Drummond.[54] Irving, forthwith, published several prophetical sermons.[55]

---

[52] Probably, the greatest Puritan influence came from Irving reading the writings of John Owen. Graham McFarlane, *Christ and the Spirit: The Doctrine of the Incarnation According to Edward Irving* (Carlisle: Paternoster Press, 1996), pp. 160-61, 166-67. Actually, Irvin was reared in a non-conformist environment, walking six miles as a young lad to attend a separatist congregation, a Church of the Seceders; this non-conformist attitude continued throughout his life and ministry. Dallimore, *The Life of Edward Irving*, pp. 4-6; Walker, *History*, p. 550.

[53] These two became friends and Coleridge often attended services to hear Irving preach. Along with Schleiermacher, Coleridge was a prominent philosophical writer and proponent of Romanticism. Regarding Coleridge's influence on Irving, see Dallimore, *The Life of Edward Irving*, pp. 45-49, 58-59, 77; Drummond, *Edward Irving and His Circle*, pp. 66-69, 108, 128, 163; Whitley, *Blinded Eagle*, pp. 20-21, 38-40. For overviews of Coleridge's writings and Romantic philosophy in its nineteenth-century context see Livingston, *Modern Christian Thought*, I, pp. 86-93; Welch, *Protestant Thought*, I, pp. 108-26. For an overview of Irving's life and his theological connection with the Romantic Movement of that day, see A.J. Carlyle, 'The Centenary of Edward Irving', *Modern Churchman* 24 (1935), pp. 588-97.

[54] Irving attended the conferences dedicated to the subject of prophecy hosted by Drummond at his estate in Surrey, Albury Park, which were held annually for 5 years (1826–30). Irving emerged as the leading voice from this conference proclaiming that Christ's coming is near, the Antichrist is about to appear, and an outpouring of the Spirit will signal the season of the 'latter rain', the time of harvest; also, the periodical *The Morning Watch* arose from these conferences as a means of propagating their prophetical views. Dallimore, *The Life of Edward Irving*, pp. 61-63, 93-94; Merricks, *Edward Irving*, pp. 86-90; Drummond, *Edward Irving and His Circle*, pp 125-27, 133-35; David D. Bundy, 'Irving, Edward', *NIDPCM*, p. 803; David W. Faupel, *The Everlasting Gospel: The Significance of Eschatology in the Development of Pentecostal Thought* (JPTSup 10; Sheffield, England: Sheffield Academic Press, 1996), pp. 93-94; Whitley, *Blinded Eagle*, pp. 25-26, 40-43; Mark Patterson, 'Creating a Last Day's Revival: The Premillennial Worldview and the Albury Circle', in Andrew Walker and Kristin Aune (eds.), *On Revival: A Critical Examination* (Carlisle: Paternoster Press, 2003), pp. 87-102. 'The Spirit ripened the spiritual seed which the Son of man had sown; gave at Pentecost the first-fruits; and is yet to give the latter rain upon the earth: after which cometh the harvest.' Edward Irving, 'The Doctrine of the Incarnation Opened in Six Sermons', in Gavin Carlyle (ed.), *CW* (5 vols.; London: Alexander Strahan & Co., 1864), V, p. 266.

[55] *For the Oracles of God, Four Orations, And for Judgment to Come, an Argument in Nine Parts* (1823); *Babylon and Infidelity Foredoomed of God: A Discourse on the Prophecies of Daniel and the Apocalypse which Relate to these Latter Times, and Until the Second Advent* (1826); *On Subjects National and Prophetical, Seven Discourses*, in *Sermons Lectures and Occasional Discourse* (1828); *The Last Days: A Discourse on the Evil Character of these Our Times: Proving them to Be the 'Perilous Times' of the 'Last Days'* (1828); *The Church and State Responsible to Christ, and to One Another: A Series of Discourses on Daniel's Vision of the Four Beasts* (1829); *Exposition of the Book of Revelation, in a Series of Lec-*

Though Irving's prophetical writings caused some disagreement and tension with certain missionary societies, they were not the catalyst for a quarrel, but not long after moving into the Regent Square Church, controversy erupted regarding his sermons about the Holy Spirit's relationship to Christ's life and ministry. The two controversies, which led to his disposition, concerned two motifs of Irving's incarnational Christology: (1) the Holy Spirit's relation with regard to Christ's human nature and (2) the doctrine of Spirit baptism and gifts of the Spirit.[56]

The initial controversy arose from the Rev. Henry Cole's allegation that Irving taught christological heresy: that Christ possessed a sinful human nature and a mortal corruptible human body.[57] Regarding these charges, Irving responded and clarified his christological position in his publication *The Doctrine of the Incarnation Opened in Six Sermons* (1828).[58] In the document's preface, Irving stated the matter in dispute with his opponents.

> The point at issue is simply this: Whether Christ's flesh had the grace of sinlessness and incorruption from its proper nature, or

---

tures (1831); he also translated from Spanish and published, with his own extensive introduction, and apocalyptic monograph, *The Coming of the Messiah in Glory and Majesty, by Juan Josafat Ben-Ezra a Converted Jew: Translated from Spanish, with a Preliminary Discourse by Edward Irving* (1827). Cf. Whitley, *Blinded Eagle*, pp. 45-52.

[56] According to Gordon Strachan,

> His writings on the Holy Spirit in relation to the new humanity of Jesus Christ, correspond to his writings on the two controversies which led to his trials and deposition; first, over the human nature of Christ and second over the gifts of the Holy Spirit. His understanding of the former was preliminary and preparatory to his understanding of the latter. His doctrine and experience of the latter confirmed and authenticated the former.

Gordon Strachan, *The Pentecostal Theology of Edward Irving* (Peabody, MA: Hendrickson Publishers, 1988), p. 21. For an overview of Irving's Christology during these controversies and the documents involved, see Dorries, *Incarnational Christology*, pp. 297-450.

[57] Dorries, *Incarnational Christology*, pp. 30-41; Dallimore, *The Life of Edward Irving*, pp. 77-82; Merricks, *Edward Irving*, pp. 98-117; Drummond, *Edward Irving and His Circle*, pp. 112-13; Strachan, *Pentecostal Theology*, pp. 26-29; Whitley, *Blinded Eagle*, pp. 27-28.

[58] In defense of his Christology, Irving also published *Orthodox and Catholic Doctrine of Our Lord's Human Nature* (1830); *The Opinions Circulating Concerning Our Lord's Human Nature, Tried by the Westminster Confession of Faith* (1830); *Christ's Holiness in Flesh, the Form, Fountain Head, and Assurance to Us of Holiness in Flesh* (1831). Any Spirit christological references in these treatises will be noted as they correspond to the texts in *The Doctrine of the Incarnation*.

from the indwelling of the Holy Ghost. I say the latter. I assert that in its proper nature it was as the flesh of His mother, but, by virtue of the Holy Ghost's quickening and inhabiting of it, it was preserved sinless and incorruptible.[59]

Irving freely admitted that he advocated the true humanity of Christ: Christ had the same flesh as other humans. Contrary to his opponent's allegations, he denied teaching that Christ sinned in the flesh; in fact, he advocated the opposite. Actually, the point at issue concerned the source of Christ's sinlessness. His opponents considered it heresy that Irving attributed Christ's sinlessness and incorruptibility to the Holy Spirit's operation, instead of it inhering in the hypostatic union of Christ's human nature with the eternal Son. So, the central point in this controversy was really a Spirit christological issue.

As indicated by the title, Irving constructs his apology in six sermons, each one with a specific purpose and theme relative to the issue at hand. Sermon one sets forth the two causes of the incarnation. God was the fundamental cause. The incarnation did not occur in response to humanity's fall in Adam; rather, God planned the incarnation before the foundation of the world (Rev. 13.8), so that God's entire relationship with creation and humanity flowed from grace.[60] The second cause was Christ's active obedience and perfect submission to the Father's will and good pleasure in vicariously suffering for humanity in human flesh (Ps. 40.68).[61] Sermon two sets forth the proposition that the end of God's manifestation in fallen human flesh and Christ's salvific work is the glory of God (Jn 13.31).[62] Sermon three discusses the method of incarnation, Deity's assumption of fallen human flesh (Lk. 1.35).[63] Sermon four examines the redemptive value of Christ's humiliation in flesh, death, and descent into hell (Jn 1.14).[64] Sermon five depicts grace and peace as the fruits of the incarnation, and describes their propagation

---

[59] Irving, 'Incarnation', *CW*, V, p. 4. *The Doctrine of the Incarnation Opened in Six Sermons* was originally published in vol. 1 of *Sermons Lectures and Occasional Discourse* (3 vols; London: R. B. Seeley and W. Burnside, 1828).

[60] Irving, 'Incarnation', *CW*, V, pp. 9-22. Cf. McFarlane, *Christ and the Spirit*, p. 25. The Scripture references indicate which text Irving chose for each sermon.

[61] Irving, 'Incarnation', *CW*, V, pp. 23-58.

[62] Irving, 'Incarnation', *CW*, V, pp. 59-113.

[63] Irving, 'Incarnation', *CW*, V, pp. 114-257.

[64] Irving, 'Incarnation', *CW*, V, pp. 258-311.

through preaching and their personal application to believers (Eph. 1.2).[65] In sermon six Irving draws his conclusions about the incarnation from the foregoing sermons (Jn 1.18).[66] Since sermon three represents the heart of Irving's rejoinder, and it contains the majority of Spirit christological references in this sermon series, the focus of this inquiry will rest here.

Sermon three has 3 main points. First, Irving examines the composition of Christ's person.

> And what is this wonderful constitution of the Christ of God? It is the substance of the Godhead in the person of the Son, and the substance of the creature in the state of fallen manhood, united, yet not mixed, but most distinct forever ... The fallen humanity could not have been sanctified and redeemed by the union of the Son alone; which directly leadeth unto in-mixing and confusing of the Divine with the human nature, that pestilent heresy of Eutyches. The human nature is thoroughly fallen; and without a thorough communication, inhabitation, and empowering of a Divine substance, it cannot again be brought up pure and holy. The mere apprehension of it by the Son doth not make it holy. Such a union leads directly to the apotheosis or deification of the creature and this again does away with the mystery of a Trinity in the Godhead. Yet do I not hesitate to assert, that this is the idea of the person of Christ generally set forth: and the effect has been to withdraw from the eye of the Church the work of the Holy Spirit in incarnation ... The Holy Ghost sanctifying and empowering the manhood of Christ even from His mother's womb, is the manifestation both of the Father and of the Son in His manhood, because the Holy Ghost testifieth of the Father and of the Son.[67]

Irving attests to the hypostatic union of the divine Son and human nature, while maintaining a clear distinction between the divine and human natures;[68] this constitutes the one person of Christ. According to Irving, for redemptive purposes, Christ of necessity must as-

---

[65] Irving, 'Incarnation', *CW*, V, pp. 312-97.
[66] Irving, 'Incarnation', *CW*, V, pp. 389-446.
[67] Irving, 'Incarnation', *CW*, V, pp. 123-24.
[68] The clear distinction between divine and human natures is fundamental to Irving's Christology. Dorries, *Incarnational Christology*, pp. 79-82, 115-18, 457-59.

sume fallen human nature: what is not assumed is not healed.[69] Moreover, if as his opponents claim Christ's sinlessness inheres from the human nature's union with the divine Son,[70] then, Irving argues, this does not delineate an incarnate union but a mixing of the divine and human natures, resulting in the deification of Christ's humanity, thereby impugning the redemptive value of Christ's humanity. Although Irving concedes that his opponents hold the common contemporary view, he warns them of the outcome of their opinions: the agency of the Holy Spirit in Christology insipidly fades away, and the trinitarian mystery is expunged from Christology. To the contrary, Irving asserts that his Christology supports the orthodox doctrine of trinitarian functions.[71] Irving, therefore, claims the synchronousness of his Christology with the ancient church fathers and councils; accordingly, he claims solidarity with the apostle John and Irenaeus contravening Gnosticism, the Cappadocians

---

[69] Cf. McFarlane, *Christ and the Spirit*, pp. 135-38. The assumption of fallen human nature constitutes an integral part of Irving's Christology. Dorries, *Incarnational Christology*, pp. 82-88, 118-25, 351-57, 459-60.

[70] Cole contended that sinlessness could not be attributed to Christ apart from the immediate impartation of immaculate holiness to the substance of Mary's humanity prior to Christ's conception. He acknowledged the Spirit's function in thus preparing an immortal flesh for Christ. However, no continuing role of the Spirit during Christ's manhood was necessary, since sinlessness was an inherent property of his humanity.

Dorries, *Incarnational Christology*, p. 314. For an overview of Cole's correspondence and the writings of other opponents of Irving during the controversy, see Dorries, *Incarnational Christology*, pp. 297-300, 303-306, 328-32, 340-42, 367-76. Friedrich Schleiermacher also addresses this issue, 'Closely connected with this doctrine of the essential sinlessness of Christ is the idea of the *natural immortality* of Christ – namely, that Christ would not have been subject to death in virtue of His human nature'. Schleiermacher, *The Christian Faith*, p. 416. Regarding this issue, he sides with Irving:

nothing more can be inferred from the sinlessness of Christ than that death can have been no evil for Christ. We must hold to this position, and instead of the idea in question take our side with those who acknowledge that immortality was conferred upon Christ's human nature only with the Resurrection.

Schleiermacher, *The Christian Faith*, p. 416. Irving also places the impartation of immortality to Christ's human nature during Christ's third anointing by the Spirit at the resurrection. v.i. pp. 401-402.

[71] Cf. Irving, 'Incarnation', *CW*, V, pp. 87-88, 122-23, 407-10; McFarlane, *Christ and the Spirit*, pp. 162-63, 167-68; Jim Purves, *The Triune God and the Charismatic Movement: A Critical Appraisal of Trinitarian Theology and Charismatic Experience from a Scottish Perspective* (Carlisle: Paternoster, 2004), pp. 132-37.

withstanding Apollinaris, as well as Theodoret and Gregory refuting the heresy of Eutyches.[72]

According to Irving, Christ's constitution was such that the Spirit could anoint the human nature.

> Now, of this anointing there is a threefold act to be noticed in Christ's life; the first being from the time of the existence of His body, – indeed, it was this anointing with the Holy Ghost which gave His body existence … He was not merely filled with the Holy Ghost, but the Holy Ghost was the author of His bodily life, the quickener of that substance which He took from fallen humanity: or, to speak more correctly, the Holy Ghost uniting Himself forever to the human soul of Jesus, in virtue and in consequence of the Second Person of the Trinity having united Himself thereto, this threefold spiritual substance, the only-begotten Son, the human soul, and the Holy Spirit – (or rather twofold, one of the parts being twofold in itself; for we may not mingle the divine nature with the human nature, nor may we mingle the personality of the Holy Ghost with the personality of the Son) – the Eternal Son, therefore, humbling Himself to the human soul, and the human soul taken possession of by the Holy Ghost, this spiritual substance (of two natures only, though of three parts) did animate and give life to the flesh of the Lord Jesus; which was flesh in the fallen state, and liable to all the temptations to which flesh is liable: but the soul of Christ, thus anointed with the Holy Ghost, did ever resist and reject the suggestion of evil. I wish it to be clearly understood – and this is the proper place for declaring it – that I believe it to be necessary unto salvation that a man should believe that Christ's soul was so held in possession by the Holy Ghost, and so supported by the Divine nature, as that it never assented unto an evil suggestion, and never originated an evil suggestion.[73]

---

[72] Irving, 'Incarnation', *CW*, V, pp. 215-16. Cf. Irving, 'Incarnation', *CW*, V, pp. 164-71. His opponents, likewise, charged Irving with dividing the person of Christ, which he adamantly denied. Irving, 'Incarnation', *CW*, V, p. 169. Cf. Dorries, *Incarnational Christology*, pp. 316-19. For an overview of how Irving's Christology correlates with the early church and early reformers, see Dorries, *Incarnational Christology*, pp. 143-207.

[73] Irving, 'Incarnation', *CW*, V, p. 126. Cf. Irving, 'Incarnation', *CW*, V, pp. 126-29.

Several observations can be gleaned from this text. First, the Holy Spirit conceived Christ's human nature, taking its substance from Mary; hence, Christ possessed a fallen human nature, body and soul, like other humans. Second, the human nature is united to divine nature, and the place of union is Christ's human soul.[74] The Son in humility hypostatically united with Christ's soul and supported it in a quiescent manner,[75] whereas the Holy Spirit possessed the soul and mediated the *communicatio idiomatum*.[76] Third, although during the earthly sojourn Christ possessed a fallen human nature, susceptible to temptations common to all humans, neither did the human soul sin nor did temptation originate in Christ's mind because it was anointed and possessed by the Spirit.[77]

In Christ's life and ministry Irving posited three events in which the Spirit anointed Christ. The first anointing mediated the incarnation and Christ's sinlessness. The second anointing of the Spirit occurred during Christ's reception of the Spirit at the Jordan.

> That Christ, from the moment He was baptized with water and anointed with the Holy Ghost sent down from heaven, was set apart from his former occupation as a tradesman in Nazareth, to the divine mission of redeeming a lost and abject world.[78]

---

[74] Cf. McFarlane, *Christ and the Spirit*, pp. 156-59, 164-65; Purves, *The Triune God and the Charismatic Movement*, pp. 137-39. Although Irving uses Origen's idea of the soul being the place of union, he carefully rejects the concept of the preexistence of souls.

> From the time that Christ was conceived by the Holy Ghost in the womb of the Virgin was He both body and soul of man. He was not soul of man before He was body of man; but He was soul and body of man from the moment of conception. From which moment also the Holy Ghost abode in Him and sanctified Him.

Irving, 'Incarnation', *CW*, V, p. 121.

[75] For in order to prepare for the mediatorial office which He had undertaken, He needed to divest Himself of His celestial state, to lay down His supercelestial glory, to make Himself of no reputation, to take upon Himself the form of a servant, and to be found in fashion as a man; and that power which He resigned, He, not in appearance but in truth, resigned.

Edward Irving, 'The Temptation', *CW*, II, p. 194. According to Dorries, this idea of a quiescent deity in union with Christ's human nature is also a vital part of Irving's Christology. Dorries, *Incarnational Christology*, pp. 88-97, 125-31, 357-58, 460-62.

[76] Cf. Irving, 'Incarnation', *CW*, V, pp. 134-35.

[77] Irving, 'Incarnation', *CW*, V, pp. 121, 320-22, 428.

[78] Irving, 'The Temptation', *CW*, II, p. 192.

Commissioning Christ for his salvific mission, the Spirit anointed him to preach the Gospel, to perform miracles, and preserved him as the sinless sacrificial Lamb of God (Lk. 4.18-19; Jn 1.29-33).[79] Drawing from Jesus' experience and corollary examples from the Book of Acts, Irving distinguished between water baptism and Spirit baptism.

> There is yet a higher mystery, in that baptism with the Holy Ghost which Christ received at His baptism with water, besides that which we have opened above: it did not only constitute Him the Prophet and possess Him with all prophetic gifts ... but, moreover, this baptism with the Holy Ghost was to Him truly and literally that same baptism of power and holiness with which He was afterwards to baptize His Church.[80]

Irving, consequently, depicts Jesus' Spirit baptism as a paradigm for believers' Spirit baptism: it is a baptism of power and holiness which water baptism anticipates.[81] The Spirit's second anointing, thereupon, marks Jesus as prophet, the sin bearer and sacrifice, and the one who baptizes with the Holy Spirit.[82]

---

[79] Irving, 'Incarnation', *CW*, V, pp. 229-34. Cf. Edward Irving, *The Day of Pentecost, or the Baptism with the Holy Ghost* (Edinburg: John Lindsay, 1831), pp. 69-70.

[80] Irving, 'Incarnation', *CW*, V, p. 132.

[81] Cf. Irving, 'Incarnation', *CW*, V, pp. 130, 268-69. It is important to note that Irving accepts the practice of paedobaptism. See Irving, 'The Sealing Virtue', *CW*, II, pp. 270-72.

[82] The concept of Jesus as receiver of the Spirit is crucial to Irving's Spirit Christology. Dorries, *Incarnational Christology*, pp. 97-105, 131-39, 313-16, 358-60, 462-64. It is, also, worthy of noting that at this time in Irving's ministry, he addresses the lack of spiritual gifts in the contemporary age.

> 'And ye shall receive the Holy Ghost.' By which, they say, we ought to understand, not the outward gift of power, which hath ceased, but the inward gift of sanctification and fruitfulness ... But for my own part, I am inclined to understand both; for I cannot find by what writ of God any part of the spiritual gift was irrevocably removed from the Church.

Irving, 'The Sealing Virtue', *CW*, II, p. 276. Cf. Strachan, *Pentecostal Theology*, pp. 55-56. Irving, therefore, opposes the cessationist view regarding spiritual gifts. Irving attributes the lack of these manifestations of the Spirit to a lack of faith; actually, guided by his eschatology, Irving believed the lack of spiritual gifts among believers were a sign of the end of the age and the impending judgment of God. Irving, 'The Sealing Virtue', *CW*, II, p. 277-79. Cf. Strachan, *Pentecostal Theology*, pp. 15, 56-58; Merricks, *Edward Irving*, pp. 146-48.

The third occurrence of the Spirit anointing Christ was on the occasion of his resurrection. In response to his opponent's accusation, that Irving advocated Christ's flesh was mortal and corruptible, he replied that Christ's death and burial proved what kind of flesh the savior bore: it was mortal and corruptible.[83] The Spirit, nevertheless, preserved Christ's body from corruption.

> But when the Holy Ghost, inhabiting His separate soul, which was united unto the Godhead, did come unto His dead body that was kept from seeing corruption, and quicken it with eternal and immortal life, instantly all mortality and corruption were thenceforward expelled from it ... Now the High Priest's anointing was complete.[84]

In the resurrection, by the power of the Spirit, Jesus Christ's humanity experienced a vital transformation: the mortal put on immortality and corruptible put on incorruption. The third anointing glorified Christ and constituted him High Priest and Lord of creation.[85]

The sermon's second point considers the universal reconciliation Christ's death and resurrection achieves, and the particular election Christ ministers as High Priest. Irving disputed the doctrines of limited atonement, held by the majority of his Reformed colleagues, and the imputation of sin laid upon Christ during the crucifixion. Instead, he argued that the incarnation itself was redemptive: Christ bore humanity's sin and suffered in fallen human nature. Christ's at-one-ment, then, was universal, reconciling creation and humanity unto God.[86] Christ was anointed and received the priesthood after he ascended into heaven by receiving the promise of power from the Father for the elect.[87]

> Regeneration, therefore, or the baptism with the Holy Ghost, which Christ, by the gift of the Father, doth bestow upon the creatures who, by His redemption, have their way opened to the Father, and the Father's way open unto them ... Regeneration of

---

[83] Irving, 'Incarnation', *CW*, V, p. 136.
[84] Irving, 'Incarnation', *CW*, V, p. 143.
[85] Irving, 'Incarnation', *CW*, V, pp. 143-46.
[86] Irving, 'Incarnation', *CW*, V, pp. 146-79, 153-61, 218-21. Cf. Dorries, *Incarnational Christology*, pp. 263-94, 306-13.
[87] Irving, 'Incarnation', *CW*, V, pp. 180-83.

the Holy Ghost is nothing more that the fulfilling, or accomplishing, or bringing into being the Father's purpose of election.[88]

At this point in Irving's ministry, apparently, Spirit baptism and regeneration are synonymous.[89] According to Irving, Christ's functions as High Priest to accomplish the decree of election: to baptize believers with the Spirit. Election is particular in the sense only those who receive the seal of election, the Spirit, are among the elect. In other words, to impart unto humanity the higher life in the Spirit has been God's plan and purpose from the beginning, when he elected the incarnation before the foundation of the world.[90]

The sermon's third point depicts the abrogation of the law and Christ as the grace of God.[91] This section recapitulates the purposes of the three-fold anointing Christ experienced. The first anointing from conception to Christ's reception of the Spirit at the Jordan was under the law to redeem and reconcile creation and humanity to God. The second anointing from Christ's reception of the Spirit at the Jordan to Christ's resurrection was a paradigm for believers to receive the Spirit: Christ was baptized with the Spirit so that believers could receive Spirit baptism. The Spirit's third anointing resurrected Christ, glorified him, and constituted him as High Priest to send forth the promise of the Father upon believers, the proleptic power of their resurrection and glorification.[92] 'Thus the work of the Holy Ghost is substantiated and realized in the person of Christ.'[93]

By the time Irving penned these sermons, during the first crucial controversy of his ministry, most theologians separated trinitarian theology from Christology;[94] then, the christological task focused on

---

[88] Irving, 'Incarnation', *CW*, V, p. 191.
[89] Irving, 'Incarnation', *CW*, V, pp. 150-51.
[90] Irving, 'Incarnation', *CW*, V, pp. 185-202, 228-29, 235. Cf. Purves, *The Triune God and the Charismatic Movement*, pp. 139-41.
[91] Irving, 'Incarnation', *CW*, V, pp. 202-37.
[92] Irving, 'Incarnation', *CW*, V, pp. 224-37.
[93] Irving, 'Incarnation', *CW*, V, p. 237. Cf. Jim Purves, 'The Interaction of Christology & Pneumatology in the Soteriology of Edward Irving', *Pneuma* 14 (1992), pp. 81-90.
[94] According to Graham McFarlane,
 what is so significant about Irving is the fact that he wrote at a time when most people believed that the proper procedure was to separate the doctrine of the Trinity from what could be said about Christ. By the time of Schleier-

recovering the historical Jesus, so the doctrine of incarnation received little attention, the role of the Holy Spirit had been obscured, and the gifts of the Spirit were relegated to the past.[95] Some theologians, such as Rev. Cole, responded to liberal theology's emphasis on Christ's humanity by strengthening their arguments favoring Christ's deity; however, these arguments often bordered on Docetism.[96] In this theological context, Irving formulated his incarnational Spirit Christology set within a trinitarian framework, which advocated the Holy Spirit as the mediator of the conception, formation, sinlessness, empowerment, and glorification of Christ's fallen and mortal human nature. The publication of his sermons on the incarnation caused many to side with Cole and increased opposition to Irving's Christology. In 1830 the Scots Presbytery of London tried Irving for heresy and convicted him of teaching that Jesus Christ was a sinner. The congregation and Trustees of Regent Square, however, stood solidly behind their pastor, and Irving denied the London Presbytery's jurisdiction over him since his ordination came from Annan in Scotland, nullifying the verdict against him.[97]

The second controversy erupted when Irving allowed manifestations of glossolalia and prophecy to continue during the worship services at Regent Square, over the objections of several church

---

macher, such a distinction was taken as a given. Irving, then, stands out sharply as one who opposed such procedure. Rather, he sought to unite the two in a perhaps more radical manner than has hitherto been presented within his own Western, theological tradition.

McFarlane, *Christ and the Spirit*, p. 12. Cf. McFarlane, *Christ and the Spirit*, pp. 13, 131.

[95] Irving, 'Incarnation', *CW*, V, pp. 87, 95-96, 215. Cf. McFarlane, *Christ and the Spirit*, pp. 22, 50-51, 98, 131-34, 176.

[96] Dorries examines the original tract Cole wrote opposing Irving's view, *The True Signification of the English Adjective Mortal* (1827), and concludes,

immediately obvious from our examination of this original tract are the undisguised docetic tendencies characterizing his treatment of Christ's Person. It was from the Christological vantage point expressed in this tract that Cole was launched into his controversy with Irving's doctrine.

Dorries, *Incarnational Christology*, p. 300. Cf. McFarlane, *Christ and the Spirit*, pp. 70-71.

[97] The Regent Square Trust Deed required its minister to be ordained by a Presbytery in Scotland. Dorries, *Incarnational Christology*, pp. 35-41; Dallimore, *The Life of Edward Irving*, pp. 93-97; Drummond, *Edward Irving and His Circle*, pp. 117-19; Strachan, *Pentecostal Theology*, pp. 13, 41-45.

trustees. A revival in the West of Scotland had been accompanied with glossolalia and miraculous healings (1830). When Irving heard of these charismatic manifestations, he carefully made inquiry into their authenticity and decided they were the genuine restoration of spiritual gifts to the church.[98] Soon, glossolalia and prophecy manifested in Regent Square worship (1831), to the anxiety of the Trustees. With the majority of Regent Square Trustees supporting the charge, Irving was tried for breaching the worship forms of the Church of Scotland; later, the Annan Presbytery charged Irving with heresy and deposed him from ministry in the Church of Scotland.[99] In attempting to vindicate himself before the Presbytery, Irving defended his doctrine of Spirit baptism and manifestation of spiritual gifts by following his treatise *The Day of Pentecost or The Baptism with the Holy Ghost* (1831).[100]

---

[98] Strachan, *Pentecostal Theology*, pp. 61-75; David W. Dorries, 'Catholic Apostolic Church', *NIDPCM*, pp. 1189-92; Whitley, *Blinded Eagle*, pp. 29-30.

[99] The London Presbytery first received the complaint from the Regent Square Trustees, on the condition that the Trustees would recognize their former verdict of heresy against Irving, and tried Irving, finding him guilty of breaching the Trust Deed and the worship decorum of the Church of Scotland (26 April–2 May 1832). Since the original charge of heresy was recognized by the Regent Square Trustees, the General Assembly of Scotland instructed the Annan Presbytery to charge Irving with heresy, so the Presbytery tried him, finding him guilty (13 March 1833). Merricks, *Edward Irving*, pp. 144-356; Dorries, *Incarnational Christology*, pp. 41-59; Drummond, *Edward Irving and His Circle*, pp. 136-228; Dallimore, *The Life of Edward Irving*, pp. 99-150; Whitley, *Blinded Eagle*, pp. 30-33. The majority of the Regent Square congregation remained faithful to Irving, which resulted in the founding of the Catholic Apostolic Church. Dorries, 'Catholic Apostolic Church', *NIDPCM*, p. 459; Whitley, *Blinded Eagle*, pp. 72-85. Although the doctrines of the Catholic Apostolic Church and modern Pentecostalism bear similarities, Gordon Strachan asserts, 'For all their striking similarities these two movements were ignorant of each other's existence'. Strachan, *Pentecostal Theology*, p. 19. Cf. Larry Christensen, 'Pentecostalism's Forgotten Forerunner', in Vinson Synan (ed.), *Aspects of Pentecostal-Charismatic Origins* (Plainfield, NJ: Logos International, 1975), pp. 15-37. David Faupel, nevertheless, points to similarities between Irving's teaching and John Alexander Dowie's Pentecostal theology and suggests the possibility of Dowie serving as the connecting link between Irving and modern Pentecostals. Faupel, *The Everlasting Gospel*, pp. 133-34, n. 60.

[100] Addressing the London Presbytery, Irving stated,

It is for the name of Christ, as 'baptizer with the Holy Ghost', that I am this day called into question before this court; and it is for that name, which God deemed so sacred and important as to give it to the Baptist to proclaim – which the Son of God deemed so important as not to permit his disciples to go forth to preach until they had received the substance of it – it is for that name, even the name of 'Jesus, the baptizer with the Holy Ghost', that I stand

The Day of Pentecost or The Baptism with the Holy Ghost is composed of an introduction and three parts. In introducing his subject, Irving accentuates four points about Christ as the one who baptizes in the Holy Spirit (Jn 1.33). First, it is Christ's *nobile officium* to baptize with the Spirit; it is the telos of all preceding redemptive activity,[101] so it is the church's most precious inheritance and message. Second, Christ's resurrection was not the restoration of Adam's life; rather, in the resurrection the Spirit glorified Christ, deifying Christ's humanity, and instituted him into the noble office of Spirit baptizer. Third, the Day of Pentecost was the inaugural event of Christ functioning in this office (Acts 1.4-5; Jn 7.37-39). Fourth, the experience of baptism with the Holy Spirit and the descriptive phrases receiving 'the promise of the Father' and 'power from on high' synonymously render the same event.[102]

The first section distinguishes the various operations of the Holy Spirit from Spirit baptism: what is not Spirit baptism. First, the phrase 'promise of the Father' does not mean this is what the Father has promised; instead, the Father is the promise and Christ the promisor.

> The Father took up his abode in him immediately upon his baptism, coming in the form of a dove. Then Christ was baptized with the Holy Ghost; then he received the promise of the Fa-

---

here before you, Sir, and before this court, and before you all, called into question this day.

William Harding, *The Trial of the Rev. Edward Irving, M.A. Before the London Presbytery; Containing the Whole of the Evidence; Exact Copies of the Documents; Verbatim Report of the Speeches and Opinions of the Presbyters, Etc.* (London: W. Harding, 1832), p. 20. Quoted in Strachan, *Pentecostal Theology*, pp. 157-58. Cf. Strachan, *Pentecostal Theology*, pp. 157-65. Irving also published other documents which respond to these issues, as well as containing Spirit christological references, the Spirit christological references in these other documents will be noted as they correlate with the texts under examination. These documents were originally published as *The Church, with Her Endowment of Holiness and Power* and *On the Gifts of the Holy Ghost Commonly Called Supernatural* were originally published in *The Morning Watch*, 2 (1830).

[101] *To baptize with the Holy Ghost*, therefore, whatever that is, is the great thing which Christ is announced to perform. Other things connected with, subservient to, and in preparation for this, he may perform, but this is his noble office ... This is by distinction THE end unto which all other work he wrought.

Irving, *The Day of Pentecost*, p. 2. Cf. Strachan, *Pentecostal Theology*, pp. 119-20.

[102] Irving, *The Day of Pentecost*, pp. 1-12. Cf. Irving, *The Day of Pentecost*, pp. 77-78; Dorries, *Incarnational Christology*, pp. 408-12.

ther; then also he was anointed with the Holy Ghost and with power: and from that time he went forth preaching the Gospel, and 'healing all that were oppressed with the devil, for God was with him' (Acts 10.28) ... The Father baptizeth him with the Holy Ghost, and he becomes the holy man inhabited with the Spirit of the Almighty God, and ever after speaks of his words and actings as not his own, but the Father's, which had sent him.[103]

Incarnation, to recover man's original righteousness, is the work of the Son; and inhabitation of God thereupon, to glorify the righteous man with his own mind and power, is the work of the Father. And in these two, incarnation and inhabitation, standeth the whole work of Godhead for the redemption, regeneration, and glorification of man. Of which two gracious and glorious works though the Father and Son be the personal actors, and they be done under their hand, to shew forth their personal offices in the blessed Godhead, yet as surely is the Holy Ghost the substance and life of each operation.[104]

From these texts, several inferences can be drawn from Irving's premise: the Father is the promise in the phrase 'promise of the Father'. First, when Jesus was baptized with the Spirit, he received the indwelling of the Father: Spirit baptism and indwelling of the Father are synonymous. Second, during Christ's reception of the Spirit at the Jordan, 'power from on high' descended upon Christ, anointing and equipping him to preach the gospel and perform miraculous deeds; accordingly, these Spirit anointed words and deeds were neither attributed to the Holy Spirit nor to Christ, but the Father who indwelled Christ. Third, Christ promised that after his ascension, he would send the promise of the Father: his disciples would partake of the same oneness with the Father which dwelled in him, empowering them to do the things that the Father enabled him to do (John 14–16).[105] Fourth, the incarnation of the Son and the indwelling of

---

[103] Irving, *The Day of Pentecost*, pp. 16-17.
[104] Irving, *The Day of Pentecost*, p. 18. Cf. Strachan, *Pentecostal Theology*, pp. 123-24.
[105] Cf. Irving, *The Day of Pentecost*, p. 15. 'To be partakers of his glory, is to share with him the inhabitation and in-working of the Father, which he had a measure of from his baptism, which he hath without and beyond measure since his resurrection and ascension into glory.' Irving, *The Day of Pentecost*, pp. 19-20.

the Father, which circumscribe God's salvific plan, are mediated by the Holy Spirit: these are redemptive events attributed to the perichoretic activity of the triune God.[106] The 'promise of the Father' and 'power from on high', then, is the indwelling of the Father through the agency of the Spirit.

Second, signaling a development in his thinking since his discussion of Spirit baptism in his work regarding the incarnation, Irving asserts that Spirit baptism is different from regeneration.[107]

> This operation of the Holy Ghost, to manifest in a believing man the power and presence, the word and work of God the Father, is altogether another and higher operation than that by which he bringeth us to believe on the Lord Jesus Christ, and enableth us to close with and stand in him. It is the consequence of union, and not the antecedence or the sustenance of it. As the operation of the Holy Ghost brought Christ into manhood, which is generation; so the continuance of that kind of operation brings the elect and believing ones of the Father forth from the bosom of his counsels unto Christ; and this is regeneration, conducted properly under the hand of the Father. Being brought unto Christ, another operation of the Holy Ghost doth wash and cleanse ... And this is under the hand of the Son, being the continuance of that which he put forth upon himself in the days of his flesh, and by which he continually resisted and overcame temptation, and presented himself holy ... Then cometh the third and last operation of the Holy Ghost, which is baptism with the Holy Ghost, bringing into the believer, thus united with Christ, the fullness of that inhabitation of the Father which Christ now enjoys.[108]

Irving, now, posits a three-fold sequential operation of the Spirit: regeneration, sanctification, and Spirit baptism. First, the Spirit's generation of Christ's humanity and uniting it to the divine nature corresponds to the Spirit regenerating believers and uniting them to Christ: regeneration continues the pneumatic power of the incarnation. Second, the Spirit's agency in sanctifying Christ's human na-

---

[106] Cf. Purves, *The Triune God and the Charismatic Movement*, pp. 142-49, 152-53.

[107] Cf. Edward Irving, 'The Church with Her Endowment of Holiness and Power', *CW*, V, 452-58.

[108] Irving, *The Day of Pentecost*, p. 21. Cf. Strachan, *Pentecostal Theology*, p. 125.

ture, preserving it immaculate, accords with the Spirit sanctifying believers: it is the continuation of the pneumatic power of holiness to overcome temptation and sin. Third, believers' Spirit baptism dovetails with Christ's baptism with the Spirit: it is the prolongation of pneumatic power bestowing the indwelling of the Father. According to Irving, glossolalia is the Spirit's attestation to a believer receiving Spirit baptism: 'the baptism with the Holy Ghost, whose standing sign, if we err not, is the speaking in tongues'.[109] Irving's Spirit Christology, therefore, has developed into the parameters of modern Pentecostal theology.[110]

The treatise's second section proceeds to delineate what Spirit baptism is.[111] According to Irving, humans are created in the image of God so that the Father may indwell them; to this end, the incarnation provided a human nature in which the fullness of the Godhead indwelt, disclosing the Father's will, words, and deeds.[112]

> To do this, was in his case the baptism with the Holy Ghost ... What was done in Christ was done in him as man; he became man in order that it might be done in him. For this end He, who was the Creator of all things, became the creature man, that in the creature man he might receive those things which had been intended for man from the time of his creation, yea, before the world was made ... To make a question, therefore, whether what Christ in his manhood attained to in the world, be not the privilege and property of other men as well as he, is not to understand the doctrine of the incarnation at all.[113]

> No doubt Christ entered into a fullness of the Holy Ghost upon his resurrection, whereof the gift at his baptism was but to him

---

[109] Irving, *The Day of Pentecost*, p. 28. Cf. Irving, 'Gifts of the Holy Ghost', *CW*, V, pp. 544-52; Irving, 'Holiness and Power', *CW*, V, pp. 488-99; Irving, *The Day of Pentecost*, pp. 65-68; Strachan, *Pentecostal Theology*, p. 18; Strachan, *Pentecostal Theology*, p. 127.

[110] According to Gordon Strachan, 'Irving today can be understood as the first Reformed-Pentecostal theologian'. Strachan, *Pentecostal Theology*, p. 21. For similarities between Irving's doctrine and modern Pentecostalism, see Strachan, *Pentecostal Theology*, pp. 19-21.

[111] 'We now come to examine what it is. And the answer is very simple: "All beyond the created powers and faculties of man, which man hath ever possessed, doth now possess, or shall ever possess."' Irving, *The Day of Pentecost*, p. 30.

[112] Irving, *The Day of Pentecost*, pp. 30-32.

[113] Irving, *The Day of Pentecost*, pp. 32-33.

the first-fruits, as the baptism of the Holy Ghost given to us now is but the first-fruits of that full harvest which at our resurrection we shall enter into.[114]

That the baptism of the Holy Ghost doth bring to every believer the presence of the Father and the power of the Holy Ghost, according to that measure, at the least, in which Christ during the days of his flesh possessed the same. My idea, therefore, concerning the baptism of the Holy Ghost, or the promise of the Father, is simply this, that it is a superhuman supernatural power, or set of powers, which God did from the beginning purpose to place in man.[115]

Christ in his human nature received the indwelling of the Father and supernatural power: the eternal inheritance and legacy the Father bequeathed to humanity.[116] Spirit baptism, moreover, is available to believers in the same measure of the Spirit's anointing which Christ possessed to preach the gospel and to do the Father's mighty works.[117] Christ's Spirit baptism was completed in his resurrection and glorification, as he received the fullness of the Father's promise and entered the *nobile officium* of baptizer with the Spirit;[118] likewise, believers' Spirit baptism is fulfilled in their resurrection and glorification. Irving, thus, conjoins creation, incarnation, redemption, and Spirit baptism into one divine movement of grace: Spirit baptism completes and is the apex of the Father's salvific purpose.[119]

---

[114] Irving, *The Day of Pentecost*, pp. 35-36.

[115] Irving, *The Day of Pentecost*, p. 39.

[116] Irving, *The Day of Pentecost*, pp. 15-16, 19, 30-31, 45. Cf. Strachan, *Pentecostal Theology*, pp. 128-32.

[117] 'On his ascension to the Father, they received on the day of Pentecost the full share thereof, to the extent of this body's power to contain.' Irving, *The Day of Pentecost*, p. 36. Cf. Irving, *The Day of Pentecost*, pp. 37-39, 43-45, 81-86, 101-16; Irving, 'Gifts of the Holy Ghost', *CW*, V, pp. 523-24. For a discussion about gifts of the Spirit, see Irving, 'Holiness and Power', *CW*, V, pp. 471-99; Irving, 'Gifts of the Holy Ghost', *CW*, V, pp. 533-44.

[118] Cf. Irving, *The Day of Pentecost*, pp. 1-4, 11-12, 17, 32, 46; Purves, *The Triune God and the Charismatic Movement*, pp. 153-55.

[119] Cf. Irving, *The Day of Pentecost*, pp. 1-9, 43, 49-54. Section three of the treatise surveys various Scriptures regarding Spirit baptism: (1) Scriptures from the Hebrew Scriptures which promise Spirit baptism and finds fulfillment in various New Testament texts, (2) gospel texts, and (3) the words of Jesus. Since the Spirit christological texts found in this section are a bit redundant, they have been noted in the appropriate places. Irving, *The Day of Pentecost*, pp. 55-114. Cf. Strachan, *Pentecostal Theology*, pp. 133-40.

Within the structure of trinitarian theology, Irving's incarnational Christology supports a Spirit christological paradigm of pneumatic mediation which integrates Logos Christology.[120] In point of fact, the Spirit mediates Christ's entire life and salvific mission: the conception of human nature and its union with the eternal Son, the *communicatio idiomatum* between the human and divine natures, the sinlessness of Christ's fallen human nature, the indwelling of the Father through Spirit baptism, and the glorification of Christ's human nature in the resurrection. After Christ's ascension, he begins his high priestly ministry as Spirit baptizer. In Spirit baptism, the Spirit mediates the Father's indwelling of believers, which is the telos of the redemptive movement; consequently, incarnation, Spirit baptism, and inhabitation of the Father, circumscribe God's soteriological activity.

Initially, Irving made no distinction between regeneration, sanctification, and Spirit baptism effectively bringing all these soteriological categories under the umbrella of Spirit baptism. However, after he authenticated the charismatic manifestations in the West of Scotland, he modified his theology. According to Irving, the Spirit's mediation in incarnation – conceiving, forming, generating the human nature, and preserving Christ's human nature immaculate – corresponds to the pneumatic power that regenerates and sanctifies believers. Christ's Spirit baptism is paradigmatic of believers' Spirit baptism; it is subsequent to regeneration and sanctification, and it is the pneumatic power mediating the Father's indwelling. While Spirit baptism holds a significant place in Irving's soteriology – the completion and goal of the soteriological movement – it remains a distinct experience in the salvific journey, not the designation of the entire redemptive schema; in fact, Irving attests to glossolalia as the 'standing sign' of this distinct experience. Irving' Spirit Christology, therefore, developed into a harbinger of Pentecostal theology.

---

[120] According to Graham McFarlane, 'Irving's is no Spirit christology. The agent of incarnation is not an inspired man; he is at all times the divine Son'. McFarlane, *Christ and the Spirit*, p. 182. Apparently, McFarlane is operating under the common assumption that a non-incarnational Spirit christological paradigm of pneumatic inspiration is the only form of Spirit Christology; however, as the research in this inquiry demonstrates, this is not the case.

Conclusion

The *Pryguny* and Edward Irving supported a Spirit christological paradigm of pneumatic mediation, structured in a triadic framework. The Spirit, thus, mediated the incarnation of the divine Son and Christ's entire life and ministry; however, regarding the Spirit's anointing, both placed the emphasis on Christ's Spirit baptism at the Jordan. This was a genuine experience of the Spirit in the life of Christ, which commissioned him to his salvific mission and endued him with power to accomplish it; hence, Christ's Spirit baptism is paradigmatic of believers' Spirit baptism. Obviously, this is not the Augustinian form of the paradigm of pneumatic mediation.

Both the *Pryguny* and Irving taught that Spirit baptism was the *telos* of the redemptive movement; history has been one salvific journey from the primal humans losing the Spirit to the ascended Christ functioning in his high priestly role of Spirit baptizer bestowing the Spirit upon the eschatological community. In point of fact, both of these proto-Pentecostal groups designated *glossolalia* as the evident sign of someone having received Spirit baptism; furthermore, the *Pryguny* asserted that this sign distinguished the bride – the sun-clothed woman – of Christ, setting it apart as the true church sealed by the Spirit.

With little variation, these proto-Pentecostals' theologies, which anteceded the Azusa Street Revival by more than seventy years, could easily fit within the boundaries of early Pentecostal theology. Common among them was the desire to recover and maintain genuine apostolic experience and doctrine. Apostolic experience meant they had received the same pneumatic experience, power, and authority the apostles enjoyed. Thereupon, they affirmed a doctrine of Spirit baptism subsequent to conversion-initiation.

16

THE EMERGENCE OF PENTECOSTALISM FROM HOLINESS REVIVALISM

Pentecostalism emerged from the *ethos* of nineteenth century Holiness and restorationist revivalism. From this revivalism emerged two forms of the 'full gospel', the fourfold and fivefold, forming the *gestalt* from which Pentecostalism emerged.[1] This chapter, accordingly, consists of two divisions: (1) it surveys the development of the fourfold gospel and (2) examines the unfolding of the fivefold version of the 'full gospel' for traces of Spirit Christology.

The Development of the Fourfold Full Gospel

Any discussion regarding the theological roots of Pentecostalism usually begins with the taproot, John Wesley.[2] Wesley's theology

---

[1] Our analysis there led to the identification of four Christological themes defining the basic *gestalt* of Pentecostal thought and ethos: Christ as Savior, as Baptizer with the Holy Spirit, as Healer, and as Coming King. This description was confirmed by an explication of the logic with which these themes are intertwined in Pentecostal rhetoric ... By the end of the century, the Holiness movement proper was preoccupied not only with the Pentecostal reformation of Wesleyan doctrine, but also more specifically ... with the themes of the four-fold gospel.'
Donald W. Dayton, *Theological Roots of Pentecostalism* (Peabody, MA: Hendrickson, 1987), pp. 173-74. It should be noted that Dayton designating the second *motif* as Baptizer in the Holy Spirit does not contradict my assigning the same *motif* as Sanctifier; rather, as it will be demonstrated in this inquiry, it indicates the shift in nomenclature due to Pentecostal terms being applied to Wesleyan doctrine.

[2] According to Vinson Synan, 'John Wesley, the indomitable founder of Methodism, was also the spiritual and intellectual father of the modern holiness

demonstrates a curious blend of Protestant, Pietistic, Catholic, and Eastern Orthodox influences.³ His soteriology primarily had an Arminian bent, and, arguably, because of Eastern influence, Wesley emphasized the recovery of the likeness of God, participation in the divine nature, experience, and therapeutic metaphors, producing the *double cure*: justification and sanctification.⁴ Justification forgave or pardoned the sins of the repentant, so that believers might participate in the divine nature, while sanctification dealt with the root of sin in the human affections.⁵ Sanctification, accordingly, affected the turning of the believer's affections to love of God and neighbor.⁶ According to Wesley, sanctification began in conversion and

---

and Pentecostal movements, which arose from Methodism'. Vinson Synan, *The Holiness-Pentecostal Tradition: Charismatic Movements in the Twentieth Century* (Grand Rapids: Eerdmans 2nd edn, 1997), p. 1. Regarding the Methodist roots of Pentecostalism, see Dayton, *Theological Roots*, pp. 35-60; Synan, *The Holiness-Pentecostal Tradition*, pp. 1-13; Synan, *The Century of the Holy Spirit*, pp. 146-52.

³ Albert C. Outler, 'The Place of John Wesley in the Christian Tradition', in Kenneth E. Rowe (ed.), *The Place of John Wesley in the Christian Tradition* (Metuchen, NJ: Scarecrow Press, 1976), pp. 26-50; Anderson, *An Introduction to Pentecostalism*, pp. 25-26; Synan, *The Holiness-Pentecostal Tradition*, pp. 2-5. For general treatments of Wesley's theology, see Outler, *John Wesley*; Maddox, *Responsible Grace*; Oden, *John Wesley's Scriptural Christianity*; Harald Gustaf Åke Lindström, *Wesley and Sanctification: A Study in the Doctrine of Salvation* (Grand Rapids: Francis Asbury Press, 1980); Albert Cook Outler, *Theology in the Wesleyan Spirit* (Nashville: Discipleship Resources, 1975); Albert Cook Outler, Thomas C. Oden, and Leicester R. Longden, *The Wesleyan Theological Heritage: Essays of Albert C. Outler* (Grand Rapids: Zondervan, 1991).

⁴ For information about Eastern influence in Wesley's theology, see Randy L. Maddox, 'John Wesley and Eastern Orthodoxy Influences, Convergences and Differences', *AsTJ* 45 (1990), pp. 29-53; Michael J. Christensen, 'Theosis and Sanctification: John Wesley's Reformulation of a Patristic Doctrine', *Wesleyan Theological Journal* 31 (1996), pp. 71-94; Mark T. Kurowski, 'The First Step toward Grace: John Wesley's Use of the Spiritual Homilies of Macarius the Great', *Methodist History* 36 (1998), pp. 113-24; K. Steve McCormick, 'Theosis in Chrysostom and Wesley: An Eastern Paradigm on Faith and Love', *Wesleyan Theological Journal* 26 (1991), pp. 38-103; Howard A. Snyder, 'John Wesley and Marcarius the Eyptian', *AsTJ* 45 (1990), pp. 55-59.

⁵ Wesley's explication of the distinction between justification and sanctification as well as the ground and effect of justification can be found in John Wesley, 'Justification by Faith', *The Works of John Wesley* (14 vols.; Grand Rapids: Baker Book House, 2002 repr.; London: Wesleyan Methodist Book Room, 3rd edn, 1872), V, pp. 53-64.

⁶ Concerning the recovery of holy affections (tempers) as the goal of religion, see John Wesley, 'On Charity', *The Works of John Wesley*, VII, pp. 45-57. For Wesley's understanding of the affections as the basis for holy actions and the affections' relationship to love encompassing the sum of sanctification, see John Wesley, 'On Patience', *The Works of John Wesley*, VI, pp. 484-92.

developed, and, at some point subsequent to the new birth, it was possible to experience an entire sanctification – Christian perfection – and the believer developed in grace after this experience. So, sanctification was an experience with prior and subsequent development.[7] Notably, Wesley affirmed that the believer would experience the Spirit's restored presence and witness to their justification,[8] and the Spirit would empower growth in holiness along the salvific journey, so that sanctification was the work of the Holy Spirit. Wesley's *way* of salvation, therefore, explicitly provided two *motifs* of the fourfold gospel, a dynamic view of justification and sanctification, a doctrine of an experience of grace *subsequent* to justification, a *two blessing* vocabulary, and an emphasis on the operation of the Holy Spirit producing experiences of *purity* and *power*.[9]

During the Holiness revivals of antebellum America, several developments occurred in Wesleyan *second blessing* theology (1830–61).[10] First, Phoebe Palmer developed her 'shorter way' within the Wesleyan Holiness tradition: the altar, which is Christ, sanctifies the gift. There were three components to Palmer's altar theology: (1) believers make a full consecration at the altar, (2) by faith they are instantaneously sanctified, and (3) they testify to having received the

---

[7] Regarding Wesley's view of sanctification and Christian growth in grace, see Wesley, 'Christian Perfection', VI, pp. 1-22. For Wesley's mature and most comprehensive discussion of sanctification, see John Wesley, 'A Plain Account of Christian Perfection, as Believed and Taught by the Reverend Mr. John Wesley, from the Year 1725 to the Year 1777', *The Works of John Wesley*, XI, pp. 366-446. Cf. Synan, *The Holiness-Pentecostal Tradition*, pp. 6-7; Land, *Pentecostal Spirituality*, 48.

[8] For his sermons on the witness of the Spirit, see John Wesley, 'The Witness of the Spirit', *The Works of John Wesley*, I, Discourses 1, 2, pp. 111-34.

[9] On occasion, Wesley came close to postulating a form of Spirit Christology: Wesley, *Notes*, Mt. 1.16, p. 404; Mt. 3.16, p. 406; Lk. 1.35, pp. 434-35; Lk. 4.18, pp. 436-37; Acts 10.38, p. 481. Nevertheless, Wesley steered away from making this connection; if pressed, at the expense of Christ's human nature, Wesley would accentuate Christ's deity almost to the point of affirming a Monophysite position. John Deschner, *Wesley's Christology: An Interpretation* (Dallas: Southern Methodist University Press, 1985), pp. 14-38; Maddox, *Responsible Grace*, pp. 114-18. Undoubtedly, influenced by Eastern mystical theology, Wesley professed a pneumatically permeated Logos Christology.

[10] Melvin Dieter, 'Wesleyan-Holiness Aspects of Pentecostal Origins', in Vinson Synan (ed.), *Aspects of Pentecostal-Charismatic Origins* (Plainfield, NJ: Logos International, 1975), pp. 59-67; Dayton, *Theological Roots*, pp. 63-84; John Thomas Nichol, *Pentecostalism* (New York: Harper & Row, 1966), pp. 5-7; Hollenweger, *The Pentecostals*, pp. 21, 322-23.

experience, with or without the Spirit's witness.¹¹ This essentially circumvented Wesley's paradigm of sanctification as a process beginning in the moment of a crisis experience and adding grace upon grace; indeed, sanctification is received *instantaneously* and *entirely* in a crisis moment. Second, holiness perfectionism as depicted by Palmer integrated with American revivalism. Its primary proponents Phoebe Palmer, Asa Mahan, and Charles G. Finney spread the message of Christian perfection across North America and Europe calling believers to an immediate response to receive sanctification.¹² Third, these revivalists began using Pentecostal semantics to describe the effects of the revival (1857–58), by speaking of the ushering in of the dispensation of the Spirit and receiving Spirit baptism, which was joined to sanctification.¹³ Antebellum American revivalism, therefore, produced the expectation of an instantaneous recep-

---

¹¹ Palmer presents herself as an earnest inquirer, asking is there a 'shorter way' of getting into the path of holiness? How will she know *when* God *accepts* her sacrifice, and in what *manner* does God accept it? Phoebe Palmer, *The Way of Holiness, with Notes by the Way: Being a Narrative of Religious Experience Resulting from a Determination to Be a Bible Christian* (From the Thirty-Fourth American Edition; London: Paternoster-Row, 1856 repr.; New York: Lane and Tippett, 1845), pp. 1-7. In her search for answers to these questions, she reaches three conclusions. First, because she had depended on *feeling* for her assurance, this had hindered her progress; she had required feeling, the fruit of faith, before exercising faith. Second, faith is simply taking God at his word, so she resolved to believe and trust the word of God regardless of any lack of evidence, change, or emotional confirmation. Third, after examining how God accepted sacrifices offered on the altar, she concluded that Christ was the genuine altar, and when anyone consecrated themselves on this altar, the altar sanctified the gift. Fourth, this 'shorter way' is the only way to enter the way of holiness. Palmer, *The Way of Holiness*, pp. 19-48. Cf. Synan, *The Holiness-Pentecostal Tradition*, pp. 17-19; Dayton, *Theological Roots*, p. 69.

¹² Asa Mahan, *Scripture Doctrine of Christian Perfection; with Other Kindred Subjects, Illustrated and Confirmed in a Series of Discourses Designed to Throw Light on the Way of Holiness* (Boston: D.S. King, 1839). Cf. Dieter, 'Wesleyan-Holiness Aspects of Pentecostal Origins', pp. 60-62; Dayton, *Theological Roots*, pp. 68-71; Synan, *The Holiness-Pentecostal Tradition*, pp. 14-15. Asa Mahan and Charles Finney served and taught at Oberlin College in Ohio.

¹³ Phoebe Palmer, *The Promise of the Father* (New York: Garland, 1985 repr.; Boston: H.V. Degen, 1859). Palmer's publication not only testifies to believers receiving Spirit baptism or baptism in fire during her revivals, but it also accentuates that the Spirit has rested on women throughout history empowering them to preach and minister. Cf. Dieter, 'Wesleyan-Holiness Aspects of Pentecostal Origins', pp. 65-67; Dayton, *Theological Roots*, pp. 71-77; Synan, *The Holiness-Pentecostal Tradition*, p. 15; Anderson, *An Introduction to Pentecostalism*, pp. 26-27.

tion of sanctification and the Spirit, engendering a shift to Pentecostal nomenclature.[14]

During the period after the American Civil War extending to the last decades of the nineteenth century, certain shifts and developments occurred in restorationist revivalism theology, which formed the final *motifs* of the fourfold gospel. First, Pentecostal semantics intensified, facilitating a continual shifting from perfectionist language to the concept of Pentecostal sanctification. Sanctification and Spirit baptism, thus, became synonymous designations of the fourfold gospel's second *motif*.[15] Second, stemming from this pneumatological emphasis, the Holiness movement shifted its eschatology from postmillennial to a premillennial worldview; thus, the *motif* of Jesus as Coming King became part of the 'full gospel'.[16] Third,

---

[14] Pentecostal semantics and its association with sanctification had previously been supplied by John Fletcher, Wesley's designated successor who died before fulfilling that role. Fletcher identified sanctification with Spirit baptism. John Fletcher, *The Works of the Rev. John Fletcher* (6 vols.; Philadelphia: Joseph Crukshank, American edn, 1791), I, pp. 120-21, 168, 261; II, p. 118. Cf. Synan, *The Holiness-Pentecostal Tradition*, p. 7. Wesley rejected this supposition as spurious teaching. See John Wesley, ' A Letter to John Fletcher', in John Telford (ed.), *Letters of the Rev. John Wesley* (8 vols.; London: Epworth, 1931), V, pp. 214-15; VI, p. 146. Cf. Dayton, *Theological Roots*, pp. 49-51; Maddox, *Responsible Grace*, p. 177. Fletcher was also the source from which flowed the concept of three dispensations: the Father, Son, and Holy Spirit.

[15] According to W.E. Boardman, perfectionist language was a 'stumbling stone' hindering people from entering the way of holiness. 'This one word perfectionism has kept, and is now keeping, thousands from examining into the matter at all. It is high time this stumbling stone was gathered out of the way.' W.E. Boardman, *The Higher Christian Life* (1871 repr.; Boston: Henry Hoyt, 1859), p. 60. For Boardman's rejection of perfectionist language, see Boardman, *The Higher Christian Life*, pp. 59-67. Boardman concludes his examination of the higher Christian life with the following affirmation regarding sanctification and Spirit baptism: 'If I have any advice to give to Christians, it is to cease to discuss the subtleties and endless questions arising from entire sanctification of Christian perfection, and all cry mightily to God for the baptism of the Holy Spirit'. Boardman, *The Higher Christian Life*, p. 305. For Boardman's rendition of Pentecostal sanctification, see Boardman, *The Higher Christian Life*, pp. 164-306. Cf. Donald W. Dayton, "Christian Perfection' to the 'Baptism of the Holy Ghost", in Vinson Synan (ed.), *Aspects of Pentecostal-Charismatic Origins* (Plainfield, NJ: Logos International, 1975), pp. 39-54; Dayton, *Theological Roots*, pp. 87-106; Synan, *The Holiness-Pentecostal Tradition*, pp. 50-51; Edith L. Blumhofer, *Restoring the Faith: The Assemblies of God, Pentecostalism, and American Culture* (Urbana, IL: University of Illinois Press, 1993), pp. 26-29; Synan, *The Century of the Holy Spirit*, pp. 26-28.

[16] For a thorough discussion of this *motif* and eschatological shift, see Faupel, *The Everlasting Gospel*, pp. 13-158. Cf. Dayton, *Theological Roots*, pp. 143-67; Blumhofer, *Restoring the Faith*, pp. 11-19.

the 'full gospel' *motif*, Jesus as Healer, developed with the teaching and practice of healing by faith, reaching prominence in the ministries of Charles Cullis, W.E. Broadman, and Carrie Judd Montgomery (1870's–80's), and further developing into the doctrine of divine healing in the atonement (1880's) as a corollary to sanctification in Holiness doctrine; A.B. Simpson and A.J. Gordon became leading advocates of divine healing in the atonement.[17] Fourth, in the preaching of such figures as Charles Finney, Dwight L. Moody, and R.A. Torrey, the experience connected to Spirit baptism shifted from purity to an empowerment for service.[18] Hence, the shift to

---

[17] Charles Cullis, *Faith Cures; or, Answers to Prayer in the Healing of the Sick* (Boston: Willard Tract Repository, 1879); Charles Cullis, *Dr. Cullis and His Work: Twenty Years of Blessing in Answer to Prayer* (The Higher Christian Life; New York: Garland Publishing, 1985 repr.; Boston: Willard Tract Repository, 1885); Carrie Judd Montgomery, *The Prayer of Faith* (Buffalo, NY: H.H. Otis, 1880); Jennifer Miskov, *Life on Wings: The Forgotten Life and Theology of Carrie Judd Montgomery (1858–1946)* (Cleveland, TN: CPT Press, 2012); W.E. Boardman, *The Lord That Healeth Thee* (London: Morgan and Scott, 1881); A.J. Gordon, *The Ministry of Healing: Miracles of Cure in All Ages* (Boston: H. Gannett, 1882); A.B. Simpson, *The Gospel of Healing* (Camp Hill, PA: Christian Publications, 1886). The most comprehensive examination of the doctrine of Pentecostal healing and the development of this *motif* of the 'full gospel' is the work of Kimberly Ervin Alexander, *Pentecostal Healing: Models in Theology and Practice* (JPTSup 29; Blandford Forum, UK: Deo, 2006). For these developments, see Alexander, *Pentecostal Healing*, pp. 1-63; Dayton, *Theological Roots*, pp. 115-37; Anderson, *An Introduction to Pentecostalism*, pp. 30-33; Blumhofer, *Restoring the Faith*, pp. 19-24.

[18] Dieter, 'Wesleyan-Holiness Aspects of Pentecostal Origins', pp. 69-73; Blumhofer, *Restoring the Faith*, pp. 24-25, 29-34; Synan, *The Century of the Holy Spirit*, pp. 29-32; Anderson, *An Introduction to Pentecostalism*, pp. 28-30. By 1876, Finney exclusively referred to Spirit baptism as an endowment of power subsequent to conversion and justification.

> The disciples were Christians before the day of Pentecost, and as such had a measure of the Holy Spirit. They must have had the *peace* of sins forgiven, and of a justified state; but yet they had not the enduement of *power* necessary to the accomplishment of the work assigned to them.'

C.G. Finney and Asa Mahan, 'The Endument of Power', *The Baptism of the Holy Ghost* (London: Elliot Stock, 1876), p. 234. For a full exposition of Finney's position, see Finney and Mahan, 'The Endument of Power', pp. 231-54. Moody and Torrey were influenced by Keswick Higher Life Movement and imported it into America. Dayton, *Theological Roots*, pp. 100-106. The Keswick movement takes its name from the English village where annual conferences regarding the

> higher Christian life began convening in 1875. These meetings were the results of the evangelistic efforts in England by such persons as Charles Finney, Asa Mahan, W.E. Broadman, Hannah Whitall Smith, Robert Pearsall Smith, and Charles Cullis. The Keswick view of sanctification teaches that power for service is its principle fruit which suppresses sinful desires rather than eradicating them.

pneumatology occasioned the final developments of the fourfold gospel, anteceding the rise of Pentecostalism.

Although the inherent nature of this form of the 'full gospel' articulates an intimate relationship between Christ and the Spirit in the lives of believers, the question remains: do any of the proponents of the fourfold gospel support a genuine form of Spirit Christology Christ? Indeed, they did. In order to present a good account of Spirit Christology among these writers and to investigate the place and importance Spirit Christology held in the fourfold gospel and the emergence of Pentecostalism, this inquiry will focus on the writings of A.B. Simpson, as representative of this Spirit christological trajectory, the first writer actually to articulate in writing the fourfold gospel paradigm.[19]

Albert Benjamin Simpson

A.B. Simpson's life and writings reflect his spiritual journey into the 'full gospel'.[20] A fecund writer, Simpson produced approximately

---

David D. Bundy, 'Keswick Higher Life Movement', *NIDPCM*, pp. 820-21; C.E. Jones, 'Holiness Movement', *NIDPCM*, pp. 727-28. For comprehensive examinations of the Keswick movement, see Steven Barabas, *So Great Salvation: The History and Message of the Keswick Convention* (Westwood, NJ: Fleming H. Revell, 1952); J.B. Figgis, *Keswick from Within* (The Higher Christian Life; New York: Garland Publishing, 1985 repr.; London: Marshall Brothers, 1914); John Charles Pollock, *The Keswick Story: The Authorized History of the Keswick Convention* (London: Hodder and Stoughton, 1964). Vinson Synan states,

> Although the Pentecostal movement had its beginning in the United States, much of its basic theology was rooted in earlier British perfectionistic and charismatic movements. At least three of these – the Methodist holiness movement, the Catholic Apostolic movement of Edward Irving, and the British Keswick 'Higher Life' movement – prepared the way for what appeared to be a spontaneous outpouring of the Holy Spirit in America.

Synan, *The Century of the Holy Spirit*, p. 2. Cf. Anderson, *An Introduction to Pentecostalism*, pp. 35-38. For a discussion regarding non-Wesleyan influences on the rise and formation of Pentecostalism, see William W. Menzies, 'The Non-Wesleyan Origins of the Pentecostal Movement', in Vinson Synan (ed.), *Aspects of Pentecostal-Charismatic Origins* (Plainfield, NJ: Logos International, 1975), pp. 81-98.

[19] Other proponents of Spirit Christology and their writings among the fourfold gospel folk will be noted along the way.

[20] A.B. Simpson (1843–1919) was reared in a Scottish Presbyterian home, deeply influenced by Puritan tradition. During his youth, Simpson imbibed from the wells of such Puritan classics as Thomas Boston's *Human Nature and its Fourfold Estate* (1720), Philip Doddridge's *The Rise and Progress of Religion in the Soul* (1745), and Richard Baxter's *The Saints' Everlasting Rest* (1650). As an adolescent, Simpson confessed Jesus as his Savior (1858) during a powerful revival. Although his father had chosen A.B. Simpson's elder brother to pursue a ministerial voca-

120 hymns and numerous books, sermons, and a multivolume commentary of Christ in the Bible.[21] Since Spirit christological references are scattered throughout the corpus of his writings, this inquiry will focus on two publications: *The Four-Fold Gospel* and *The Holy Spirit or Power from on High*. Simpson published his collection of sermons, *The Four-Fold Gospel* (1890), to articulate his guiding be-

---

tion and could only afford to send one son to college for theological training, convinced of a divine calling, he was undeterred from pursuing his calling and education and soon matriculated into theological training at Knox College at the University of Toronto, Canada (1861–65). As an adolescent theological student, Simpson frequently preached in various churches and acquired a reputation as a great preacher. After graduation, he served as the pastor of three eminent North American Presbyterian churches: Knox Presbyterian Church in Hamilton, Ontario (1856–73); Chestnut Street Church in Louisville, Kentucky (1874–79); Thirteenth Street Presbyterian Church in New York City (1879–81). During his second pastorate in Louisville, KY, after reading W.E. Boardman's publication *The Higher Christian Life* (1858), Simpson became convinced of the *second blessing* and received sanctification/Spirit baptism (1874), experiencing the second *motif* of the 'full gospel'. While pastoring in New York City, Simpson became acquainted with the work and teaching of Charles Cullis. Through Cullis' influence, Simpson embraced the doctrine of divine healing, was healed of a chronic heart disorder (1881), and established a healing home in his residence (1883), thus, integrating the third component of his fourfold gospel. By the late 1870's, Simpson had abandoned postmillennial eschatology and shifted to a premillennial position, so that by 1880 he began publishing a missionary magazine, *The Gospel in All Lands*, espousing his premillennial view that the preaching of this gospel to all the world was 'the great unfulfilled condition of the Lord's return'. A.B. Simpson, 'Editorial', *The Gospel in All Lands* 1 (Feb. 1880), p. 60. Cited in Charles Nienkirchen, *A.B. Simpson and the Pentecostal Movement: A Study in Continuity, Crisis, and Change* (Peabody, MA: Hendrickson, 1992), p. 23. According to A.E. Thompson, this publication 'was the first illustrated missionary magazine on the American continent, and, with one exception, the first in the world'. A.E. Thompson, *A.B. Simpson: His Life and Work* (Harrisburg, PA: Christian Publications, Revised edn, 1960), p. 152. Thus, the fourth component to the fourfold gospel was appropriated into Simpson's theology. Recognizing that his vision of a missionary oriented church did not correlate with the vision of the church which he pastored and he had come to doubt many of the Presbyterian doctrines he had preached and defended, he resigned his position as pastor of the Thirteenth Street Presbyterian Church and established an independent church (1881), the Gospel Tabernacle, to evangelize the unsaved masses of New York City. This move became the impetus for the development of the Christian Missionary Alliance (1885) which Simpson led. Simpson, also, established a missionary training school at Nyack, New York. For information about Simpson's life, ministry, and teaching, see Thompson, *Simpson*; Nienkirchen, *Simpson and the Pentecostal Movement*; Bernie A. Van De Walle, *The Heart of the Gospel: A.B. Simpson, the Fourfold Gospel, and Late Nineteenth-Century Evangelical Theology* (PTMS 106; Eugene, OR: Pickwick, 2009); Charles Nienkirchen, 'Simpson, Albert Benjamin', *NIDPCM,* pp. 1069-70.

[21] For an overview of Simpson's work as an author and editor, see Thompson, *Simpson*, pp. 150-59.

liefs.²² The structure follows the christocentric order of Jesus as Savior, Sanctifier, Healer, and Coming Lord. The contents of the two-volume collection of sermons, *The Holy Spirit or Power from on High* (1895–96),²³ were originally preached to the congregants of the Gospel Tabernacle in New York City and published in the *Alliance Weekly*,²⁴ to honor and arouse interest in the Holy Spirit.²⁵ Though in volume one Simpson surveys the ministry of the Holy Spirit in

---

22 According to Charles Nienkirchen,

> The motto 'Fourfold Gospel' was first coined by Simpson at the outset of the March 1890 convention held at the Gospel Tabernacle in New York City. It was intended to crystallize and convey publicly the distinctive doctrinal convictions of his movement – Christ as Savior, Sanctifier, Healer, and Coming King. Understood in terms of historical development, the expression provides the interpretive key to understanding the integral relationship between those crisis experiences that energized the spiritual journeys of Simpson and his associates and the statement of faith they formulated.

Nienkirchen, *Simpson and the Pentecostal Movement*, p. 2. According to Bernie Van De Walle,

> Few if any of A.B. Simpson's numerous and impressive achievements were unique in their day, and Simpson himself was neither a theological anomaly nor a theological innovator. Even that aspect most closely identified with Simpson – the Fourfold Gospel – was peculiar to neither him nor the C&MA. Rather the Fourfold Gospel was simply an encapsulation of the central theological themes of the late nineteenth-century evangelicalism.

Van De Walle, *The Heart of the Gospel*, p. 22. Van De Walle is correct that Simpson's fourfold gospel encapsulates the theological ethos of the late nineteenth century, but to use evangelicalism in a broad sense is not correct. It seems more proper to narrow the focus to the theological ethos of the Holiness Movement; after all, before Simpson coined the term, the Holiness proponents of this 'full gospel' had been *pushed out* of most mainstream denominations or *come out* to the margins.

23 A.E. Thompson lauds this work as 'the fullest and clearest general survey on the person and ministry of the Holy Spirit that can be found in religious literature'. Thompson, *Simpson*, p. 156.

24 Originally, this began as a missionary magazine, *The Word, Work, and World* (1882). The name of this magazine changed to *The Christian Alliance* (1888) and later to *The Christian Alliance and Foreign Missionary Weekly* (1889). Since that time, it often appeared under the title of *The Alliance Weekly*. Thompson, *Simpson*, pp. 152-53.

25 It is worthy of noting that Stephen Merritt who penned the introduction to volume one was an acquaintance of A.J. Tomlinson. After his conversion (1892), A.J. Tomlinson – who was elected as the first General Overseer of the Church of God, Cleveland, TN (1914) – went about the country visiting places experiencing visitations of the Spirit, which brought him to New York City where he spent time with Merritt who was a close associate of Simpson and considered to have an extensive expertise in pneumatology. A.J. Tomlinson, *Diary of A.J. Tomlinson* (3 vols.; Queen's Village, NY: Church of God, 1949), I, pp. 23-24.

the Hebrew Scriptures and often interprets it christologically, the focus will narrow to the 28 sermons in volume two. The inquiry will proceed by examining each *motif* of *The Four-Fold Gospel*, presenting any Spirit christological references found therein, and integrating parallel passages from *The Holy Spirit or Power from on High*.[26]

In his discussion of Christ as Saviour, Simpson elucidates what salvation effects for humans, the process by which Christ bestows the blessings of salvation and how these blessings are received, the biblical designations for salvation, why the gospel is good news, human accountability, and the urgent need to respond in faith.[27] The first texts of interest are located in the context of the Spirit's relation to Christ in the salvific experience of regeneration.[28]

> Our Lord was born of the Holy Spirit. The announcement by the angel to Mary connects the Divine Spirit directly with the conception and incarnation of Christ ... The very fact that she was an imperfect and sinful woman adds to the glory of this mystery and makes it the more perfect type of the experience through which we also come into fellowship with our living Head. For just as Jesus was born of the Spirit, so we, the disciples of Jesus, must also be born of the Holy Ghost ... The mystery of the incarnation is repeated every time a soul is created anew in Christ Jesus ... Like Him we are born of the Holy Ghost and become sons of God, not by adoption, but by divine regeneration.[29]

---

[26] Along the way, Spirit christological references in other publications will also be noted.

[27] A.B. Simpson, *The Four-Fold Gospel* (BiblioLife repr.; New York: Christian Alliance Publishing, 1890), pp. 7-41.

[28] 'Salvation gives us a new heart. It brings to us regeneration of the soul. Every spark of life from the old polluted nature is worthless, and the divine nature is born in us as part of our very being.' Simpson, *The Four-Fold Gospel*, p. 21. Cf. Simpson, *The Four-Fold Gospel*, p. 29.

[29] A.B. Simpson, *The Holy Spirit or Power from on High: An Unfolding of the Doctrine of the Holy Spirit in the Old and New Testaments* (2 vols.; Harrisburg, PA: Christian Publications, 1896), II, pp. 13-14. Cf. Simpson, *Power from on High*, II, pp. 50-51, 195-203; A.B. Simpson, *The Gentle Love of the Holy Spirit* (An Undated and Edited Version of the Former Title, Walking in the Spirit repr.; Camp Hill, PA: Christian Publications, 1983), pp. 9, 80-82; A.J. Gordon, *The Ministry of the Spirit* (Philadelphia, PA: American Baptist Publication Society, 1895), pp. 53-55, 100-107.

Three noteworthy observations emerge from these texts. First, the Spirit functioned as the agent of conception, incarnation, and birth of Jesus Christ. Second, Mary was not immaculate; the Spirit was the source of Christ's sinless human nature. Third, Jesus' birth of the Spirit paradigmatically depicts the Spirit's salvific agency in the regeneration of human souls; thereupon, Simpson carefully distinguishes between becoming sons of God by adoption and regeneration.

Simpson, thus, includes the Spirit's function in the process of Christ's redemptive mission: salvation comes through Christ's righteous obedience, death, resurrection, intercession, and grace of the Holy Spirit.[30]

> First, we have the witnessing Spirit. In Romans 1.3, 4, the Lord Jesus is said to have been 'of the seed of David according to the flesh, and declared to be the Son of God with power, according to the Spirit of holiness, by the resurrection from the dead'. The Spirit of holiness has been interpreted to mean the divine nature of Jesus Christ, but it is quite proper and, indeed, a more simple interpretation to apply it directly to the Holy Ghost as a divine Person, witnessing to the divinity of the Lord Jesus Christ, by raising Him from the dead according to the will of the Father. The Holy Ghost was ever the witness to Christ's divinity, and the Spirit Who had so distinct a part in the offering up of His sacrifice (for it was 'by the eternal Spirit that He offered Himself to God without spot') had surely as important part in His resurrection.[31]

---

[30] Simpson, *The Four-Fold Gospel*, pp. 24-26.
[31] Simpson, *Power from on High*, II, p. 99. Cf. Gordon, *The Ministry of the Spirit*, pp. 107-108; Asa Mahan, *The Baptism of the Holy Ghost* (London: Elliot Stock, 1876 repr.; New York: W.C. Palmer, jr., 1870), p. 16. Regarding other Spirit christological references to the Spirit's witness to Christ's divinity in his salvific work, see the discussion of justification in the Spirit according to 1 Tim. 3.16 in Simpson, *Power from on High*, II, pp. 184-85; concerning the Spirit's function in Christ's death, see the discussion of Heb. 9.14 in Simpson, *Power from on High*, II, p. 204. In depicting the Spirit's relation to Christ in his roles as the anointed of God, the Lamb of God, and the altar, it appears that Phoebe Palmer implicitly held a Spirit Christology; however, her emphasis remained on the role of the Spirit in relation to Christ and believers after Pentecost. See Palmer, *The Way of Holiness*, pp. 35-36, 40, 42-43.

Here, Simpson sharply distinguishes between Christ's humanity and deity: flesh and Spirit. The Spirit's relation to Christ's identity functions as the definitive witness to and validation of Christ's divinity: by the Spirit, Christ offered himself as a sinless sacrifice for sin, and the Spirit resurrected Christ. These texts attest to the Spirit's relation and function in every aspect of Christ's identity and salvific mission; hence, Simpson rooted the *motif* Jesus as Savior in Spirit Christology.

Next, in his examination of sanctification, he carefully differentiates between regeneration and sanctification by affirming sanctification as a subsequent crisis experience by depicting what is not sanctification, what constitutes sanctification, how sanctification is received, and the source of sanctification.[32]

> It comes through the personal indwelling of Jesus. He does not put righteousness into the heart simply, but He comes there personally Himself to live ... It is something more than regeneration and forgiveness. It is the living God come to live in the new heart. It is the Holy Spirit dwelling in the heart of flesh that God has given ... As we are thus possessed by the Holy Spirit, we are made partakers of the Divine nature.[33]

> In the Old Testament age the Holy Ghost came rather as the Spirit of the Father, in the glory and majesty of the Deity, while under the New Testament He comes rather as the Spirit of the Son, to represent Jesus to us, and to make Him real in our experience and life. Indeed, the Person of the Holy Ghost was not fully constituted under the Old Testament. It was necessary that He should reside for three and a half years in the heart of Jesus of Nazareth, and become, as it were, humanized, colored, and brought nearer to us by His personal union with our Incarnate Lord. Now He comes to us as the same Spirit that lived, and loved, and suffered, and wrought, in Jesus Christ.[34]

According to Simpson, sanctification consists of more than regeneration; it is partaking of the divine nature which he depicts through

---

[32] Simpson, *The Four-Fold Gospel*, pp. 42-74.
[33] Simpson, *The Four-Fold Gospel*, pp. 61-66. Cf. Simpson, *Power from on High*, II, pp. 22, 93-95.
[34] Simpson, *Power from on High*, II, p. 12. Cf. Simpson, *Love of the Holy Spirit*, pp. 29-31.

synonymous phrases and experiences: the personal indwelling of Christ and the possession of the Spirit. Hence, Simpson makes no distinction between Christ and the Spirit indwelling believers. This is because Simpson asserted that the Spirit entered personal union with Christ's humanity and experienced the passions of human nature, forming the personal nature of the Spirit as the Spirit of the Son. In the OT age the Spirit came *upon* humans, but now in the NT age the Spirit dwells *in* believers as the agent of personal union with God, so that they partake of the divine nature.[35]

Simpson, moreover, affirms that sanctification is an experience subsequent to regeneration; the Spirit falls upon and possesses only those believers entirely consecrated to God. He uses the disciples' Spirit baptism as an example. Simpson, accordingly, designates this sanctifying experience of the Spirit by the designation, baptism with the Holy Spirit.[36]

> Jesus was baptized by the Holy Spirit. Not only did He derive His person and His incarnate life from the Holy Ghost, but when at thirty years of age He consecrated Himself to His ministry of life and suffering and service, and went down into the waters of the Jordan, in token of His self-renunciation and His assumption of death, the heavens were opened and the Holy

---

[35] Simpson, *Power from on High*, II, p. 12.
> First, we have the Holy Spirit in relation to the Lord Jesus. In John 1.32, we see the Spirit descending from heaven like a dove, and abiding upon Him, and in John 3.34, we are further told that God giveth not the Spirit by measure unto Him. Up to this time all men had received the Spirit by measure; that is, they had received some of His gifts, influences, and power; but Christ received the Spirit Himself in His personal presence and immeasurable fullness, and since then the Spirit has resided in the world in His boundless and infinite attributes. Christ first received Him as a pattern for His followers, and then gave Him forth to them, from His own very heart, as the Spirit had resided in Him, and comes to us softened by His humanity and witnesses to His person.

Simpson, *Power from on High*, II, p. 49. Cf. Gordon, *The Ministry of the Spirit*, pp. 19-32. According to Simpson's discussion of Gal. 5.25, the promise of the Spirit is the substance of the covenant with Abraham and the supreme blessing of Christ's redemptive mission; it is the sum of all blessings of Christ and the covenant. Simpson, *Power from on High*, II, pp. 134-43.

[36] In Simpson's nomenclature baptism with the Holy Spirit, second blessing, crisis sanctification, the anointing of the Spirit, the sealing of the Spirit, receiving the Spirit, and the indwelling Christ all denote the same experience. Nienkirchen, *Simpson and the Pentecostal Movement*, p. 59. Asa Mahan follows suite, Mahan, *The Baptism of the Holy Ghost*, p. 11.

Ghost, by whom He had been born, now came down and personally possessed His being and henceforth dwelt within Him. No one can for a moment deny that this was something transcendently more than the incarnation of Christ. Up to this time there had been one personality, henceforth there were two; for the Holy Ghost was added to the Christ, and in the strength of this indwelling Spirit, henceforth He wrought His works, and spake His words, and accomplished His ministry on earth. But this also has its parallel in the experience of the disciples of Christ. It is not enough for us to be born of the Holy Ghost, [*sic*] we must also be baptized with the Holy Ghost.[37]

Henceforth, all His teachings, all His works, all His miracles of power were attributed directly to the Holy Ghost ... The Holy Ghost in us is the same Holy Ghost that wrought in Christ. We yield to none, in honor to the Son of God. He was truly the eternal God, 'very God of very God'. But when He came down from yonder heights of glory, he suspended the direct operation of His own independent power and became voluntarily dependent upon the power of God through the Holy Ghost.[38]

---

[37] Simpson, *Power from on High*, II, pp. 14-15. For similar Spirit christological texts, see Simpson, *Love of the Holy Spirit*, pp. 9-12, Mahan, *The Baptism of the Holy Ghost*, pp. 19-22. A.J. Gordon speaks of the Jordan event in a Spirit christological manner:

> The antitype first appears in Christ our Lord, baptized in water at the Jordan, and then baptized in the Holy Ghost which 'descended from heaven like a dove and abode upon him.' Then it recurred again in the waiting disciples, who besides the baptism of water, which had doubtless already been received, now were baptized 'in the Holy Ghost and in fire.'

Gordon, *The Ministry of the Spirit*, p. 57.

[38] Simpson, *Power from on High*, II, p. 19. Cf. Simpson, *Love of the Holy Spirit*, pp. 69-70. In his discussion of Jn 3.34, Asa Mahan asks the following Spirit christological questions:

> Did the development or manifestation of the spiritual life in Christ depend on the baptism, the indwelling, and influence of the Holy Spirit, the same in all essential particulars as in us? Did he seek and secure this Divine anointing as the necessary conditions and means of 'finishing the work which the Father had given him to do' – just as we are necessitated to seek and secure the same 'enduement of power from on high,' as the same means and conditions of our finishing the work which Christ has given us to do?'

Mahan, *The Baptism of the Holy Ghost*, p. 16. Mahan finds his answers in the Spirit's relation to Christ's identity and salvific mission:

Simpson bases his doctrine of Spirit baptism/sanctification on Christ's Spirit baptism during the Jordan event. Several important conclusions can be gleaned from this paradigm. First, Simpson posits two divine persons existing in perichoretic unity in Christ: the eternal divine Son and the Holy Spirit. In the incarnation the Spirit conceived, formed, and united Christ's human nature to the divine person of the Son, but the Spirit did not indwell the human nature until the Jordan event, when the Spirit was personally joined to Christ's human nature through Spirit baptism. Second, it appears that Simpson thinks of the divine Son indwelling Christ's humanity in a quiescent manner: the divine Son voluntarily deferred to the Holy Spirit the communication of divine attributes to Christ's humanity. Third, Christ's Spirit baptism, at the Jordan, empowered him for his salvific mission. Likewise, Spirit baptism is a crisis experience, an empowerment for service subsequent to regeneration;[39] in

---

> The fact that Christ was thus baptized of the Spirit implies that He needed that baptism, an [*sic*] that without it, in the relations in which He then was, He could not have 'finished the work which the Father had given Him to do.' In seeking, and obtaining, and acting under that baptism, Christ is our Exemplar in respect to the spiritual and divine life which is required of us ... In John 3.34, we are told, for example, that the reason Christ spake *as* He did, and *what* He did, was owing to the measureless effusion and power of the Spirit which was vouchsafed to Him ... God does not bestow gifts or influences where and when they are not needed. Christ received this measureless effusion of the Spirit at the beginning and during the progress of His mission, because it was a necessity to Him – just as similar baptisms are a necessity for us in our life mission.

Mahan, *The Baptism of the Holy Ghost*, pp. 17-18.

> We must carefully distinguish between the state of Christ when, as the eternal Word, He dwelt with the Father, and when, as the same Word, He 'was made flesh and dwelt among us.' In the former state, He had infinite all-sufficiency in Himself; in the latter, He 'was in all respects made like unto His brethren,' and had the same need of the baptism of the Spirit that we have, and obtained 'power from on high' on the same conditions on which the same blessing is promised to us.

Mahan, *The Baptism of the Holy Ghost*, p. 18.

[39] See Simpson's sermon 'The Baptism with the Holy Ghost (Mt. 3.11),' *Power from on High*, II, pp. 21-28. For his understanding of Spirit baptism as power for service, see his sermon regarding 'The Parable of the Pounds, or, Power for Service', *Power from on High*, II, pp. 37-48. Cf. Simpson, *Power from on High*, II, p. 100; A.B. Simpson, *The Fourfold Gospel: Albert B. Simpson's Conception of the Complete Provision of Christ for Every Need of the Believer – Spirit, Soul and Body* (Camp Hill, PA: Christian Publications, Updated and edited edn, 1984), pp. 77-78.

positing this position, Simpson makes a clear distinction between two classes of believers, with Spirit baptism being the deciding factor.[40] Fourth, Spirit baptism comes in response to one's entire consecration to God's will and service. Fifth, since contemporary believers have received the same Spirit baptism that Christ experienced and are privy to the same miraculous power, the church's mission should be conducted in the same apostolic power.[41] In Simpson's fourfold gospel, indubitably, the second *motif's* infrastructure is Spirit Christology.

In Simpson's deliberations on Jesus as Healer, he rejects any notion that divine healing is connected with medical treatment, metaphysical healing, spiritualism, or human will power;[42] rather, its doctrinal premise stands on the redemptive work of Christ, and it is

---

Simpson's espousal of a normative two-step pattern of Christian initiation, biblically legitimized by the experience of Christ, the apostles, and the early church, dictated his trenchant opposition to any doctrine of progressive sanctification which undermined the importance of Spirit baptism subsequent to conversion-regeneration.

Nienkirchen, *Simpson and the Pentecostal Movement*, pp. 62-63. Cf. Gordon, *The Ministry of the Spirit*, pp. 67-96. It should be noted that Gordon understood that at Pentecost the entire body of Christ was baptized in the Spirit as a permanent condition, yet this gift must be individually appropriated by each believer as an experience subsequent to justification.

[40] See Simpson's sermon regarding the distinction between the wise and foolish virgins in Matthew chapter 25 in which he argues that those virgins, believers, who have not received Spirit baptism will not be ready as the bride to meet the bridegroom and go to the marriage supper when the Lord returns. Simpson, 'The Wise and Foolish Virgins, or, the Holy Spirit and the Coming of the Lord (Mt. 25.1-4)', *Power from on High*, II, pp. 29-36.

[41] 'Oh, if the Son of God did not presume to begin His public work until He had received this power from on high, what presumption it is that we should attempt in our own strength to fulfill the ministry committed to us and the witnesses unto Him!' Simpson, *Power from on High*, II, p. 16. Cf. Simpson's sermon 'Power from on High', *Power from on High*, II, pp. 77-89. Cf. Simpson, *Love of the Holy Spirit*, pp. 70-71; Mahan, *The Baptism of the Holy Ghost*, pp. 8, 30-33. According to A.J. Gordon, 'Christ, who is our example in this as in all things, did not enter upon his ministry till he had received the Holy Ghost. Not only so, but we see that all his service from his baptism to his ascension was wrought in the Spirit'. Gordon, *The Ministry of the Spirit*, p. 75. Cf. Gordon's discussion of Christ being sealed with the Spirit referring back to the Jordan event, as well as his discussions regarding the fullness of the Spirit, and the anointing of the Spirit. Gordon, *The Ministry of the Spirit*, pp. 77-96. It was also the Spirit which sustained Christ during the wilderness temptations. Simpson, *Power from on High*, II, pp. 16-18. Cf. Simpson, *Power from on High*, II, pp. 49-50, 68, 208.

[42] Simpson, *The Four-Fold Gospel*, pp. 75-91.

experienced through the agency of the Holy Spirit quickening human bodies with an infusion of divine power.[43]

> Divine healing comes to us through the life of Jesus Christ, who rose from the dead in his own body. He has gone up to heaven with His living body. You can see Him there this morning, with hands and feet of living flesh and bones, which you could handle ... We are healed by the life of Christ in our body. It is a tender union with Him: nearer than the bond of communal oneness, so near that the very life of His veins is transfused into yours. That is divine healing.[44]

> It is the work of the Holy Spirit, quickening the body. When Christ healed the sick while He was upon earth, it was not by the Deity that dwelt in His humanity. He said, 'If I cast out devils by the Spirit of God, then the Kingdom of God is come unto you'. Jesus healed by the Holy Ghost. 'The Spirit of the Lord is upon me, because He hath anointed me to preach the Gospel to the poor, to heal the broken hearts.' The Holy Ghost is the agent, then, by which this great power is wrought. Especially should we expect to see His working in these days, because they are the days of His own Dispensation, the days in which it has been prophesied that there shall be signs and wonders.[45]

From these texts, Simpson defines two facets of his doctrine of divine healing: the roles of Christ's human nature and the Holy Spirit. First, Christ's humanity is foundational to Simpson's teaching on divine healing because he places it in Christ's redemptive work, specifically, in Christ's physical suffering of Calvary, bodily resurrection, ascension, and mystical union with believers in which Christ

---

[43] Simpson, *The Four-Fold Gospel*, pp. 91-109.
[44] Simpson, *The Four-Fold Gospel*, pp. 99-100. Cf. Simpson, *Love of the Holy Spirit*, pp. 71-75. In discussing Rom. 8.11, Simpson states,

> The Holy Spirit is next revealed as the Spirit of quickening and healing in our mortal flesh ... He is the Spirit that raised up Christ from the dead, and He dwells in our mortal bodies as a quickening life. This is not the immortal body of the resurrection, but the mortal frame of the present life which feeds upon the divine life. And this is the secret of living on the life of God. It is thus that our bodies are the temples of the Holy Ghost, and our frames are the members of Christ, and partake of the life of our living Head.

Simpson, *Power from on High*, II, pp. 100-101.
[45] Simpson, *The Four-Fold Gospel*, pp. 100-101.

infuses physical life and health into believers. So, Simpson's doctrine of divine healing accentuates both the physical nature of Christ's suffering atonement and the communication of the benefits available to believers through the continuation of his corporeality in glorification. Second, the Holy Spirit is the agent of divine healing. The Spirit's role in divine healing functions in relation to Christ's redemptive mission the same in his ascended state as it did in the earthly. Here, Simpson clearly distinguishes Christ's divine and human natures. During the earthly phase of Christ's mission, deity indwelling his humanity did not manifest divine power in healing the sick; instead, the Spirit which anointed Christ's human nature healed the sick.[46] Likewise, the Spirit infuses into believers the life of Christ and healing, which are redemptive benefits of his glorified human nature. Furthermore, for Simpson, the contemporary agency of the Spirit in healing the sick affirmed to him that he was living in the dispensation of the Spirit when the Spirit would be poured out upon believers with apostolic power and authority, in anticipation of the *Parousia*.[47] The third *motif* of Simpson's fourfold gospel, Christ as Healer, therefore, rests upon the relationship of the Spirit anointing Christ's humanity in his redemptive mission: Spirit Christology.

Simpson, then, proceeds to explain the meaning of Christ's coming and millennial reign, a premillennial view of the order of events,

---

[46] For a discussion regarding the Spirit anointing Christ, see Simpson, *Power from on High*, II, pp. 126-29. Carrie Judd Montgomery presents a form of Spirit Christology in her discussion of the importance of the Spirit anointing Christ in her teaching on divine healing; specifically, in addressing the question: in praying for the sick, why should the sick be anointed with oil? She answers the query by affirming,

> both the sacrifices and priests were, of course, typical of Christ's atonement and Priesthood, and the significance of the typical anointing is made clear to us in passages like the following: St. Peter says, 'That word, I say, ye know ... how God anointed Jesus of Nazareth with the Hold Ghost and with power. Who went about doing good and healing all that were oppressed of the devil, for God was with Him.' The wonderful and blessed anointing of the Holy Spirit, first poured upon Jesus Christ, and then through His mediatorial office, shed forth on His faithful followers, was the precious fulfilling of the Levitical foreshadowing.

Montgomery, *The Prayer of Faith*, p. 73. In placing both the healing of believer's soul and body in the atonement, she integrates the Spirit anointing Christ with believers' Pentecostal sanctification. Montgomery, *The Prayer of Faith*, pp. 72-78.

[47] Cf. Mahan, *The Baptism of the Holy Ghost*, pp. vi, 11, 79-97, 193-94; Gordon, *The Ministry of the Spirit*, pp. 13-16.

the signs and blessings of Christ's coming, and the lessons it teaches. He, moreover, asserts that the fourth component, Christ our Coming Lord, is the culmination of the apostolic gospel, and it encompasses the previous three components.[48]

> The Holy Ghost has not undertaken to convert the world, but to call out of it the Church of Christ and prepare a people for His name ... He Himself has told her that when the message of salvation has been proclaimed to all the world, then shall the end come.[49]

> And so, while we must still recognize the supernatural ministry of the Spirit, which never was intended to be interrupted, and ought to be expected yet more wonderfully in these last days before the coming of the Lord Jesus Christ, let us never make the mistake of regarding it as an end, or allowing it to take the place of the higher truths that relate to our spiritual life. At the same time, let us not ignore it. The church is one through all the ages. 'Jesus Christ is the same yesterday, and today, and forever'; the Holy Spirit is unchanged, and the constitution of the church is identical with the twelfth chapter of First Corinthians and the plan which God gave at Pentecost.[50]

According to Simpson, in light of the Lord's premillennial return, the ministries of the church and Holy Spirit coalesce into one mission: to bring the 'full gospel' message to the entire world before the eschaton. This mission is to be carried out in demonstration of the Spirit and apostolic power; furthermore, the outpouring of the Spirit and increase of the charismata, signs, wonders, and miracles

---

[48] Simpson, *The Four-Fold Gospel*, pp. 110-52.

[49] Simpson, *The Four-Fold Gospel*, pp. 130-32. 'The Spirit of missions is His Spirit. The crowning revelation of the Holy Ghost in this sublime epistle is the Spirit of evangelization for the whole world.' Simpson, *Power from on High*, II, p. 106. Cf. Simpson, *Power from on High*, II, pp. 186-89.

[50] Simpson, *Power from on High*, II, pp. 83-84. Cf. Simpson, *The Four-Fold Gospel*, p. 101.

> The Holy Spirit of hope and anticipation of the coming glory is next seen. And so we read in verse 23, 'And not only they, but ourselves also, who have the first fruits of the Spirit, even we ourselves groan within ourselves, waiting for the adoption, to *wit*, the redemption of our body.' That is, the Holy Spirit awakens the consciousness and brings the earnest of the coming glory, and calls forth our eager longing and outreach for it.

Simpson, *Power from on High*, II, p. 103.

are all prodigies of the Lord's return, placing the fourth *motif* of the fourfold gospel in the environs of Spirit Christology.

The edifice of Simpson's fourfold gospel, therefore, is laid on a Spirit christological foundation. All four components coalesce around the Spirit's paradigmatic relation and function in Christ's identity and mission. Christ's incarnation and birth of the Spirit correlates with believers' regeneration by the Spirit. Christ's Spirit baptism becomes the model for believers' empowerment for service, subsequent to regeneration. The indwelling Christ/Spirit infuses believers with the bodily benefits of participating in the divine nature and Christ's resurrected and ascended physical nature: divine healing. The Spirit awakens in believers the eschatological consciousness of the coming king and kingdom and provides the impetus and power to proclaim the full gospel with the signs of the kingdom. In other words, as the Spirit mediates every facet of Christ's salvific mission, the Spirit also mediates each component of the 'full gospel', its proclamation, and experience. To construct his Spirit Christology, Simpson appears to have retrieved, from the time before the third ecumenical council in the East and before Augustine in the West, a patristic Spirit christological paradigm of pneumatic mediation which integrates Logos Christology.

Simpson's rendition of the 'full gospel' might not represent the views of all proponents of the Holiness fourfold gospel; nonetheless, he was a major figure who competently delineated a version of the fourfold gospel with a Spirit christological trajectory. This is the point: among the proponents of this trajectory, the Holiness movement and American restorationist revivalism's shift in nomenclature to a pneumatic accent flowed from a relocation of the fourfold gospel's christological nexus, from a pneumatically permeated Logos Christology to Spirit Christology. Simpson's articulation of the fourfold gospel represents this *shift* to Spirit Christology in forming the theological *ethos* from which Pentecostalism emerged.[51]

---

[51] Charles Nienkirchen has accentuated several aspects of Simpson's teachings which demonstrate continuity with Pentecostalism. First, his restorationist interpretation of history previsioned an outpouring of the Spirit, the latter rain, which presaged the closing of the present age. Second, he rejected the fundamentalist dispensational assertion that the *charismata* ceased with the close of the apostolic period; instead, Simpson argued that the power of the Spirit depicted in the Book of Acts delineated the spiritual norm for Christians. Third, Simpson's hermeneutical method drew out doctrinal truth from narrative readings of the texts; for

The Unfolding of the Fivefold Full Gospel

With the integration of Pentecostal sanctification, the quandary facing the Holiness movement concerned how to maintain the Wesleyan themes of perfection and purity since power now dominated the exposition of sanctification and Pentecostal biblical texts. In response, several holiness leaders argued for maintaining the traditional Wesleyan 'second blessing' doctrine of entire sanctification while positing a 'third blessing' of power through Spirit baptism;[52] thus, setting the stage for the addition of the fifth *motif* to the 'full gospel. For example, R.C. Horner, G.D. Watson, B.H. Irwin, C.F. Parham, and W.J. Seymour held this position.

Ralph Cecil Horner

Albeit R.C. Horner authored a treatise on *Bible Doctrines*, an autobiography,[53] and numerous holiness publications from a Wesleyan

---

example, Simpson pointed to three events of Pentecost (Acts chs. 2; 8; 19) to validate his attestation that Spirit baptism was a *second blessing* or *crisis sanctification* subsequent to regeneration. Nienkirchen, Simpson, *Simpson and the Pentecostal Movement*, pp. 52-72; Nienkirchen, 'Simpson', *NIDPCM*, p. 1069. Apparently, Simpson's theology had either directly or indirectly influenced several early Pentecostal pioneers, such as Charles Parham, Agnes Ozman, A.J. Tomlinson, Thomas Barratt, Andrew Argue, Alice Flower, Alice Garrigus, Lilian Yeomans, Aimee Semple McPherson, and George Jefferys. Nienkirchen, *Simpson and the Pentecostal Movement*, pp. 26-41. In fact, Nienkirchen has demonstrated that through his training school in Nyack, NY, most of the early leaders of the Assembly of God came under Simpson's influence. Nienkirchen, *Simpson and the Pentecostal Movement*, pp. 41-51.

[52] Donald Dayton rightly assesses the context:

> A party that found the synthesis above too easy argued instead for three works or 'blessings' in which the second work of the dominant Holiness position was broken into two separate blessings. This party, however, was not the fanatical fringe that it appeared to be to Holiness leaders then and since. It pointed to the fundamental difficulty in expressing Wesleyan theology in Pentecostal dress.

Dayton, *Theological Roots*, p. 95. Cf. Synan, *The Holiness-Pentecostal Tradition*, p. 50.

[53] According to R.C. Horner, he 'was born in a revival' and was never called to ministry; rather, he was divinely called to evangelism. R.C. Horner, *Ralph C. Horner, Evangelist: Reminiscences from His Own Pen, Also Reports on Five Typical Sermons* (Brockville ON: Standard Church Book Room, n.d.), p. 20. R.C. Horner (1854–1921) was saved and received the 'second blessing' of sanctification (1872) near Shawville, Quebec. He attended Victoria College (1882–85) to prepare for evangelism in the Methodist Church of Canada. With some difficulty, Horner was ordained in the Montreal Conference of the Methodist Church of Canada (1887). During his ordination examination, Horner's dislike for the phrase 'office of a minister' postponed and almost blocked his ordination. Horner acknowledged

perspective, this inquiry will focus on his monograph devoted to explicating his position regarding Pentecostal power, *Pentecost* (1891).[54] His purpose for writing this work is threefold: (1) to argue that Spirit baptism is empowerment for service, (2) this blessing is for all of God's children, and (3) Christ's disciples 'can do nothing without the baptism of fire'.[55]

In explicating these premises, Horner makes his three blessings position clear.

> The Scriptures present regeneration, entire sanctification, and the baptism of power, as separate, definite blessings to be definitely sought and obtained by faith. Those who hold that they are one, [*sic*] must have come to that conclusion without a proper investigation of the subject ... Most writers on the subject of holiness have been careful and explicit, [*sic*] they have not attempted to make holiness and the baptism of the Holy Ghost one and the same blessing.[56]

---

that he had accepted an *irregular* ordination which granted ministerial privileges to carry out his evangelistic mandate. Of course, the Methodist Conference never agreed to any form of *irregular* ordination. It was not long before Horner's evangelistic methods, his talk of 'cyclones of power', and the physical manifestations – ecstasy, immoderate laughter, and prostrations – exhibited in his tent meetings ran afoul of his Methodist peers. Consequently, the Methodist Conference censured his activity. Unfailing in his resolve, Horner continued his methods which resulted in his trail and deposition (1894). According to the Methodist Conference, Horner ran afoul of the hierarchy because he neither respected district lines nor the authority of his peers; often he would set up his tent without contacting the local minister. According to the Methodist view, at his trial the primary concern of the Conference regarded his attitude toward its authority, and the physical manifestations were only secondary concerns. However, Horner's view of the proceedings is dramatically different. For overviews of Horner's life and ministry, see Brian R. Ross, 'Ralph Cecil Horner: A Methodist Sectarian Deposed, 1887 – 1895', *Journal of the Canadian Church Historical Society* 19 (1977), 94-103; Horner, *Evangelist*.

[54] Horner constructs the argument of this book through nine chapters: (1) The Upper Room To-day, (2) The Upper Room in Jerusalem, (3) Testimony of John the Baptist, (4) The Christ Anointed, (5) The Experience of the Apostles, (6) Power of Conviction, (7) What Is Power?, (8) Power Relative to Our Brethren, and (9) History of the Doctrine.

[55] R.C. Horner, *Pentecost* (Toronto: William Briggs, 1891), pp. iv-v.

[56] Horner, *Pentecost*, p. 135.

> There is power received when the soul is regenerated, and much more power when it is sanctified wholly; still there is a special anointing of the Spirit, which is not received with either of these experiences. This baptism is to be 'filled with power by the Spirit of the Lord' ... It is power for service.

In distinguishing between sanctification and Pentecostal power, Horner appealed to the precedent of John Wesley. According to Horner, Wesley did not integrate holiness commandments in the Scripture with Jesus' command for his disciples to be endued with power (Lk. 24.49).[57] Jesus' disciples, accordingly, experienced justification and sanctification as distinct salvific events prior to receiving power on the day of Pentecost.[58] Horner, therefore, stanchly defended the Wesleyan view of sanctification as a 'second blessing' and affirmed the baptism in the Holy Ghost with power as a definite and distinct 'third blessing.'[59]

Horner based his doctrine of Spirit baptism as an enduement of power for service on Jesus Christ's experience of the Spirit.

Horner, *Pentecost*, p. 86. Cf. Horner, *Pentecost*, pp. 86-92.

[57] Wesley did not quote this command given by the Lord Jesus to the disciples. The question is why he did not? Simply because he knew that they had received holiness, and this command was for the special anointing for service, which they received on the day of Pentecost. Wesley taught that holiness was salvation from inbred sin, and he knew that the disciples were not told to wait for cleansing. He collected and quoted prayers that had been offered up for the entire sanctification of God's people, but he did not intimate that any of these prayers were answered on the day of Pentecost.

Horner, *Pentecost*, pp. 137-38. Cf. Dayton, *Theological Roots*, p. 98. Horner refutes Phoebe Palmer's understanding of Wesleyan sanctification and her altar theology. See Ralph C. Horner, 'To, before, and on the Altar', *From the Altar to the Upper Room* (Higher Christian Life; New York: Garland Publishing, 1984 repr.; Toronto: William Briggs, 1891), pp. 28-30. He lays out his doctrine of consecration in Ralph C. Horner, 'What Is Consecration', *From the Altar to the Upper Room*, pp. 3-12. Horner presents his doctrine of entire consecration in Horner, 'Entire Consecration', *From the Altar to the Upper Room*, pp. 7-116. Horner also defended the Wesleyan 'second blessing' theology against a polemical attack by Jeremiah Boland. See R.C. Horner, *Notes on Boland; or, Mr. Wesley and the Second Work of Grace* (Boston: McDonald and Gill, 1893).

[58] Horner discusses how the apostles received these three distinct experiences in Horner, *Pentecost*, pp. 52-74.

[59] Horner, *Pentecost*, pp. 21-36. According to Horner, the intense desire to acquire power to win souls led him to understand the baptism in the Holy Spirit as a third definite and distinct experience of power, so that this 'extra gift for soul winning has been the aggressive element in my experience. It brought all the dormant powers of my soul into activity and energized all my facilities for efficiency in the vineyard of the Lord'. Horner, *Evangelist*, pp. 13-14. Cited in Dayton, *Theological Roots*, p. 99. According to Vinson Synan, 'The most far-reaching effect of Horner's teaching was to separate in time and purpose the experiences of second-blessing sanctification and the "third blessing" of "baptism in the Holy Spirit," a theological distinction that became crucial to the development of Pentecostalism'. Synan, *The Holiness-Pentecostal Tradition*, p. 50.

Why was Jesus baptized with the Holy Ghost and with power, when He had no sin to be purged away? Why was it necessary for him to be baptized with the Holy Ghost? Was he not perfect God as well as perfect man? The baptism of the Holy Ghost was not designed by God to save His people from their sins. The soul must be fully saved from inbred sin, as well as actual sins, before it is anointed for service. Jesus, having no sin to he saved from, was fully prepared for the anointing of the Holy Ghost.[60]

He had a human body and soul to be operated upon. He had human affections which were energized by the Holy Ghost. He had a body, which was pregnated [*sic*] by the power of God, and so permeated, that it became strengthened for the purpose of suffering, and accomplishing the work He came to do ... If it was absolutely necessary for Jesus to be baptized with the Holy Ghost, how much more His frail creatures, with their fallibility, infirmities, ignorances, [*sic*] etc. He had more than a perfect human nature; He had a perfect divine nature in the same body.[61]

Jesus came to take away our sins and give us many baptisms of the Holy Ghost. It is not just one baptism. It is one baptism after another increasing in power, as the capacity for receiving it has been developed.[62]

According to Horner, Jesus was immaculate, so his experience of Spirit baptism had no sanctifying effect; in fact, the Jordan event demonstrates that only those entirely sanctified are fit candidates for Spirit baptism.[63] Spirit baptism endued Jesus with power – not holiness, wisdom, or faith – to endure, suffer, and accomplish his redemptive mission. Furthermore, if Spirit baptism was an essential endowment of power for Jesus to accomplish his salvific calling, the same experience and power is necessary for his disciples to continue

---

[60] Horner, *Pentecost*, p. 47.

[61] Horner, *Pentecost*, p. 49. 'Jesus was led into the wilderness by the Spirit to fast for forty days, and then to be tempted of the devil. He needed this anointing for such a trial. It gave Him power to endure.' Horner, *Pentecost*, p. 48.

[62] Horner, *Pentecost*, p. 133. According to Horner, Jesus 'did not remain satisfied with one anointing of the Spirit'. Horner, *Pentecost*, p. 48.

[63] 'The special anointing of the Spirit for service will be received as soon as it is known to be the privilege of the sanctified soul.' Horner, 'On the Altar', *From the Altar to the Upper Room*, p. 30.

his work in the earth.⁶⁴ After the believer has experienced the initial Spirit baptism, Horner, advocated for multiple baptisms in the Spirit, so that one could gain more power and deeper experiences in the Spirit. Horner, also, deliberated on the Spirit's relation to the divine and human natures in the one person of Christ, placing the discussion in the environs of Spirit Christology. Horner attested to the reality of Christ's divine nature,⁶⁵ which needed no anointing of the Spirit, yet he carefully distinguished the human nature, allowing place for the Spirit to anoint Christ's humanity: soul, affections, and body. So, the Spirit functioned as the agent of power anointing Christ's humanity to fulfill the salvific ministry.

Horner, therefore, grounds his 'third blessing' doctrine in Spirit Christology. Christ's Spirit baptism during the Jordan event is paradigmatic of his disciples receiving this anointing subsequent to their regeneration and sanctification. For Horner, Spirit baptism has nothing to do with acquiring holiness but everything to do with power for service. This is the point: Christ's humanity needed and received power from the Spirit, which vitally affected Jesus Christ, so that the Spirit's anointing was essential for Christ to fulfill his ministry, agreeing with the axioms of Spirit Christology. Since Horner positions his christological reflections within trinitarian theology and clearly affirms that the eternal divine Son was incarnated in Christ, he postulates a Spirit Christology set within a triune framework which integrates Logos Christology, fitting nicely into a Spirit christological paradigm of pneumatic mediation.

George Douglas Watson

G.D. Watson was a fecund writer, publishing numerous monographs pertaining to history, prophecy, eschatology, and holiness issues, as well as regularly contributing articles to J.M. Pike's *Way of Faith* holiness periodical.⁶⁶ Attention will concentrate on Watson's

---

⁶⁴ 'Wait before God for the holy anointing. God will come; He will not tarry. He will come speedily. He will baptize with the Holy Ghost. The promise cannot fail. The fire will come upon you and go through us. We shall be anointed for service.' Horner, 'Entire Consecration', *From the Altar to the Upper Room*, p. 49.

⁶⁵ Cf. Horner, 'Entire Consecration', *From the Altar to the Upper Room*, pp. 103-104.

⁶⁶ G.D. Watson (1845–19?) was reared in a Methodist family in antebellum Virginia. At the tender age of six, George Watson felt the convicting power of the Spirit, and at the age of thirteen he was called to preach, but he did not surrender fully to Christ until 1863, while serving in the Southern army during the Ameri-

work which advocates a 'third blessing' of power within the parameters of Spirit Christology, *The Secret of Spirit Power* (1894).[67]

Watson's fundamental premise regarding the secret of power stands within the axioms of Spirit Christology.

> The power that Jesus used in working miracles, in preaching sermons, in healing diseases, in casting our demons, in saving souls was not the power of His sinless soul, but it was the power flowing from the baptism of the Spirit upon His pure humanity. This is distinctly marked in the two periods of His life. From His infancy to His baptism in Jordan He was entirely holy, but wrought no miracles, but when the Holy Ghost descended on Him, from that time on, He was the Anointed One, and worked under the perpetual unction that flowed through Him from the Holy Spirit.[68]

---

can Civil War (1861–65), when his regiment experienced a revival, so he began his ministry holding prayer meetings with the young soldiers. Watson received his theological training at the Biblical Institute at Concord, NH. He sought and confessed to having received entire sanctification at a National Camp Meeting in 1869; however, due to his presiding elder's opposition to the doctrine, he soon lapsed into his old habits. To fill his intellectual hunger Watson studied philosophy and science, while aimlessly playing with repression and Zinzendorf theories of sanctification to satisfy his spiritual hunger. Though a popular and successful preacher, Watson did not receive his entire sanctification until December, 1876. Subsequently, Watson became an adroit defender of Wesleyan 'second blessing' sanctification and a proponent of a 'third blessing' baptism of power. Sometime around 1896 Watson shifted from postmillennial to premillennial eschatology. Regarding his eschatology, see Stephen J. Lennox, 'The Eschatology of George D. Watson', *Wesleyan Theological Journal* 29 (1994), pp. 111-26. For information about his life and ministry, see S. Olin Garrison and G.D. Watson, *Forty Witnesses: Covering the Whole Range of Christian Experience* (New York: Eaton and Mains, 1888), pp. 100-106; Eva M. Watson, *Glimpses of the Life and Work of George Douglas Watson* (Salem, OH: Schmul, 1974 repr.; Cincinnati: God's Bible School and Revivalist, 1929); Lennox, 'Eschatology', pp. 111-12.

[67] Watson constructs his book with thirty chapters. The first six chapters explicate essential ingredient conditions to spiritual power: (1) the Holy Spirit being joined to the sanctified soul, (2) the crucifixion of self, (3) the perpetual ignoring of our creature ability, (4) the salvific role of truth, (5) the willingness to suffer apparent failure for Jesus' sake, and (6) the constant recognition of the Holy Spirit's presence. G.D. Watson, *The Secret of Spiritual Power* (Boston: Christian Witness, 1894), pp. 1-29. The remainder of the book enlarges on these themes and examines certain related issues.

[68] Watson, *Spiritual Power*, pp. 2-3.

We are told that when Jesus had gotten through with the temptation of the wilderness, He 'returned to Galilee in the power of the Holy Ghost.' This ex-

> We sometimes hear it said that 'holiness is power,' and that all the power we need for the work of God is heart purity, but these remarks are not entirely correct according to the Word of God. It is true that heart purity is power in the creature sense of power, but it is not the power of the Holy Ghost in the Scripture sense of it. Jesus is our example, and we read that He received in addition to His pure humanity the power of the Holy Ghost, and that it was 'through the eternal Spirit He offered Himself without spot unto God.'[69]
>
> Now, if Jesus needed the Holy Ghost united with His holy creature nature in order to give Him the peculiar secret or power in His mission, and if He is our example, how much more do we need that we should have our sanctified hearts and our mental faculties in vital union with the Holy Spirit, that by that union we may do the work of God.[70]

Watson uses Christ as an example to argue that holiness is one thing and power is another. Here, Watson is refuting Phoebe Palmer's solution to the conundrum Pentecostal sanctification presents Wesleyan theologians: 'holiness is power.'[71] Although he does agree that in a limited sense purity is power, the Pentecostal endowment of power is an experience distinct from sanctification; in fact, Christ best demonstrates this distinction. Christ lived an immaculate life, yet he performed no acts of power until he received Spirit baptism during the Jordan event. Through the Spirit's power, not purity of nature, Christ healed the sick, exorcised demons, performed miracles, and offered himself as a sacrifice for humanity's sin. This is the point: holiness is a prerequisite for power.[72] If Christ, who was holy,

---

pression of returning in the 'power of the Holy Ghost,' implies that there was added unto Him a power which He did not possess as a mere pure man.' Watson, *Spiritual Power*, p. 3.

[69] Watson, *Spiritual Power*, p. 3.

[70] Watson, *Spiritual Power*, p. 4. 'Thus the secret of power is in having the Holy Ghost unite Himself to our souls.' Watson, *Spiritual Power*, p. 5. 'The power is identified with the Holy Ghost, and is spoken of as a current or wave which gushes out from the conjunction of the Holy Spirit and the human soul.' Watson, *Spiritual Power*, p. 4.

[71] Palmer, *The Promise of the Father*, p. 206. Cf. Dayton, *Theological Roots*, p. 97.

[72] 'Another condition essential to the full enduement of spiritual power is the *crucifixion of self* in order that we may be united with the Holy Ghost.' Watson, *Spiritual Power*, p. 7.

needed the Spirit's power to conduct his ministry, so do his followers. According to Watson, the fundamental secret of power is that the Holy Spirit must be conjoined with a sanctified soul.[73] Clearly, Watson avers the Wesleyan 'second blessing' sanctification doctrine and the 'third blessing' of power through Spirit baptism.[74]

The lineaments of Watson's doctrine of Spirit baptism reveal his underlying Spirit Christology. According to Watson, Jesus' life and ministry fell into two distinct epochs divided by the Jordan event. Antecedent to the Jordan event Christ performed no works of power; nonetheless, Christ's human nature existed in a state of purity, which is an example for believers achieving sanctification through the cleansing agency of the Holy Spirit.[75] The Jordan event, more specifically Christ's Spirit baptism, was the transition for Christ into a new epoch of power and mission; henceforth, Christ

---

The spirit of consecration is a part of the new life imparted to the soul in regeneration; but in order to receive the full baptism of the Spirit, the principle of consecration must be carried to completeness. Just as long as consecration is defective on any point, or in any degree, the experience of complete cleansing and filling cannot be received.

Watson, *Spiritual Power*, p. 65. Cf. Watson, *Spiritual Power*, pp. 7-11, 60-74.

[73] 'In the first place, the secret of spiritual power consists in the union of the Holy Ghost with the purified faculties and natural energies of the human soul.' Watson, *Spiritual Power*, p. 1. 'However holy a man is, there must be joined on to him a divine current, a supernatural energy which is emphatically divine, of which he is the vehicle and conductor.' Watson, *Spiritual Power*, p. 2.

[74] Watson attested that

I have observed that some teach the receiving of the full baptism of the Spirit, while at the same time, strongly denying the destruction of inward sin. But, according to the Word of God, the two things are utterly contrary to each other, and I have never in all my travels found or heard of a person actually receiving the baptism of the Spirit under such teaching.

Watson, *Spiritual Power*, p. 71. 'If we want Pentecostal power we must pay Pentecostal prices.' Watson, *Spiritual Power*, p. 74. 'The word sanctification does not imply the full baptism of the Holy Ghost; it simply means to *cleanse* the heart. But there is another side, and that is the full baptism of the Holy Ghost, the enduement of power, the anointing of "that which remaineth."' G.D. Watson, *The Seven Overcomeths; and Other Expositions from the Revelation* (Boston: Christian Witness, 1889), p. 20. True to Wesleyan theology Watson states, 'The Bible represents us as having a double disease, and over against this is presented a double cure'. G.D. Watson, *White Robes: Garments of Salvation* (Boston: Christian Witness, 1883), p. 18. Regarding fuller explications of Watson's Wesleyan 'second blessing' doctrine of sanctification, see Watson, *White Robes*, pp. 7-31, 47-65, 77-93. Concerning his further exposition of second-blessing sanctification and 'third blessing' enduement of power, see Watson, *The Seven Overcomeths*, pp. 9-25.

[75] Watson, *Spiritual Power*, p. 130.

accomplished his soteriological mission through the power of the Spirit.[76] The secret of Christ's spiritual power was that his human soul was united with the Holy Spirit.

Watson, therefore, constructs his 'third blessing' of power doctrine on the foundation of Spirit Christology: Christ's experience of the Spirit stands as the example of believers' sanctification and Spirit baptism. Watson adheres to trinitarian theology and the doctrine of the incarnation of the eternal divine Son in Jesus Christ; nevertheless, he sharply distinguishes between the divine and human natures in Christ, permitting the Spirit to empower the human nature. Christ's works of power were, thus, assigned to the Spirit's agency functioning in his human nature, rather than the Logos. It appears, then, that Watson's 'third blessing' theology is supported by a Spirit christological paradigm of pneumatic mediation which integrates Logos Christology within a trinitarian framework.

Benjamin Hardin Irwin

Although information about B.H. Irwin's early life is a bit thin, his ministry, holiness views, and doctrine of multiple pneumatic experiences are well documented.[77] After preaching second blessing sanctification for several years,[78] the turning point in his ministry oc-

---

[76] Watson, *Spiritual Power*, p. 127.

[77] Information about the life of B.H. Irwin (1853–1917) can be gleaned from snippets of autobiographical information given by Irwin in the official organ of the Fire-Baptized Church, *Live Coals of Fire*: B.H. Irwin, *LCF,* 1.9 (Dec. 29, 1899), p. 1; 1.12 (Feb. 9, 1900), p. 2; 1.14 (March 9, 1900), p. 5; 1.15 (March 23, 1900), p. 1; 1.20 (June 1, 1900), p. 4. Cf. Vinson Synan, *Oldtime Power: A Centennial History of the International Pentecostal Holiness Church* (Franklin Springs, GA: LifeSprings, Centennial edn, 1998), pp. 45-56; Synan, *The Holiness-Pentecostal Tradition*, pp. 51-54; Vinson Synan, 'Irwin, Benjamin Hardin', *NIDPCM*, pp. 804-805. Educationally, Irwin studied botany and law, and his early vocational life was spent as a lawyer. Irwin was converted in Tecumseh, NE (1879) and became the pastor of a local Baptist church. B.H. Irwin, 'Editorial Correspondence', *LCF* 1.9 (Dec. 29, 1899), p. 1. Nevertheless, after several encounters with various preachers representing the Iowa Holiness Association, Irwin received the 'second blessing' sanctification experience (1891). B.H. Irwin, 'Definite Experiences', *LCF* 1.12 (Feb. 9, 1900), p. 2. Cf. J.M. Pike (ed.), *WF* (Nov. 13, 1895), p. 2. Irwin, then, served as an evangelist in the Wesleyan Methodist Church, spreading the message of the 'double cure' throughout Nebraska, Iowa, and Kansas (1892–95).

[78] Irwin was thoroughly inundated with the teachings of John Wesley and John Fletcher, referring to them in almost every one of the 21 issues of *Live Coals of Fire* while he was editor (Oct. 6, 1899–June 15, 1900). Irwin continued teaching a Wesleyan form of sanctification throughout his ministry, and he disdained the Keswick form of sanctification. See B.H. Irwin, 'The Eradication of Sin', *LCF* 1.5

curred when he received a third distinct experience, a baptism in fire (1895);[79] subsequently, Irwin began proclaiming this 'third blessing' with significant results: people received the experience with dynamic physical manifestations.[80] Because Irwin preached this bap-

---

(Nov. 3, 1899), pp. 5, 8. Cf. Irwin, *LCF*, 1.8 (Dec. 15, 1899), p. 3; 1.18 (May 4, 1900), p. 8. Irwin also offered a critique of Phoebe Palmer's altar theology in B.H. Irwin, 'Theoretical Holiness', *LCF* 1.9 (Dec. 29, 1899), p. 1.

[79] Irwin received this experience in Enid, OK, in 1895. According to Irwin, he had already received sanctification and Spirit baptism, yet there remained

> inexpressible longings after the deeper and greater things of God ... I was being led every step of the way by the personal Holy Ghost. Intuitively I knew that I was approaching a great crisis in my experience. Many things had led me down to this point. The loss of property, declining health, disappointments, persecutions, betrayals, and the slander of many [*sic*] ... I had been reading Upham's 'Life of Madame Guyon' and Dr. Watson's 'Coals of Fire.' I know that some of my brethren in the ministry, and in the ranks of the laity as well, professed to have an experience of fire which I had never known. Moreover I had been praying for fire all summer in my camp meeting, and had seen the need of it in many places. And as I read the word alone on my knees, the Holy Ghost seemed to direct my mind continually to those passages where fire is spoken of, and especially to Mt. 3.11 – 'and with fire.' And to that wonderful Scripture in Rev. 15.2, 'A sea of glass mingled with fire' ... everything seemed to gather about that single word FIRE ... I became convinced and satisfied that there was an experience of fire for me, and that it was my privilege and duty to ask and receive it ... I saw in the room above me a cross of pure, transparent fire. It was all fire ... No fire that ever was kindled on earth was half so pure, so beautiful, so divinely transparent as that. In a few moments the whole room where we were lying seemed to be all luminous with seven fold light (Isa. 30.26), and a little later still the very heavens were all aglow with transparent flame. The very walls of the room seemed to be on fire. But as yet there was no sense of heat connected with it ... all at once I became conscious of the fact that I was literally on fire ... I felt that I was in the very midst of a burning fiery presence. At no time in my life have I known or felt such unutterable ecstatic bliss. For five hours I felt that I should certainly be consumed.

B.H. Irwin, 'The Baptism of Fire', *WF* (Nov. 13, 1895), p. 2. Cf. Irwin, 'Definite Experiences', p. 2; J.H. King, 'History of the Fire-Baptized Holiness Church', *PHA* (Mar. 21, 1921), p. 4; Synan, *Oldtime Power*, p. 46. It is worth noting G.D. Watson's influence on Irwin; for example, Irwin testifies that reading Watson's *Coals of Fire* helped prepare and convince him to seek this baptism of fire. Both Irwin and Watson were regular contributors to the *Way of Faith*. Not only did Irwin read Watson's publications, but he sold Watson's books during his revivals, see Irwin, *WF* (Dec. 28, 1896), p. 1. According to Irwin, 'I believe Dr. Watson to be the ablest and profound writer on the inner life that lives today'. Irwin, *WF* (July 22, 1896), p. 1.

[80] 'His service soon began to draw large crowds, a special attraction being the renewed exhibition of the emotional phenomena that characterized the Cane Ridge revivals earlier in the century.' Synan, *The Holiness-Pentecostal Tradition*, p. 52. There were exhibitions of spiritual ecstasy, the holy dance, weeping, laughing,

tism of fire and consistently criticized the holiness standards of the holiness associations,[81] the central stream of the holiness movement reprobated his teachings, labeling them fanaticism, delusion, and the 'third blessing heresy'.[82] Because of the emerging controversy over the baptism of fire, Irwin and the Iowa Holiness Association parted ways; consequently, Irwin formed the Fire-Baptized Holiness Association (FBHA) in Olmitz, Iowa, (1895).[83] By 1898, the movement

---

shaking, jerking, laughing, shouting, prostrations, and other manifestations: Irwin, *WF* (July 22, 1896), p. 5; (July 29, 1896), p. 1; (Sept. 2, 1896), p. 1; (Dec. 28, 1896), p. 1; (Oct. 20, 1897), p. 2. Cf. G.F. Taylor, *PHA* (May 22, 1930), p. 8.

[81] Irwin and other ministers in the FBHA consistently condemned the following practices of other ministers: eating pork, drinking coffee, tobacco chewing, belonging to the lodge, attending theatres, and such demonstrations of pride as parting their hair in the middle, wearing neckties, wearing jewelry, and Sabbath breaking which included preachers riding in cars on Sunday. Certain of these restrictions caused critics to accuse the FBHA with law-keeping and legalism. The FBHA rejected this charge:

> Our adversary, the devil, has been trying to convince inquiring minds that the fire-baptized people are trying to live under the law. We are not under the law, nor are we trying to make laws; and we praise God that we are not under the Levitical law, 'which could not make the comers thereunto perfect,' for being without grace they could not keep the law. We are under God, the Holy Ghost being His executive agent in this dispensation of the last days. The points wherein we are accused of becoming legal were established by God Himself *before the law was given*.

E.D. Wells, 'Tithing', *LCF* 1.19 (May 18, 1900), p. 6.

[82] Irwin defended his doctrine of baptism with fire against his critics in B.H. Irwin, 'Pyrophobia', *WF* (Oct. 28, 1896), p. 2. One such critic of the experience responded to Irwin: J.A. Porter, 'Is a Third Blessing Necessary?', *WF* (Nov. 11, 1896), p. 4. J.M. Pike the editor of the *Way of Faith* wrote an amicable article regarding Irwin's experience and teachings: J.M. Pike, 'The Baptism of Fire', *WF* (Nov. 13, 1895), p. 4. For denunciations of Irwin see Synan, *The Holiness-Pentecostal Tradition*, p. 53, n. 21; Synan, *Oldtime Power*, pp. 47-48.

[83] Irwin and his fellow Fire-Baptized evangelists spread the message and experience across Texas, Oklahoma, and Kansas. Beginning in 1896, the Fire-Baptized gospel swept across the Southeast, as well as into Ontario and Manitoba, Canada. Also, in 1899, land was donated to the FBHA to found a school for training missionaries, The School of the Prophets, and a national headquarters in Beniah, TN, located about nine miles north of Cleveland. See, Irwin, *LCF* 1.5 (Nov. 3, 1899), p. 6; 1.6 (Nov. 10, 1899), p. 4. 'We have seventy-five acres of fine land, and it may be covered with cottages subject to the regulations of the Board of Trustees, and thereby Beniah may be made a great center of fire-baptized holiness. We expect to make Beniah the seat of fire-baptized holiness learning, and the center of our evangelistic and missionary work. From Beniah we expect to send forth evangelists and missionaries into every part of the earth, who will teach and preach the gospel of the fire and the dynamite.' Irwin, *LCF* 1.10 (Jan. 12, 1900), p. 1. By 1899, FBHA congregations existed in 13 states and two nations, with plans to send missionaries to Africa and Cuba. Irwin, *LCF* 1.5 (Nov. 3, 1899), p. 6; 1.7

had purchased a publishing facility in Lincoln, Nebraska; in October 1899, the first issue of the movement's official publication, *Live Coals of Fire* was printed with Irwin serving as the editor.[84]

During a sermon he preached Nov. 8, 1898 in Toronto, Canada, Irwin depicted how he associated the 'third blessing' with baptism in fire in his exposition of the seraphic cry of Isa. 6.3: 'Holy, holy, holy is the Lord of hosts; the whole earth is full of his glory'.

> It is an ascription of praise to the holy Trinity. Holy Father! Holy Son! Holy Spirit! The first 'holy' also means justification; the second 'holy,' entire sanctification: and the third 'holy,' the baptism with fire! ... And so, beloved, when Jesus gives us the mighty baptism of fire, He floods the whole earth with His glory![85]

Continuing the sermon regarding God's question, 'whom shall I send'? (Isa. 6.8), Irwin correlated the seraphim taking a burning coal off the celestial altar and placing it on Isaiah's lips (Isa. 6.7) with the calling to preach the fire-baptized gospel.[86]

(Dec. 1, 1899), p. 3; 1.12 (Feb. 9, 1900), p. 5; 1.13 (Feb. 23, 1900), p. 5; 1.14 (Mar. 9, 1900), p. 2. Though the FBHA was poised to become a national and international influence, in the spring of 1900, Irwin confessed to living in gross sin, a devastating blow to the movement. J.H. King succeeded Irwin as General Overseer of the movement and editor of *Live Coals of Fire* (1900). In 1902 the name of the movement was changed to the Fire-Baptized Holiness Church, and in 1906 the doctrine of a definite and distinct baptism of fire subsequent to baptism in the Holy Spirit was dropped. In 1911, the Fire-Baptized Church merged with the Pentecostal Holiness Church. Synan, *Oldtime Power*, pp. 44-65; Synan, *The Holiness-Pentecostal Tradition*, pp. 51-60; King, 'History of the Fire-Baptized Holiness Church', *PHA* (Mar. 31, 1921), pp. 10-11; Joseph E. Campbell, *The Pentecostal Holiness Church, 1898 – 1948* (Franklin Springs, GA: Publishing House of the Pentecostal Holiness Church, 1951), pp. 194-97; Douglas Beacham, *A Brief History of the Pentecostal Holiness Church* (Franklin Springs, GA: Advocate Press, 1983), pp. 43-49.

[84] *Live Coals of Fire* was published by the FBHA, in Lincoln, Nebraska, with B.H. Irwin serving as its editor for the first 21 issues (Oct. 6, 1899–June 15, 1900), until J.H. King succeeded him after Irwin's fall. The focus will rest on the issues which Irwin served as editor. The periodical began as a weekly publication, for the first 6 issues, but beginning Dec. 1, 1899 it became a biweekly publication. It consisted of 8 pages, except for issues 4 and 21 which contained only 4 pages, which included Irwin's editorial comments and sermons, as well as various preachers and laity contributing sermons, articles, letters, and testimonies. Since Irwin edited *Live Coals of Fire* and determined which material was included for publication, if someone's writing made it into the periodical, it can be assumed that it represented Irwin's and the movement's view.

[85] B.H. Irwin, 'Sermon', *LCF* 1.1 (Oct. 6, 1899), p. 5.

[86] It is noteworthy that G.D. Watson argues that

And this call includes the mighty three-fold salvation of justification, entire cleansing, and the two-fold baptism with the Holy Ghost and fire.[87]

According to Irwin, the 'third blessing' encompasses Jesus' two-fold baptism: in the Spirit and in fire (Mt. 3.11). Though these are pneumatic experiences distinct in time and purpose,[88] they constitute two parts of the 'third blessing'. Spirit baptism fills sanctified vessels with the person of the Holy Spirit, while fire-baptism reveals God's glory in the earth in and through the fire-baptized saints. God's glory is revealed through saints preaching the fire-baptized gospel, striking fear and conviction in sinner's hearts and setting in motion judgment and destruction upon apostate churches.[89] Fire-baptism, also, reveals God's glory in saints bringing them into mystical communion with the triune God,[90] so that visions of fire,

---

the seraphim refer to redeemed men fully baptized of the Holy Ghost ... So in this passage from Isaiah, the seraphim, elsewhere called the 'living creatures,' representing the fire-baptized heralds of salvation, intimate that when the holiness of God is proclaimed and accepted, this will fill the earth with His glory.

G.D. Watson, *Coals of Fire: Being Expositions of Scripture on the Doctrine, Experience, and Practice of Christian Holiness* (Salem, OH: Schmul Publishers repr.; Boston: Christian Witness, 1886), pp. 10-13.

[87] Irwin, 'Sermon', *LCF* 1.1 (Oct. 6, 1899), p. 8.

[88] 'We desire to say that the central idea of the Fire-Baptized Holiness Movement is that **the baptism with fire is a definite experience**.' B.H. Irwin, 'The Central Idea', *LCF* 1.6 (Nov. 10, 1899), p. 4. Cf. *LCF* 1.1 (Oct. 6, 1899), p. 3.

[89] When you speak in the demonstration of the Spirit and power, there will be a setting in motion, and a stirring among the dry and dead bones, hallelujah! The very foundations of things will be shaken up. The devil will rage, and carnal professors storm and threaten, and timid, unsanctified church members will tremble and expostulate, fearing the whole ecclesiastical fabric will tremble to ruins upon their heads!

Irwin, 'Sermon', *LCF* 1.1 (Oct. 6, 1899), p. 5. Again, the influence of G.D. Watson seems to appear, see Watson, *Coals of Fire*, pp. 13-15.

[90] We received the experience of the baptism with fire as **a definite experience**. We sought it as such. It came to us in the marvelous revelation of the adorable Holy Trinity. It marked an epoch in our personal history ... His Threefold splendor and glory was fully risen in our soul, and now we had the conscious personal acquaintance of each of the Eternal Three.

Irwin, 'The Central Idea', *LCF* 1.6 (Nov. 10, 1899), p. 4. This mystical triune communion was essential to Irwin's doctrine of baptism in fire, see *LCF* 1.2 (Oct. 13, 1899), pp. 3, 6; 1.3 (Oct. 20, 1899), p. 5; 1.5 (Nov. 3, 1899), pp. 1, 5, 7;

lightening, and divine light are expected.⁹¹

Fire-baptism, thus, serves as a portal into deeper experiences with the triune God, potentially, opening space for subsequent pneumatic experiences of increased anointing and power. This is vividly attested to in Irwin's ruminations concerning power. Since the word dynamite was derived from the Greek word for power (δύναμις) in Acts 1.8, Irwin translated this text as a promise to receive dynamite subsequent to baptism in fire.

> The apex – the acme, of this Pentecostal experience is the mighty dynamite of God. Jesus did not tell them to tarry till they got the Holy Ghost and fire, but the dynamite is mentioned ... I see depths and heights and divine experiences out beyond the fire line, and away out beyond entire sanctification; and I am going in for them; and while I am going in for them I am keeping true to the fire, and sanctification, and justification, and divine

---

1.8 (Dec. 15, 1899), p. 2; 1.9 (Dec. 29, 1899), pp. 6, 7; 1.10 (Jan. 12, 1900), pp. 2, 4, 7; 1.13 (Feb. 23, 1900), pp. 2, 4; 1.14 (Mar. 9, 1900), p. 4; 1.15 (Mar. 23, 1900), pp. 3, 7; 1.18 (May 4, 1900), pp. 1, 4, 7, 8; 1.19 (May 18, 1900), p. 8. Commenting on Isa. 6.3 G.D Watson states: 'His soul discovered the blessed Trinity ... Jesus told the disciples that when they received the abiding Comforter, they should know the Trinity, not as a dogma, but as an inward revelation to the heart. "The Spirit of Truth shall be in you, and ye shall know that I am in my Father" (Jn 14.17-20)'. Watson, *Coals of Fire*, pp. 26-27. Writing from Beniah, Tennessee, where he and Irwin were conducting a revival, John Dull affirmed 'I received the baptism with fire as a third, definite and distinct work of grace upon my soul ... I was sanctified wholly and had the personal Holy Ghost within me, and had had for some time before I received this wonderful revelation of the Trinity in the experience of the baptism with fire'. John E. Dull, 'The Third Blessing', *LCF* 1.3 (Oct. 20, 1899), p. 5.

> Much has been said about the *third blessing* people, and ever since the fire-baptized movement has been organized into an independent organization, they have been termed the third blessing people, and a great deal of opposition has come to them from this fact. Now the writer never heard a fire-baptized prophet yet preach the baptism of fire as a *third* blessing, but they have always used the scriptural language and called it what God calls it: 'The baptism with fire.' Yet 'The third blessing' is just as scriptural as the 'second' blessing.

Dull, *LCF* 1.3 (Oct. 20, 1899), p. 5.

⁹¹ For descriptions of divine fire, lightening, and light see *LCF* 1 (Oct. 6, 1899), pp. 5, 7; 1.2 (Oct. 13, 1899), pp. 3, 8; 1.3 (Oct. 20, 1899), p. 7; 1.5 (Nov. 3, 1899), p. 1; 1.6 (Nov. 10, 1899), pp. 1, 2, 3; 1.7 (Dec. 1, 1899), pp. 1, 2, 4; 1.8 (Dec. 15, 1899), pp. 1, 3, 4; 1.9 (Dec. 29, 1899), pp. 3, 4 ,6, 7; 1.10 (Jan. 12, 1900), pp. 1, 2, 3, 6, 7, 8; 1.11 (Jan. 26, 1900), p. 1; 1.12 (Feb. 9, 1900), pp. 1, 5; 1.13 (Feb. 23, 1900), p. 8; 1.14 (Mar. 9, 1900), pp. 2, 4, 5; 1.15 (Mar. 23, 1900), p. 4; 1.16 (April 6, 1900), pp. 1, 3, 4, 5, 8; 1.17 (April 20, 1900), p. 2.

healing, and the premillennial coming of the Lord ... I am glad this dynamite locates the devil and tears up his works.[92]

In Luke 9.1, we read that Jesus gave them (the disciples) *power* and authority over all devils, and to cure disease. Here we have the word dynamite again ... Jesus was so wonderfully charged with this dynamite that whole multitudes were healed, and miracles wrought in casting out devils, raising the dead, etc. The literal rendering of Luke 6.19 is: 'there went dynamite out of him and healed them all.'[93]

He bare record and gave testimony of Jesus Christ that He was the Son of God by descending and remaining upon Him immediately after His baptism, and it was by *this* testimony that the Holy Ghost bore to Christ that John knew that He had power to baptize with a *peculiar* baptism with the Holy Ghost and with fire.[94]

Several observations emerge. First, Irwin posited a version of the fivefold gospel, though he did not use this specific designation, and he was determined to remain anchored in it as he plumed the infinite depths of divine experiences.[95] Second, from the baptism of fire flowed the pneumatic experience of dynamite, a greater anointing of power to destroy the devil's strongholds.[96] Third, receiving dynamite became the zenith of fire-baptized testimony.[97] Fourth,

---

[92] B.H. Irwin, 'The Dynamite', *LCF* 1.6 (Nov. 10, 1899), p. 2. During a revival in Moonlight, Kansas (Aug. 18, 1899), Irwin preached this sermon, 'The Dynamite,' from Acts 1.8 about receiving power. Cf. *LCF* 1.19 (May 18, 1900), p. 2.

[93] G.M. Henson, 'Dynamite', *LCF* 1.2 (Oct. 13, 1899), 7. 'Jesus by the Spirit of God cast out devils and healed the sick.' Irwin, 'Comment', *LCF* 1.1 (Oct. 6, 1899), p. 6.

[94] John E. Dull, 'The Trinity', *LCF* 1.17 (April 20, 1900), p. 5. Cf. *LCF* 1.18 (May 4, 1900), p. 7.

[95] For similar testimonies depicting a fire-baptized form of the fivefold gospel, see *LCF* 1.1 (Oct. 6, 1899), p. 2; 1.2 (Oct. 13, 1899), pp. 2, 3; 1.3 (Oct. 20, 1899), p. 3; 1.6 (Nov. 10, 1899), p. 2.

[96] 'The same hell shaking, earth-quaking, devil destroying power or dynamite is in the gospel of Christ as it always was, and it only needs a fire-baptized apostle, today, to carry it out in the devil's ranks, and the Holy Ghost to give it the *jar* to explode this heavenly dynamite to prove this.' Henson, 'Dynamite', *LCF* 1.2 (Oct. 13, 1899), p. 7.

[97] In Col. 1.11, 'Paul prays that they be "strengthened with all might," or "dynamited with all dynamite."' Henson, 'Dynamite', *LCF* 1.2 (Oct. 13, 1899), p. 7. Hence, the fire-baptized testimony would include: 'I am saved, sanctified, baptized with the Holy Ghost and fire, and dynamited with all dynamite'. Testimo-

Emergence of Pentecostalism   447

the basis for Christ's disciples receiving dynamite was Christ's experience of the Sprit empowering dynamite. Irwin affirmed Christ's deity, yet he asserted, during the Jordan event, Christ's human nature received the Spirit,[98] identifying him as the one who will baptize his disciples with the Holy Spirit and with fire, so that Christ fulfilled his salvific mission through the dynamite; accordingly, Irwin bases this dynamic continuum of spiritual experience in Spirit Christology.

The baptism of fire was, therefore, an entryway into a two-fold deeper spiritual experience: divine power and divine mystical communion. Soon, these experiences proliferated into multiple pneumatic experiences.[99] Since the fire-baptized saints needed power to wage spiritual warfare, Irwin adopted the two most powerful and destructive explosives known to him at that time as epithets of pneumatic power: dynamite and lyddite;[100] whereas, the experiences of oxidite and selenite elevated them into more intimate mystical trinitarian communion, revealing deity and conforming them more to the image of God.[101] These experiences were not designated de-

---

nies of fire-baptized saints receiving the dynamite experience permeates every issue of *Live Coals of Fire*.

[98] In another rendition of 'The Third Blessing', John Dull compares the Spirit anointing David with the activity of the Spirit in the life and ministry of Jesus Christ, see *LCF* 1.6 (Nov. 10, 1899), p. 5. Regarding the reality of temptations to Christ's human nature, see *LCF* 1.9 (Dec. 29, 1899), pp. 2, 3. For Irwin's Christology, see *LCF* 1.15 (Mar. 23, 1900), pp. 2, 3.

[99] Answering his critic's rejection of multiple experiences, Irwin replied: 'So you may call it a fourth blessing if you want to. If you were to talk about the **fifth, sixth, or seventh blessings you could not frighten me. I am in for all the blessings there are for me, no matter how many there may be**'. B.H. Irwin, 'The Pentecostal Church', *LCF* 1.20 (June 1, 1900), p. 2.

[100] Lyddite was used by the British army during the Boer War in South Africa during this time. There is an account of its devastating effects in this context in *LCF* 1.19 (May 18, 1900), pp. 1, 8. For testimonies of fire-baptized saints receiving the experience of lyddite, see *LCF* 1.13, (Feb. 23, 1900), p. 4; 1.14 (Mar. 9, 1900), pp. 1, 6; 1.15 (Mar. 23, 1900), pp. 1, 6, 8; 1.16 (April 6, 1900), pp. 1, 5, 6; 1.17 (April 20, 1900), p. 3; 1.18 (May 4, 1900), pp. 1, 5, 7, 8; 1.19 (May 18, 1900), pp. 1, 2, 6, 8.

[101] Apparently Irwin derived the term oxidite from oxidize (to unite with oxygen). According to Irwin, because all of creation was corrupted by the fall, the very air humans breathe is also corrupted; in the eschaton the air will be restored to its primordial paradisiacal purity, yet even now the experience of oxidite enables the fire-baptized saint to partake of the unpolluted vivifying atmosphere of heaven. When used in the form of a thin plate, selenite polarizes light in the microscope; hence, the experience of selenite illuminates and reveals the invisible

grees of pneumatic power and charismata; rather, they were *distinct* and *definite* experiences of divine energy and presence, flowing from the same source.

According to B.H. Irwin's son, Stewart Toombs Irwin, these experiences coalesced in the disciples at Pentecost.

> Then came – and that in rapid order – the dynamite and lyddite, for they *spake* with other tongues as the Spirit gave them *utterance*. This utterance of speech was beyond understanding by those who witnessed that awful scene, and they were utterly confounded and greatly amazed. This was not strange for they were 'strengthened with all might,' and bursting forth with articulations of heavenly lyddite. They were actually viewing the heavenly inhabitants – had the selenite; and were breathing the pure atmosphere of heaven – had the oxidite. Hallelujah! O the grandeur of being in heavenly places, viewing heavenly things and breathing heavenly atmosphere![102]

Under the one umbrella of Pentecost all four experiences are conjoined in a single pneumatically inspired witness: *glossolalia*. Whereas *glossolalia* manifested the devastating power of dynamite and lyddite – blasting away Jewish traditions and prejudice, as well as amazing, perplexing, and opening the hearts of the people gathered in Jerusalem – the celestial language mystically conjoined heaven and earth, so that the disciples participated in an eschatological in-breaking of the kingdom of God. Although Irwin did not designate *glossolalia* as the initial evidence of Spirit baptism,[103] *glossolalia* seemed to be de-

---

things to the fire-baptized saints, allowing them participation in these things. *LCF* 1.20 (June 1, 1900), p. 1.

[102] S.T. Irwin, 'The Breath of Jesus', *LCF* 1.20 (June 1, 1900), p. 6. Likewise, B.H. Irwin commenting on Acts 2.4, during a sermon he preached at Royston, Georgia, (April 5, 1899) affirmed, 'These were tongues of fire. The dialects were another thing. God put mighty power upon these people, and the Holy Ghost enabled them to speak with other tongues'. Irwin, 'The Pentecostal Church', 1.20 (June 1, 1900), p. 3. For other references to the connection of *glossolalia* with the dual motifs of divine power and divine communion, see *LCF* 1.3 (Oct. 20, 1899), p. 4; 1.5 (Nov. 3, 1899), p. 7; 1.12 (Feb. 9, 1900), p. 5.

[103] *Glossolalia* was not uncommon in either Irwin's revivals or the FBHA ministers' revivals. For example, it was reported more than 100 people experienced glossolalia during a revival at Shearer Schoolhouse located at Camp Creek in Cherokee County, North Carolina (1896). The congregation there, then known as the Christian Union, was the nucleus of the modern Church of God, Cleveland, Tennessee. For an account of this revival from a Church of God perspective, see

veloping into an integral part of the continuum of pneumatic experiences on the eve of Irwin's fall and deposition.

B.H. Irwin's doctrine of multiple pneumatic experiences furthered the development of the fivefold gospel and preparation for the emergence of Pentecostalism. Although neither Irwin nor FBHA ministers coined the term fivefold gospel, they implicitly taught it; their teaching was known as the 'three blessing heresy,' and they were known as the 'three blessing' people. Their doctrine of baptism with Spirit and with fire as a 'third blessing' distinct, separate, and subsequent to justification and sanctification contributed to the emergence of the full gospel's fifth *motif*. Furthermore, the integrating effect of *glossolalia* with the distinct pneumatic experiences of divine power and divine mystical communion, conjoining them into one witness of the Spirit in the event of Pentecost, seems to be an incipient form of the doctrine affirming tongues as the initial evidence of Spirit baptism.[104] Important to this study is the fact

---

Charles W. Conn, *Like a Mighty Army, Moves the Church of God, 1886–1955* (Cleveland, TN: Church of God Publishing House, 1955), pp. 16-27. Although Church of God historian Charles Conn did not acknowledge any affiliation of the evangelists – William Martin, Joe M. Tipton, and Milton McNabb – with the FBHA, Vinson Synan asserts that these men left the Methodist and Baptist churches in the Coker Creek Community near the North Carolina border to join the FBHA in 1896. Synan, *The Holiness-Pentecostal Tradition*, p. 72; Synan, *Oldtime Power*, pp. 52-53. It is certain about three years subsequent to the revival Irwin attested to the fact that in the area of Beniah, Tennessee, 'Bros. Martin, Porter, and Tipton have done faithful work in this region. The fire and the dynamite are here to stay, and will continue to spread in spite of the devil's devices'. B.H. Irwin, 'Editorial', *LCF* 1.3 (Oct. 20, 1899), p. 1. Also, it is noteworthy that in a letter Stewart Irwin states that as part of his ministry in the Beniah area as a 'circuit rider' he will preach at Bryant's school house, an obvious reference to W.F Bryant functioning as pastor of the congregation. *LCF* 1.16 (April 6, 1900), p. 5. However, the Christian Union under the leadership of W.F Bryant and R.G. Spurling rejected the teaching of many baptisms of fire and fanatical holiness restrictions, such as forbidding the eating of pork, and changed its name to The Holiness Church at Camp Creek (1902). Conn, *Like a Mighty Army*, pp. 41-45. Regarding the question of FBHA influence on the development of the Church of God, see Daniel G. Woods, 'Daniel Awrey, the Fire-Baptized Movement, and the Origins of the Church of God: Toward a Chronology of Confluence and Influence', *Cyberjournal for Pentecostal-Charismatic Research* 19 (2010), http://www.pctii.org.cyberj/index.html (5/8/2012), pp. 1-15.

[104] For affirmations of Irwin's contribution to the emergence of Pentecostalism, see Synan, *Oldtime Power*, pp. 60-63; Synan, *The Holiness-Pentecostal Tradition*, pp. 59-60; Carl Brumback, *Suddenly ... From Heaven: A History of the Assemblies of God* (Springfield, MO: Gospel Publishing House, 1961), pp. 9, 99; Klaud Kendrick, *The Promise Fulfilled* (Springfield, MO: Gospel Publishing House, 1959),

that Irwin's doctrine of multiple pneumatic experiences has been laid on the foundation of Spirit Christology; specifically, a Spirit christological paradigm of pneumatic mediation which integrates Logos Christology.

Charles Fox Parham

With Charles Parham's formulation of Spirit baptism, the fivefold gospel had reached the completion of its unfolding.[105] The formula seems to have emerged in Parham's thinking, owing to various influences, as Parham's ministry developed.[106] Early on, the holiness

---

pp. 33, 177-82; Campbell, *The Pentecostal Holiness Church*, p. 195; Nichol, *Pentecostalism*, p. 104. The most comprehensive analysis is found in Wade H. Phillips, *The Significance of the Fire-Baptized Holiness Movement (1895–1900) in the Historical and Theological Development of the Wesleyan-Pentecostal-Charismatic Metamorphosis*, presented at the Second Annual Meeting of the Historical Society of Church of God Movements (Cleveland, TN, May 24, 2003). Furthermore, it should be noted that the manifestations of tongues in Irwin's teachings is *glossolalia* and not the notion of *xenolalia* postulated by Charles Parham; in point of fact, FBHA missionaries prepared for the mission field by learning the language of the country where they were going, so that they could preach to the people in their indigenous language. *LCF* 1.7 (Dec. 1, 1899), p. 7; 1.13 (Feb. 23, 1900), p. 5.

[105] Parham taught *xenolalia* as the biblical evidence of Spirit baptism. Also, he taught an array of doctrines. His doctrine of apostolic renewal was stanchly anti-creedal. Parham taught there were several functions of the Spirit, regarding the anointing, so he distinguished between the anointing that abideth (sanctification) and Spirit baptism. He distinguished between the church, the bride, and the man-child of the sun-clothed woman (Rev. 12.1-5); those Spirit baptized believers who constitute the man-child are the only ones rapture-ready. Parham taught water baptism is not the essential baptism; instead, Spirit baptism fills this sacramental role. Furthermore, early on, he taught water baptism conducted in 'Jesus name' was the correct formula, for a candidate is identified with Jesus' death, burial, and resurrection. He taught the conditional immortality for the redeemed and annihilation of the unredeemed at death. Parham taught an Anglo-Israel theory that the cultured Anglo-Saxon nations represented the lost 10 tribes of Israel, and the blessings of Joseph's sons have passed on to England (Ephraim) and America (Manasseh). For Parham's theology, see Charles F. Parham, 'Kol Kare Bomidbar: A Voice Crying in the Wilderness', *The Sermons of Charles F. Parham* (The Higher Christian life; New York: Garland Publishing, 1985 repr.; Baxter Springs, KS: R.L. Parham, 1944); Charles F. Parham, 'The Everlasting Gospel', *The Sermons of Charles F. Parham* (The Higher Christian life; New York: Garland Publishing, 1985 repr.; Baxter Springs, KS: Apostolic Faith Bible College, 1911); Douglas G. Jacobsen, *Thinking in the Spirit: Theologies of the Early Pentecostal Movement* (Bloomington: Indiana University Press, 2003), pp. 17-50.

[106] Charles Parham was born in Muscatine Iowa (1873–1929), and from the age of five, he grew up on the rough nineteenth century Kansas plains. Though he felt the call to preach at the tender age of nine, he neglected the calling until the death of his mother (1885) which occasioned his true conversion. While studying at Southwest Kansas College (1890–93), Parham struggled with his call to

movement influenced Parham, so that as a Methodist evangelist he preached the doctrines of 'second blessing' sanctification and pre-millennial eschatology.[107] While wrestling with college studies, his call to preach, and life-threatening sickness, Parham received a miraculous healing; thus, the doctrine of divine healing in the atonement became part of the gospel Parham preached.[108] After initiating an independent holiness ministry,[109] garnering a reputation as a heal-

---

preach, so for a time he quit his ministerial studies and pursued the idea of becoming a doctor; however, after battling rheumatic fever and experiencing divine healing, he reaffirmed his ministerial calling and became a staunch advocate of the doctrine of divine healing. Leaving school, Parham served as a supply pastor for the Methodist church (1893). Finding the authority of the Methodist church too confining and restrictive, Parham began an independent holiness ministry (1895), which promoted divine healing with great success. Parham married Sarah Thistlethwaite (1896) the granddaughter of a Quaker, David Baker, through Baker's influence Parham accepted the doctrine of the conditional immortality of the righteous and total annihilation of the wicked at death. Although Parham's doctrinal formulation of Spirit baptism was an essential impetus to early Pentecostal theology and evangelism, he lost his influence with the majority of early Pentecostals because of his disapproval of the direction the Azusa Street Revival took and charges of moral failure brought against him (1907). For overviews of the life and ministry of Charles Parham, see Sarah E. Parham, *The Life of Charles F. Parham, Founder of the Apostolic Faith Movement* (The Higher Christian life; New York: Garland Publishing, 1985 repr.; Joplin, MO: Hunter Printing, 1930); James R. Goff, *Fields White Unto Harvest: Charles F. Parham and the Missionary Origins of Pentecostalism* (Fayetteville: University of Arkansas Press, 1988); James R. Goff, 'Parham, Charles Fox', *NIDPCM*, pp. 955-57.

[107] Parham, *The Life of Charles F. Parham*, pp. 1-26; Goff, *Fields White Unto Harvest*, pp. 33-35, 51-53; Kendrick, *The Promise Fulfilled*, pp. 38-45; Robert Mapes Anderson, *Vision of the Disinherited: The Making of American Pentecostalism* (Peabody, MA: Hendrickson, 1979), pp. 45-49. For Parham's doctrine of sanctification, see Parham, 'The Everlasting Gospel', pp. 10-16, 70, 108. For Parham's pneumatically informed eschatology, see Parham, 'The Everlasting Gospel', pp. 29-31, 74-76, 90-91, 98-110; Parham, 'Kol Kare Bomidbar', pp. 27, 30-31, 34-35, 69-80, 86-138. Furthermore, according to James Goff, similar to Ralph Horner and George Watson, Parham supported a doctrine of Spirit baptism of divine power distinct from sanctification. Goff, *Fields White Unto Harvest*, pp. 34-35.

[108] Parham, *The Life of Charles F. Parham*, pp. 27-40; Goff, *Fields White Unto Harvest*, pp. 38-44, 53-54; Synan, *The Holiness-Pentecostal Tradition*, p. 89. Parham taught there are 3 sources of disease: (1) inherited, (2) acquired through the environment, and (3) sins of omission and commission. Since healing is in the atonement, according to Parham, sanctification not only delivers from inbred sin but also inbred disease, and healing is attained for the other two causes of disease through repentance, prayer, and the unction of the Spirit. For Parham's doctrine of divine healing, see Parham, 'Kol Kare Bomidbar', pp. 39-52. Cf. Parham, 'Kol Kare Bomidbar', p. 19; Parham, 'The Everlasting Gospel', p. 14.

[109] Goff, *Fields White Unto Harvest*, pp. 35-37; Parham, *The Life of Charles F. Parham*, pp. 31-38; Faupel, *The Everlasting Gospel*, pp. 158-61.

ing evangelist, and being influenced by the coeval practices of those advocating divine healing, Parham established in Topeka, Kansas the Bethel Healing Home (1898) and a holiness periodical, *Apostolic Faith* (1899), to publicize the successes of the healing home and his ministry.[110]

Although it remains uncertain to what extent, two specific figures seem to have influenced Parham's thinking regarding Spirit baptism: B.H. Irwin and Frank W. Sandford. When Parham arrived in Topeka the FBHA had been organized in Kansas for almost three years, so Parham encountered Irwin's 'third blessing' doctrine of the twofold baptism of Jesus: baptism with Spirit and with fire.[111] In the early issues of *Apostolic Faith*, Irwin's doctrine of multiple pneumatic experiences received favorable press.[112] Parham, however, neither testified to having received the fire nor emphasized it in his preaching, and with the fall of Irwin, Parham expunged it from his publications; nevertheless, his thinking was being influenced toward working out the difficulties of Irwin's concept of a 'third blessing'.[113]

---

[110] Parham, *The Life of Charles F. Parham*, pp. 39-50; Goff, *Fields White Unto Harvest*, pp. 44-51, 53-54; Synan, *The Holiness-Pentecostal Tradition*, p. 90; Faupel, *The Everlasting Gospel*, pp. 161-64; Blumhofer, *Restoring the Faith*, pp. 46-47; Kendrick, *The Promise Fulfilled*, pp. 45-46; Anderson, *Vision of the Disinherited*, pp. 49-50.

[111] Goff, *Fields White Unto Harvest*, pp. 54-57.

[112] In fact, the first issue of *Apostolic Faith* included it as an accepted belief of the Bethel Healing School: 'salvation by faith; healing by faith, laying on of hands and prayer; sanctification by faith; coming (pre-millennium) of Christ; the baptism of Holy Ghost and Fire, which seals the Bride and bestows the gifts'. *AF* (Topeka; Mar. 22, 1899), p. 8. Cited in Goff, *Fields White Unto Harvest*, p. 55. Parham, therefore, had published an implicit form of the fivefold gospel based on the twofold baptism of Jesus which directly connected the Pentecostal experience of Acts ch. 2 with reception of divine power. Parham also included in *Apostolic Faith* testimonies of people describing their reception of baptism with fire. *AF* (Topeka; June 7, 1899), pp. 5-6.

[113] According to Vinson Synan,

> How deeply Parham was impressed with Irwin's premise of the separate Holy Ghost baptism we do not know; but it is likely that the Fire-Baptized doctrine was largely influential in shaping the climate for the Pentecostal phenomenon in Topeka, Kansas, when Agnes Ozman, later a Fire-Baptized Holiness preacher, received the Pentecostal experience accompanied by glossolalia in 1901. Parham was definitely impressed and somewhat repelled by the demonstrations seen in Irwin's meetings. According to Parham, they would scream 'until you could hear them for three miles on a clear night, and until the blood vessels stood out like whipcords.' Irwin explained to Parham that when the Holy Ghost and fire fell, 'a tremendous power took hold of us until we nearly

During the summer of 1900, Parham visited several holiness centers, including Frank Sandford's school in Shiloh Maine. It is certain that prior to arriving at Sandford's 'Holy Ghost and Us' bible school, for his six weeks stay, Parham was aware of the discussion in Sandford's periodical, *Tongues of Fire*, regarding the manifestation of *xenolalia* and its potential impact in the missionary ministry of Jennie Glassey. According to reports in *Tongues of Fire*, through the empowerment of the Holy Spirit Jennie Glassey received the gift to speak, write, and sing in several languages (1895), equipping her for missionary evangelism in Africa.[114] Parham had enthusiasti-

---

screamed our heads off.' The boisterous emotional demonstrations of the Fire-Baptized services pointed to an inherent weakness in the movement – the desire for ever greater experiences of religious excitement.

Synan, *Oldtime Power*, pp. 54-55. Synan is quoting Parham's encounter with Irwin from Parham's AF (Baxter Springs; April 25, 1925), pp. 3, 9-14. 'An interested observer of Irwin's meetings was Charles Parham, the patriarch of the Pentecostal movement, who was repelled by the noise and emotion of the meetings but was impressed by Irwin's "third blessing" doctrine.' Synan, *The Holiness-Pentecostal Tradition*, p. 56, n. 26. Cf. Harold Hunter, 'Beniah at the Apostolic Crossroads: Little Noticed Crosscurrents of B.H. Irwin, Charles Fox Parham, Frank Sandford, A.J. Tomlinson', *Cyberjournal for Pentecostal-Charismatic Research* 1 (1997), http://www.pctii.org.cyberj/index.html (5 May 2012), pp. 3-4.

[114] *Tongues of Fire* 4.12 (June 15, 1898), pp. 92-93.

One foreign language after another has been given her. She has sung in the Spirit African tunes, and even written strange characters which the Holy Ghost taught her as an alphabet. The most striking confirmation of one of these dialects has taken place. There was an old sailor named Jack, who was years ago taken and held prisoner for some time by one of the African tribes, thus becoming somewhat acquainted with their language. After much search he was found, and asked Miss Glassey a certain question in that dialect. She answered him at once, and told him what he had said. He asked a second question. She answered promptly, and told him what he had said. The old sailor's face had a startled look at the intelligent reply to his first question, and as the second one was answered, his face grew pale and white. The power of God settled upon him, and then and there he broke down, confessed his sins, and became a Christian ... The same power that drove the arrow of conviction into the hardened heart of an old sailor as he listened to a young girl speaking a language she had never heard in the power of the Holy Ghost, that same power will convict unconverted people, even as it did on the day of Pentecost. God almighty is raising up such a movement, and the last mighty billow that is to sweep over this globe and prepare the way for the coming of the Son of Man, is the movement that will 'Tarry Until'.

Frank Sandford, 'Tarry Until', *TF* 3.5 (Mar. 1, 1897), p. 38. Cf. *TF* 4.12 (June 15, 1898), pp. 92-94; 4.14 (July 15, 1898), p. 107. For Sandford's positive assessment of tongues, see *TF* 3.6 (Mar.15, 1897), p. 45; 3.7 (Apr. 1, 1897), p. 54.

cally reported her experience in the *Apostolic Faith*.[115] It is also possible that Parham encountered *glossolalia* while at Shiloh.[116] It remains uncertain to what extent Sandford influenced Parham's doctrinal formulation of Spirit baptism, but it is certain that they disagreed about the theological significance of tongues.[117]

---

[115] Glassy [*sic*] now in Jerusalem, received the African dialect in one night ... She received the gift while in the Spirit in 1895, but could read and write, translate and sing the language while out of the trance or in a normal condition, and can until now. Hundreds of people can testify to the fact, both saint and sinner, who heard her use the language. She was also tested in Liverpool and Jerusalem. Her Christian experience is that of a holy, consecrated woman, filled with the Holy Ghost. Glory to our God for the return of the apostolic faith.

Apostolic Faith, (Topeka; May 3, 1899), p. 5. Cited in Goff, *Fields White Unto Harvest*, p. 73. Cf. Parham, 'Kol Kare Bomidbar', p. 29. According to James Goff,

Parham speculated that Glassey's experience provided the key to world evangelization in the last days. By April 1900 he had wholeheartedly accepted the premise and reported to his *Apostolic Faith* readers that a 'Brother and Sister Hamaker' were staying at Beth-el waiting for Jesus to 'give them a heathen tongue, and then they will proceed to the missionary field.'

Goff, *Fields White Unto Harvest*, p. 73. Goff was quoting from *AF* (Topeka; Apr. 1, 1900), p. 7.

[116] According to a personal interview Charles Shumway conducted with Charles Parham, during his stay at Shiloh, Parham heard Sandford's students speaking in tongues as they emerged from the school's Prayer Tower; furthermore, Shumway believed that Parham conceived his concept of missionary tongues at Shiloh. Charles William Shumway, 'A Critical History of Glossolalia' (PhD dissertation, Boston University, 1919), p. 111. Cf. Hunter, 'Beniah at the Apostolic Crossroads', pp. 2-3; Goff, *Fields White Unto Harvest*, pp. 73-74; Parham, *The Life of Charles F. Parham*, p. 48; Synan, *The Holiness-Pentecostal Tradition*, p. 90.

[117] According to Shirley Nelson,

the lines were being drawn in what had not yet been a serious issue – the viability of speaking in tongues, or ecstatic language. In fact, a student at Shiloh, Charles Parham, who had come with the Tacoma Party, had recently broken fellowship with Sandford over the very issue and had gone back to the Midwest to found his own school, where speaking in tongues soon began to be practiced. Sandford, who believed the phenomenon of tongues was simply the gift of dialects sometimes given to missionaries in foreign lands, repudiated Parham for gross error.

Shirley Nelson, *Fair, Clear, and Terrible: The Story of Shiloh, Maine* (Latham, NY: British American Publishing, 1989), p. 157. 'Although few of his adherents would later embrace the Pentecostal movement, Sandford's major contribution to Pentecostalism came through his impact on the theology and practice of Charles Fox Parham.' Faupel, *The Everlasting Gospel*, p. 158. For an overview of Sandford's contribution to the theological context and influence on Pentecostalism, see Faupel, *The Everlasting Gospel*, pp. 136-58.

Parham returned from his trip convinced of an impending outpouring of the Spirit;[118] correspondingly, he founded a bible school in Topeka (Sept. 1900), after the order of Shiloh, to prepare missionaries evangelists for the outpouring of the Spirit that would empower them to carry the full gospel to the world before the eschaton.[119] According to Parham, the doctrinal formulation of *xenolalia* as the biblical evidence for Spirit baptism arose from among the students. After teaching and examining the students on the essential doctrines of holiness, strategically directing them to Acts ch. 2,[120] Parham assigned the students the task of determining the bible evidence for Spirit baptism, while he was absent on a three day journey (Dec. 1900). Upon his return, the students had reached a consensus: *xenolalia* was the biblical evidence of Spirit baptism, and Spirit baptism was the impetus of apostolic missions. During a watch-night service, Agnes Ozman received Spirit baptism with the accompanying sign of *xenolalia* (Jan. 1, 1901), and in the forthcoming days Parham and 34 students likewise received this 'third blessing,' equip-

---

[118] Parham seemed unsatisfied with the doctrinal formulations and experiences of the Spirit he found on his trip: 'I returned home fully convinced that while many had obtained real experiences in sanctification and the anointing that abideth, there still remained a great outpouring of power for the Christians who were to close this age'. Parham, *The Life of Charles F. Parham*, p. 48.

Pursuing our studies, we visited institutions of deep religious thought, which were reported as having the power of the Holy Ghost; yet these all failed to tally with the account in Acts. After careful study, we returned from an extended trip through the east and Canada with profound conviction that no one in these days was really enjoying the power of personal Pentecost.

Parham, 'Kol Kare Bomidbar', pp. 30-31. Cf. Kendrick, *The Promise Fulfilled*, pp. 46-47.

[119] Parham, *The Life of Charles F. Parham*, pp. 48-51; Faupel, *The Everlasting Gospel*, pp. 165-70; Leslie D. Callahan, 'Charles Parham: Progenitor of Pentecostalism', in Henry H. Knight (ed.), *From Aldersgate to Azusa Street: Wesleyan, Holiness, and Pentecostalism Visions of the New Creation* (Eugene, OR: Wipf and Stock, 2010), p. 212; Blumhofer, *Restoring the Faith*, pp. 47-50; Kendrick, *The Promise Fulfilled*, pp. 47-50; Anderson, *Vision of the Disinherited*, pp. 50-52. Parham had left the Healing Home in the charge of two unnamed holiness preachers who were unwilling to relinquish control to Parham when he returned; thus, Parham easily transitioned to founding a bible school to train workers for the harvest.

[120] According to Parham, 'We had reached in our studies a problem. What about the 2nd Chapter of Acts? I had felt for years that any missionary going to the foreign field should preach in the language of the natives. That if God had ever equipped His ministers in that way [*sic*] He could do it today'. Parham, *The Life of Charles F. Parham*, p. 51. Cf. Goff, *Fields White Unto Harvest*, pp. 74-77; Faupel, *The Everlasting Gospel*, pp. 170-71; Anderson, *Vision of the Disinherited*, p. 53.

ping them for missionary evangelism, according to the language they received.¹²¹ So, the formulation of the fifth *motif* of the fivefold gospel was essentially complete, based on biblical evidence and the experience of Parham and his students.¹²²

Charles Parham, therefore, was a great synthesizer of the various concepts floating around about Spirit baptism. The doctrine of Pentecostal sanctification was unacceptable to those maintaining a Wesleyan holiness view of 'second blessing' sanctification, but these holiness advocates accepted the notion of a 'third blessing' of power for service through Spirit baptism. Parham adroitly gathered up these 'third blessing' streams anticipating the latter rain of the Spirit into a conceptual framework of Spirit baptism, distinct and separate from justification and sanctification, with corollary attestations of definite biblical evidence and personal experience. Thus, with Parham's formulation of Spirit baptism, the fivefold gospel unfolded into its complete *gestalt*.

William Joseph Seymour

Parham's attempt at Topeka to initiate a global Pentecostal missionary effort was less than gratifying; undaunted, he successfully spread the message of Spirit baptism through his evangelistic ministry of divine healing, garnering several thousand Spirit baptized members into his Apostolic Faith movement.¹²³ Endeavoring to spark the

---

¹²¹ Parham, *The Life of Charles F. Parham*, pp. 51-74; Parham, 'Kol Kare Bomidbar', pp. 31-38; Synan, *The Holiness-Pentecostal Tradition*, pp. 90-92; Goff, *Fields White Unto Harvest*, pp. 78-81; Faupel, *The Everlasting Gospel*, pp. 173-76; Blumhofer, *Restoring the Faith*, pp. 50-52; Nichol, *Pentecostalism*, pp. 27-29; Brumback, *Suddenly from Heaven*, pp. 21-25; Anderson, *An Introduction to Pentecostalism*, pp. 33-34; Kendrick, *The Promise Fulfilled*, pp. 50-54; Anderson, *Vision of the Disinherited*, pp. 53-58. 'In the close of the age, God proposes to send forth men and women preaching in languages they know not a word of, which when interpreted the hearers will know is truly a message from God, spoken through lips of clay by the power of the Holy Ghost.' Parham, 'Kol Kare Bomidbar', p. 31. Cf. Parham, 'The Everlasting Gospel', pp. 63-71, 75.

¹²² Faupel, *The Everlasting Gospel*, p. 185; Callahan, 'Charles Parham', p. 216. For a thorough discussion of Parham's doctrine of tongues as initial evidence, see James R. Goff, 'Initial Tongues in the Theology of Charles Fox Parham', in Gary B. McGee (ed.), *Initial Evidence: Historical and Biblical Perspectives on the Pentecostal Doctrine of Spirit Baptism* (Eugene, OR: Wipf and Stock, 2007 repr.; Peabody, MA: Hendrickson, 1991), pp. 57-71.

¹²³ Parham, *The Life of Charles F. Parham*, pp. 59-124; Goff, *Fields White Unto Harvest*, pp. 87-100; Nichol, *Pentecostalism*, pp. 29-32; Synan, *The Holiness-Pentecostal Tradition*, pp. 92-93; Faupel, *The Everlasting Gospel*, pp. 176-80; Kendrick, *The Promise Fulfilled*, pp. 54-63; Blumhofer, *Restoring the Faith*, pp. 53-54. By the time of

worldwide Pentecostal outpouring, Parham established a missionary training school in Houston, Texas (Dec. 1905).

Although the missionary evangelists emerging from this school in Texas had certain measures of success spreading the Pentecostal message, with William Seymour, during the Azusa Street Revival, the message of Pentecostal power flowered into global missionary evangelism.[124] Owing to Southern racial mores, African Americans could not sit in the same classroom as Caucasians, so Seymour attended Parham's bible school for several months while either sitting in an adjoining room or the hallway.[125] These obstacles notwithstanding, Seymour incorporated Parham's doctrine of Spirit baptism into his Wesleyan holiness theology.[126]

---

the Azusa Street revival in 1906, there were at least 1,000 Pentecostals in Texas alone and at least 10,000 in the United States. For this information, see Goff, *Fields White Unto Harvest*, pp. 115, 169-70.

[124] Parham, *The Life of Charles F. Parham*, pp. 131-46; Goff, *Fields White Unto Harvest*, pp. 106-15; Larry Jay Martin, *The Life and Ministry of William J. Seymour: And a History of the Azusa Street Revival* (Joplin, MO: Christian Life Books, 1999), pp. 21-27; Rufus G.W. Sanders, *William Joseph Seymour: Black Father of the 20th Century Pentecostal/Charismatic Movement* (Sandusky, OH: Xulon Press, 2003), pp. 61-73; Callahan, 'Charles Parham', pp. 212-14; Anderson, *An Introduction to Pentecostalism*, pp. 34-35; Kendrick, *The Promise Fulfilled*, pp. 63-64; Blumhofer, *Restoring the Faith*, p. 55; Anderson, *Vision of the Disinherited*, pp. 58-61.

[125] William J. Seymour (1870–1922) was born in Centerville, Louisiana, in St. Mary's Parish. Seymour left the South in 1895 and stayed in Indianapolis and Cincinnati, beginning his ministry during his sojourn in the North, before returning to the South to visit family in Houston Texas (1902). Seymour evangelized in the South and visited such African American holiness leaders as Charles Price Jones and Charles Harrison Mason (1902–1904). Seymour moved to Houston, Texas in 1905 and attended an African American holiness church pastored by Mrs. Lucy Farrow. Through the persuasion of Mrs. Farrow, Seymour began attending Parham's bible school. Seymour and Parham seemed to have enjoyed an amicable relationship, and at times, they ministered together. This relationship, however, was strained and broken during the Azusa Street revival. For information about Seymour's context, life, teachings, and ministry, see Martin, *The Life and Ministry of William J. Seymour*; Sanders, *William Joseph Seymour*; Vinson Synan and Charles R. Fox, *William J. Seymour: Pioneer of Azusa Street Revival* (Alachua, FL: Bridge-Logos Publishers, 2012), pp. 15-167; Cecil M. Robeck, 'Seymour, William Joseph', *NIDPCM*, pp. 1053-58; Cecil M. Robeck, *The Azusa Street Mission and Revival: The Birth of the Global Pentecostal Movement* (Nashville: Nelson Reference & Electronic, 2006), pp. 17-52; Synan, *The Holiness-Pentecostal Tradition*, pp. 92-95.

[126] Martin, *The Life and Ministry of William J. Seymour*, pp. 88-93; Sanders, *William Joseph Seymour*, pp. 72-73; Parham, *The Life of Charles F. Parham*, pp. 137, 161; Synan and Fox, *William J. Seymour*, pp. 56-62; Robeck, *The Azusa Street Mission and Revival*, pp. 46-50.

After receiving an invitation from an African American holiness church in Los Angeles (Feb. 1906), Seymour traveled to California to spread the Pentecostal message in a context that was well prepared for revival,[127] though he had not yet received the experience.[128] The leaders of the congregation, however, were unconvinced of the veracity of Seymour's Pentecostal message and refused it; consequently, he and Edward S. Lee began cottage prayer meetings in Lee's home,[129] and subsequently the meetings moved to the home of Richard and Ruth Asberry at 214 North Bonnie Brae Street. At this location, several people received the experience he preached (Apr. 9, 1906): they were baptized in the Spirit and spoke in tongues as the Spirit gave utterance.[130] Soon, the Asberry home could no longer accommodate the number of people either seeking or investigating the Pentecostal experience, so the meeting moved to 312 Azusa Street (Apr. 15, 1906). Here, a three-year revival began

---

[127] For example, through books and periodicals people in Los Angeles had received reports of the great Welsh revival (1904–1905), which prompted them to seek an outpouring of the Spirit, so the context was ready for revival when Seymour arrived. Regarding the ingredients and contributors to the spiritual climate and anticipation of revival in this context, see Synan, *The Holiness-Pentecostal Tradition*, pp. 84-88; Robeck, *The Azusa Street Mission and Revival*, pp. 53-60; Martin, *The Life and Ministry of William J. Seymour*, pp. 119-31; Sanders, *William Joseph Seymour*, pp. 77-84; Anderson, *An Introduction to Pentecostalism*, pp. 35-37; Faupel, *The Everlasting Gospel*, pp. 190-94; Anderson, *Vision of the Disinherited*, pp. 44-46, 62-64; Blumhofer, *Restoring the Faith*, pp. 57-59; Brumback, *Suddenly from Heaven*, pp. 34-35. Cf. Frank Bartleman's first-hand account of the spiritual context of Los Angeles, Frank Bartleman, *Azusa Street* (2000 repr.; New Kensington, PA: Whitaker House, 1982), pp. 7-38.

[128] Martin, *The Life and Ministry of William J. Seymour*, pp. 94-95; Brumback, *Suddenly from Heaven*, p. 35. Sarah Parham reports that Charles Parham had expected Seymour to carry the Pentecostal gospel to the African Americans in Texas, but when he understood that Parham had determined to go to California: 'Mr. Parham made up his car fare and we bid him God's-speed to the western coast'. Parham, *The Life of Charles F. Parham*, p. 142. Cf. Martin, *The Life and Ministry of William J. Seymour*, p. 94; Robeck, *The Azusa Street Mission and Revival*, pp. 50-51.

[129] Robeck, *The Azusa Street Mission and Revival*, pp. 60-64; Martin, *The Life and Ministry of William J. Seymour*, pp. 139-44; Sanders, *William Joseph Seymour*, pp. 84-86; Nichol, *Pentecostalism*, p. 32; Kendrick, *The Promise Fulfilled*, pp. 64-65. Both the Lee and Asberry families were African American.

[130] Robeck, *The Azusa Street Mission and Revival*, pp. 64-69; Martin, *The Life and Ministry of William J. Seymour*, pp. 146-50; Sanders, *William Joseph Seymour*, pp. 86-87; Synan, *The Holiness-Pentecostal Tradition*, p. 96; Faupel, *The Everlasting Gospel*, pp. 200-202; Anderson, *Vision of the Disinherited*, pp. 65-66; Nichol, *Pentecostalism*, p. 33; Brumback, *Suddenly from Heaven*, pp. 35-36; Bartleman, *Azusa Street*, p. 39; Kendrick, *The Promise Fulfilled*, pp. 65-66.

which launched a global Pentecostal outpouring of the Spirit. People came to the Azusa Street Mission to seek their Pentecostal experience, and forthwith traveled to various parts of the world spreading the message and experience of the fivefold gospel.[131]

Undoubtedly, Seymour preached Parham's formulation of Spirit baptism, yet Seymour allowed space for more diversity than Parham. When Parham arrived in Los Angeles (Oct. 1906) to take control of the revival and consolidate it into his Apostolic Faith movement,[132] he detested what he found.[133] It appears that Parham essentially objected to three manifestations occurring during the Azusa Street revival. First, though Parham had previously participated in interracial meetings, his paternal racism would not allow for the extent of racial equality demonstrated among participants of the revival.[134] Second, Parham considered vulgar the various displays of

---

[131] Visitors came from across the USA and from various parts of the world to experience their Pentecost. Many returned to their homelands carrying the Pentecostal message; others went as missionary evangelists empowered by the Spirit; leaders of several holiness movements received Spirit baptism and led these movements into Pentecostalism. In short, in some way, the Azusa Street revival influenced every early Pentecostal movement. Regarding the significance of the Azusa Street revival, see Harold D. Hunter and Cecil M. Robeck (eds.), *The Azusa Street Revival and Its Legacy* (Cleveland, TN: Pathway Press, 2006); Robeck, *The Azusa Street Mission and Revival*, pp. 1-16, 187-280, 313-25; Martin, *The Life and Ministry of William J. Seymour*, pp. 155-240; Sanders, *William Joseph Seymour*, pp. 93-99; Synan, *The Holiness-Pentecostal Tradition*, pp. 97-100, 103-42; Faupel, *The Everlasting Gospel*, pp. 202-203, 212-27; Joe Creech, 'Visions of Glory: The Place of the Azusa Street Revival in Pentecostal History', *CH* 65.3 (1996), pp. 405-24; Nichol, *Pentecostalism*, pp. 33-53; Bartleman, *Azusa Street*, pp. 40-68; Grant McClung, *Azusa Street and Beyond: Pentecostal Missions and Church Growth in the Twentieth Century* (Gainesville, FL: Bridge-Logos Publishers, 1986); Brumback, *Suddenly from Heaven*, pp. 36-47, 64-87; Blumhofer, *Restoring the Faith*, pp. 59-87; Anderson, *Vision of the Disinherited*, pp. 66-78; Kendrick, *The Promise Fulfilled*, pp. 66-70; Vinson Synan, *In the Latter Days: The Outpouring of the Holy Spirit in the Twentieth Century* (Ann Arbor: Servant, 1984).

[132] Supposedly, Seymour had written letters to Parham requesting his presence in Los Angeles to take the leadership of the revival and to set the work in order as part of the Apostolic Faith movement. Parham, *The Life of Charles F. Parham*, pp. 154-56; Martin, *The Life and Ministry of William J. Seymour*, pp. 267-68; Faupel, *The Everlasting Gospel*, pp. 205-206.

[133] Parham, *The Life of Charles F. Parham*, pp. 163-70; Parham, 'The Everlasting Gospel', pp. 72-73; Martin, *The Life and Ministry of William J. Seymour*, pp. 268-71; Sanders, *William Joseph Seymour*, pp. 108-10; Synan, *The Holiness-Pentecostal Tradition*, pp. 102-103; Robeck, *The Azusa Street Mission and Revival*, pp. 127-28; Faupel, *The Everlasting Gospel*, pp. 206-209.

[134] Goff, *Fields White Unto Harvest*, pp. 130-33; Parham, *The Life of Charles F. Parham*, pp. 162-63; Martin, *The Life and Ministry of William J. Seymour*, pp. 269-70;

emotionalism.[135] Third, though Seymour taught the fundamental premise of missionary tongues, during the Azusa Street revival, *glossolalia* had implicitly become accepted as evidence of Spirit baptism alongside of *xenolalia*.[136] It should be noted that due to failure of

---

Sanders, *William Joseph Seymour*, p. 109; Faupel, *The Everlasting Gospel*, pp. 210-12. In describing worship during the revival, Parham's racism is evident in his own words:

> Men and women, whites and blacks knelt together or fell across one another. Frequently, a white woman, perhaps of wealth and culture, could be seen thrown back into the arms of a big black nigger, and held tightly thus as she shivered and shook in a freak imitation of Pentecost.

Shumway, 'Glossolalia', p. 178. Cited in Sanders, *William Joseph Seymour*, p. 6. No doubt Parham's view of white racial superiority was supported by his Anglo-Israel theory that Anglo-Saxons held a distinct place in salvific history and miscegenation brought God's judgment in Noah's day.

> Thus began the woeful inter-marriage of races for which cause the flood was sent in punishment, and has ever been followed by plagues and incurable diseases upon the third and fourth generation, the offspring of such marriages. Were time to last and inter-marriage continue between the whites, the blacks, and the reds in America, consumption and other diseases would soon wipe the mixed bloods off the face of the earth.

Parham, 'Kol Kare Bomidbar', pp. 83-84. Regarding Parham's Anglo-Israel theory, see Parham, 'Kol Kare Bomidbar', pp. 106-107. Cf. Parham, 'Kol Kare Bomidbar', pp. 91-100. For discussions of Parham's racial philosophy, see Goff, *Fields White Unto Harvest*, pp. 107-11, 131-32, 220; Allan Anderson, 'The Dubious Legacy of Charles Parham: Racism and Cultural Insensitivites among Pentecostals', *Pneuma* 27.1 (2005), pp. 51-64.

[135] Similar to Parham's rejection of the physical demonstrations of emotion among Irwin's FBHA, Parham considered these 'manifestations of the flesh, fits and spasms, wild-fire, fanaticism' and he concluded that 'the falling under the power in Los Angeles has, to a large degree, been produced through a hypnotic, mesmeric, magnetic current'. Parham, *The Life of Charles F. Parham*, pp. 163, 164, 166, 168, 169. 'But by a careful study of Acts 1.8, we find that the power was to make them witnesses. The modern idea of shouting, groaning and screaming, performed in imitation of supposed drunken disciples is a misinterpretation of their actions.' Parham, 'Kol Kare Bomidbar', p. 28. Cf. Parham, 'Kol Kare Bomidbar', p. 62; Martin, *The Life and Ministry of William J. Seymour*, p. 269; Sanders, *William Joseph Seymour*, pp. 72-73, 108-109; Faupel, *The Everlasting Gospel*, p. 210.

[136] Parham described the *glossolalic* manifestations as 'chattering, jabbering, sputtering, speaking no language at all, and counterfeit experiences of tongues achieved through the suggestion of words and sounds, the working of the chin, or the massage of the throat'. Parham, *The Life of Charles F. Parham*, pp. 163, 165, 169; Goff, *Fields White Unto Harvest*, pp. 132-34. 'Two-thirds of this tongue stuff over the country is not Pentecost. The counterfeits have no real languages, and fleshly controls of spiritualistic origin have destroyed their soul-saving power.' Parham, 'The Everlasting Gospel', p. 31. Cf. Parham, 'The Everlasting Gospel', pp. 16, 32, 63-64, 71-73; Martin, *The Life and Ministry of William J. Seymour*, p. 269;

xenolalia on the mission field, by 1910 most Pentecostals had adopted *glossolalia* as the biblical sign of Spirit baptism,[137] but Parham and the Apostolic Faith movement adamantly maintained *xenolalia* as the evidence of Spirit baptism and missionary calling.[138]

Conclusion

By the last decades of the nineteenth century, the development of the fourfold paradigm of the 'full gospel' was complete, and an ex-

---

Faupel, *The Everlasting Gospel*, p. 212. Seymour's doctrine of Spirit baptism also carried an ethical emphasis along with his view of 'tongues', so that sanctification was a prerequisite to Spirit baptism. See Synan and Fox, *William J. Seymour*, pp. 196-206. Cecil Robeck argues that during the Azusa Street revival Seymour moved away from Parham's doctrine of tongues as the bible evidence of Spirit baptism. Cecil M. Robeck, 'William J. Seymour and "the Bible Evidence"', in Gary B. McGee (ed.), *Initial Evidence: Historical and Biblical Perspectives on the Pentecostal Doctrine of Spirit Baptism* (Eugene, OR: Wipf and Stock, 2007 repr.; Peabody, MA: Hendrickson, 1991), p. 82. Renea Brathwaite refutes Robeck's analysis of Seymour's view of tongues and initial evidence. Renea Barthwaite, 'Tongues and Ethics: William J. Seymour and the "Bible Evidence": A Response to Cecil M. Robeck, Jr.', *Pneuma* 32 (2010), pp. 203-22.

[137] Goff, *Fields White Unto Harvest*, p. 16. Cf. Grant Wacker, *Heaven Below: Early Pentecostals and American Culture* (Cambridge, MA: Harvard University Press, 2001), pp. 40-51; Faupel, *The Everlasting Gospel*, p. 228. Aaron Friesen argues that

> Parham held a very similar doctrine to the doctrine of initial evidence that firmly planted itself in the movement. However, what exactly Parham meant by the words is different from the meaning given to those words by the majority of Pentecostals after 1908. Rather than attribute the founding of the Pentecostal doctrine of initial evidence to Parham, it may be more appropriate to say that Parham inaugurated the application of a distinct hermeneutic to the book of Acts.

Aaron Friesen, 'The Called out of the Called Out: Charles Parham's Doctrine of the Spirit Baptism', *JEPTA* 29 (2009), p. 53.

[138] According to Parham,

> Scores have been sent to foreign fields by so-called messages, who have no language but their own; many of them have returned; others stayed to graft the Home Missions support; some tried to learn the languages or took positions in those countries. If the Holy Spirit had sent out these workers, they would have been endowed with real tongues. This is a patent fact ... No one in the true Apostolic work ever claims the Baptism of the Holy Spirit until he speaks fluently and smoothly in another language, and then have it proven by some disinterested foreigner witnessing to the fact that they really used a language. No repetition of sounds or chattering are ever accepted unless it occurs at the first reception of the baptism, but must then speedily give away to a clear real language that you are able to use without any undue emotions or unnatural action of the body.

Parham, 'The Everlasting Gospel', p. 71.

pectation of an outpouring of the Spirit and apostolic power permeated its *ethos*. The context was well prepared for the emergence of Pentecostalism. The fourfold gospel, furthermore, was christocentric and intrinsically pneumatological. Each *motif* accentuated the identity and mission of Jesus Christ, yet the Holy Spirit's effectual agency functioned in an intimate relationship with Christ in their application. It appears, therefore, that the Holiness movement and American restorationist revivalism's shift in nomenclature to a pneumatological emphasis flowed from a relocation of the fourfold gospel's christological nexus, from a pneumatically permeated Logos Christology to Spirit Christology; specifically, they advocated a Spirit christological paradigm of pneumatic mediation which integrated aspects of Logos Christology. This *shift* to Spirit Christology seems to be an essential component in forming the theological *ethos* from which Pentecostalism emerged.

Moreover, among Parham's and Seymour's holiness predecessors, teaching a 'third blessing' doctrine – Ralph Horner, George Watson, and B.H. Irwin – Spirit Christology functioned as the basis for theology; specifically, these protagonists of a 'third blessing' of spiritual power through Spirit baptism advocated a Spirit christological paradigm of pneumatic mediation which integrated Logos Christology. Nevertheless, Horner, Watson, and Irwin cannot be designated Pentecostals.

With Parham's doctrinal formulation of Spirit baptism, the fivefold gospel budded into fruition, providing the impetus to incipient Pentecostalism, yet the rigid environs constituting his theological schema limited further growth; therefore, Pentecostal doctrine and experience unfolded into flowerage with William Seymour.[139] Its

---

[139] There has been much debate about who should be given the honor of being dubbed 'the Father of Pentecostalism,' Charles Parham or William Seymour. See, Hollenweger, *Pentecostalism*, pp. 18-24; Goff, *Fields White Unto Harvest*, pp. 10-16, 160-66; Leonard Lovett, 'Perspective on the Black Origins of the Contemporary Pentecostal Movement', *Journal of the Interdenominational Theological Center* 1.1 (1973), pp. 36-49; James S. Tinney, 'William J. Seymour [1855?–1920?]: Father of Modern-Day Pentecostalism', *Journal of the Interdenominational Theological Center* 4.1 (1976), pp. 34-44; Sanders, *William Joseph Seymour*, pp. 5-15; Leonard Lovett, 'Black Origins of the Pentecostal Movement', in Vinson Synan (ed.), *Aspects of Pentecostal-Charismatic Origins* (Plainfield, NJ: Logos International, 1975), pp. 123-68; Anderson, *An Introduction to Pentecostalism*, pp. 41-45; Steven J. Land, 'William J. Seymour: The Father of the Holiness-Pentecostal Movement', in Henry H. Knight (ed.), *From Aldersgate to Azusa Street: Wesleyan, Holiness, and*

doctrine of Spirit baptism, however, positioned Pentecostalism on the margins of theological discussion.[140] It should be noted, however, among the extant writings of Parham, Spirit Christology does not appear. So, the question remains: are there traces of Spirit Christology among early Pentecostals; furthermore, if Spirit Christology has appeared among them, how well does Spirit Christology and early Pentecostal theology correlate? To answer these questions, attention will turn to an examination of early Pentecostal periodical literature.

Pentecostalism Visions of the New Creation (Eugene, OR: Wipf and Stock, 2010), pp. 218-26. It seems to this author that both men should be given due honor for their respective contributions. Parham completed the doctrinal formulation, albeit with a misguided emphasis on *xenolalia*, of the full gospel's fifth motif, Spirit baptism, while Seymour took Parham's formulation and liberated it from Parham's constraints – racial, emotional and physical manifestations, and *glossolalia*, though it does not appear that Seymour taught *glossolalia* as biblical evidence of Spirit baptism – allowing Pentecostalism the freedom and providing the impetus for a global Pentecostal revival.

[140] Pentecostalism, now, positioned itself as an opponent of the Protestant liberal tradition – protesting the desiccation of the church, encroachment of worldliness, Darwinism, and liberalism in the church – and on the fringe of the holiness tradition, averring that the latter rain *motif*, in which the Spirit would be poured out on all flesh to bring in the eschatological harvest before the Lord's return, was fulfilled in Pentecostalism's experience of Spirit baptism. Although Pentecostalism quickly grew through the network of holiness associations, when Pentecostals asserted that Spirit baptism was separate and distinct from sanctification and *glossolalia* was the bible evidence, this was not well received among the majority of the holiness tradition. Furthermore, Pentecostalism also emerged as a critique of Princeton Fundamentalism's rejection of spiritual gifts and divine healing. For a discussion of the hermeneutical issues, see Kenneth J. Archer, *A Pentecostal Hermeneutic for the Twenty-First Century: Spirit, Scripture and Community* (JPTSup 28; London: T. & T. Clark, 2004), pp. 9-126. Regarding the Pentecostal view of the Latter Rain Covenant, see Wesley Myland, 'The Latter Rain Covenant and Pentecostal Power: With Testimony of Healings and Baptism', in Donald W. Dayton (ed.), *Three Early Pentecostal Tractates* (New York: Garland Publishing, 1985 repr.; Chicago: Evangel Publishing House, 1910). Much has been written about the social, cultural, and psychological aspects of the rise of Pentecostalism. See Anderson, *Vision of the Disinherited*; Wacker, *Heaven Below*; Blumhofer, *Restoring the Faith*; Kilian McDonnell, *Charismatic Renewal and the Churches* (New York: Seabury, 1976).

17

EARLY PENTECOSTAL PERIODICAL LITERATURE

This chapter will examine Pentecostalism as it appeared on the horizon of the North America theological context for indications of the presence of Spirit Christology. Pentecostalism emerged from the ethos of nineteenth century Holiness and restorationist revivalism.[1] The upshot of this revivalism was the coalescing of four christological *motifs* into a fourfold gospel – comprised of Jesus as Savior, Sanctifier, Healer, and Coming King – which its proponents asserted was the restoration of the 'full gospel' of the apostolic era. This fourfold 'full gospel' formed the *gestalt* from which Pentecostalism emerged. With the outpouring of the Spirit and the accession of the fifth *motif*, baptism in the Holy Spirit, to the fourfold gospel, the fivefold 'full gospel' message depicted Pentecostalism's theological *heart*. Here, I am in agreement with Walter Hollenweger and Steve Land that the first ten years of the Pentecostal movement depicts its 'heart and not the infancy' of the movement, so any contemporary historical inquiry or attempts at Pentecostal theological reflection should consider the *heart* of the tradition's spirituality and theology.[2] If Steve Land has correctly assessed Pentecostal spiritual-

---

[1] For presentations of the historical development of Pentecostalism, see Synan, *The Holiness-Pentecostal Tradition*; Faupel, *The Everlasting Gospel*. Regarding Pentecostalism's theological development, see Dayton, *Theological Roots*.

[2] Steven J. Land, *Pentecostal Spirituality: A Passion for the Kingdom* (JPTSup 1; Sheffield, England: Sheffield Academic Press, 1993), p. 47. In fact, Hollenweger regards 'the early Pentecostal spirituality as the norm by which I measure its subsequent history'. Walter J. Hollenweger, 'Pentecostals and the Charismatic

ity and its relationship to the 'full gospel', more than likely, Spirit Christology will be present: 'This spirituality is Christocentric precisely because it is pneumatic; its "fivefold gospel" is focused on Christ because of its starting point in the Holy Spirit'.[3]

This chapter, accordingly, canvasses early Pentecostal literature for traces of Spirit Christology. The focus rests upon the early North American Pentecostal publications of certain movements which were formed or transformed into Pentecostal organizations because of the Azusa Street revival's influence. Initially, this literature advocated Pentecostalism's fivefold gospel; however, with the rise of the 'Finished Work' controversy (1910) propagated by William Durham, which rejected the Wesleyan doctrine of 'second blessing' sanctification and coalesced sanctification with justification in conversion, Pentecostalism bifurcated into fivefold and fourfold gospel streams.[4] This section, accordingly, will examine the literature of these streams of early Pentecostalism. Since each Pentecostal movement usually published a periodical, methodologically, this inquiry will examine these periodicals for any vestiges of Spirit Christology.[5]

The Fivefold Gospel Stream

This part will examine five periodicals representing – Jesus as Savior, Sanctifier, Spirit Baptizer, Healer, and Coming King – the Wes-

---

Movement', in C. Jones, G. Wainwright, and E. Yarnold (eds.), *The Study of Spirituality* (New York: Oxford University Press, 1986), p. 551. Therefore, I will primarily focus on the periodicals produced during this period of time.

[3] Land, *Pentecostal Spirituality*, p. 23. Actually, it seems to have appeared among Holiness groups, so that accompanying the shift in pneumatic emphasis was a corollary shift from a pneumatically permeated Logos Christology to a Spirit christological basis for the fourfold gospel; consequently, Spirit Christology should be present in the fivefold gospel.

[4] Synan, *The Holiness-Pentecostal Tradition*, pp. 149-56; Faupel, *The Everlasting Gospel*, pp. 229-70.

[5] Early Pentecostals as well as subsequent Spirit movements owe much of their success to periodicals. 'Each of them looks at the printed page as an important tool to evangelize, indoctrinate, introduce distinctives, inspire, promote their ministries, and offer leadership helps.' W.E. Warner, 'Periodcals', *NIDPCM*, p. 982. For an overview of Pentecostal/Charismatic periodicals and discussion of their importance, see Warner, 'Periodcals', *NIDPCM*, pp. 974-82; Alexander, *Pentecostal Healing*, pp. 67-72. As Spirit Christology is found among the early Pentecostal periodicals, this inquiry will note corresponding Spirit christological references that may be found in monographs by the same author.

leyan stream of Pentecostalism: *The Apostolic Faith*, *The Bridegroom's Messenger*, *The Church of God Evangel*, *The Whole Truth*, and *The Pentecostal Holiness Advocate*.

Apostolic Faith

This examination of early Pentecostal literature begins with the official publication of the Azusa Street revival, *Apostolic Faith*, in Los Angeles, California. Consisting of four pages, there were thirteen issues of the *Apostolic Faith* published (Sept. 1906–May 1908),[6] spreading the Pentecostal testimonies and teachings of the Azusa Street revival.[7] Five issues of *Apostolic Faith* contain seven articles with Spirit christological references; six are unsigned, and William Seymour initialed the other one, W.J.S.[8] By examining Seymour's article and noting the corresponding references in the other articles, Seymour's Spirit Christology will come to light, along with the bent of the *Apostolic Faith*.

The title and subject of the article is 'The Baptism of the Holy Ghost'.[9] It begins with an introduction and explains Seymour's teaching of Spirit baptism through five points: the Holy Ghost is power; tarry in one accord; the baptism falls on a clean heart; Jesus' first sermon after his baptism; the Holy Ghost flows through pure channels. The introduction, moreover, provides the article's scriptural basis (Acts 1.5, 8; 2.4; Lk. 24.49) and thesis: 'Jesus gave the church at Pentecost the great lesson of how to carry on a revival, and it would be well for every church to follow Jesus' standard of the baptism of the Holy Ghost and fire'.[10] So, Seymour's purpose is

---

[6] In 1907 the February and March issues were combined into one eight page issue. After Seymour married Jennie Moore in May 1908 the editor of the *Apostolic Faith*, Clara Lum, absconded with the mailing list for the periodical, and along with Florence Crawford published the *Apostolic Faith* in Portland, Oregon. Sanders, *William Joseph Seymour*, pp. 110-14.

[7] Charles Parham originated the *Apostolic Faith* periodical; nonetheless, Seymour and the editorial staff publishing the Azusa Street periodical kept the same name.

[8] It was not unusual for authors of articles in *Apostolic Faith* to omit their names; they emphasized their teaching was from God, not humans or dead creeds. Jacobsen, *Thinking in the Spirit*, p. 61. Vinson Synan has gathered into one location all of Seymour's signed articles in *Apostolic Faith*. Vinson Synan and Charles R. Fox, *William J. Seymour*, pp. 169-241.

[9] Synan includes this article in Synan and Fox, *William J. Seymour*, pp. 241-47.

[10] W.J.S., 'The Baptism of the Holy Ghost', *AF* 2.13 (May 1908), p. 3.

to instruct the church about how to experience revival: by obeying Jesus' command to receive Spirit baptism.

> In all Jesus' great revivals and mircles [*sic*], the work was wrought by the power of the Holy Ghost flowing through His sanctified humanity.[11]

> Jesus is our example. 'And Jesus being full of the Holy Ghost, returned from Jordan, and was led by the Spirit.' We find in reading the Bible that the baptism with the Holy Ghost and fire falls on a clean, sanctified life, for we see according to Scriptures that Jesus was 'holy, harmless, undefiled,' and filled with wisdom and favor with God and man, before God anointed Him with the Holy Ghost and power ... Beloved, if Jesus who was God Himself, needed the Holy Ghost to empower Him for His ministry and His miracles, how much more do we children need the Holy Ghost baptism today.[12]

> Jesus was the Son of God and born of the Holy Ghost and filled with the Holy Ghost from His mother's womb; but the baptism of the Holy Ghost came upon His sanctified humanity at the Jordan. In his humanity, He needed the Third Person of the Trinity to do His work.[13]

---

[11] W.J.S., 'The Baptism of the Holy Ghost', *AF* 2.13 (May 1908), p. 3. 'Jesus came to destroy all the works of the devil, and He said He would give us power, the Holy Ghost coming upon us, the same power that He had.' *AF*, 1.2 (Oct. 1906), p. 3.

[12] W.J.S., 'The Baptism of the Holy Ghost', *AF* 2.13 (May 1908), p. 3.

> There is nothing sweeter, higher or holier in this world than sanctification. The baptism with the Holy Ghost is the gift of power upon the sanctified soul, giving power to preach the Gospel of Jesus Christ and power to go to the stake. It seals you unto the day of redemption, that you may be ready to meet the Lord Jesus at midnight or any time, because you have oil in your vessel with your lamp. You are partaker of the Holy Ghost in the Pentecostal baptism, just as you are partaker of the Lord Jesus Christ in sanctification. You become partaker of the eternal Spirit of God in the baptism with the Holy Ghost. Jesus was a God before He received the baptism, sanctified and sent into the world, but yet He could not go on His great mission, fighting against the combined forces of hell, until He received the baptism with the Holy Ghost. If He needed it, how much more we as His servants ought to get the same thing.

AF 1.6 (Feb.–Mar. 1907), p. 6. Cf. *AF* 1.5 (1907), p. 3.

[13] W.J.S., 'The Baptism of the Holy Ghost', *AF* 2.13 (May 1908), p. 3.

Several conclusions emerge from these references. First, Seymour affirmed a trinitarian position and Christ's deity: the eternal Son was incarnated in Christ. Second, Seymour attested to two natures in the one person of Christ, divine and human. Third, he sharply distinguished between Jesus' divine and human natures, allowing space for the Spirit to sanctify the human nature in conception and anoint it. Fourth, at the Jordan, Christ received Spirit baptism because his human nature needed an enduement of power to fulfill his salvific mission. Fifth, Christ's human nature performed miracles through the power of the Spirit. Sixth, Christ's Spirit baptism is paradigmatic for his followers' Spirit baptism: Spirit baptism is separate and distinct from sanctification, and it is a subsequent experience of power. When someone receives Spirit baptism, they receive the witness of speaking in tongues, as Christ received the witness of Spirit.[14] Thus, according to Seymour, to experience great revivals and miracles believers must obey Christ's command and follow his example of receiving Spirit baptism, so that the power of the Holy Spirit flows through their sanctified humanity.

William Seymour and the *Apostolic Faith* periodical supported a form of Spirit Christology. In point of fact, they based their doctrine of Spirit baptism on Christ's experience of the Spirit; the Spirit sanctified and empowered Christ's life and ministry. Seymour carefully affirmed triune theology and the incarnation of the eternal divine Son in Christ, but this Logos Christology was integrated into a

---

> The abiding anointing, which is the Spirit of Christ, is holy; but it is not the third Person of the Trinity. You have the Father, Son and Holy Ghost in sanctification, but you have not the enduement of power until you are baptized with the Holy Spirit. Then you receive the baptism that Christ received on the banks of Jordan. He had the fullness of the Godhead, but He had to be baptized for His great work. Jesus was anointed with the Holy Ghost and power and went about doing good. If we put sanctification for the Holy Ghost, then we would have Jesus with carnality in Him up to His baptism.

'Pentecostal Notes', *AF* 1.10 (Sept. 1907), p. 3.

[14] Praise God for a salvation that brings a witness. God gives us a witness that we are justified, the Spirit witnesses that we are sanctified and when we receive the Holy Ghost, He witnesses through us, as recorded in Acts 2.4, the speaking in other tongues. Jesus has a witness for everything. When He was born, the angels sang on Bethlehem's plain, when He was baptized with the Holy Ghost, He had the witness of the heavenly dove and the voice from Heaven ... Why not have the Bible witness, a supernatural witness that people will not have to take your word for?

AF 1.2 (Oct. 1906), p. 4.

Spirit christological paradigm of pneumatic mediation. Spirit Christology, therefore, stood at the hermeneutical and theological center of, the Azusa Street revival, the impetus of global Pentecostal missionary evangelism.[15]

The Bridegroom's Messenger

After Gaston Barnabas Cashwell received Spirit baptism at the Azusa Street revival,[16] he returned to Dunn, North Carolina and began (Dec. 31, 1906) a Pentecostal revival producing tremendous results; subsequently, he canvassed the South conducting Pentecostal revivals, earning him the designation the 'Apostle of Pentecost' to the South.[17] Through these revivals and a periodical he published, *The Bridegroom's Messenger*, Cashwell influenced numerous constituents, leaders, and entire holiness movements to join the ranks of Pentecostalism.[18] Cashwell initiated this periodical (Oct. 1,

---

[15] According to Douglas Jacobsen, 'The theology articulated during the heyday of the revival seems for the most part to have reflected the general consensus of the leadership of the mission. Understood in this way, to speak of Seymour's theology is to speak of the theology of the mission as a whole'. Jacobsen, *Thinking in the Spirit*, p. 61. For overviews of Seymour's theology and the Azusa Mission, see Jacobsen, *Thinking in the Spirit*, pp. 61-84; Synan and Fox, *William J. Seymour*, pp. 63-105.

[16] After hearing of the Azusa Street revival in California, Gaston Barnabas Cashwell traveled from Dunn, North Carolina to Los Angeles, inquiring into the validity of the Pentecostal experience; whereupon, he received Spirit baptism. Cashwell's testimony can be found in 'Came 3,000 Miles for His Pentecost', *AF* 1.4 (Dec. 1906), p. 3.

[17] For example, Cashwell conducted revivals in North Carolina, South Carolina, Virginia, Tennessee, Georgia, and Alabama.

[18] G.B. Cashwell (1862–1916) was born in Sampson County near Dunn, North Carolina. At an early age, he became a minister in the North Carolina Conference of the Methodist Episcopal Church. Influenced by A.B. Crumpler, he transitioned into the holiness movement (1903). Cashwell, forthwith, became a prominent evangelist in the holiness movement, garnering a significant amount of influence along the way. After receiving the baptism with the Holy Spirit at the Azusa Street Revival, Cashwell spread the Pentecostal message across the South. Through Cashwell's influence, several holiness movements came under the umbrella of Pentecostalism: The Fire-Baptized Holiness Church (1907), The Holiness Church of North Carolina which renamed itself the Pentecostal Holiness Church (1908), and the Church of God (Cleveland, TN 1908). Concerning Cashwell's life, ministry and influence, see Synan, *The Holiness-Pentecostal Tradition*, pp. 112-24; Synan, *Oldtime Power*, pp. 85, 97-110; Vinson Synan, 'Cashwell, Gaston Barnabas', *NIDPCM*, pp. 457-58.

1907) in Atlanta, Georgia and served as its editor until Elizabeth A. Sexton succeeded him as proprietor and editor (June 1908).[19]

Considering the influence of *The Bridegroom's Messenger* in southern Pentecostalism, it is significant that in the early years of its publication (1907–16) there are at least 23 Spirit christological references, encompassing Christ's life and ministry.[20] Elizabeth Sexton, for example, comments on the uniqueness of Christ.

> Jesus was the God-man, born of the Holy Ghost. He was a very different man from even the first Adam.[21]

Here, Sexton accentuates the divine and human natures in the one person of Christ while stressing his unique birth: the human nature was conceived in the incarnation and born by the Holy Spirit. Regarding Christ's divine nature Sexton references a Jewish scholar, who discovered the triune revelation in the Hebrew Scriptures, to validate her trinitarian position against the Oneness Pentecostal position.

> I have never doubted the existence of Him who said, 'If I be a Father, where is my honor' (Mal. 1.6), but I have been led by a power, once unknown to me, into the inquiry how the other two Spirits have revealed themselves. In what manner the Holy Spirit and the Spirit which is the middle pillar in the Godhead have been manifested. I found that the Spirit, which is the middle Spirit of the Godhead, has revealed Himself as the 'Word of God,' as the uncreated, self-existing Word, to which the Holy Scripture ascribes the holy name, 'Jehovah,' and all the attributes of God.[22]

Sexton affirms the consubstantial nature of the Father, Word, and Holy Spirit: the one divine essence of the Godhead is Spirit. Christ's divine nature, therefore, is Spirit, but existing as a distinct subsistence from either the Holy Spirit or the Father. Divine Spirit, thus,

---

[19] The first two issues of *The Bridegroom's Messenger* were published monthly; then, it became a bi-monthly publication until October 1, 1914, when it reverted back to monthly issues.

[20] Instead of presenting these references according to how they chronologically appear in the various issues, they will appear as they pertain to the life and ministry of Christ. To avoid repetition, several references will be located in footnotes.

[21] 'His Word Like as a Fire', *TBM* 8.168 (Mar. 1, 1915), p. 1.

[22] 'His Name Shall Be Called Wonderful', *TBM* 9.182 (May 1, 1916), p. 1.

unites with human nature in the incarnation, attesting to Christ's uniqueness.

The distinction of the divine and human natures come into view when discussing Christ's Spirit baptism.

> Christ received the baptism of the Spirit at His baptism at the Jordan, but on the cross He was baptized or immersed in suffering.[23]

> When the Holy Ghost descended upon Jesus, it revealed his character and mission as well as introducing Him to the Jewish nation for the gentle dove of peace crowned Him the great Prince of Peace, and throughout His dispensation His mission was to make peace between God and man, and in like manner, on the day of Pentecost, when the Holy Ghost descended from heaven in fulfillment of the promise of Jesus, who was manifested as He who baptized with the Holy Ghost.[24]

> Prayer brought the anointing upon Jesus that made Him the public Man, Master and Miracle Worker that He was.[25]

> The Holy Ghost baptism is power to witness ... Is the baptism given to only sanctified souls? Yes; the Holy Ghost is the same anointing that Jesus received and He was holy. We must be holy in order for the Spirit to take possession of His temple and abide in us ... What is the difference between sanctification and the

---

[23] J.H. King, 'Answers to Questions as Requested', *TBM* 1.4 (Dec. 15, 1907), p. 2. Cf. *TBM* 2.27 (Dec. 1, 1908), p. 4.

[24] J.A. Culbreth, 'The Baptism and Evidence of Pentecost Foreshadowed', *TBM* 1.8 (Feb. 15, 1908), p. 2.

> Jesus selected tongues controlled, emblematical of love and its powers, and when His spiritual kingdom was to be officially announced, when the day of Pentecost was fully come, Jesus witnessed to the Holy Ghost baptism having come as clearly as God witnessed to Jesus being His beloved Son in whom He was well pleased, as Jesus' baptism, Mt. 3.7.

Eli Gardner, 'God's Banner over them Was Love – Cant. 2.4', *TBM* 2.40 (June 15, 1909), p. 4. Cf. *TBM* 6.135 (June 15, 1913), p. 1.

[25] A.S. Copley, 'The Prayer of the Righteous', *TBM* 2.35 (Apr. 1, 1909), p. 2. Cf. *TBM* 3.60 (Apr. 15, 1910), p. 4. 'Prayer does not cease with the coming of the Comforter. Jesus received the Spirit while praying Lk. 3.21, so, also, the disciples Lk. 11.13 and Acts 1.14. But the anointing was just the beginning of Jesus' prayer life.' A.S. Copley, 'Why We Need the Baptism', *TBM* 2.31 (Feb.1, 1909), p. 2.

baptism? Sanctification is holiness and the baptism is the enduement of power.[26]

Several inferences can be drawn from these texts. First, Christ's human nature was baptized in the Spirit; the Spirit empowering him and working miracles. Second, these writers distinguished between baptism in water, Spirit, and suffering: neither water baptism nor baptism in suffering on the cross was synonymous with Christ's Spirit baptism. Third, Christ's Spirit baptism revealed his salvific identity and mission: to reconcile humanity to God, and to baptize them with the Holy Spirit.[27] Fourth, prayer was essential to Jesus' ministry: through prayer Jesus expressed his relationship with the Father, received the Spirit, and fulfilled his ministry. Fifth, the writers clearly demarcate between sanctification and Spirit baptism: holiness and enduement of power. Sixth, Jesus' humanity was sanctified before receiving Spirit baptism. The Spirit's agency in Christ's sanctification and Spirit baptism, accordingly, accentuates the distinction between Christ's human and divine natures: the divine nature needed neither sanctification nor power. Christ's human nature, however, experienced an integral relationship with the Spirit in fulfilling his salvific mission. Through the Spirit Jesus resisted temptation and learned obedience,[28] so believers are privy to a pneumatic epistemology based on Jesus' pneumatic experience.[29]

According to Elizabeth Sexton, Christ is the sanctified altar which sanctifies all who consecrate themselves upon it.

---

[26] Unknown contributor, 'The Baptism of the Holy Ghost', *TBM* 5.107 (Apr. 1, 1912), p. 2.

[27] 'The Son, under the mighty effulgence of the power of the Holy Spirit, is now seen as "the express image of His person" (the Father). With this mighty baptism in full revealing power, the fullness of the Godhead bodily is magnified in Jesus, the Christ, in one great revelation.' J.O. Lehman, 'Pentecostal Revelation', *TBM* 3.70 (Sept. 15, 1910), p. 4.

[28] Regarding the Spirit's agency in assisting Jesus' humanity to overcome temptation, see *TBM* 1.12 (Apr. 15, 1908), p. 4; 5.107 (Apr. 1, 1912), p. 1. 'We need the Holy Spirit that we may learn to obey God … Jesus, "Though being a Son, He learned obedience from the things which He suffered" Heb. 5.8. But this was after He was anointed with the Spirit. O, if our Saviour learned anything, how much more our need!' A.S. Copley, 'Why We Need the Baptism', *TBM* 2.31 (Feb.1, 1909), p. 2. Cf. *TBM* 5.120 (Nov. 1, 1912), p. 1.

[29] 'The Holy Ghost is given, not to make preachers of all of us at once, but to teach us, "that we might know the things that are freely given to us of God."' A.S Copley, 'Power from on High', *TBM* 2.27 (Dec. 1, 1908), p. 4.

The essential and fundamental attribute of the altar was its power of imparting sanctity to the offerings placed upon it ... It was cleansed by a sin offering for atonement, which symbolized the spotlessness of Him it foreshadowed. It was then 'anointed' and 'sanctified' with the holy oil which was compounded by God's order and recipe, and was used in anointing the highest priest and his sons when consecrated to their office. It symbolized the anointing of the Holy Ghost for a holy office. It was after this ceremony that the altar possessed its sanctity and sanctified every gift that touched it. Here we see a beautiful type of the divine One who, in the fullness of time, through the eternal Spirit, offered Himself without spot to God.[30]

The anointing of the Spirit sanctifying Christ's humanity enabled him to be offered as a spotless sacrifice and consecrated him as the altar, the sanctifier.[31] Ultimately, it was the Spirit who has functioned as the agent of Christ's resurrection, the eschatological presence of the kingdom in power, and transformation of mortal bodies and creation at his coming.[32]

Although Christ stands at the center and is the focus of the fivefold gospel – Jesus is Savior, Sanctifier, Holy Spirit Baptizer, Healer, and Coming King – the Spirit permeates these *motifs* and functions as the empowering agent. In other words, in *The Bridegroom's Messenger* the basis of the fivefold gospel rests on a Spirit christological paradigm of pneumatic mediation which integrates Logos Christology, structured within the lineaments of trinitarian theology.

The Church of God Evangel

With its origin extending back to 1886, the Church of God (Cleveland, Tennessee) was a holiness movement that transitioned to Pentecostalism.[33] Although the movement had experienced an outpour-

---

[30] Elizabeth Sexton, 'The Altar Sanctifies the Gift', *TBM* 9.179 (Feb. 1, 1916), p. 1.

[31] 'Being immersed into this element of death, similar to the immersion of the body of water, some person must perform the operation. This Person is the Holy Spirit Himself submerging us into death as He did Christ on the cross, for it was "through the Eternal Spirit Christ offered Himself."' J.H. King, 'Answers to Questions as Requested', *TBM* 1.4 (Dec. 15, 1907), p. 2.

[32] *TBM* 2.35 (Apr. 1, 1909), p. 1.

[33] The Church of God originally began under the name The Christian Union (August 19, 1886), organizing under the leadership of R.G. Spurling with 9 members in a mill at Barney Creek in Monroe County, Tennessee. The impetus of its

ing of the Spirit with glossolalic manifestations in 1896, it did not enter the ranks of Pentecostalism until its General Moderator, A.J. Tomlinson,[34] was baptized in the Spirit while G.B. Cashwell was preaching in a Church of God (January 12, 1908).[35] Subsequently,

---

emergence was an aversion to the creedalism, ritualism, and desiccation of the institutional churches. Early leadership of the movement passed to R.G. Spurling Jr. and W.F. Bryant. The name of the church was changed to The Holiness Church at Camp Creek (May 15, 1902). A.J. Tomlinson joined the movement and became its pastor (June 13, 1903), providing dynamic leadership and growth. The center of the movement's activities moved from Camp Creek to Cleveland, Tennessee in 1906. Finally, the movement's name was changed to the Church of God during its second annual General Assembly (January 9–13 1907). The office of General Moderator of the church, to serve continuously through the year, was established during the fourth General Assembly (January 6–9 1909), and A.J. Tomlinson was elected to serve in this position; Tomlinson had moderated the previous General Assemblies. The name of this office was changed to General Overseer in 1910, and A.J. Tomlinson filled this position until 1923. For the history of the Church of God during this era, see, A.J. Tomlinson, *The Last Great Conflict* (Cleveland, TN: Walter E. Rodgers Press, 1913), pp. 184-98; Conn, *Like a Mighty Army*, pp. 3-183; Alexander, *Pentecostal Healing*, pp. 95-97.

[34] Ambrose Jessup Tomlinson (1865–1943) was born to a Quaker family near Westfield, Indiana; however, it was not until he was almost hit by lightning, at the age 24, that he professed allegiance to the gospel, and began contributing to the growth of the local Quaker congregation. Tomlinson was well traveled; his journeys brought him into contact with such figures as Stephen Merritt, D.L. Moody, A.B. Simpson, George D. Watson, and Frank W. Sandford. Finally, after several years of contact with the people of the Holiness Church at Camp Creek; he joined the church (June 13, 1903), proclaiming that this was the Church of God of the Bible. Of the four congregations in the movement, by 1904 Tomlinson was serving as pastor of three. Tomlinson served as the chief executive bishop of the Church of God (1909–23), inspiring growth, until a dispute with the council of Elders regarding a charge of misappropriation of funds caused a parting of the ways (1923). Although Tomlinson was legally exonerated by the courts of any financial impropriety, the die was already cast; Tomlinson and at least 2,000 followers began the Church of God of Prophecy. Nevertheless, Tomlinson left an indelible imprint on the Church of God. For Tomlinson's life, teaching, and ministry, see Daniel D. Preston, *The Era of A.J. Tomlinson* (Cleveland, TN: White Wing Publishing House, 1984); R.G. Robins, *A.J. Tomlinson: Plainfolk Modernist* (Religion in America Series; Oxford: Oxford University Press, 2004); Lillie Duggar, *A.J. Tomlinson: Former General Overseer of the Church of God* (Cleveland, TN: White Wing Publishing House, 1964); Tomlinson, *Diary of A.J. Tomlinson*; Tomlinson, *The Last Great Conflict*; A.J. Tomlinson, *A.J. Tomlinson, God's Anointed – Prophet of Wisdom: Choice Writings of A.J. Tomlinson in Times of His Greatest Anointings* (Cleveland, TN: White Wing Publishing House, 1943); A.J. Tomlinson, *God's Twentieth Century Pioneer: A Compilation of Some of the Writings of A.J. Tomlinson* (Cleveland, TN: White Wing Publishing House, 1962); Harold Hunter, 'Tomlinson, Ambrose Jessup', *NIDPCM*, pp. 1143-45.

[35] According to Tomlinson,

the Church of God became an ardent proponent of fivefold gospel Pentecostalism and missionary evangelism.[36]

Publication of *The Church of God Evangel* began (March 1, 1910), with A.J. Tomlinson serving as editor (1910–22), as a biweekly eight page publication; by January 1914, it was published weekly, and beginning with the December 12, 1914 issue its page count was reduced to four.[37] *The Church of God Evangel* served as a means of communication between the General Overseer, ministers, and laity; it included the editorials of the General Overseer, ministerial sermons, revival reports, missionary reports, various poems, and testimonies. The contributors to *The Church of God Evangel* focused on the ministry of the Spirit in the life and ministry of the church, often relating this to their ecclesiology; nevertheless, this periodical contains numerous Spirit christological references.

In January, 1907, I became more fully awakened on the subject of receiving the Holy Ghost as He was poured out on the day of Pentecost. That whole year I ceased not to preach that it was our privilege to receive the Holy Ghost and speak in tongues as they did on the day of Pentecost. I did not have the experience, so I was almost always among the seekers at the altar ... By the end of the year I was so hungry for the Holy Ghost that I scarcely cared for food, friendship or anything else. I wanted one thing – the Baptism with the Holy Ghost. I wrote G.B. Cashwell, who had been to Los Angeles, Cal., and received the baptism there, and asked him to come to our place for a few days. He arrived January 10, 1908. He preached on Saturday night, and on Sunday morning, January 12, while he was preaching, a peculiar sensation took hold of me, and almost unconsciously I slipped off my chair in a heap on the rostrum at Brother Cashwell's feet. I did not know what such an experience meant. My mind was clear, but a peculiar power so enveloped and thrilled my whole being that I concluded to yield myself up to God and await results.

Tomlinson, *The Last Great Conflict*, pp. 210-11. Following these comments, Tomlinson continues with a description of an amazing testimony of his Spirit baptism. For his complete testimony, see Tomlinson, *The Last Great Conflict*, pp. 209-19.

[36] The time has come now for christians [*sic*] to conform completely to the Bible teaching. We can't plead ignorance any longer. Light and knowledge are increasing rapidly as the last message is going forth. The Holy Ghost is our great teacher ... The Holy Ghost is constantly testifying of Jesus as Saviour and healer and coming King ... Wonderful advancements have been made in this direction in the last four years, since the falling of the 'latter rain.' The advances will no doubt be more rapid in the next four years if the Lord tarries. To accept Christ in these last days means to take Him for all He is, viz., Saviour, sanctifier, baptizer with the Holy Ghost, healer and coming King.

A.J. Tomlinson, 'Healing in the Atonement', *COGE*, 1.19 (Dec. 1, 1910), p. 2.

[37] The periodical began as *The Evening Light and Church of God Evangel*, and in 1911 the name was shortened to *The Church of God Evangel*.

Tomlinson frequently linked the Spirit's relationship with Christ's humanity to the Spirit's vinculum with the church as the body of Christ. According to Tomlinson, functioning with a theocratic government, the true church existed in a visible form on earth as the body of Christ, the Church of God, confirmed by signs and wonders.[38] Tomlinson affirmed the consubstantial triune nature of God: the Father, Son, and Holy Spirit exist in one divine essence which is Spirit.[39] Though the eternal Son existed as Spirit, through the incarnation he existed on earth with a tangible human body; likewise, the Holy Spirit exists on earth in a body, the church.[40] Moreover, the church has received the same anointing of the Spirit which Christ experienced.

> Fiery trials come to God's servants in olden times, and even to Jesus, Himself, our great exemplar, and as God pours out His Spirit and gives special revelation of His truth and power in these last days, the fiery trials will come too ... Jesus, on the occasion of our text had just been anointed with the Holy Ghost, God had spoken from heaven setting His approval on this wonderful scene of Jesus' baptism, when He was ushered into the life-work which he came to earth to perform.[41]

Christ's humanity received the Spirit's anointing to overcome trials, temptations, and empower his ministry; if Christ depended on the Spirit's power to fulfill his mission, so must the church. Christ's relationship with the Spirit, therefore, constitutes a model for the church's relationship with the Spirit.

---

[38] See Tomlinson, 'The Church of God', *COGE* 7.27 (July 1, 1916), pp. 1, 4; J.B. Ellis, 'The Church Literal or Invisible', *COGE* 7.24 (June 10, 1916), p. 3. When these articles appeared in the *COGE*, they stirred up some controversy. A writer for the *Apostolic Evangel* (July 19, 1916) challenged the Church of God's claim to represent the visible body of Christ on the earth. Tomlinson defended his position in an article containing several parts and published in three issues of the *COGE*: Tomlinson, 'Another Good Opportunity for Correction, Explanation and Instruction', *COGE* 7.33 (Aug. 12, 1916), p. 1; *COGE* 7.34 (Aug. 19, 1916), p. 1; *COGE* 7.35 (Aug. 26, 1916), p. 1.

[39] *COGE* 5.8 (Feb. 21, 1914), p. 2; 7.31 (July 29, 1916), p. 1.

[40] 'Did Jesus come here in a spirit? No he came in a tangible body. So in Eph. 5.23, we find that He is the head of the Church, then if the head is tangible the body must be tangible also.' J.B. Ellis, 'The Church Literal or Invisible', *COGE* 7.24 (June 10, 1916), p. 3. Cf. *COGE* 7.30 (Dec. 9, 1916), p. 1; Tomlinson, *The Last Great Conflict*, pp. 91-92.

[41] Sam Perry, 'The Fiery Trial', *COGE* 5.8 (Feb. 21, 1914), p. 6.

The *COGE* presents Jesus' empowerment of the Spirit serving as a paradigm for the Spirit empowered church under two parallel themes. First, to reject the manifestations of power among modern Pentecostalism is dangerous.

> If it was a fearful sin to ascribe the works of Jesus done in the power of the Holy Spirit, to Satan, must it not be a horrible sin to ascribe to Satan the works of the Spirit in those who are filled with His Holy Presence ... The Spirit is the special Revealer of Christ, and One Who executeth His work on the earth, and to reject the Spirit is to reject, in a very deep sense, Christ Himself.[42]

Jesus performed his mighty works – exorcisms, healings, and miracles – through the power of the Spirit; accordingly, the church's witness is validated in the power of the Spirit with exorcisms, signs, and wonders. Since it is the Spirit's mission to mediate Christ's ministry and mission,[43] to reject the demonstration of the Spirit's power is tantamount to rejecting Christ the Savior.

Second, Jesus' example of obedience to the Father functions as a model of the church's obedience to Christ. Jesus as a human learned obedience through the Spirit; consequently, the Spirit teaches his followers obedience.[44]

> If Jesus is our pattern and we are His followers then we are to be sanctified ... Then we should next be filled with the Holy Ghost.[45]

In obedience to God's command to be holy Christ was sanctified, so that the church might be sanctified. Christ, also, received Spirit baptism at the Jordan and conducted his ministry in the power of

---

[42] A.S. Worrell, 'The Crisis Now On', *COGE* 1.16 (Oct. 15, 1910), p. 5. Cf. *COGE* 5.4 (Jan. 24, 1914), p. 7; F.J. Lee, 'Darkness and Light', *COGE* 5.5 (Jan. 31, 1914), p. 7; *COGE* 5.8 (Feb. 21, 1914), p. 2.

[43] 'Jesus suffered outside the gate that He might sanctify the people with His own blood, Heb. 13.12 But there must be a force or power to perform the work with that blood, so that is the mission of the Holy Ghost.' A.J. Tomlinson, 'The Holy Ghost: His Great Mission Is Fully Explained in the Bible', *COGE* 6.21 (May 22, 1915), p. 1.

[44] A.J. Tomlinson, 'Obedience to Jesus', *COGE* 6.12 (Mar. 20, 1915), p. 1.

[45] J.M. Scarbrough, 'Why Should We Be Sanctified', *COGE* 6.23 (June 5, 1915), p. 3. Cf. *COGE* 6.12 (Mar. 20, 1915), p. 2; *COGE* 7.16 (Apr. 15, 1916), p. 4.

the Spirit as a pattern for the church's ministry. The inference is clear: if the early church received Spirit baptism in obedience to Christ's command to be endued with power, the modern church should also be obedient to Christ.

In accordance with the *ethos* of the fivefold gospel, the Church of God's Christology is pneumatically permeated. The Christology is set within a trinitarian framework: the Father, Son, and Holy Spirit exist in consubstantial relationship in one divine essence which is Spirit. The divine Son was incarnated in human flesh, so that two distinct natures joined in the one person of Christ: divine Spirit and human. Christ's relationship with the Holy Spirit in his life and mission demonstrates that the Spirit sanctified, empowered, and taught his human nature; in fact, the Spirit's distinct mission comes to light: to mediate Christ's ministry and mission in his life and in the church through the empowerment of the Spirit. The *COGE*, therefore, depicts a Spirit christological paradigm of pneumatic mediation which acknowledges and freely integrates Logos Christology.

The Whole Truth

With roots extending back to 1897, the Church of God In Christ (COGIC), with headquarters in Memphis, Tennessee, was led into Pentecostalism by its founder Charles Harrison Mason after he had received Spirit baptism at the Azusa Street Mission. The majority of the COGIC constituents accepted Mason's full gospel of Pentecostalism and reorganized the COGIC as a Pentecostal movement (September 1907). Mason was elected General Overseer, and the movement's official periodical, *The Whole Truth*, began publication at Argenta, Arkansas.[46] The original editor was D.J. Young and Justus

---

[46] C.H. Mason (1866–1961) was born on a farm in a community – today known as Bartlett, Tennessee – nearby Memphis, Tennessee. Mason's parents, who were former African American slaves, reared him in the environment of a Missionary Baptist home. Mason was baptized at the age of 13 and began giving testimony as a lay preacher. He was licensed as an ordained minister in 1891, and in 1893 he received the experience of sanctification and began studies at Arkansas Baptist College. After being disillusioned with the higher criticism taught at the college, Mason left the institution in 1894. In 1895 Mason became acquainted with C.P. Jones who also had experienced sanctification. Mason and Price began (1896–99) holding holiness conventions, preaching, and publishing in periodicals proclaiming sanctification as a 'second blessing' subsequent to justification, which caused much debate among Baptists; eventually, this led to Mason and Jones establishing a new African American holiness movement (1897), the Church of God In Christ (COGIC). After hearing about the Pentecostal outpouring at Az-

Bowe succeeded him. The periodical consisted of four pages and was published 'at no set time, but at such times as the Lord leads and provides the means'.[47] The COGIC insisted that its content 'shall be strictly based upon the plain teaching of the Holy Scriptures, and with testimonies of what God is truly doing for us and through us in fulfilling his word of promise'.[48]

Though only one extant issue of *The Whole Truth* remains, it reveals a Spirit christological bent in Mason's theology; especially, apropos to his view of the Spirit's anointing and Spirit baptism.

> 'The Spirit of the Lord God is upon me; because the Lord hath anointed me to preach good tidings unto the meek,' Isaiah 61.1. The prophet, speaking by the Spirit of God, prophesied of Jesus and his office as a minister of God, showing that this office can only be filled by those who have been anointed of the Lord and have the Spirit poured out upon them. It is one thing to be anointed of the Lord, and to have the Spirit of the Lord upon you is another ... Jesus was anointed or sanctified when he came

---

usa Street, Mason traveled to Los Angeles to investigate the reports (March 1907). During his five weeks participation in the revival, he received Spirit baptism; then, he returned to Memphis preaching the full gospel of Pentecostalism, which caused a division between Mason and Charles Price Jones, the co-founder of the COGIC. The followers of Jones remained within the holiness movement, while Mason and his supporters reorganized the COGIC as a Pentecostal movement (September 1907). It is important to note that this was an interracial movement, for it contained Caucasian members, and several white congregations merged with the COGIC (1910–14). These congregations, however, left the COGIC in 1914, joining in founding the Hot Springs organizational meeting of the Assemblies of God. Mason served as General Overseer of the COGIC from 1907–61, so basically the story of C.H. Mason and the history of the COGIC are synonymous. For information about Mason's life and ministry and the history of the COGIC, see Mary Mason, *The History and Life Work of Elder C.H. Mason Chief Apostle and His Co-Laborers* (1987 repr.; No publisher or location, 1924); Ithiel C. Clemmons, *Bishop C.H. Mason* (Bakersfield, CA: Pneuma Life Publishing, 1996); Synan, *The Holiness-Pentecostal Tradition*, pp. 125-26; Elnora L. Lee, *A Life Fully Dedicated to God* (No publisher or location, 1967); Elsie Mason, *The Man, Charles Harrison Mason (1866–1961)* (Wayne M. and W.L. Porter. Memphis, TN: Pioneer Series Publication, 1979 repr.; No publisher, location or date); J.O. Patterson, German R. Ross, and Julia Mason Atkins, *History and Formative Years of the Church of God in Christ with Excerpts from the Life and Works of Its Founder – Bishop C.H. Mason* (Memphis, TN: Church of God in Christ Publishing House, 1969); J.C. Clemmons, 'Mason, Charles Harrison', *NIDPCM*, pp. 865-67.

[47] *TWT* 4.4 (Oct. 1911), p. 2.
[48] *TWT* 4.4 (Oct. 1911), p. 2.

into the world, but after he was baptized of John the Father sent the Holy Spirit upon him while he prayed.[49]

Some observations emerge from this text. First, Mason distinguishes between being anointed by the Spirit in sanctification and receiving Spirit baptism, even though whomever the Spirit baptizes operates in the Spirit's anointing. The Spirit anointed Jesus in the incarnation; nonetheless, at the Jordan the Spirit came upon Jesus or baptized him in the Spirit. Likewise, the Spirit anoints or sanctifies Christians prior to receiving Spirit baptism. Second, this text discloses the Spirit's agency in Christ's ministry. The empowering of the Spirit enabled and validated Jesus' ministry; correspondingly, Spirit baptism becomes a requisite experience for ministerial office. The Spirit, therefore, was integral to Christ's life and ministry.

Mason based his Christology and fivefold gospel on a Spirit christological foundation. The Spirit anointed Jesus in the incarnation; probably, this refers to the Western Spirit christological tradition of ascribing to the Spirit the conception of Christ's human nature and joining it to the divine nature. The Spirit, thus, sanctified or anointed Christ's human nature. Jesus' Spirit baptism, however, was a real event of empowerment, equipping him for ministry. Mason, accordingly, supports a Spirit christological paradigm of pneumatic mediation.

The Pentecostal Holiness Advocate

The Pentecostal Holiness Church was founded through the amalgamation of three holiness groups (1911–15): the Fire Baptized-Holiness Church, Pentecostal Holiness Church, and Tabernacle Presbyterian Church.[50] The General Convention of the Pentecostal

---

[49] C.H. Mason, 'The Spirit of God upon Us', *TWT* 4.4 (Oct. 1911), p. 4.

[50] The Fire-Baptized Holiness Association originated in 1895 and was led by its founder B.H. Irwin. After Irwin confessed to living in sin in 1900, J.H. King picked up the mantle of leadership, and the name of the movement was changed to the Fire-Baptized Holiness Church in 1902. Through the influence of G.B. Cashwell, King and several ministers received Spirit baptism in 1907, and in 1908 the movement included the Pentecostal doctrine of tongues in its expression of faith. After receiving second blessing sanctification in 1890, A.B. Crumpler (1863–1952) became a strong proponent of the holiness movement while remaining a minister in the Methodist Church. Through his efforts the North Carolina Holiness Association was formed in 1897, with Crumpler serving as president. After parting ways with the Methodist Church in 1898, Crumpler founded the Pentecostal Holiness Church in 1900 and began publishing *The Holiness Advocate*. Pentecostal was dropped from this designation in 1901, but after the church be-

Holiness Church in 1917 produced at least two monumental decisions. J.H. King (1869–1946), the former General Overseer of the Fire-Baptized Holiness Church, was elected as General Superintendent and continued to provide strong capable leadership until his death in 1946.[51] Also, *The Pentecostal Holiness Advocate* began weekly publication, consisting of 16 pages, as the official organ of The Pentecostal Holiness Church, with G.F. Taylor appointed to serve as editor. The first issue was produced May 3, 1917 in Falcon, North Carolina, and the place of publication moved to Franklin Springs, Georgia in 1918.

Although most early Pentecostal periodicals were reluctant to discuss ancient creedal statements, King and Taylor did not shy away from discussing these intricate issues in the *PHA*, in a manner depicting Pentecostalism as a restoration of apostolic faith and practice. These deliberations, containing several Spirit christological references, are found in several articles by King, and Taylor's presentation of the 'Basis of Union' – the doctrinal basis for the union of the Pentecostal Holiness Church and the Fire-Baptized Church – and a series of 'Sunday School Lessons' covering the

---

came part of the Pentecostal movement in 1908, over Crumpler's protests, in the wake of the Azusa Street Revival and Cashwell's evangelistic efforts, Pentecostal was reattached to the its name in 1909. Needless to say Crumpler did not retain leadership of this group; rather, A.H. Butler took the reign of leadership. The Fire-Baptized Church and the Pentecostal Holiness Church united in 1911, with S.D. Page elected to serve as its General Superintendent. After serving as the pastor of Second Presbyterian Church of Greenville, South Carolina, from 1892 through 1895, N.J. Holmes (1847–1919) received second blessing sanctification in 1896. Subsequently, he founded a holiness church (1896), the Tabernacle Presbyterian Church, and the Holmes Bible and Missionary Institute in 1898. Accepting the Pentecostal message Cashwell preached, Holmes was baptized in the Spirit and the entire Bible Institute entered the Pentecostal movement in 1907. In 1915 the Tabernacle Presbyterian Church merged with the Pentecostal Holiness Church; thus, the amalgamation was complete. Synan, *Oldtime Power*, pp. 43-149; Synan, *The Holiness-Pentecostal Tradition*, pp. 54-60, 62-64, 118-23; Alexander, *Pentecostal Healing*, pp. 123-27; Synan, 'Irwin', *NIDPCM*, pp. 804-805; Vinson Synan, 'Crumpler, Ambrose Blackman', *NIDPCM*, p. 566; Vinson Synan, 'Holmes, Nickels John', *NIDPCM*, p. 730.

[51] For information about King's life, ministry, and teachings, see J.H. King, *Yet Speaketh: Memoirs of the Late Bishop Joseph H. King* (Franklin Springs, GA: The Publishing House of the Pentecostal Holiness Church, 1949); J.H. King, *From Passover to Pentecost* (Memphis, TN: H.W. Dixon, 1914); J.H. King, *Christ – God's Love Gift* (Selected Writings of Joseph Hillery King 1; Franklin Springs, GA: Advocate Press, 1969); J.H. King, 'My Experience, *PHA*, 30.4 (May 23, 1946), pp. 6-7, 11-13, 16; Vinson Synan, 'King, Joseph Hillery', *NIDPCM*, pp. 822-23.

same topics, as well as his responses to certain questions posed by the readers. Regarding trinitarian theology, in his presentation of the 'Basis of Union' concerning Jesus Christ, Taylor affirms the veracity of the Nicean Creed, affirming the consubstantial nature of the Son and Father,[52] and the full personality of the Holy Spirit attested to by the first Council of Constantinople.[53] Interestingly, there appears to be some Eastern influence on Taylor's trinitarian theology; in agreement with early Syrian writers he affirms the inclusion of divine motherhood in trinitarian theology.[54] With regard to the immanent and economic Trinity, both King and Taylor support a form of trinitarian mystical fellowship.

> We note first its origin. It flows from heaven, and proceeds from the heart of the Father through that of the Son, and reaching our hearts by the inflow of the current of love. Love is but the exchange of hearts, and is the current that carries the essence and fullness of the one to the other; infinite, unutterable, eternal love, is the band that unites the heart of the Father and the Son in absolute, indissoluble, unity ... The unity existing in Godhead is reproduced in us, and the fellowship that is enjoyed between the Father and the Son is imparted to us ... The love current, fathomless and limitless in Godhead, marks the activity of the Holy Ghost ... The incoming of the Holy Ghost as a constant, ceaseless love current is the establishment and continuance of

---

[52] *PHA* 1.26 (Oct. 25, 1917), p. 4.

[53] *PHA* 1.37 (Jan. 10, 1918), pp. 4-5.

[54] Wisdom is the first product of the divine mind, and this personification is another name of Jesus Christ ... We hear much about the Fatherhood of God, but have heard but little concerning the Motherhood of God. There is a Fatherhood in God, and there is a Motherhood in God. Otherwise, there would be no births from above.

G.F. Taylor, 'Two Remarkable Women', *PHA* 1.12 (July 19, 1917), p. 8. 'What is wisdom, as it is used in Proverbs 8? Wisdom is the first product of the divine mind. It often refers to Christ. It carries the idea of the motherhood of God. There is a motherhood in God as well as a fatherhood.' G.F. Taylor, 'Question Box', *PHA* 1.37 (Jan. 10, 1918), p. 7. Though the idea of the motherhood of God was also prominent in Gnostic soteriology, given Taylor's position of the two natures of Christ, which will be examined shortly, more than likely, Taylor was influenced by early Syrian writers rather than Gnosticism.

this holy fellowship. The Pentecostal outpouring of the Spirit is the beginning of this in its fullness.[55]

Regarding the immanent Trinity, triune fellowship exists in love. Love is the band of unity in the Godhead, uniting the Father and Son and communicating the divine essence and fullness. The current of love flowing in the Godhead distinguishes the person of the Holy Spirit in immanent triune relationship and economic mission; it is the Spirit's mission to draw believers into the continuance of triune fellowship. Spirit baptism, therefore, ushers one into the fullness of this mystical triune fellowship.

According to Taylor, in the 'Basis of Union' regarding Spirit baptism, the premise for believers' Spirit baptism and initiation into triune fellowship is Jesus' experience of the Spirit in his life and mission.

> It is said (John 3.34) that Jesus received the Holy Spirit without measure, and this implies that we receive Him by measure. The prophet Joel spoke of a day when the Spirit would be given in a measure unknown to men of old (Joel 2.28). Joel's prophecy was fulfilled on the day of Pentecost (Acts 2.16) ... The Baptism of the Holy Spirit brings Him in a measure never received by man before the day of Pentecost ... We are also told (John 7.37-39) that this measure of the Spirit could not be given until Jesus was glorified ... Inasmuch as it was first received on the day of Pentecost, our Basis of Union calls it 'The Pentecostal baptism of the Holy Ghost and fire.' This Pentecostal Baptism establishes a relationship between man and God such as he has never had before. It brings to the heart a revelation of the Son of God. It is

---

[55] J.H. King, 'Fellowship', *PHA* 1.17 (Aug. 23, 1917), p. 2. Taylor repeats almost verbatim what King says in this article and extends it by stating,

> The Holy Spirit comes into us as a constant, ceaseless, love current to establish and continue this holy fellowship. The Baptism of the Spirit is the beginning of this in its fullness. There is a fellowship before the Baptism is received, but without the Baptism the fellowship cannot be enjoyed in its fullness. The Holy Spirit makes you know the fellowship that is in the Father and in the Son. Those who are living in the fullness of the Pentecostal experience are drawn into the infinite circuit of love's current flowing through ineffable Godhead.

G.F. Taylor, 'Sunday School Lessons', *PHA* 3.12, 13 (July 17, 24, 1919), p. 2.

the glorified Jesus coming back to dwell in us. It is Jesus crowned within. It is a revelation of the Trinity to the soul.[56]

Jesus received the Holy Spirit without measure so that believers through Spirit baptism could partake of the Spirit and the divine nature in a fuller manner than previously possible. Spirit baptism is the catching up of humans in the perichoretic dance of the divine; it is the indwelling of the triune God. Noticeably, Christ's humanity received the person of the Spirit at the Jordan, and in the Pentecostal experience it is the glorified Jesus returning to dwell in humans through the Spirit; in Christ's resurrection and glorification the Spirit assumed the nature of Christ, so that the indwelling of the Spirit and the glorified Jesus are synonymous.

To validate his position concerning Jesus' reception of the Spirit, Taylor cites the christological creed of Chalcedon, affirming two natures in one person. Taylor rejects the idea of the divine taking up humanity into itself and deifying Christ's humanity, so that Christ did not possess a human body like other humans and no room was left for the operation of the human will. His argument is summed up in his exposition of the 'Basis of Union' regarding Jesus Christ.[57] According to Taylor, Jesus is the human name given the savior, signifying his mission as the instrument of salvation, while the name Christ denotes the Spirit's anointing for that mission.

---

[56] G.F. Taylor, 'Basis of Union, ch. 14, The Baptism of the Holy Ghost', *PHA* 1.38 (Jan. 17, 1918), pp. 8-9. Cf. *PHA* 2.51 (Apr. 17, 1919), pp. 2-3; *PHA* 3.7, 8, (June 12, 19, 1919), p. 11.

> His baptism: This refers to both his baptism in water and the baptism of the Holy Ghost. He lived in all purity from infancy to manhood, till the time that he came to John to be baptized. No sin had ever been committed by him, no sin had any place in him. He possessed the spirit of perfect loyalty to God the Father, and his will was solely in the hands of God. He was to fulfill all things. Yea, all the righteousness of the law in the Spirit and in the letter also. On this ground he was baptized. It was an example of perfect obedience. And this was the ground of his Spirit baptism also … We are not purified by the baptism of the Holy Ghost, but we receive him because we are pure. Purity is not effected by the baptism but is a preparation for it. The Trinity was manifested in his baptism … Pentecost is a revelation of the Trinity in us. This is its distinctive feature.

King, *From Passover to Pentecost*, pp. 104-105.

[57] G.F. Taylor, 'Basis of Union, ch. 3, Jesus Christ', *PHA* 1.26 (Oct. 25, 1917), pp. 4-5.

Properly speaking, it can apply to Him only after He was anointed by the Father. He was anointed in the womb of the virgin, and from that moment was the Christ. His divine Sonship did not begin in the womb, in fact, it had no beginning; still this title points to His divinity, and implies His consecration and qualification for the work He undertook (John 10.36); while 'Son of God' is applicable to Him from eternity. 'Son of Man' is another phrase which the New Testament applies to Him. This name is applicable only from the point of conception. It refers directly to His humanity. The angel said to Mary: 'The Holy Ghost shall come upon thee, and the power of the Highest shall overshadow thee: therefore also that holy thing which shall be born of thee shall be called the Son of God.' This cannot mean that He is the *Son of God* by virtue of His conception in the womb of the virgin, for His conception was by the Holy Ghost. 'The *Holy Ghost* shall come upon thee;' and if it was by virtue of this act of the Holy Ghost that His divine Sonship is declared, then He is the Son of the Holy Spirit. Needless to say this is contrary to all revelation … He is the only begotten Son of the Father from all eternity, and He was conceived (incarnated) in the virgin Mary by the Holy Spirit. Mary was human, was MAN herself, and so she conceived 'that holy thing' (the humanity of Jesus), He was the Son of MAN.[58]

Here, Taylor sounds remarkably like several Syrian Antiochene theologians who supported a form of Spirit Christology within the boundaries of the christological confession of Chalcedon. Christ signifies the union of two natures in one person: the divine Son of God and the human nature, the Son of Man, conceived and anointed by the Spirit in the virgin's womb. The divine sonship did not begin in Mary's womb; rather, he eternally existed as the only begotten of the Father, so the Holy Spirit is not the progenitor of the Son of God. The Spirit, however, did anoint Christ in the virgin's womb; arguably, this refers to the Spirit's agency in the grace of un-

---

[58] G.F. Taylor, 'Basis of Union, ch. 3, Jesus Christ', *PHA* 1.26 (Oct. 25, 1917), pp. 4-5. Cf. G.F. Taylor, 'Sunday School Lessons', *PHA* 2.49 (Apr. 3, 1919), pp. 2-3.

ion, in which the Spirit conceives and sanctifies the human nature uniting it to the divine nature.[59]

Although the Spirit's anointing was present with Christ from conception, Taylor's emphasis on Christ's distinct human nature allows for the subsequent reception of the Spirit at the Jordan empowering him for his mission and overcoming temptation.[60]

> When Christ healed the sick while He was upon earth, it was not by the Deity that dwelt in His humanity. He said, 'If I cast out devils by the Spirit of God, then the Kingdom of God is come unto you.' Jesus healed by the Holy Ghost.[61]

Christ's miracles, accordingly, were wrought through the Spirit empowering his humanity. In fact, in Christ's life and ministry the Holy Spirit is the agent of 'the holy conception, Luke 1.35, anointing Him for service, Luke 4.14-18, raising Him from the dead, Rom. 8.11, so much so was He the executive power of God in the plan of redemption'.[62] In other words, the Spirit was the active agent mediating Christ's life and ministry.

The *PHA* affirms a Spirit Christology which fits within the boundaries of Chalcedon's christological confession, similar to the Antiochene position. The triune nature of God is affirmed, along with a position regarding the dual natures of Christ which allows for the Holy Spirit's agency in the conception of Christ's human nature and union with the divine nature, as well as anointing the human nature, empowering Christ for his salvific mission. Christ's experience of the Spirit becomes paradigmatic of believers' Spirit baptism and empowerment for service; moreover, when believers experience Spirit baptism, they receive the glorified Christ in the person of the Spirit. The Pentecostal experience, thus, catches up believers

---

[59] 'He was born of the Spirit, or we could say he was constituted man by the Holy Ghost. Everything in his nature was formed by the Spirit in connection with, and by, the use of the laws of nature in the virgin.' King, *From Passover to Pentecost*, p. 103. It is interesting to note that King posits that Christ was also sanctified during his circumcision, denoting the pattern for believers to follow: birth of the Spirit, circumcision of the heart in sanctification, and Spirit baptism. See, King, *From Passover to Pentecost*, pp. 102-105.

[60] *PHA* 1.2 (May 10, 1917), p. 4; 1.20 (Sept. 13, 1917), pp. 2, 13; 1.46 (Mar. 14, 1918), p. 4; 4.3 (May 20, 1920), p. 8.

[61] A.B. Simpson, 'Divine Healing', *PHA* 3.47 (Mar. 18, 1920), p. 4.

[62] R.B. Beall, 'The Holy Spirit as a Person', *PHA* 1.3 (May 17, 1917), p. 2. Cf. *PHA* 1.37 (Jan. 10, 1918), pp. 4-5; 3.41 (Feb. 5, 1920), p. 4.

in the perichoretic dance of triune fellowship. The *PHA*, therefore, depicts a Spirit Christology which amicably integrates Logos Christology into a paradigm of pneumatic mediation.

As the examination of the fivefold stream of early Pentecostal periodical literature closes, noteworthy is the fact that Spirit Christology seems to serve as the common basis of Pentecostal Christology and pneumatology.

The Fourfold Gospel Stream

With the emergence of William Durham's 'Finished Work' doctrine, in 1910, controversy ensued regarding the doctrine of sanctification as a second blessing; consequently, Pentecostalism divided into two steams. Those maintaining their roots in Wesleyan holiness continued to preach Pentecostalism's fivefold gospel, while those adhering to the 'Finished Work' doctrine coalesced justification and sanctification into the initial conversion experience, so that a fourfold gospel arose among Pentecostals: Jesus as Savior, Spirit Baptizer, Healer, and Coming King. This part will present three periodicals, which contain Spirit christological references, representing the 'Finished Work' stream of Pentecostalism: *The Latter Rain Evangel*, *The Pentecost*, and *The Pentecostal Testimony*. Then, it culminates in an examination of Oneness Pentecostalism.

The Latter Rain Evangel

William Hamner Piper (1868–1911), who served as a prominent and influential elder in Alexander Dowie's movement and Zion City, after disassociating himself from Dowie, moved to Chicago and founded the Stone Church (1906). Though early on Piper rejected the message and experience of Pentecostalism, he received Spirit baptism (Feb. 1908), and led the constituency of Stone Church into the Pentecostal movement.[63] Piper initiated *The Latter Rain Evangel* (Oct. 1908) as a monthly publication of the Stone Church, consisting of 24 pages, propagating Pentecostal teaching through printing

---

[63] Beginning in October 1908, the publication continued until June 1939. Piper served as editor until Anna C. Reiff succeeded him as editor. For information about Piper, see Edith L. Blumhofer, 'Piper, William Hamner', *NIDPCM*, pp. 989-90.

sermons, missionary and revival reports, and short theological treatises.[64]

In a sermon explicating the greater blessings of the Spirit available to believers after Christ's ascension, Piper credits the Spirit's agency in the incarnation of the divine Son. He begins by acknowledging the activity of the Son and Holy Spirit in ancient dispensations: they were in the world in a secondary sense, so that they were *with* and *upon* humans but not *in* them. Nevertheless, at the appropriate time the Son and Spirit became incarnate in human flesh.

> The incarnation of the Son is no more a reality than the incarnation of the Holy Spirit, and as heaven has been the abode of the Son for the last nineteen hundred years, just so has the church on earth been the abiding place of the Holy Spirit during the same time. The Holy Spirit became incarnate on the day of Pentecost; the Son of God became incarnate when conceived by the Holy Ghost and born of the Virgin Mary.[65]

It is important to note that Piper is not advocating a Spirit Christology of pneumatic inspiration, but an actual incarnation of the divine Son *abiding* in human flesh through the Spirit mediating the act of conception. The incarnation of the Spirit in Christ's disciples, however, is not as clear. Here, it seems that Piper is distinguishing between the Spirit *inspiring* and *anointing* humans before Pentecost and the *abiding* presence of the Spirit in Christ's disciples after Pentecost constituting an incarnation of the Spirit. According to Piper, this incarnation of the Spirit is synonymous with Christ dwelling in the believer.[66]

---

[64] The periodical effectively elevated Stone Church's importance and extended its influence among Pentecostals, so that it hosted the second and seventh general councils of the Assemblies of God.

[65] W.H. Piper, 'The Expediency of Christ's Ascension: How Could His Departure Result in Greater Blessing to His Disciples?', *LRE* 1.8 (May 1909), p. 3.

[66] *LRE* 1.8 (May 1909), pp. 3-4. 'Christ was on the earth in His human body for only a short time, but at Pentecost He came through the Holy Spirit to stay.' M.B. Woodworth-Etter, 'Blasphemy against the Holy Ghost: God's Cyclone of Power a Great Leveler', *LRE* 5.11 (Aug. 1913), p. 20. It is significant that in later issues when discussing the Spirit's role in the incarnation, the emphasis shifts more toward a Logos form of Christology accenting the Son as the Word while the stress on the Spirit's activity diminishes. See *LRE* 6.5 (Feb. 1914), p. 2; 6.9 (June 1914), p. 21.

The two natures of Christ, divine and human, are readily confessed along with the Spirit enduing the human nature with power to accomplish Christ's ministry: overcoming temptations, performing miracles, and the resurrection.[67] An article by A.B. Simpson addresses these issues by comparing the lives and ministries of Elisha, after receiving a double portion of the Spirit, with Jesus Christ. Of course, the pivotal point of their ministries was the reception of the Spirit at the Jordan.

> Such an experience came to Christ Himself as He stood upon the banks of the Jordan and the heavens opened; a new presence and a new personality came into His life, and He went forth, no longer one person, but two, united with the mighty Holy Ghost, and from that hour everything He did was through that anointing and indwelling Holy Spirit.[68]

According to Simpson, though Christ is one person, two divine personalities – the Holy Spirit and divine Son – unite in Christ, but Christ's humanity fulfills its mission through the agency of the Spirit's anointing. The Spirit's indwelling and empowering Christ, thus, becomes the example of his disciples fulfilling the church's mission in the Spirit.[69]

---

[67] Jesus took upon Himself this human nature of ours that He might enter into sympathetic relationship with you and me and know what it was to be tempted, and to know also the power of victory in this life ... Immediately after His baptism being full of the Holy Ghost, Jesus was led of the Spirit into the wilderness and there for forty days and forty nights, while fasting and praying, He was subjected to temptation.

A.L. Fraser, 'All Things Shall Be Subdued Unto God', *LRE* 7.4 (Jan. 1915), p. 3.

But if the Spirit of Him that raised up Jesus from the dead dwell in you, He that raised up Christ from the dead shall also quicken (or add life to) your mortal bodies by His Spirit that dwelleth in you. In a sense, two persons were raised from the dead; Jesus the human, and Christ the divine, and because Jesus was the Christ and now lives on the throne as our human brother, we may have His resurrection life in our mortal bodies, healing and preserving them.

D. Wesley Myland, 'In Deaths Oft', *LRE* 2.2 (Nov. 1909), p. 16.

[68] A.B. Simpson, 'The Double Portion: Striking Lessons from the Life of Elisha', *LRE* 2.2 (Nov. 1909), p. 6. It is significant to note that in later issues the stress on Christ's reception of the Spirit at the Jordan shifts to a *realization* of what he already possessed. *LRE* 8.9 (July 1916), p. 3. This corresponds more to the form of Spirit Christology advocated by Augustine.

[69] *LRE* 3.9 (June 1911), pp. 21-22; 5.11 (Aug. 1913), p. 19; 6.12 (Sept. 1914), p. 18.

The Latter Rain Evangel posits a Spirit Christology corresponding to an early form in the Western tradition. Since trinitarian theology is stringently affirmed, the *LRE* integrates Logos Christology with Spirit Christology. The Spirit functions as the agent of Christ's incarnation, ministry, and resurrection. The *LRE* supports a Spirit christological paradigm of pneumatic mediation set within a triune framework.

The Pentecost

The Pentecost began as a monthly eight-page publication in Indianapolis, Indiana edited by J. Roswell Flower.[70] By early 1909 Flower had moved to Kansas City, Missouri and continued publication of the periodical, and A.S. Copley joined him as co-editor.[71] In 1910, the November-December issue rolled from the press with Copley as the sole editor of the periodical, and in 1911 Copley changed the name of the publication to *Grace and Glory*. In agreement with previous articles published by Copley and included in this inquiry, Copley's contributions to *The Pentecost* and editorship demonstrate support for Spirit Christology.

The bulk of the Spirit christological references are included in two series of articles. The first series, 'The Seven Dispensational Parables', drawn from Mt. ch. 13, sets forth Jesus' teaching concerning the mysteries of the kingdom of God and connects these parables with seven dispensations of God's redemptive schema.[72] The second series, 'Pentecost in Type', depicts how the Pentecostal experience was foreshadowed in the Hebrew Scriptures.[73] Both se-

---

[70] J. Roswell Flower (1888–1970) rose to prominence in the Assemblies of God, serving as its secretary-treasurer and assistant superintendent. For information about Flower's life and ministry, see Gary B. McGee, 'Flower, Joseph James Roswell', *NIDPCM*, pp. 642-43.

[71] Copley's ministry was located in Kansas City, and Flower moved there and assisted Copley's ministry. Flower described this move as being in the will of God and receiving confirmation after his arrival in Kansas City. For Flower's report about the move and Copley's welcoming response, see, *The Pentecost* 1.6 (April-May 1909), p. 6.

[72] This series begins in *The Pentecost* 1.3 (Nov. 1908), p. 1 and continues through 1.7 (June 1909), p. 7.

[73] This exposition continues through eight articles, beginning in *The Pentecost* 1.8 (July 1909), p. 7 and continues through 2.3 (Feb. 1910), p. 5. Seven articles present seven types of Pentecost: the dove, fire, oil, wine, wind, water, and the eyes of the Lord. The eight article summaries the previous seven.

ries acknowledge his baptism in the Jordan as the point of Jesus' reception of the Spirit and the Spirit empowering Jesus for ministry.

> Briefly stated, these four gospel records set forth the character, life, labors and destiny of Jesus anointed from four points of view, viz: 'Jesus as King' (by Matthew), 'Jesus as Servant' (by Mark), 'Jesus as Man (by Luke), 'Jesus as God' (by John).[74]

> Then the Spirit came upon Jesus, who, 'through the Eternal Spirit, offered Himself without spot to God,' whereby the waters of just divine wrath were assuaged.[75]

> As truly as you need Christ the Saviour, so truly you need the Holy Spirit the Comforter. If Jesus needed the anointing with the Holy Spirit and power (Acts 10.38) and the infant assembly needed the baptism with the Spirit, the enduement with power, how much less do we need that baptism today?[76]

> It was through the presence and power of the Spirit that the Son of God endured the sufferings in the garden and the cross ... All of Christ's toil and teaching were through the Spirit, and no blessing of God can come to us apart from Him ... The oil was a sign and seal ... Concerning Jesus, the Father said: 'This is my beloved Son.' The descent of the Holy Spirit upon Him was the sign and seal of the divine selection, 'for Him hath God the Father sealed,' Jn 6.28 [sic].[77]

---

[74] A.S. Copley, 'The Seven Dispensational Parables', *The Pentecost* 1.3 (Nov. 1908), p. 1.

[75] A.S. Copley, 'Pentecost in Type, The First Type – The Dove', 1.8 (July 1909), p. 7. Copley picks up on Noah releasing the dove three times from the ark. The first time the dove was released it found no place to rest, so it returned to the ark. The second time it returned with an olive branch. The third time it did not return. Using these events as types of Pentecost, Copley assigns the first release of the dove to correlate with the Spirit finding very few humans on which the Spirit could rest. Corresponding to this quotation, the second release of the dove correlates with the Spirit's descent and resting in Jesus Christ, so that Christ performs his salvific ministry in the power of the Spirit and presents the olive branch of peace, in behalf of humanity, to the Father. The third release of the Spirit correlates with the Spirit's descent on the Day of Pentecost, so the Spirit has not yet returned to the Father but remains in the church.

[76] A.S. Copley, 'Pentecost in Type, The Second Type – Fire', *The Pentecost* 1.9 (Aug. 1909), p. 8.

[77] A.S. Copley, 'Pentecost in Type, The Third Type – Oil', *The Pentecost* 1.10 (Sept. 1909), pp. 5, 6. (The correct Johannine reference is Jn 6.27.) 'Jesus enjoyed

Jesus was born of the Spirit. Thirty years later, He was just as really anointed with the Spirit. From His birth He was 'holy, harmless, undefiled, separate from sinners' and lived in victory for these thirty years. But at the age of thirty, He received power from on high to live and labor for others – Acts 10.37 [*sic*] ... Hence He must receive the anointing of which the anointing, of the high priest, the prophets and kings were types.[78]

Several conclusions emerge from these texts. First, the Spirit's descent upon Jesus sealed him, identifying him as the chosen messiah and revealing him as the divine Son of God. Second, the four gospels depict Jesus fulfilling varying roles anointed by the Spirit. Third, the Spirit's anointing upon Jesus' human nature was essential to every aspect of Christ's ministry: teaching, toil, miracles, overcoming temptation, and sufferings. Fourth, the Spirit's anointing established him in the offices of priest, prophet, and king; the anointing functioned as the divine commissioning to service. Fifth, Christ's anointing for ministry is paradigmatic for fulfilling the church's mission; the same power is essential for the contemporary church to conduct ministry.[79] So, the descent of the Spirit, at the Jordan, was not merely symbolic; rather, Christ received a definite empowering experience of the Spirit.

The Spirit's agency permeates every aspect of Christ's life and ministry. The Spirit is the agent of the incarnation; Christ is born of the Spirit. Christ fulfilled his mission in the power of the Spirit, salvifically offering his life as a sacrifice for sin. After Pentecost, the Spirit mediates the fullness of Christ in believers through the Pentecostal experience, so that the church accomplishes its ministry in the Spirit. *The Pentecost*, therefore, supports a Spirit christological paradigm of pneumatic mediation, while integrating Logos Christology.

---

perfect victory for thirty years before he received His anointing with the Spirit.' A.S. Copley, 'Sanctification', *The Pentecost* 1.2 (Sept. 1908), p. 7. Cf. *The Pentecost* 1.1 (Aug. 1908), p. 5.

[78] A.S. Copley, 'Contrasts Worthy of Study', *The Pentecost* 2.9-10 (Sept.-Oct. 1910), p. 16.

[79] In fact, to receive the fullness and power of the Spirit is to receive the fullness of Jesus. *The Pentecost* 1.1 (Aug. 1908), p. 8; 1.4 (Dec. 1908), p. 10.

The Pentecostal Testimony

William H. Durham received Spirit baptism at the Azusa Street Mission in 1907 and returned to Chicago with the message of Pentecost, so that the church he pastored, the North Avenue Mission, became a major center of Pentecostalism in the Midwest.[80] Durham's notoriety among Pentecostals increased when he began publishing and editing *The Pentecostal Testimony* in 1909; varying in lengths (12-16 pages), publication continued sporadically until Durham's death in 1912. Although Durham had previously accepted and preached the 'second blessing' sanctification doctrine, by 1910 he began preaching his Finished Work doctrine which conjoined justification and sanctification in the conversion experience.[81]

---

[80] William H. Durham (1873–1912) was converted in 1898 as a member of the Baptist Church and forthwith entered full-time ministry. He began serving as pastor of the North Avenue Mission in Chicago in 1901. After receiving Spirit baptism (March 2, 1907), the church he pastored became an international center for the propagation of Pentecostalism, and he garnered much personal influence. Although his Finished Work doctrine caused great controversy among Pentecostals, it had little effect among the Southern Pentecostal movements: Church of God (Cleveland, TN), Church of God in Christ, and the Pentecostal Holiness Church. Charles Parham and William Seymour vigorously opposed Durham's doctrine. Seymour had Durham locked out of the Azusa Street Mission. Also, it is reported that Charles Parham prophesied Durham's untimely death, before the event, as judgment for teaching this 'heresy'. For overviews of Durham's life, ministry, and role in the Finished Work controversy, see Synan, *The Holiness-Pentecostal Tradition*, pp. 149-52; Faupel, *The Everlasting Gospel*, pp. 229-45; Richard M. Riss, 'Durham, William H.', *NIDPCM*, pp. 594-95; Brumback, *Suddenly ... From Heaven*, pp. 98-106; Anderson, *Vision of the Disinherited*, pp. 166-67.

[81] According to Durham's testimony in the *AF*, it appears that he affirms his own experience of sanctification subsequent to conversion, placing him in the Wesleyan Holiness camp before he received his Spirit baptism:

> Nine years ago I was deeply convicted of sin, through the Bible and the Spirit moving upon me, which He continued to do till I truly repented of my sins, and earnestly sought the Lord, finally yielding all to Him, and pleading His mercy. He revealed to my heart Christ dying on the cross, and His voice whispered to me, 'Christ died for your sins.' Instantly my heart believed, and His peace flooded my soul, and the joy of His salvation was wonderful to me. Later I saw and grasped by faith the truth of sanctification, and the Spirit witnessed to my heart that the work was done, and the Holy Ghost wonderfully wrought in my life.

W.H. Durham, 'A Chicago Evangelist's Pentecost', *AF* 1.6 (Feb.-Mar. 1907), p. 4. In a later testimony regarding his conversion, his testimony remains fairly consistent, but Durham denies the reality of receiving second-blessing sanctification:

> I was a new creature and knew it, and God was with me all the time and was so real and precious to me, and for months I walked in a heavenly state; till finally I began to lose the victory on some lines and again to set my face to

Along with making occasional evangelistic treks to Los Angeles to reinvigorate the Pentecostal revival there and to persuade Pentecostals to accept his Finished Work doctrine, *The Pentecostal Testimony* functioned as a major tool to spread Durham's Finished Work teaching; in fact, Durham used the *PT* as a polemical forum to refute fivefold Pentecostalism.[82]

Within the six extant issues of the periodical, there are two clear Spirit christological references. The first occurrence is found in a theological treatise regarding the sealing function of the Spirit. Throughout this article, Durham argues that the Spirit sealing believers has nothing to do with regeneration or sanctification but everything to do with Spirit baptism.

> Even of Christ it is said in John 6.27, 'Him the Father, even God, hath *sealed*.' The context shows this sealing does not refer to God's saving or regenerating the Son, for he never needed this, but to an act by which God bestowed on the Son *authority* to give men 'food which abideth unto eternal life.' This sealing with authority was through the anointing of the Holy Spirit, for Jesus 'by the Spirit of God cast out demons' and gave 'com-

---

seek God. I was told that sanctification was what I needed, and I sought this blessing the best I knew how for a long time. Sometimes I would think the work was done, then again would realize that it was not, till finally, some three years after my conversion, God gave me light and grace to definitely trust the blood of Christ and rest my faith on His finished works. And when I did this the Spirit witnessed that I was sanctified.

William Durham, 'Personal Testimony of Pastor Durham', *PT* 1.1 (n.d.), pp. 5-6. Cf. Alexander, *Pentecostal Healing*, p. 150.

[82] Durham's challenge to the fivefold gospel paradigm contained four central premises. First, Scripture does not contain any example of sanctification occurring as a second definite work of grace. Second, the advocates of second blessing sanctification appeal to John Wesley for authority to teach the doctrine instead of the authority of Scripture. Third, though Wesley concedes that sanctification begins in conversion, Wesley's teaching on the subject is based on experience, not Scripture; likewise, teachers of sanctification as a second definite work of grace base their teaching on experience. Fourth, the Scriptures teach that believers are sanctified 'in Christ' at conversion, which is the true biblical teaching; they are 'identified' with Christ. See William Durham 'Sanctification, the Bible Does Not Teach that It Is a Second Work of Grace', *PT*, 1.8 (Aug. 1911), pp. 1-3. Here, Durham presents his confession of the 'Finished Work' doctrine in response to the correspondence and reaction he received from an earlier article he published in the previous issue of the *PT* 1.7 (since this issue is not extant, and the periodical was not published on regular basis, the date of publication is uncertain). This polemical tone permeates the various issues of the periodical.

mandments through the Holy Spirit unto the apostles,' and on the cross 'through the eternal Spirit offered Himself without blemish unto God' to provide this eternal life for us. Now it was immediately after Jesus was baptized in water by John that God bestowed on Him the Holy Spirit and bore testimony of His sonship ... Beyond all doubt this is the time when the 'Father anointed and sealed the Son with the Spirit and power.'[83]

According to Durham, when Christ received the Spirit at the Jordan, the Father sealed Christ with the Spirit. This sealing was not a symbolic event but a vital experience in Christ's life and ministry, bearing witness to Christ's deity and bestowing authority and power upon Christ's humanity to confirm and fulfill his salvific ministry. Moreover, the sealing function of the Spirit in Christ's life and ministry serves as a paradigm for believers' pneumatic empowerment for ministry.

The other text is found in a theological discussion about false doctrines; specifically, Durham was refuting a doctrine that taught that Spirit baptism and the new birth were synonymous: since the fullness of the Godhead dwells in Christ bodily, when someone receives Christ, they also receive the Holy Spirit.[84] Durham, neverthe-

---

[83] William Durham, 'Sealed with the Spirit', *PT* 1.1 (n.d.), p. 12.

[84] Durham states that about four years prior to this article, there appeared among Pentecostals the teaching that the new birth and Spirit baptism was synonymous, but Pentecostal leaders withstood this doctrine by affirming that the Holy Spirit will not dwell in an unclean temple, so that only a 'saved' person could receive Spirit baptism. According to Durham, at the time of his writing this article, this doctrine reappeared in two forms:

> One form of this teaching is to the effect that, as in Christ dwells all the fulness of the Godhead bodily, and as Christ is received when a man is saved, all who receive Christ at the same time receive the Holy Spirit. In other words they claim that it means one and the same thing to receive Christ, and to receive the Holy Spirit. This is a false interpretation of Scripture ... Every one we have met that taught the above wrong doctrine has seemed to be afraid to come out boldly with it. With one breath they will teach it, and with the next breath deny that they believe it. Sometimes they say they do not think it is time to preach it yet ... Another branch of this doctrine is that the baptism in the Spirit is *the* witness of the Spirit, that only those who have the baptism in the Spirit have the witness of the Spirit to their acceptance with God. Both these doctrines mean the same thing – that men are not saved till they are baptized in the Holy Spirit. Both are equally and wholly false.

William Durham, 'False Doctrines', *PT* 2.2 (May 1912), p. 6. It is also interesting to note that in this same article, according to Durham,

less, asserts that although the triune God is one, the Scripture refers to the members of the Godhead as distinct persons.

> On different sides we hear people, when they get in a corner, cry out, 'You cannot divide the Trinity.' Go with us to the Jordan, where Jesus was baptized, Mt. 3.16-17. Here we see the Trinity. Jesus Christ, the second Person of the Trinity, was baptized. When he came up from the water the Holy Spirit fell on Him ... It is one thing to receive Jesus Christ, and it is another thing to receive the Holy Spirit.[85]

So, Durham's refutation asserted that the Spirit descending upon Christ's humanity distinguished the person of the Spirit from the person of the eternal Son incarnated in Christ. This event also distinguished the divine and human natures of the one person of Christ. Christ's human nature received the Spirit's anointing. Noteworthily, the Spirit also anoints and mediates the role of the divine nature in Christ. The Spirit descended upon the eternal Son, delineating the kenotic and perichoretic relationship of the Holy Spirit and the eternal divine Son in Christ's salvific mission: the Spirit pours into the Son, revealing the Son's identity and taking the lead in the divine dance. Christ's reception of the Spirit at the Jordan, moreover, elucidates and distinguishes the sequential salvific order: a person receives Christ in conversion; subsequently, that person can receive Spirit baptism.

Similar to other Pentecostals, Durham stresses the significance of Christ's reception of the Spirit in his life and ministry: the Spirit seals Christ with authority and power to cast out devils, heal the

---

> Another doctrine which we believe should be classed as false is the teaching that converts should be baptized in the name of Jesus only. In Mt. 28.19 Jesus, after His resurrection, gives His instructions to His Disciples just before leaving them, and He said, 'Baptizing them into the Name of the Father and of the Son and of the Holy Spirit.' To our mind there is no conflict between this plain command and those in Acts, where it is only mentioned that they were baptized into the Name of Jesus. One who is baptized into the Name of the Father, Son and Holy Spirit is baptized into the Name of Jesus.

William Durham, 'False Doctrines', *PT* 2.2 (May 1912), p. 7. Durham concludes this article by stating that 'the object of our paper is not to see how many false doctrines we can run down, but to set forth God's real message for today, which consists of the Finished Word of Calvary, and the truth concerning the baptism in the Holy Spirit'. William Durham, 'False Doctrines', *PT* 2.2 (May 1912), p. 7.

[85] William Durham, 'False Doctrines', *PT* 2.2 (May 1912), p. 6.

sick, and be offered as a sacrifice for sin. Durham, therefore, posits a Spirit Christology of pneumatic mediation which integrates Logos Christology and triune doctrine.

Owing to his untimely death, Durham never authored a monograph he had planned explicating his christocentric doctrine,[86] so Durham's Finished Work doctrine remained somewhat undeveloped, bequeathing to Pentecostalism a troubling legacy. His doctrine marked the first and second major schisms in Pentecostalism. First, Pentecostalism divided into two streams: Wesleyan Holiness and Finished Work. Afterward, various groups which followed Durham's teaching amalgamated in 1914 forming the Assemblies of God. Within this group's early periodicals there was a definite shift away from Spirit Christology to Logos Christology with a pneumatological emphasis.[87] Arguably, among the majority of Finished

---

[86] *PT* 2.3 (July 1912), p. 16.

[87] I make this conclusion because after examining the early periodicals, during this period, associated with this movement – *Word and Witness*, *The Christian Evangel*, and *The Weekly Evangel* which is the official publication of the Assemblies of God – I could not find any clear references bearing the characteristics of Spirit Christology. Perhaps, the following quote from E.N. Bell, who edited these publications, expresses their concern in this shift to Logos Christology:

> No one is more glad at the present Latter Rain outpouring of the Holy Ghost than this writer; yet I fear that some of our dear brethren are making the Holy Spirit practically our Savior. Whenever that is done Christ is obscured, and the vision of Him as the only Redeemer of mankind is dimmed. Faith is directed to the wrong place. The object of this article is to uncover Christ Jesus, to bring Him more fully to light, to give Him His rightful place in our mind and in our preaching, to exalt Him and give Him the honor due unto His great and glorious name.

E.N. Bell, 'Jesus the Great Life-Giving Spirit: The Holy Ghost Not a Savior, Christ Our Life, *WE*, 99 (July 17, 1915), p. 2. Cf. *WW*, 12.8 (Aug. 1915), p. 4. The concerns that Bell expresses in this article are classical rejoinders which proponents of Logos Christology use to diminish the influence of Spirit Christology: Spirit Christology obscures and denigrates the salvific vision of Christ, so that the Holy Spirit intrudes into Christ's rightful place of exaltation, honor, worship, and faith. More than likely, this move was a reaction to the 'New Issue' and its development. For example, several members of the Assemblies of God presbytery released a personal statement stating their position in preparation for a council (Oct. 10–11, 1915) regarding the 'New Issue'. Of the seven topics discussed, three of them depict their opinions concerning the Spirit's role in Christ's life and ministry: (1) the new birth and Spirit baptism are not synonymous, (2) the Holy Spirit is not the blood of Christ, and (3) the word Christ does not mean the Holy Ghost. 'Personal Statement', *WE*, 108 (Sept. 18, 1915), p. 2. Cf. 'Resolution on Doctrinal Matters', *WE*, 145 (June 24, 1916), p. 8; 'Personal Statement', *WW*, 12.10 (Oct. 1915), p. 4.

498   Spirit Christology

Work proponents, as Durham's doctrine developed it would alter the pneumatic-christological center, which had emerged in the ethos of early Pentecostalism, to a christocentric focus on Christ's atonement and Logos Christology. Second, Oneness Pentecostalism emerged within the Assemblies of God around 1914 and because of the ensuing controversy parted ways in 1916. Although maintaining a focus on Logos Christology, Oneness Pentecostalism with its christocentric piety and radical emphasis on Jesus' name retained space for Spirit Christology in their theological schema.

Oneness Pentecostalism

Oneness Pentecostalism emerged in the midst of the theological flux created by Durham's *unfinished* Finished Work doctrine.[88] In coalescing the new birth and sanctification into the conversion experience he had posited it as identification with Christ, according to Romans chapter six, and this identification was demonstrated through water baptism by using the Acts 2.38 formula.[89] Identifica-

---

[88] For overviews of the various influences which contributed to the rise of Oneness Pentecostalism, see David Reed, *'In Jesus' Name': The History and Beliefs of Oneness Pentecostals* (JPTSup 31; Blandford Forum, UK: Deo, 2008), pp. 9-135; David Reed, 'Aspects of the Origins of Oneness Pentecostalism', in Vinson Synan (ed.), *Aspects of Pentecostal-Charismatic Origins* (Plainfield, NJ: Logos International, 1975), pp. 143-68; David K. Bernard, *A History of Christian Doctrine* (3 vols.; Hazelwood, MO: Word Aflame Press, 1995), III, pp. 9-63; Thomas A. Fudge, *Christianity without the Cross: A History of Salvation in Oneness Pentecostalism* (Parkland, FL: Universal Publishers), pp. 9-45, 58-59; Talmadge L. French, *Our God Is One: The Story of Oneness Pentecostals* (Indianapolis: Voice & Vision Publications, 1999), pp. 31-56; Fred J. Foster, *Think It Not Strange: A History of the Oneness Movement* (St. Louis: Pentecostal Publishing House, 1965), pp. 9-51; Daniel L. Butler, *Oneness Pentecostalism: A History of the Jesus Name Movement* (Cerritos, CA: Daniel A. Butler, 2004), pp. 19-82; David Reed, 'Oneness Pentecostalism', *NIDPCM*, pp. 936-37; Faupel, *The Everlasting Gospel*, pp. 270-80; Doug Hogsten, 'The Monadic Formula of Water Baptism: A Quest for Primitivism Via a Christocentric and Restorationist Impulse', *JPT* 17 (2008), pp. 70-95.

[89] According to Durham,

When we appeal the case to the Scriptures, we see that They teach to repent and be baptized and receive the Holy Spirit, Acts 2.38-39. All through the Acts and the Epistles of Paul, we see this order of teaching. Not one single Scripture ever mentions any second work of grace. But the rule laid down by Peter on the day of Pentecost is continually followed, both in teaching and practice ... In Paul's letter to the Romans and the sixth chapter, he makes the teaching so clear and plain that a child can readily understand it ... He proceeds to ask them, if they do not know that all who are baptized into Jesus Christ are baptized into His death. He then illustrates, in the most beautiful and yet the most simple way possible, the real plan of salvation. A death, bur-

tion with Christ through baptism in Jesus' name was essential to the rise of Oneness Pentecostalism; in fact, this 'New Issue' arose among the Finished Work stream of Pentecostalism through the teachings of Durham's closest associates.[90] R.E. McAlister raised the issue of baptizing in the name of Jesus during a sermon he preached in a camp meeting (April 1913) at Arroyo Seco, outside Los Angeles.[91] According to McAlister, though with certain variations, the Book of Acts records water baptism being performed with the christological formula in the name of the Lord-Jesus-Christ, which is the christological equivalent of the triune name Father, Son, Holy Spirit.[92] The sermon stirred a mixed reaction among the congrega-

---

ial and a resurrection clearly expresses it. Christian baptism is a beautiful symbol of it. Identification is the plain teaching of this Scripture.

William Durham, 'The Finished Work of Calvary, Identification with Jesus Christ Saves and Sanctifies', *PT* 2.1 (Jan. 1912), p. 3. Cf. Reed, *In Jesus' Name*, pp. 87-94; Bernard, *Christian Doctrine*, III, pp. 43-52. It is interesting to note that originally the masthead of *The Pentecostal Testimony* carried Acts 2.4 as its Scriptural theme but later it changed to Acts 2.38. According to Daniel Butler, 'Durham had established water baptism and immersion, and inadvertently laid the ground work for the Oneness doctrine'. Butler, *Oneness Pentecostalism*, p. 87. David Bernard depicts five ways Durham influenced the rise of the Oneness movement. Bernard, *Christian Doctrine*, III, pp. 60-63. Faupel's assessment seems close to the mark:

More than half of the Pentecostal movement had recently followed Durham's lead in jettisoning their old understanding of entire sanctification in order to seek complete identification with the *person* of Jesus in his Finished Work of Calvary. It should come as little surprise that many would now be inclined to identify with the *name* of Jesus in the waters of baptism. Indeed the surprise is that so many Finished Work advocates did not'.

Faupel, *The Everlasting Gospel*, p. 306.

[90] Reed, *In Jesus' Name*, pp. 105-10. According to Reed, the list of close associates include: Frank Ewart, R.E. McAlister, Glen A. Cook, and Garfield T. Haywood. Cf. Butler, *Oneness Pentecostalism*, pp. 87-88.

[91] R.E. McAlister was a Canadian Finished Work proponent and was connected to Durham through Frank Ewart. Ewart was Durham's associate pastor at the Seventh Street Mission in Los Angeles and successor in ministry; McAlister became Ewart's associate and co-editor of *The Good Report* after Durham's death.

[92] The initial impetus of the Oneness movement occurred in Apr. 1913 at a highly publicized international pentecostal camp meeting in Arroyo Seco, outside Los Angeles. The moment came in a baptismal sermon by Canadian evangelist R.E. McAlister, in which he proposed that the reason the apostles baptized in the name of the Lord Jesus Christ (variations in Acts) instead of the triune name commanded by Jesus (Mt. 28.19) was that they understood 'Lord-Jesus-Christ' to be the christological equivalent of 'Father-Son-Holy Spirit.'

Reed, 'Oneness Pentecostalism', *NIDPCM*, p. 937. Cf. Bernard, *Christian Doctrine*, III, p. 64.

tion. After spending the night in prayer, John G. Scheppe proclaimed that he had received a revelation of the power of Jesus' name, and all true believers should be baptized in Jesus' name.[93]

Subsequently, Frank J. Ewart spent about one year formulating a foundation for a theology of Jesus's name. After Ewart preached his Oneness doctrine publically for the first time (April 15, 1914), several eminent Pentecostal ministers joined with him in quickly spreading this message throughout Finished Work Pentecostalism.[94] The leaders of the movement published three prominent periodicals to spread Oneness doctrine: Frank Ewart's *Meat in Due Season*, G.T. Haywood's *Voice in the Wilderness*, and D.C.O. Opperman's *The Blessed Truth*. These journals, however, are not accessible, so other sources will be employed. Several tracts written by Frank J. Ewart, Andrew D. Urshan, and Garfield T. Haywood are available.[95] The inquiry will proceed by narrowing the focus to Haywood's tract, *The Victim of the Flaming Sword*,[96] to mark out a cursory outline of One-

---

[93] Reed, *In Jesus' Name*, pp. 136-41; Bernard, *Christian Doctrine*, III, pp. 63-65; Fudge, *Christianity without the Cross*, pp. 45-46; Synan, *The Holiness-Pentecostal Tradition*, pp. 156-57; French, *Our God Is One*, pp. 57-58; Butler, *Oneness Pentecostalism*, pp. 83-85; Foster, *Think It Not Strange*, pp. 51-52; Faupel, *The Everlasting Gospel*, pp. 280-81; Brumback, *Suddenly from Heaven*, p. 191; Alexander, *Pentecostal Healing*, pp. 182-84; Anderson, *Vision of the Disinherited*, pp. 176-77.

[94] For the spread and development of Oneness Pentecostalism, see Reed, *In Jesus' Name*, pp. 136-66; Bernard, *Christian Doctrine*, III, pp. 65-75; Fudge, *Christianity without the Cross*, pp. 46-54; French, *Our God Is One*, pp. 59-159; Foster, *Think It Not Strange*, pp. 52-63; Reed, 'Oneness Pentecostalism', *NIDPCM*, pp. 936-40; Faupel, *The Everlasting Gospel*, pp. 290-301; Brumback, *Suddenly from Heaven*, pp. 191-210; Anderson, *Vision of the Disinherited*, pp. 177-94.

[95] These tracts can be found in Donald W. Dayton (ed.), *Seven 'Jesus Only' Tracts* (HCL; New York: Garland Publishing, 1985). Here, I am following the lead of Kimberly Alexander in getting at the sources:

> A tributary flowing out of the Finished Work stream is the Oneness Pentecostal movement. The leaders of this movement published prolifically, though no journals as such are extant. Therefore, in order to hear from this part of the tradition, other resourses are utilized.

Alexander, *Pentecostal Healing*, p. 70.

[96] Haywood notes in the introduction to this tract that these articles were originally published in the periodical *Voice in the Wilderness* and other publications. Garfield T. Haywood (1880–1931), an African American, was one of the most prominent and influential leaders of the early Pentecostal movement. Garfield blessed the movement as a pastor, denominational leader, and song composer. He received Spirit baptism (1908) through the influence of Henry Prentiss, who had received his Pentecost during the Azusa Street revival; subsequently, Haywood succeeded Prentiss as pastor in the Pentecostal work in Indianapolis (late 1908), which became a large and eminent church among Pentecostals. Haywood

ness Pentecostal theology and delineate any Spirit christological references.[97]

The Victim of the Flaming Sword consists of nine chapters, depicting the greatness of Jesus Christ. In chapter one, Haywood reiterates how, after the fall of humanity into sin, God placed angelic creatures in the Garden of Eden wielding flaming swords to prevent humanity from accessing the tree of life. Christ, therefore, endured being the victim of the flaming sword to gain humanity access to

---

joined the Oneness movement in Jan. 1915 and quickly became a prominent leader. For overviews of Haywood's life, ministry, and theology, see Garfield T. Haywood, *The Life and Writings of Elder G.T. Haywood* (Oneness Pentecostal Pioneer Series; Portland, OR: Apostolic Book Publishers, 1968); Jacobsen, *Thinking in the Spirit*, pp. 196-232; Cecil M. Robeck, 'Haywood, Garfield Thomas', *NIDPCM*, pp. 693-94.

[97] Any corresponding references in the tracts written by Ewart and Urshan will be noted along the way. Frank J. Ewart (1876–1947) began his ministry in Australia as a Baptist missionary. Later, he migrated to Canada (1903) and became the pastor of a Baptist church; however, he parted ways with this church after he received Spirit baptism (1908). Then, through the invitation of William Durham, Ewart became Durham's assistant pastor in Los Angeles (1911). Owing to Durham's untimely demise, Ewart became the pastor of this church (1912), placing him in a role of prominence among Finished Work Pentecostals. Ewart was present and approving of R.E. McAlister's baptismal sermon regarding the name of Jesus (1913) at the Arroyo Seco camp meeting. It was Ewart, however, who first formulated and preached the message which gave impetus to the Oneness movement. According to Thomas Fudge,

> There is no evidence to suggest that anyone else was actively working on such a theological interpretation at that time. Ewart must be seen as the originator of a new direction within early Pentecostal history. The work of Frank J. Ewart yielded up a theology of the Name of Jesus which functioned as a hermeneutical key in the validation of a new religious experience.

For information about Ewart's life, ministry, and theology, see Fank J. Ewart, *The Phenomenon of Pentecost* (Hazelwood, MO: Word Aflame Press, 1975 repr.; St. Louis: Pentecostal Publishing House, Revised edn, 1947); J.L. Hall, 'Ewart, Frank J.', *NIDPCM*, pp. 623-24. Andrew David Urshan (1884–1967) was born in Iran to a Presbyterian pastoral family, which was part of a Nestorian community. After migrating to the United States (1901) and living for a while in New York City, he settled in Chicago. Subsequent to receiving Spirit baptism he planted a Persian mission. After William Durham ordained him in 1910, Urshan returned, as a missionary, to Iran (1914). While a refugee in Russia during WWI (1915–16), Urshan planted Pentecostal churches in Tiflis, Armaear, and Leningrad. Although he was baptized in the name of Jesus during his time in Leningrad, he did not officially join the ranks of the Oneness movement until 1918. For overviews, of Urshan's life, ministry, and theology, see Andrew D. Urshan, *The Story of My Life* (St. Louis: Gospel Publishing House, n.d.); Jacobsen, *Thinking in the Spirit*, pp. 232-59; J.L. Hall, 'Urshan, Andrew David', *NIDPCM*, p. 1167. The best contemporary work regarding Urshan is Daniel Lee Seagraves, 'Andrew D. Urshan: A Theological Biography' (PhD Dissertation, Regent University, 2010).

the abundant life the tree provided. The subsequent chapters delineate Christ's deity.

According to Haywood, there is only one God, and the fullness of the Godhead dwells in Jesus Christ; therefore, trinitarian theology is an unscriptural creedal confession of polytheism, depicting the apostasy of the church. Triune terminology designates the titles and manifestations of the Godhead, as well as plurality of attributes, but not distinct persons. Father designates the deity of Jesus Christ, Spirit the transcendent nature and substance of God, and Son refers to Jesus' humanity; moreover, there is only one deity revealed as Father *in* the Son and as Spirit *through* the Son.[98] God had revealed himself through his name in the Hebrew Scriptures, and the name Jesus is the ultimate means of divine self-revelation and salvation.[99]

The references bearing Spirit christological characteristics appear in discussions regarding three areas of the christological mission: the incarnation, Christ's reception of the Spirit at the Jordan, and

---

[98] Garfield T. Haywood, 'The Victim of the Flaming Sword', in Donald W. Dayton (ed.), *Seven 'Jesus Only' Tracts* (HCL; New York: Garland Publishing, 1985 repr.; Indianapolis: Christ Temple Book Store, n.d.), pp. 12-13, 55-59, 64-66. Cf. Haywood, 'The Finest of the Wheat', pp. 35-36; Fank J. Ewart, 'The Revelation of Jesus Christ', in Donald W. Dayton (ed.), *Seven 'Jesus Only' Tracts* (HCL; New York: Garland Publishing, 1985 repr.; St. Louis: Pentecostal Publishing House, n.d.), pp. 6-7, 14-15.

[99] Haywood, 'Flaming Sword', pp. 12-20, 25-34, 64-65. Cf. Haywood, 'Divine Names', pp. 1-19; Ewart, 'The Revelation of Jesus Christ', pp. 13-15; Andrew D. Urshan, 'The Almighty God in the Lord Jesus Christ', in Donald W. Dayton (ed.), *Seven 'Jesus Only' Tracts* (HCL; New York: Garland Publishing, 1985 repr.; Los Angeles: Apostolic Book Corner, 1919), pp. 27-31, 42-46, 75-81. Accordingly, under the rubric of Jesus' name Oneness Pentecostals teach a three-fold soteriological schema: (1) repentance which is faith acting in obedience, (2) water baptism in Jesus' name identifies the convert with Christ by binding them with the name and demonstrates true obedience, and (3) Spirit baptism with glossolalic evidence. This synopsis by no means covers the extent and complexities of Oneness Pentecostalism. For overviews of Oneness Pentecostal theology, see Reed, *In Jesus' Name*, pp. 227-363; French, *Our God Is One*, pp. 161-225; Butler, *Oneness Pentecostalism*, pp. 88-191; Fudge, *Christianity without the Cross*, pp. 64-199; Reed, 'Oneness Pentecostalism', pp. 940-44; Faupel, *The Everlasting Gospel*, pp. 282-90; Alexander, *Pentecostal Healing*, pp. 187-94. For thorough examinations of Oneness theology, see David K. Bernard, *The Oneness of God* (Hazelwood, MO: Word Aflame Press, 1983); David K. Bernard, *The Oneness View of Jesus Christ* (Hazelwood, MO: Word Aflame Press, 1994); David K. Bernard, *In the Name of Jesus* (Hazelwood, MO: Word Aflame Press, 1992); David K. Bernard, *Essentials of the New Birth* (Hazelwood, MO: Word Aflame Press, 1987); David K. Bernard, *Essentials of Oneness Theology* (Hazelwood, MO: Word Aflame Press, 1984).

Pentecost. The first matter concerns the nature of deity in the incarnation.

> He was God in the 'likeness of men'; the Lord and Master in the 'form of a servant;' The Everlasting Father 'as a son'; the Eternal Spirit 'manifest in flesh.'[100]

> Touching the Doctrine of the Trinity, the Apostles knew of no such thing; they knew nothing about three Spirits; they had no knowledge of three separate Persons in the Godhead; they had not been informed that the Holy Ghost, the Spirit of God, and the Spirit of Christ were the Spirits of three separate Persons. They knew of but One God, One Spirit and One Lord. They knew that God was a Spirit (John 4.24) and that the Lord was that Spirit (2 Cor. 3.17), and that Jesus Christ was that Lord.[101]

Haywood grounded his doctrine on apostolic testimony to validate his monotheistic pneumatic position. Jesus Christ was not the incarnation and revelation of a *single* person of the Godhead; rather, Jesus manifested the *fullness* of the Godhead. Jesus, therefore, revealed the entire substance or nature of deity, which is Spirit.

Jesus is also the Son of God. This designation, however, does not refer to a triune person existing in hypostatic union; it denotes Jesus' humanity.[102] Jesus' body serves as the temple of deity, so that when people behold him, they have encountered the habitation of the mighty God of the patriarchs.[103] Jesus' life and ministry as Son

---

[100] Haywood, 'Flaming Sword', p. 44. 'The Eternal Spirit, who had no visible form, took possession of the body of Jesus, spoke out of it, worked through it, gave it His name and nature.' Ewart, 'The Revelation of Jesus Christ', p. 43. Cf. Haywood, 'The Finest of the Wheat', p. 34.

[101] Haywood, 'Flaming Sword', p. 56. Cf. Ewart, 'The Revelation of Jesus Christ', pp. 14, 18; Haywood, 'Divine Names', pp. 12-15.

[102] Haywood, 'Flaming Sword', pp. 12-13. Cf. Andrew D. Urshan, 'The Doctrine of the New Birth or the Perfect Way to Eternal Life', in Donald W. Dayton (ed.), *Seven 'Jesus Only' Tracts* (HCL; New York: Garland Publishing, 1985 repr.; Cochrane, WI: Witness of God Publishers, 1921), pp. 11, 14.

[103] Haywood, 'Flaming Sword', pp. 20-23.

> In explaining the mystery of the incarnation he says, 'And the word was made flesh and dwelt among us ... full of grace and truth.' That there should be no doubt as to the divinity of Jesus, and that no attempt to be made to make God and the Son of God separate persons, the Apostle places in parenthesis these words (and we beheld His [God's] glory, the glory as of the only begotten of the Father).

of God, furthermore, functions as a pattern,[104] which brings forth the next interrelated areas of discussion, Christ's reception of the Spirit at the Jordan and Pentecost.

> At the river Jordan he showed us how to fulfill the righteousness of God, saying, 'Thus it becometh us to fulfill all righteousness,' and when he came forth out of the water, the spirit of God descended in the bodily form of a dove and abode on him. And a voice from came heaven saying, 'This is my Beloved Son in whom I am well pleased.' It was thus that he demonstrated the manner in which we should come to be sons of God, and that, by being brought forth of the water and Spirit.[105]

Christ's reception of the Spirit at the Jordan functioned as a pattern for conversion-initiation into sonship. Jesus was baptized in water and Spirit; accordingly, Haywood's soteriology requires the status of sonship to be achieved by a convert through water and Spirit baptism. So, one must be born of water and the Spirit; essentially, the new birth and Spirit baptism is one experience.[106]

Christ's reception of the Spirit also was Jesus' point of entry into the ministry function of high priest.[107]

> He entered by the door into the sanctuary at the River Jordan, when He was baptized in water and Spirit. After the resurrection He went into the Holy of Holies, of heaven itself. On the day of Pentecost He came out in the person of the Holy Spirit and gave

---

Haywood, 'Flaming Sword', p. 20. Cf. Ewart, 'The Revelation of Jesus Christ', pp. 26, 37; Urshan, ' Almighty God', pp. 85-88.

[104] Haywood, 'Flaming Sword', p. 18.

[105] Haywood, 'Flaming Sword', p. 14.

[106] Cf. 'That to be born of the Spirit is to be baptized with the Holy Ghost, is the conclusion drawn from the word of God by every close student of the Holy Scriptures.' Haywood, 'The Birth of the Spirit', p. 14. 'The birth of the Spirit and the baptism of the Spirit are synonymous ... According to the apostolic record, all who were baptized with the Holy Spirit spoke with other languages as the Spirit gave them utterance.' Haywood, 'The Birth of the Spirit', p. 16. Cf. Haywood, 'The Finest of the Wheat', p. 3. For thorough treatments of this subject, see Haywood, 'The Birth of the Spirit', pp. 1-40; Urshan, 'The Doctrine of the New Birth', pp. 3-48.

[107] Haywood, 'Flaming Sword', pp. 35-38.

us 'power to become the sons of God' that we might minister in the true sanctuary (Acts 1.8; John 1.12).[108]

On the day of Pentecost Peter declared Jesus to be 'both' the LORD and the ANOINTED of the LORD, saying, 'God hath made this Jesus, who ye have crucified, "both" Lord and Christ.' In other words, 'The Spirit (John 4.24) has proven this Jesus … to be both JEHOVAH and His Anointed.' It was this revelation, no doubt, that caused Peter to proclaim baptism in the 'name of JESUS CHRIST' as identical to the commission to 'baptize in the name of the Father, and of the Son, and of the Holy Ghost.'[109]

At the Jordan, the Spirit's anointing upon the Son, the human nature, commissioned him into the salvific role as priest to offer sacrifice for sin, reconciling the world unto himself.[110] The resurrected Son ascended into the heavenly Holy of Holies to continue his salvific priestly function by baptizing converts in the Spirit, empowering them to become sons of God.[111] Christ's reception of the Spirit at the Jordan, therefore, is proleptic of Pentecost, and Pentecost verifies the Son's experience of the Spirit at the Jordan, and the two events are conjoined in the revelation of Jesus Christ: he is the Lord and the anointed of the Lord; he is Lord and Christ. Thus, baptism in the name of the Lord (Father)-Jesus (Son)-Christ (Spirit) is equivalent to the triune baptismal formula Father, Son, and Holy Spirit. Only one divine personality, therefore, is revealed as the Father *in* the Son and as Spirit *through* the Son.

Oneness Pentecostalism posits a form of Spirit Christology which integrates Logos Christology. Oneness Christology often ex-

---

[108] Haywood, 'Flaming Sword', p. 36. 'The personal, visible form of God was Jesus Christ, and today the Christ with us and in us is "that Holy Spirit."' Haywood, 'The Finest of the Wheat', p. 35.

[109] Haywood, 'Flaming Sword', pp. 69-70. Cf. Urshan, 'The Doctrine of the New Birth', p. 26.

[110] 'The Lord from heaven never attempted to preach the Gospel until He was anointed with the Holy Spirit at the Jordan.' Haywood, 'The Finest of the Wheat', pp. 50-51.

[111] Similar to Marcellus of Ancyra's Christology, Haywood posits that the glorified humanity of the Son will continue its ministry until the telos of history: 'When the "last enemy is destroyed" the Sonship that God assumed will come to an end. The full work of redemption will have been completed'. Haywood, 'Flaming Sword', p. 42.

presses the preexistent Logos as the thought of God which emerges or is revealed in the divine activity of creation and redemption, so that Spirit denotes the transcendent eternal divine nature and Logos designates God's immanent presence and relationship in time. In the incarnation the non-corporeal Spirit assumes human flesh through the Logos, providing a clear distinction between the divine and human natures. The divine nature is the undivided eternal substance of God, which is Spirit, and the human nature is the Son. Consequently, certain acts are attributed to the divine nature and other acts to the human nature; thus, at the Jordan, Jesus is anointed with the Spirit, which is paradigmatic of his disciples' new birth and Spirit baptism. Nonetheless, only one divine person is present in these revelations; the fullness of the Godhead, which is Spirit, dwells in Jesus Christ. Oneness theology, therefore, supports a monotheistic pneumatic Christology, a Spirit christological paradigm of pneumatic incarnation.

Conclusion

This inquiry has traced the presence of Spirit Christology in early Pentecostal periodical literature and demonstrated that Spirit Christology has abundantly appeared in all three streams of the Pentecostal tradition. The central Spirit christological premises, which have emerged, postulate that Spirit Christology depicts the Spirit's relationship in the life and mission of Jesus Christ, and Christ's experience of receiving the Spirit at the Jordan is paradigmatic of believers' Spirit baptism. So, when the various Spirit christological paradigms are compared to the early forms of Pentecostal theology – trinitarian and Oneness – how well do they correlate?

The Spirit christological paradigm of pneumatic mediation and early trinitarian Pentecostal theology appear to correlate very well. Both of their doctrines of God affirm the one divine essence, which is Spirit, eternally exists in triune relationship as Father, Son, and Holy Spirit. Both of their Christologies delineate the Spirit's relationship in Christ's entire life and ministry. For example, both of them attest to the incarnation of the eternal divine Son in Mary's virgin womb and the Spirit's agency in conceiving Christ's humanity and uniting it to deity, so that two distinct natures, divine and human, constitute the one person of Christ. Likewise, both of them acknowledge the Spirit's role as sanctifier of Christ's humanity in the grace of union, forming the human nature and uniting it to deity in the incarnation, and in subsequent sanctifying experiences as his humanity grew into maturity. The one as well as the other agree concerning the importance of Jesus' Spirit baptism at the River Jordan. The Spirit identified and revealed Christ's deity; furthermore, the Spirit's anointing commissioned and empowered Christ for his salvific mission: through the Spirit's power Jesus endured temptations, performed exorcisms, healed the sick, was offered as sacrifice for sin, was resurrected, and entered his priestly function as baptizer in the Holy Spirit. Accordingly, Jesus' Spirit baptism at the Jordan is paradigmatic of believers' Spirit baptism and empowerment for mission to the world. Consequently, there does not appear to be any opposition between early Pentecostal theology and the Spirit christological paradigm of pneumatic mediation; therefore, they have existed in an amicable relationship.

The Spirit christological paradigm of pneumatic incarnation and Oneness Pentecostal theology appear to parallel one another. In point of fact, their doctrines of God and incarnation dovetail: God is Spirit, and this divine Spirit was incarnated in Jesus Christ. Although both use triadic terminology, they adhere to a strict form of monotheism and reject triune theology as apostate. Accordingly, Father refers to Christ's divine nature, Son denotes the human nature, and Spirit designates God's transcendent nature. The Spirit, thus, conceived, sanctified, and empowered the human nature in its entire life, ministry, death, and resurrection. Both agree that Christ's Spirit baptism at the Jordan is paradigmatic of believers' Spirit baptism. According to Oneness Pentecostalism, repentance, water baptism, the new birth, and Spirit baptism sacramentally coalesce. Nevertheless, nothing in this conjoining of salvific doctrine in Oneness Pentecostal theology is incongruent with the Spirit christological paradigm of pneumatic incarnation; therefore, there has existed an amicable relationship between them.

However, not all Spirit christological paradigms correlate well with every form of early Pentecostal theology. Although historically certain points of agreement have existed between the Spirit christological paradigms of pneumatic incarnation and pneumatic mediation, problems immediately present themselves when either juxtaposing Oneness Pentecostalism with pneumatic mediation or trinitarian Pentecostalism with pneumatic incarnation; in other words, certain parts do not fit together. Furthermore, the Spirit christological paradigm of pneumatic inspiration did not fare well with either form of early Pentecostal theology. Even though Pentecostals consistently accentuated the Spirit anointing Christ's humanity, inspiring and empowering it for ministry, they did not think of Jesus simply as a human uniquely inspired by the Spirit; in all the early periodical literature examined by this inquiry, Pentecostals explicitly affirmed Christ's deity and an incarnational model of Christology. Actually, Pentecostalism stood in opposition to the Spirit christological paradigm of pneumatic inspiration.

Hence, it would not be proper to draw the general conclusion: Spirit Christology and early Pentecostal theology correlate well with one another. Instead, a more specific conclusion seems appropriate: certain Spirit christological paradigms have existed in amicable relationships with some forms of early Pentecostal theology.

18

SUMMARY/CONCLUSION TO PART THREE

As the third part of this inquiry concludes, the survey will assess its purposes: to trace Spirit Christology's presence, or lack thereof, and to identify the Spirit christological paradigms and their relationships with doctrinal development in the Christian tradition.

All of these groups surveyed in this part of the inquiry protested the desiccation of the institutional church, sought to further ecclesiastical reforms, and most rejected creedalism as detrimental to love and fellowship; moreover, they returned to the early church's experience of the Spirit and Jesus' experience of the Spirit revealed in Scripture to formulate their doctrines of Spirit baptism. Accompanying this reemergence and doctrinal development of Spirit baptism among these groups was a shift in christological terms and symbols to a Spirit christological center. The central Spirit christological premises, therefore, have emerged among these groups surveyed: Spirit Christology depicts the Spirit's relationship in the life and mission of Jesus Christ, and Christ's experience of receiving the Spirit at the Jordan is paradigmatic of believers' Spirit baptism.

These various groups and writers, therefore, speak through Spirit christological voices, speaking in unison regarding certain issues and distinction about other issues. Noteworthily, with little variation, proto-Pentecostals' theologies, which anteceded the Azusa Street Revival by more than seventy years, could easily fit within the boundaries of early Pentecostal theology. Common among them and early Pentecostalism was the desire to recover and maintain genuine apostolic experience and doctrine. Apostolic experience meant they had received the same pneumatic experience, power, and authority the apostles enjoyed. Apostolic doctrine affirmed the centrality of Christology to their theology, viewed through a pneumatic prism of Christ's relationship to the Spirit in his life and mission, which affected all other doctrines. So, maintaining Christ's true humanity, they rejected the notion that Jesus' reception of Spirit baptism had only typological significance; rather, it was a vital experience in Christ's identity, life, and ministry, and it functioned paradigmatically for his followers' relationship to the Spirit. So, these proto-Pentecostals and early Pentecostals unequivocally maintained Christ's deity, but also staunchly affirmed that he was a man anointed by the Spirit: because Christ was baptized in the Spirit, so should his followers be endowed with power.

The diversity among them arose from the distinct Spirit christological paradigms they advocated: pneumatic mediation and pneumatic incarnation. On the one hand, the *Pryguny*, Edward Irving, and early trinitarian Pentecostals taught a Spirit Christology of pneumatic mediation which integrated Logos Christology. It should be noted that though Irving and some early Pentecostals espoused traditional trinitarian theology, the *Pryguny's* doctrine of God looked more like an early form of economic Trinity which subordinated the Son and Spirit to the Father; however, they all affirmed the incarnation of the Son. Although they recognized the Son as Christ's divine nature, they allowed space for the Spirit to anoint, commission, and empower the human nature. Consequently, they posited the Spirit's agency in mediating Christ's entire life and mission. On the other hand, Oneness Pentecostalism delineated a Spirit christological paradigm of pneumatic incarnation. Though they used trinitarian language, Oneness proponents rejected triune doctrine as apostasy. The various titles – Father, Son, and Holy Spirit – depict manifestations of the one God. Father denotes the deity of Jesus Christ, Son signifies Jesus' humanity, and Spirit expresses the transcendent nature and substance of God which had become incarnated in Jesus. This pneumatic incarnation is central to Oneness doctrine: for the fullness of the Godhead dwelled in the Lord Jesus Christ, so that believers have received the revelation of the 'Mighty God' in Christ.

The Holiness writers' various versions of the 'full gospel' formed the *ethos* from which Pentecostalism emerged. Stemming from Wesley's doctrine of sanctification, Holiness revivalism taught an experience of sanctification subsequent to justification, which was thoroughly a pneumatic event, providing a doctrine of subsequent pneumatic experience in Pentecostal terms. Along with the doctrine of Pentecostal baptism, a shift in eschatology to a premillennial view, and the emerging emphasis on divine healing, there seemed to be a shift in nomenclature to a pneumatological accent. Corresponding to this shift to pneumatic terminology, Holiness christological foundations appeared to have shifted from Logos Christology to Spirit Christology. Moreover, with the emergence of the 'third blessing' doctrine of Pentecostal baptism of power, distinct from sanctification, among Holiness writers, the terminology and doctrinal environment was prepared for the appearance of early Pentecostalism.

This monograph has examined early Pentecostal periodical literature and found Spirit Christology present in all three streams – Wesleyan Holiness, Finished Work, and Oneness – of early Pentecostal theology: in sermon, song, and testimony. The following conclusions, therefore, seem appropriate. Spirit Christology, seemingly, permeated early Pentecostal writings; indeed, Spirit christological precepts were integral to early Pentecostal theology and spirituality. Accordingly, with its christological center and pneumatic starting point, the *heart* of early Pentecostal spirituality and theology existed in amicable relationships with certain Spirit christological paradigms.

19

CONTRIBUTIONS AND IMPLICATIONS

Consisting of two parts, this chapter attempts to set forth several significant conclusions and contributions this research offers to the fields of Historical Theology, Spirit Christology, and Pentecostal Theology as well as several implications for Pentecostal theology.

Contributions

The fundamental purposes of this inquiry have been achieved: to trace Spirit Christology's presence, or lack thereof, and to identify the Spirit christological paradigms and their relationships with doctrinal development in the Christian tradition.

This inquiry has examined Spirit Christology from the earliest patristic sources to the rise of Pentecostalism in the twentieth-century. Although Spirit Christology was prominent in the ancient church and held strong positions in the councils of Nicea and Constantinople I, its influence diminished in the councils of Ephesus and Chalcedon, losing ground to Logos Christology, and Logos Christology replaced it in the central Christian tradition at the Council of Constantinople II; henceforth, Spirit Christology appeared only sporadically until its emergence in the twentieth-century. Nonetheless, a large body of research, representing Spirit Christology, has been gathered revealing the historical identification of various groups and writers, and their primary writings have been educed; previously, several of these writers were neither included in historical surveys nor conversations regarding Spirit Christology. Indeed, this investigation has produced a plethora of new texts to consider; moreover, this study has translated many of these texts into English, unavailable anywhere else. This monograph, accordingly, contributes to the fields of historical theology and Spirit Christology as the most comprehensive historical theological inquiry of Spirit Christology to date.

This inquiry has demonstrated that Spirit Christology has played an instrumental role in the doctrinal development of the Christian tradition. I use the phrase 'Christian tradition' inclusively, because this inquiry does not limit itself to the central tradition; rather, it includes a respectful and discerning hearing of those voices on the margins of the tradition. Arguably, these marginal voices have helped define, identify, and enclose the central tradition, like the banks of a mighty river. This is especially true regarding Spirit Christology; at times, its presence only continued among these groups, yet its influence affected the central tradition. On the one hand, Spirit Christology emerged in the central tradition and was pressed onto the margins; for example, Spirit christological issues were integral to the first five ecumenical councils of the church. Arius posited a form of Spirit Christology at Nicea. Apollinarius' Spirit Christology contributed to convoking Constantinople I. The Syrian Antiochene model of Spirit Christology was central to the councils of Ephesus, Chalcedon, and Constantinople II; seven of Cyril's twelve anathemas focused on Spirit christological issues present in these councils. On the other hand, Spirit Christology has existed on the margins and migrated into the central tradition, bringing significant influence and transformation; for example, Pentecostalism existed on the cultural and theological margins in the early twentieth-century and acclimated into the central tradition during the latter part of the century. This inquiry, thus, has demonstrated that Spirit Christology was integral to christological and trinitarian doctrinal development in the Christian tradition.

Arguably, this inquiry's most important contribution to the fields of Historical Theology and Spirit Christology is its identification of the various historical streams of Spirit Christology by classifying them paradigmatically according to their distinct pneumatic traits.

First, this research has validated part of this document's introductory thesis statement: Spirit Christology is very fluid in nature and transcends rigid boundaries, so several paradigms are necessary to account for its presence in the Christian tradition. This inquiry has identified the diverse characteristics of Spirit Christology, so that three paradigms have emerged: pneumatic inspiration, pneumatic incarnation, and pneumatic mediation.[1] Pneumatic inspiration is a non-incarnation paradigm, viewing Jesus as a human anointed, empowered, and deified by the Spirit. The other two are incarnational paradigms. Pneumatic incarnation and pneumatic mediation agree regarding Christ's two natures: flesh and Spirit. Flesh designates Christ's genuine and complete humanity, and Spirit marks his deity, the divine essence of God. Here, the paradigm of pneumatic mediation developed and distinguished itself from pneumatic incarnation. The latter attests to a modalist view of the incarnation of divine Spirit, the fullness of the Godhead dwelling bodily in Jesus, while the former supports trinitarian belief in the incarnation of the divine Logos: the Spirit mediates Christ's virgin birth, life, ministry, death, resurrection, and continuing presence in the church. Though, some overlap exists among them, these paradigmatic classifications provide assistance in identifying and defining Spirit Christology. Thus, this inquiry contributes paradigmatic clarification and challenges scholarship to broaden its scope of study regarding Spirit Christology.

Second, although all three paradigms bear historical evidence, they are not equal in usefulness. The paradigm of pneumatic inspiration does not appear to come down on the right side of history or Scriptural veracity. The paradigm of pneumatic incarnation has lim-

---

[1] Ralph Del Colle briefly presents three paradigms: pneumatic inspiration, pneumatic incarnation, and pneumatic communication. However, Del Colle limits these models to his discussion regarding Spirit Christology in the 'pre-conciliar church'; specifically, he focuses on the Christologies of the Ebionites and the Shepherd of Hermas to delineate these three models of Spirit Christology. Del Colle, *Christ and the Spirit*, pp. 158-60. Then he compares them to Geoffrey Lampe's pneumatic Christology:

> For the moment we simply note how this contemporary Spirit-christology takes up the different dimensions of pneumatic christology present in the ancient church. Pneumatic inspiration, incarnation, and communication all inform what we can designate as Lampe's post-Chalcedonian christology.

Del Colle, *Christ and the Spirit*, p. 164. Cf. Del Colle, *Christ and the Spirit*, pp. 161-64. Obviously, since the paradigm of pneumatic mediation in this work supports a full trinitarian theology and integrates Logos Christology, there is much difference in our respective classifications: pneumatic mediation and communication. Also, I would only identify the paradigm of pneumatic inspiration in Lampe's Spirit Christology, suggesting further differences in how Del Colle and I define and apply these models of Spirit Christology.

ited usefulness because it is only amicable to modalist theology. The paradigm of pneumatic mediation appears more useful than the paradigms of pneumatic inspiration and incarnation because it can account for certain essential aspects of these two modalist paradigms – the Spirit's anointing inspiring and empowering Christ's humanity, affirmation of the incarnation of the divine Logos or Spirit, while maintaining a monotheistic view of deity – within a triune framework.

This inquiry has demonstrated that two distinct branches of the paradigm of pneumatic mediation have emerged; so, the question arises: which form of pneumatic mediation is more useful? One branch stemming from Augustine taught that the Spirit's agency in the incarnation of the divine Logos completed Christ's anointing of the Spirit, so Christ remained anointed for his entire ministry, and all subsequent experiences of the Spirit, such as Christ receiving the Spirit at the Jordan, were merely typological, having no genuine effect on Christ. The other branch stemming from the ancient church – through such figures as Justin Martyr, Tertullian, Irenaeus, Cyril of Jerusalem, Athanasius, the Cappadocian Fathers, Ambrose, Hilary, Eustathius, Nestorius, and Theodoret of Cyrus – and continuing through the *Pryguny*, Edward Irving, and some early Pentecostals, affirmed the Spirit's mediation of Christ's virgin birth and all subsequent experiences of the Spirit as actual experiences in Christ's life and ministry; thus, at the Jordan Christ received the Spirit as a genuine and proper experience of the Spirit in Christ's life and ministry empowering him for mission, which is paradigmatic for believers' Spirit baptism and empowerment for mission. The latter form, consequently, delineates a more ancient heritage in the Christian tradition and a more robust form of pneumatic mediation than the Augustinian form. So, scholars who advocate an Augustinian form of pneumatic mediation, as well as paradigms of pneumatic inspiration and incarnation need to reassess the strength of their proposals in light of this ancient and robust form of pneumatic mediation.

Third, this inquiry has demonstrated that the paradigm of pneumatic mediation proffers a Spirit christological model that fully *integrates* Logos Christology's triune theology and doctrine of the incarnation of the eternal divine Son into its christological schema, thus, affirming another part of this document's thesis statement: not all Spirit christological paradigms are antithetical to Logos Christology.

This conclusion is important because often modern Spirit christological proponents attempt to offer a model of Spirit Christology which *complements* Logos Christology, in a sense cherry-picking between two distinct and seemingly antithetical christological models to form their theological postulates. The paradigm of pneumatic mediation, however, is neither antithetical to Logos Christology nor obliged to function in a *complementary* role to Logos Christology; rather, it can stand alone on its own merits as a model in which the essential aspects of pneumatic Christology and Logos Christology coalesce, offering a Spirit christological model which is in no wise *subordinate* to nor *determined* by Logos Christology. This postulate, consequently, requisitions a reappraisal of contemporary thinking regarding the relationship of Spirit Christology and Logos Christology.

This inquiry, moreover, has made at least two significant contributions to Pentecostal Theology. First, it has traced the presence of Spirit Christology in early Holiness literature and Pentecostal literature; arguably, this is the most comprehensive survey of proto-Pentecostal, Holiness, and early Pentecostal writers regarding Spirit Christology to date. Second, after examining the periodical literature of all three steams of early Pentecostalism – Wesleyan Holiness, Finished Work, and Oneness – it has delineated the various Spirit christological paradigms present among these writers and how well these paradigms correlate with various forms of early Pentecostal theology.

Implications for Pentecostal Theology

Furthermore, these conclusions present several significant implications for contemporary Pentecostal theology. First, this investigation has demonstrated an abundance of Spirit christological characteristics in early Pentecostal periodical literature; specifically, the Spirit christological paradigms of pneumatic mediation and incarnation were present. Hence, this inquiry has juxtaposed early Pentecostalism's trinitarian theology with the paradigm of pneumatic mediation and Oneness theology with pneumatic incarnation, demonstrating their correlation respectively. However, not all Spirit christological paradigms correlate with early Pentecostal theology. Indeed, neither does the trinitarian paradigm of pneumatic mediation match Oneness theology, nor does the paradigm of pneumatic incarnation correspond with trinitarian Pentecostal theology; furthermore, the paradigm of pneumatic inspiration did not find any acceptance among early Pentecostals. Therefore, in affirmation of part of this document's thesis statement, this research has demonstrated that some forms of early Pentecostal theology have existed in amicable relationships with certain Spirit christological paradigms. Pentecostal scholars, therefore, should give attention to the presence of these Spirit christological paradigms and their roles in the primary sources of early Pentecostalism; in other words, contemporary historical inquiry into Pentecostalism or attempts at Pentecostal theological reflection should consider the *heart* of the tradition's spirituality and theology.

Second, scholars seeking to formulate Pentecostal theology should consider the historical presence of Spirit Christology in the Christian tradition. For example, the paradigm of pneumatic inspiration appeared often in the early Christian tradition; usually, in the modern Spirit christological discussion, it has emerged among liberal Protestant theologians, such as Geoffrey Lampe.[2] Pentecostals readily affirm Christ's genuine humanity, and that Jesus went about his mission as a man anointed by the Spirit after his Spirit baptism at the Jordan: by the indwelling inspiration and power of the Spirit, Jesus performed his mighty works and spoke with authority. Although the Spirit's anointing is a significant part of Pentecostal theology, the dangers which the paradigm of pneumatic inspiration has presented to Christology and soteriology should not be overlooked: it denies Christ's deity, so that Jesus was merely a man anointed by the Spirit, and it undermines the foundations of Christian soteriology. The Spirit christological paradigm of pneumatic inspiration has lacked historical validation in the Christian tradition; moreover, it is not found in early Pentecostal literature. Therefore, even though the Spirit's anointing is an integral part of Pentecostal theology and serves an essential function in the Spirit christological paradigms of pneumatic incarnation and pneumatic mediation, the Spirit's inspiration is not paradigmatic in the early Pentecostal tradition.

---

[2] For an overview and analysis of Lampe's Spirit Christology, see Dorman, 'The Spirit Christology of Geoffrey Lampe'.

Third, scholars seeking to build trinitarian Pentecostal theology on the foundation of Spirit Christology need to consider this inquiry's conclusions regarding the Spirit christological paradigm of pneumatic mediation: (1) this paradigm integrates triune theology and the doctrine of the incarnation of the eternal divine Son, so that the paradigm of pneumatic mediation can stand on its own merits as a fully trinitarian model of Spirit Christology; therefore, it is neither antithetical to Logos Christology nor obliged to function in a *complementary* role to Logos Christology; and (2) two forms or branches of this paradigm has appeared in the Christian tradition.

Frequently, when modern Pentecostal scholars work with trinitarian theology and Spirit Christology, it produces two results: they either seek to formulate a Spirit Christology which *complements* Logos Christology[3] or follow the trinitarian Spirit christological branch of pneumatic meditation, stemming from Augustine, posited by such scholars as David Coffey and Ralph Del Colle.[4] Granted the Augustinian form of pneumatic mediation correlates well with Logos Christology, yet it does not allow for any actual subsequence experiences of the Spirit in Christ's life and ministry. Accordingly, incarnation and Jesus' reception of the Spirit at the Jordan are two ways of expressing the same event, one from a descending christological perspective and the other from an ascending christological perspective.[5] The Spirit anointed Christ's humanity in the incarnation when the Spirit formed the human nature and joined it to deity

---

[3] Clark Pinnock sets an example of formulating Spirit Christology to *complement* Logos Christology. Pinnock, *Flame of Love*. Frank Macchia is an example of a Pentecostal scholar building Pentecostal theology implicitly *using* Spirit Christology in a *complementary* fashion to Logos Christology. Macchia, *Baptized in the Spirit*; Macchia, *Justified in the Spirit*.

[4] Coffey, 'The Holy Spirit as the Mutual Love', pp. 193-229; Coffey, *Deus Trinitas*; Coffey, 'Spirit Christology and the Trinity', pp. 315-38; Coffey, 'Proper Mission', pp. 227-50; Coffey, *Grace: The Gift of the Holy Spirit*; Coffey, 'The Theandric Nature of Christ', pp. 405-31; Coffey, 'The "Incarnation" of the Holy Spirit in Christ', pp. 466-80; Del Colle, *Spirit-Christology*. Amos Yong is an example of a Pentecostal scholar who *uses* this form of Spirit Christology to construct Pentecostal theology, and Skip Jenkins is an example of a Pentecostal scholar who *follows* this method and *builds* on it. Yong, *Spirit-Word-Community*, pp. 50-72; Yong, *The Spirit Poured out on All Flesh*, pp. 86-88, 109-12, 203-204; Jenkins, 'The Human Son of God and the Holy Spirit'.

[5] 'The Incarnation and the anointing are two ways of presenting the same event, the one in the perspective of descending, the other in the perspective of ascending, Christology'. Coffey, 'Proper Mission', p. 241.

in Mary's womb, and any seeming subsequent anointings were merely typological without any genuine effect on Christ.[6] Likewise, believers receive Spirit baptism at conversion and any subsequent manifestations of the charismata are latent endowments stemming from their initial experience. Hence, this position does not seem adequate to demonstrate the Pentecostal point of view.

More than likely, Pentecostal scholars use this Spirit christological paradigm because of its triadic framework and incarnational perspective, or perhaps they are unaware of the other branch of pneumatic mediation. This inquiry has demonstrated that a more ancient and pneumatically robust form of the paradigm of pneumatic mediation than the Augustinian form has existed in the Christian tradition and in early Pentecostal periodical literature, which *integrates* trinitarian and incarnational theology. Indeed, it has accentuated the mediation of the Spirit in conceiving Christ's humanity and joining it to deity in the incarnation, and it has allowed space for a subsequent anointing of the Spirit at the Jordan which genuinely affected Christ empowering him for his salvific mission, which is paradigmatic of believers' Spirit baptism. This position, therefore, appears to represent more adequately the early Pentecostal perspective.

There are several reasons why trinitarian Pentecostals, attempting to construct Pentecostal theology on the basis of Spirit Christology, should accept and work from this latter form of pneumatic mediation. First, if Jesus' Spirit baptism at the Jordan is paradigmatic of believers' Spirit baptism, Pentecostals would expect this event to be an actual experience of anointing and enduement of power. Second, this point of view supports a doctrine of experiences of the Spirit subsequent to the initial experience of the Spirit, especially Spirit baptism. Third, in the Christian tradition, this paradigm's roots extend back to the ancient church where it can be found in its incipient form as early as Ignatius; this correlates well with the Pentecostal desire to share the experience and doctrine of the primitive

---

[6] Christ's supernatural operations flow not from habitual grace as with us, but directly from the hypostatic union itself. There is no room in this scheme for a habitual grace in Christ ... If Jesus' human nature was theandric, there was no place in him for habitual grace, for the radical sanctification of his human nature by the Holy Spirit terminated in its union with the divine Son. Coffey, 'Theandric Nature', pp. 426-27.

church.⁷ Fourth, it is the only trinitarian paradigm of pneumatic Christology found in the writings of early Pentecostal periodical literature, demonstrating its close relationship to early Pentecostal spirituality and theology. Fifth, Pentecostal spirituality and doctrine is inherently Christocentric and pneumatically permeated; its full gospel 'is focused on Christ because of its starting point in the Holy Spirit'.⁸ In fact, early Pentecostal spirituality and theology had no problem integrating Spirit Christology and Logos Christology in a pneumatically permeated christological schema set within a trinitarian framework. This form of the Spirit christological paradigm of pneumatic mediation, therefore, awaits its recognition among modern Pentecostal scholars and its implementation in building Pentecostal theology.

From this discussion of implications for Pentecostal theology, questions arise regarding further research. First, since the paradigm of pneumatic mediation integrates Logos Christology, what doctrinal impact would a theology constructed solely on pneumatic mediation make? Second, owing to the fact that Oneness Pentecostal Christology bears the characteristics of the paradigm of pneumatic incarnation, how would Oneness doctrine be affected by consciously embracing this paradigm as a basis to build theology? Third, how does Spirit Christology provide ecumenical ground for trinitarian and Oneness Pentecostals dialogue?

---

⁷ R.G. Spurling, *The Lost Link* (Turtletown, TN, np., 1920), pp. 20-35; Jacobsen, *Thinking in the Spirit*, pp. 53-54.

⁸ Land, *Pentecostal Spirituality*, p. 23.

BIBLIOGRAPHY

Abramowski, Luise, *Untersuchungen Zum Liber Heraclidis Des Nestorius* (Louvain: CSChO 242, 1963).
Alexander, Kimberly Ervin, *Pentecostal Healing: Models in Theology and Practice* (JPTSup 29; Blandford Forum, UK: Deo, 2006).
Alexandria, Clement of, 'Fragments', in Alexander Roberts and James Donaldson (eds.), *ANF; Translations of the Writings of the Fathers Down to A.D. 325* (trans. William Wilson; 10 vols.; Grand Rapids: Eerdmans, American reprint of the Edinburgh edn, 1956), II, pp. 569-87.
Alexandria, Cyril of, *Letters* (trans. John I. McEnerney; FC: A New Translation Washington: Catholic University of America Press, 1987).
Alfaro, Sammy, *Divino Compañero: Toward a Hispanic Pentecostal Christology* (PTMS 147; Eugene, OR: Wipf and Stock, 2010).
Alfeyev, Hilarion, *St. Symeon the New Theologian and Orthodox Tradition* (OECS; Oxford: Oxford University Press, 2000).
Allert, Craig D., *Revelation, Truth, Canon and Interpretation: Studies in Justin Martyr's Dialogue with Trypho* (VCSup 64; Leiden: E.J. Brill, 2002).
Ambrose, *Theological and Dogmatic Works* (trans. Joseph Roy Deferrari; FC: A New Translation; Washington: The Catholic University of America Press, 1963).
—'On the Holy Spirit', in Philip Schaff and Henry Wace (eds.), *NPNF, Second Series* (trans. H. De Romestin; 14 vols.; American reprint of the Edinburgh edn.; Grand Rapids: Eerdmans, 1997), X, pp. 91-158.
—'Select Works and Letters', in Philip Schaff and Henry Wace (eds.), *NPNF, Second Series* (trans. H. De Romestin; 14 vols.; American reprint of the Edinburgh edn.; Grand Rapids: Eerdmans, 1997), X, pp. 409-73.
Anastos, Thomas L., 'Gregory Palamas' Radicalization of the Essence, Energies, and Hypostasis Model of God', *SVTQ* 38 (1993), pp. 335-49.
Anatolios, Khaled, 'The Soteriological Significance of Christ's Humanity in St. Athanasius', *SVTQ* 40 (1996), pp. 265-86.
—*Athanasius: The Coherence of His Thought* (London: Routledge, 1998).
—*Athanasius* (ECF; London: Routledge, 2004).
Anderson, Allan, *An Introduction to Pentecostalism: Global Charismatic Christianity* (Cambridge: Cambridge University Press, 2004).
—'The Dubious Legacy of Charles Parham: Racism and Cultural Insensitivites among Pentecostals', *Pneuma* 27.1 (2005), pp. 51-64.
Anderson, Robert Mapes, *Vision of the Disinherited: The Making of American Pentecostalism* (Peabody, MA: Hendrickson, 1979).

Anderson, Vladimir, *Staroobriadchestvo I Sektantstvo* (St. Petersburg: Gubinsky, 1909).

Angold, Michael, 'Byzantium and the West, 1204–1453', in Michael Angold (ed.) *CHC: Eastern Christianity* (9 vols.; Cambridge: Cambridge University Press, 2006), V, pp. 53-78.

'Aphrahat', in F.L. Cross and Elizabeth A. Livingstone (eds.), *ODCC* (Oxford: Oxford University Press, 3rd edn, 1997), p. 82.

Aphrahat, 'Demonstrations ', in Philip Schaff and Henry Wace (eds.), *NPNF, Second Series* (trans. John Gwynn; 14 vols.; Grand Rapids: Eerdmans, 1997), XIII, pp. 344-412.

'Apollinarius and Apollinarianism', in F.L. Cross and Elizabeth A. Livingstone (eds.), *ODCC* (Oxford: Oxford University Press, 3rd edn, 1997), p. 86.

Archer, Kenneth J., *A Pentecostal Hermeneutic for the Twenty-First Century: Spirit, Scripture and Community* (JPTSup 28; London: T. & T. Clark, 2004).

'Aristides', in F.L. Cross and Elizabeth A. Livingstone (eds.), *ODCC* (Oxford: Oxford University Press, 3rd edn, 1997), p. 101.

Aristides, 'The Apology of Aristides', in Allan Menzies (ed.) *ANF; Translations of the Writings of the Fathers Down to A.D. 325* (trans. D.M. Kay; 10 vols.; Grand Rapids: Eerdmans, American reprint of the Edinburgh edition edn, 1994), IX, pp. 259-79.

Arndt, William et al., *A Greek-English Lexicon of the New Testament and Other Early Christian Literature: A Translation and Adaptation of the Fourth Revised and Augmented Edition of Walter Bauer's Griechisch-Deutsches Wörterbuch Zu Den Schriften Des Neuen Testaments Und Der Übrigen Urchristlichen Literatur* (Chicago: University of Chicago Press, 2nd rev. and augmented edn, 1979).

Ashwin-Siejkowski, Piotr, *Clement of Alexandria: A Project of Christian Perfection* (London: T. & T. Clark, 2008).

Athanasius, *The Letters of Saint Anthanasius Concerning the Holy Spirit* (trans. C.R.B. Shapland; London: Epworth Press, 1951).

—'Four Discourses against the Arians', in Philip Schaff and Henry Wace (eds.), *NPNF, Second Series* (14 vols.; Grand Rapids: Eerdmans, American reprint of the Edinburgh edn, 1994), IV, pp. 303-447.

Athenagoras, 'A Plea for the Christians', in Alexander Roberts, James Donaldson and A. Cleveland Coxe (eds.), *ANF: Translations of the Writings of the Fathers Down to A.D. 325* (trans. B.P. Pratten; 10 vols.; Grand Rapids: Eerdmans, American reprint of the Edinburgh edition edn, 2001), II, pp. 127-48.

Atkinson, William, 'Pentecostal Responses to Dunn's Baptism in the Holy Spirit: Luke-Acts', *JPT* 6 (1995), pp. 87-131.

—'Pentecostal Responses to Dunn's Baptism in the Holy Spirit: Pauline Literature', *JPT* 7 (1995), pp. 49-72.

Atkinson, William P., *Baptism in the Holy Spirit: Luke-Acts and the Dunn Debate* (Eugene, OR: Wipf and Stock, 2011).

Augustine, 'The Anti-Pelagian Writings', in Philip Schaff (ed.) *NPNF, First Series* (trans. Peter Holmes and Robert Ernest Wallis; 14 vols.; Grand Rapids: Eerdmans, American reprint of the Edinburgh edn, 1989), V, pp. 373-434.

—'The Writings against the Manichaeans and against the Donatists', in Philip Schaff (ed.) *NPNF, First Series* (trans. Richard Stothert, Albert H. Newman

and J.R. King; 14 vols.; Grand Rapids: Eerdmans, American reprint of the Edinburgh edn, 1996), IV, pp. 3-365.
—'Homilies on the Gospel of John', in Philip Schaff (ed.) *NPNF, First Series* (trans. John Gibb and James Innes; 14 vols.; Edinburgh: Eerdmans, American reprint of the Edinburgh edn, 1997), VII, pp. 459-529.
—'On the Predestination of the Saints', in Philip Schaff (ed.) *NPNF, First Series* (trans. Peter Holmes and Robert Ernest Wallis; 14 vols.; Grand Rapids: Eerdmans, American reprint of the Edinburgh edn, 1997), V, pp. 493-519.
—'The Enchiridion', in Philip Schaff (ed.) *NPNF, First Series* (trans. J.F. Shaw; 14 vols.; Grand Rapids: Eerdmans, American reprint of the Edinburgh edn, 1998), III, pp. 237-76.
—'On the Holy Trinity', in Philip Schaff (ed.) *NPNF, First Series* (trans. J.F. Shaw; 14 vols.; Grand Rapids: Eerdmans, American reprint of the Edinburgh edn, 1998), III, pp. 1-228.
Ayele, Teklehaymanot, *La Dottrina Della Chiesa Etiopica Dissidente Sull'unione Ipostatica* (Roma: Pont. Institutum Orientalium Studiorum, 1956).
—*The Ethiopian Church and Its Christological Doctrine* (trans. Teklehaymanot Ayele; Addis Ababa: Graphics Printers, Revised English edn, 1982).
Aymro, Wondmagegnehu, and Joachim Motovu (eds.), *The Ethiopian Orthodox Church* (Addis Ababa: Ethiopian Orthodox Mission, 1970).
Badcock, Gary D., *Light of Truth and Fire of Love: A Theology of the Holy Spirit* (Grand Rapids: Eerdmans, 1997).
Baelz, Peter R., 'A Deliberate Mistake?', in Stephen Sykes and John Powell Clayton (eds.), *Christ, Faith and History: Cambridge Studies in Christology* (London: Cambridge University Press, 1972), pp. 13-34.
Baillie, D.M., *God Was in Christ: An Essay on Incarnation and Atonement* (New York: Scribner, 1955).
Bandrés, J.L., and U. Zanetti, 'Christology', in S. Uhlig (ed.), *Encyclopedia Æthiopica* (Wiesbaden: Harrassowitz Verlag, 2003), I, pp. 728-32.
Barabas, Steven, *So Great Salvation: The History and Message of the Keswick Convention* (Westwood, NJ: Fleming H. Revell, 1952).
Barclift, Philip L., 'The Shifting Tones of Pope Leo the Great's Christological Vocabulary', *CH* 66 (1997), pp. 221-39.
Barnard, L.W., *Justin Martyr: His Life and Thought* (Cambridge: Cambridge University Press, 1967).
Barnes, Timothy D., 'The Chronology of Montanism', *JTS* 21 (1970), pp. 403-408.
Barnes, Timothy David, *Tertullian: A Historical and Literary Study* (2005 repr.; Oxford: Clarendon Press, 1971).
Barriger, Lawrence, 'The Legacy of Constantinople in the Russian Liturgical Tradition', *GOTR* 33 (1988), pp. 387-416.
Barth, Karl, *Protestant Thought: From Rousseau to Ritschl; Being the Translation of Eleven Chapters of Die Protestantische Theologie Im 19. Jahrhundert* (trans. Brian Cozens; New York: Simon and Schuster, 1969).
—*The Theology of Schleiermacher: Lectures at Göttingen, Winter Semester of 1923/24* (trans. Geoffrey W. Bromiley; Grand Rapids: Eerdmans, 1982).

Barthwaite, Renea, 'Tongues and Ethics:William J. Seymour and the "Bible Evidence": A Response to Cecil M. Robeck, Jr.', *Pneuma* 32 (2010), pp. 203-22.

Bartleman, Frank, *Azusa Street* (2000 repr.; New Kensington, PA: Whitaker House, 1982).

Basil, *Exegetical Homilies* (trans. Agnes Clare Way; FC: A New Translation Washington: Catholic University of America Press, 1963).

—*On the Holy Spirit* (trans. David Anderson; Crestwood, NY: St. Vladimir's Seminary Press, 1980).

Basil, St., 'On the Spirit', in Philip Schaff and Henry Wace (eds.), *NPNF, Second Series* (trans. Blomfield Jackson; 14 vols.; Grand Rapids: Eerdmans, American reprint of the Edinburgh edition edn, 1996), VIII, pp. 1-50.

Bathrellos, Demetrios, *The Byzantine Christ: Person, Nature, and Will in the Christology of Saint Maximus the Confessor* (OECS; Oxford: Oxford University Press, 2004).

Bauer, Walter, Robert A. Kraft, and Gerhard Krodel, *Orthodoxy and Heresy in Earliest Christianity* (Philadelphia: Fortress Press, 1971).

Beacham, Douglas, *A Brief History of the Pentecostal Holiness Church* (Franklin Springs, GA: Advocate Press, 1983).

Beatus, and Etherius, *Beati Liebanensis Et Eterii Oxomensis Adversus Elipandum Libri Duo* (CChr Continuatio Mediaevalis 59; Turnholti: Brepols, 1984).

Beckwith, Carl L., *Hilary of Poitiers on the Trinity: From De Fide to De Trinitate* (OECS; Oxford: Oxford University Press, 2008).

—'Suffering without Pain: The Scandal of Hilary of Poitiers' Christology', in Peter William Martens (ed.) *In the Shadow of the Incarnation: Essays on Jesus Christ in the Early Church in Honor of Brian E. Daley, S.J* (Notre Dame: University of Notre Dame Press, 2008), pp. 69-96.

Bede, *The Venerable Bede Commentary on the Acts of the Apostles* (trans. Lawrence T. Martin; CSS; 117; Kalamazoo, MI: Cistercian, 1989).

—*Homilies on the Gospels* (trans. Lawrence T. Martin and David Hurst; CSS; 110-11; 2 vols.; Kalamazoo, MI: Cistercian, 1991).

Beeley, Christopher A., *Gregory of Nazianzus on the Trinity and the Knowledge of God: In Your Light We Shall See Light* (Oxford Studies in Historical Theology; Oxford: Oxford University Press, 2008).

—'Gregory of Nazianzus on the Unity of Christ', in Peter William Martens (ed.) *In the Shadow of the Incarnation: Essays on Jesus Christ in the Early Church in Honor of Brian E. Daley, S.J* (Notre Dame: University of Notre Dame Press, 2008), pp. 97-120.

Bellinzoni, A.J., *The Sayings of Jesus in the Writings of Justin Martyr* (NovTSup 17; Leiden: E.J. Brill, 1967).

Berkhof, Hendrikus, *The Doctrine of the Holy Spirit* (Richmond, VA: John Knox Press, 1964).

—*The Christian Faith: An Introduction to the Study of Faith* (Grand Rapids: Eerdmans, 1979).

Berkhof, Louis, *The History of Christian Doctrines* (2002 repr.; Carlisle, PA: Banner of Truth Trust, 1937).

Bernard, David K., *The Oneness of God* (Hazelwood, MO: Word Aflame Press, 1983).

—*Essentials of Oneness Theology* (Hazelwood, MO: Word Aflame Press, 1984).
—*Essentials of the New Birth* (Hazelwood, MO: Word Aflame Press, 1987).
—*In the Name of Jesus* (Hazelwood, MO: Word Aflame Press, 1992).
—*The Oneness View of Jesus Christ* (Hazelwood, MO: Word Aflame Press, 1994).
—*A History of Christian Doctrine* (3 vols.; Hazelwood, MO: Word Aflame Press, 1995).
Bethune-Baker, J.F., *An Introduction to the Early History of Christian Doctrine: To the Time of the Council of Chalcedon* (London: Methuen, 8th edn, 1949).
—*Nestorius and His Teaching: A Fresh Examination of the Evidence* (Cambridge: Cambridge University Press, 1908).
Bigg, Charles, *The Christian Platonists of Alexandria: Eight Lectures Preached before the University of Oxford in the Year 1886 on the Foundation of the Late Rev. John Bampton* (New York: AMS Press, 1970).
Bindley, T. Herbert, and F. W. Green (eds.), *The Oecumenical Documents of the Faith* (Westport, CT: Greenwood Press, 1980).
Bingham, D. Jeffrey, *Irenaeus' Use of Matthew's Gospel in Adversus Haereses* (Traditio Exegetica Graeca 7; Leuven: Peeters, 1998).
Blumhofer, Edith L., *Restoring the Faith: The Assemblies of God, Pentecostalism, and American Culture* (Urbana, IL: University of Illinois Press, 1993).
—'Piper, William Hamner', in Stanley M. Burgess and Ed M. Van der Maas (eds.), *NIDPCM* (Grand Rapids: Zondervan, Rev. and expanded edn, 2002), pp. 989-90.
Blunt, A.W.F., *The Apologies of Justin Martyr* (Eugene, OR: Wipf and Stock, 2006 repr.; Cambridge: Cambridge University Press).
Bobrinskoy, Boris, 'The Indwelling of the Spirit in Christ: "Pneumatic Christology" in the Cappadocian Fathers', *SVTQ* 28.01 (2001), pp. 49-65.
Boardman, W.E., *The Lord That Healeth Thee* (London: Morgan and Scott, 1881).
—*The Higher Christian Life* (1871 repr.; Boston: Henry Hoyt, 1859).
Boers, Hendrikus, 'Religionsgeschichtliche Schule', in John Haralson Hayes (ed.), *DBI* (2 vols.; Nashville: Abingdon Press, 1999), II, pp. 383-87.
Bolshakoff, Serge, *Russian Nonconformity: The Story of "Unofficial" Religion in Russia* (Philadelphia: Westminster Press, 1950).
Bonaventure, 'The Tree of Life', in *Bonaventure* (trans. Ewert H. Cousins; CWS; New York: Paulist Press, 1978), pp. 117-75.
—*Saint Bonaventure's Disputed Questions on the Knowledge of Christ* (trans. Zachary Hayes; Works of St. Bonaventure 4; 2005 repr.; St. Bonaventure, NY: Franciscan Institute Publications, 1992).
—*St. Bonaventure's Commentary on the Gospel of Luke: Chapters 1–8* (trans. Robert J. Karris; Works of St. Bonaventure 8; St. Bonaventure, NY: Franciscan Institute Publications, 2001).
Bonaventure, and Ewert H. Cousins, *Bonaventure* (CWS; New York: Paulist Press, 1978).
Bonner, Campbell, *The Homily on the Passion by Melito, Bishop of Sardis, and Some Fragments of the Apocryphal Ezekiel* (SD; Philadelphia: University of Philadelphia Press, 1940).
Bonner, Gerald, *St Augustine of Hippo: Life and Controversies* (London: SCM Press, 1963).

Bossakov, Joseph, 'The Iconoclastic Controversy: Historical Perspectives', *GOTR* 38 (1993), pp. 215-30.

Bougerol, Jacques Guy, *Introduction to the Works of Bonaventure* (trans. José de Vinck; Paterson, NJ: St. Anthony Guild Press, 1964).

Bousset, Wilhelm, *Kyrios Christos: A History of the Belief in Christ from the Beginnings of Christianity to Irenaeus* (trans. John E. Steely; Nashville: Abingdon, 1970).

Bouyer, Louis, *Orthodox Spirituality and Protestant and Anglican Spirituality* (trans. Barbara Wall; HCS; 3 vols.; London: Burns & Oates, 1968).

Boyle, Majorie O'Rouke, 'Christ the EIKON, in the Apologies for Holy Icons of John of Damascus', *GOTR* 15 (1970), pp. 175-86.

Braaten, Carl E., 'Modern Interpretations of Nestorius', *CH* 32 (1963), pp. 251-67.

Braaten, Carl E., and Roy A. Harrisville, *The Historical Jesus and the Kerygmatic Christ: Essays on the New Quest of the Historical Jesus* (New York: Abingdon Press, 1964).

Bradshaw, Paul F., 'Who Wrote the Apostolic Tradition: A Response to Alistair Stewart-Sykes', *SVTQ* 48.2 (2004), pp. 195-206.

Brent, Allen, *Hippolytus and the Roman Church in the Third Century: Communities in Tension before the Emergence of a Monarch-Bishop* (VCSup 31; Leiden: E.J. Brill, 1995).

Brown, George Hardin, *Bede the Venerable* (Twayne's English Authors Series 443; Boston: Twayne, 1987).

Brown, Peter Robert Lamont, *Augustine of Hippo: A Biography* (London: Faber, 1967).

Brown, Raymond Edward, *The Birth of the Messiah: A Commentary on the Infancy Narratives in the Gospels of Matthew and Luke* (ABRL; New York: Doubleday, New updated edn, 1993).

Brumback, Carl, *Suddenly ... From Heaven: A History of the Assemblies of God* (Springfield, MO: Gospel Publishing House, 1961).

Buchsel, Friedrich, 'εἰμί, ὁ ὤν', *TDNT* (1999), II, pp. 398-400.

Buckley, Jorunn Jacobsen, 'A Cult-Mystery in the Gospel of Philip', *JBL* 99 (1980), pp. 569-81.

Bucur, Bogdan Gabriel, *Angelomorphic Pneumatology: Clement of Alexandria and Other Early Christian Witnesses* (VCSup 95; Leiden: E.J. Brill, 2009).

Bundy, David D., 'Irving, Edward', in Stanley M. Burgess and Ed M. Van der Maas (eds.), *NIDPCM* (Grand Rapids: Zondervan, Rev. and expanded edn, 2002), pp. 803-804.

—'Keswick Higher Life Movement', in Stanley M. Burgess and Ed M. Van der Maas (eds.), *Encyclopedia Keswick Higher Life Movement* (Grand Rapids: Zondervan, Rev. and expanded edn, 2002), pp. 820-21.

Burge, Gary M., *The Anointed Community: The Holy Spirit in the Johannine Tradition* (Grand Rapids: Eerdmans, 1987).

Burgess, Stanley M., *The Holy Spirit: Ancient Christian Traditions* (2002 repr.; Peabody, MA: Hendrickson, 1984).

—*The Holy Spirit: Eastern Christian Traditions* (2000 repr.; Peabody, MA: Hendrickson, 1989).

—*The Holy Spirit: Medieval Roman Catholic and Reformation Traditions* (Peabody, MA: Hendrickson 1997).

—'Holy Spirit, Doctrine Of: The Ancient Fathers', in Stanley M. Burgess and Ed M. Van der Maas (eds.), *NIDPCM* (Grand Rapids: Zondervan, Rev. and expanded edn, 2002), pp. 730-46.
—*Christian Peoples of the Spirit: A Documentary History of Pentecostal Spirituality from the Early Church to the Present* (New York: New York University Press, 2011).
Burns, J. Patout, 'Christ and the Holy Spirit in Augustine's Theology of Baptism', in Joanne McWilliam (ed.) *Augustine: From Rhetor to Theologian* (Waterloo, Ont: Wilfrid Laurier University Press, 1992), pp. 161-71.
Burns, Paul C., *The Christology in Hilary of Poitiers' Commentary on Matthew* (Studia Ephemeridis Augustinianum 16; Roma: Institutum Patristicum Augustinianum, 1981).
Butler, Daniel L., *Oneness Pentecostalism: A History of the Jesus Name Movement* (Cerritos, CA: Daniel A. Butler, 2004).
Cabasilas, Nicolas, *Life in Christ* (trans. Margaret I. Lisney; Worthing: Churchman Publishing, 1989).
Campenhausen, Hans von, *The Fathers of the Church* (2 vols.; Peabody, MA: Hendrickson, The Combined Edition of The Fathers of the Greek Church and The Fathers of the Latin Church edn, 2000).
Carlton, C. Clark, 'The Temple That Held God: Byzantine Marian Hymnography and the Christ of Nestorius', *SVTQ* 50 (2006), pp. 99-125.
Carlyle, A.J., 'The Centenary of Edward Irving', *Modern Churchman* 24 (1935), pp. 588-97.
Callahan, Leslie D., 'Charles Parham: Progenitor of Pentecostalism', in Henry H. Knight (ed.) *From Aldersgate to Azusa Street: Wesleyan, Holiness, and Pentecostalism Visions of the New Creation* (Eugene, OR: Wipf and Stock, 2010), pp. 210-17.
Campbell, Joseph E., *The Pentecostal Holiness Church, 1898–1948* (Franklin Springs, GA: Publishing Hous of the Pentecostal Holiness Church, 1951).
Cavadini, John C., *The Last Christology of the West: Adoptionism in Spain and Gaul, 785–820* (Middle Ages Series; Philadelphia: University of Pennsylvania Press, 1993).
Cerrato, J.A., 'The Association of the Name Hippolytus with a Church Order Now Known as the *Apostolic Tradition*', *SVTQ* 48.2 (2004), pp. 179-94.
Chabannes, Jacques, *St. Augustine* (trans. Julie Kernan; Garden City, NY: Doubleday, 1962).
Chadwick, Henry, 'The Fall of Eustathius of Antioch', *JTS* 49 (1948), pp. 27-35.
—'Eucharist and Christology in the Nestorian Controversy', *JTS* 2 (1951), pp. 145-64.
Chaillot, Christine, *The Ethiopian Orthodox Tewahedo Church Tradition: A Brief Introduction to Its Life and Spirituality* (Paris: Inter-Orthodox Dialogue, 2002).
Chesnut, Robert, 'The Two Prosopa in Nestorius' Bazaar of Heracleides', *JTS* 29 (1978), pp. 392-409.
Christensen, Michael J., 'Theosis and Sanctification: John Wesley's Reformulation of a Patristic Doctrine', *Wesleyan Theological Journal* 31 (1996), pp. 71-94.
Christensen, Larry, 'Pentecostalism's Forgotten Forerunner', in Vinson Synan (ed.) *Aspects of Pentecostal-Charismatic Origins* (Plainfield, NJ: Logos International, 1975), pp. 15-37.

Clarke, Clifton Roy, 'Faith in Christ in Post-Missionary Africa: Christology among Akan African Indigenous Churches in Ghana' (PhD Thesis; Birmingham, UK: University of Birmingham, 2002).
—'Towards a Functional Christology among AICs in Ghana', *Mission Studies* 22 (2005), pp. 287-318.
Clay, J. Eugene, 'The Woman Clothed in the Sun: Pacifism and Apocalyptic Discourse among Russian Spiritual Christian Molokan-Jumpers', *CH* 80 (2011), pp. 109-38.
Clayton, Paul B., *The Christology of Theodoret of Cyrus: Antiochene Christology from the Council of Ephesus (431) to the Council of Chalcedon (451)* (OECS; Oxford: Oxford University Press, 2007).
Clement, *The Second Epistle of Clement to the Corinthians* (trans. Kirsopp Lake; The Apostolic Fathers, LCL; 2 vols.; London: Heinemann, 1912).
—*Clement of Alexandria* (trans. George William Butterworth; LCL; 2 vols.; London: Heinemann, 1919).
—'Clement of Alexandria: Christ the Educator', in Joseph Roy Deferrari (ed.) *FC: A New Translation* (trans. Simon Wood; Washington: Catholic University of America Press, 1954).
—'The Second Epistle of Clement', in Alexander Roberts and James Donaldson (eds.), *ANF; Translations of the Writings of the Fathers Down to A.D. 325* (trans. M.B. Riddle; 10 vols.; Grand Rapids: Eerdmans, American reprint of the Edinburgh edition edn, 1994), VII, pp. 509-23.
—*Clementis Alexandrini Protrepticus* (VCSup 34; Leiden: E.J. Brill, 1995).
—'Recognitions of Clement', in Alexander Roberts and James Donaldson (eds.), *ANF; Translations of the Writings of the Fathers Down to A.D. 325* (trans. Thomas Smith; 10 vols.; Grand Rapids Eerdmans, American reprint of the Edinburgh edn, 1995), VIII, pp. 75-211.
—*Clementis Alexandrini Paedagogus* (VCSup 61; Leiden: E.J. Brill, 2002).
Clemmons, Ithiel C., *Bishop C.H. Mason* (Bakersfield, CA: Pneuma Life Publishing, 1996).
Clemmons, J.C., 'Mason, Charles Harrison', in Stanley M. Burgess and Ed M. Van der Maas (eds.), *NIDPCM* (Grand Rapids: Zondervan, Rev. and expanded edn, 2002), pp. 865-67.
Coffey, David, *Grace: The Gift of the Holy Spirit* (Manly: Catholic Institute of Sydney, 1979).
—'The "Incarnation" of the Holy Spirit in Christ', *TS* 45 (1984), pp. 466-480.
—'A Proper Mission of the Holy Spirit', *TS* 47 (1986), pp. 227-250.
—'The Holy Spirit as the Mutual Love of the Father and the Son', *TS* 51 (1990), pp. 193-229.
—*Deus Trinitas: The Doctrine of the Triune God* (New York: Oxford University Press, 1999).
—'The Theandric Nature of Christ', *TS* 60 (1999), pp. 405-31.
—'Spirit Christology and the Trinity', in Bradford E. Dabney Hinze, D. Lyle (ed.) *Advents of the Spirit: An Introduction to the Current Study of Pneumatology* (Milwaukee: Marquette University Press, 2001), pp. 315-38.
Coggins, R.J., *Samaritans and Jews: The Origins of Samaritanism Reconsidered* (Atlanta: John Knox Press, 1975).

Cohen, Leonardo, 'Visions and Dreams: An Avenue of Ethiopians' Conversion to Catholicism at the Beginning of the Seventeenth Century', *Journal of Religion in Africa* 39 (2009), pp. 4-29.

Cohick, Lynn H., *The Peri Pascha Attributed to Melito of Sardis: Setting, Purpose, and Sources* (BJS 327; Providence: Brown Judaic Studies, 2000).

Colless, Brian, *The Wisdom of the Pearlers: An Anthology of Syriac Christian Mysticism* (CSS 216; Kalamazoo, MI: Cistercian Publications, 2008).

Collins, Roger, *Early Medieval Spain: Unity in Diversity, 400-1000* (New York: St. Martin's Press, 1983).

—*Early Medieval Europe, 300–1000* (New York: St. Martin's Press, 1991).

Congar, Yves, *I Believe in the Holy Spirit* (3 vols.; New York: Seabury, 1983).

—*The Word and the Spirit* (San Francisco: Harper & Row, 1986).

Conn, Charles W., *Like a Mighty Army, Moves the Church of God, 1886–1955* (Cleveland, TN: Church of God Publishing House, 1955).

Conybeare, F.C., *Russian Dissenters* (Harvard Theological Studies 10; Cambridge: Harvard University Press, 1921).

Copleston, Frederick C., *A History of Philosophy* (9 vols.; New York: Doubleday, Image Books edn, 1994).

Corwin, Virginia, *St. Ignatius and Christianity in Antioch* (Yale Publications in Religion 1; New Haven: Yale University Press, 1960).

Cowley, Roger W., *Ethiopian Biblical Interpretation: A Study in Exegetical Tradition and Hermeneutics* (University of Cambridge Oriental Publications 38; Cambridge: Cambridge University Press, 1988).

Coxe, A. Cleveland, 'Tertullian, Introductory Note', in Alexander Roberts and James Donaldson (eds.), *ANF: Translations of the Writings of the Fathers Down to A.D. 325* (10 vols.; Grand Rapids: Eerdmans, 1997 repr.; Buffalo: The Christian Literature Publishing Company, 1885), III, pp. 1-15.

Creech, Joe, 'Visions of Glory: The Place of the Azusa Street Revival in Pentecostal History', *CH* 65.3 (1996), pp. 405-24.

Cross, F.L. (ed.), *St. Cyril of Jerusalem's Lectures on the Christian Sacraments: The Procatechesis and the Five Mystagogical Catecheses* (trans. R.W. Church; Crestwood, NY: St. Vladimir's Seminary Press, 1995).

Crouzel, Henri, *Origen* (trans. A.S. Worrall; San Francisco: Harper & Row, 1989).

Crummey, Donald, *Priests and Politicians: Protestant and Catholic Missions in Orthodox Ethiopia, 1830-1868* (Oxford Studies in African Affairs; Oxford: Clarendon Press, 1972).

—'Church and Nation: The Ethiopian Orthodox Täwahedo Church', in Michael Angold (ed.) *CHC: Eastern Christianity* (9 vols.; Cambridge: Cambridge University Press, 2006), V, pp. 457-87.

Cullen, Christopher M., *Bonaventure* (Great Medieval Thinkers; Oxford: Oxford University Press, 2006).

Cullis, Charles, *Faith Cures; or, Answers to Prayer in the Healing of the Sick* (Boston: Willard Tract Repository, 1879).

—*Dr. Cullis and His Work: Twenty Years of Blessing in Answer to Prayer* (The Higher Christian Life; New York: Garland Publishing, 1985 repr.; Boston: Willard Tract Repository, 1885).

Cyprian, *Treatises* (trans. Roy J. Deferrari; FC: A New Translation; New York: Catholic University of America Press, 1958).

Cyril, *Catecheses 1-12* (trans. Leo P. McCauley; FC: A New Translation; Washington: Catholic University of America Press, 1968), LXI.

—*Catecheses 13-18* (trans. Leo P. McCauley; FC: A New Translation; Washington: Catholic University of America Press, 1970), LXIV.

—*On the Unity of Christ* (trans. John Anthony McGuckin; Crestwood, NY: St. Vladimir's Seminary Press, 1995).

Daley, Brian, *Gregory of Nazianzus* (ECF; London: Routledge, 2006).

Daley, Brian E., 'One Thing and Another: The Persons in God and the Person of Christ in Patristic Theology', *ProEccl* 15 (2006), pp. 17-46.

Dallimore, Arnold, *The Life of Edward Irving: Fore-Runner of the Charismatic Movement* (Edinburgh: Banner of Truth Trust, 1983).

Damascus, St. John of, *Three Treatises on the Divine Images* (trans. Andrew Louth; Press Popular Patristics Series; Crestwood: St. Vladimir's Seminary Press, 2003).

Daniélou, Jean, *Origen* (New York: Sheed and Ward, 1955).

Daniélou, Jean, and John A. Baker, *The Theology of Jewish Christianity* (London: Darton Longman & Todd, 1964).

Daniels, Richard, *The Christology of John Owen* (Grand Rapids: Reformation Heritage Books, 2004).

Davidson, Ivor J., '"Not My Will but Yours Be Done": The Ontological Dynamics of Incarnational Intention', *IJST* 7 (2005), pp. 178-204.

Davis, Leo Donald, *The First Seven Ecumenical Councils (325–787): Their History and Theology* (Theology and Life Series 21; Collegeville, MN: Liturgical Press, 1990).

Day, Adrian D., 'The Spirit in the Drama: Balthasar's *Theo-Drama* and the Relationship between the Son and the Spirit' (PhD dissertation; Marquette: Marquette University, 2001.

Dayton, Donald W., "Christian Perfection' to the 'Baptism of the Holy Ghost'", in Vinson Synan (ed.) *Aspects of Pentecostal-Charismatic Origins* (Plainfield, NJ: Logos International, 1975), pp. 39-54.

—*Theological Roots of Pentecostalism* (Peabody, MA: Hendrickson, 1987).

Declerck, José H. (ed.), *Evstathii Antiocheni, Patris Nicaeni, Opera Qvae Svpersvnt Omnia* (CCHr 51; Turnhout: Brepols Publishers, 2002).

DeConick, April D., 'The True Mysteries', *VC* 55 (2001), pp. 225-61.

'Deism', in F.L. Cross and Elizabeth A. Livingstone (eds.), *ODCC* (Oxford: Oxford University Press, 3rd edn, 1997), p. 465.

Deissmann, Adolf, *The Religion of Jesus and the Faith of Paul: The Selly Oak Lectures, 1923, on the Communion of Jesus with God & the Communion of Paul with Christ* (trans. William Ernest Wilson; London: Hodder and Stoughton, 1923).

—*Paul: A Study in Social and Religious History* (trans. William E. Wilson; Harper Torchbooks 15; New York: Harper & Brothers, 1957).

Del Colle, Ralph, 'Spirit Christology: Dogmatic Foundations for Pentecostal-Charismatic Spirituality', *JPT* 3 (1993), pp. 91-112.

—*Christ and the Spirit: Spirit-Christology in Trinitarian Perspective* (New York: Oxford University Press, 1994).

—'Oneness and Trinity: A Preliminary Proposal for Dialogue with Oneness Pentecostalism', *JPT* 10 (1997), pp. 85-110.
—'A Response to Jürgen Moltmann and David Coffey', in Bradford E. Dabney Hinze, D. Lyle (ed.) *Advents of the Spirit: An Introduction to the Current Study of Pneumatology* (Milwaukee: Marquette University Press, 2001), pp. 339-46.
Deschner, John, *Wesley's Christology: An Interpretation* (Dallas: Southern Methodist University Press, 1985).
Dever, Mark, *Richard Sibbes: Puritanism and Calvinism in Late Elizabethan and Early Stuart England* (Macon, GA: Mercer University Press, 2000).
Dewart, J. McWilliam, 'The Influence of Theodore of Mopsuestia on Augustine's Letter 187', *Augustinian Studies* 10 (1979), pp. 113-32.
Dibelius, Martin, *Der Hirt Des Hermas* (Die Apostolischen Väter; 4 vols.; Tübingen: Mohr, 1923).
Dieter, Melvin, 'Wesleyan-Holiness Aspects of Pentecostal Origins', in Vinson Synan (ed.) *Aspects of Pentecostal-Charismatic Origins* (Plainfield, NJ: Logos International, 1975), pp. 57-80.
Dix, Gregory, and Henry Chadwick (eds.), *The Treatise on the Apostolic Tradition of St. Hippolytus of Rome: Bishop and Martyr* (1992 repr.; Alban: London, 1937).
Dobroklonsky, A.P., *Rukovodstvo Po Istorii Russkoi Tserkvi* (Material for the History of the Church 25; Moscow: Society of Friends of Church History, 2001 repr.; Moscow: Moscow University Press, 1893).
Donfried, Karl Paul, *The Setting of Second Clement in Early Christianity* (NovTSup 38; Leiden: E.J. Brill, 1974).
Dorman, David A., 'The Spirit Christology of Geoffrey Lampe: A Critical Analysis' (PhD dissertation; Pasadena, CA: Fuller Theological Seminary, 1992).
Dorries, David W., 'Catholic Apostolic Church', in Stanley M. Burgess and Ed M. Van der Maas (eds.), *NIDPCM* (Grand Rapids: Zondervan, Rev. and expanded edn, 2002), pp. 459-60.
—*Edward Irving's Incarnational Christology* (Fairfax, VA: Xulon, 2002).
Doval, Alexis James, *Cyril of Jerusalem, Mystagogue: The Authorship of the Mystagogic Catecheses* (North American Patristic Society: Patristic Monograph Series 17; Washington: Catholic University of America Press, 2001).
Drijvers, Jan Willem, *Cyril of Jerusalem* (VCSup 72; Leiden: Brill, 2004).
Drummond, Andrew Landale, *Edward Irving and His Circle* (London: J. Clarke & Co., 1937).
Duckett, Eleanor Shipley, *Alcuin, Friend of Charlemagne: His World and His Work* (New York: Macmillan, 1951).
Duggar, Lillie, *A.J. Tomlinson: Former General Overseer of the Church of God* (Cleveland, TN: White Wing Publishing House, 1964).
Dunn, Geoffrey D., 'Divine Impassibility and Christology in the Christmas Homilies of Leo the Great', *TS* 62 (2001), pp. 71-85.
—*Tertullian* (ECF; London: Routledge, 2004).
Dunn, James D.G., *Baptism in the Holy Spirit: A Re-Examination of the New Testament Teaching on the Gift of the Spirit in Relation to Pentecostalism Today* (London: S.C.M. Press, 1970).
—'2 Corinthians 3.17 "the Lord Is the Spirit"', *JTS* 21 (1970), pp. 309-20.
—'Spirit and Kingdom', *ExpTim* 82 (1970-71), pp. 36-40.

—'1 Corinthians 15.45—Last Adam, Life-Giving Spirit', in Barnabas Lindars and Stephen S. Smalley (eds.), *Christ and the Spirit in the New Testament* (Cambridge: Cambridge University Press, 1973), pp. 127-41.

—'Jesus – Flesh and Spirit: An Exposition of Romans 1.3-4', *JTS* 24 (1973), pp. 40-68.

—*Jesus and the Spirit: A Study of the Religious and Charismatic Experience of Jesus and the First Christians as Reflected in the New Testament* (NTL; London: S.C.M. Press, 1975).

—*Unity and Diversity in the New Testament: An Inquiry into the Character of Earliest Christianity* (Philadelphia: Westminster Press, 1977).

—*Christology in the Making: A New Testament Inquiry into the Origins of the Doctrine of the Incarnation* (Philadelphia: Westminster Press, 1980).

—*The Evidence for Jesus* (Philadelphia: Westminster Press, 1985).

—'Spirit, Holy Spirit', in Colin Brown (ed.), *NIDNTT* (4 vols.; Grand Rapids: Zondervan, 1986), III, pp. 693-707.

—'Christology', in David Noel Freedman (ed.) *ABD* (6 vols.; New York: Doubleday, 1992), I, pp. 979-91.

—'Incarnation', in David Noel Freedman (ed.), *ABD* (6 vols.; New York: Doubleday, 1992), III, pp. 397-404.

—'Baptism in the Holy Spirit: A Response to Pentecostal Scholarship on Luke-Acts', *JPT* 3 (1993), pp. 3-27.

—*The Theology of Paul the Apostle* (Grand Rapids: Eerdmans, 1998).

Edwards, Denis, *Breath of Life: A Theology of the Creator Spirit* (Maryknoll: Orbis Books, 2004).

Edwards, Jonathan, 'A History of the Work of Redemption ', in John F. Wilson (ed.) *Works of Jonathan Edwards* (23 vols.; New Haven: Yale University Press, 1989), IX, pp. 204-375.

Edwards, M.J., 'Clement of Alexandria and His Doctrine of the Logos', *VC* 54 (2000), pp. 159-77.

Epiphanius, *The Panarion of St. Epiphanius, Bishop of Salamis: Selected Passages* (trans. Philip R. Amidon; New York: Oxford University Press, 1990).

Ervin, Howard M., *Conversion-Initiation and the Baptism in the Holy Spirit: A Critique of James D.G. Dunn, Baptism in the Holy Spirit* (Peabody: Hendrickson, 1984).

Eusebius, 'The Church History of Eusebius', in Philip Schaff and Henry Wace (eds.), *The NPNF, Second Series* (trans. Authur Cushman McGriffert; 14 vols.; Grand Rapids: Eerdmans, American reprint of the Edinburgh edn, 1997), I, pp. 73-403.

'Eusebius, Bishop of Nicomedia', in F.L. Cross and Elizabeth A. Livingstone (eds.), *ODCC* (Oxford: Oxford University Press, 3rd edn, 1997), p. 547.

Evalenko, Alexander M., *The Message of the Doukhobors: A Statement of True Facts by 'Christians of the Universal Brotherhood' and by Prominent Champions of Their Cause* (New York: International Library Publishing Company, 1913).

Evans, Craig A., *Life of Jesus Research: An Annotated Bibliography* (New Testament Tools and Studies 13; Leiden: E.J. Brill, 1989).

Ewart, Fank J., *The Phenomenon of Pentecost* (Hazelwood, MO: Word Aflame Press, 1975 repr.; St. Louis: Pentecostal Publishing House, Revised edn, 1947).

—'The Revelation of Jesus Christ', in Donald W. Dayton (ed.) *Seven 'Jesus Only' Tracts* (HCL; New York: Garland Publishing, 1985 repr.; St. Louis: Pentecostal Publishing House, n.d.)

Faupel, David W., *The Everlasting Gospel: The Significance of Eschatology in the Development of Pentecostal Thought* (JPTSup 10; Sheffield, England: Sheffield Academic Press, 1996).

Ferguson, Everett, 'Baptism According to Origen', *EvQ* 78 (2006), pp. 117-35.

Ferguson, Sinclair B., 'John Owen and the Doctrine of the Person of Christ', in Robert W. Oliver (ed.) *John Owen: The Man and His Theology: Papers Read at the Conference of the John Owen Centre for Theological Study, September 2000* (Darlington: Evangelical Press, 2002), pp. 69-99.

'The Fifth Ecumenical Council: The Second Council of Constantinople', in Philip Schaff and Henry Wace (eds.), *NPNF, Second Series* (trans. Henry R. Percival; 14 vols.; Grand Rapids: Eerdmans, American reprint of the Edinburgh edn, 1997), XIV, pp. 297-323.

Figgis, J.B., *Keswick from Within* (The Higher Christian Life; New York: Garland Publishing, 1985 repr.; London: Marshall Brothers, 1914).

Filson, Floyd V., 'New Greek and Coptic Gospel Manuscripts', *BA* 34 (1961), pp. 2-18.

Finney, C.G., and Asa Mahan, 'The Endument of Power', in *The Baptism of the Holy Ghost* (London: Elliot Stock, 1876), pp. 231-54.

Fitzmyer, Joseph A., 'The Qumran Scrolls, the Ebionites, and Their Literature', in Krister Stendahl and James H. Charlesworth (eds.), *The Scrolls and the New Testament* (New York: Crossroad, 1992), pp. 208-231.

Fletcher, John, *The Works of the Rev. John Fletcher* (6 vols.; Philadelphia: Joseph Crukshank, American edn, 1791).

Foster, Fred J., *Think It Not Strange: A History of the Oneness Movement* (St. Louis: Pentecostal Publishing House, 1965).

Foster, Paul, 'The Epistles of Ignatius of Antioch', in Paul Foster (ed.) *The Writings of the Apostolic Fathers* (London: T. & T. Clark, 2007), pp. 81-107.

'The Fourth Ecumenical Council: The Council of Chalcedon', in Philip Schaff and Henry Wace (eds.), *NPNF, Second Series* (trans. Henry R. Percival; 14 vols.; Grand Rapids: Eerdmans, American reprint of the Edinburgh edn, 1997), XIV, pp. 243-96.

Franklin, Lloyd David, 'The Spiritual Gifts in Tertullian' (PhD dissertation; St. Louis: St. Louis University, 1989).

Franzmann, Majella, *Jesus in the Nag Hammadi Writings* (Edinburgh: T. & T. Clark, 1996).

Frei, Hans W., *The Eclipse of Biblical Narrative: A Study in Eighteenth and Nineteenth Century Hermeneutics* (New Haven: Yale University Press, 1974).

French, Talmadge L., *Our God Is One: The Story of Oneness Pentecostals* (Indianapolis: Voice & Vision Publications, 1999).

Frend, W.H.C., *The Rise of Christianity* (Philadelphia: Fortress Press, 1984).

Friesen, Aaron, 'The Called out of the Called Out: Charles Parham's Doctrine of the Spirit Baptism', *JEPTA* 29 (2009), pp. 43-55.

Fudge, Thomas A., *Christianity without the Cross: A History of Salvation in Oneness Pentecostalism* (Parkland, FL: Universal Publishers).

Garrison, S. Olin, and G.D. Watson, *Forty Witnesses: Covering the Whole Range of Christian Experience* (New York: Eaton and Mains, 1888).

Goff, James R., *Fields White Unto Harvest: Charles F. Parham and the Missionary Origins of Pentecostalism* (Fayetteville: University of Arkansas Press, 1988).

—'Initial Tongues in the Theology of Charles Fox Parham', in Gary B. McGee (ed.) *Initial Evidence: Historical and Biblical Perspectives on the Pentecostal Doctrine of Spirit Baptism* (Eugene, OR: Wipf and Stock, 2007 repr.; Peabody, MA: Hendrickson, 1991), pp. 57-71.

—'Parham, Charles Fox', in Stanley M. Burgess and Ed M. Van der Maas (eds.), *NIDPCM* (Grand Rapids: Zondervan, Rev. and expanded edn, 2002), pp. 955-57.

González, Justo L., *A History of Christian Thought: From the Beginnings to the Council of Chalcedon* (3 vols.; 1987 repr.; Nashville: Abingdon Press, 2nd English edn, 1970).

—*A History of Christian Thought: From Augustine to the Eve of the Reformation* (3 vols.; 1987 repr.; Nashville: Abingdon Press, 2nd English edn, 1971).

—*A History of Christian Thought: From the Protestant Reformation to the Twentieth Century* (3 vols.; 1987 repr.; Nashville: Abingdon Press, 2nd English edn, 1975).

Goodenough, Erwin Ramsdell, *The Theology of Justin Martyr: An Investigation into the Conceptions of Early Christian Literature and Its Hellenistic and Judaistic Influences* (Amsterdam: Philo Press, 1968).

Goodwin, Thomas, 'Christ the Mediator', in *The Works of Thomas Goodwin* (14 vols.; Grand Rapids: Reformation Heritage Books, 2006 repr.: James Nichol, 1861–66), V, pp. 59-60.

—'The Work of the Holy Ghost in Our Salvation', in *The Works of Thomas Goodwin* (14 vols.; Grand Rapids: Reformation Heritage Books, 2006 repr.: James Nichol, 1861-66), VI, pp. 11-13.

Goranson, Stephen, 'Ebionites', in David Noel Freedman (ed.), *ABD* (6 vols.; New York: Doubleday, 1992), II, pp. 261-62.

'The Gospel of Philip', in James M. Robinson and Richard Smith (eds.), *NHL* (trans. Wesley W. Isenberg; San Francisco: HarperSanFrancisco, 3rd completely rev. edn, 1990), pp. 139-60.

'The Gospel of Truth', in James M. Robinson and Richard Smith (eds.), *NHL* (trans. Harold W. Attridge and George W. MacRae; San Francisco: HarperSanFrancisco, 3rd completely rev. edn, 1990), pp. 38-51.

Gordon, A.J., *The Ministry of Healing: Miracles of Cure in All Ages* (Boston: H. Gannett, 1882).

—*The Ministry of the Spirit* (Philadelphia, PA: American Baptist Publication Society, 1895).

Grant, Robert M., *Greek Apologists of the Second Century* (Philadelphia: Westminster Press, 1988).

—'Aristides', in David Noel Freedman (ed.), *ABD* (6 vols.; New York: Doubleday, 1992), I, p. 382.

Grant, Robert M., Graham, Holt H., *The Apostolic Fathers: A New Translation and Commentary* (6 vols.; London: Thomas Nelson, 1965).

Grant, Robert McQueen, *Gnosticism: A Source Book of Heretical Writings from the Early Christian Period* (New York: Harper & Row, 1961).

—*Gnosticism and Early Christianity* (New York: Columbia University Press, 2nd edn, 1966).
—*Irenaeus of Lyons* (ECF; London; New York: Routledge, 1997).
Grass, Konrad, *Die Geheime Heilige Schrift Der Skopzen* (trans. Konrad Grass; Leipzig: J.C. Hinrichs, 1904).
—*Die Russischen Sekten* (2 vols.; Leipzig: J.C. Hinrichs, 1905–14).
Green, Bernard, *The Soteriology of Leo the Great* (OTM; Oxford: Oxford University Press, 2008).
Greer, Rowan A., and Margaret Mary Mitchell, *The 'Belly-Myther' of Endor: Interpretations of 1 Kingdoms 28 in the Early Church* (SBLWGRW 16; Atlanta: Society of Biblical Literature, 2007).
Gregg, Robert C., 'Cyril of Jerusalem and the Arians', in *Arianism: Historical and Theological Reassessments: Papers from the Ninth International Conference on Patristic Studies, September 5-10, 1983, Oxford, England* (Patristic Monograph Series 11; Cambridge, MA: Philadelphia Patristic Foundation, 1985), pp. 85-109.
—(ed.), *Arianism: Historical and Theological Reassessments* (Patristic Monograph Series; Eugene, OR: Wipf and Stock, 2006 repr.; Philadelphia: The Philadelphia Patristic, 1985).
Gregg, Robert C., and Dennis Groh, *Early Arianism—A View of Salvation* (London: SCM Press, 1981).
Greggs, Tom, 'Exclusivist or Universalist? Origen the 'Wise Steward of the Word' (*Commrom*. V.1.7) and the Issue of Genre', *IJST* 9 (2007), pp. 315-27.
Grenz, Stanley, and Roger E. Olson, *20th Century Theology: God & the World in a Transitional Age* (Downers Grove: InterVarsity Press, 1992).
Grillmeier, Aloys, *Christ in Christian Tradition: From the Apostolic Age to Chalcedon (451)* (trans. John Bowden; 2 vols.; Atlanta: John Knox Press, Second Revised edn, 1975).
—*Christ in Christian Tradition: From the Council of Chalcedon (451) to Gregory the Great (590–604)* (trans. Dean O.C.; 2 vols.; London: Mowbrays, 1975).
Grosart, Alexander Balloch, 'Memoir of Richard Sibbes', in Alexander Balloch Grosart (ed.) *Works of Richard Sibbes* (7 vols.; 1973 repr.; Edinburgh: Banner of Truth Trust, 1862–64), I, pp. xix-cxxxi.
Gunkel, Hermann, *The Influence of the Holy Spirit: The Popular View of the Apostolic Age and the Teaching of the Apostle Paul* (trans. Roy A. Harrisville and Philip A. Quanbeck; Philadelphia: Fortress Press, 1979).
'Gunkel, Hermann', in F.L. Cross and Elizabeth A. Livingstone (eds.), *ODCC* (Oxford: Oxford University Press, 3rd edn, 1997), p. 722.
Gwatkin, Henry Melvill, *Studies of Arianism: Chiefly Referring to the Character and Chronology of the Reaction Which Followed the Council of Nicaea* (New York: AMS, 1978).
—*The Arian Controversy* (New York: AMS Press, 1979).
Gwynn, David M., *The Eusebians: The Polemic of Athanasius of Alexandria and the Construction of the 'Arian Controversy'* (OTM; Oxford: Oxford University Press, 2007).
Habets, Myk, 'Spirit Christology: Seeing in Stereo', *JPT* 11 (2003), pp. 199-234.
—*The Anointed Son: A Trinitarian Spirit Christology* (PTMS 129; Eugene, OR: Wipf and Stock, 2010).

Hadjiantoniou, George A., *Protestant Patriarch: The Life of Cyril Lucaris, 1572–1638, Patriarch of Constantinople* (Richmond: John Knox Press, 1961).

Haight, Roger, 'The Case for Spirit Christology', *TS* 53 (1992), pp. 257-87.

—*Jesus, Symbol of God* (Maryknoll, NY: Orbis Books, 1999).

Haile, Getatchew, 'Religious Controversies and the Growth of Ethiopic Literature in the Fourteenth and Fifteenth Centuries', *Oriens Christianus* 65 (1981), pp. 102-36.

—'Materials on the Theology of Qebat or Unction', in G. Goldenberg (ed.) *Ethiopian Studies: Proceedings of the Sixth International Conference, Tel-Aviv, 14–17 April 1980* (Rotterdam: A.A. Balkema, 1986), pp. 205-50.

—*The Faith of the Unctionists in the Ethiopian Church* (CSChO, Scriptores Æthiopici 91; Leuven: Peeters, 1990).

—*The Faith of the Unctionists in the Ethiopian Church* (trans. Haile Getatchew; CSChO, Scriptores Æthiopici 92; Leuven: Peeters, 1990).

Hall, J.L., 'Ewart, Frank J.', in Stanley M. Burgess and Ed M. Van der Maas (eds.), *NIDPCM* (Grand Rapids: Zondervan, Rev. and expanded edn, 2002), pp. 623-24.

—'Urshan, Andrew David', in Stanley M. Burgess and Ed M. Van der Maas (eds.), *NIDPCM* (Grand Rapids: Zondervan, Rev. and expanded edn, 2002), p. 1167.

Hall, Stuart George (ed.), *Melito of Sardis: On Pascha and Fragments* (OECT; Oxford: Clarendon Press, 1979).

Han, Sang-Ehil, 'A Revisionist Spirit-Christology in Korean Culture' (PhD dissertation; Atlanta: Emory University, 2004).

—'Journeying into the Heart of God: Rediscovering Spirit-Christology and Its Soteriological Ramifications in Korean Culture', *JPT* 15 (2006), pp. 107-26.

—'Weaving the Courage of God and Human Suffering: Reorienting the Atonement Tradition', in Steven J. Land, Rickie Moore and John Christopher Thomas (eds.), *Passover, Pentecost, and Parousia: Studies in Celebration of the Life and Ministry of R. Hollis Gause* (JPTSup 35; Blandford Forum: Deo, 2010), pp. 171-90.

Hansen, Olaf, 'Spirit Christology: A Way out of the Dilemma?', in Paul D. Opsahl (ed.) *The Holy Spirit in the Life of the Church: From Biblical Times to the Present* (Minneapolis: Augsburg, 1978), pp. 172-203.

Hanson, R.P.C., 'The Source and Significance of the Fourth Oratio Contra Arianos Attributed to Athanasius', *VC* 42 (1988), pp. 257-66.

—*The Search for the Christian Doctrine of God: The Arian Controversy, 318–81* (Grand Rapids: Baker Academic, 2005).

Harding, William, *The Trial of the Rev. Edward Irving, M.A. Before the London Presbytery; Containing the Whole of the Evidence; Exact Copies of the Documents; Verbatim Report of the Speeches and Opinions of the Presbyters, Etc.* (London: W. Harding, 1832).

Harnack, Adolf von, *History of Dogma* (trans. Neil Buchanan; 7 vols.; Eugene, OR: Wipf and Stock, 1997 repr.; Boston: Little, Brown, 3rd edn., 1901).

Harris, J. Rendel, and J. Armitage Robinson (eds.), *The Apology of Aristides on Behalf of the Christians: From a Syriac Ms. Preserved on Mount Sinai, with an Appendix Con-

taining the Main Portion of the Original Greek Text (Piscataway, NJ: Gorgias Press, 2004).
Hayes, Zachary, *Bonaventure: Mystical Writings* (The Crossroad Spiritual Legacy Series; New York: Crossroad, 1999).
Haykin, Michael A.G., 'John Owen and the Challenges of the Quakers', in Robert W. Oliver (ed.) *John Owen: The Man and His Theology: Papers Read at the Conference of the John Owen Centre for Theological Study, September 2000* (Darlington: Evangelical Press, 2002), pp. 131-55.
Haywood, Garfield T., *The Life and Writings of Elder G.T. Haywood* (Oneness Pentecostal Pioneer Series Portland, OR: Apostolic Book Publishers, 1968).
—'The Birth of the Spirit in the Days of the Apostles', in Donald W. Dayton (ed.) *Seven 'Jesus Only' Tracts* (HCL; New York: Garland Publishing, 1985 repr.; Indianapolis: Christ Temple Book Store, n.d.).
—'Divine Names and Titles of Jehovah', in Donald W. Dayton (ed.) *Seven 'Jesus Only' Tracts* (HCL; New York: Garland Publishing, 1985 repr.; Indianapolis: Christ Temple Book Store, n.d.).
—'The Finest of the Wheat', in Donald W. Dayton (ed.) *Seven 'Jesus Only' Tracts* (HCL; New York: Garland Publishing, 1985 repr.; Indianapolis: Christ Temple Book Store, n.d.).
—'The Victim of the Flaming Sword', in Donald W. Dayton (ed.) *Seven 'Jesus Only' Tracts* (HCL; New York: Garland Publishing, 1985 repr.; Indianapolis: Christ Temple Book Store, n.d.).
Heard, Albert F., *The Russian Church and Russian Dissent: Comprising Orthodoxy, Dissent, and Erratic Sects* (New York: Harper & Brothers, 1887).
Hector, Kevin W., 'The Mediation of Christ's Normative Spirit: A Constructive Reading of Schleiermacher's Pneumatology', *Modern Theology* 24 (2008), pp. 1-22.
Hefelbower, Samuel Gring, *The Relation of John Locke to English Deism* (Chicago: The University of Chicago Press, 1918).
Heine, Ronald E., *The Montanist Oracles and Testimonia* (Macon, GA: Mercer University Press, 1989).
'Henoticon', in F.L. Cross and Elizabeth A. Livingstone (eds.), *ODCC* (Oxford: Oxford University Press, 3rd edn, 1997), p. 750.
Henry, Patrick, 'What Was the Iconoclastic Controversy About?', *CH* 45 (1976), pp. 16-31.
Hermas, 'The Pastor of Hermas', *ANF*; *Translations of the Writings of the Fathers Down to A.D. 325* (trans. F. Crombie; 10 vols.; American reprint of the Edinburgh Edition repr.; Grand Rapids: Eerdmans, 2001). II, pp. 9-55.
'Hesychasm', in F.L. Cross and Elizabeth A. Livingstone (eds.), *ODCC* (Oxford: Oxford University Press, 3rd edn, 1997), pp. 763-64.
Hick, John, 'Jesus and the World Religions', in John Hick (ed.) *The Myth of God Incarnate* (Philadelphia: Westminster, 1977), pp. 167-85.
—'An Inspiration Christology for a Religiously Plural World', in Stephen T. Davis (ed.) *Encountering Jesus: A Debate on Christology* (Atlanta: John Knox, 1988), pp. 5-22.
—*Disputed Questions in Theology and the Philosophy of Religion* (New Haven: Yale University Press, 1993).

—*The Metaphor of God Incarnate: Christology in a Pluralistic Age* (Louisville, KY: Westminster/John Knox Press, 1993).

Hilary, *The Trinity* (trans. Stephen McKenna; FC: A New Translation; Washington: Catholic University of America Press, 1954).

—'On the Trinity', in Philip Schaff and Henry Wace (eds.), *The NPNF, Second Series* (trans. E.W. Watson and L. Pullan; 14 vols.; Grand Rapids: Eerdmans, American reprint of the Edinburgh edn, 1997), IX, pp. 40-233.

Hildebrand, Stephen M., *The Trinitarian Theology of Basil of Caesarea: A Synthesis of Greek Thought and Biblical Truth* (Washington: Catholic University of America Press, 2007).

Hinze, Bradford E., and D. Lyle Dabney, *Advents of the Spirit: An Introduction to the Current Study of Pneumatology* (Milwaukee: Marquette University Press, 2001).

'Hippolytus', in F.L. Cross and Elizabeth A. Livingstone (eds.), *ODCC* (Oxford: Oxford University Press, 3rd edn, 1997), pp. 773-74.

Hippolytus, 'Against the Heresy of One Noetus', in Alexander Roberts and James Donaldson (eds.), *ANF; Translations of the Writings of the Fathers Down to A.D. 325* (trans. J.H. MacMahon; 10 vols.; Grand Rapids: Eerdmans, American reprint of the Edinburgh edn, 1995), V, pp. 223-31.

—'The Refutation of All Heresies', in Alexander Roberts and James Donaldson (eds.), *ANF* (trans. J.H. MacMahon; 10 vols.; Grand Rapids: Eerdmans, American reprint of the Edinburgh edn, 1995), V, pp. 9-241.

Hippolytus, and Burton Scott Easton, *The Apostolic Tradition of Hippolytus* (Cambridge: Cambridge University Press, 1934).

Hippolytus, and Alistair Stewart-Sykes, *On the Apostolic Tradition* (Popular Patristics Series; Crestwood, NY: St. Vladimir's Seminary Press, 2001).

Hocken, Peter D., 'Charismatic Movement', in Stanley M. Burgess and Ed M. Van der Maas (eds.), *NIDPCM* (Grand Rapids: Zondervan, Rev. and expanded edn, 2002), pp. 477-519.

Hoek, Annewies van den, 'The "Catechetical" School of Early Christian Alexandria and Its Philonic Heritage', *HTR* 90.1 (1997), pp. 59-87.

Hogsten, Doug, 'The Monadic Formula of Water Baptism: A Quest for Primitivism Via a Christocentric and Restorationist Impulse', *JPT* 17 (2008), pp. 70-95.

Holder, Arthur G., 'Bede and the Tradition of Patristic Exegesis', *ATR* 72 (1990), pp. 399-411.

Hollenweger, Walter J., *The Pentecostals: The Charismatic Movement in the Churches* (Minneapolis: Augsburg, 1972).

—'Pentecostals and the Charismatic Movement', in C. Jones, G. Wainwright and E. Yarnold (eds.), *The Study of Spirituality* (New York: Oxford University Press, 1986), pp. 549-53.

—*Pentecostalism: Origins and Developments Worldwide* (Peabody, MA: Hendrickson Publishers, 1997).

Holmes, Michael W., *The Apostolic Fathers in English* (trans. Michael W. Holmes; after the earlier version of Lightfoot, J.B. and Harmer, J.R. repr.; Grand Rapids: Baker Book House, 3rd edn, 2006).

Hook, Norman, *Christ in the Twentieth Century: A Spirit Christology* (London: Lutterworth, 1968).

—'A Spirit Christology', *Theology* 75 (1972), pp. 226-32.
Horner, R.C., *Pentecost* (Toronto: William Briggs, 1891).
—*Notes on Boland; or, Mr. Wesley and the Second Work of Grace* (Boston: McDonald and Gill, 1893).
—*Ralph C. Horner, Evangelist: Reminiscences from His Own Pen, Also Reports on Five Typical Sermons* (Brockville Ont: Standard Church Book Room, n.d.).
—'Entire Consecration', in *From the Altar to the Upper Room* (The Higher Christian life; New York: Garland Publishing, 1984 repr.; Toronto: William Briggs, 1891), pp. 7-116.
—'To, before, and on the Altar', in *From the Altar to the Upper Room* (Higher Christian Life; New York: Garland Publishing, 1984 repr.; Toronto: William Briggs, 1891), pp. 11-30.
—'What Is Consecration', in *From the Altar to the Upper Room* (The Higher Christian Life; New York: Garland Publishing, 1984 repr.; Toronto: Willian Briggs, 1891), pp. 3-12.
Howson, Barry H., 'The Puritan Hermeneutics of John Owen: A Recommendation', *WTJ* 63 (2001), pp. 351-76.
Hulse, Erroll, *Who Are the Puritans?: And What Do They Preach?* (Darlington, England: Evangelical Press, 2000).
Humphrey, Edith McEwan, *The Ladies and the Cities: Transformation and Apocalyptic Identity in Joseph and Aseneth, 4 Ezra, the Apocalypse and the Shepherd of Hermas* (JSPSup 17; Sheffield: Sheffield Academic Press, 1995).
Hunter, Harold, 'The Resurgence of Spirit Christology', *European Pentecostal Theological Association Bulletin* 11 (1992), pp. 50-57.
—'Tomlinson, Ambrose Jessup', in Stanley M. Burgess and Ed M. Van der Maas (eds.), *NIDPCM* (Grand Rapids: Zondervan, Rev. and expanded edn, 2002), pp. 1143-45.
—'Spirit Christology Dilemma and Promise (1)', *HeyJ* 24 (1983), pp. 127-40.
—'Spirit Christology Dilemma and Promise (2)', *HeyJ* 24 (1983), pp. 266-77.
—'Beniah at the Apostolic Crossroads: Little Noticed Crosscurrents of B.H. Irwin, Charles Fox Parham, Frank Sandford, A.J. Tomlinson', *Cyberjournal for Pentecostal-Charismatic Research* 1 (1997), pp. 1-25.
Hunter, Harold D., and Cecil M. Robeck (eds.), *The Azusa Street Revival and Its Legacy* (Cleveland, TN: Pathway Press, 2006).
Hurtado, Larry W., *Lord Jesus Christ: Devotion to Jesus in Earliest Christianity* (Grand Rapids: Eerdmans, 2003).
Hussey, Edmund M., 'Persons: Energy Structure in the Theology of St. Gregory Palamas', *SVTQ* 18 (1974), pp. 22-43.
Hyatt, Harry Middleton, *The Church of Abyssinia* (The Oriental Research Series 4; London: Luzac, 1928).
Irenaeus, *The Scandal of the Incarnation: Irenaeus against the Heresies, Selected and with an Introduction by Hans Urs Von Balthasar* (trans. John Saward; San Francisco: Ignatius Press, 1990).
—'Against Heresies', in Alexander Roberts and James Donaldson (eds.), *ANF; Translations of the Writings of the Fathers Down to A.D. 325* (trans. M. Dods; 10 vols.; Grand Rapids: Eerdmans, American reprint of the Edinburgh edn, 1995), I, pp. 309-567.

Irving, Edward, *The Day of Pentecost, or the Baptism with the Holy Ghost* (Edinburg: John Lindsay, 1831).
—'The Church with Her Endowment of Holiness and Power', in Gavin Carlyle (ed.) *CW* (5 vols.; London: Alexander Strahan & Co., 1864), V, pp. 449-506.
—'The Doctrine of the Incarnation Opened in Six Sermons', in Gavin Carlyle (ed.) *CW* (5 vols.; London: Alexander Strahan & Co., 1864), V, pp. 9-446.
—'On the Gifts of the Holy Ghost Commonly Called Supernatural', in Gavin Carlyle (ed.) *CW* (5 vols.; London: Alexander Strahan & Co., 1864), V, pp. 509-61.
—'The Sealing Virtue', in Gavin Carlyle (ed.) *CW* (5 vols.; London: Alexander Strahan & Co., 1864), II, pp. 270-89.
—'The Temptation', in Gavin Carlyle (ed.) *CW* (5 vols.; London: Alexander Strahan & Co., 1864), II, pp. 191-243.
Isenberg, Wesley W., 'Philip, Gospel Of', in David Noel Freedman (ed.), *ABD* (6 vols.; New York: Doubleday, 1992), V, pp. 312-13.
Jackson, Pamela, 'Cyril of Jerusalem's Use of Scripture in Catechesis', *TS* 52 (1991), pp. 431-50.
Jacobsen, Douglas G., *Thinking in the Spirit: Theologies of the Early Pentecostal Movement* (Bloomington: Indiana University Press, 2003).
Jefford, Clayton N., *The Apostolic Fathers: An Essential Guide* (Nashville: Abingdon Press, 2005).
Jenkins, S.D.L., 'The Human Son of God and the Holy Spirit: Toward a Pentecostal Incarnational Spirit Christology' (PhD dissertation; Marquette: Marquette University, 2004.
'Jesus Prayer', in F.L. Cross and Elizabeth A. Livingstone (eds.), *ODCC* (Oxford: Oxford University Press, 3rd edn, 1997), p. 875.
Jevtich, Atanasije, 'Between the "Nicaeans" and the "Easterners": The Catholic Confession of Saint Basil', *SVTQ* 24 (1980), pp. 235-52.
Jonas, Hans, *The Gnostic Religion: The Message of the Alien God and the Beginnings of Christianity* (Boston: Beacon Press, 2nd edn, 1963).
Jones, C.E., 'Holiness Movement', in Stanley M. Burgess and Ed M. Van der Maas (eds.), *Encyclopedia Holiness Movement* (Grand Rapids: Zondervan, Rev. and expanded edn, 2002), pp. 726-29.
Jones, F. Stanley, 'Clementines, Pseudo-', in David Noel Freedman (ed.), *ABD* (6 vols.; New York: Doubleday, 1992), I, pp. 1061-62.
—*An Ancient Jewish Christian Source on the History of Christianity: Pseudo-Clementine Recognitions 1.27-71* (Atlanta: Scholars Press, 1995).
Jones, Marvin D., *Athanasius' Concept of Eternal Sonship as Revealed in Contra Arianos* (Lewiston, NY: Edwin Mellen Press, 2006).
'The Journey into Refuge from the Transcaucasus and Transcaspia to America', in Ivan Gureivich Samarin and Daniel H. Shubin (eds.), *Spirit and Life—Book of the Sun: Divine Discourses of the Preceptors and the Martyrs for the Word of God, the Faith of Jesus, and the Holy Spirit, of the Religion of the Spiritual Christian Molokan-Jumpers, Including a History of the Religion* (trans. John W. Volkov; 1983 repr.; USA: Daniel H. Shubin, 1928)
Justin, *The First and Second Apologies* (trans. Leslie W. Barnard; ACW 56; New York: Paulist Press, 1997).

Kalleres, Dayna S., 'Cultivating True Sight at the Center of the World: Cyril of Jerusalem and the Lenten Catechumenate', *CH* 74 (2005), pp. 431-59.

Kannengiesser, Charles, *Arius and Athanasius: Two Alexandrian Theologians* (Brookfield, VT: Gower, 1991).

Kant, Immanuel, *Foundations of the Metaphysics of Morals: What Is Enlightenment? And a Passage from the Metaphysics of Morals* (Chicago: University of Chicago Press, 1950).

—'The Critique of Practical Reason', in Mortimer Jerome Adler, Clifton Fadiman and Philip W. Goetz (eds.), *GBWW* (trans. Thomas Kingsmill Abbott; 61 vols.; Chicago: Encyclopedia Britannica Inc., 2nd edn, 1990), XXXIX, pp. 289-361.

—'The Critique of Pure Reason', in Mortimer Jerome Adler, Clifton Fadiman and Philip W. Goetz (eds.), *GBWW* (trans. J.M.D. Meiklejohn; 61 vols.; Chicago: Encyclopedia Britannica Inc., 2nd edn, 1990), XXXIX, pp.1-250.

Kärkkäinen, Veli-Matti, *Pneumatology: The Holy Spirit in Ecumenical, International, and Contextual Perspective* (Grand Rapids: Baker Academic, 2002).

—*Christology: A Global Introduction* (Grand Rapids: Baker Academic, 2003).

—(ed.), *Holy Spirit and Salvation: The Sources of Christian Theology* (Louisville, KY: Westminster / John Knox Press, 2010).

Kasper, Walter, *Jesus Der Christus* (Mainz: Matthias Grunewald-Verlag, 1974).

—*Jesus the Christ* (trans. V. Green; New York: Paulist Press, 1976).

—*The God of Jesus Christ* (trans. Matthew J. O'Connell; New York: Crossroad, 1994).

Kearsley, Roy, *Tertullian's Theology of Divine Power* (Rutherford Studies in Historical Theology; Carlisle: Paternoster, 1998).

Keating, Daniel, 'The Baptism of Jesus in Cyril of Alexandria: The Re-Creation of the Human Race', *ProEccl* 8 (1999), pp. 201-22.

Kelly, J.N.D., *Early Christian Doctrines* (San Francisco: Harper & Row, 1960).

Kelsey, Catherine L., *Thinking About Christ with Schleiermacher* (Louisville: Westminster John Knox Press, 2003).

Kendrick, Klaud, *The Promise Fulfilled* (Springfield, MO: Gospel Publishing House, 1959).

'Kenotic Theories', in F.L. Cross and Elizabeth A. Livingstone (eds.), *ODCC* (Oxford: Oxford University Press, 3rd edn, 1997), p. 923.

The Key of Truth: A Manual of the Paulician Church of Armenia (trans. F.C. Conybeare; Oxford: Clarendon Press, 1898).

Kidane, Habtemichael, 'The Holy Spirit in the Ethiopian Orthodox Church Täwahedo Tradition', in Teresa Berger and Bryan D. Spinks (eds.), *The Spirit in Worship, Worship in the Spirit* (Collegeville, MN: Liturgical Press, 2009), pp. 179-205.

King, J.H., *From Passover to Pentecost* (Memphis, TN: H.W. Dixon, 1914).

—*Yet Speaketh: Memoirs of the Late Bishop Joseph H. King* (Franklin Springs, GA: The Publishing House of the Pentecostal Holiness Church, 1949).

—*Christ—God's Love Gift* (Selected Writings of Joseph Hillery King 1; Franklin Springs, GA: Advocate Press, 1969).

—'History of the Fire-Baptized Holiness Church', *PHA*.

Kissinger, Warren S., *The Lives of Jesus: A History and Bibliography* (Garland Reference Library of the Humanities; New York: Garland, 1985)

Kitromilides, Paschalis M., 'Orthodoxy and the West: Reformation to Enlightenment', in Michael Angold (ed.) *CHC: Eastern Christianity* (9 vols.; Cambridge: Cambridge University Press, 2006), V, pp. 187-209.

Klubnikin, Efim Gerasimovich, 'Articles and Plans of Efim Gerasimovich Klubnikin', in Ivan Gureivich Samarin and Daniel H. Shubin (eds.), *Spirit and Life—Book of the Sun: Divine Discourses of the Preceptors and the Martyrs for the Word of God, the Faith of Jesus, and the Holy Spirit, of the Religion of the Spiritual Christian Molokan-Jumpers, Including a History of the Religion* (trans. John W. Volkov; 1983 repr.; USA: Daniel H. Shubin, 1928)

Knott, John R., *The Sword of the Spirit: Puritan Responses to the Bible* (Chicago: University of Chicago Press, 1980).

Kontzevitch, I.M., *The Acquisition of the Holy Spirit in Ancient Russia* (trans. Olga Koshansky; The Acquisition of the Holy Spirit in Russia Series; Platina, CA: St. Herman of Alaska Brotherhood, 1988).

Kraft, Robert A., *The Apostolic Fathers: A New Translation and Commentary* (6 vols.; London: Thomas Nelson, 1965).

Krivocheine, Basil, *In the Light of Christ: Saint Symeon the New Theologian (949-1022) Life-Spirituality-Doctrine* (trans. Anthony P. Gythiel; Crestwood, NY: St. Vladimir's Seminary Press, 1986).

Kurowski, Mark T., 'The First Step toward Grace: John Wesley's Use of the Spiritual Homilies of Macarius the Great', *Methodist History* 36 (1998), pp. 113-24.

Kutepov, Konstantin, *Sekty Khlystov I Skoptsov* (Kazan: Imperial University, 1882).

L'Huillier, Peter, *The Church of the Ancient Councils: The Disciplinary Work of the First Four Ecumenical Councils* (Crestwood, NY: St. Vladimir's Seminary Press, 1995).

Lactantius, *The Divine Institutes, Books I–VII* (trans. Mary Francis McDonald; FC: A New Translation; Washington: Catholic University of America Press, 1964).

Lake, Kirsopp, *The Apostolic Fathers* (trans. Kirsopp Lake; LCL; 2 vols.; London: Heinemann, 1912-13).

Lambert, Malcolm, *Medieval Heresy: Popular Movements from Bogomil to Hus* (New York: Holmes & Meier Publishers, 1977).

—*Medieval Heresy: Popular Movements from the Gregorian Reform to the Reformation* (Oxford: Blackwell, 2nd edn, 1992).

—*The Cathars* (Malden, MA: Blackwell Publishers, 1998).

Lampe, G.W.H., 'The Holy Spirit and the Person of Christ', in Stephen Sykes and John Powell Clayton (eds.), *Christ, Faith and History: Cambridge Studies in Christology* (London: Cambridge University Press, 1972), pp. 111-130.

—*God as Spirit* (Oxford: Clarendon Press, 1977).

Lancel, Serge, *Saint Augustine* (trans. Antonia Nevill; London: SCM Press, 2002).

Land, Steven J., *Pentecostal Spirituality: A Passion for the Kingdom* (JPTSup 1; Sheffield, England: Sheffield Academic Press, 1993).

—'William J. Seymour: The Father of the Holiness-Pentecostal Movement', in Henry H. Knight (ed.) *From Aldersgate to Azusa Street: Wesleyan, Holiness, and Pentecostalism Visions of the New Creation* (Eugene, OR: Wipf and Stock, 2010), pp. 218-26.

Latourette, Kenneth Scott, *A History of Christianity* (2 vols.; New York: Harper & Row, Rev. edn, 1975).
Lawson, John, *A Theological and Historical Introduction to the Apostolic Fathers* (New York: Macmillan, 1961).
Lee, Elnora L., *A Life Fully Dedicated to God* (n.p., 1967).
Leo, *Letters* (trans. Edmund Hunt; FC: A New Translation; Washington: Catholic University of America Press, 1957).
—*Sermons* (trans. Jane Patricia Freeland and Agnes Josephine Conway; FC: A New Translation; Washington: Catholic University of America Press, 1996).
Lennox, Stephen J., 'The Eschatology of George D. Watson', *Wesleyan Theological Journal* 29 (1994), pp. 111-26.
Levison, John R., *Filled with the Spirit* (Grand Rapids: Eerdmans, 2009).
Liddell, Henry George, and Robert Scott, 'συντρέχω', *An Intermediate Greek-English Lexicon, Founded upon the Seventh Edition of Liddell and Scott's* (Oxford: Oxford University Press repr.; New York: Harper & Brothers, 1889), p. 781.
Lienhard, Joseph T., 'Marcellus of Ancyra in Modern Research', *TS* 43 (1982), pp. 486-503.
—'The Epistle of the Synod of Ancyra, 358: A Reconsideration', in Robert C. Gregg (ed.) *Arianism: Historical and Theological Reassessments: Papers from the Ninth International Conference on Patristic Studies, September 5-10, 1983, Oxford, England* (Patristic Monograph Series 11; Cambridge, MA: Philadelphia Patristic Foundation, 1985), pp. 313-19.
—'The "Arian" Controversy: Some Categories Reconsidered', *TS* 48 (1987), pp. 415-37.
—'Basil of Caesarea, Marcellus of Ancyra, and "Sabellius"', *CH* 58 (1989), pp. 157-67.
—'Did Athanasius Reject Marcellus?', in Michel R. Barnes and Daniel H. Williams (eds.), *Arianism after Arius: Essays on the Development of the Fourth Century Trinitarian Conflicts* (Edinburgh: T. & T. Clark, 1993), pp. 65-80.
—'"The Glue Itself Is Charity": Ps.62.9 in Augustine's Thought', in Joseph T. Lienhard, Earl C. Muller and Roland J. Teske (eds.), *Augustine: Presbyter Factus Sum* (Collectanea Augustiniana; New York: Peter Lang, 1993), pp. 375-84.
—*Contra Marcellum: Marcellus of Ancyra and Fourth-Century Theology* (Washington: Catholic University of America Press, 1999).
Lietzmann, Hans, *Apollinaris Von Laodicea Und Seine Schule: Texte Und Untersuchungen* (Hildesheim: Georg Olms, 1970 repr.; Tübingen: J.C.B. Mohr [Paul Siebeck], 1904).
Lightfoot, J.B., *The Apostolic Fathers: A Revised Text with Introductions, Notes, Dissertations, and Translations* (trans. J.B. Lightfoot; 2 parts in 5 vols.; Peabody, MA: Hendrickson, 1984).
Lindström, Harald Gustaf Åke, *Wesley and Sanctification : A Study in the Doctrine of Salvation* (Grand Rapids: Francis Asbury Press, 1980).
Livingston, James C., *Modern Christian Thought: The Enlightenment and the Nineteenth Century* (2 vols.; Upper Saddle River, NJ: Prentice Hall, 2nd edn, 1997).
Livingston, James C., and Francis Schèussler Fiorenza, *Modern Christian Thought: The Twentieth Century* (2 vols.; Upper Saddle River, NJ: Prentice-Hall, 2nd edn, 2000).

Lodahl, Michael, *Shekhinah/Spirit: Divine Presence in Jewish and Christian Religion* (New York: Paulist Press, 1992).

Loewe, William P., 'Two Revisionist Christologies of Presence; Roger Haight and Piet Schoonenberg', in Michael Horace Barnes and William P. Roberts (eds.), *A Sacramental Life: A Festschrift Honoring Bernard Cooke* (Milwaukee: Marquette University Press, 2003), pp. 93-115.

Logan, B.H., 'Marcellus of Ancyra and the Councils of AD 325: Antioch, Ancyra, and Nicaea', *JTS* 43 (1992), pp. 428-46.

Loofs, Friedrich, *Nestoriana: Die Fragmente Des Nestorius Gesammelt, Untersucht Und Herausgegeben* (Halle: Max Niemeyer, 1905).

—*Nestorius and His Place in the History of Christian Doctrine* (Cambridge: Cambridge University Press, 1914).

—*Theophilus Von Antiochien Adversus Marcionem Und Die Anderen Theologischen Quellen Bei Irenaeus* (TUGAL 46; Leipzig: Hinrichs, 1930).

Lossky, Vladimir, *The Mystical Theology of the Eastern Church* (trans. Members of the Fellowship of St. Alban and St. Sergius; Crestwood, NY: St Vladimir's Seminary Press, 1976 repr.; London: J. Clarke, 1957).

—*In the Image and Likeness of God* (Crestwood, NY: St. Vladimir's Seminary Press, 1985).

Louth, Andrew, *Maximus the Confessor* (ECF; London: Routledge, 1996).

—*St. John Damascene: Tradition and Originality in Byzantine Theology* (OECS; New York: Oxford University Press, 2002).

Lovett, Leonard, 'Perspective on the Black Origins of the Contemporary Pentecostal Movement', *Journal of the Interdenominational Theological Center* 1 (1973), pp. 36-49.

—'Black Origins of the Pentecostal Movement', in Vinson Synan (ed.) *Aspects of Pentecostal-Charismatic Origins* (Plainfield, NJ: Logos International, 1975), pp. 143-68 .

Ludlow, Morwenna, 'Theology and Allegory: Origen and Gregory of Nyssa on the Unity and Diversity of Scripture', *IJST* 4 (2002), pp. 45-66.

Lyman, J. Rebecca, 'Substance Language in Origen and Eusebius', in Robert C. Gregg (ed.) *Arianism: Historical and Theological Reassessments: Papers from the Ninth International Conference on Patristic Studies, September 5-10, 1983, Oxford, England* (Patristic Monograph Series 11; Eugene, OR: Wipf and Stock, 2006 repr.; Cambridge, MA: Philadelphia Patristic Foundation, 1985), pp. 257-66.

—*Christology and Cosmology: Models of Divine Activity in Origen, Eusebius, and Athanasius* (OTM; Oxford: Clarendon Press, 1993).

Macchia, Frank D., 'Salvation and Spirit Baptism: Another Look at James Dunn's Classic', *Pneuma* 24.1 (Spring 2002), pp. 1-6.

—*Baptized in the Spirit: A Global Pentecostal Theology* (Grand Rapids: Zondervan, 2006).

—*Justified in the Spirit: Creation, Redemption, and the Triune God* (Pentecostal Manifestos; Grand Rapids: Eerdmans, 2010).

MacKenzie, Iain M., and Irenaeus, *Irenaeus's Demonstration of the Apostolic Preaching: A Theological Commentary and Translation* (trans. J. Armitage Robinson; Aldershot, Hants, England Burlington, VT: Ashgate, 2002).

Maddox, Randy L., *Responsible Grace: John Wesley's Practical Theology* (Nashville: Kingswood, 1994).

—'John Wesley and Eastern Orthodoxy Influences, Convergences and Differences', *AsTJ* 45 (1990), pp. 29-53.

Mahan, Asa, *Scripture Doctrine of Christian Perfection; with Other Kindred Subjects, Illustrated and Confirmed in a Series of Discourses Designed to Throw Light on the Way of Holiness* (Boston: D.S. King, 1839).

—*The Baptism of the Holy Ghost* (London: Elliot Stock, 1876 repr.; New York: W.C. Palmer, jr., 1870).

Malchion, 'The Epistle Written by Malchion, in the Name of the Synod of Antioch, against Paul of Samosata', in Alexander Roberts and James Donaldson (eds.), *ANF; Translations of the Writings of the Fathers Down to A.D. 325* (trans. S.D. Salmond; 10 vols.; Grand Rapids: Eerdmans, American reprint of the Edinburgh edn, 1997), VI, pp. 169-72.

Martin, Larry Jay, *The Life and Ministry of William J. Seymour: And a History of the Azusa Street Revival* (Joplin, MO: Christian Life Books, 1999).

Martyr, Justin, 'Dialogue with Trypho, a Jew', in Alexander Roberts and James Donaldson (eds.), *ANF; Translations of the Writings of the Fathers Down to A.D. 325* (trans. M. Dods; 10 vols.; Grand Rapids: Eerdmans, American reprint of the Edinburgh edn, 1995), I, pp. 194-270.

—'The First Apology of Justin', in Alexander Roberts and James Donaldson (eds.), *ANF; Translations of the Writings of the Fathers Down to A.D. 325* (trans. M. Dods; 10 vols.; Grand Rapids: Eerdmans, American reprint of the Edinburgh edition edn, 1995), I, pp. 163-87.

Mason, Elsie, *The Man, Charles Harrison Mason (1866–1961)* (Wayne M. and W.L. Porter. Memphis, TN: Pioneer Series Publication, 1979 repr.; n.p., n.d.).

Mason, Mary, *The History and Life Work of Elder C.H. Mason Chief Apostle and His Co-Laborers* (1987 repr.; n.p., 1924).

Maurer, Christian, 'σκεῦος', in Geoffrey W. Bromiley (ed.), *TDNT* (trans. Geoffrey W. Bromiley; Grand Rapids: Eerdmans, 1999), VII, pp. 358-67.

Maxwell, David R., 'What Was "Wrong" with Augustine? The Sixth-Century Reception (or Lack Thereof) of Augustine's Christology', in Peter William Martens (ed.) *In the Shadow of the Incarnation: Essays on Jesus Christ in the Early Church in Honor of Brian E. Daley, S.J* (Notre Dame: University of Notre Dame Press, 2008), pp. 212-27.

McClung, Grant, *Azusa Street and Beyond: Pentecostal Missions and Church Growth in the Twentieth Century* (Gainesville, FL: Bridge-Logos Publishers, 1986).

McCormick, Bruce L., 'Karl Barth's Christology as a Resource for a Reformed Version of Kenoticism', *IJSTheo* 8 (2006), pp. 244-45.

McCormick, K. Steve, 'Theosis in Chrysostom and Wesley: An Eastern Paradigm on Faith and Love', *Wesleyan Theological Journal* 26 (1991), pp. 38-103.

McDonnell, Kilian, 'A Trinitarian Theology of the Holy Spirit', *TS* 46 (1985), pp. 191-27.

—*The Baptism of Jesus in the Jordan: The Trinitarian and Cosmic Order of Salvation* (Collegeville: Liturgical Press, 1996).

—*Charismatic Renewal and the Churches* (New York: Seabury, 1976).

McDonnell, Kilian, and George T. Montague, *Christian Initiation and Baptism in the Holy Spirit: Evidence from the First Eight Centuries* (Collegeville, MN: Liturgical Press, 1990).

McFarland, Ian A., 'Developing an Apophatic Christocentrism: Lessons from Maximus the Confessor', *ThTo* 60 (2003), pp. 200-14.

—'Fleshing out Christ: Maximus the Confessor's Christology in Anthropological Perspective', *SVTQ* 49 (2005), pp. 417-36.

McFarlane, Graham, *Christ and the Spirit: The Doctrine of the Incarnation According to Edward Irving* (Carlisle: Paternoster Press, 1996).

McGee, Gary B., 'Flower, Joseph James Roswell', in Stanley M. Burgess and Ed M. Van der Maas (eds.), *NIDPCM* (Grand Rapids: Zondervan, Rev. and expanded edn, 2002), pp. 642-43.

McGrath, Alister E., *The Making of Modern German Christology, 1750–1990* (Eugene, OR: Wipf and Stock, 2005 repr.; London: Inter-Varsity Press, 2nd edn, 1994).

McGuckin, John Anthony, 'Did Augustine's Christology Depend on Theodore of Mopsuestia?', *HeyJ* 31 (1990), pp. 39-52.

—*St. Cyril of Alexandria: The Christological Controversy: Its History, Theology, and Texts* (VCSup 23; Leiden: E.J. Brill, 1994).

McGuire, Anne, 'Conversion and Gnosis in the Gospel of Truth', *NovT* 28 (1986), pp. 338-55.

McKim, Donald K., *Westminster Dictionary of Theological Terms* (Louisville: Westminster / John Knox Press, 1996).

McKinley, David J., 'John Owen's View of Illumination: An Alternative to the Fuller-Erickson Dialogue', *Bibliotheca Sacra* 154 (1997), pp. 93-104.

McLynn, Neil B., *Ambrose of Milan: Church and Court in a Christian Capital* (Berkeley: University of California Press, 1994).

Menzies, Robert P., *The Development of Early Christian Pneumatology: With Special Reference to Luke-Acts* (JSNTSup; 54; Sheffield: *JSOT* Press, 1991)

—'Luke and the Spirit: A Reply to James Dunn', *JPT* 4.2 (Apr 1994), pp. 115-38.

—*Empowered for Witness: The Spirit in Luke-Acts* (JPTSup; 6; Sheffield: Sheffield Academic Press, 1994)

Menzies, William W., 'The Non-Wesleyan Origins of the Pentecostal Movement', in Vinson Synan (ed.) *Aspects of Pentecostal-Charismatic Origins* (Plainfield, NJ: Logos International, 1975), pp. 81-98.

Meredith, Anthony, *The Cappadocians* (Crestwood, NY: St. Vladimir's Seminary Press, 1995).

Meredith, Anthony, and Gregory, *Gregory of Nyssa* (ECF; London: Routledge, 1999).

Merricks, William S., *Edward Irving: The Forgotten Giant* (East Peoria, IL: Scribe's Chamber Publications, 1983).

'Messalians', in F.L. Cross and Elizabeth A. Livingstone (eds.), *ODCC* (Oxford: Oxford University Press, 3rd edn, 1997), p. 1075.

'Messalians; Paulicians; Bogomils, Cathari, Albigenses; Patarenes', in F.L. Cross and Elizabeth A. Livingstone (eds.), *ODCC* (Oxford: Oxford University Press, 3rd edn, 1997), p. 1075.

Metzger, Bruce Manning, *The Early Versions of the New Testament: Their Origin, Transmission, and Limitations* (Oxford: Clarendon Press, 1977).

Meyendorff, John, 'The Doctrine of Grace in St. Gregory Palamas', *SVTQ* 2 (1954), pp. 17-26.
—*Christ in Eastern Christian Thought* (Washington, DC: Corpus Books, 1969).
—*Byzantine Theology: Historical Trends and Doctrinal Themes* (New York: Fordham University Press, 1974).
—*St. Gregory Palamas and Orthodox Spirituality* (trans. Fiske Adele; Crestwood, NY: St. Vladimir's Seminary Press, 1974).
—*Christ in Eastern Christian Thought* (Crestwood, NY: St. Vladimir's Seminary Press, 1975).
Migne, J.P. (ed.), *PG* (Paris, 1857-66).
Miller, Patricia Cox, 'Words with an Alien Voice', *JAAR* 57 (1989) pp. 459-82.
Minns, Denis, *Irenaeus* (Washington, DC: Georgetown University Press, 1994).
Miskov, Jennifer, *Life on Wings: The Forgotten Life and Theology of Carrie Judd Montgomery (1858–1946)* (Cleveland, TN: CPT Press, 2012).
Moltmann, Jürgen, *The Spirit of Life: A Universal Affirmation* (trans. Margaret Kohl; Minneapolis: Fortress, 1992).
—*The Crucified God: The Cross of Christ as the Foundation and Criticism of Christian Theology* (Minneapolis: Fortress, 1993).
—*God in Creation: A New Theology of Creation and the Spirit of God* (Gifford Lectures; 1984–85; Minneapolis: Fortress, 1993).
—*The Trinity and the Kingdom: The Doctrine of God* (Minneapolis: Fortress, 1993).
—*The Way of Jesus Christ: Christology in Messianic Dimensions* (Minneapolis: Fortress Press, 1993).
—'The Trinitarian Personhood of the Holy Spirit', in Bradford E. Hinze, Dabney, D. Lyle (ed.) *Advents of the Spirit: An Introduction to the Current Study of Pneumatology* (trans. D. Lyle Dabney; Milwaukee: Marquette University Press, 2001), pp. 302-314.
'Monarchianism', in F.L. Cross and Elizabeth A. Livingstone (eds.), *ODCC* (Oxford: Oxford University Press, 3rd edn, 1997), p. 1102.
'Montanism', in F.L. Cross and Elizabeth A. Livingstone (eds.), *ODCC* (Oxford: Oxford University Press, 3rd edn, 1997), pp. 1107-08.
Montgomery, Carrie Judd, *The Prayer of Faith* (Buffalo, NY: H.H. Otis, 1880).
Mühlen, Heribert, *Der Heilige Geist Als Person* (Münster Westfalen: Aschendorffsche Verlagsbuchhandlung, 1963).
—*Una Mystica Persona* (Paderborn: Ferdinand Schöningh, 1964).
Munro-Hay, S., 'Christianity, History of Christianity', in S. Uhlig (ed.), *Encyclopedia Æthiopica* (Wiesbaden: Harrassowitz Verlag, 2003), I, pp. 717-23.
Murray, Russel, 'Mirror of Experience: Palamas and Bonaventure on the Experience of God—A Contribution to Orthodox-Roman Catholic Dialogue', *JES* 44 (2009), pp. 432-60.
Myland, Wesley, 'The Latter Rain Covenant and Pentecostal Power: With Testimony of Healings and Baptism', in Donald W. Dayton (ed.) *Three Early Pentecostal Tractates* (New York: Garland Publishing, 1985 repr.; Chicago: Evangel Publishing House, 1910)
Nazianzus, Gregory of, 'Prolegomena', in Philip Schaff and Henry Wace (eds.), *NPNF, Second Series* (14 vols.; Grand Rapids: Eerdmans, American reprint of the Edinburgh edition edn, 1996), VII, pp. 187-202.

—'Select Letters', in Philip Schaff and Henry Wace (eds.), *NPNF, Second Series* (trans. Charles Gordon Browne and James Edward Swallow; 14 vols.; American reprint of the Edinburgh edition repr.; Grand Rapids: Eerdmans, 1996), VII, pp. 437-82.

—'Select Orations', in Philip Schaff and Henry Wace (eds.), *NPNF, Second Series* (trans. Charles Gordon Browne and James Edward Swallow; 14 vols.; Grand Rapids: Eerdmans, American reprint of the Edinburgh edition edn, 1996), VII, pp. 203-434.

Need, Stephen W., *Truly Divine and Truly Human: The Story of Christ and the Seven Ecumenical Councils* (London: SPCK, 2008).

Nelson, Shirley, *Fair, Clear, and Terrible: The Story of Shiloh, Maine* (Latham, NY: British American Publishing, 1989).

Nestorius, *The Bazaar of Heracleides* (trans. Godfrey Rolles Driver and Leonard Hodgson; Eugene, OR: Wipf and Stock, 2002 repr.; Oxford: Oxford University Press, 1925).

Neusner, Jacob, *Judaism, Christianity, and Zoroastrianism in Talmudic Babylonia* (Studies in Judaism; Lanham, MD: University Press of America, 1986).

Newman, Paul W., *A Spirit Christology: Recovering the Biblical Paradigm of Christian Faith* (Lanham, MD: University Press of America, 1987).

Nichol, John Thomas, *Pentecostalism* (New York: Harper & Row, 1966).

Nielsen, J.T., *Adam and Christ in the Theology of Irenaeus of Lyons: An Examination of the Function of the Adam-Christ Typology in the Adversus Haereses of Irenaeus, against the Background of the Gnosticism of His Time* (Assen: Van Gorcum, 1968).

Nienkirchen, Charles, *A.B. Simpson and the Pentecostal Movement: A Study in Continuity, Crisis, and Change* (Peabody, MA: Hendrickson, 1992).

—'Simpson, Albert Benjamin', in Stanley M. Burgess and Ed M. Van der Maas (eds.), *Encyclopedia Simpson, Albert Benjamin* (Grand Rapids: Zondervan, Rev. and expanded edn, 2002), pp. 1069-70.

Norris, Frederick W., and Gregory, *Faith Gives Fullness to Reasoning: The Five Theological Orations of Gregory Nazianzen* (trans. Lionel Wickham and Frederick Williams; VCSup 13; Leiden: E.J. Brill, 1990).

Norris, Richard A., *Manhood and Christ: A Study in the Christology of Theodore of Mopsuestia* (Oxford: Clarendon Press, 1963).

—*The Christological Controversy* (Sources of Early Christian Thought; Philadelphia: Fortress Press, 1980).

Nuttall, Geoffrey F., *The Holy Spirit in Puritan Faith and Experience* (Chicago: University of Chicago Press, 1992).

Nyssa, Gregory of, 'Against Eunomius', in Philip Schaff and Henry Wace (eds.), *NPNF, Second Series* (trans. H.A. Wilson; 14 vols.; Grand Rapids: Eerdmans, American reprint of the Edinburgh edition edn, 1994), V, pp. 33-248.

O'Collins, Gerald, *Christology: A Biblical, Historical, and Systematic Study of Jesus* (Oxford: Oxford University Press, 2nd edn, 2009).

O'Keefe, John J., 'Impassible Suffering? Divine Passion and Fifth-Century Christology', *TS* 58 (1997), pp. 39-60.

Obolensky, Dimitri, *The Bogomils: A Study in Balkan Neo-Manichaeism* (2004 repr.; Cambridge: Cambridge University Press, 1st pbk. edn, 1948).

Oden, Thomas C., *John Wesley's Scriptural Christianity* (Grand Rapids: Zondervan, 1994).
Oliver, Robert W., 'John Owen: His Life and Times', in Robert W. Oliver (ed.) *John Owen: The Man and His Theology: Papers Read at the Conference of the John Owen Centre for Theological Study, September 2000* (Darlington: Evangelical Press, 2002), pp. 9-39.
Olson, Mark Jeffrey, *Irenaeus, the Valentinian Gnostics, and the Kingdom of God (A.H. Book V): The Debate about 1 Corinthians 15.50* (Lewiston, NY: Mellen Biblical Press, 1992).
Olson, Roger E., *The Story of Christian Theology: Twenty Centuries of Tradition & Reform* (Downers Grove, IL: InterVarsity Press, 1999).
Origen, *Contra Celsum* (trans. Henry Chadwick; Cambridge: Cambridge University Press, 1980).
—*Commentary on the Gospel According to John: Books 1–10* (trans. Ronald E. Heine; Fathers of the Church; Washington: Catholic University of America Press, 1989).
—*Commentary on the Gospel According to John: Books 13–32* (trans. Ronald E. Heine; FC; Washington: Catholic University of America Press, 1993).
—'Commentary on Matthew', in Alexander Roberts and James Donaldson (eds.), *ANF; Translations of the Writings of the Fathers Down to A.D. 325* (trans. Allan Menzies; 10 vols.; Grand Rapids: Eerdmans, American reprint of the Edinburgh edn, 1994), IX, pp. 413-512.
—*Contra Celsum: Libri VIII* (VCSup 54; Leiden: Brill, 2001).
Origen, and Paul Koetschau, *On First Principles: Being Koetschau's Text of the De Principiis Translated into English* (trans. G.W. Butterworth; New York: Harper & Row, 1966).
Osborn, Eric Francis, *Irenaeus of Lyons* (Cambridge: Cambridge University Press, 2001).
—*Clement of Alexandria* (Cambridge: Cambridge University Press, 2005).
Osiek, Carolyn, 'The Genre and Function of the Shepherd of Hermas', *Semeia* 36 (1986), pp. 113-21.
Osiek, Carolyn, and Helmut Koester, *Shepherd of Hermas: A Commentary* (Hermeneia—A Critical and Historical Commentary on the Bible; Minneapolis: Fortress Press, 1999).
Outler, Albert C., *John Wesley* (New York: Oxford University Press, 1964).
—'The Place of John Wesley in the Christian Tradition', in Kenneth E. Rowe (ed.) *The Place of John Wesley in the Christian Tradition* (Metuchen, NJ: Scarecrow Press, 1976)
—*Theology in the Wesleyan Spirit* (Nashville: Discipleship Resources, 1975).
Outler, Albert C., Thomas C. Oden, and Leicester R. Longden, *The Wesleyan Theological Heritage: Essays of Albert C. Outler* (Grand Rapids: Zondervan, 1991).
Owen, John, 'Christologia, or a Declaration of the Glorious Mystery of the Person of Christ – God and Man', in William H. Goold (ed.) *The Works of John Owen* (16 vols.; London: Banner of Truth Trust, 1965), I, pp. 1-272.
—Communion with God the Father, Son, and Holy Ghost, Each Person Distinctly, in Love, Grace, and Consolation', in William H. Goold (ed.) *The Works of John Owen* (16 vols.; London: Banner of Truth Trust, 1965), II, pp. 1-274.

—'Pneumatologia, or a Discourse Concerning the Holy Spirit', in William H. Goold (ed.) *The Works of John Owen* (16 vols.; London: Banner of Truth Trust, 1965), III, pp. 39-381.
—'Vindiciae Evangelicae, or the Mystery of the Gospel Vindicated and Socinianism Examined', in William H. Goold (ed.) *The Works of John Owen* (16 vols.; London: Banner of Truth Trust, 1965), XII, pp. 1-590.
—*The Holy Spirit: His Gifts and Power* (2007 repr.; Fearn, Scotland: Christian Focus Publications, 2004).
—*Communion with the Triune God* (Wheaton, IL: Crossway Books, 2007).
'Owen, John', in F.L. Cross and Elizabeth A. Livingstone (eds.), *ODCC* (Oxford: Oxford University Press, 3rd edn, 1997), p. 1203.
Pagels, Elaine H., *The Gnostic Gospels* (New York: Random House, 1979).
Paget, James Carleton, 'The Epistle of Barnabas', in Paul Foster (ed.) *The Writings of the Apostolic Fathers* (London: T. & T. Clark, 2007), pp. 72-80.
Palamas, Gregory, *The Triads* (trans. Nicholas Gendle; CWS; New York: Paulist Press, 1983).
Palmer, Phoebe, *The Way of Holiness, with Notes by the Way: Being a Narrative of Religious Experience Resulting from a Determination to Be a Bible Christian* (From the Thirty-Fourth American Edition; London: Paternoster-Row, 1856 repr.; New York: Lane and Tippett, 1845).
—*The Promise of the Father* (New York: Garland, 1985 repr.; Boston: H.V. Degen, 1859).
Palmer, Richard E., *Hermeneutics: Interpretation Theory in Schleiermacher, Dilthey, Heidegger, and Gadamer* (Northwestern University Studies in Phenomenology & Existential Philosophy; Evanston: Northwestern University Press, 1969).
Palmieri, Aurelio, 'The Russian Doukhobors and Their Religious Teachings', *HTR* 8 (1915), pp. 62-81.
Parham, Charles F., 'The Everlasting Gospel', in *The Sermons of Charles F. Parham* (HCL; New York: Garland Publishing, 1985 repr.; Baxter Springs, KS: Apostolic Faith Bible College, 1911).
—'Kol Kare Bomidbar: A Voice Crying in the Wilderness', in *The Sermons of Charles F. Parham* (HCL; New York: Garland Publishing, 1985 repr.; Baxter Springs, KS: R.L. Parham, 1944).
Parham, Sarah E., *The Life of Charles F. Parham, Founder of the Apostolic Faith Movement* (HCL; New York: Garland Publishing, 1985 repr.; Joplin, MO: Hunter Printing, 1930).
Parvis, Paul, '2 Clement and the Meaning of the Christian Homily', in Paul Foster (ed.) *The Writings of the Apostolic Fathers* (London: T. & T. Clark, 2007), pp. 32-41.
Parvis, Sara, *Marcellus of Ancyra and the Lost Years of the Arian Controversy 325–45* (OECS; Oxford: Oxford University Press, 2006).
Patterson, J.O., German R. Ross, and Julia Mason Atkins, *History and Formative Years of the Church of God in Christ with Excerpts from the Life and Works of Its Founder—Bishop C.H. Mason* (Memphis, TN: Church of God in Christ Publishing House, 1969).

Patterson, Mark, 'Creating a Last Day's Revival: The Premillennial Worldview and the Albury Circle', in Andrew Walker and Kristin Aune (eds.), *On Revival: A Critical Examination* (Carlisle: Paternoster Press, 2003), pp. 87-104.
'Paul of Samosata', in F.L. Cross and Elizabeth A. Livingstone (eds.), *ODCC* (Oxford: Oxford University Press, 3rd edn, 1997), p. 1242.
Pearson, Birger A., 'Gnostic Interpretation of the Old Testament in the Testimony of Truth (NHC IX, 3)', *HTR* 73 (1980), pp. 311-19.
—'Truth, Testimony Of', in David Noel Freedman (ed.), *ABD* (6 vols.; New York: Doubleday, 1992), VI, pp. 668-69.
Pearson, Lori, 'Schleiermacher and the Christologies Behind Chalcedon', *HTR* 96 (2003), pp. 349-67.
Pelikan, Jaroslav, *The Christian Tradition: A History of the Development of Doctrine, the Emergence of the Catholic Tradition (100–600)* (5 vols.; Chicago: University of Chicago Press, 1971–89).
Peppiatt, Lucy, 'Spirit Christology and Mission' (PhD thesis; Otago, NZ: University of Otago, 2010).
Pernveden, Lage, *The Concept of the Church in the Shepherd of Hermas* (Lund: C.W.K. Gleerup, 1966).
Peters, Edward, *Heresy and Authority in Medieval Europe: Documents in Translation* (Philadelphia: University of Pennsylvania Press, 1980).
Petriano, Thomas, 'Spirit Christology or Son Christology?: An Analysis of the Tension between the Two in the Theology of Walter Kasper' (PhD dissertation; New York: Fordham University, 1998).
Pettersen, Alvyn, *Athanasius* (Harrisburg, PA: Morehouse, 1995).
Phillips, Wade H., *The Significance of the Fire-Baptized Holiness Movement (1895–1900) in the Historical and Theological Development of the Wesleyan-Pentecostal-Charismatic Metamorphosis*; in *Second Annual Meeting of the Historical Society of Church of God Movements* (ed.; Cleveland, TN, May 24, 2003).
'Photinus', in F.L. Cross and E. A. Livingston (eds.), *ODCC* (Oxford: Oxford University Press, 1997), p. 1283.
Pinnock, Clark H., *Flame of Love: A Theology of the Holy Spirit* (Downers Grove, IL: InterVarsity, 1996).
Piper, Otto A., 'Change of Perspective', *Interpretation* 16 (1962), pp. 402-17.
Pollock, John Charles, *The Keswick Story: The Authorized History of the Keswick Convention* (London: Hodder and Stoughton, 1964).
'Praxeas', in F.L. Cross and Elizabeth A. Livingstone (eds.), *ODCC* (Oxford: Oxford University Press, 3rd edn, 1997), p. 1315.
Preston, Daniel D., *The Era of A.J. Tomlinson* (Cleveland, TN: White Wing Publishing House, 1984).
Pritz, Ray, *Nazarene Jewish Christianity: From the End of the New Testament Period until Its Disappearance in the Fourth Century* (Studpb 37; Leiden E.J. Brill, 1988).
'Prolegomena', in Philip Schaff and Henry Wace (eds.), *NPNF, Second Series* (trans. William Moore and Henry Austin Wilson; 14 vols.; Grand Rapids: Eerdmans, American reprint of the Edinburgh edition edn, 1997), V, pp. 1-32.
Purves, Jim, 'The Interaction of Christology & Pneumatology in the Soteriology of Edward Irving', *Pneuma* 14 (1992), pp. 81-90.

—*The Triune God and the Charismatic Movement: A Critical Appraisal of Trinitarian Theology and Charismatic Experience from a Scottish Perspective* (Carlisle: Paternoster, 2004).

Quasten, Johannes, *Patrology* (4 vols.; Christian Classics, Notre Dame, IN. Ave Maria Press repr.; Utrecht: Spectrum Publishers, 1950).

Ramelli, Ilaria L.E., 'Christian Soteriology and Christian Platonism: Origen, Gregory of Nyssa, and the Biblical and Philosophical Basis of the Doctrine of Apokatastasis', *VC* 61 (2007), pp. 313-56.

Ramsey, Boniface, *Ambrose* (Early Church Fathers; London: Routledge, 1997).

Rankin, David, *Tertullian and the Church* (Cambridge: Cambridge University Press, 1995).

Raven, Charles E., *Apollinarianism: An Essay on the Christology of the Early Church* (Cambridge: Cambridge University Press, 1923).

Redeker, Martin, *Schleiermacher: Life and Thought* (trans. John Wallhausser; Philadelphia: Fortress Press, 1973).

Reed, David, 'Aspects of the Origins of Oneness Pentecostalism', in Vinson Synan (ed.) *Aspects of Pentecostal-Charismatic Origins* (Plainfield, NJ: Logos International, 1975), pp. 143-68.

—'Oneness Pentecostalism', in Stanley M. Burgess and Ed M. Van der Maas (eds.), *NIDPCM* (Grand Rapids: Zondervan, Rev. and expanded edn, 2002), pp. 936-44.

—*In Jesus' Name: The History and Beliefs of Oneness Pentecostals* (JPTSup 31; Blandford Forum, UK: Deo, 2008).

Reedy, Gerard, 'Socinians, John Toland, and the Anglican Rationalists', *HTR* 70 (1977), pp. 285-304.

Reimarus, H.S., *Fragments from Reimarus: Consisting of Brief Critical Remarks on the Object of Jesus and His Disciples as Seen in the New Testament* (trans. G.E. Lessing; London: Williams and Norgate, 1879).

'Reimarus, Hermann Samuel', in F.L. Cross and Elizabeth A. Livingstone (eds.), *ODCC* (Oxford: Oxford University Press, 3rd edn, 1997), p. 1378.

Reno, R.R., 'Origen and Spiritual Interpretation', *ProEccl* 15 (2006), pp. 108-26.

Richardson, Cyril Charles, *Early Christian Fathers* (New York: Macmillan, 1970).

Riss, Richard M., 'Durham, William H.', in Stanley M. Burgess and Ed M. Van der Maas (eds.), *NIDPCM* (Grand Rapids: Zondervan, Rev. and expanded edn, 2002), pp. 594-95.

Robeck, Cecil M., *Prophecy in Carthage: Perpetua, Tertullian, and Cyprian* (Cleveland, Ohio: Pilgrim Press, 1992).

—'Haywood, Garfield Thomas', in Stanley M. Burgess and Ed M. Van der Maas (eds.), *NIDPCM* (Grand Rapids: Zondervan, Rev. and expanded edn, 2002), pp. 693-94.

—'Seymour, William Joseph', in Stanley M. Burgess and Ed M. Van der Maas (eds.), *NIDPCM* (Grand Rapids: Zondervan, Rev. and expanded edn, 2002), pp. 1053-58.

—*The Azusa Street Mission and Revival: The Birth of the Global Pentecostal Movement* (Nashville: Nelson Reference & Electronic, 2006).

—'William J. Seymour and "the Bible Evidence"', in Gary B. McGee (ed.) *Initial Evidence: Historical and Biblical Perspectives on the Pentecostal Doctrine of Spirit*

Baptism (Eugene, OR: Wipf and Stock, 2007 repr.; Peabody, MA: Hendrickson, 1991), pp. 72-95.

Robins, R.G., *A.J. Tomlinson: Plainfolk Modernist* (Religion in America Series; Oxford: Oxford University Press, 2004).

Robinson, David Charles, 'Informed Worship and Empowered Mission: The Integration of Liturgy, Doctrine, and Praxis in Leo the Great's Sermons on Ascension and Pentecost', *Worship* 83 (Worship), pp. 524-40.

Robinson, James M. (ed.), *The NHL in English* (trans. and intro. by members of the Coptic Gnostic Library Project of the Institute for Antiquity and Christianity; San Francisco: Harper San Francisco 3rd completely rev. edn, 1990).

—(ed.), *The Coptic Gnostic Library: A Complete Edition of the Nag Hammadi Codices* (trans. The Institute of Antiquity and Christianity; 5 vols.; Leiden: Brill, 2000).

Robinson, John A.T., *Honest to God* (Philadelphia: Westminster Press, 1963).

—'Need Jesus Have Been Perfect?', in Stephen Sykes and John Powell Clayton (eds.), *Christ, Faith and History: Cambridge Studies in Christology* (London: Cambridge University Press, 1972), pp. 39-54.

—*The Human Face of God* (Philadelphia: Westminster Press, 1973).

Rock, Stella, 'Russian Piety and Orthodox Culture, 1380-1589', in Michael Angold (ed.) *CHC: Eastern Christianity* (9 vols.; Cambridge: Cambridge University Press, 2006), V, pp. 253-75.

Rosato, Philip J., 'Spirit Christology: Ambiguity and Promise', *TS* 38 (1977), pp. 423-49.

Ross, Brian R., 'Ralph Cecil Horner: A Methodist Sectarian Deposed, 1887-95', *Journal of the Canadian Church Historical Society* 19 (1977), pp. 94-103.

Rousseau, Philip, *Basil of Caesarea* (TTCH 20; Berkeley: University of California Press, 1994).

Rowe, J. Nigel, *Origen's Doctrine of Subordination: A Study in Origen's Christology* (New York: Peter Lang, 1987).

Rudolph, Kurt, *Gnosis: The Nature and History of Gnosticism* (trans. Robert McLachlan Wilson; 1987 repr.; San Francisco: Harper & Row, 1977).

Rudometkin, Maxim Gavrilovich, 'Divinely-Inspired Discourses of Maxim Gavrilovich Rudometkin, King of Spirits and Leader of the People of Zion, the Spiritual Christian Molokan Jumpers', in Ivan Gureivich Samarin and Daniel H. Shubin (eds.), *Spirit and Life—Book of the Sun: Divine Discourses of the Preceptors and the Martyrs for the Word of God, the Faith of Jesus, and the Holy Spirit, of the Religion of the Spiritual Christian Molokan-Jumpers, Including a History of the Religion* (trans. John W. Volkov; 1983 repr.; USA: Daniel H. Shubin, 1928), pp. 167-631.

Runciman, Steven, *The Medieval Manichee: A Study of the Christian Dualist Heresy* (1969 repr.; Cambridge: Cambridge University Press, 4 edn, 1960).

Runia, David T., 'Clement of Alexandria and the Philonic Doctrine of the Divine Power(S)', *VC* 58 (2004), pp. 256-76.

Russell, Norman, *Cyril of Alexandria* (ECF; London: Routledge, 2000).

Samarin, Ivan Gureivich, and Daniel H. Shubin (eds.), *Spirit and Life—Book of the Sun: Divine Discourses of the Preceptors and the Martyrs for the Word of God, the Faith of Jesus, and the Holy Spirit, of the Religion of the Spiritual Christian Molokan-Jumpers,*

Including a History of the Religion (trans. John W. Volkov; 1983 repr.; USA: Daniel H. Shubin, 1928).

Sample, Robert, 'The Christology of the Council of Antioch (268 CE) Reconsidered', *CH* 48 (1979), pp. 18-26.

Samuel, V.C., 'One Incarnate Nature of God the Word', *GOTR* 10 (1964–65), pp. 37-53.

—'The Faith of the Church', in Sergew Hable Selassie (ed.) *The Church of Ethiopia: A Panorama of History and Spiritual Life* (Addis Ababa: Ethiopian Orthodox Church, 1970), pp. 43-54.

Sanders, Rufus G.W., *William Joseph Seymour: Black Father of the 20th Century Pentecostal/Charismatic Movement* (Sandusky, OH: Xulon Press, 2003).

Sandidge, Jerry L., 'A Pentecostal Response to Roman Catholic Teaching on Mary', *Pneuma* Fall (1982), pp. 33-42.

Schaff, Philip, *History of the Christian Church* (8 vols.; Grand Rapids: Eerdmans, 1910).

—'Prolegomena: St. Augustin's Life and Work', in Philip Schaff (ed.) *NPNF, First Series* (14 vols.; Grand Rapids: Eerdmans, American reprint of the Edinburgh edn, 2001), I, pp. 1-27.

—(ed.), *The Creeds of Christendom* (3 vols.; Grand Rapids: Baker Book House, 2007 repr.; New York: Harper & Row, Sixth edn, 1931).

Scheeben, Matthias Joseph, *Die Mysterien Des Christentums* (Freiburg: Herder, 1941).

Schleiermacher, Friedrich, *The Life of Jesus* (Lives of Jesus Series; Philadelphia: Fortress Press, Gilmour, Jack C. edn, 1975).

—*On Religion: Speeches to Its Cultured Despisers* (trans. John Oman; Louisville, KY: Westminster/John Knox Press, translated from 3rd German edn, 1994).

—*The Christian Faith* (trans. H.R. Mackintosh and J.S. Stewart; Berkeley, CA: Apocryphile Press, 2011).

Schleiermacher, Friedrich, and Keith Clements, *Friedrich Schleiermacher: Pioneer of Modern Theology* (The Making of Modern Theology 1; Minneapolis: Fortress Press, 1991 repr.; London: Collins, 1987).

Schoedel, William R., *Ignatius of Antioch: A Commentary on the Letters of Ignatius of Antioch* (Hermeneia—a Critical and Historical Commentary on the Bible; Philadelphia: Fortress Press, 1985).

Schoeps, Hans-Joachim, *Jewish Christianity: Fractional Disputes in the Early Church* (Philadelphia: Fortress, 1969).

Scholasticus, Socrates, 'Ecclesiastical History', in Philip Schaff and Henry Wace (eds.), *NPNF, Second Series* (14 vols.; 1997 repr.; Edinburgh: T. & T. Clark: Grand Rapids: Eerdmans), II, pp. 1-178.

Schoonenberg, Piet J.A.M., *Covenant and Creation* (Notre Dame: University of Notre Dame Press, 1969).

—*The Christ: A Study of the God-Man Relationship in the Whole of Creation and in Jesus Christ* (trans. Della Couling; New York: Herder and Herder, 1971).

—'Trinity-the Consummated Covenant: Thesis on the Doctrine of the Trinity', *SR* 5 (1975–76), pp. 111-16.

—'Spirit Christology and Logos Christology', *Bijdr* 38 (1977), pp. 350-75.

Schweitzer, Albert, *The Mysticism of Paul the Apostle* (New York: H. Holt and Co., 1931).

—*The Quest of the Historical Jesus: A Critical Study of Its Progress from Reimarus to Wrede* (trans. William Montgomery; New York: MacMillan, 1948).

Scullion, J.J., 'Gunkel, Johannes Heinrich Hermann', in John Haralson Hayes (ed.), *DBI* (2 vols.; Nashville: Abingdon Press, 1999), I, pp. 472-73.

Seagraves, Daniel Lee, 'Andrew D. Urshan: A Theological Biography' (PhD dissertation; Virginia Beach, VA: Regent University, 2010).

Seeberg, Reinhold, and Charles Ebert Hay, *Text-Book of the History of Doctrines* (trans. Charles E. Hay; 2 vols.; Eugene, OR: Wipf and Stock, 1997 repr.; Philadelphia: Lutheran Publication Society, 1905).

Segelberg, Eric, 'The Coptic-Gnostic Gospel According to Philip and Its Sacramental System', *Numen* 7 (1960), pp. 189-200.

Selassie, Sergew Hable, 'The Establishment of the Ethiopian Church', in Sergew Hable Sellassie (ed.) *The Church of Ethiopia: A Panorama of History and Spiritual Life* (Addis Ababa: Ethiopian Orthodox Church, 1970)

—'The Period of Reorganization', in Sergew Hable Sellassie (ed.) *The Church of Ethiopia: A Panorama of History and Spiritual Life* (Addis Ababa: Ethiopian Orthodox Church, 1970), pp. 31-41.

Sellers, Robert Victor, *Eustathius of Antioch and His Place in the Early History of Christian Doctrine* (Cambridge: The University Press, 1928).

—*The Council of Chalcedon: A Historical and Doctrinal Survey* (London: SPCK, 1953).

—*Two Ancient Christologies: A Study in the Christological Thought of the Schools of Alexandria and Antioch in the Early History of Christian Doctrine* (London: SPCK, 1954).

Shakarian, Demos, John L. Sherrill, and Elizabeth Sherrill, *The Happiest People on Earth: The Long-Awaited Personal Story of Demos Shakarian* (Old Tappan, NJ: Chosen Books: Distributed by F.H. Revell Company, 1975).

Shedd, William G.T., *A History of Christian Doctrine* (2 vols.; Eugene, OR: Wipf and Stock, 1999 repr.; New York: Charles Scribner, 1864).

Shenk, Calvin E., 'The Ethiopian Orthodox Church: A Study in Indigenization', *Missiology* 16 (1988), pp. 259-65.

—'Reverse Contextualization: Jesuit Encounter with the Ethiopian Orthodox Church', *Direction* 28 (1999), pp. 88-100.

Shotwell, Willis A., *The Biblical Exegesis of Justin Martyr* (London: SPCK, 1965).

Shubin, Daniel H., *A History of Russian Christianity* (4 vols.; New York: Algora Publishing, 2005).

Shumway, Charles William, 'A Critical History of Glossolalia', Ph.D. dissertation, Boston University, 1919.

Sibbes, Richard, 'Christ's Sufferings for Man's Sin', in Alexander Balloch Grosart (ed.) *Works of Richard Sibbes* (7 vols.; 1973 repr.; Edinburgh: Banner of Truth Trust, 1862–64), I, pp. 851-69.

—'Description of Christ', in Alexander Balloch Grosart (ed.) *Works of Richard Sibbes* (7 vols.; 1973 repr.; Edinburgh: Banner of Truth Trust, 1862–64), I, pp. 1-31.

—'The Excellency of the Gospel above the Law', in Alexander Balloch Grosart (ed.) *Works of Richard Sibbes* (7 vols.; 1983 repr.; Edinburgh: Banner of Truth Trust, 1862–64), IV, pp. 201-305.

Sideris, Theodore, 'Theological Position of the Iconophiles during the Iconoclastic Controversy', *SVTQ* 17 (1973), pp. 210-26.

Simpson, A.B., *The Gospel of Healing* (Camp Hill, Pa.: Christian Publications, 1886).

—*The Four-Fold Gospel* (BiblioLife repr.; New York: Christian Alliance Publishing, 1890).

—*The Holy Spirit or Power from on High: An Unfolding of the Doctrine of the Holy Spirit in the Old and New Testaments* (2 vols.; Harrisburg, PA: Christian Publications, 1896).

—*The Fourfold Gospel: Albert B. Simpson's Conception of the Complete Provision of Christ for Every Need of the Believer—Spirit, Soul and Body* (Camp Hill, PA: Christian Publications, Updated and edited edn, 1984).

—'Editorial', *The Gospel in All Lands* 1 (February, 1880).

—*The Gentle Love of the Holy Spirit* (An Undated and Edited Version of the Former Title, *Walking in the Spirit* repr.; Camp Hill, PA: Christian Publications, 1983).

Siker, Jeffery S., 'Gnostic Views on Jews and Christians in the Gospel of Philip', *NovT* 31 (1989), pp. 274-88.

Skarsaune, Oskar, *The Proof from Prophecy: A Study in Justin Martyr's Proof-Text Tradition: Text-Type, Provenance, Theological Profile* (NovTSup 55; Leiden: E.J. Brill, 1987).

—'Justin and His Bible', in Sara Parvis and Paul Parvis (eds.), *Justin Martyr and His Worlds* (Minneapolis: Fortress Press, 2007)

Slusser, Michael (ed.), *St. Justin Martyr: Dialogue with Trypho* (trans. Thomas B. Falls; FC; Washington: Catholic University of America Press, Revised with a New Introduction by Thomas P. Halton edn, 2003).

Snyder, Howard A., 'John Wesley and Marcarius the Eyptian', *AsTJ* 45 (1990), pp. 55-59.

Socinus, Faustus, 'Epitome of a Colloquium Held in Raków in the Year 1601', in George Huntston Williams (ed.) *The Polish Brethren: Documentation of the History and Thought of Unitarianism in the Polish-Lithuanian Commonwealth and in the Diaspora, 1601–85* (trans. George Huntston Williams; 2 vols.; Missoula, MT: Scholars Press, 1980).

Speller, Lydia, 'New Light on the Photinians: The Evidence of Ambrosiaster', *JTS* 34 (1983), pp. 99-113.

Spence, Alan, *Incarnation and Inspiration: John Owen and the Coherence of Christology* (London: T. & T. Clark, 2007).

Spoerl, Kelly McCarthy, 'Apollinarian Christology and the Anti-Marcellan Tradition', *JTS* 45 (1994).

—'Two Early Nicenes: Eustathius of Antioch and Marcellus of Ancyra', in Peter William Martens (ed.) *In the Shadow of the Incarnation: Essays on Jesus Christ in the Early Church in Honor of Brian E. Daley, S.J.* (Notre Dame: University of Notre Dame Press, 2008), pp. 121-48.

Stewart-Sykes, Alistar, *The Lamb's High Feast: Melito, Peri Pascha and the Quartodeciman Paschal Liturgy at Sardis* (VCSup 42; Leiden: E.J. Brill, 1998).

Stibbe, Mark W.G., and et al., 'A Global Pentecostal Dialogue with Jurgen Moltmann's *the Spirit of Life: A Universal Affirmation*', *JPT* 4 (1994), pp. 5-70.
Stoyanov, Yuri, *The Other God: Dualist Religions from Antiquity to the Cathar Heresy* (Yale Nota Bene; New Haven: Yale University Press, 2000).
Strachan, Gordon, *The Pentecostal Theology of Edward Irving* (Peabody, MA: Hendrickson Publishers, 1988).
Strimple, Robert B., *The Modern Search for the Real Jesus: An Introductory Survey of the Historical Roots of Gospels Criticism* (Philipsburg, NJ: P&R Publishing, 1995).
Stronstad, Roger, *The Charismatic Theology of St. Luke* (Peabody: Hendrickson, 1984).
Studebaker, Steven M., 'Integrating Pneumatology and Christology: A Trinitarian Modification of Clark H. Pinnock's Spirit Christology', *Pneuma* 28 (2006), pp. 5-20.
Studite, Theodore the, *On the Holy Icons* (trans. Catharine P. Roth; Crestwood, NY: St. Vladimir's Seminary Press, 1981).
Sullivan, Francis Aloysius, *The Christology of Theodore of Mopsuestia* (Romae: Apud Aedes Universitatis Gregoriana, 1956).
Swete, Henry Barclay, *The Holy Spirit in the Ancient Church: A Study of Christian Teaching in the Age of the Fathers* (Eugene, OR: Wipf and Stock, 1997 repr.; London: Macmillan, 1912).
Sykes, S.W., 'The Theology of the Humanity of Christ', in Stephen Sykes and John Powell Clayton (eds.), *Christ, Faith and History: Cambridge Studies in Christology* (London: Cambridge University Press, 1972), pp. 53-72.
Sykes, Stephen, *Friedrich Schleiermacher* (Richmond, VA: John Knox Press, 1971).
Symeon, *The Sin of Adam and Our Redemption: Seven Homilies* (trans. Nicetas Stethatos; OTT 2; Platina, CA: Saint Herman of Alaska Brotherhood, 1979).
—*The Discourses* (trans. C.J. deCatanzaro; CWS; New York: Paulist Press, 1980).
—*The Practical and Theological Chapters and the Three Theological Discourses* (trans. Paul McGuckin; CSS 41; Kalamazoo, MI: Cistercian Publications, 1982).
—*On the Mystical Life: The Ethical Discourses* (trans. Alexander Golitzin; 3 vols.; Crestwood, NY: St. Vladimir's Seminary Press, 1995).
Synan, Vinson, *In the Latter Days: The Outpouring of the Holy Spirit in the Twentieth Century* (Ann Arbor: Servant, 1984).
—*Under His Banner* (Costa Mesa, CA: Gift Publications, 1992).
—*The Holiness-Pentecostal Tradition: Charismatic Movements in the Twentieth Century* (Grand Rapids: Eerdmans 2nd edn, 1997).
—*Oldtime Power: A Centennial History of the International Pentecostal Holiness Church* (Franklin Springs, GA: LifeSprings, Centennial edn, 1998).
—*The Century of the Holy Spirit: 100 Years of Pentecostal and Charismatic Renewal, 1901-2001* (Nashville: Thomas Nelson Publishers, 2001).
—'Cashwell, Gaston Barnabas', in Stanley M. Burgess and Ed M. Van der Maas (eds.), *NIDPCM* (Grand Rapids: Zondervan, Rev. and expanded edn, 2002), pp. 457-58.
—'Crumpler, Ambrose Blackman', in Stanley M. Burgess and Ed M. Van der Maas (eds.), *NIDPCM* (Grand Rapids: Zondervan, Rev. and expanded edn, 2002), p. 566.

—'Holmes, Nickels John', in Stanley M. Burgess and Ed M. Van der Maas (eds.), *NIDPCM* (Grand Rapids: Zondervan, Rev. and expanded edn, 2002), p. 730.
—'Irwin, Benjamin Hardin', in Stanley M. Burgess and Ed M. Van der Maas (eds.), *NIDPCM* (Grand Rapids: Zondervan, Rev. and expanded edn, 2002), pp. 804-805.
—'King, Joseph Hillery', in Stanley M. Burgess and Ed M. Van der Maas (eds.), *NIDPCM* (Grand Rapids: Zondervan, Rev. and expanded edn, 2002), pp. 822-23.
Synan, Vinson, and Charles R. Fox, *William J. Seymour; Pioneer of Azusa Street Revival* (Alachua, FL: Bridge-Logos Publishers, 2012).
Tabbernee, William, *Montanist Inscriptions and Testimonia: Epigraphic Sources Illustrating the History of Montanism* (Macon, GA: Mercer University Press, 1997).
Tallman, Matthew William, *Demos Shakarian: The Life, Legacy, and Vision of a Full Gospel Business Man* (The Asbury Theological Seminary Series in World Christian Revitalization Movements in Pentecostal/Charismatic Studies; Lexington, KY: Emeth Press, 2010).
Tamrat, Taddesse, 'Persecution and Religious Controversies', in Sergew Hable Selassie (ed.) *The Church of Ethiopia: A Panorama of History and Spiritual Life* (Addis Ababa: Ethiopian Orthodox Church, 1970), pp. 27-41.
—Revival of the Church', in Sergew Hable Selassie (ed.) *The Church of Ethiopia: A Panorama of History and Spiritual Life* (Addis Ababa: Ethiopian Orthodox Church, 1970), pp. 17-25
Tatian, 'Address to the Greeks', in Alexander Roberts, James Donaldson and A. Cleveland Coxe (eds.), *ANF; Translations of the Writings of the Fathers Down to A.D. 325* (trans. J.E. Ryland; 10 vols.; Grand Rapids: Eerdmans, American reprint of the Edinburgh edn, 1994), II, pp. 65-83.
Telfer, William (ed.), *Cyril of Jerusalem and Nemesius of Emesa* (LCL 4; Philadelphia:' Westminster Press, 1955).
Tertullian, 'Against Praxeas', in Alexander Roberts and James Donaldson (eds.), (*ANF; Translations of the Writings of the Fathers Down to A.D. 325*; (trans. Michael W. Holmes; 10 vols.; Grand Rapids: Eerdmans, American reprint of the Edinburgh edn, 1997), III, pp. 597-632.
—'The Five Books against Marcion', in Alexander Roberts, James Donaldson and A. Cleveland Coxe (eds.), *ANF; Translations of the Writings of the Fathers Down to A.D. 325*; (trans. Michael W. Holmes; 10 vols.; Grand Rapids: Eerdmans, American reprint of the Edinburgh edn, 1997), III, pp. 269-475.
—'On the Flesh of Christ', in Alexander Roberts and James Donaldson (eds.), *ANF; Translations of the Writings of the Fathers Down to A.D. 325* (trans. Michael W. Holmes; 10 vols.; Grand Rapids:' Eerdmans, American reprint of the Edinburgh edn, 1997), III, p. 521-43.
TeSelle, Eugene, *Augustine the Theologian* (London: Burns & Oates, 1970).
Tesfazghi, Uqbit, *Current Christological Positions of Ethiopian Orthodox Theologians* (Orientalia Christiana Analecta 196; Rome: Pont. Institutum Studiorum Orientalium, 1973).
'The Testimony of Truth', in James M. Robinson and Richard Smith (eds.), *NHL* (trans. Soren Giverson and Birger A. Pearson; San Francisco: HarperSanFrancisco, 3rd completely rev. edn, 1990), pp. 448-59.

Theodoret, 'The Counter-Statements of Theodoret', in Philip Schaff and Henry Wace (eds.), *NPNF, Second Series* (trans. Blomfield Jackson; 14 vols.; Grand Rapids: Eerdmans, American reprint of the Edinburgh edition edn, 1996), III, pp. 26-31.

—'Eranistes', in Philip Schaff and Henry Wace (eds.), *NPNF, Second Series* (trans. Blomfield Jackson; 14 vols.; Grand Rapids: Eerdmans, American reprint of the Edinburgh edition edn, 1996), III, pp. 160-244.

—'Letters', in Philip Schaff and Henry Wace (eds.), *NPNF, Second Series* (trans. Blomfield Jackson; 14 vols.; Grand Rapids: Eerdmans, American reprint of the Edinburgh edition edn, 1996), III. pp. 250-348.

—*Commentary on the Psalms: Psalms 1–72* (trans. Robert C. Hill; FC: A New Translation; Washington: Catholic University of America Press, 2000).

—*Eranistes* (trans. Gerard H. Ettlinger; FC: A New Translation; Washington: Catholic University of America Press, 2003).

'Theodotus', in F.L. Cross and Elizabeth A. Livingstone (eds.), *ODCC* (Oxford: Oxford University Press, 3rd edn, 1997), p. 1602.

Theophilus, 'Theophilus to Autoclycus', in Alexander Roberts, James Donaldson and A. Cleveland Coxe (eds.), *ANF. Translations of the Writings of the Fathers Down to A.D. 325* (trans. Marcus Dods; 10 vols.; Grand Rapids: Eerdmans, 2001 repr.; Grand Rapids: Eerdmans, American reprint of the Edinburgh edn, 2001), II, pp. 85-121.

'The Third Ecumenical Council: The Council of Ephesus', in Philip Schaff and Henry Wace (eds.), *NPNF, Second Series* (trans. Henry R. Percival; 14 vols.; Grand Rapids: Eerdmans, American reprint of the Edinburgh edn, 1997), XIV, pp. 191-242.

Thomas, John Christopher, 'The Spirit in the Fourth Gospel: Narrative Explorations', in Terry L. Cross and Emerson B. Powery (eds.), *The Spirit and the Mind: Essays in Informed Pentecostalism* (Lanham: University Press of America, 2000), pp. 157-74.

Thomasius, Gottfried, 'Christ's Person and Work; Part II: The Person of the Mediator', in Claude Welch (ed.) *God and Incarnation in Mid-Nineteenth Century German Theology* (trans. Claude Welch; A Library of Protestant Thought; New York: Oxford University Press, 1965), pp. 31-101.

Thompson, A.E., *A.B. Simpson: His Life and Work* (Harrisburg, PA: Christian Publications, Revised edn, 1960).

Thomson, Andrew, 'Life of Owen', in William H. Goold (ed.) *The Works of John Owen* (16 vols.; London: Banner of Truth Trust, 1965), I, pp. xix-cxxii.

Tice, Terrence N., *Schleiermacher* (Abingdon Pillars of Theology; Nashville: Abingdon, 2006).

Tinney, James S., 'William J. Seymour [1855?–1920?]: Father of Modern-Day Pentecostalism', *Journal of the Interdenominational Theological Center* 4.1 (1976), pp. 34-44.

Tollefsen, Torstein, *The Christocentric Cosmology of St. Maximus the Confessor* (OECS; Oxford: Oxford University Press, 2008).

Tomlinson, A.J., *The Last Great Conflict* (Cleveland, TN: Walter E. Rodgers Press, 1913).

—*A.J. Tomlinson, God's Anointed—Prophet of Wisdom: Choice Writings of A.J. Tomlinson in Times of His Greatest Anointings* (Cleveland, TN: White Wing Publishing House, 1943).
—*Diary of A.J. Tomlinson* (3 vols.; Queen's Village, NY: Church of God, 1949).
—*God's Twentieth Century Pioneer: A Compilation of Some of the Writings of A.J. Tomlinson* (Cleveland, TN: White Wing Publishing House, 1962).
Torrance, Alexis, 'Precedents for Palamas' Essence-Energies Theology in the Cappadocian Fathers', *VC* 63 (2009), pp. 47-70.
Torrance, Thomas F., *The Doctrine of Grace in the Apostolic Fathers* (Grand Rapids: Eerdmans, 1960).
Trevett, Christine, *Montanism: Gender, Authority, and the New Prophecy* (Cambridge: Cambridge University Press, 1996).
Trigg, Joseph Wilson, *Origen: The Bible and Philosophy in the Third-Century Church* (Atlanta: John Knox Press, 1983).
Trueman, Carl R., 'John Owen's Dissertation on Divine Justice: An Exercise in Christocentric Scholasticism', *CTJ* 33 (1998), pp. 87-103.
—'John Owen as a Theologian', in Robert W. Oliver (ed.) *John Owen the Man and His Theology: Papers Read at the Conference of the John Owen Centre for Theological Study, September 2000* (Darlington: Evangelical Press, 2002), pp. 41-68.
Tschiflianov, Blagoy, 'The Iconoclastic Controversy: A Theological Perspective', *GOTR* 38 (1993), pp. 231-64.
Turcescu, Lucian, *Gregory of Nyssa and the Concept of Divine Persons* (American Academy of Religion Academy Series; Oxford: Oxford University Press, 2005).
Tzamalikos, Panayiotis, *Origen: Philosophy of History & Eschatology* (VCSup 85; Leiden: E.J. Brill, 2007).
Upton, Liam, "Our Mother and Our Country': The Integration of Religious and National Identity in the Thought of Edward Irving', in Robert Pope (ed.) *Religion and National Identity: Wales and Scotland C. 1700–2000* (Cardiff: University of Wales Press, 2001), pp. 242-67.
Urshan, Andrew D., 'The Almighty God in the Lord Jesus Christ', in Donald W. Dayton (ed.) *Seven 'Jesus Only' Tracts* (HCL; New York: Garland Publishing, 1985 repr.; Los Angeles: Apostolic Book Corner, 1919)
—'The Doctrine of the New Birth or the Perfect Way to Eternal Life', in Donald W. Dayton (ed.) *Seven 'Jesus Only' Tracts* (HCL; New York: Garland Publishing, 1985 repr.; Cochrane, WI: Witness of God Publishers, 1921)
—*The Story of My Life* (St. Louis: Gospel Publishing House, n.d.).
Van De Walle, Bernie A., *The Heart of the Gospel: A.B. Simpson, the Fourfold Gospel, and Late Nineteenth-Century Evangelical Theology* (PTMS 106; Eugene, OR: Pickwick, 2009).
van Dusen, Henry P., *Spirit, Son, and Father: Christian Faith in the Light of the Holy Spirit* (New York: Charles Scribner's Sons, 1958).
Verghese, Paul, 'The Monothelete Controversy: A Historical Survey', *GOTR* 13 (1968), pp. 196-211.
Verheyden, Joseph, 'The Shepherd of Hermas', in Paul Foster (ed.) *The Writings of the Apostolic Fathers* (London: T. & T. Clark, 2007), pp. 63-71.

'Victorinus Afer, Caius (or Fabius) Marius', in F.L. Cross and Elizabeth A. Livingstone (eds.), *ODCC* (Oxford: Oxford University Press, 3rd edn, 1997), p. 1694.
Victorinus, Marius, *Theological Treatises on the Trinity* (trans. Mary T. Clark; FC; Washington: Catholic University of America Press, 1981).
Vinzent, Markus (ed.), *Markell Von Ankyra: Die Fragmente; Der Brief an Julius Von Rom* (trans. Markus Vinzent; VCSup 39; Leiden: E.J. Brill, 1997).
Wacker, Grant, *Heaven Below: Early Pentecostals and American Culture* (Cambridge, MA: Harvard University Press, 2001).
Walker, Williston, *A History of the Christian Church* (New York: Charles Scribner's Sons, 1918).
Ward, Benedicta, *The Venerable Bede* (Outstanding Christian Thinkers; Harrisburg, PA: Morehouse, 1990).
Ware, Timothy, *The Orthodox Church* (London: Penguin Group, 1964).
Warner, W.E., 'Periodicals', in Stanley M. Burgess and Ed M. Van der Maas (eds.), *NIDPCM* (Grand Rapids: Zondervan, Rev. and expanded edn, 2002), pp. 974-82.
Watson, Eva M., *Glimpses of the Life and Work of George Douglas Watson* (Salem, OH: Schmul, 1974 repr.; Cincinnati: God's Bible School and Revivalist, 1929).
Watson, G.D., *White Robes: Garments of Salvation* (Boston: Christian Witness, 1883).
—*Coals of Fire: Being Expositions of Scripture on the Doctrine, Experience, and Practice of Christian Holiness* (Salem, OH: Schmul Publishers repr.; Boston: Christian Witness, 1886).
—*The Seven Overcometh; and Other Expositions from the Revelation* (Boston: Christian Witness, 1889).
—*The Secret of Spiritual Power* (Boston: Christian Witness, 1894).
Watts, Thomas, 'Two Wills in Christ? Contemporary Objections Considered in the Light of a Critical Examination of Maximus the Confessor's *Disputation with Pyrrhus*', *WTJ* 71 (2009), pp. 455-87.
Weedman, Mark, *The Trinitarian Theology of Hilary of Poitiers* (VCSup 89; Leiden: E.J. Brill, 2007).
Weinandy, Thomas G., *Athanasius: A Theological Introduction* (Great Theologians Series; Burlington, VT: Ashgate, 2007).
Welch, Claude, *Protestant Thought in the Nineteenth Century* (2 vols.; New Haven: Yale University Press, 1972).
—(ed.), *God and Incarnation in Mid-Nineteenth Century German Theology* (trans. Claude Welch; A Library of Protestant Thought; New York: Oxford University Press, 1965).
Wendel, Susan, 'Interpreting the Descent of the Spirit: A Comparison of Justin's Dialogue with Trypho and Luke-Acts', in Sara Parvis and Paul Parvis (eds.), *Justin Martyr and His Worlds* (Minneapolis: Fortress Press, 2007)
Wesley, John, 'Christian Perfection', in *The Works of John Wesley* (14 vols.; Grand Rapids: Baker Book House, 2002 repr.; London: Wesleyan Methodist Book Room, 3rd edn, 1872), VI, pp. 1-22.
—'Justification by Faith', in *The Works of John Wesley* (14 vols.; Grand Rapids: Baker Book House, 2002 repr.; London: Wesleyan Methodist Book Room, 3rd edn, 1872), V, pp. 53-64.

—'On Charity', in *The Works of John Wesley* (14 vols.; Grand Rapids: Baker Book House, 2002 repr.; London: Wesleyan Methodist Book Room, 3rd edn, 1872), VII, pp. 45-57.
—'On Patience', in *The Works of John Wesley* (14 vols.; Grand Rapids: Baker Book House, 2002 repr.; London: Wesleyan Methodist Book Room, 3rd edn, 1872), VI, pp. 484-92.
—'A Plain Account of Christian Perfection, as Believed and Taught by the Reverend Mr. John Wesley, from the Year 1725 to the Year 1777', in *The Works of John Wesley* (14 vols.; Grand Rapids: Baker Book House, 2002 repr.; London: Wesleyan Methodist Book Room, 3rd edn, 1872), XI, pp. 366-446.
—'The Witness of the Spirit', in *The Works of John Wesley* (14 vols.; Grand Rapids: Baker Book House, 2002 repr.; London: Wesleyan Methodist Book Room, 3rd edn, 1872), V, Discourses 1, 2, pp. 111-44.
—A Letter to John Fletcher', in John Telford (ed.) *Letters of the Rev. John Wesley* (8 vols.; London: Epworth, 1931), V, pp. 214-15; VI, p. 146.
—*Wesley's Notes on the Bible* (Grand Rapids: Zondervan, 1987).
Wessel, Susan, *Cyril of Alexandria and the Nestorian Controversy: The Making of a Saint and of a Heretic* (The OECS; Oxford: Oxford University Press, 2004).
—*Leo the Great and the Spiritual Rebuilding of a Universal Rome* (VCSup 93; Leiden: E.J. Brill, 2008).
White, L. Michael, 'Harnack, Karl Gustav Adolf Von', in John Haralson Hayes (ed.), *DBI* (2 vols.; Nashville: Abingdon Press, 1999), I, pp. 481-83.
Whitley, Henry Charles, *Blinded Eagle: An Introduction to the Life and Teaching of Edward Irving* (London: SCM Press, 1955).
Wiles, Maurice, 'Eternal Generation', *JTS* 12 (1961), pp. 284-91.
—'The Nature of the Early Debate about Christ's Human Soul', *JEH* 16 (1965), pp. 139-51.
—'Does Christology Rest on a Mistake?', in Stephen Sykes and John Powell Clayton (eds.), *Christ, Faith and History: Cambridge Studies in Christology* (London: Cambridge University Press, 1972), pp. 3-12.
—'Christianity without Incarnation?', in John Hick (ed.) *The Myth of God Incarnate* (Philadelphia: Westminster Press, 1977), pp. 1-10.
—'Myth in Theology', in John Hick (ed.) *The Myth of God Incarnate* (Philadelphia: Westminster Press, 1977), pp. 148-66.
—'Person or Personification? A Patristic Debate About Logos', in L.D. Hurst and N.T. Wright (eds.), *The Glory of Christ in the New Testament: Studies in Christology in Memory of George Bradford Caird* (Oxford: Clarendon Press, 1987), pp. 281-89.
—'Attitudes to Arius in the Arian Controversy', in Michel R. Barnes and Daniel H. Williams (eds.), *Arianism after Arius: Essays on the Development of the Fourth Century Trinitarian Conflicts* (Edinburgh: T. & T. Clark, 1993), pp. 31-43.
—*Working Papers in Doctrine* (London: SCM Press, 1976).
—*The Christian Fathers* (New York: Oxford University Press, 1982).
—*Archetypal Heresy: Arianism through the Centuries* (Oxford: Clarendon Press, 1996).
Williams, Daniel H., *Ambrose of Milan and the End of the Nicene—Arian Conflicts* (OECS; Oxford: Clarendon Press, 1995).

Williams, Michael A., 'Realized Eschatology in the Gospel of Philip', *ResQ* 14 (1971), pp. 1-17.

Williams, Robert R., *A Guide to the Teachings of the Early Church Fathers* (Grand Rapids: Eerdmans, 1960).

Williams, Rowan, *Arius: Heresy and Tradition* (Grand Rapids: Eerdmans, Revised edn, 2001).

Wilson, John Christian, *Toward a Reassessment of the Shepherd of Hermas: Its Date and Its Pneumatology* (Lewiston, NY: Mellen Biblical Press, 1993).

Wilson, John Elbert, *Introduction to Modern Theology: Trajectories in the German Tradition* (Louisville: Westminster / John Knox Press, 2007).

Wilson, R. McL., *The Gospel of Philip: Translated from the Coptic Text, with an Introduction and Commentary* (London: A. R. Mowbray & Co., 1962).

Wolfson, Elliot R., 'Inscribed in the Book of the Living: *Gospel of Truth* and Jewish Christology', *JSJ* 38 (2007), pp. 234-71.

Wolfson, Harry Austryn, *The Philosophy of the Church Fathers: Faith, Trinity, Incarnation* (Structure and Growth of Philosophic Systems from Plato to Spinoza; 3 vols.; Cambridge: Harvard University Press, 3rd, rev. edn, 1970).

Wood, Laurence W., 'From Barth's Trinitarian Christology to Moltmann's Trinitarian Pneumatology: A Methodist Perspective', *AsTJ* 48 (Spring 1993), pp. 49-80.

Woods, Daniel G., 'Daniel Awrey, the Fire-Baptized Movement, and the Origins of the Church of God: Toward a Chronology of Confluence and Influence', *Cyberjournal for Pentecostal-Charismatic Research* 19 (2010), pp. 1-15.

Wright, David F., 'Why Were the Montanists Condemned?', *Themelios* 2 (1976), pp. 15-22.

—'Ebionites', in Ralph P. Martin and Peter H. Davids (eds.), *Encyclopedia Ebionites* (Downers Grove, IL: InterVarsity Press, 1997), pp. 313-17.

Wright, N.T., 'Jesus, Quest for the Historical ', in David Noel Freedman (ed.), *ABD* (6 vols.; New York: Doubleday, 1st edn, 1992), III, pp. 796-802.

Yarnold, Edward, *Cyril of Jerusalem* (ECF; London: Routledge, 2000).

Yesehaq, Archbishop, 'The Ethiopian Church and Its Living Heritage', *Journal of the Interdenominational Theological Center* 16 (1988– 89), pp. 84-96.

Yesseyevich, David, 'Book of Zion', in Ivan Gureivich Samarin and Daniel H. Shubin (eds.), *Spirit and Life—Book of the Sun: Divine Discourses of the Preceptors and the Martyrs for the Word of God, the Faith of Jesus, and the Holy Spirit, of the Religion of the Spiritual Christian Molokan-Jumpers, Including a History of the Religion* (trans. John W. Volkov; 1983 repr.; USA: Daniel H. Shubin, 1928), pp. 77-107.

Yong, Amos, *Spirit-Word-Community: Theological Hermeneutics in Trinitarian Perspective* (Aldershot, England: Ashgate, 2002).

—*The Spirit Poured out on All Flesh: Pentecostalism and the Possibility of Global Theology* (Grand Rapids: Baker, 2005).

Young, Francis, 'A Cloud of Witnesses', in John Hick (ed.) *The Myth of God Incarnate* (Philadelphia: Westminster Press, 1977), pp. 13-47.

Young, Pauline V., *The Pilgrims of Russian-Town* (Chicago: University of Chicago Press, 1932).

Zachariadou, Elizabeth A., 'The Great Church in Captivity, 1453–1586 ', in Michael Angold (ed.) *CHC: Eastern Christianity* (9 vols.; Cambridge: Cambridge University Press, 2006), V, pp. 169-86.

Zander, Valentine, *St. Seraphim of Sarov* (trans. Gabriel Anne; Crestwood, NY: St. Vladimir's Seminary Press, 1975).

Zaprometova, Olga, 'Experiencing the Holy Spirit: A Pentecostal Reading of ECF Part 2: Isaac of Nineveh and Simeon the New Theologian', *JEPTA* 30 (2010), pp. 1-19.

Ziemke, Donald C., 'Echoes of the Ancient Gnostic Heresy', *LQ* 14 (1962), pp. 148-57.

Index of Biblical (and Other Ancient) References

Old Testament

Genesis
2.7   23

Numbers
11.17   160
11.25   368

Psalms
1.3-6   53
2.2   292
2.7   95
34.11-17   47-48
40.68   395
44   187
44.8   243, 244, 292
45.7   143, 207, 219, 255, 303
45.7-8   150
62.9   223
104.29-30   23

Proverbs
8   482
8.22-25 154

Canticles
2.4   471

Isaiah
5.5   245
6.3   443, 445
11.1-3   255
11.2   242, 313
30.26   441
42.1   242
42.1-2   320
45.5   100, 107
61.1   292
61.1-3   244
66.7, 8 443
66.12   53

Jeremiah
2.13   53

Ezekiel
47.1, 7, 12   53

Daniel
9.25   292

Joel
2.28   483

Malachi
1.6   470

New Testament

Matthew
1.1-16   361
1.16   414
1.18   242
1.20   192, 242
2.1-13   361
3.1-17   361
3.7   471
3.11   304-305, 426, 441, 444
3.16   292, 414
3.16-17   12, 496
3.17   321
5.3   91
12.18-19 320
12.28   242
13   490
16.17   88
18.18   361
25.1-4   427
28.18   359
28.19   496, 499
28.20   159

Mark
1.9-11   12

Luke
1.26-38   361
1.34-35   242
1.35   108, 313, 395, 414, 486
2.1-13   361
3.21   471
3.21-22   12
3.22   315
4.1   313
4.13   471
4.14-18   486
4.17   242
4.18   292, 312, 313, 414
4.18-19   400
4.21   242
6.19   446
9.1   446
24.49   434, 466

John
1.1   133
1.9   185
1.13   323
1.14   178, 193, 395
1.16   323
1.18   396
1.29-33   400
1.32   305
1.32-33   12
1.33   242, 405
3.34   243
4.1-11   53

John cont'd	
4.24	222
6.27	491
6.28	491
6.55	128
7.37-39	53, 405, 425
10.30	100, 107, 144, 206
13.31	395
14.9-10	100, 107
14.17-20	445
16.14	239
16.28	120
17.11	144
20.19-23	361
20.22	168
20.23	361

Acts	
1.1-5	302, 361
1.4-5	361, 405
1.5	302, 466
1.8	445, 446, 460, 466, 505
1.14	471
2	432, 452, 455
2.1-21	361
2.1-33	302
2.4	448, 466, 468, 499
2.4-11	302
2.16	483
2.33	303
2.38	498, 499
2.38-39	498
2.47	292
3	303
4	303
4.1-26	303
4.27	303
6.1-8	361
8	432
8.26-39	287
10.28	406
10.34	313
10.34-37	304
10.34-48	304
10.37	492
10.37-38	313
10.38	242, 266, 304, 305, 414, 491
10.48	305
11.17	349
13.1-6	3.61
15.8	349
19	432

Romans	
1.3-4	13, 422
6	498
8.11	428, 486

1 Corinthians	
6.17	351
12	209
15.24-28	157
15.44-45	13, 14
15.45	351

2 Corinthians	
3.17	185, 351, 503
3.17-18	324

Galatians	
5.25	424

Ephesians	
1.2	396
5.23	476

Philippians	
2	203
2.5-11	193
2.6-7	206
2.6-8	307, 344
2.7	308
2.9-10	143

Colossians	
1.11	446
1.15	156

1 Thessalonians	
5.23	179

1 Timothy	
3.16	422
5.21	171

Hebrews	
1.9	242, 292
2.14-18	242
5.8	331, 472
9.14	422
10.5	254, 321
13.12	477
13.17-21	361

Revelation	
7.4-8, 9	382
12.1-5	387, 450
12.1-17	382
13.8	395
15.2	441

Other Ancient References

Acacius of Constantinople
Henoticon 262, 263

Adamantius
Dialogue
5.11   200

Ambrose of Milan
Fid.
1.4.32	249
2.7.56	218, 219
2.7.58	219
2.8.62	249
2.8.64	249
2.9.75	218
3.8.58	162
4.4.38	220
4.4.45	218
4.8.92	217

Index of Biblical (and Other Ancient) References

Fid. cont'd			6.12-15	160		9	180
4.9.97-116	217		6.14	159, 160		13	180
5.8	163		6.15	160			
5.14.171	218		11–13	158		Aristides of Athens	
5.15.182-87		218	15–19	158		*Apology*	64
5.35	249		21	158		15	65
5.35-45	218		23	158		66	65
6.47-48	249		17.1	158			
7.63-69	218		17.2	158		Arius	
7.67-68	249		18.10	160		*Letter to Alexander of*	
7.72-77	218		21.9	161		*Alexandria*	141
8.84	217		21.10	160			
9.89-102	217		23.61	160		*Letter to Emperor Constan-*	
9.103-16	218		23.63	160		*tine*	141
Spir.			Apollinarius of Laodicea			*Letter to Eusebius of Ni-*	
1.3.43-45	305		*Faith*			*comedia*	141
1.3.44	218		32	180			
1.6.76-80	219					*Thalia*	141, 142
1.8.93	219		*Fragments*				
1.9.100-10	219		9.26-28	178		Asterius	
1.9.105	217		19	177		*General Letter*	152
1.9.107	249		22	179, 180			
1.13.132-59		218	25	179		Athanasius	
1.13.156-58		218,	28	179		*C. Ar.*	
	251		29	179		1.2.5	141, 143
2.1.17-18	218		41	177		1.2.5-6	143
2.35.38	218		69-72	180		1.5.15-16	143
3.1.2	219		74	180		1.11.37	143
3.1.5-6	219, 251		76	180		1.11.38-39	143
3.1.8	218, 251		83	179		1.12.46	144
3.7.44	219, 251		89	179		1.12.46-47	175
3.11.79	218		111	179		1.12.47	144, 173
3.14.101-103		218	116	180		1.12.47-49	144
3.22.168	249		128	180		2.15.13	144
			149	179		3.15.15	172
Aphrahat						2.15.18	174
Dem.			*Recapitulatio*		176	3.25.10	145
1.3	159		16.4-5	177		3.25.17	144-45
1.5	159					3.25.24	145, 175
5.25	160		*Union*			3.26.26	144
6.9	159		2	177		3.30-31	144
6.10	159		5	177		4.2-3	101
6.11	160		6	178		4.25	101
6.12	160		8	178		4.30-36	98

C. Ar., cont'd		Tom.		Basil of Caesarea	
9	102, 143	7	144	DSS	
13-17	102			1.3	184
		Athenagoras		4	184
Ep. Serap.		A Plea for the Christians		5	184
1.1	171	10	76	5.7	184
1.2	172, 174			5.9	186
1.3	171	Augustine		6.13	184
1.3-10	171	Enchir.		6.15	184
1.6	173	34	225, 250	9.22	185
1.9	173	35	225, 250	12.28	186, 187
1.10	171	36	250	14.31	186
1.10-14	171	40	250	15.35-36	186
1.14	172			16.39	186
1.15-16	174	Praed.		16.39-40	187
1.16	174	30	226, 251	17.43	185, 187
1.17	171	31	226, 251	18.44-47	185
1.19	174			18.46	187
1.20	172, 174	Tract. Ev. Jo.		18.47	185
1.23	175	1.4.7	222	19.48	187
1.23-24	175	74.3	224, 249-50	19.48-50	185
1.26-27	171	78.3	249-50	19.49	186, 187
1.28	172			21.52	185, 187
1.30	175	Trin.		22.53	187
1.31	171, 172, 175	1.5.8	222	26.62	187
1.33	175	1.11.22	224	26.64	188
3.1	172	1.11.22-12.27	225, 250		
3.2	174			Chrysostom	
3.3	175	4.20.28	224	Hom. Jo.	
3.5	175	4.21.30	222	5.1	196
3.6	172, 175	4.30	250	11.2	197
4.1	174	5.11.12	223	17.2-3	195
4.2	174	6.5.7	223	30.2	196
4.3	175	9.2.2	222	52.3	197
4.4	174, 175	9.3.3	222	54.2	197
4.5-6	174	9.4.4	222	75.2	197
4.6	174	10.3.5-4.6	222	78.1	197
		10.10.13	222	78.2	195
Syn.		10.11.17	222		
15	141	10.11.18	222	Hom. Matt.	
16	141	11.1.1-11.18	222	4.6	194
22	169	14.6.8-8.11	222	11.6	195
26	98, 162, 163	15.15.27	223	12.2	195
27	162	15.18.32-19.37	223		
50	175	15.26.46	224, 250, 303, 305		

Hom. Phil.
7   197

Clement of Alexandria
Excerpts from Theodotus
     125

Paed.
1.1	126
1.1.1.4	126
1.5.12.1	126
1.5.24	129
1.8.71	129
1.8.74	126
1.6	128
1.6.26	128
1.6.26.1	127
1.6.43	128
1.9.83-84.3	127
2.8.61	130
2.2.19	129

Protr.
1–4	126
5–8	126
9–12	126
1.5.3	129
1.8	129
8.79	129
11	126
11.2	129

Salvation of the Rich 125

Strom.
1.1.11, 1.4.28	128
1.5.28	127
2.4.14	127
2.20.117	130
4.20	130
4.21.23	127
4.25	130
4.25.155	127
5.3.16	127
5.13	130
6.9.71	129-30
6.9.78	127
6.15	127
7.2.29	129
7.9.68	128

Clement of Rome
1 Clem.
22.1-8	48

2 Clem.
1.1	60
9.1-3	60
9.5	61
10.3	60
14.4	61

Clementine Literature
The Two Letters Addressed to Virgins   59

Homilies 59, 92, 93
2.38–52	92
3.15	95
3.20	95
3.22–27	94
3.47	92
3.50-57	92
8.15	92
9.23	92
15.7-10	92
16.15–17	94

Recognitions 59, 92, 93
1.16	94
1.24	94
1.27–71	93
1.40	94
1.43	95
1.45	94, 95
1.47	94, 95
1.48	94
1.49	94
2.56–60	94
3.24	94
3.59–61	94
5.9	94
5.10	94
8.55	94
8.59	94
10.51	94

Cyprian
Idol.
11	139

Cyril of Alexandria
Ad Reginas 234

De Recta Fide   234

Explanation of the Twelve Anathemas 243-44

Ep. Nestorius
3.3-4	239
3.4-6	239
3.8	239
3.10	239

Five Tomes against Nestorius   234

Letter to John of Antioch   246-47, 258

Letter to Pope Celestine   234

Monks
7.9	238
10-11	238
11	238
13-14	238
15	238
16	238
19-20	238
26	238
21-27	239

On the Unity of Christ   230, 232-38, 248

Twelve Anathemas 202, 235-40, 243-46, 248, 253, 256-57, 261-62, 266-67, 513
1   240-41, 248
2   239, 243, 248
4   239, 248
5   239, 248
7   196, 244, 248
9   196, 240, 241-42, 244, 248
10 242, 248

Cyril of Jerusalem
Sermon on the Paralytic
        163

Letter to Constantius
        163

Procatechesis 163, 164

Catecheses 163, 164
3.2   167
3.7   167
10.5   166
11.5   165
11.7   165
16.4   166
17.9   166
17.10 166
17.12 168
17.13-19 168
17.14 168
17.15-16 168
17.20-32 168
17.34 165
17.35-37 167

Mystagogical Catecheses
        163
2.6   167
2.7   165
3.1   167

3.2   166
3.3-5 168

Dead Sea Scrolls 92

Didymus
Trin.
3.41   105

Dionysius of Alexandria
Epistle to Dionysius Bishop of Rome
1.4   139

Ephrem the Syrian
Hymns for the Feast of the Epiphany
3.1   200

Hymns on the Faith
10.17 200
40.3   200

Hymns on Virginity
4.8   200

Epiphanius
Pan.
4.1   157
16.4-7 92
29   91
30.3.4-5, 30.3.6 95
30.14.4 94
30.15.3 93
30.16.2 94
30.16.8-9 93
30.17.1-3 91
30.18.4-6 94
48.11 105
51.3.1-6 95
51.33.1-3 104
54.3.1 97
57.1.8 99
57.2.9 99
62.1.4 101
62.1.6-9 102
62.1.8 102

64.63   133
65.1.3-4 97
65.1.5-8 98
69.6   141
69.7-8   141
71.1.1   162
71.1.3   162

Epistle of Barnabas 52, 53
1.1-3   54
1.5   52
2–17   52
5.5   54
5.6   54
6.12   54
6.14   54
7.2   54
7.3   53, 54
9.2   54
11.1   53
11.2   53
11.8   53
11.9   53, 54
11.10-11 53
16.6-8 54
16.9   54
18–21   53

Eusebius of Caesarea
Hist. eccl.
1.3.13   145
5.24.5   72
15.16.17 105

Eustathius of Antioch
Fragments
2.18-20 149
2.18-24 150
3.1-9   150
6.1-14   148
7.12-15 147, 148
10.1-5   148
17.6-8   148
19a.20-28 147-48
19a.23-25 148
19b.1-6 148
19.10-14 149

Index of Biblical (and Other Ancient) References 571

Fragments, cont'd		Antirrheticus	176	3.4	204
20.20	149			3.23	204
21.19	149	On Not Three Gods	186	5.4	206
21.21	149			7.3	162
32.3	149	On the Holy Spirit	185,	7.5	206
44.5-7	149		186	7.7	163
48.2	149			7.11	204
50.20-29	149	Gregory of Thaumatur-		7.14	204
50.30	149	gus		7.27	204
56-58	149	A Detailed Confession of		7.31	206
57.1	149	Faith	176	8.19–20	205
65a.3-8	149			8.21	205
65–81	149	Orations		8.23	205
66.4	149	29.2	186	8.24–25	206
68.1-2	149	30.18-21	184	8.27	205
72	151	30.21	186, 187	8.29	209
74	151	31.3	185	8.29–34	209, 251
75	151	31.12	185	8.30	209
82.3	149	31.14	185	8.31	209
85.2-3	149, 150	31.25-29	186	8.33	209
88	151	31.28	185	8.34	209
		31.29	186, 187	8.40	163
Evagrius Ponticus		39.16	186	9	207
The Gnostic 79		41.5	187	9.3	206
Gospel of the Hebrews		41.11	187	9.4	249
	91			9.14	206, 249
				9.38	206, 249
Gospel of Mary	81	Hilary of Poitiers		9.57	204
		Syn.		10	207
Gregory of Nazianzus		38	162	10.6	204
Letters		48	208	10.7	206, 249
101	183			10.9–49	207
		Trin.		10.22	208
Gregory of Nyssa		1.16–19	203	10.50–51	208
Against Eunomius		1.26	162	10.55	207, 249
1.26	187	2.4	163	10.56–71	207
1.36	185, 188	2.4–23	203, 205	11.6	206, 249
2.2	186, 187	2.24	206, 208	11.9	208
2.14	184, 187	2.26	206	11.13	206
4.1	186	2.30	205	11.17	206
4.6	185	2.31–32	205	11.18	207, 249
5.2	185	2.34	209	11.19	208, 249
7.1	185	3.3	204	11.39–40	208

Hilary, *Trin.*, cont'd		9.1	51	3.6.2	118
12.1–8	204	18.2	50	3.9.3	117
12.8	204			3.18.1	116
12.14	204	*Magn.*		3.22.4	116
12.21	204	6.1	51	4.20.3	115
12.55–57	203	7.2	51	4.38.1	117
		8.2	49, 51	4.38.1-4	118
Hippolytus		8-10	49	5.1.1	117
Haer.		9.1-2	51	5.1.3	115
7.32	96, 97	13.1-2	49-50	5.14.2	116
8.19	105	15	50	5.21.2	116
9.2	98				
9.4-5	99	*Phld.*		*Trin.*	
9.5	99	6.1	49	1.16–19	203
9.5–7	119	7.1-2	51	1.26	162
10.13	119			2.4	163
10.23	99	*Pol.*		2.4–23	163, 205
10.25-26	105	2.2	51	2.24	206, 208
				2.26	206
Noet.		*Rom.*		2.30	205
1	120	Superscription	51	2.31–32	205
4	121, 122			2.34	209
2	99	*Smyrn.*		3.3	204
7	120	Superscription	51	3.4	204
8	120, 121	2.5	49	3.23	204
11	120	3.1-3	50	5.4	206
11–12	123	8.1	51	5.40	163
12	121, 122			6.35	204
14	120, 121, 122	*Trall.*		7.3	162
15	121	10.1	49	7.5	206
16	120, 122			7.7	163
17	122	Irenaeus		7.11	204
		Epid.		7.14	204
Trad. ap.		1	116	7.27	204
2.1–3.7	123	5	115	7.31	206
3.3	124	9.17	117	8.19–20	205
3.5	124	22	116	8.21	205
4.4-6	121	47	117	8.23	205
8.1-5	123	51	115	8.24–25	206
9.10-12	123-24	53	117	8.27	205
10.1-2	124	71	116	8.29	209
15	124			8.29–34	209, 251
35.3	124	*Haer.*		8.30	209
		1.1-6	80	8.31	209
Ignatius		1.26.2	91	8.33	209
Eph.		3.1.9	82	8.34	209
7.2	50	3.4.3	82	9	207

Index of Biblical (and Other Ancient) References

Irenaeus, *Trin.*, cont'd			
9.3	206
9.4	249
9.14	206, 249
9.38	206, 249
9.57	204
10	207
10.6	204
10.7	206, 249
10.9–49	207
10.22	208
10.50–51	208
10.55	207, 249
10.56–71	207
11.6	206, 249
11.9	208
11.13	206
11.17	206
11.18	207, 249
11.19	208, 249
11.39–40	208
12.1–8	204
12.8	204
12.14	204
12.21	204
12.55–57	203

Journeys of Peter 91

Preaching of Peter 91

Justin Martyr
First Apology
1–3	65
4–12	66
6.1-2	66
13–68	66
13.3	67
33–53	66
33.5	68
33.6	68
36.1	68
46.2-3	66
46.5	68
59	66
63	67
64.5	67
66.2	68

Second Apology 65

Dialogue with Trypho 65, 68
1–8	69
9–31	69
32–110	69
55.1	69
56–63	69
61.2	70
61.2-3	69-70
63	70
75.6–88.1	70
87	71
87.2	70
87.5	70
88.4	70
111–42	69

Lactantius
Inst.
| 4.12 | 139 |
| 4.13 | 139 |

Leo the Great
Letters 250, 251, 257
16	250-51
28	252
20–38	252
38	252

Sermons 250, 251

Tome to Flavian 252, 253, 257, 258, 262

Life of Saint Anthony 221

Malchion
Epistle 97

Marcellus of Ancyra
Contra Asterium 151, 152, 153
3	155
5	155
7	155
10	154
26	154
36	154
48	154, 156
51-56	156
57	154
57-60	155
61	155
65	155
66	154
70	156
72	155
73	156
74	154
75	154
79	156
87	156
91	156
92	154
94	155
97	154, 156
104	156, 157
113	154
117	154
120	154
124	154
125	154
126-28	156

Letter to Julius of Rome 151, 152, 153

Melito of Sardis
Fragments 72
| 15 | 74, 75 |

New Fragments	73	71.4-11	89	*Treat. Res.*	
20	74	71.16-21	89	44.14-19	80
II, 4	74	73.14-15	88		
II, 23	75	74.11-16	88	*Tri. Trac.*	
		75.2-11	80	50.12	81
Peri Pascha	72, 73			51.5-57.8	80
1-10	73	*Gos. Truth*	81, 82, 84	74.17	80
8	74	16.31-17.4	82	80.11	80
9-10	74	17.4-24.9	82	118.14	83
11-45	73	18.16-21	83	122.12	83
45	74	22.13-15	80	138.27	81
46-65	73	24.9-33.32	82		
47	74	24.10-16	83	Nestorius	
65	74	26.30-32	83	*Bazaar of Heracleides*	
66-67	74	26.35-27.4	83		191-96, 232
66-105	73	27.29	84		
100	74	30.16	84	Novatian	
105	74, 75	30.17-26	84	*Treatise Concerning the Trinity*	
				24	139
Nag Hammadi Tractates		*Hyp. Arch.*			
Ap. John		94.5-19	80	Origen	
1.1-5.22	80			*Princ.*	
9.26-19.15	80	*Orig. World*		Preface.1	137
19.16-32.8	81	98.7-100.9	80	Preface.1-3	132
				Preface.4	135, 137
Gos. Phil.	81, 86, 87	*Testim. Truth*	81, 84	Preface.4-10	132
55.18-22	88	29.6-9	85	1.1.1-9	132
55.23-26	88	29.9-31.22	85	1.2.4	133
55.23-36	88	30.18-31.5	86	1.2.8	133
55.24	89	31.22	85	1.2.13	133
55.27-28	88	32.22-24	86	1.3.4	133, 136
55.32-36	88	35.27-41.4	85	1.3.5	135
57.6-8	90	38.27	85	1.3.8	132
57.28	90	39.22-23	86	1.6.1-4	134
58.10	90	39.24-40.1	85	2.3.1-7	134
59.35-60	89	41.4-45.6	85	2.6.3	134, 135
64.22-27	89	45.6-18	86	2.6.4	135, 136
66.7-23	80	45.6-22	85	2.6.5	135
67.3-6	89	45.23	85	2.7.1	137
67.9-21	90	49.10	85	2.8.1-5	134
67.9-30	89	50.11	85	2.9.8	134
68.22-26	87	55.1-74.30	85	3.6.1-9	134
69.4-8	88			4.11-13	132
70.6-9	89	*Thom. Cont.*		4.28	133
70.10-22	87	138.1-7	80		
70.34-71.3	88	138.19-22	80		

Index of Biblical (and Other Ancient) References 575

Cels.
1.32	135
1.33	135
1.43	136
1.46	136
1.56	136
2.9	136
3.2	136
4.5	136
6.17	136
6.19	137
6.65	136
6.69-73	135
6.75-77	135
7.17	133
8.15	133
8.18	138
8.72	134

Comm. Jo.
1.191-97	136
1.230-33	135
1.236-39	136
2.1-20	133
2.76	133, 138
2.77	138
2.81	136
2.83-85	136
6.217-21	135
6.220	137

Comm. Matt.
10.17	135
14.6	136

Paulinus of Milan
The Life of Saint Ambrose
216

Qumran Scrolls 91

Shepherd of Hermas
Man. 55

Sim.
V	58
5.5.1-5	56
V:6:5-7	58
IX	58
IX:1:1	58
9.1.1	59
9.13.2-5	59

Vis.
3	59
3.3.3	59

Socrates Scholasticus
Hist. eccl.
4.23	79

Sozomenus
Hist. eccl.
2.27	141
4.6	162

Sulpitius Severus
Sacred History
2.36	162

Tatian
Address to the Greeks
76

Sophia of Jesus 81

Tertullian
Apol.
21	111, 249

Carn. Chr.
1	201
5	111, 201
5.18	249
9	201
10–13	201
14	111
18	111
19	111

Marc.
1.19	90
3.8	90
3.15	111
5.8	110, 111
5.17	111

Prax.
1	100
2	100, 201
5	100
7	100, 201
9–10	100
15	100
20	100
21	100
26	201
27	100, 201, 249
29	100, 201

Theodore of Mopsuestia
On the Incarnation
5.1	195, 197, 267
7.2	194
7.3	194, 196, 265
7.4	194
7.6	196, 267
7.7	197
12.11	193

Theodoret of Cyrus
Commentary on the Psalms
255, 266

Defense of Diodore of Tarsus and Theodore of Mopsuestia 253, 256

Eranistes 252, 253, 254, 255, 266

Fragments 256
15 256

Hist. eccl.
1.4	141
1.6	146
1.7	148

Spirit Christology

Letters	253, 256	Victorinus of Pettau		3.1-2	213
113	246	*Commentary on the Apoca-*		3.3	214
151	239, 241-42,	*lypse of the Blessed John*		3.6	213
	246	4.1	139	3.7	212, 213
163–71	237			3.8	213
171–78	248	Victorinus of Rome		3.9	212, 213
		Ad. Ar.		3.11	211
On the Holy and Vivifying		1a.8	214	3.11-12	214
Trinity	240	1a.12	212, 215	3.14-16	215, 251
		1a.16	212	3.17	213
On the Incarnation of the		1a.17	212, 214	3.18	213, 251
Lord	240	1a.18	212	4.4-5	213
		1a.21-22	213	4.6-7	214
Commentary on the Psalms		1a.28-32	213	4.7	214
	255, 266	1a.31	213	4.8	213
1–72	255	1.31	213	4.9-10	213
45	253, 255	1a.44	214	4.11	214
45.6	255	1b.49	211	4.17	215
		1b.50	211	4.18	214, 215
Refutation of the Twelve		1b.51	214	4.19	211
Anathemas against Nesto-		1b.52	212	4.19-20	213
rius	240-44, 256	1b.53	214, 251	4.21-29	213
		1b.54	212, 213	4.23	211
The Counter Statements of		1b.55	213		
Theodoret	241	1b.58	214, 251	*Ad. Cand.*	
		1b.59	213	2.1-13	211
Theophilus		1b.61	222	2.17-30	213
Autol.		2.1	211, 215		
2.10	76	2.7	213	Vigilius, Pope	
2.15	76	2.10	212	*Judicatum*	263

Index of Names

Abramowski, L. 191
Abunä M. 291
Acacius of Beroea 245
Acacius of Constantinople 262, 263
Acacius of Melitene 237
Acca of Hexham 301-302
Achilleus 141
Adam 4, 13-14, 30-31, 87, 89, 93, 115-16, 122, 177, 243, 245, 280-81, 341, 358-60, 362, 372, 384, 395, 398, 405, 470
Adamantius 200,
Aelurus, T. 261
Aetius 170
Alcuin 210, 306
Alexander, K.E. xiii, 417, 465, 474, 481, 494, 500, 502,
Alexander of Alexandria 140-41, 169, 203
Alfaro, S. 36-37
Alfeyev, H. 280
Allert, C.D. 69-70
Ambrose of Milan 162, 216-21, 228, 242, 249, 251, 271, 303, 305, 308, 312, 375, 515
Amphilochius of Iconium 242
Anastos, T.L. 283
Anatolios, K. 169-75
Anawim 91
Anderson, A. 32-33, 413, 415, 417-18, 456-58, 460, 462
Anderson, R.M. 451-52, 455-59, 463, 493, 500
Anderson, V. 363-66, 368, 380-81
Andrew of Samosata 189
Angold, M. 285
Anselm 311
Aphrahat 158-61, 198-200

Apollinarius of Laodaceia 156, 176-81, 191, 198-200, 231, 239, 264, 513
Arator 303
Archer, K. xiii, 463
Argue, A. 432
Aristides of Athens 64-66, 76
Aristotle 210, 285, 311
Arius 140-48, 150, 152, 155, 169-70, 198-200, 202-203, 206, 271, 291, 513
Asberry, R. 458
Ashwin-Siejkowski, P. 125, 128
Asterius the Sophist 141, 152-56
Athanasius 96, 98, 101-102, 141-45, 148, 151-54, 157, 162-63, 169-76, 198, 200, 202, 217, 234, 242, 252, 271, 287, 375, 515
Athanasius of Anazarbus 141
Athenagoras 76
Atkins, J.M. 479
Atkinson, W.P. 13
Atticus of Constantinople 242
Aquinas, T. 19, 285, 311
Augustine 18, 21, 131, 210, 216, 220-28, 234, 249, 251-52, 264, 271, 300, 303, 305, 308-309, 311-13, 316, 375, 431, 489, 515, 518
Aurelius, M. 72
Auxentius of Milan 170, 216
Auxentius of Durostorum 170
Awerjan 365
Awrey, D. 449
Ayele, T. 287-92, 298
Aymro, W. 287-89, 291
Badcock, G. 317, 338-40, 342
Baelz, P. 2
Bagratuni, S. 357

Baillie, D.M. 3
Baker, D. 451
Baker, J.A. 47, 91-92
Bandrés, J.L. 288-89, 294, 298
Barabas, S. 418
Barclift, P.L. 250
Barlaam the Calabrian 282
Barnard, L.W. 66-69, 71
Barnes, M.H. 10
Barnes, M.R. 157, 170
Barnes, T.D. 103, 105-106
Barratt, T. 432
Barriger, L. 364
Barth, K. 22, 27, 35, 334, 336-38, 342, 344
Barthwaite, R. 461
Bartleman, F. 458-59
Basil of Ancyra 203, 270
Basil of Caesarea 96, 98, 101-102, 157, 176, 181-88, 203, 217, 242, 270
Basilides 126, 131
Bathrellos, D. 276
Bauer, W. 92, 94
Baxter, R. 418
Beacham, D. 443
Beatus of Liebana 306-309
Beckwith, C.L. 202-203, 207
Bede, The Venerable 210, 301-305, 312-16, 374
Beeley, C.A. 182-83, 186, 189
Bell, E.N. 497
Bellinzoni, A.J. 68
Berkhof, H. 3, 62
Berkhof, L. 63, 98-99, 102
Bernard of Clairvaux 311-12
Bernard, D.K. 498-500, 502
Bethune-Baker, J.F. 189-94, 196, 230, 233, 235-36, 242, 252-53, 257-60, 263
Biddle, J. 325
Bigg, C. 125-26, 128-35
Bindley, T.H. 240-42, 252, 258-60
Bingham, D.J. 117
Biscop, B. 301
Blumhofer, E.L. 416-17, 452, 455-59, 463, 487

Blunt, A.W.F. 67, 69
Bobrinskoy, B. 182-85, 188-89, 283-84
Boardman, W.E. 416-19
Boethius 210
Bolshakoff, S. 286, 363-66, 368-71, 380-81
Bonaventure 314-16, 374
Bonner, C. 72, 75
Bonner, G. 220-21
Bossakov, J. 277
Boston, T. 418
Bougerol, J.G. 310, 312
Bousset, W. 11, 50, 113, 352-53
Bouyer, L. 363-64
Bowe, J. 478-79
Boyle, M. 277
Braaten, C.E. 192, 336
Bradshaw, P.F. 123
Brent, A. 119
Brown, G.H. 301-302
Brown, P.R.L. 220
Brown, R.E. 91
Bruce, F.F. 28
Brumback, C. 449, 456, 458-59, 493, 500
Bryant, W.F. 449, 474
Buckley, J.J. 87
Bucur, B.G. 158-61
Bulgakov, F.O. 382
Bundy, D.D. 393, 418
Burge, G.M. 34
Burgess, S.M. xiii, 55, 88, 95, 98, 102-103, 124, 167-69, 280-84, 288, 298, 301, 303, 310-11, 317, 356, 363, 391
Burns, J.P. 225
Burns, P.C. 204-205, 208
Butler, A.H. 481
Butler, D.L. 498-500, 502
Cabasilas, N. 283-84
Callistus of Rome 100-101, 119
Campbell, J.E. 443, 450
Campenhausen, H. 169
Candidian 235-36
Candidus 211
Carlton, C.C. 232-33

Index of Names   579

Carlyle, A.J.   393
Callahan, L.D.   455-57
Campbell, J.E.   443, 450
Cashwell, G.B.   469, 474-75, 480-81
Cassian, J.   197, 234
Cassianus, J.   84
Cassiodorus   210
Cavadini, J.C.   306-309
Celestine   233-36, 249
Cerinthus   95
Cerrato, J.A.   123
Chabannes, J.   220
Chadwick, H.   119, 123-24, 146, 190, 246
Chaillot, C.   287, 289
Chalmers, T.   392
Charlemagne   306
Charles I   319
Charlesworth, J.H.   91,
Chesnut, R.   191-92, 231
Christensen, M.J.   404, 413
Chrysaphius   249, 257
Chrysostom, J.   189-90, 194-97, 239, 242, 413
Cicero   210
Clay, J.E.   380-83, 391
Clayton, P.B.   256
Clement of Alexandria   78, 81, 84, 125-30, 138-39, 271, 375
Clement of Rome   47-48, 55, 59, 60, 93
Clemmons, I.C.   479
Clemmons, J.C.   479
Clements, K.   337-39, 341-42
Clifton R.C.   37-38
Coffey, D.   16-22, 34-35, 226, 245, 518-19
Coggins, R.J.   93
Cohen, L.   288-89
Cohick, L.   72-73
Cole, H.   394, 397, 403
Coleridge, S.T.   337, 393
Colless, B.   158-60
Collins, R.   306-308
Congar, Y.   18-20
Conn, C.W.   449, 474
Constans   153, 202

Constantine   141, 146, 151-52, 170
Constantine V   277
Constantius   163, 202
Conybeare, F.C.   357-66, 368-71, 380-81
Cook, G.A.   499
Copleston, F.C.   336, 338
Copley, A.S.   471-72, 490-92
Corwin, V.   49
Cotton, J.   319
Cowley, R.W.   292, 294
Creech, J.   459
Crawford, F.   466
Cromwell, O.   325
Cross, F.L.   164-67
Crouzel, H.   131-35
Crummey, D.   286, 288-91, 298
Crumpler, A.B.   469, 480-81
Culbreth, J.A.   471
Cullen, C.M.   309-11, 314
Cullis, C.   417, 419
Cyprian   139, 242, 252
Cyril of Alexandria   190-93, 196-98, 200, 226, 229, 231-49, 251-58, 261-68, 271-72, 276, 284, 288-90, 294, 300, 513
Cyril of Jerusalem   163-69, 198-200, 271, 375, 515
Cyril of White Lake   363
Dabney, D.L.   17, 20, 26, 33
Daley, B.   98-100, 119, 156, 181-84, 207, 226, 231, 241
Dallimore, A.   392-94, 403-404
Damasus of Rome   242
Daniélou, J.   47, 91-92, 131-37
Daniels, R.   326-31
Davidson, I.J.   276
Davis, L.D.   141, 152-53, 182, 190, 230, 232-38, 245-47, 249, 251, 253, 256-60, 262-65, 275-77
Day, A.D.   22
Dayton, D.W.   412-17, 432, 434, 438, 463-64, 502-503
Declerck, J.H.   147-50
DeConick, A.D.   87-90
Deferrari, J.R.   125, 139
Deissmann, A.   11, 352-53

Del Colle, R. 8, 17-18, 20, 22, 34-35, 39-41, 514, 518
Deschner, J. 414
Dever, M. 319-20
Dewart, J.M. 225
Dibelius, M. 58
Didymus of Alexandria 105, 206, 217
Dieter, M. 414-15, 417
Diodore of Tarsus 176-77, 189, 200, 233, 253, 256, 263
Dionysius of Alexandria 101, 139
Dionysius a presbyter 176
Dionysius, Pseudo 276, 311
Dionysius of Rome 139
Dioscorus of Alexandria 249, 251-53, 257-58, 291
Dix, G. 119, 123-24
Doddridge, P. 418
Domnus of Antioch 249, 252-53, 258
Donfried, K.P. 60
Donskoi, D. 365
Dorman, D.A. 3, 34, 434, 517
Dorner, I.A. 345
Dorotheus 234
Dorries, D.W. 392, 394, 396-401, 403-405
Doval, A.J. 163-64
Dowie, J.A. 404, 487
Drijvers, J.W. 163-64
Drummond, A.L. 392-94, 403-404
Drummond, H. 393
Duckett, E.S. 306
Duggar, L. 474
Dull, J.E. 445-47
Dunn, G.D. 105-106, 109, 231
Dunn, J.D.G. 10-16, 20, 34-35, 39
Durham, W.H. 465, 487, 492, 494-501
Edwards, D. 28, 40
Edwards, J. 320, 333
Edwards, M.J. 129
Eli the priest 93
Elipandus 306-309, 316, 374
Ellis, J.B. 476
Ephraim of Antioch 261

Ephrem the Syrian 200, 242
Epignous 100
Epiphanius 81, 91-99, 101-102, 104-105, 110, 114, 131, 141, 157, 162
Ervin, H.M. 12
Etherius 306-309
Eudoxia 234
Eudoxius 170
Eunomius 170
Eusebius of Caesarea 48, 72, 91, 96-97, 105, 113-14, 132, 141, 145-46, 152-53, 155, 170, 182
Eusebius of Dorylaeum 252-53
Eusebius of Nicomedia 141, 152
Eustathius of Antioch 146-52, 177, 189, 198-200, 242, 270, 515
Eutyches 249, 251-53, 255, 257-58, 262, 264, 396, 398
Evagrius Ponticus 79, 264, 276
Evalenko, A.M. 380
Evans, C.A. 336
Eve 87, 116, 384
Ewart, F.J. 499-504
Ezana 287
Farrow, L. 457
Fäsiladas 289, 291-92
Faupel, D.W. 393, 404, 416, 451-52, 454-56, 458-61, 464-65, 493, 498-500, 502
Felix III 262
Felix of Urgel 306
Ferguson, E. 137
Ferguson, S.B. 326, 328
Figgis, J.B. 418
Filson, F.V. 81-82, 86-87
Finney, C.G. 415, 417
Fiorenza, F.S. 348
Fitzmyer, J.A. 91-93
Flavian of Antioch 189
Flavian of Constantinople 191-92, 242, 249, 251-53, 258
Fletcher, J. 416, 440
Flower, A. 432
Flower, J.R. 490
Foster, F.J. 498, 500
Foster, P. 48-49, 52, 56, 60
Fox, C.R. 457, 461, 466, 469

Index of Names 581

Franklin, L.D. 105-107, 110
Franzmann, M. 81-82, 86, 88, 90
Fraser, A.L. 489
Hans W. 336, 338
Finney, C.G. 415, 417
Francis of Assisi 309
French, T.L. 498, 500, 502
Frend, W.H.C. 82-83, 87, 98, 102, 112, 114, 116, 118-20, 125-27, 129-34, 153, 162, 169, 176, 178, 180, 202, 216, 221, 231, 233-38, 240, 245, 247-49, 252-53, 257-59, 261, 263-64
Friesen, A. 461
Fudge, T.A. 498, 500-502
Fulgentius 308
Frumentius 287
Gardner, E. 471
Garrigus, A. 432
Garrison, S.O. 437
Germinius of Sirmium 170
Glassey, J. 453-54
Goff, J.R. 451-52, 454-57, 459-62
González, J.L. 49, 63, 94, 96, 98-99, 112, 114, 116, 118-20, 125-28, 130-35, 142, 148, 170, 173, 180, 182, 192, 201, 203, 218, 221-22, 225, 230-32, 234-37, 246, 249, 253, 257-59, 261-64, 275-77, 281-82, 285-86, 288, 301, 306-307, 310, 312, 334, 336-41, 356, 363-64
Goodenough, E.R. 68, 71
Goodwin, T. 333
Goranson, S. 91
Gordon, A.J. 417, 421,-22, 424-25, 427, 429
Graham, H.H. 61
Grant, R.M. 61, 63-66, 72, 79, 81-82, 114-15
Grass, K. 365-71
Gratian 217
Green, B. 234, 249-53, 257, 263, 268
Green, F.W. 240-42, 252-60
Greer, R.A. 147
Gregg, R.C. 141-46, 167
Greggs, T. 134

Gregory of Nazianzus 176, 181-87, 234, 242, 280
Gregory of Nyssa 132, 134, 157, 176, 181-88, 242
Gregory X 311
Gregory of Thaumaturgus 176, 181
Grenz, S. 318, 334, 336-38, 340
Grillmeier, A. 50, 54, 58, 67, 74, 109, 113-14, 116, 120-23, 133, 135-36, 142, 148-49, 153, 155, 157-59, 162,-63, 173, 178-79, 183, 197, 204, 206-208, 214, 218, 225, 231-34, 236, 240-41, 246-47, 249-53, 256, 258-60, 262-64, 266, 268, 288-89, 298, 300
Groh, D. 142-45
Grosart, A.B. 319-20
Grotius, H. 325
Gunkel, H. 351-52
Guyon, M. 441
Gwatkin, H.M. 140-42, 152, 155
Gwynn, D.M. 154
Habets, M. 32, 41
Hadjiantoniou, G.A. 286
Hadrian 64
Hadrian I 306
Haight, R. 6, 10, 40
Haile, G. 290-98
Hall, J.L. 501
Hall, S.G. 72-75
Han, S.E. 35-36
Hansen, O. 6
Hanson, R.P.C. 140-42, 146, 148-55, 157, 162-63, 165-67, 169-74, 181-84, 202-208, 210-15, 217-18
Harding, W. 405
Harnack, A. 58, 71, 76, 79, 81, 92-93, 96-98, 101-102, 114, 116, 118, 120-21, 125-26, 128, 132-35, 142, 170-71, 180, 183, 192, 222-23, 225, 232-36, 246, 249, 252-53, 257-59, 261-65, 277, 306-308
Harris, J.R. 64-66
Harrisville, R.A. 336, 348
Hay, C.E. 51, 58, 61, 79, 91, 96-100, 102, 114, 121, 128, 130, 132-35,

142, 170, 174, 180, 190, 206, 222, 225, 310-11, 314
Hayes, Z. 309-12, 314
Haykin, M.A.G. 327
Haywood, G.T. 499-505
Heard, A.F. 286, 364-65, 368-69, 371
Hector, K.W. 342
Hefelbower, S.G. 334
Hegel, G.W.F. 343
Heine, R.E. 104-106, 136
Henry, P. 277
Henson, G.M. 446
Heraclites 98
Herbert, Lord of Cherbury 334
Hermas 55-59, 514
Hick, J. 2, 3, 6
Hilary of Poitiers 98, 162-63, 202-209, 217, 222, 228, 249, 251-52, 271, 303, 308, 375, 515
Hildebrand, S.M. 181-82, 189
Hinze, B.E. 17, 20, 26, 33
Hippolytus of Rome 81, 91, 96-99, 105, 114, 118-24, 138-39, 157, 242
Hocken, P.D. 33
Hogsten, D. 498
Holder, A.G. 302
Hollenweger, W.J. 33, 414, 462, 464
Holmes, M.W. 50, 52
Holmes. N.J. 481
Hook, N. 3, 38-39, 41
Horner, R.C. 432-36, 451, 462
Howson, B.H. 327
Hulse, E. 319-20
Humphrey, E.M. 55
Hunter, H. 34, 39, 41, 453-54, 459, 474
Hurst, L.D. 153, 303-304
Hussey, E.M. 283
Hyatt, H.M. 287-89, 292, 298
Ibas of Edessa 253, 258, 262-63
Ignatius of Antioch 47-51, 114, 242, 271, 333, 519
Ildefonsus 308
Irenaeus 29-30, 32, 35, 80-82, 91, 113-19, 123, 138-39, 157-58, 175, 242, 252, 271, 375, 397, 515

Irwin, B.H. 432, 440-50, 452-53, 460, 462, 480-81
Irwin, S.T. 448-49
Irving, E. 35, 379, 392-411, 418, 510, 515
Isaac of Nineveh 281
Isenberg, W.W. 87-88
Isidore of Seville 210, 303, 308
Isidore of Russia 286
Ivan III 286
Ivanov, A. 366
Jackson, P. 164
Jacobsen, D.G. 87, 450, 466, 469, 501, 520
Jemeljan, I. 365
Jefferys, G. 432
Jefford, C.N. 47, 62
Jenkins, S.D.L. 35, 518
Jerome 91, 176, 303, 308, 312
Jevtich, A. 98
Joachim of Fiore 310
John of Antioch 235-37, 240, 245-47, 256, 258
John of Damascus 277, 284
John the Evangelist 13, 108, 123, 129, 136, 280, 397
John of Jerusalem 163
John of Parma 310
Jonas, H. 79-82
Jones, C. 465
Jones, C.E. 418
Jones, C.P. 457, 478-79
Jones, F.S. 93-94
Jones, M.D. 170
Joseph of Volokolamsk 364
Jovian 176
Julius of Rome 151-53, 176
Justin 262-63
Justinain 104, 262-63, 355
Justin Martyr 66-72, 74, 76, 104, 113-14, 262,-63, 271, 333, 355, 375, 515
Kakhavski 380
Kalleres, D.S. 164
Kannengiesser, C. 140, 170
Kant, I. 318, 336-37
Kapustin, S. 380

Index of Names 583

Kärkkäinen, V.   xiii, 304, 314, 323, 339-41
Kasper, W.   16-18, 26
Kearsley, R.   109
Keating, D.   245
Kelly, J.N.D.   38, 57-58, 65, 74, 94, 97-98, 100-102, 114, 119, 120-23, 130, 135, 142, 146, 148, 155-57, 164, 167-68, 170, 174, 178, 180, 182-83, 192, 201, 207, 211-12, 217-19, 221, 223, 225, 231-36, 240, 246-47, 249-52, 255, 257-60
Kelsey, C.L.   338-41
Kendrick, K.   449, 451-52, 455-59
Kenyon, F.   72
Kidane, H.   291
King, J.H.   441, 443, 471, 473, 480-84, 486
Kissinger, W.S.   336
Kitromilides, P.M.   286
Klubnikin, E.G.   382, 391
Knott, J.R.   320
Kolesnikov, S.   379
Kontzevitch, I.M.   286, 363-64
Koetschau, P.   131, 133, 135-37
Koester, H.   55-56
Kraft, R.A.   52-54, 92, 94
Krivocheine, B.   280-81
Krodel, G.   92, 94
Kurowski, M.T.   413
Kutepov, K.   366-71
L'Huillier, P.   238, 258
Lactantius,   139
Lake, K.   48-53, 55-57, 59-61
Lambert, M.   356-57
Lampe, G.W.H.   3-6, 10, 34, 38-39, 353, 514, 517
Lancel, S.   220
Land, S.J.   xiii, 36, 414, 464-65, 520
Latourette, K.S.   276-79, 306, 310, 356, 363-64
Laud, W.   319
Laurentius   222
Lawson, J.   49, 52-53, 61
Lee, E.L.   479
Lee, E.S.   458

Lee, F.J.   477
Lehman, J.O.   472
Lennox, S.J.   437
Leo I, the Great   191-92, 197, 231, 234, 246, 249-53, 257-58, 262-63, 268, 291, 308
Leo III   277, 306
Leo V   278
Leontius of Byzantium   261
Leporius   234
Lessing, G.E.   335
Levison, J.R.   348-49
Liddell, H.G.   260
Lienhard, J.T.   151-57, 162, 223
Lietzmann, H.   176-77, 179
Lightfoot, J.B.   50
Lindström, H.G.Å.   413
Livingston, J.C.   318, 334-38, 340-41, 348, 393
Locke, J.   334
Lodahl, M.   6, 40
Loewe, W.P.   10
Logan, B.H.   151-52
Lombard, P.   310
Longden, L.R.   413
Loofs, F.   158, 160-61, 189-92, 194
Lossky, V.   279-80, 282-83
Louth, A.   276-77
Lovett, L.   462
Lucaris, C.   286
Lucian of Antioch   189
Ludlow, M.   132
Luke the Evangelist   312, 358, 491
Lum, C.   466
Luther, M.   194
Lyman, J.R.   132-35, 146
Macchia, F.D.   xiii, 13, 35, 518
MacKenzie, I.M.   115-17
Maddox, R.L.   29, 413-14, 416
Magnentius   202
Mahan, A.   415, 417, 422, 424-27, 429
Makeda   287
Malchion   96-97, 189
Macarius   279, 413
Macedonius   291

Marcellus of Ancyra 146, 151-54, 156-57, 162-63, 176, 178, 198-200, 505
Marcian 257, 262
Marcion 85, 90, 95, 110, 119, 131
Maris the Persian 263
Martin, L.J. 457-60
Martin, W. 449
Mary the virgin 8, 23, 50, 86-88, 100, 109, 116, 122, 150, 159, 163, 167, 172, 190, 192-95, 197, 201, 209, 214, 226, 230, 232-33, 235, 238-39, 241-42, 246-48, 254, 259, 264, 295-97, 304-306, 316, 329, 352, 356, 358-59, 362, 368, 372, 375, 385, 397, 399, 421-22, 485, 488, 506, 519
Mason, C.H. 457, 478-80
Mason, E. 479
Mason, M. 479
Matthew the Evangelist 287, 491
Maurer, C. 54
Maximilla 103, 105
Maximus of Jerusalem 163
Maximus the Confessor 276
Maxwell, D.R. 225-26
McAlister, R.E. 499, 501
McClung, G. 459
McCormick, B.L. 344
McCormick, K.S. 413
McDonnell, K. 22, 50, 72, 74, 104, 106, 109, 117, 130, 137, 143, 161, 166, 168,-69, 187, 196, 208-209, 463
McFarland, I.A. 276
McFarlane, G. 393, 395, 397, 399, 402-403, 410
McGee, G.B. 456, 461, 490
McGrath, A.E. 318, 336-40, 344-45, 348
McGuckin, J.A. 226, 229-40, 243-48, 251, 253, 257-60, 263, 265
McGuire, A. 84
McKim, D.K. 312
McKinley, D.J. 328
McLynn, N.B. 216

McNabb, M. 449
McPherson, A.S. 432
Meletius of Antioch 242
Melito of Sardis 72-77
Memnon of Ephesus 236-37
Menelik 287
Menzies, R.P. 12-13
Menzies, W.W. 418
Meredith, A. 181-84, 189
Merricks, W.S. 392-94, 400, 404
Merritt, S. 420, 474
Methodius of Patara 242
Metzger, B.M. 287-88, 292
Meyendorff, J. 230-31, 252-53, 259-65, 276-80, 282-84
Michael II 278
Migne, J.P. 242-45
Miller, P.C. 82-84
Minns, D. 114, 116, 118
Miskov, J. 417
Molokan 365, 378, 380-83, 391
Moltmann, J. 20, 22-28, 30, 34, 40, 71
Montague, G.T. 72, 104, 106, 137, 166, 168-69, 196, 208-209
Montanus 102-105, 110
Montgomery, C.J. 417, 429
Moody, D.L. 417, 474
Moore, J. 466
Motovu, J. 287-89, 291
Mühlen, H. 7
Munro-Hay, S. 287-89, 298
Murray, R. 311
Myland, D.W. 463, 489
Napoleon 337
Narcissus of Neronius 152
Need, S.W. 230-33, 237, 249, 252-53, 257-60, 262-65, 276-77
Nelson, S. 454
Nestorius 189-200, 206, 226, 229-40, 245-46, 248, 250, 256, 258, 261-63, 266-67, 270-71, 291, 375, 515
Neusner, J. 158
Newman, P.W. 6, 39
Nicephorus 278
Nichol, J.T. 414, 450, 456, 458-59

Index of Names 585

Nielsen, J.T.   116
Nienkirchen, C.   419, 420, 424, 427, 431-32
Nikon   364, 367
Nilus of Sora   364
Noah   93, 166, 287, 460, 491
Noetus of Symrna   98-100, 119-23
Norris, F.W.   181-84, 186
Norris, R.A.   177-80, 194, 196, 232
Novalis   337
Novatian   139, 190
Nuttall, G.F.   326-27, 331
O'Collins, G.   231-32, 236, 246, 253, 258-60, 262-63, 265, 275-76
O'Keefe, J.J.   231
Obolensky, D.   356-57
Oden, T.C.   29, 68, 71, 413
Oliver, R.W.   325-27
Olson, M.J.   114
Olson, R.E.   63, 126-28, 318, 334, 336-40
Opperman, D.C.O.   500
Origen   78, 91, 118, 125-26, 130-39, 142, 146-47, 181, 261, 264, 271, 276, 375, 399
Osborn, E.F.   115-18, 125-26, 128-30
Osiek, C.   55-56
Outler, A.C.   29, 413
Owen, J.   319, 325-33, 352, 393
Ozman, A.   432, 452, 455
Paez, P.   289, 294
Page, S.D.   481
Pagels, E.H.   81, 84-85, 88
Paget, J.C.   52
Palamas, G.   279, 282-84, 311, 363
Palladius of Ratiaria   170
Palmer, P.   414-15, 422, 434, 438, 441
Palmer, R.E.   338
Palmieri, A.   380-81
Pantaenus   125
Parham, C.F.   432, 450-63, 466, 493
Parham, S.E.   451-52, 454-60
Parvis, P.   60, 67, 72
Parvis, S.   67, 72, 152-53
Patterson, J.O.   479

Patterson, M.   393
Paul the Apostle   11, 13-14, 52, 93, 209-10, 307-308, 348-52, 357, 446, 498
Paul of Emesa   245
Paul of Samosata   97-98, 144, 150, 162, 189, 191, 355, 357, 362
Paulinus of Milan   216
Paulinus of Tyre   141, 152
Pearson, B.A.   84-85
Pearson, L.   340
Pelagius   234
Pelikan, J.   57-58, 68, 75, 79, 91, 95, 97-100, 102-103, 110, 120, 124-26, 129-30, 132, 134, 156, 171-73, 177, 182-83, 193-95, 197, 206, 218, 221, 253, 259-60, 262-64, 275-77, 279-80, 283, 286, 303, 306-308, 318, 336-38, 340, 356
Peppiatt, L.   38
Pernveden, L.   58
Perry, S.   476
Peter the Apostle   91, 93, 175, 186, 301, 303-304, 313, 361, 429, 498, 505
Peter III   366
Peters, E.   306
Pettersen, A.   169, 172
Philip the Evangelist   287
Philip of Rome   237
Philippov, D.   365-69, 373
Phillips, W.H.   xiii, 450
Philo   68, 126
Philogonius   146
Philoxenus of Mabbug   261, 263
Photinus   162-63, 191, 198-200, 203
Pike, J.M.   436, 440, 442
Pinnock, C.H.   28-34, 40, 518
Piper, W.H.   487-88
Piper, O.A.   82
Pius, A.   64, 66
Pius, Pope   55
Plato   48, 67, 285
Plethon, G.G.   285
Plotinus   210
Pobirokin, I.   379-80
Pollock, J.C.   418

Polycarp of Smyrna 48, 51, 66, 242
Porphyry 210
Porter, J.A. 442, 449
Praxeas 99-100, 106-109
Prentiss, H. 500
Preston, D.D. 474
Priscilla 103
Pritz, R. 91
Proclus 233, 249, 256
Prosper 222
Pulcheria 230, 234, 235, 257
Purves, J. 397, 399, 402, 407, 409
Quasten, J. 47-48, 52, 59, 63, 65, 72, 79, 82, 84, 93, 96-97, 105-107, 113-14, 116, 119, 121, 123, 125-27, 131, 133-35, 141-42, 146, 148, 151-52, 163-67, 170-71, 173, 176-78, 180, 182-84, 189-91, 202-205, 210-13, 215-17, 221-23, 225, 230-34, 237, 240, 245, 250-51, 254-56
Rahner, K. 16-17, 19
Ramelli, I.L.E. 134
Ramsey, B. 216-17
Rankin, D. 105-106
Raven, C.E. 176-80
Redeker, M. 338
Reed, D. 498-500, 502
Reedy, G. 334
Reiff, A.C. 487
Reimarus, H.S. 334-36
Reno, R.R. 132
Richard of St. Victor 311
Richardson, C.C. 48, 61
Riss, R.M. 493
Ritschl, A. 334, 342, 348, 350
Robeck, C.M. 103-104, 106, 110, 457-59, 461, 501
Roberts, W.P. 10
Robins, R.G. 474
Robinson, D.C. 252
Robinson, J.M. 79-85, 87-89
Robinson, J.A.T. 2, 64-66
Rock, S. 286, 363-64
Rosato, P.J. 16, 34, 41
Ross, B.R. 433
Ross, G.R. 479
Rousseau, P. 182

Rowe, J.N. 133
Rowe, K.E. 413
Rudolph, K. 79, 81
Rudometkin, M.G. 381-90
Rufinus 131-32, 176
Runciman, S. 355-57
Runia, D.T. 130
Russell, N. 230-31, 233-37, 244-46, 248
Sabellius 101-102, 157, 291
Samarin, I.G. 381-83, 391
Sample, R. 97
Samuel, V.C. 264, 291
Samson 93
Sanders, R.G.W. 457-60, 462, 466
Sandford, F.W. 452-54, 474
Sandidge, J.L. 233
Scarbrough, J.M. 477
Schaff, P. 48, 52, 64, 66, 72, 79, 82, 91, 93, 95-96, 98-104, 110, 113-14, 119, 125, 127, 131, 152, 155, 162-64, 169, 176, 180, 189-90, 202, 205, 216, 220-23, 230, 235-37, 247, 249, 250-53, 257-60, 262-64, 275-78, 301, 306-308, 356
Scheeben, M.J. 7, 16
Scheppe, J.G. 500
Schlegel, F. 337
Schleiermacher, F. 113, 337-44, 347, 353, 393, 397
Schoedel, W.R. 48, 51
Schoeps, H. 91-93
Scholasticus, S. 79
Schoonenberg, P.J.A.M. 7-10, 17, 19, 21, 41
Schweitzer, A. 11, 335-36, 339, 352, 354
Scott, R. 260
Scullion, J.J. 348
Seagraves, D.L. 501
Seeberg, R. 51, 58, 61, 79, 91, 96-100, 102, 114, 121, 128, 130, 132-35, 142, 170, 174, 180, 190, 206, 222, 225, 310-11, 314
Segelberg, E. 89
Selassie, S.H. 287-88, 290-92, 294, 298

Index of Names 587

Selivanov, K. 366, 368
Sellers, R.V. 146-51, 178-80, 189-90, 192-94, 230-32, 239, 241, 247, 249, 251-53, 256, 258-65
Seraphim of Sarov 363
Serapion 170-71
Severus of Antioch 261
Severus, S. 125
Sexton, E.A. 470, 472-73
Seymour, W.S. 432, 456-63, 466-69, 493
Shakarian, D. 391
Sheba, Queen of 288
Shedd, W.G.T. 68, 92, 98, 120, 133, 154, 170, 180
Shenk, C.E. 286-89, 294
Shenoute 264
Shotwell, W.A. 68
Shubin, D.H. 381-83, 391
Shumway, C.W. 454, 460
Sibbes, R. 319-25, 333, 352
Sideris, T. 277
Simon Magus 93
Simpson, A.B. 417-32, 474, 486, 489
Siker, J.S. 87
Sixtus III 249
Skarsaune, O. 67, 69, 70, 71
Slusser, M. 69-70
Smith, H.W. 417
Smith, R.P. 417
Snyder, H.A. 413
Socinus, F. 327
Sokolov, L.P. 382
Solomon King of Israel 287-88
Sophia of Russia 286
Sophronius 191
Sozomenus 141, 162, 176
Speller, L. 162-63
Spence, A. 326-33
Spoerl, K.M. 146, 148-49, 151, 156, 178
Spurling, R.G. 449, 473-74, 520
Spurling Jr., R.G. 474
Stephen 280-281
Stewart-Sykes, A. 72-73, 123-24
Stibbe, M.W.G. 23
Stoyanov, Y. 356

Strachan, G. 394, 400, 403-409
Stendahl, K. 91
Strimple, R.B. 335-36
Stronstad, R. 12
Studebaker, S.M. 32
Sullivan, F.A. 196, 200
Sulpitius Severus 162
Suseneyos 289, 290, 292, 294
Suslov, I. 368
Susneos 289, 294
Swete, H.B. 52
Sykes, S.W. 2, 3, 5, 338
Symeon the New Theologian 279-81, 284
Symmachus 91-92
Synan, V. xiii, 33, 391, 404, 412-18, 432, 434, 440-43, 449, 451-59, 461-62, 464-66, 469, 479, 481, 493, 498, 500
Tabbernee, W. 103-104
Taheb 93
Tallman, M.W. 391
Tamrat, T. 288, 290
Taylor, G.F. 442, 481-86
Tatian 76
Telfer, W. 163-64
Tertullian 81, 90-91, 96, 100, 103-106, 147, 157, 192, 201, 249, 252, 271, 375, 515
TeSelle, E. 225
Tesfazghi, U. 288-90, 292-93, 295, 298
Tewofelos 291
Theodore of Mopsuestia 176-77, 189, 193-97, 200, 225-26, 235, 257, 263, 265-67
Theodore the Studite 278
Theodoret of Cyrus 141, 146, 148, 176, 189, 196, 206, 235-37, 239-44, 246, 248-49, 251-58, 261-63, 266-67, 270-71, 375, 398, 515
Theodosius I 233
Theodosius II 189-90, 230, 235, 237, 243, 245, 252, 257
Theodotus 96-97, 125, 357
Theognis 141
Theophilus of Alexandria 190, 229

Theophilus of Antioch 76, 113, 122, 158, 160-61, 190, 229, 278
Theophilus, Emperor 278
Thistlethwaite, S.E. 451
Thomas, J.C. xiii, 34
Thomasius, G. 343-47, 353
Thomson, A. 325-26
Tice, T.N. 337-38
Tillotson, J. 334
Tindal, M. 334
Tinney, J.S. 462
Tipton, J.M. 449
Tollefsen, T. 276
Tomlinson, A.J. 420, 432, 453, 474-77
Torrance, A. 283
Torrance, T.F. 51
Torrey, R.A. 417
Trevett, C. 103, 104, 106, 110
Trigg, J.W. 131, 134-35
Trueman, C.R. 325-26
Trypho 66, 69-72
Tschiflianov, B. 277
Turcescu, L. 181-83
Tzamalikos, P. 131-32, 134
Uklein, S.M. 380, 389
Ulfilas 170
Upton, L. 392
Ursacius of Singidunum 170
Urshan, A.D. 500-505
Valens of Mursa 170, 202
Valentinus 82, 126, 131
Valentinian 216
Van De Walle, B.A. 419-20
Van Den Hoek, A. 125
Van Dusen, H.P. 50
Verghese, P. 276
Verheyden, J. 56, 339
Victor of Rome 96, 99
Victorinus, M. 210-15, 221-22, 228, 251
Victorinus of Pettau 139
Vigilius 263
Vinzent, M. 152-57
Voltaire 334
Wacker, G. 461, 463
Wainwright, G. 465

Walker, W. 230-33, 235, 246, 249, 252-53, 257-59, 261-64, 275-77, 306, 310, 318, 334-38, 356, 392-93
Ward, B. 301-302
Ware, T. 285-86, 290, 364
Warner, W.E. 465
Watson, E.M. 437
Watson, G.D. 432, 436-41, 443-45, 451, 462, 474
Watts, T. 276
Weedman, M. 202-208, 210-13
Weinandy, T.G. 170, 172-75
Welch, C. 334, 336-39, 343-45, 393
Wendel, S. 72
Wesley, J. 29, 35-36, 412-18, 432, 434, 437-40, 494, 510
Wessel, S. 230-31, 233-38, 245-50, 252-53, 257-58
Whitley, H.C. 392-94, 404
Wiles, M. 2, 3, 109, 114, 116, 121-23, 129, 133, 135, 142, 147, 153-55, 170, 173, 178, 232
Williams, D.H. 157, 170, 216
Williams, G.H. 327
Williams, M.A. 89
Williams, R.R. 51
Williams, R. 140-42
Wilson, J.C. 55-58
Wilson, J.E. 336-39
Wilson, J.F. 333
Wilson, R.M. 87
Wolfson, E.R. 82-83
Wolfson, H.A. 48, 61, 65, 121-22, 124, 128-29, 135
Wood, L.W. 27
Woods, D.G. 449
Woodworth-Etter, M.B. 488
Worrell, H.S. 477
Wright, D.F. 92, 104, 110
Wright, N.T. 153, 336
Yarnold, E. 163-64, 465
Yeomans, L. 432
Yesehaq 287
Yesseyevich, D. 382
Yong, A. 34-35, 518
Young. D.J. 478
Young, F. 2

Young, P.V.   381, 391
ZäDengel   289
Zachariadou, E.A.   285
Zander, V.   363
Zanetti, U.   288-89, 294, 298

Zaprometova, O.   281
Zeno   262
Zephyrinus   101, 119
Ziemke, D.C.   81
Zinzendorf,   437

Printed by Amazon Italia Logistica S.r.l.
Torrazza Piemonte (TO), Italy